MOON

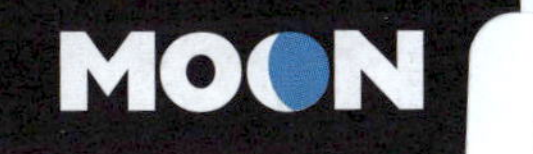

I0762714

Colombia

OCEAN MALANDRA

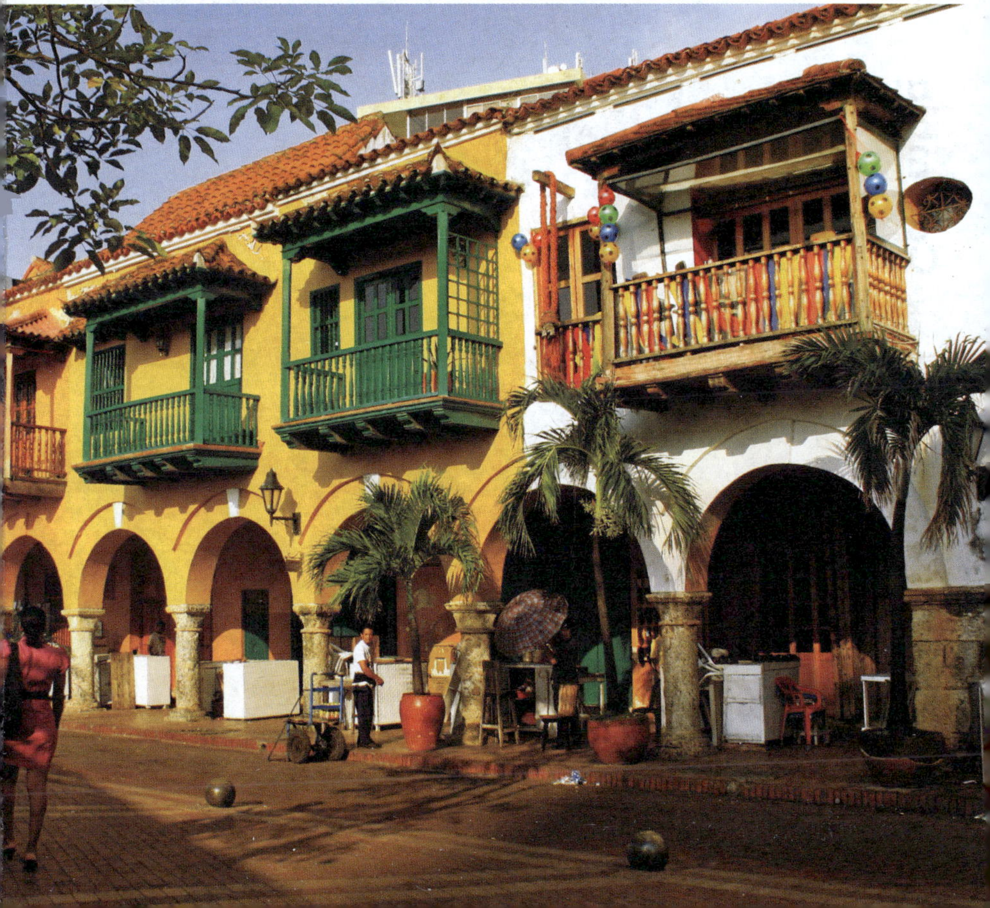

Colombia

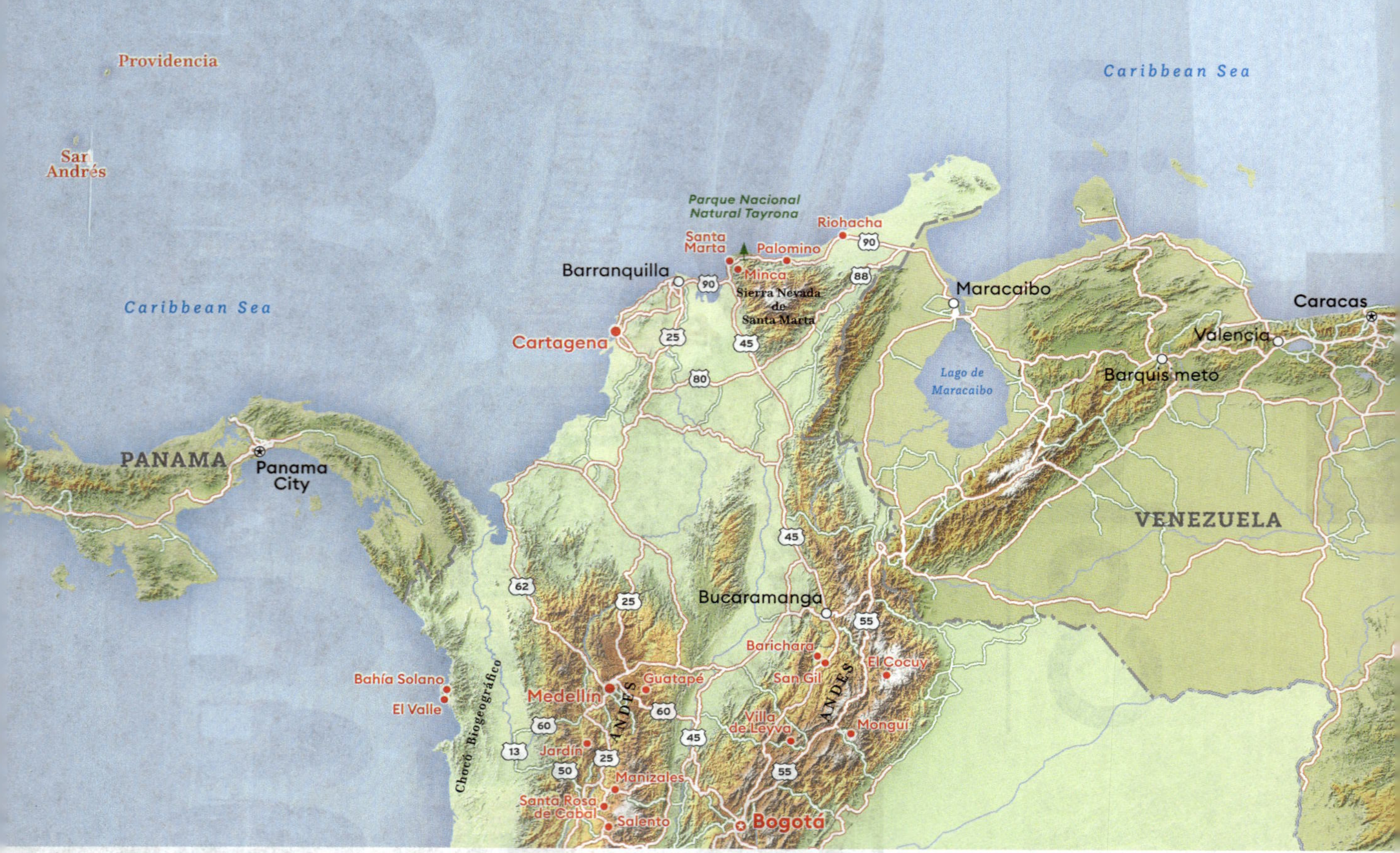
Providencia
San Andrés
Caribbean Sea
Caribbean Sea
Parque Nacional Natural Tayrona
Riohacha
Santa Marta
Palomino
Minca
Sierra Nevada de Santa Marta
Barranquilla
Cartagena
Maracaibo
Lago de Maracaibo
Caracas
Valencia
Barquismeto
VENEZUELA
PANAMA
Panama City
Bucaramanga
Barichara
San Gil
El Cocuy
ANDES
Villa de Leyva
Monguí
Bogotá
Guatapé
Medellín
ANDES
Bahía Solano
El Valle
Chocó Biogeográfico
Jardín
Manizales
Santa Rosa de Cabal
Salento
90
88
25
45
80
62
25
45
55
60
60
45
13
50
25
55

PACIFIC
OCEAN
La Barra
Buenaventura
San Cipriano
Cali
Pueblo Pance
40
COLOMBIA
Inírida
Villavieja
Silvia
San Andrés de Pisimbalá
Popayán
Coconuco
25
San Agustín
45
Pasto
Mitú
Quito
ANDES
ECUADOR
Guayaquil
PERU
Río Amazonas
Puerto Nariño
Leticia
Río Amazonas
BRAZIL
Río Javari
0
100 miles
0
100 km

CONTENTS

mango tree, Santa Marta

Guatapé

WELCOME TO

COLOMBIA

WITH WHITE-SAND CARIBBEAN BEACHES, snow-capped Andean peaks, lush Amazon rainforest, and a lost-in-time rugged Pacific coast all packed into one country, Colombia is unparalleled when it comes to natural splendor. In fact, measured by square foot, it's the most biodiverse country on earth. Add in the kaleidoscope of different cultures that make their home here and their unique musical and gastronomical traditions, and what emerges is a destination so multifaceted it can rightly be called the crown jewel of South America.

Magical realism pervades all of Colombia's varied landscapes, whether it's the fairy-tale streets of colonial Cartagena, the bird-filled cloud forests outside Bogotá, or the steamy dance floors of Cali's legendary salsa clubs. From historic pueblo-hopping to immersions into Amazonian Indigenous communities, the hardest decision a visitor to Colombia has to make is what to include and what to leave for next time.

In between the planned itinerary, the abundance of exotic fruits and traditional delicacies, the local fiestas and festivals that often rage till the break of dawn, and the warm hospitality and friendliness of the Colombian people themselves often steal the show and become the highlight of the trip. A passion for life that is profoundly exuberant, even by Latin American standards, is on full display at every turn and usually set to music.

So, pack up that sunscreen and that umbrella, the Gabriel García Márquez novel you always wanted to read, and those dancing shoes: Colombia is going to put them all to good use. Whether it's a weeklong beach break or a multiple-month pilgrimage across the entire country, Colombia will steal your heart and capture your imagination like nowhere else on earth.

Cerro de Monserrate, Bogotá

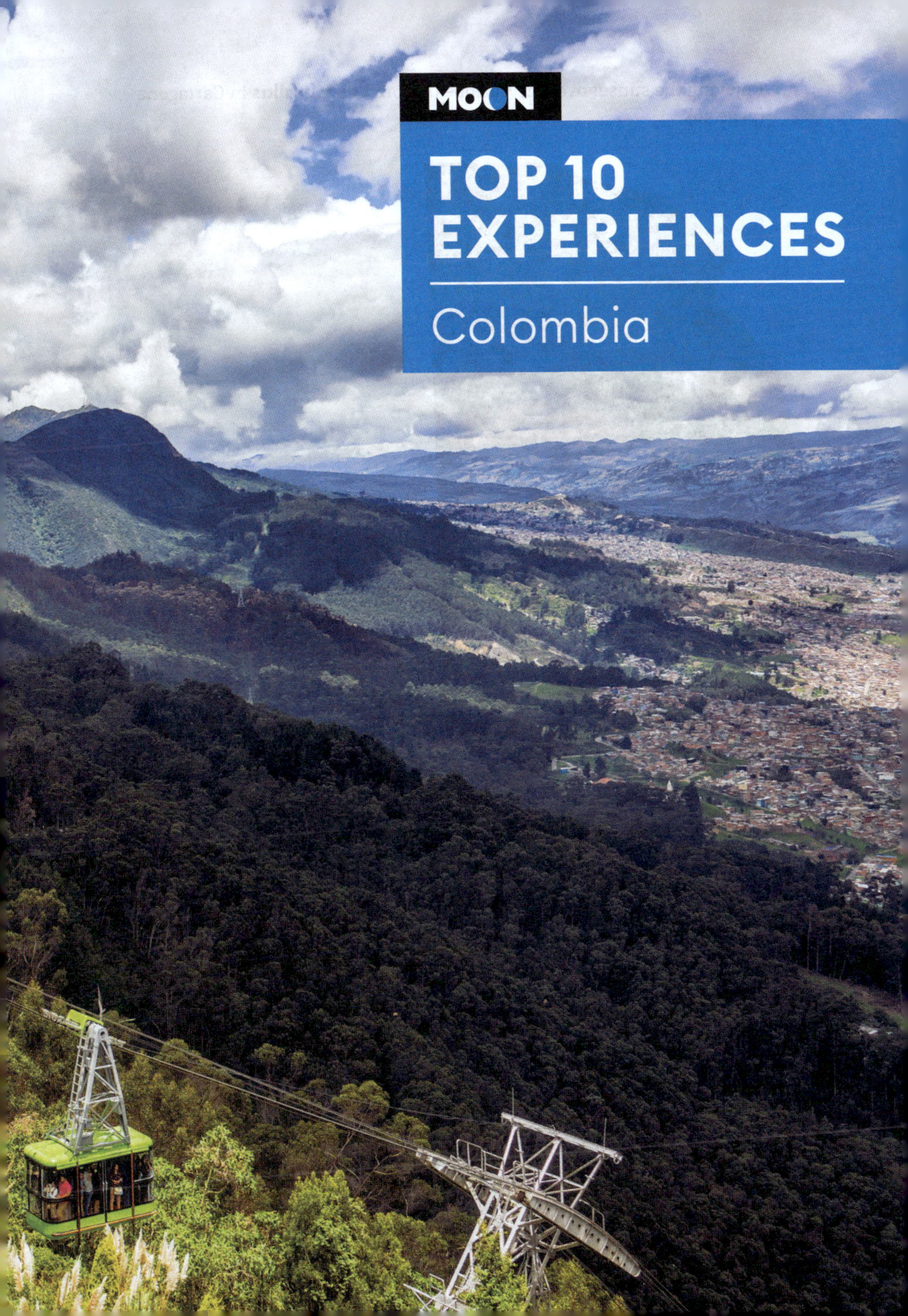
MOON
TOP 10 EXPERIENCES
Colombia

Enjoying the sunset over the Caribbean from **Las Murallas** in Cartagena (page 56).

2 Exploring Colombia's legendary **coffee culture at a farm-stay** in the coffee region (page 270).

Relaxing on the wilderness beaches of **Parque Nacional Natural Tayrona** (page 106).

4 Marveling at the stone statues of **San Agustín,** the largest pre-Columbian archaeological site in the country (page 335).

5 Joining the **Ciclovía** and biking your way through mountain-high Bogotá (page 148).

Taking in the masterpieces of the **Museo de Antioquia** in Medellín (page 228).

Diving the pristine coral reefs of the **Seaflower Biosphere Reserve** (page 358).

8

Wandering through **Barichara,** the most beautiful pueblo in Colombia (page 211).

9 **Salsa dancing** in Cali, the Salsa Capital of the World (page 308).

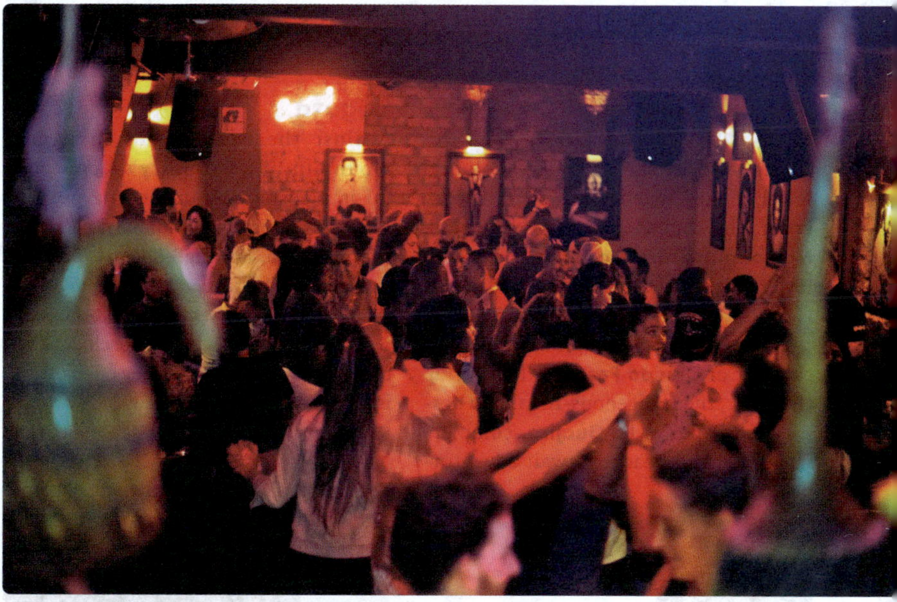

10 Cruising up the **Amazon River** (page 385).

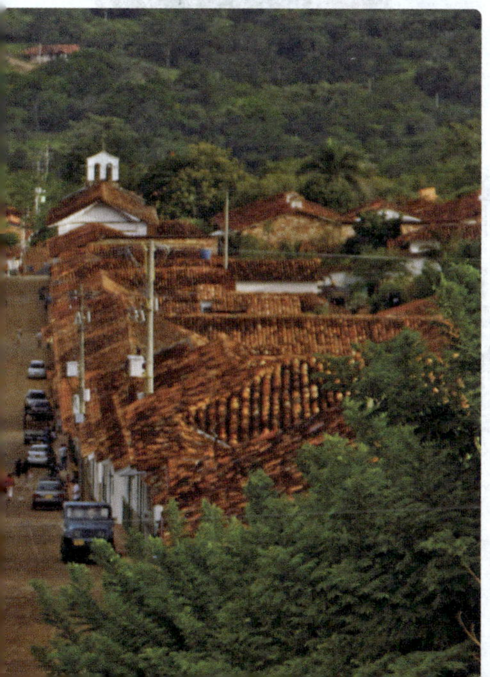

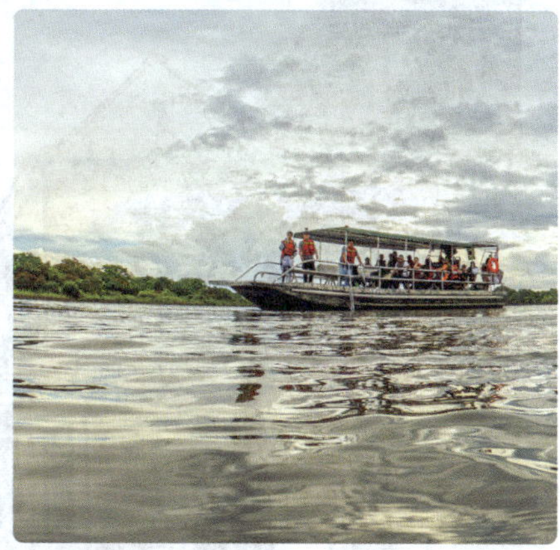

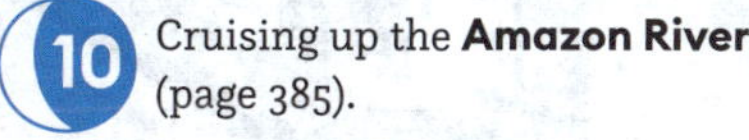

PLANNING YOUR TRIP

WHERE TO GO

Cartagena and the Caribbean Coast

Cartagena is the seductive colonial jewel of the Caribbean. Moving up the coast, the rugged coastline of **Parque Nacional Natural Tayrona** is just the lower reaches of the snow-capped **Sierra Nevada de Santa Marta,** which holds the ruins of the Tayrona Indigenous settlement of **Ciudad Perdida.** Farther up the coast, the Indigenous-inhabited desert landscapes of **La Guajira,** complete with red-sand beaches, await adventurous travelers.

Bogotá

Against the backdrop of the Andes Mountains, the country's cool capital is a cosmopolitan melting pot. It's a city of stunning colonial and modern **architecture,** cutting-edge art, progressive culture, fantastic **shopping,** five-star **dining,** and euphoric **nightlife.** Just outside Bogotá, towering waterfalls, fascinating archaeological sites, picturesque pueblos, and incredible national parks await.

Boyacá and Santander

The cradle of Colombian independence, the mountainous departments of Santander

Cartagena

Providencia
San Andrés
San Andrés and Providencia
Caribbean Sea
Cartagena and the Caribbean Coast
Maracaibo
Cartagena
Lago de Maracaibo
Caribbean Sea
Barquisimeto
Panama City
PANAMA
VENEZUELA
Boyacá and Santander
Medellín
Medellín and the Coffee Region
PACIFIC OCEAN
Bogotá
Bogotá
Buenaventura
Cali
COLOMBIA
Popayán
Cali and Southwest Colombia
Mitú
Pasto
BRAZIL
Quito
ECUADOR
Guayaquil
PERU
The Amazon
Leticia
0
100 miles
0
100 km

town of Jardin

and Boyacá are graced with stunning countryside, from the awe-inspiring desertlike **Cañón del Chicamocha** to the snow-capped peaks of the **Sierra Nevada del Cocuy. San Gil** is the outdoor adventure capital, while nearby **Barichara** is one of the most beautiful colonial pueblos in the country. The sacred **Iguaque lagoon** and the nearby town of **Villa de Leyva,** with its serene whitewashed buildings and cobblestone streets, are truly picturesque.

Medellín and the Coffee Region

Ambitious Medellín is known for its temperate climate, excellent public transportation, fun nightlife, and world-class art museums. Photogenic coffee region pueblos abound, with **Jardín** and **Salento** some of the most colorful. Stay at one of several **coffee farm-stays** in the lush rolling hills. The landscape is dotted with towering wax palms and brightly colored birds. The snow-covered volcanic peaks of **Parque Nacional Natural Los Nevados** beckon mountain climbers.

The Pacific is Colombia's wild coast, where the thick rainforest of **Chocó** meets the beaches and endless ocean at wonderfully remote **Bahía Solano.** Warm Pacific water is a playground for **humpback whales** that spend July-October here. Sea turtles are also return visitors.

Cali and Southwest Colombia

Colombia's third-largest city is a joyous one, filled with music and dance. When the sun goes down it's hard to resist Cali's hypnotic salsa rhythms. To the west, beyond the endless sugarcane fields of the **Valle de Cauca,** stands the White City of **Popayán,** a historic colonial city of presidents and poets. Tucked into the fertile valleys of the Macizo Colombiano, the archaeological sites of **Tierradentro** and **San Agustín** beckon.

San Andrés and Providencia

The paradise of English-speaking San Andrés and Providencia offers everything you'd expect from a Caribbean island vacation. Fantastic **diving** will keep you occupied for days off sunny San Andrés. The daily routine of lounging on **remote beaches,** eating fresh seafood, lazing in hammocks, and **stargazing** on the beach in rustic Providencia will have you hooked.

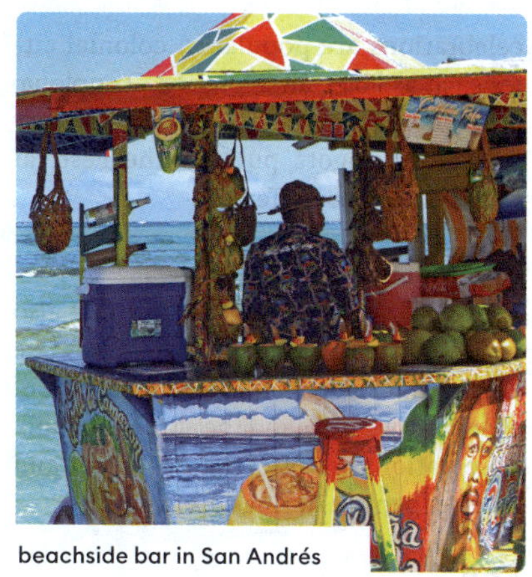

beachside bar in San Andrés

The Amazon

The Amazon **rainforest** is the lungs of the world. Enjoy the cuisine and nightlife of the triple border town of **Leticia.** Visit an ecolodge on the **Río Javari,** where you can take canoe rides above the treetops in the flooded forest. Observe birds and pink dolphins by day and look for crocodiles as darkness falls. Spend a couple of days in the blissfully car-free and Indigenous-run hamlet of **Puerto Nariño.**

WHEN TO GO

Because Colombia straddles the equator, the temperature and the length of the day are nearly constant year-round. What gives variation is altitude: It is always hot and humid in low-lying and coastal areas, and it is always crisp and often downright cold in the high Andes. There are, however, distinct dry and rainy seasons throughout the year. In most of the country, December-February and July-August are considered **verano (dry season). Invierno (rainy season)** is usually April-May and again September-November.

In San Andrés and Providencia, June-November is rainy and February-April is drier. In the Amazon the drier months are June-September and the rainy season is December-May. It's worth a visit during either season. In the Pacific coast region, it rains year-round.

Tourism **high season** corresponds with North American winter (December-March) and also summer break for students (June-August). **Humpback whales** make their appearance off the Pacific coast **July-October.**

Spring

Spring is a great time to visit, especially the coastal regions where there is little rain. **Semana Santa (Easter week)** celebrations are popular in colonial cities such as Popayán, Mompox, Pamplona, and Tunja, while during that time every two years Bogotá puts on the Festival Iberoamericano de Teatro.

Summer

Summertime is high season, but that also means lots of festivals in major cities like Bogotá and Medellín that take advantage of the sunny weather and the absence of rain. Reservations are often harder to get and more expensive during this time.

Fall

Fall is off-season, meaning there are plenty of travel deals, but it is rainy, especially along the Caribbean coast. For much of the rest of the country, this is an excellent time to travel, and deals abound.

Winter

Winter is high season and dry season, with locals heading out for vacation and international visitors flooding the top destinations. Many of the major **festivals and celebrations** take place December-February: the Feria de Cali, the Carnaval de Negros y Blancos in Pasto, Hay Festival in Cartagena, and the Carnaval de Barranquilla.

If You Have . . .

7 DAYS

With a full week you can fly into Cartagena, get a couple of days of beach and partying in, and then head up the coast to Parque Nacional Natural Tayrona and do the Ciudad Perdida trek or explore the coffee farms and waterfalls of Minca.

10 DAYS

With 10 days in Colombia you can add a trip to the coffee region to your beach break, hitting up the pueblo of Salento, hiking through the wax palm-studded Valle de Cocora, and visiting an authentic coffee farm-stay.

BEFORE YOU GO

Passports and Visas

Travelers to Colombia who intend to visit for tourism for less than 90 days need only a valid passport on entry to the country. You may be asked to show proof of a return ticket. Tell the immigration officer if you intend to stay up to 90 days as otherwise they may give you a stamp permitting a stay of 60 days. Language schools and universities will be able to assist those who may require a yearlong student visa.

Vaccinations

There are no obligatory vaccination requirements for visiting Colombia. However, proof of the **yellow fever vaccination** may be requested on arrival at Parque Nacional Natural Tayrona or at the Leticia airport in the Amazon. This vaccination can be obtained at Red Cross clinics throughout the country.

The US Centers for Disease Control and Prevention recommends that travelers have all the basic vaccinations updated. In addition, for most travelers to Colombia, the CDC recommends **hepatitis A** and **typhoid** vaccinations. **Hepatitis B, rabies,** and **yellow fever** vaccinations are recommended for some travelers. If you plan to visit the Amazon region, **antimalarial drugs** may be recommended. With infections of **mosquito-borne illnesses** such as malaria, dengue, chikungunya, and Zika possible in tropical areas of the country, visitors are encouraged to keep mosquito repellent close at hand.

14 DAYS

With two weeks at your disposal, you can add Bogotá, the fascinating capital of Colombia, where bicycle-led street-art tours and late-night parties will give you an urban fix. Also check out Villa de Leyva, a gorgeous colonial pueblo just hours from the city.

21 DAYS

Three weeks allows you to slow down and do some deep exploring in the south of the country, including the archaeological site of San Agustín and the sultry salsa clubs in the city of Cali. Alternatively, you can head to the Pacific coast or the Amazon rainforest.

Mastering a few essential Spanish expressions enhances your interactions with locals. Here are some key phrases to keep in your linguistic arsenal:

Hello, Hi	Hola
Nice to meet you	Un placer a conocerte
Thank you	Muchas gracias
Good morning	Buenos dias
Good afternoon/evening	Buenas noches
See you later	Hasta la vista
Bye!	Chau!

Transportation

There are **overland border entries** from Ecuador (to Ipiales) and **by boat** from Peru or Brazil to the Amazonian port of Leticia and, by sea, from Panama to Capurganá or Cartagena.

AIR

Most travelers arrive in Colombia by plane, with the vast majority arriving at the modern **Aeropuerto Internacional El Dorado** in Bogotá. There are numerous daily nonstop flights to Bogotá from the eastern United States as well as from Houston, Dallas, Los Angeles, and Toronto. The cities of **Medellín, Cali, Cartagena, Barranquilla,** and **Armenia** are also served by nonstop flights from the US East Coast.

Domestic flights are easy, safe, increasingly more economical, frequent, and, above all, quick.

BUS

Taking the bus to just about anywhere in the country is an inexpensive and popular but slower option. All major cities, and most smaller ones, have large modern bus terminals where a variety of bus companies compete for your business. For longer trips (like between major cities) there are often several classes of travel available, with the more expensive options including luxury seats and meals.

In the major cities, there are extensive **rapid bus networks.**

CAR

Renting a car is a viable option in several

shrine on a mountain in Boyacá

Parque Simón Bolívar, Bogotá

areas, including the **coffee region,** where roads are good, and in the mountainous Boyacá and Santander regions. Public transit is good everywhere, however, and a car is not necessary, especially in major cities.

What to Pack

For rainforest exploration, waterproof **hiking boots** and collapsible **trekking poles** are musts. For exploring the Amazon as well as the Pacific coast, a waterproof **camera bag** and **silica gel** may prevent the heartache of a ruined camera. For caving, visiting the tombs of Tierradentro, and finding your way at night, a **small flashlight or headlight** comes in handy. To spot humpbacks, birds, and other wildlife, **binoculars** are great to have. If you plan on spending much time on the coast, bring your own **snorkeling gear.** A lightweight **sleeping sack** makes rustic sleeping conditions more comfortable.

To protect against the sun, pack a wide-brimmed **hat;** against the rain, a lightweight **rain jacket** and compact **umbrella;** against mosquitoes, lightweight and light-colored long-sleeved shirts and some strong repellent. For long bus rides, earplugs, eye masks, and **luggage locks** will make the trip more relaxing. A **Latin American Spanish dictionary** will help you get your point across.

Casual attire is fine at most restaurants, theaters, and religious venues. Restaurants in Bogotá and Cartagena may expect more effort. In large cities, you'll want to **dress to impress** in bars and clubs. Shorts are generally frowned on in interior cities.

MAKE IT A GREENER TRIP

Experience all Colombia has to offer while minimizing your environmental impact. Colombia is a country with valuable and unique ecosystems, and ambitious sustainability initiatives have been implemented to protect them. As a leader in ecotourism, Colombia's efforts around sustainable travel and environmental protection are part of its new national plan. With advance planning and appropriate packing, you'll find it's easy to travel sustainably around the country.

▶ *Packing Checklist*

Reusable water bottle and shopping bag

Reusable utensils

Reef-friendly sunscreen

▶ *Sustainable Transportation*

Colombia has invested heavily in public transportation and low-emission alternatives to driving.

Bogotá's award-winning **bicycle infrastructure** and new public bike system makes getting around the capital on two wheels easy and effective.

Medellín's **Metro** rail system is a model for South American cities.

▶ *Reducing Your Impact*

By being conscious of the impact of tourism in a given area, you can make sure your presence helps and doesn't harm locals and their environments.

Shop local: Spend your money with locally owned businesses. This ensures that locals benefit directly from the tourism economy.

Slow travel: When planning where to stay, consider staying more than one night at each destination to reduce your impact on the local infrastructure as well as making a more relaxing trip.

Go green: Seek out accommodations that practice natural building, energy efficiency, and water conservation.

▶ *Eco-Tourism*

In a country like Colombia, home to precarious ecosystems like the Amazon rainforest and the Andean páramo, eco-tourism is key to the country's plan for development.

Support community tourism projects: A number of local communities in Colombia have launched ecotourism projects as a way to create a regional economy and also protect their ecological resources.

Eat regionally: Dining at the top chef-run restaurants—which use local producers and ingredients—is a great way to support regional economies and treat yourself.

Get involved: Colombia offers plenty of volunteer and educational opportunities to get involved in ecological projects and use your time here to fortify its resilience.

toucan

a giant hammock in Minca

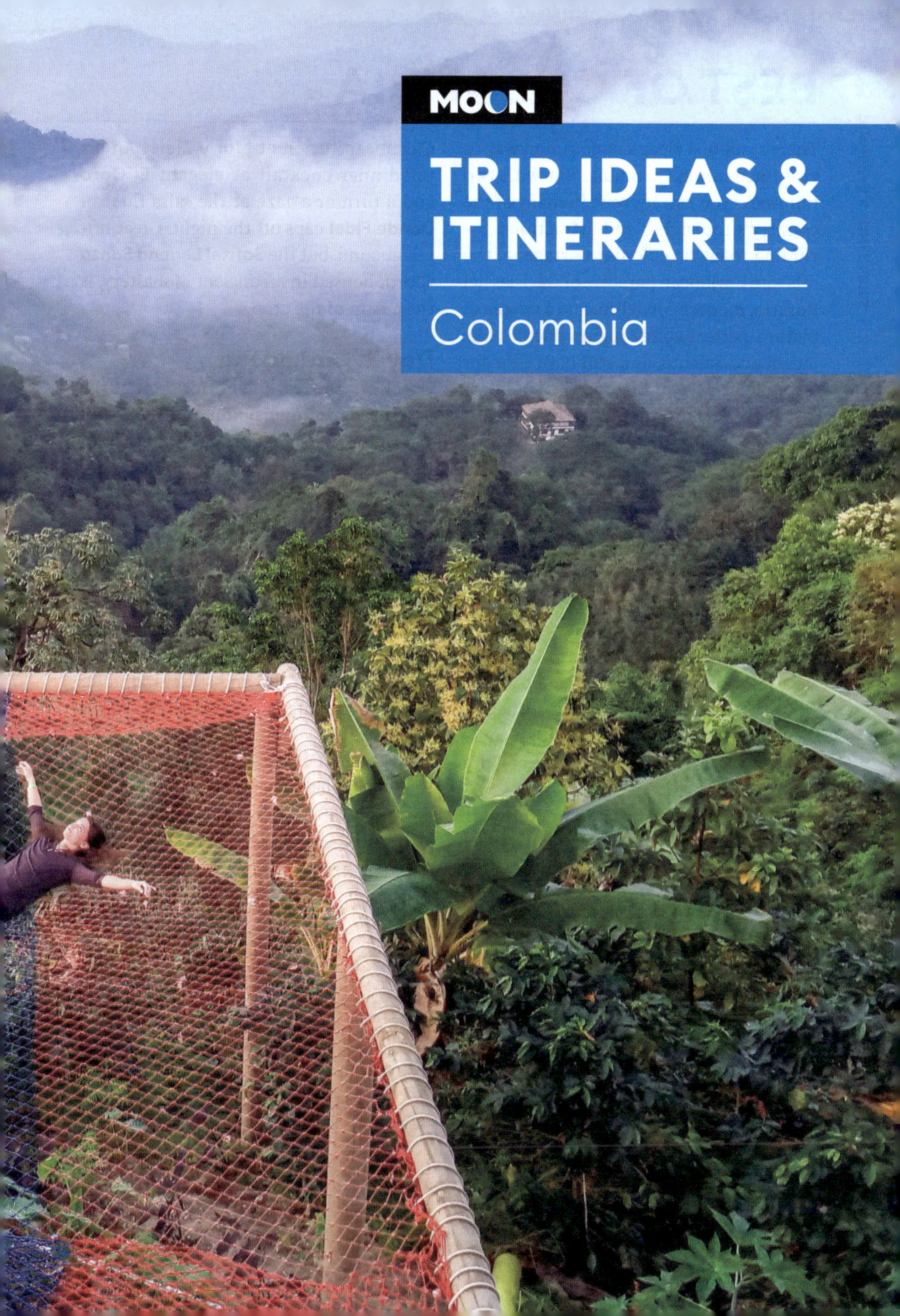
MOON
TRIP IDEAS &
ITINERARIES
Colombia

BEST OF COLOMBIA

There's not one clear-cut common way to visit uncommon Colombia. But with two full weeks you can squeeze in many of the country's top sights and attractions, including majestic colonial Cartagena, the offshore Caribbean paradise of the Islas del Rosario, modern Medellín, and a couple of picture-perfect coffee region pueblos like Jardín and Salento, and still have time for a couple of days in Bogotá, the country's fast-pasted, mile-high, über-hip cosmopolitan capital.

Day 1: Cartagena

Start your trip in **Cartagena.** Walk the Old City streets, getting lost and found again as you amble from the Torre del Reloj to the divine **Parque de Bolívar** and the **San Diego** neighborhood, stopping to admire **La Catedral de Santa Catalina de Alejandría** on the way. Don't miss a sunset stroll along **Las Murallas,** the ancient city walls, stopping to enjoy a cocktail and the Caribbean Sea breeze at **Café del Mar.**

For dinner, dive into some Peruvian Caribbean fusion at **Mar y Zielo.** An after-dinner cocktail at elegant **El Coro** and a turn or a gaze at the salsa floor of **Donde Fidel** caps off the night. Great hotels abound, but the **Sofitel Legend Santa Clara,** housed in an ancient Monastery, is the cream of the crop.

Day 2: Cartagena

Check out the real-life horror show at the **Palacio de la Inquisición** and then find some human inspiration at the **Iglesia and Claustro de San Pedro Claver.** In the afternoon, head over to the **Castillo de San Felipe** to learn the real story of the pirates of the Caribbean.

At night, head over to **Getsemaní** for a live dance show on Plaza de la Trinidad and then grab some tapas at **Lunático.** Afterward, catch the champeta class at the **Bazurto Social Club** and stick around for the live band later.

Days 3-4: Islas del Rosario

From the Muelle Turístico in town, take the 45-minute boat ride to the beaches of **Islas**

Cartagena
DAY 1

Cartagena
DAY 2

Islas del Rosario
DAYS 3-4

del Rosario, the area's finest beaches, and spend a night at an island hotel. It's worth splurging for the beachfront **Gente de Mar,** located on **Isla Grande.**

Get in some quality beach time, do some snorkeling, rent a kayak, and enjoy the fresh seafood. The next day, take the boat back to Cartagena. Have dinner at **Lobo de Mar** later that night.

Day 5: Medellín

Take an early-morning hour-long domestic flight from Cartagena to the Aeropuerto Olaya Herrera in Medellín. Check into **La Playa Hotel,** then make your way to the finest art museum in the country, the **Museo de Antioquia.** If you have time, also visit the heart-wrenching **Museo Casa de la Memoria,** the country's first museum dedicated to the memory of victims of Colombia's decades-long armed conflict.

For dinner, enjoy the creative fusion plates at one of the city's up-and-coming gastronomical stars, **Salón Centro.** After dinner, check out the hip nightlife along Calle de Cervantes and catch a live music show at **La Pascasia** or some live theater at the **Pequeño Teatro de Medellín.**

Day 6: Medellín

Take a ride on the world-class Metro to the **Metrocable gondola** network and visit the **Biblioteca España,** a boldly designed public library built on the side of a mountain. Grab a local lunch here in the barrio Santo Domingo. From there, transfer to another Metrocable line to **Parque Arví,** a huge recreational area in a lush forest setting.

At night, head to El Poblado for dinner at critically acclaimed **Carmen** or get your ramen fix on at the **Tamagotchi Ramen Bar.** Stroll the El Poblado streets, stopping at **El Social Tienda Mixta** for a drink.

Day 7: Guatapé

Take a day trip to the lakeside village of **Guatapé,** about two hours from Medellín. Catch an early morning bus and, when you arrive, enjoy a hearty brunch at **Montano.** After, stroll along the picturesque lakefront.

Grab a mototaxi to **La Piedra Peñol** and climb the 700 steps to the top to enjoy the incredible views. Back in the village of Guatapé, refuel with a freshly caught trout at one of the waterfront restaurants before taking the bus back to Medellín.

Medellín
DAY 5

Medellín
DAY 6

Guatapé
DAY 7

BEST HIKES

Parque Nacional Natural El Cocuy

CARTAGENA AND THE CARIBBEAN COAST

Ciudad Perdida Trek

52 km (32 mi); 4-6 days; strenuous

One of the most epic treks on the South American continent, this guided excursion takes you through dense coastal rainforest to ruins of the ancient Tayrona civilization (page 94).

BOGOTÁ

Cerro de Monserrate

5 km (3 mi); 2 hours; moderate-strenuous

Colombia's most famous urban hike, this strenuous but short jaunt follows stone steps up from the center of Bogotá to the gleaming white Santuario de Monserrate (page 150).

BOYACÁ AND SANTANDER

Púlpito del Diablo

17 km (11 mi); 8 hours; strenuous

The most iconic of the three hikes up the glimmering glacier-covered peaks of Parque Nacional Natural El Cocuy, this vigorous trek ends at a striking rock formation that juts up through the snow and ice (page 205).

Camino Real

10.6 km (6.6 mi); 3 hours; easy

Follow the stone-paved path once used by the Spanish empire and ancient civilizations before them through the gorgeous countryside from Barichara to the pueblo of Guane (page 214).

MEDELLÍN AND THE COFFEE REGION

Valle de Cocora

15 km (9 mi); 5 hours; moderate

Explore a majestic valley filled with wax palms, the tallest palm trees in the world, in the lower reaches of Parque Nacional Natural Los Nevados (page 278).

Days 8-9: Jardín

Take the three-hour bus ride through the southern Antioquia countryside to the picture-perfect Paisa coffee town of **Jardín.** Hang out with the locals in the sublime **Parque Principal,** a park bursting with flowers, where you can enjoy a beer or sip a locally produced coffee. Check out the in-town **Reserva Natural Jardín de Rocas** for an up-close look at the scarlet Andean cock-of-the-rock, an emblematic bird.

The next day take the **Cable Aéreo** up to the lookout at Cristo Rey. From here you can hike about an hour to get to the Cascada Escalera waterfall. Stop at **La Truchería** on the way back into town to pick your own meal out of the large tanks and have it cooked to order. Back in town, enjoy an aperitif at **Café Macanas.**

Day 10

Wake up early to take an all-day bus (or rented car) through the majestically verdant coffee region to brightly painted **Salento,** an 8.5-hour trip-from Jardín, and longer if you stop to visit local coffee farms. Alternatively, head back to Medellín to take a one-hour domestic flight from Aeropuerto Olaya Herrera to Aeropuerto Internacional El Edén in Armenia, 30 minutes by bus or taxi from Salento.

Stay at the bright orange **Tralala** hostel and have dinner at wonderful **Casa La Eliana,** followed by dessert and coffee at **Café Jesús Martín.**

Day 11

In the morning, book a Jeep Willy at the main plaza to the awe-inspiring **Valle de Cocora,** where 60-m-tall (200-ft) palm trees fill a verdant valley. In the afternoon, do the **Finca Don Eduardo coffee tour** on the outskirts of town.

Refuel with a steak and wine at **Juan Esteban Parrilla y Vinos,** on the main plaza. Before retiring for the night, stroll the atmospheric **Calle Real.**

Day 12

Take a flight from the Aeropuerto Internacional El Edén in Armenia (30 minutes from Salento by bus or taxi) to **Bogotá,** the nation's mile-high Andean capital. Spend the day exploring the ancient mural-covered colonial streets of **La Candelaria,** stopping to check out the massive **Catedral Primada** in Plaza de Bolívar and the street life at the **Chorro**

Jardín
DAYS 8-9

Salento
DAY 10

Valle de Cocora
DAY 11

de Quevado. Give yourself a couple of hours for the **Museo del Oro,** which holds artifacts from Colombia's many pre-Columbian civilizations.

At night, have dinner at **Chamanico** before heading over to **Casa Quiebracanto** for live salsa. Stay at **Casa Deco** to be close to everything.

Day 13

In the morning, hike or take the funicular to the top of **Cerro de Monserrate** for spectacular views over the city and the altiplano. Refuel with lunch at **Recetas de Abuela** in La Concordia market.

In the afternoon, grab a public bike or take a **bike tour** and explore the city's excellent system of ciclorutas (bike paths). At night, head to **Zona G** for a five-star fusion meal at **Restaurante Leo** before dancing off all those calories at **Theatrón** in the Chapinero area.

Day 14

In the morning, visit the **Jardín Botánico** for an exploration of the many ecosystems of Colombia all in one place. In the afternoon, head over to the Teusaquillo area for an Amazonian lunch at **Copoazú** and some exotic fruit-based ice cream at **Selva Nevada.** Before your flight home, do some last-minute shopping on **La Séptima,** where several arcades full of artisan and souvenir vendors are located.

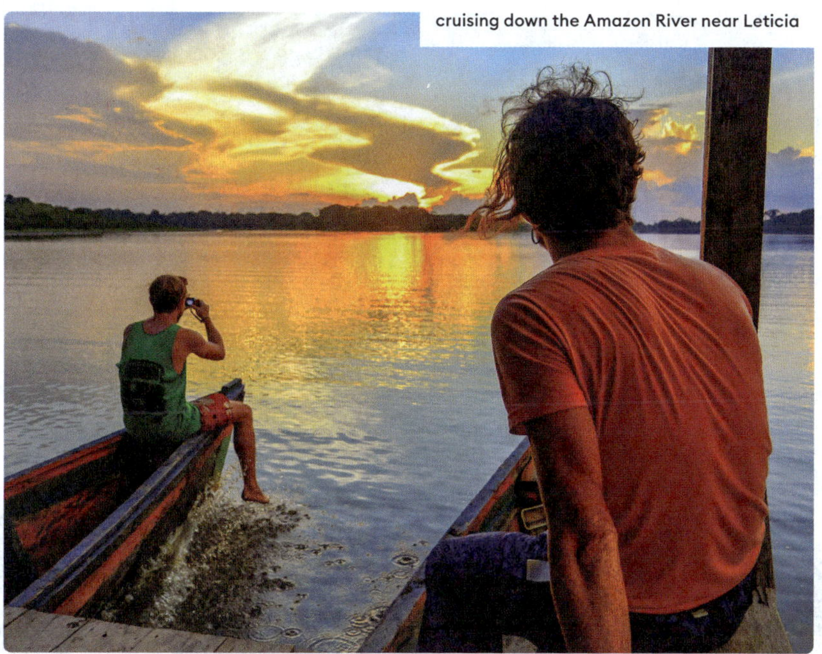

cruising down the Amazon River near Leticia

Excursions and Side Trips

SAN ANDRÉS AND PROVIDENCIA

If you're looking to get away from it all, go to the **San Andrés** Archipelago, off the coast of Nicaragua. Allot at least **four days** for some solid beach relaxation time.

Fly to San Andrés from any major Colombian city. Take a boat to the idyllic white-sand beach of **Johnny Cay,** and check out the local reggae music scene down in **San Luis.**

The pristine island of **Providencia** is a one-hour flight from here. Once in Providencia, check into a room with **Miss Elma** and then head over to **Felipe's Place,** where dive experts can take you to the lively reefs of the **Seaflower Biosphere Reserve** for a few underwater adventures.

THE AMAZON

This quick but meaningful Amazon adventure will require at least **four days.** Leticia is the gateway to the Colombian Amazon. It's a two-hour flight from Bogotá. At the **Reserva Natural Tanimboca,** you can stay in a treehouse in the rainforest, just minutes from town.

For the next couple of days, take a boat up the world's most powerful river and visit the Ticuna community of **San Martín.** Continue onward to the decidedly eco-friendly **Puerto Nariño.**

Alternatively, you can head straight to the ecolodges along the **Río Javari,** in Brazil, where you can take day and nighttime safaris, discovering the abundant life of the Amazonian rainforest and river.

Basílica Menor de la Inmaculada Concepción in Jardín

MUSIC AND DANCE FESTIVALS

procession in the Carnaval de Barranquilla

Colombia feels like a celebration year-round, but especially during these colorful music and dance festivals.

- **Carnaval de Barranquilla:** The Caribbean coast's favorite party is held each year in February. Cumbia, an intriguing mix of Indigenous, African, and Spanish musical styles, takes center stage at this multiday event of parades, concerts, and revelry (page 90).
- **Festivales al Parque:** Bogotá doesn't have just one music celebration. July-November the action takes place in the city's largest park, Parque Simón Bolívar, during the Festivales al Parque series (page 157).
- **Feria de las Flores:** Medellín's biggest festival takes place in early May and fills the streets with colorful processions and beauty pageants that last all week (page 239).
- **Festival Petronio Álvarez:** A major Cali festival worth checking out is the Festival Petronio Álvarez, an August celebration of Pacific coast music and culture (page 309).
- **Feria de Cali:** The last week of the year is Feria de Cali, a weeklong event of open-air salsa concerts, parties, and pageantry that takes all over the city (page 309).
- **Carnaval de Negros y Blancos:** A week of processions, concerts, and dancing in the streets takes over the Andean city of Pasto as festivalgoers paint their faces black and then white and join in the fun (page 343).

SPOTLIGHT ON
Bird-Watching in Colombia

▲ shining sunbeam hummingbird

Colombia is a global hot spot of biodiversity, home to more species of birds than anywhere else on the planet. The latest count found more than 2,000 species, with 80 of them endemic, meaning they are only found in Colombia. To put this in perspective, there are only 900 species of birds in all of North America and 540 in all of Europe. Nearly 20 percent of all bird species around the world are present in Colombia.

This means that for bird-watchers, Colombia is simply unparalleled. While bird-watching can be practiced almost anywhere in the country, including in major cities, where botanical gardens are always prime, there are several areas that are simply outstanding—hot spots within a hot spot.

- **Minca:** The **Sierra Nevada,** the highest coastal mountain range in the world, is a great place to catch a glimpse of Colombia's amazing bird diversity, especially on the lower forest-covered slopes near Minca. Be on the lookout for members of the emerald family of hummingbirds, which shimmer like living jewels (page 101).
- **The coffee region:** These lush mountain valleys are prime bird-watching areas. Right in the town of **Jardín** (page 255) is a reserve for the bright-red Andean cock-of-the-rock, while the wax palm-covered valleys outside **Salento** (page 274) are home to yellow-eared parrots and Andean condors.
- **Pacific coast:** The rainforests of Colombia's Pacific coast are also home to many interesting exotic bird species,

including the sword-billed hummingbird—the only bird in the world with a beak longer than its body! Stop by the 163-ha (403-acre) **Jardín Botánico de Pacífico** in Bahía Solano (page 285) for a truly stunning living showcase.

- **Parque Nacional Natural Farallones de Cali:** The rainforest-covered mountains between Cali and the Pacific coast have the highest count of bird species in the entire world—nearly 30 percent of the country's megadiversity of birds have been spotted here. Key species include the multicolored tanager and the crested eagle (page 317).
- **Amazon Rainforest:** The world's most biodiverse ecosystem is home to an extraordinary number of bird species, including the spectacular scarlet macaw and the majestic white-throated toucan. You will see bright green parrots roosting in the center of **Leticia** (page 382), but to really see the splendor, visit **Parque Nacional Natural Amacayacu** (page 396) or stay at a rainforest lodge along the **Río Javari** (page 402).

BIRD-WATCHING TOURS

Bird-watching tours are available all over Colombia and can be organized by local experts, tour agencies, and hotels. Bird-watching tours include 1-2-hour urban excursions in cities to multiday adventures that require off-road exploring in pristine wilderness areas. Prices range from COP$50,000 for a day tour to over COP$5,000,000 for an all-inclusive guided journey.

In many Colombian regions bird-watching is being heavily invested in as a form of sustainable tourism, and local youth are being trained to be expert

▼ blue-winged mountain tanager

guides. Ask at a local tourism office to be connected to a local guide or outfit.

Avistando Aves Andinos

Run by professional bird guide and Salento native Néstor Jaime Sabaria, **Avistando Aves Andinos** (tel. 322/381-8777; https://avistandoavesandinas.com) does group and private bird-watching tours all over the coffee region, including into Valle de Cocora and Parque Nacional Natural Los Nevados. An expert wilderness guide, Sabaria also offers an 18-day bird-watching journey through several ecosystems, including the Farallones de Cali mountain range, the Sierra Nevada de Santa Marta, and the Putumayo region of the Amazon rainforest. This is a rare and special opportunity to get off the beaten path and into Colombia's most gorgeous scenery.

Nature Colombia

Nature Colombia (tel. 321/373-2882; https://naturecolombia.com) is a quality locally run ecotourism outfit that offers a variety of 4-, 6-, and 10-day birding adventures around the country. Every year they offer a weeklong all-women birding adventure to top hot spots in the south of the country.

BIRD-WATCHING RESERVES

A government-funded conservation agency, **ProAves** (tel. 604/406-9776; https://proaves.org) runs 27 bird reserves in 14 departments of Colombia, from the Caribbean coast to the Amazon rainforest. All of these reserves are open to the public for bird-watching experiences, which must be booked ahead and include a professional guide (COP$120,000 pp). Eleven of the reserves offer lodging in basic but comfortable shared rooms (USD$50 pp, food included).

▼ buffy helmetcrest

BEST BEACHES

Johnny Cay, San Andrés

With both a Caribbean and a Pacific coastline plus many offshore islands, Colombia is a beach lover's dream. Here are some of the most picturesque:

- **Isla Grande, Islas del Rosario:** Just an hour offshore from Cartagena, Isla Grande beckons beach bums with powdered-sugar sand and crystal-clear water (page 64).
- **Cabo San Juan, Parque Nacional Natural Tayrona:** Giant boulders and lush rainforest frame this spectacular Caribbean beach, located in the heart of the national park (page 107).
- **Playa El Almejal, Chocó:** At this rainforest-backed wilderness beach on Colombia's Pacific coast, giant blue whales frolic just offshore (page 288).
- **Johnny Cay, San Andrés:** This picture-perfect white sand-ringed Caribbean island is just 20 minutes off the coast of San Andrés (page 355).
- **Almond Bay, Providencia:** Gently lapping waves caress the white sand of this idyllic Caribbean beach on the island of Providencia (page 368).

THE MOST MAGICAL PUEBLOS IN COLOMBIA

With all the spectacular nature and exciting urban nightlife, it's easy to overlook one of Colombia's most enchanting treasures: the country's magical historical pueblos. But not only are Colombia's pueblos living museums of colonial architecture and traditional living, many have also attracted sizable former city-dwelling populations and overflow with creative gourmet restaurants, relaxing cafés, and energetic art scenes. For many visitors, a trip to a historic pueblo is the most memorable part of their trip.

Villa de Leyva

Just three hours from Bogotá in Boyacá is the romantic pueblo of Villa de Leyva, built in the 16th century and known for its wide central plaza, ancient cobblestone streets, walled gardens, and perfectly preserved churches. It's also a bastion of the arts, with a vibrant local music scene, tons of galleries, and even its own annual film festival (page 187).

Monguí

Still off the radar for many travelers, the tiny high Andean village of Monguí in Boyacá feels like it is lost in simpler times. It has gorgeous colonial architecture and hikes into the mountains, including to the pristine Páramo de Ocetá (page 195).

Barichara

With whitewashed and terra-cotta tile-roofed houses that line cobblestone streets in a spectacular valley in the Santander region, it's no wonder that Barichara is frequently cited as the most beautiful town in Colombia. Besides a fantastic dining scene, epic country walks on the Camino Real, and some world-class day spas, the majestic 16th-century village is also home to an ecologically minded set of locals working to restore the surrounding landscape (page 211).

Jardín

With flowers blooming in spacious public plazas and lush hills surrounding it, 18th-century Jardín is quite possibly the most relaxing place in the country. Besides leisurely day hikes to waterfalls and verdant coffee farms, it's also a prime

Villa de Leyva

Barichara

bird-watching destination. It's in southern Antioquia, just two hours from Medellín (page 255).

Salento

Brightly painted 18th-century buildings, a bustling main plaza, and dozens of incredible cafés make this coffee region pueblo one of Colombia's tourism hot spots. The fact that it's the jumping-off point for visiting coffee farms, the magnificent Valle de Cocora, and Parque Nacional Natural Los Nevados just add to the appeal (page 274).

San Agustín

In the southern department of Huila, murals of local birds adorn the walls of this charming colonial farming village that dates to the 16th century. Local shops and cafés sell handmade organic products, and vegetarian restaurants abound. Known for the incredible pre-Colombian statues that dot the countryside, and designated a UNESCO World Heritage Site, San Agustín is also located above the spectacular Río Magdalena canyon and offers endless hiking opportunities (page 335).

Monguí

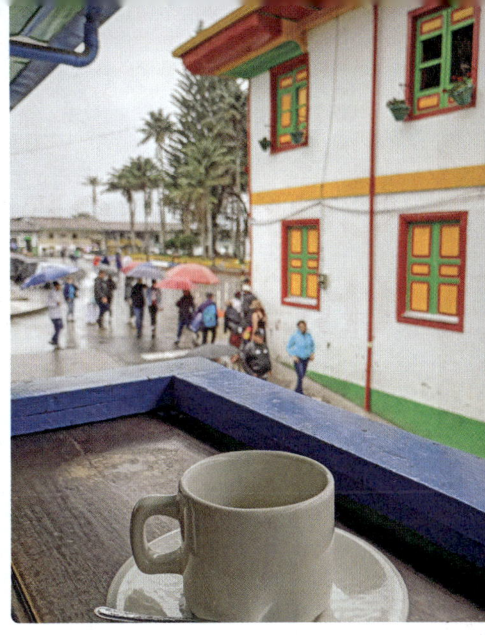

clockwise Jardín; Salento; San Agustín

Cartagena and the Caribbean Coast

 Highlights

★ **Las Murallas:** Enjoy a cerveza with the Caribbean sunset from the bars that top the ancient walls of Cartagena's historic city center (page 56).

★ **Palacio de la Inquisición:** Discover the horrors behind the colonization of the New World at this morbid museum (page 59).

★ **Islas del Rosario:** White-sand beaches await on the Rosario Islands, just a 45-minute boat ride from Cartagena (page 64).

★ **Ciudad Perdida Trek:** Make this epic five-day trek to the ruins of an ancient pre-Colombian metropolis (page 94).

★ **Minca** *(upper left)*: Hike to waterfalls, visit a coffee farm, and bird-watch to your heart's content in this mountain town (page 101).

★ **Parque Nacional Natural Tayrona:** Pitch a tent or rent a cabaña on the wilderness coastline of Colombia's most popular natural area (page 104).

★ **Cabo de la Vela** *(upper right)*: Catch the winds over the Caribbean backed by a magical desert landscape full of rich Indigenous traditions (page 118).

Look for ★ to find recommended sights, activities, dining, and lodging.

◂ Cartagena

Magical Cartagena wastes no time in seducing its visitors. Sitting pretty on the edge of the glimmering Caribbean Sea, the majestic walled city is full of magnificent churches and palaces, picturesque balcony-lined streets, and lush plazas. This romantic combo of a historic city and a tropical beach paradise makes Cartagena unrivaled in South America, and it frequently tops lists of the continent's most beautiful and coveted holiday destinations.

Cartagena is also a mecca of cultural heritage, with its roots as a major port during the transatlantic slave trade nurturing a strong musical tradition that allowed for resistance and joy even under the most horrific circumstances. From the drum-driven palenquero dancers to the urban grinding of champeta, Cartagena ranks among other African diaspora hot spots (think New Orleans and Rio de Janeiro) in terms of soul and flow.

Just a stone's throw offshore, the Islas del Rosario are a string of picture-perfect Caribbean islands easily visited by boat on day trips or epic overnight beach getaways. Moving up the coast, the rugged coastline around Parque Nacional Natural Tayrona, the country's most visited natural area, draws those looking for wilderness beaches and offers travelers the chance to chill in the laid-back backpacker meccas of Taganga, Minca, and Palomino.

Farther east, the dramatic desert coastline of La Guajira is home to wilderness beaches and Indigenous Wayúu communities.

Orientation

CARTAGENA

The focus for visitors is on two primary areas: the **Old City,** the original Spanish settlement that was once completely enclosed by massive stone walls, and **Bocagrande,** the beach area that stretches to the west of it. The Old City is divided into the **Centro,** with its magnificent walls, narrow streets, colorful bougainvillea dangling from balconies, activity-packed plazas, and myriad churches and palaces; and **Getsemaní,** the mural-lined former servants quarters that offers a more relaxed counterpart to the Centro, with more bohemian-style lodgings, restaurants, and nightlife options.

Centro and San Diego

The Centro, from *centro histórico,* also called the **Old City** or the **Walled City,** is the historic core of Cartagena and is surrounded by the most impressive sections of the city walls. Most of Cartagena's sights are here, including its most famous churches and museums. Today the Centro is where many upscale hotels, restaurants, shops, and nightclubs are found.

The northeastern half of the Centro is known as **San Diego.** The former home of the middle-class inhabitants of Cartagena, the architecture is more modest but still bursting with style and color. There are a few attractions in San Diego, but the charm of the area lies in its quieter streets and

Cartagena's Old City

Cartagena and the Caribbean Coast

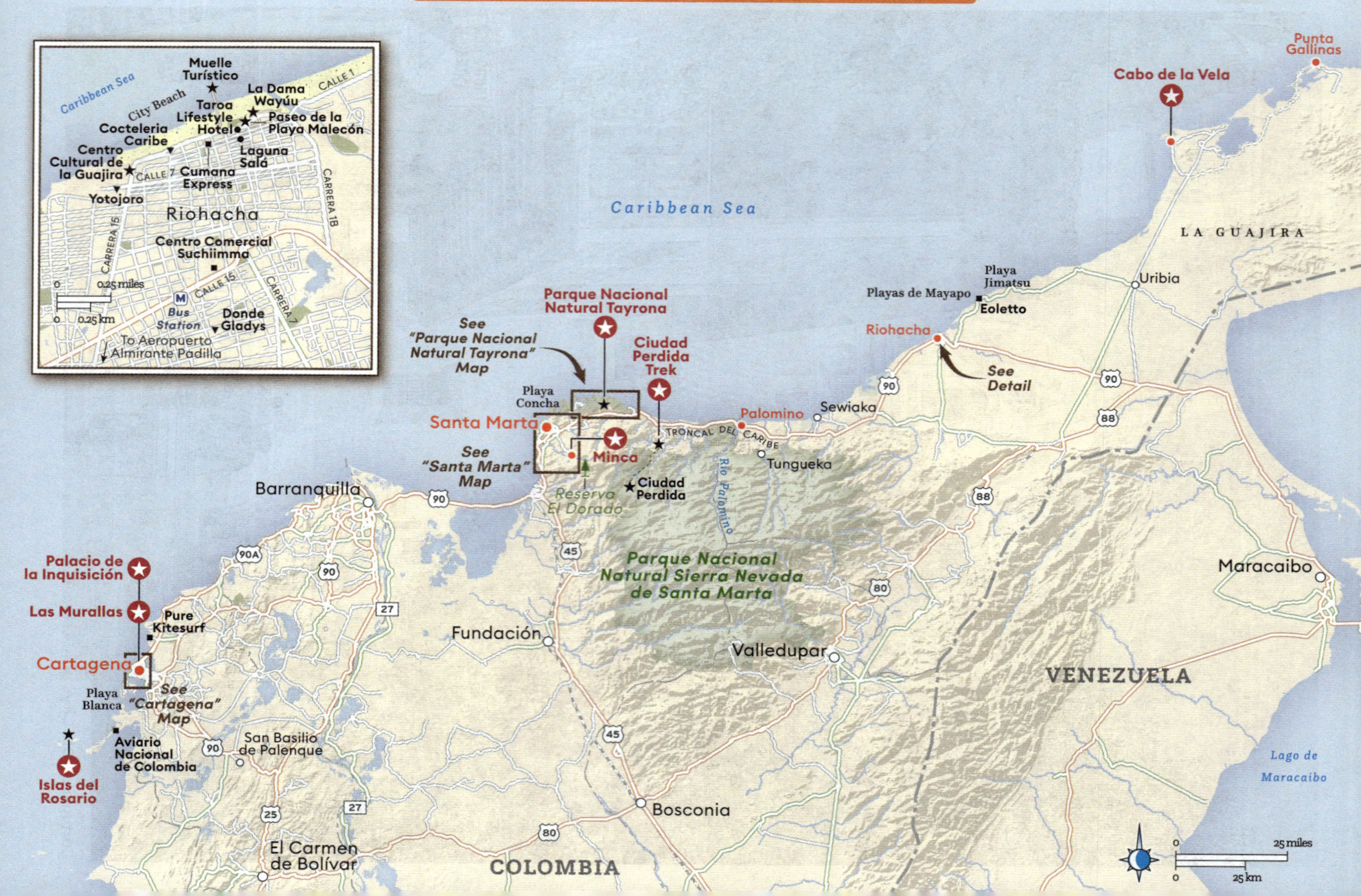

leafy plazas, including Plaza de San Diego, and its high-end restaurants and bars, many tucked into former colonial houses.

The Centro is generally organized in a grid with numerous plazas. Even many residents don't know or use the official street names as they change from block to block. Orient yourself by identifying the main squares—Torre de los Coches, Plaza de la Aduana, Plaza de Santo Domingo, Parque de Bolívar, and Plaza Fernández de Madrid—and make your way from one to the other. Walking these charming streets, and even getting lost on occasion, is a pleasure.

Getsemaní

The neighborhood of Getsemaní lies southeast of the Centro, just outside the main walls. Also walled and just as old as the Centro, it's a bohemian alternative to the Old City, with hip cafés and independent hostels tucked down narrow, winding, mural-lined passageways. The street art here is amazing. The epicenter of the neighborhood is the **Plaza de la Trinidad,** in front of Iglesia de la Santísima Trinidad, where Cartagena's independence was first declared. Backpackers, street artists, palenquero dancers, and locals mingle in the open air over cold beers on a nightly basis.

Between Getsemaní and the Old City are the docks of the Muelle de los Pegasos and the Muelle Turístico de la Bodeguita, the departure point for boats headed to the Islas del Rosario.

Manga

Southeast of Getsemaní, across the Puente Roman (Roman Bridge), is the island of Manga, a historic residential district dotted with gorgeous 19th-century mansions. A handful of hostels have popped up here recently, and it's also home to the landmark Club de Pesca restaurant, housed in the well-preserved Fuerte de San Sebastián del Pastelillo, one of many forts that once protected the bay. The boardwalk along Calle 24, with its magnificent views across the bay, is a pleasant place to walk at sunset.

Bocagrande

South of the Old City is Bocagrande, a skinny peninsula with high-rise hotels, malls, and residential buildings fronting a wide swath of golden sand and the milky-blue Caribbean Sea. The main attraction is the beaches, which get packed on weekends with vacationing Colombian families, vendors, and masseuses. The beaches in no way compare to those of the Islas del Rosario and Barú, but they're close to the city center and easy to enjoy for an afternoon. At the southern end of the Bocagrande peninsula is the Laguito neighborhood, home to more laid-back beaches that are popular with kitesurfers and other water sports enthusiasts. This is also where boats depart for the island of Tierrabomba and its much nicer white-sand beaches.

AROUND CARTAGENA

The Islas del Rosario are just off the coast of Cartagena, and the Barú peninsula, home to Playa Blanca, is just to the south. Santa Marta, the oldest city on the continent, lies three hours east along the coast. From Santa Marta, it's possible to explore the wilderness beaches of Parque Nacional Natural Tayrona, the backpacker hangouts of Taganga, Minca, and Palomino, and the magical desert landscape of La Guajira.

Planning Your Time

Cartagena is so full of sights that it feels like one big sensory indulgence. While a weekend will suffice to wander the streets of the Old City and soak up the history, beauty, and atmosphere, **3-4 days** is ideal, especially if you want to hit the beaches at Playa Blanca or the Islas del Rosario—both require at least a full day and also offer several enticing options for staying the night right at the sand.

Exploring the area of **Santa Marta** and **Parque Nacional Natural Tayrona** requires a little more time, unless you book a tour just to the park from Cartagena. Taganga, Minca, and Palomino each offer enough natural beauty and cool vibes to enchant you into spending multiple nights. Visiting La Guajira means downshifting into slow travel mode, but the red-sand beaches and authentic Wayúu communities are well worth it. Give this area at least **4-5 days.**

Weather in Cartagena is hot and humid year-round, with a distinct rainy season May-October that gets progressively wetter—September-October see constant downpours with possible hurricane warnings.

Safety

The historic **Old City** and **Getsemaní** areas of Cartagena are safe to visit and walk around, even relatively late into the night. This is because they are an island separated from the rest of the sprawling city by a couple of bridges and are well policed. Because the old streets of the center are often packed, however, keep your valuables close to your body. Also stay mindful while walking on the walls after dark, and be careful when leaving this secured area—the rest of Cartagena is one of the most insecure urban landscapes in the country due to high levels of inequality.

By far the greatest annoyances in Cartagena are persistent **street vendors,** who have even been known to latch on to walking tours. Some try to annoy you into buying something to make them go away, probably because that has worked in the past. Saying "No, gracias," and making eye contact instead of ignoring them usually helps ward off these nuisances. Don't allow them to get under your skin.

Most taxi drivers, bartenders, and vendors are honest, but there are always a few who will try to take advantage of visitors by overcharging or not returning the proper amount of change to foreign visitors who may not hold a strong grasp of the language or be confused by the currency. Always try to pay street vendors with small notes or coins when possible—keep those COP$50,000 notes only for emergencies, or break them. Request to see the menu (la carta) at bars and restaurants before ordering. Before getting into a cab, have an idea of what you'll be paying, and confirm the amount with the driver up front.

Itinerary Ideas

Three days is enough for a whirlwind tour of Cartagena. Pack in as much sightseeing, beach time, dining, and nightlife as you can. The San Diego neighborhood makes for a great base for this itinerary.

DAY 1

1 Start the day with a **historic walking tour** of the Old City to get your bearings. Begin at the clocktower and then make your way plaza by plaza, leisurely exploring the enchanting streets, to the San Diego neighborhood.

2 After working up an appetite, grab a taxi to **Playa Hollywood** for lunch at Kiosco El Bony and then spend the rest of the afternoon relaxing on the golden sand.

3 At night, enjoy a Peruvian-Caribbean fusion meal under the lighted spire of the cathedral at **Mar y Zielo.**

4 Afterward, hit up the **Bazurto Social Club** to groove out to champeta with a live band.

Itinerary Ideas

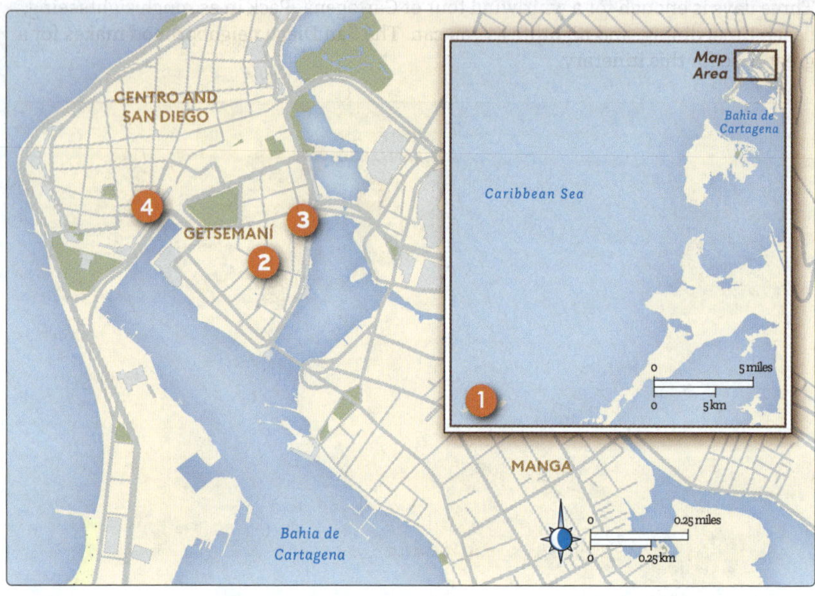

DAY 2

1. Book a day tour to **Isla Grande,** where you will enjoy a freshly caught lunch, sunbathe on the powdered-sugar sand, and snorkel in the crystal-clear Caribbean.

2. Back in the city that evening, head over to the **Plaza de la Trinidad** in Getsemaní to mingle and watch live Afro-Colombian dancers in the plaza.

3. Grab some tasty tapas based on freshly caught fish and other seafood for dinner at **Lunático.**

4. Later, join the fun on the salsa floor at **Donde Fidel.**

Isla Grande beach

street party in Getsemaní

Donde Fidel

DAY 3

1. Spend the morning checking out the **Palacio de la Inquisición** and the Claustro de San Pedro Claver.

2. Grab some street ceviche for lunch, and then do some last-minute souvenir shopping in **Las Bóvedas,** tucked into the city walls, before talking a seafront walk on Las Murallas.

3. Try to time it so that you arrive at **Café del Mar** just before sunset to toast out the end of another glorious day in Caribbean paradise.

4. Feast on creative fusion based on locally caught fare at **Lobo de Mar.**

5. If you still have more energy, head to the rooftop party at **Alquímico** to sweat it out.

Sights

 TOP EXPERIENCE

★ Las Murallas

One of the most salient features of the city, Cartagena's murallas (walls) provide epic views over Cartagena and the Caribbean Sea. A walk on the walls is a quintessential Cartagena experience, enjoyed by international visitors, Colombian honeymooners, and local high school students alike. The best time for this is in the early evening hours around sunset, when the sky casts its fiery spell over the turquoise water. Vendors sell cold beers along the wall at this time, and couples cuddle up to witness the impressive natural spectacle.

This is the largest series of fortifications in South America. The walls were built by the Spaniards after Sir Francis Drake sacked the city in 1568 in an effort to guard the gold and other goods they'd stolen from Indigenous people in Colombia. The project took almost two centuries to complete. The walls that can be seen today are mostly from the 17th-18th centuries.

The most impressive section is the stretch that runs along the Old City parallel to the sea. This includes three baluartes (bulwarks or ramparts) where Spaniards stood ready to defend the city from attack. The massive **Baluartes de San Lucas y de Santa Catalina,** built in the very north of the city to repel attacks from land, are known as Las Tenazas because they're shaped like pincers. About midway along the seafront wall is the equally impressive **Baluarte Santo Domingo,** now home to swank **Café del Mar,** where you can take it all in over a cocktail. At the southern tip of the segment facing the sea, next to the Plaza de Santa Teresa, are the **Baluartes de San Ignacio y de San Francisco Javier,** home to several other bars and lounges.

Centro and San Diego

LA CATEDRAL DE SANTA CATALINA DE ALEJANDRÍA

Calle de los Santos de Piedra, Carrera 4; no phone; mass 6am, noon, and 6:15pm Mon.-Fri., 6:30pm Sat., 8am, 10am, 6pm, and 7pm Sun.

Cartagena's most magnificent church, La Catedral de Santa Catalina de Alejandría can be seen from just about anywhere in the city thanks to its ornate domed tower, lit up with tropical colors at night. Built in 1577, it lies kitty-corner from Parque de Bolívar and contains an 18th-century gilded altar and a marble pulpit.

CLAUSTRO DE SAN PEDRO CLAVER

Plaza de San Pedro Claver No. 30-01; tel. 5/664-4991; www.sanpedroclaver.co; 8am-6pm Mon.-Fri., 8am-5pm Sat.-Sun.; COP$14,000

An outstanding example of colonial architectural majesty, the Claustro de San Pedro Claver is a massive former Jesuit monastery turned three-story museum. Saint Pedro Claver served here as a priest. The first person to be canonized as a saint in the New World, he fought for the rights of newly arrived enslaved Africans in Cartagena, calling himself the "slave of the slaves."

Cartagena
Caribbean Sea
90A
Calle 70
Rafael Núñez International Airport
Carrera 1
Ciénaga de Tesca
Carrera 14
Berlinas
Marsol
Las Murallas
See "Centro and San Diego" Map
Carrera 17
Centro and San Diego
Av. Pedro de Heredia
Palacio de la Inquisición
Getsemaní
Castillo de San Felipe
La Popa
Convento Nuestra Señora de la Candelaria
Restaurante Shwarma Khala
See "Getsemaní" Map
Club de Pesca
Calle 25
Manga
Calle 29
Veleros Colombia
Tourist Information Kiosk
Mercado de Bazurto
Carrera 2
Bocagrande
Av. Pedro de Heredia
Bocagrande
Kiosco el Bony
Playa Hollywood
Hotel Caribe
Hospital Universitario de Cartagena
Cartagena Kitesurf School
Bahia de Cartagena
Punta Arena
Namaste Beach Club
0
0.5 miles
0
0.5 km

clockwise clocktower and entrance to the walled Old City; monkey in Parque del Centenario; view from Palacio de la Inquisición

Claver is said to have baptized hundreds of thousands of enslaved people as well as personally attended to their medical needs. In addition to encompassing a spacious lush courtyard brimming with flowers and trees, the museum holds relics and art from the colonial era on the 1st floor, memorials to Saint Claver on the 2nd, including the Spartan little room where he lived and prayed, and an impressive collection of African and Afro-Colombian art on the 3rd.

Adjacent to the monastery is the towering **Iglesia de San Pedro Claver** (Plaza de San Pedro Claver No. 30-01; tel. 5/664-4991; mass 6:45am and 6pm Mon.-Sat., 7am, 10am, noon, and 6pm Sun.). Its majestic dome is one of the most prominent features of the ancient Cartagena skyline. Inside lies a beautiful marble altar, the final resting place for Saint Pedro Claver.

MUSEO DE ARTE MODERNO DE CARTAGENA DE INDIAS

Calle 30 No. 4-08, Plaza de San Pedro Claver; tel. 5/664-5815; www.mamcartagena.org; 9am-noon and 3pm-7pm Tues.-Fri., 11am-5pm Sat.-Sun.; COP$25,000

Cartagena's main art museum, the Museo de Arte Moderno de Cartagena de Indias, is on the square in front of Plaza de San Pedro Claver, which contains several metallic sculptures by Cartagenero Edgardo Carmona that depict quotidian scenes of Cartagena life. The museum has a small permanent collection of works from 20th-century Colombian artists, including native sons Alejandro Obregón and Enrique Grau. The museum is in the old Customs House.

★ PALACIO DE LA INQUISICIÓN

Parque de Bolívar; tel. 5/664-4570; www.muhca.gov.co; 9am-6pm Mon.-Sat., 10am-4pm Sun.; COP$21,000

On the south side of Parque de Bolívar is the Palacio de la Inquisición. This remarkable 18th-century structure, one of the grandest examples of colonial architecture in the city, was the headquarters of the Spanish Inquisition in Cartagena. The building housed the Tribunal del Santo Oficio, whose purpose was to exert control over Indigenous people, mestizos, and enslaved Africans not only in Nueva Granada but also in New World colonies in Central America, the Caribbean, and Venezuela. One of just three Palaces of Inquisition in the Americas (the others were in Lima and Mexico City), the tribunal was active from 1610 until the late 17th century.

The building's 1st floor is a museum displaying the weapons of torture employed by authorities as part of the Inquisition. In Cartagena as elsewhere, the most common punishable crime was "witchcraft," which could mean anything from practicing African religious rites to owning the wrong books, including science books that didn't align with church doctrine. Hundreds of supposed heretics were condemned here and dozens put to death. On the 2nd floor are exhibition spaces dedicated to the restoration of the building and to the history of Cartagena. Most explanations are written in Spanish; you may hire an English-speaking guide (COP$55,000 for a group up to 5). On your way out, take a right and then another right onto Calle de la Inquisición and look for a small window on the palace wall. This was a secret spot where citizens of colonial Cartagena could anonymously report others for various and sundry heresies.

Caribbean Sea
AV. SANTANDER
Las Bóvedas
La Comunión
CARRERA 10
Marzola Parrilla Argentina
Sofitel Legend Santa Clara
El Coro
La Serrezuela
Juan del Mar
CALLE 39
Las Murallas
La Cevichería
Cuba 1940
Diving Planet
CARRERA 2
Casa la Cartujita
3 Banderas
CARRERA 6
Ego
Lobo de Mar
Carmen
CALLE 38
CALLE 38
CENTRO AND SAN DIEGO
El Santísimo
CARRERA 9
CALLE DE DON SANCHO
CARRERA 5
Hotel Boutique Santo Toribio
Townhouse Boutique Hotel
La Mulata
Cartagena Insider
Anandá
Hostal Badillo
CALLE 36
Bettina Spitz
Casa San Agustín
AV. VENEZUELA
CALLE 36
Crazy Salsa
Abaco Libros
CL. DE LA IGLESIA
CARRERA 7
CALLE 35
Casa Blue
CARRERA 3
Café del Mar
PLAYA DE LA ARTILLERÍA
Gelateria Tramonti
Mar y Zielo
Casa Movida
CALLE 35
La Catedral de Santa Catalina de Alejandría
Artesanías de Colombia
St. Dom
Alquímico
Eivissa
Le Petit Club
CALLE 32
CALLE 33
Museo del Oro Zenú
Plaza de los Coches
Palacio de la Inquisición
Tourist Information Kiosk
Parque de Centenario
Folklore Colombian Café
Donde Fidel
CARRERA 9
CARRERA 10
CALLE 32
Hotel Charleston Santa Teresa
Paseo de los Mártires
La Movida
Claustro de San Pedro Claver
Iglesia de San Pedro Claver
CALLE MEDIA LUNA
AV. BLAS DE LEZO
Patio de Banderas Centro de Convenciones
Museo de Arte Moderno de Cartagena de Indias
CALLE 25
AV. SANTANDER
CALLE 24
0
100 yds
0
100 m

MUSEO DEL ORO ZENÚ

Carrera 4 No. 33-26, Parque de Bolívar; tel. 5/660-0778; 9am-5pm Tues.-Sat., 9am-1pm Sun.; free

The Museo del Oro Zenú, on the east side of Parque de Bolívar, exhibits gold jewelry and funerary objects from the Indigenous Zenú people, who were the original inhabitants of the Río Magdalena area and Río Sinú valley, southwest of Cartagena. It has excellent explanations in both English and Spanish. A smaller version of the Museo del Oro in Bogotá, this museum has a regional focus and is one of the few tributes to Indigenous culture in Cartagena.

Getsemaní

IGLESIA DE LA SANTÍSIMA TRINIDAD

Plaza de la Trinidad; tel. 5/664-2050; mass 6pm Mon.-Sat., 9am and 6pm Sun.

The Iglesia de la Santísima Trinidad, completed in the mid-17th century, consists of three naves and is modeled on the city's cathedral. The church is often open during the day, and visitors are welcome to sit on a pew in front of a massive fan and cool off. In the evenings the colorful Plaza de la Trinidad is a hub of activity.

statue of San Pedro Claver by Enrique Grau

PASEO DE LOS MÁRTIRES AND PARQUE DEL CENTENARIO

Paseo de los Mártires was once the main corridor that led from the Walled City to Getsemaní and today features nine marble statues of important historical figures. Adjacent to the corridor is Parque del Centenario, opened in 1911 in commemoration of Colombia's first century of independence. It's a pleasant place for a stroll, and you just might spot enormous iguanas, small monkeys, or even a sloth up in the trees. On the northern edge of the park is a series of stalls where vendors sell used books.

Greater Cartagena

CASTILLO DE SAN FELIPE

Cerro de San Lázaro, east of the Old City; tel. 5/656-6803; www.patrimoniodecartagena.com; 8am-6pm daily; COP$33,000

The largest Spanish fort on the continent, the magnificent Castillo de San Felipe must have given pirates pause as they contemplated an attack on the city. While the walls around the city fended off maritime attacks, this fort was built atop the Cerro de San Lázaro to repel attacks by land at the Media Luna gate. Construction was begun in 1639 and completed more than a century later. Tunnels enabled soldiers to quickly move around without being noticed, and cells housed the occasional unlucky prisoner.

Today, visitors ramble through 890 m (0.6 mi) of tunnels and secret passages

(a flashlight will come in handy). Views from the highest points of the fort are magnificent. The best time to visit is late afternoon, when the intense sun abates. Audio tours (COP$10,000) are available. For some, the view of the fort from a distance suffices, especially at nighttime when it's lit up. To get here, take a taxi (COP$20,000) from in front of the Torre de Reloj just outside the Old City.

LA POPA

La Popa is a 150-m-high (500-ft) hill east of Castillo de San Felipe, so named because of its resemblance to a ship's popa (stern). Panoramic views await of Cartagena below and the Caribbean stretching to the horizon. You can take a taxi here from the Old City for COP$60,000-80,000 round-trip. Arrange the fare in advance and make sure the driver will wait for you. Many visitors combine a visit to La Popa with the Castillo de San Felipe, which is relatively nearby, although not within walking distance.

Convento Nuestra Señora de la Candelaria

Carrera 20A 29D-16; tel. 5/666-0976; 9am-5:30pm daily; COP$12,000

La Popa is home to the Convento Nuestra Señora de la Candelaria, built by Augustinian monks, reportedly on a site of pagan worship. The monastery has a courtyard abloom with flowers, a small chapel where the faithful pray to the Virgen de la Candelaria, and memorabilia from Pope John Paul II's visit to the monastery in 1986. Cruise ship passengers arrive by the busload at La Popa, so be prepared for crowds.

MERCADO DE BAZURTO

Av. Pedro Heredia; 5am-4pm daily

Not for the faint of heart, a visit to the sprawling Mercado de Bazurto is the best way to connect with workaday Cartagena. Be sure to peruse the seafood area on the waterfront periphery of this covered market, where women sell the catch of the day to restaurateurs. You'll also be amazed at all the different kinds of fruit on offer. Don't be afraid to barter a little, and don't be shy: The hundreds of vendors generally enjoy interacting with foreign visitors. The market is at its liveliest in the morning, but it's also a great place to grab lunch; expect to spend a few hours here. Dress down and keep an eye on your valuables.

The market is in the Pie de la Popa neighborhood southeast of the Old City. The best way to get here is by taxi (COP$20,000). It's possible to take a bus (COP$2,200) from Avenida Santander, and there is also a TransCaribe rapid bus station here. **Beyond Colombia** (tel. 322/898-8557; https://beyondcolombia.com) offers a tour of the market (4 hours; 10am daily;

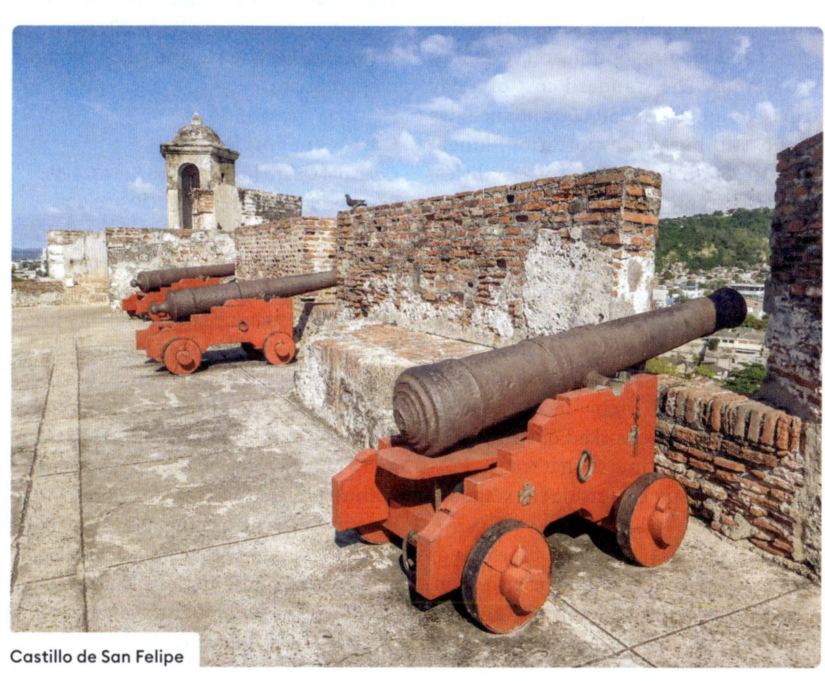

Castillo de San Felipe

COP$195,000) that includes transportation from your hotel and an in-depth look at the local fruits, vegetables, and cuisine of the Caribbean region.

★ Islas del Rosario

Part of Parque Nacional Natural Corales del Rosario y San Bernardo, the 25-plus small coral islands of the Islas del Rosario, about 25 km (16 mi) southwest of Cartagena and just off the shore of Playa Blanca, are a marine wonderland. The islands encompass spectacular white-sand beaches and crystalline Caribbean water and feel remote, even though they're just an hour's boat ride from the city. Many of the smaller islands are private, home to Colombian celebrities like Shakira and Carlos Vives, who each own their own islands, but much of this paradise is public and by far makes the best day trip or overnight escape from Cartagena.

Hotels and small resorts offer day passes and lodging options on several of the islands. The standard cost of a day trip is around COP$250,000 and includes round-trip boat transportation, lunch, and use of all hotel or resort facilities. Day trips typically depart at 8am and return by 5pm. These trips are available from any tour agency in town or at the port of Muelle Turístico de la Bodeguita. Many of the hotels rent out kayaks, snorkeling equipment, and Jet Skis, and most have on-site bars. Spending the night on the islands is also highly recommended, but this should be worked out with your lodging ahead of time so that transportation can be arranged outside the standard day tours.

Isla Grande is the largest of the islands and has the most options for visitation, whether you're day-tripping or overnighting. Some tours island-hop, but it's better to spend the day lounging in one beautiful spot rather than bouncing around among the islands. Most day-trippers have lunch included in their tours, and most overnight visitors have food included in their accommodations. There are also some very informal local eateries on the island.

Sightseeing Tours

Beyond Colombia

tel. 312/441-3171; www.beyondcolombia.com; tips

Beyond Colombia offers free walking tours of the Old City (10am and 4pm daily) and Getsemaní (10am daily) as well as food tours (4pm daily) that meet at the *Noli Me Tángere* statue in the middle of the Camellón de los Mártires plaza, just outside the Torre del Reloj and the Old City, in front of the Muelle de los Pegasos. They're easy to find; look for their red umbrellas. Tours last about two hours and are led by locals, who request a COP$50,000 donation at the end. Feel free to give what you think is appropriate.

Cartagena Insider

Calle del Quero No. 9-64; tel. 5/643-4185; www.insider.com.co; from COP$120,000

A fundraising project for the nonprofit FEM (www.femcolombia.org), Cartagena Insider takes visitors beyond the boutique hotels and fancy restaurants of the Old City to experience the "real" Cartagena and its people. Tour options include a night of salsa, a day trip to La Boquilla fishing community, a walking tour of the Mercado de Bazurto, and a tour focusing on the champeta music culture unique to Cartagena. Proceeds go directly to the nonprofit's social programs in and around the city. Tours can also be arranged to communities such as Tuchín, Córdoba, Leticia on Barú, Palmarito, and San Basilio de Palenque.

Recreation

Beaches

Cartagena boasts a seaside location with wide swaths of city beaches.

The **Bocagrande peninsula** runs west from the Old City and is lined with gray-sand beaches packed with Colombian families and plied by vendors and masseuses. Umbrella and chair rentals (around COP$23,000 pp) are required for using the beaches along Bocagrande.

Playa Hollywood

At the far southwestern end of Bocagrande is a gay-friendly section called Playa Hollywood, which also attracts those still partying from the night before. Beyond this point, the beach hangs a sharp left to the south and merges into the beaches of the Laguito neighborhood, where there are some waterfront restaurants as well as kitesurfing and windsurfing rentals.

Punta Arena

From Laguito you can get to the beaches on the nearby island of Tierrabomba, including Punta Arena, which has panoramic views over the modern high-rises of Cartagena; colectivo boats (COP$12,000) depart from in front of the Nuevo Hospital de Bocagrande. The water is clearer here than on the mainland and the crowds are much thinner than at either Bocagrande or Playa Blanca, making this an excellent option for a quality beach break. Punta Arena is also home to several resorts that offer day passes (COP$40,000) that include use of beach chairs and restrooms.

Playa Blanca

Lapped by bright blue turquoise water, Playa Blanca is on the Barú peninsula about an hour southwest of Cartagena. It's popular with Colombian travelers and gets very crowded; vendors are a constant presence. Be careful of masseuses who begin massaging you without permission: If you don't ask them to stop right away, they'll ask for money.

Playa Blanca is lined with simply styled accommodations with on-site restaurants, most charging about COP$80,000-150,000 d in high season. Most of these hotels double as beachfront restaurants serving the day crowds. The food offered on Playa Blanca is mostly freshly caught fish and is overpriced but delicious. Most visitors will have lunch included in the price of the day tour. If it's not included, expect to pay around COP$45,000 for lunch. Try negotiating for the use of the beach facilities for the rest of the day if you eat at a venue.

At the southern end of Playa Blanca is slightly more laid-back **Playa Tranquilo.** You can walk there in about 30 minutes or take a mototaxi (COP$7,000) from Playa Blanca.

The most common way to get to Playa Blanca is by bus on a day tour (8am daily; COP$100,000). These tours pick you up at your hotel in Cartagena and have you back by 5pm-6pm. Tours usually include a basic lunch on the beach. Some tour companies combine visits to Playa Blanca with some of the closer Islas del Rosario, especially Cholón, where semi-submerged bars serve overpriced cocktails and yachts pull up and blast music. A taxi from Cartagena costs COP$80,000-100,000 one-way, making joining a tour more attractive.

Punta Arena on Tierrabomba

Playa Blanca on the Barú peninsula

Bird-Watching

Aviario Nacional de Colombia

Km 14.5, Vía Barú; tel. 322/552-9134; www.aviarionacional.co; 9am-5pm daily; COP$80,000

If you are visiting Playa Blanca, consider stopping by the Aviario Nacional de Colombia, also on the Barú peninsula. The aviary is a mecca to see up close Colombia's incredible birds, the greatest diversity in the world. The aviary is home to nearly 200 endemic species, including the scarlet ibis and harpy eagle, and its 22 exhibits cover ecosystems that include mangrove forests, tropical rainforests, and desert.

Diving

Diving Planet

Calle Estanco del Aguardiente No. 5-09; tel. 5/660-0450; www.divingplanet.org; 8am-7pm Mon.-Sat.

Diving Planet offers classes and diving excursions to 25 locations throughout Parque Nacional Natural Corales del Rosario y San Bernardo. A two-day basic course costs USD$695 and the PADI training costs COP$1,200,000. Snorkeling and fun dives for certified divers are also available (from COP$150,000).

Sailing

Veleros Colombia

Carrera 23 No. 24-32; tel. 316/528-2413; www.veleroscolombia.com; 8 hours from COP$1,500,000

It doesn't get much better than renting a 13-m (43-ft) catamaran with a captain and crew and sailing around Cartagena and its nearby islands. Veleros Colombia can make that happen. It also rents out a variety of other sailboats for those who know the ropes. In addition they offer sailing courses along the Caribbean coast as well as diving excursions in the Islas del Rosario and the Islas de San Bernardo.

Biking

The best time to explore Cartagena by bike is early on Sunday morning or Sunday-Monday evening, when there is little activity and light traffic in the Old City. Many hostels and some hotels have bicycles for rent.

Bicitour Getsemaní

Calle Don Sancho, Ed. Aqua Marina; tel. 300/357-1825; COP$5,000 per hour

Bicitour Getsemaní rents out bikes and offers guided tours of the Old City, Manga, and Bocagrande.

Kitesurfing

Pure Kitesurf

Manzanillo; tel. 321/521-5110; www.purekitesurf.com

About half an hour's drive northeast of Cartagena, along the beaches of the Manzanillo neighborhood, the Swiss-run Pure Kitesurf offers kitesurfing classes with instruction available in Spanish, English, and German. Private instruction costs USD$60 per hour. A six-day all-inclusive Kite Safari tour of the Caribbean coast to La Guajira costs USD$999.

Cartagena Kitesurf School

Carrera 1B No. 1-52, Laguito; tel. 300/461-9947; https://kitesurfcartagena.odoo.com

Cartagena Kitesurf School offers a basic 10-hour course (COP$1,200,000) and a two-hour course (COP$280,000). If wind conditions are not adequate, the school will transport students up the coast to Puerto Velero, where there's always a good breeze. While the school is located in the Laguito section of Bocagrande, most classes take place on the beaches of Hotel Las Américas.

OVERNIGHTING ON A CARIBBEAN ISLAND

The white-sand beaches and turquoise waters of Barú, Tierrabomba, and the Islas del Rosario can all easily be visited by day trip from the city, but spending a night or two right on the edge of the shimmering Caribbean Sea is truly divine.

Gente de Mar

ISLAS DEL ROSARIO

Most of the accommodation options in the Islas del Rosario are located on **Isla Grande,** but you may also find houses on smaller private islands available for rent through agencies in Cartagena.

- ★ **Gente de Mar** (Isla Grande; Cartagena office: Calle Gastelbondo, No. 103; tel. 5/674-2553; www.gentedemar.co; COP$880,000 d): This tropical paradise is near several picture-perfect coves with beaches. The 21 rooms open onto an outdoor seating area next to the on-site restaurant and bar. Food is included.
- **Hotel San Pedro de Majagua** (Isla Grande; Cartagena office: Calle del Torno No. 39-114; tel. 5/650-4464; www.hotelmajagua.com; COP$1,064,000 d): This hotel offers deluxe rooms and full and junior suites with private hammock-strung patios. Food is included.
- **EcoHotel Las Palmeras** (Isla Grande; tel. 314/584-7358; COP$45,000 dorm, COP$89,000 d): Run by the native islander community, this ecohotel is an economical and culturally fascinating option, but

it requires a bit more independent exploration. Located inland, it's a few minutes from the beaches on foot or bicycle. Local-style meals (about COP$35,000) are available.

BARÚ

Many of the local-style restaurants that lined the beach at **Playa Blanca** double as hotels, but several options farther down the beach tend to be more tranquilo:

- **Media Luna Hostel** (Playa Bobo; tel. 313/536-3146; www.medialunahostel.com; COP$50,000 dorm, COP$120,000 d): Best known for its location in Cartagena, Media Luna Hostel also owns a chill beachside hostel at the southern tip of Barú. It consists of five two-story thatched-roof cabañas fronting the beach. The hostel takes care of round-trip transportation (COP$60,000) from its Getsemaní location, or you can opt for a backpacker-friendly all-inclusive deal that comes with meals (COP$150,000).
- **Aura Hotel Barú** (Ensenada del Cholón, Km. 26; tel. 314/506-6520; www.aurahotelbaru.com; COP$800,000 d): Aura Hotel Barú is nestled among the mangroves on the quiet side of the Cholón lagoon. There are three cabins with multiple rooms each for rent; all 16 or so of them are comfortable. A visit here usually includes lounging on the beach in front of the hotel or at Playa Azul, a small uninhabited island that's just a quick boat ride away.

TIERRABOMBA

Recently, a cluster of hotels have popped up on the island of Tierrabomba, many of them right on the sands of **Punta Arena.**

- **Namaste Beach Club** (Punta Arena; tel. 300/678-0848; www.namastebeachclub.com; COP$380,000 d): The upscale, holistically themed Namaste Beach Club is where you can lounge around on couch beds, drink smoothies on the sand, and even catch a yoga class. The onsite restaurant offers both vegetarian and freshly caught seafood items.

Playa Blanca

Entertainment and Events

Dance Classes

Crazy Salsa

Carrera 8 No. 8-85, Ed. Banco Santander, Ofc. 302; https://crazysalsa.net

With daily morning and evening classes in bachata, champeta, and several styles of salsa, Crazy Salsa is your one-stop shop to learn to dance to Caribbean rhythms. Located just two blocks from the clocktower, they also throw parties most nights and host live bands on the weekends.

Festivals and Events

Cartagena feels like a celebration all the time, but it's especially true November-February, when an array of cultural events are featured. Pick up a copy of *Donde*, a free monthly newspaper with Cartagena event listings. You can find it at the airport and in big hotels.

Hay Festival

www.hayfestival.com; Jan.-Feb.; prices vary

The international Hay Festival began in Wales in the 1980s. It celebrates literature, music, environmental awareness, and community and is held in various cities across the world, including in Cartagena. Bill Clinton called it the "Woodstock of the mind." In addition to talks and concerts, the festival holds educational programs for youth in the city's neighborhoods, and provides free or discounted tickets to students. Most events take place in the **Teatro Heredia** (Calle de la Chichería No. 38-10; tel. 5/664-6023 or 5/664-9631). While the festival's name is pronounced as the English *hay*, in Colombia it's often pronounced as the Spanish *hay* ("ai"). Hay Festival is thus a double entendre: *hay festival* in Spanish means "Yes, there is a festival!"

Festival Internacional de Cine de Cartagena de Indias

tel. 5/664-2345; www.ficcifestival.com; Feb.; free-COP$20,000

If you're in town during late February, the Festival Internacional de Cine de Cartagena de Indias is an excuse to escape the heat. A tradition since the 1960s, this weeklong film festival has a program of documentaries, international and Colombian films, and shorts. A series of roundtable discussions with prominent actors and directors along with educational activities take place in neighborhoods throughout the city, including historic buildings and plazas.

Carnaval of Independencia

Nov.; free

While the massive Carnaval two hours east in Barranquilla gets lots of write-ups, Cartagena was the original site of Colombia's Caribbean Carnaval celebrations. When the upstart Barranquilla took over as the coast's primary port and economic engine, the festival went with it. But Cartagena still throws the happening Carnaval of Independencia in the weeks leading up to November 11, the day the city declared its independence from Spain in 1811, eight years before the rest of the country did the same. During the day, dancers in bright colors accompany huge floats featuring live musical acts down Avenida Santander, which fronts the Caribbean Sea. At night the streets are full of raucous parties, especially around the Plaza de los Coches in Centro and Calle Media Luna in Getsemaní. The festival ends with a beauty contest that crowns the Queen of Cartagena.

Shopping

Cartagena is made for walking around and sometimes feels like you're on a movie set. The Centro is full of boutiques, many from Colombia's top designers, ready to dress you for the part.

Centro and San Diego

CRAFTS

Las Bóvedas

San Diego, northeastern corner of Las Murallas; 9am-6pm daily

The most historic place to pick up some Colombian handicrafts is Las Bóvedas. Once a military storehouse, today it's the place to buy multicolored hammocks and all kinds of Colombian artesanías (handicrafts) of varying quality.

Artesanías de Colombia

La Serrezuela, Local L-312; tel. 5/642-1785; 11am-9pm Sun.-Thurs., 11am-10pm Fri.-Sat.

Artesanías de Colombia is a government-run shop that only stocks the highest-quality handmade crafts from across the country. Intricately woven palm-frond furniture and hats are available as well as colorful home decorations.

CLOTHING

Ego

Calle Sargento Mayor 38 No. 6-107; tel. 5/668-6016; 9am-5pm Mon.-Fri.

For men, nothing says Cartagena chic like a crisp linen shirt or a Cuban-style guayabera. The typical guayabera has two vertical embroidered stripes and four pockets and can be worn to a wedding or special event, or even out to dinner at one of the elegant restaurants of the Old City. Tailor Edgar Gómez of Ego purportedly once made guayaberas for Bill Gates and the king of Spain.

Bettina Spitz

Calle de la Mantilla No. 3-37; tel. 5/660-2160; www.bettinaspitz.com; 11am-1pm and 2pm-8pm daily

Along Calle Santo Domingo are several boutiques of top Colombian designers focused on women's fashion. Bogotana Bettina Spitz sells casual, beach, and formal clothes for women as well as an array of accessories, shoes, and some men's items.

St. Dom

Calle de Santo Domingo No. 33-70; tel. 5/664-0197; 10am-8pm Mon.-Sat., noon-6pm Sun.

St. Dom is a boutique that brings together Colombian designers of accessories, clothing, handbags, and jewelry. It also has a beachfront location in Bocagrande (Calle 2 No. 15-63; tel. 5/655-2542; 10am-6pm daily).

BOOKSTORES

Abaco Libros

Calle de la Mantilla; tel. 5/664-8290; 9am-9pm Mon.-Sat., 3pm-9pm Sun.

Abaco Libros is a cozy bookshop and café with a variety of books on Cartagena, top Colombian novels, and a selection of magazines, classics, and bestsellers in English.

SHOPPING CENTERS

La Serrezuela

Carrera 11 No. 39-21; www.plazalaserrezuela.com; 9am-11pm daily

Once a bullfighting ring, La Serrezuela is an architectural masterpiece of a shopping mall, with high-end boutiques circling

hats for sale in Cartagena

the historic arena and cafés and restaurants opening onto several levels of terraces overlooking the city and seascapes. It's a great place to escape the afternoon heat and enjoy a Colombian coffee at local chains like Juan Valdez and Café Quindío in an elegant atmosphere with spectacular views.

Food

Street food is varied in Cartagena and quite inexpensive. There's no better refreshment than a cold **agua de coco** (coconut water), straight from the fruit itself. Street snacks, popular in the late morning, late afternoon, or late at night, are called **fritos** (COP$5,000-7,000). They include items like **arepa de huevo** (fried eggs in a corn arepa), **carimañola** (fried yuca-flour pastry with cheese and meat), and seafood empanadas. For a sweet bite, head to the Portal de las Dulces, a traditional sweets market near the Torre del Reloj, and try a **cocada,** made from coconut and raw sugar.

This Is Cartagena (www.ticartagena.com) offers a reservation service for many of the city's top restaurants.

Centro and San Diego

COLOMBIAN

La Mulata

Calle Quero No. 9-58; tel. 5/664-6222; noon-10pm Mon.-Sat.; COP$22,000-58,000

La Mulata specializes in Cartagena cuisine. Seafood dishes feature a perfect mound of coconut rice topped with a thin crispy slice of fried plantain to add some height to the presentation. Decorated with names of regional dishes, the restaurant walls provide a vocabulary lesson on Caribbean cuisine. Try the coconut lemonade.

La Cevichería

Calle Stuart No. 7-14; tel. 5/660-1492; 1pm-10:30pm daily; COP$32,000-60,000

Some of the freshest ceviche in town is served at La Cevichería. The restaurant has a creative menu featuring options with mango and coconut. It's located on a quiet street with pleasant outdoor seating. Get a little taste of everything by ordering the Miss-Cellanea ceviche sampler. You can also pick up a T-shirt at its little shop.

★ La Comunión

Calle de las Bóvedas No. 39-116; tel. 5/645-5301; noon-10:30pm daily; COP$36,000-60,000

The Pacific and Caribbean coasts of Colombia unite at La Comunión, housed in a cheerfully decorated space. Chef Charlie Otero spent years researching the coastlines to come up with this unique menu that features items like black tamales filled with octopus and squid and a salad made from chontaduro, a savory palm fruit said to have aphrodisiac powers.

Juan del Mar

Plaza de San Diego No. 8-12; tel. 5/664-2782; www.juandelmar.com; 12:30pm-1am daily; COP$38,000-85,000

Juan del Mar is run by a former Colombian actor and model turned chef. His namesake restaurant does fresh Caribbean-style ceviche and traditional dishes like the mofongo Caribeño, a stewed meat and plantain dish that's popular from Cuba to Puerto Rico as well as on the Colombian Caribbean coast. Right next door he also has a pizzeria, and across the plaza is his Peruvian fusion joint. Since they all have outside seating, Plaza de San Diego might have to rename itself after him at some point.

★ El Santísimo

Calle del Torno No. 39-62; tel. 5/660-1531; www.elsantisimo.com; noon-11pm daily; COP$55,000-90,000

Open since 1998, El Santísimo is one of Cartagena's original fine-dining restaurants and has elevated Caribbean cuisine to an art form. It remains popular and is a great place to indulge in thoughtful takes on Cartagena standards like cazuela de mariscos (seafood stew) in coconut milk. The decor has a religious theme, with candles and an austere interior design.

CARIBBEAN FUSION

★ Lobo de Mar

Calle del Santísimo No. 8-15; tel. 318/615-0434; 12:30pm-3pm and 7pm-11pm daily; COP$45,000-60,000

Lobo de Mar is a stylish Mediterranean-Caribbean restaurant owned by the same local team behind discos La Movida and La Jugada Club House. Well-prepared plates include mixed seafood paella and slow-cooked pork ribs, while the trendy bar up front attracts a crowd for cocktails and light bites. If you dine here, ask for a pass to one of the clubs.

★ Mar y Zielo

Carrera 5 34-63; tel. 317/391-1393; www.maryzielo.com; noon-4pm and 7pm-11pm Sun.-Thurs., noon-4pm and 7pm-midnight Fri.-Sat.; COP$45,000-110,000

Seafood meets the Andes at Mar y Zielo, a fusion restaurant owned and managed by Peruvian chef Mariano Cerna. One of the most visually stunning restaurants in the city, it's located in the Casa de la Escribana, a historic mansion. The elegantly decked-out dining room hosts live Latin music nightly as well as a rooftop terrace fantastically perched right under La Catedral de Santa Catalina de Alejandría, which is lit up at night. The food is as good as the ambience, with plates like the Caribbean tiradito (Peruvian-style sashimi) smothered in leche de tigre (the lime-and-fish juice left over from ceviche) and pumpkin puree, securing the restaurant's reputation as one of the best Colombian-Peruvian marriages on the continent.

Carmen

Calle de Santísimo, Calle 38 No. 8-19; tel. 5/664-5116; www.carmencartagena.com; noon-3pm and 6pm-11pm Mon.-Tues., noon-11pm Wed.-Sun.; à la carte COP$65,000-85,000

Fabulous Carmen blends Caribbean with Asian and Middle Eastern cuisine, offering a five-course tasting menu (COP$189,000) that includes wine hand-selected by a Cordon Bleu-certified chef trained in San Francisco, California. An à la carte menu is also available. Impeccable service and an unforgettable meal await. Seating is indoors or out on the patio. Reservations are required.

INTERNATIONAL

★ Marzola Parrilla Argentina

Carrera 7 No. 38; tel. 5/660-2403; noon-midnight daily; COP$55,000-88,000

The mischievous smiles of tango crooners like Carlos Gardel watch over diners at Marzola Parrilla Argentina. A small menu lists only the essentials: a trio of thick juicy steaks done Buenos Aires-style and two high-quality bottles of wine from the Mendoza region of Argentina. The house-made chimichurri sauce comes in both classic green and paprika-infused red; be sure to ask for both.

CAFÉS, BAKERIES, AND QUICK BITES

Folklore Colombian Cafe

Calle 32 No. 4-17; tel. 5/668-5057; www.folklorecolombiancafe.com; 7:30am-8:30pm daily; COP$8,000

Beans from top coffee regions in Colombia are freshly ground and brewed at Folklore Colombian Cafe. A quiet oasis just off Plaza de la Aduana, it also serves an impressive house-made triple-layer ganache chocolate cake.

★ Gelateria Tramonti

Calle 35 No. 480; tel. 5/664-9354; 9am-1am daily; COP$10,000

Run by two Italian brothers, one of whom actually graduated from a gelato-making university, Gelateria Tramonti offers sensual treats that you won't soon forget. Flavors include fruit juice-sweetened local delights like maracuya (passionfruit) and zapote, a creamy deep-orange fruit that's much like a sweet avocado, as well as a

SEAFOOD IN CARTAGENA

mixed seafood ceviche

Seafood reigns supreme in Cartagenan cuisine. Popular fish are **pargo rojo** (red snapper), **corvina** (sea bass), **dorado** (mahimahi), and **sierra** (swordfish). Shellfish include **langosta** (lobster), **langostinos** (prawns), and **chipi chipis** (tiny clams). These main dishes are often accompanied by delicious coconut rice and patacones (fried plantains). You will find these on the menu at most beachside restaurants in Bocagrande, Tierrabomba, and Barú, and in most cases, they will serve you right at your beach chair.

Cartagena also is known for its fresh seafood **ceviches,** which are more like what we think of as a "cocktail" than a Peruvian- or Mexican-style ceviche. Vendors hawk ceviche up and down the beach at Bocagrande, and it is a deliciously refreshing light meal on a hot afternoon. You will find better prices and high quality at the row of street cevicherías (Av. Venezuela and Calle 34; 10am-6pm daily; COP$12,000-25,000) just across the street from the Torre del Reloj outside of the city walls. Freshly mixed shrimp, oyster, crab, conch, and octopus ceviche await, with sidewalk seating under ancient trees.

dark chocolate (80 percent cacao) that will leave you buzzing.

Getsemaní

COLOMBIAN

Restaurante Coroncoro

Carrera 10 No. 39-22; tel. 314/541-0393; 7:30am-10pm daily; COP$16,000

Restaurante Coroncoro has been serving freshly caught mojarra (local whitefish), posta negra (a beef dish featuring a molasses-based marinade), and other Cartagena classics to locals since the 1970s. It has the best budget lunch special (COP$16,000) in town. Everything has the homemade taste of grandma's kitchen.

CARIBBEAN FUSION

★ Lunático

Av. Pedregal No. 29-225, 2nd Fl.; tel. 310/238-5804; https://lunaticoexperience.com; 11am-10pm Mon.-Sat.; COP$30,000-75,000

At brightly lit Lunático, freshly caught local Caribbean seafood is masterfully utilized in classic Spanish tapas and Mediterranean fusion plates. Giant paella and fideuà (Spanish noodles) bursting with shellfish are meant to be shared and make an excellent and decently priced gourmet dinner. The restaurant's bottomless mimosa brunch special (COP$58,000) includes a three-course meal and is available daily.

SEAFOOD

Marea Barra & Comida

Centro de Convenciones, Calle 24 No. 8A-344; tel. 5/654-4205; www.mareacartagena.com; noon-3pm and 7pm-10pm Tues.-Sat., 4pm-10pm Sun.; COP$75,000-120,000

Marea Barra & Comida is an ultra-chic

grilled octopus at Lunático

seafood restaurant that is the brainchild of the Rausches, two brother chefs from Bogotá. Specialties include tuna tartare and prawns in a coconut and saffron sauce. This restaurant has excellent views of the bay and the Torre del Reloj.

BAKERIES AND CAFÉS

★ Cafe del Mural

Calle San Juan No. 25-60; tel. 321/288-9323; 8am-8pm daily

For a real Colombian coffee-tasting experience, hit up Cafe del Mural. With outside garden seating under a street mural and an artsy indoor area, this bohemian Getsemaní institution also offers a wide variety of brewing methods and hosts regular coffee tastings and classes.

Manga

SEAFOOD

Club de Pesca

Fuerte de San Sebastián del Pastelillo; tel. 5/660-4594; noon-11pm daily; COP$49,000-80,000

The Club de Pesca is a Cartagena classic in the old San Sebastián del Pastelillo fort, with magnificent views of the bay that are best enjoyed in the evening. It's a favorite spot for wedding banquets, and some guests arrive in yachts. Freshly caught pargo, served whole with coconut rice, is a favorite, but other seafood dishes like the jaiba gratinada (crab au gratin) often steal the show. They have an extensive wine list.

INTERNATIONAL

★ Restaurante Shwarma Khala

Calle 26 No. 18; tel. 5/660-5382; 10am-9pm daily; COP$18,000-33,000

Authentic Middle Eastern specialties await at Restaurante Shwarma Khala, a true hidden gem that is both inexpensive and top quality. From falafel and shawarma wraps to full plates featuring Middle Eastern delights, this is the place to get your hummus fix without breaking the budget.

Bocagrande

COLOMBIAN

★ Kiosco el Bony

Playa Hollywood, Carrera 1; no phone; 8am-10pm daily; COP$28,000-55,000

A Cartagena institution since the 1980s, right on the beach at Playa Hollywood, Kiosco el Bony serves freshly caught fish in a variety of styles as well as classic ceviches and cocteles. Run by ex-boxing champ Bonifacio Ávila Berrío (El Bony), the restaurant does a house special cazuela de mariscos (seafood stew) that's packed with shellfish and secret spices to recharge body and soul. Bony's has both indoor and outdoor dining rooms with views over the packed beach.

Bars and Nightlife

Cartagena's nightlife rages seven nights a week thanks to the steady river of visitors who pour into town. Bars tend to close at 2am-3am weekdays, and some stay open until 5am on weekends. Expect to pay a cover charge for larger discos and places with live music; those in groups can ask for a discount. The two most concentrated nightlife areas are around **Plaza de los Coches** in the Old City and **Calle Media Luna** in Getsemaní. The city's favorite music styles are Latin crossover rhythms, such as reggaetón and salsa, along with the Afrobeats of homegrown champeta. More upscale places tend to play electronic music and Top 40 hits mixed in with Latin beats.

Public drinking—legal throughout the city—is a popular sport all over Cartagena, and there are several other excellent spots to down a cold one in the open air. **Plaza de la Trinidad** in Getsemaní is a great place to go after sunset to warm up for the evening. As the nexus of several hip mural-lined streets, it's the beating heart of the neighborhood and stays lively until late at night, although the action slows after midnight or so. Cheap beers (COP$5,000) are sold by vendors, and street performers and dance groups, including palenquero dancers, perform about 7pm-10pm. Mingling with locals and other travelers is easy here. Several bars also front the plaza and offer sidewalk seating for those who prefer a more formal front-row seat.

Centro and San Diego

BARS AND LOUNGES

Café del Mar

Baluarte Santo Domingo; tel. 5/664-6515; 5pm-3am daily; no cover

With the Caribbean breeze kissing your face and the city and coast spread before you, enjoying a drink on Las Murallas is an experience that shouldn't be missed. Sunset is especially divine, and that's when the crowds gather at Café del Mar, on the wall just two blocks from the Plaza de Santo Domingo. A live DJ plays lounge-style electronic music, and it stays busy until late.

El Coro

Calle del Torno No. 39-29; tel. 5/650-4700; 5pm-2am Sun.-Thurs., 5pm-3am Fri.-Sat.; no cover

If you're looking for atmosphere, head to El Coro at the Hotel Sofitel Legend Santa Clara. At this posh bar in a former 17th-century convent, crisply dressed bartenders serve Caribbean cocktails to hotel guests and others while Latin jazz plays in the background. Of the larger convent complex, El Coro is located in the chorus area, where the resident nuns sang while mass was celebrated in the adjacent chapel. Ask to see the crypt, which was an inspiration for Gabriel García Márquez as he wrote *Of Love and Other Demons*.

Cuba 1940

Calle Stuart No. 7-46; tel. 304/680-7301; 11am-midnight daily; no cover

With sidewalk seats fronting charming Plaza de San Diego, Cuba 1940 is a classy Latin jazz joint decked out like an old-school Havana living room. Live bands play most nights of the week, and the friendly owners like to come around and chat with guests between sets.

DANCE CLUBS

Alquímico

Calle del Colegio No. 34-24; tel. 318/845-0433; www.alquimico.com; 6pm-2am Sun.-Thurs., 6pm-3am Fri.-Sat.; no cover

Three stories of tropical cool at their finest make Alquímico the place for top-notch mixology in an inspiring setting. Housed in a restored colonial mansion, the 1st floor wraps around a large central bar and is great for mingling, and the 2nd floor looks down on the 1st and is decked out with couches and tables that make for more intimate conversations. Up on the rooftop, dance tunes get the crowd bumping and grinding in the humid open air.

La Movida

Calle Baloco No. 2-14; tel. 310/636-4472; 9pm-4am Tues.-Sat.; cover COP$40,000

La Movida is the hippest disco in Cartagena at the moment, and for good reason. Located just across from the sea-fronting ancient walls in the Old City, the Euro-chic gay-friendly disco has a large indoor dance floor and lounge decked out with retro furnishings along with a two-level garden patio. Each space hosts its own DJ, playing everything from electronica to Latin club hits. It locks the doors after 3am and keeps the party going into the after hours—you can leave, but you can't get back in.

Eivissa

Calle Portocarrero No. 7-33; tel. 301/623-2336; 9pm-4am daily; cover COP$20,000

Right on the Plaza de los Coches, Eivissa is a two-story club that's a favorite with international travelers and the locals who want to meet them. Downstairs a DJ spins Top 40 and Latin beats, often accompanied by professional dancers, while on the rooftop live bands play over sweeping views of the Torre del Reloj and the waterfront. Many hostels offer free passes to Eivissa, so it's worth asking.

SALSA

Colombia moves and grooves to the rhythm of salsa everywhere you go, and Cartagena is no exception. In fact it's one of the country's salsa meccas and gave birth to Colombia's most famous salsa singer, Joe Arroyo. You will no doubt hear his greatest hit, "Rebelión," a protest against enslavement and a tribute to Afro-Colombian history, all over town in taxis and supermarkets during your stay.

Donde Fidel

Plaza de los Coches; tel. 5/664-3127; noon-2am Sun.-Thurs., noon-3am Fri.-Sat.; no cover

Donde Fidel is a large old-school salsa lovers' spot that spans three storefronts on Plaza de los Coches near the Torre de Reloj. The bar's name means "where Fidel is," and the walls are covered with photos of owner Fidel posing with salsa stars from all over Latin America. Good times and cold beer can be found every night of the week.

LGBTQ+

Le Petit Club

Calle del Candilejo No. 32-34; tel. 5/664-3645; 5pm-2am Wed.-Sat.

A landmark LGBTQ+ hangout, Le Petit Club has a pub-like atmosphere in the immediate post-work hours but transforms into a full-fledged disco come late night. Expect everything from Shakira to electronica on the small but packed dance floor. Sometimes there's a cover, but not usually.

Getsemaní

In Getsemaní, nightlife ground zero is Calle Media Luna, which is lined with bars and nightclubs that cater to both locals and visitors.

BARS AND LOUNGES

La Caponera

Calle 24 No. 25-100; tel. 5/664-1372; 11am-3:30am daily

Local creatives and international travelers rub shoulders at La Caponera, a funky and down-to-earth bar located across from the Getsemaní Convention Center. With a row of outdoor tables and inexpensive drinks, the place tends to get packed later in the evening, when the tight indoor dance floor spills out onto the sidewalk. Located just below The City Club, the city's top LGBTQ+ venue, there is considerable crossover between the two bars, and a friendly open vibe in general.

Casa de la Cerveza

Calle Arsenal No. 24; tel. 316/291-4644; www.casadelacerveza.com; 5pm-1am daily

For a chilled-out version of Café del Mar, check out Casa de la Cerveza. It's located on top of the Baluarte el Reducto, an ancient battle station on the wall in Getsemaní. The outdoor beer garden overlooks the bay and offers bed-style lounges for enjoying Colombian-brewed red, golden, or black beers on tap.

Demente

Plaza de la Trinidad; tel. 311/831-9839; www.demente.com.co; 4pm-2am Mon.-Sat.

The Plaza de la Trinidad is the beating heart of happening Getsemaní and home to some swanky spots perfect for a small meal and a couple of drinks. Cool Demente specializes in cocktails and tapas. It's an open-air spot with a retractable roof, where the music is funky, the cocktails are chic, and the cigars are Cuban. On the back patio is a beer garden, complete with twinkling lights, serving wood-oven pizza and craft beer. It's a fun place for an evening of small plates and drinks.

DANCE CLUBS

Bazurto Social Club

Carrera 9 No. 30-42; tel. 317/648-1183; www.bazurtosocialclub.com; 8pm-3am Wed.-Sat.; cover COP$20,000 after 11pm Fri.-Sat.

Bazurto Social Club is a colorful, fun restaurant and dance club that offers free champeta dance classes at 10:30pm. Stick around until midnight to practice with the live house band, the Bazurto All Stars, and visiting performers. The friendly bohemian vibe is great for mingling, so feel comfortable coming solo. Food is also served, with dishes such as shrimp empanadas and paella.

La Santa

Calle Larga 25 No. 8B-90; tel. 302/453-3732; 7pm-4am Tues.-Sat., 2pm-4am Sun.; cover COP$50,000

There is a large cluster of nightclubs over by Calle del Arsenal, on the Getsemaní waterfront, that are popular with younger Colombians on vacation. La Santa is the standout here; it's been voted best electronic club in the country several years in a row. The huge dance floor has two levels and is carefully tended to by an award-winning in-house DJ. The Sunday pool party at La Santa is a Cartagena partygoer institution.

SALSA

Quiebra Canto

Carrera 28B No. 25-110; tel. 5/664-1372; 7pm-2am Tues.-Thurs. and Sun., 7pm-4am Fri.-Sat.; no cover

Overlooking the gorgeous skyline of the Old City from a wraparound balcony, Quiebra Canto is the epitome of classy

Colombian salsa joints. A Cartagena institution founded in 1979, live bands play nightly, the walls are covered with photos of salsa legends, and the friendly regulars are always up for a dance.

Café Havana

Calle Media Luna and Calle del Guerrero; tel. 314/556-3905 or 310/610-2324; www.cafehavanacartagena.com; 8:30pm-3am Thurs.-Sat., cover COP$40,000

Located on the Media Luna strip, Café Havana famously received an endorsement from Hillary Clinton on her trip to Colombia in 2012, when she was US Secretary of State. This is a place for expensive rum drinks and all-night dancing backed by live orchestras, many of which travel from Cuba to perform here.

LGBTQ+

The City Club

Carrera 8B No. 24-16; tel. 305/466-2899; 9pm-4am Fri.-Sat.; cover COP$20,000 Fri.-Sat.

The hottest gay disco in Cartagena is The City Club, in Getsemaní near the convention center. Two dance floors, one playing electronic music and the other reggaetón, open onto balconies overlooking the street below. Because it's located above La Caponera bar, there's a mixing of clientele as people go down and then head back up again.

Accommodations

As the top travel destination in Colombia, Cartagena boasts a large and diverse hotel sector. Centro and Getsemaní are the top neighborhoods for small high-end boutique hotels, often occupying well-restored colonial-era homes; many feature rooftop terraces and swimming pools, which go together quite nicely. Being pampered at one of these luxury options, even for just a few nights, will be a highlight of your visit.

Hostels proliferate in the city, especially in Getsemaní. The vast majority offer private rooms with air-conditioning, but these tend to go fast, so plan to reserve at least a few weeks in advance. Some hostel dorm rooms don't have air-conditioning. Bocagrande, with its high-rise hotels and condos, is more popular with Colombian families than with international visitors. Staying here means proximity to Bocagrande's beaches and several shopping malls.

In general, prices are higher in Cartagena than in the rest of the country.

Centro and San Diego

COP$70,000-200,000

★ Casa Movida

Calle del Tablón; tel. 318/707-5378; www.casamovidahostel.com; COP$95,000 dorm, COP$260,000 d

With a rooftop bar that is pumping every night and a coworking space on the ground floor, Casa Movida offers both capsule-style dorms and 13 private rooms in a colorfully restored colonial mansion right near all the nightlife of the Torre de Reloj. Owned by the same local team that runs Lobo de Mar restaurant and La Movida disco, this is the place to connect instantly with Cartagena's fast-moving nightlife and dining scenes.

Hostal Badillo

Carrera 7 No. 36-58, 2nd Fl.; tel. 5/651-3724; COP$184,000 d

On the 2nd floor of a busy shop in barrio San Diego, this basic but comfy family-owned hotel has only a half dozen rooms, all with private baths. For price and location, it can't be beat.

COP$200,000-500,000

Casa Blue

Plaza Fernández de Madrid, Calle del Curato No. 38-08; tel. 5/668-6501; COP$360,000 d

Previously a hostel, Casa Blue is in the Walled City just a few blocks from the Plaza de Santo Domingo and Parque Simón Bolívar. The 40 rooms are private, and the hotel markets itself to the budget-conscious business crowd. Its location on a popular plaza means you should expect some noise in the evenings.

★ 3 Banderas

Calle Cochera del Hobo No. 38-66; tel. 5/660-0160; www.hotel3banderas.com; COP$380,000 d

A midrange option with a guesthouse feel is 3 Banderas. This hotel is housed in a 200-year-old building with two interior patios and a rooftop terrace with a tiny pool. Some of the 24 rooms are small, but it's generally a good value. Request one of the rooms with a small balcony.

OVER COP$500,000

★ Hotel Boutique Santo Toribio

Calle Segunda del Badillo No. 36-87; tel. 317/893-6464; www.hotelsantotoribio.com; COP$750,000 d

With just eight rooms, a pleasant rooftop terrace, a cool wading pool for relaxing in the afternoons, and a delicious breakfast included in the morning, Hotel Boutique Santo Toribio checks all the boxes for a comfortable stay in the San Diego neighborhood. Lounge music adds an air of chicness. Bikes are available for rent.

Casa la Cartujita

Calle del Curato No. 38-53; tel. 5/660-5248; www.casalacartujita.com; COP$800,000 d, 2-night minimum

The two-story colonial-era Casa la Cartujita has seven bright-white minimalist rooms and a lovely terrace, a jetted tub, a dipping pool, and a pleasant reading room. Rent the entire house and you'll have a personal chef at your service.

★ Anandá

Calle del Cuartel No. 36-77; tel. 5/664-4452; COP$950,000 d

Good taste reigns at Anandá, whose name means "maximum state of happiness" in Hindi. It's certainly close to the truth at this gorgeous meticulously restored 16th-century home. There are 23 rooms of three different styles and a pool, a jetted tub, and daybeds on the rooftop. Anandá is home to the restaurant Carmen.

Hotel Charleston Santa Teresa

Plaza de Santa Teresa; tel. 5/664-9494; www.hotelcharlestonsantateresa.com; COP$1,219,000 d

The 89-room Hotel Charleston Santa Teresa is in front of the El Baluarte San Francisco section of Las Murallas. It was built in the 17th century as a convent for Carmelita nuns. There are two wings to this historic hotel, a colonial one and a republican-era one dating from the early 20th century. The 86 rooms are nothing short of luxurious, with accommodations in the colonial wing a notch above the more modern ones. The two inner courtyards are lovely, with astounding and ever-changing floral displays, and the front courtyard is so large it is almost its own plaza. Concierges can arrange any excursion you'd like. The hotel's many amenities, including four restaurants, one run by renowned chef Harry Sasson, a rooftop pool, a spa, and a gym, ensure a relaxing stay.

Townhouse Boutique Hotel

Carrera 7 No. 36-88; tel. 5/664-9100; www.townhousecartagena.com; COP$1,400,000 d

Party animals will love the rooftop bar of the 36-room Boutique Hotel, where champagne is served at private swimming pools and the electronic music pumps out over views of the historic skyline. A jazz piano bar is located on the ground floor, which attracts an artsy crowd, and rooms are individually decorated by local Colombian artists. Townhouse also runs the Blue Apple Beach House on the island of Tierrabomba, just 30 minutes away by boat. Guests can visit for the day for free or stay the night at discounted rates.

★ Sofitel Legend Santa Clara

Calle del Torno No. 39-29; tel. 5/650-4700; www.sofitel.com; COP$1,900,000 d

An iconic Old City classic in San Diego, the 122-room Sofitel Legend Santa Clara is synonymous with class and luxury, though it once served as a monastery for nuns. The stunning central colonial courtyard features tropical plants, a fountain, and modern sculptures, all dotted with tables where guests wine and dine. The gorgeous chapel is available for weddings. Be sure to request a tour of the hotel from a staff member to see remnants of the convent. Make time for drinks at the on-site bar El Coro. The pool area is spacious; an on-site spa offers individual and couples treatments, and the hotel can arrange exclusive trips to the Islas del Rosario.

★ Casa San Agustín

Calle de la Universidad No. 36-44; tel. 5/681-0000; www.hotelcasasanagustin.com; COP$2,260,000 d

The result of a meticulous restoration of three adjacent 17th-century houses, the Casa San Agustín is easily one of the most luxurious addresses in Cartagena, if not all of Colombia. Among the amenities are an inviting pool on the main floor, complimentary afternoon tea in the library, a terrace with a fabulous view, 21 spacious rooms with exposed wood-beamed ceilings, 10 private suites, a cozy bar, and the original stone walls. This hotel is a member of Leading Hotels of the World.

Getsemaní

UNDER COP$70,000

Media Luna Hostel

Calle de la Media Luna No. 10-46; tel. 5/664-3423; www.medialunahostel.com; COP$55,000 dorm, COP$220,000 d

The Shangri-la of backpacker accommodations in Cartagena is the famous Media Luna Hostel. Located on the heart of Getsemaní, it's a high-energy place with socializing (and flirting) centered on the medium-size pool in the courtyard. If you're looking to break out of your shell, this may be the place. It has a capacity of more than 100, with just a couple of private rooms; book early for those. The staff organizes lots of activities, and bikes are available to rent. Then there's the bar, only open Wednesday nights for the famous Visa por un Sueño party, also open to nonguests. Media Luna also runs a beachfront hostel on the end of Barú near Playa Tranquilo and can set up transportation to and from it.

★ Casa del Pozo

Carrera 10B No. 5-95; tel. 5/679-9066; COP$60,000 dorm, COP$180,000 d

Casa del Pozo is a "boutique hostel" that opens onto Plazuela del Pozo, where tables fill with diners from surrounding restaurants come sundown. With an outdoor swimming pool, a comfy book-filled common area, and a street-front café that serves breakfast and lunch, this is one of the nicer backpacker options in town. Dorms are private capsule-style with individual outlets, lighting, and curtains.

COP$200,000-500,000

Casa Relax

Calle del Pozo No. 25-105; tel. 310/443-1505; www.cartagenarelax.com; COP$375,000 d

Casa Relax has a friendly hostel-like vibe with lots of common spaces, yet all 12 rooms are private with ensuite baths. Here you can make use of the kitchen, have a cocktail by the groovy pool, and socialize a bit—a great bet for solo travelers.

★ Casa Pizarro

Carrera 10B No. 2556; tel. 5/643-6867; www.hotelcasapizarro.com; COP$433,000 d

Casa Pizarro is almost hidden from street view behind the massive trees fronting it, making it a true sanctuary in the middle of frenetic Cartagena. Most of the 15 rooms in this lovingly restored colonial mansion have private walled garden patios, some with hot tubs as well as comfy outdoor sofas and beds. A long narrow pool occupies the ground-floor courtyard, while the rooftop hosts a lounge restaurant and sundeck.

OVER COP$500,000

Hotel Capellán

Calle de La Sierpe No. 29-52; tel. 5/660-9562; www.hotelcapellandegetsemani.com; COP$852,000 d

The most luxurious option in Getsemaní is the 30-room Hotel Capellán. A poolside bar graces the rooftop terrace, an on-site spa offers pampering treatments, and a top-floor duplex suite might be just right for families or a group of friends. Period details abound, but the rooms are mostly minimalist and modern.

Bocagrande

Hotel Caribe

Carrera 1 No. 2-87; tel. 5/650-1160; www.hotelcaribe.com; COP$445,000 d

Bocagrande's most classic digs are to be found at the Hotel Caribe. The historic Spanish-style complex comprises three large buildings across from Playa Hollywood and has a beach club exclusively for guests. The hotel's nicest feature is the lush garden, complete with resident parrots and deer. The 360 medium-size rooms have views of the sea or the garden. Most visitors enjoy lounging by the pools and drinking a fruity cocktail.

Information and Services

Tourist Information

In addition to locations at the airport and at the cruise ship terminal, there are city-run **tourist information kiosks** (no phone; 9am-noon and 1pm-6pm Mon.-Sat., 9am-5pm Sun.) near the Torre del Reloj as well as an air-conditioned main office in the historic **Casa del Marqués Plaza de la Aduana** (tel. 5/660-1583; 9am-noon and 1pm-6pm Mon.-Sat., 9am-5pm Sun.).

Emergency and Medical Services

In case of an emergency, call the **police** at tel. 112. For medical emergencies, call an **ambulance** by dialing tel. 125.

Hospital Universitario de Cartagena

Calle 29 No. 50-50; tel. 5/669-7308; 24 hours daily

Hospital Universitario de Cartagena is a public hospital that provides around-the-clock emergency and urgent care as well as fully specialized on-site clinics.

Money

ATMs are easy to come by in Cartagena—there are several located right on the Plaza de La Aduana in the Walled City. There are several money-changing outfits on Carrera 7 just off of the Plaza de los Coches, but watch the exchange rate closely.

Transportation

Getting There

AIR

Rafael Núñez International Airport

CTG; tel. 5/656-9202; www.sacsa.com.co

Cartagena's Rafael Núñez International Airport is east of the city, about a 12-minute cab ride from Cartagena. Taxis from the airport to the Old City are reliable and regulated. The current fixed rate is COP$20,000. There are some public transportation options, but they're not advised.

Delta (www.delta.com) has nonstop service to Cartagena from Atlanta. **JetBlue** (www.jetblue.com) and **Avianca** (www.avianca.com) operate flights between New York City's JFK and Cartagena. Nonstop flights from Florida are offered by **Spirit Airlines** (www.spirit.com) from Fort Lauderdale and by Avianca from Miami. **Copa Airlines** (www.copaair.com) serves Cartagena from its hub in Panama City, Panama. Charter carrier **Air Transat** (www.airtransat.com) flies nonstop from Montreal to Cartagena December-March.

The main domestic carriers, Avianca and **LATAM Airlines** (www.latam.com), operate many flights each day to Cartagena from various Colombian cities. **Clic Air** (www.clicair.co) offers inexpensive flights between Cartagena and Medellín, Bogotá, Cali, and Pereira.

BUS

Regular bus service connects Cartagena

THE UNCONQUERABLE TOWN OF SAN BASILIO DE PALENQUE

palenque dancers

Cartagena was one of the main slave ports in Spanish America during the colonial era, and enslaved people who escaped created free communities, known as **palenques.** The largest, oldest, and most famous of these is the inland town of San Basilio, just 50 km (30 mi) southeast of Cartagena, yet a world apart.

Founded in the 16th century by **Benkos Biohó,** an African king who was enslaved and later escaped, it soon became a refuge for other enslaved people who escaped from Cartagena. After years of skirmishes with the Spanish, the outlaw town signed a peace treaty with the governor of Cartagena in 1605 and won its right to exist. Although Biohó was betrayed by the Spanish in 1621—he was captured and executed—San Basilio de Palenque remained unconquered and was finally declared free by royal decree of the king of Spain in 1691. This makes San Basilio de Palenque the **first free African town in the Americas,** a historical distinction that was honored by UNESCO in 2005 with its placement on the Representative List of the Intangible Cultural Heritage of Humanity.

As a free and independent city, San Basilio de Palenque nurtured many of the African traditions that were stamped out in other diaspora hot spots. Over the centuries, this little Africa would exert a major influence on Cartagena: After Colombia banned slavery in 1851, many **palenqueros** retuned to Cartagena and infused it with their African-influenced culture and music. Palenqueros to this day are an integral part of the city's cultural fabric. You'll see dancers performing to drum-driven music around the city and brightly dressed women selling fruits and posing for photos.

GETTING THERE

Day tours to San Basilio de Palenque run only on Sunday, and although these trips are sold all over town, it's best to go with a company that has a connection to the community. The best of these is **Fundación TuCultura** (Carrera 10C No. 25-51, Getsemaní; tel. 300/317-8355; https://tucultura.co), a nonprofit cultural tourism organization founded in 2009 by Merly Beltrán Vargas with the mission to use tourism to promote the culture and traditional art forms of Cartagena. Its daylong tour (COP$185,000) includes round-trip transportation from your hotel at 8am, lunch at a typical restaurant, visits to major historical sites in San Basilio de Palenque, and an expert tour guide, before returning to Cartagena around 5pm.

with all major and coastal cities. The **Terminal de Transportes** (Diag. 56 No. 57-236; tel. 5/663-0454; www.terminaldecartagena.com) is a 20-30-minute cab ride from the Centro (about COP$30,000). It's not advised to take public transportation to get here; take a cab.

The Terminal de Transportes offers bus service to Bogotá (18 hours), Medellín (14 hours), Cali (30 hours), and other interior cities. However, if you are making your way along the coast, it's quicker and easier to get to Santa Marta or Barranquilla by taking one of the fast hourly busetas (large vans) that serve the main Caribbean cities. **Marsol** (Carrera 2A No. 43-11; tel. 5/656-0302; www.transportesmarsol.net) and **Berlinas** (Calle 46C No. 3-80; tel. 5/693-0006; www.berlinasdelfonce.com) are the top choices and have pickup sites near the Centro in the Marbella neighborhood. Marsol even offers puerta-puerta service (door-to-door). The last buseta leaves Cartagena around 8pm. It's a decent option to travel after dark—the roads are in good condition and it's safe—as the roadside scenery isn't that impressive, there's less traffic, and you might as well spend the remaining daylight hours enjoying a mojito in the Old City.

CAR OR MOTORCYCLE

Consider renting a car or motorcycle for overland travel. Hertz and National, as well as local companies, have pickup and drop-off locations at the airport. This could be a good option if you are planning to take your time getting to know the Caribbean coast or are continuing onward to Colombia's interior. The main road to Barranquilla is mostly four lanes but shrinks to two lanes closer to Santa Marta. These roads are all well-traveled and maintained.

Getting Around

Walking is the best way to get around the Centro and Getsemaní. Thanks to its narrow streets, scarce parking, and heavy traffic, the Centro is not particularly car friendly.

TAXI AND RIDE-HAILING APP

For short hops between neighborhoods, cabs are quick and easy. Taxis do not have meters, so it's possible you won't get the local rate. Before hopping in a cab, ask a local or two the standard rate. Or just use **Easy Taxi** (https://cabify.com), an app run by Cabify; it connects you with a taxi and allows you to see the fare up front. From the Old City to Bocagrande, expect to pay around COP$16,000. A ride to the airport will cost COP$20,000, and a trip to the beaches at Las Américas will be COP$25,000. Tipping is not customary. **Uber** (www.uber.com) works just about everywhere.

BUS

To hop on a buseta to Bocagrande from the Old City, walk down to Avenida Santander along the sea and flag down just about any bus you see (or look for a sign in the window that reads "Bocagrande"). The ride will set you back COP$2,600, and the driver can make change. There are a few options for getting off: As you board, tell the bus driver where you would like to be let off; belt out "¡Parada!" as you approach your destination; or discreetly exit behind someone else. Riding the busetas into the interior of Cartagena is not advised due to safety issues. Use TransCaribe instead.

TransCaribe

www.transcaribe.gov.co

The TransCaribe bus system employs organized stations rather than standard bus stops. It caters mostly to residents but may be useful for visitors interested in traveling out of the Centro to the city's southern neighborhoods. Some of the major stops are at Muelle de la Bodeguita, La Matuna, Chambacú (Castillo de San Felipe), and Mercado de Bazurto.

The bright-orange bus stations are located along Avenida Venezuela, a thoroughfare between the Centro and La Matuna that extends into the southern neighborhoods. Expect to pay COP$2,600 for the comfortable ride. Change is given by a station agent.

Santa Marta

Founded in 1525, Santa Marta is Colombia's oldest city. Although its architectural glory seems paltry next to grandiose Cartagena, the city's pleasant pedestrian-only streets and historic plazas exude a tropical cool and friendly local vibe. It's also the jumping off point for visits to Parque Nacional Natural Tayrona, the Ciudad Perdida trek, and the backpackers hangouts of Taganga, Minca, and Palomino.

ORIENTATION

The **Centro Histórico** extends from busy Calle 22 (Avenida Santa Rita) in the south to Avenida del Ferrocarril in the north, and from the same Avenida del Ferrocarril in the east to the malecón (Carrera 1C/Avenida Rodrigo de Bastidas) to the west. The focal point of the Centro is lovely Parque de los Novios, bounded by Carreras 2A-3 and Calles 19-20, with pedestrian streets (Calle 19 and Carrera 3) intersecting on its eastern side. Most sights are within a smaller range of streets, from Carrera 5 to the water and between Calles 20 and 14.

The **Rodadero district,** also known as Colombia's Miami Beach, is lined with beachfront condos and hotels. It is just southwest of town, and local buses continuously ply the stretch between the Centro Histórico and Rodadero.

Sights

The compact **Centro Histórico** in Santa Marta feels like a living museum thanks to its mix of colonial and republican-era architecture. All major sights, save for the Quinta de San Pedro Alejandrino, are located here and can be visited in one day. The best way to get around the Centro Histórico is on foot.

CATEDRAL BASÍLICA DE SANTA MARTA

Plaza de La Catedral, Carrera 4; tel. 315/678-2845

Built in 1760, Santa Marta's glorious cathedral opens onto a wide activity-filled plaza and features a unique Byzantine-style cupola. Inside is a grave that holds the ashes of Simón Bolívar.

QUINTA DE SAN PEDRO ALEJANDRINO

Mamatoco; tel. 5/433-2995; www.museobolivariano.org.co; 9am-4:30pm daily; COP$27,000

Simón José Antonio de la Santísima Trinidad Bolívar y Palacios, better known as Simón Bolívar, was instrumental in bringing independence to several countries in Latin America, including Venezuela, Colombia, Ecuador, Peru, and Bolivia. While awaiting exile to Europe, he died at the age of 47 in Santa Marta at the Quinta de San Pedro Alejandrino. This country estate is now a museum where visitors can see the bedroom in which Bolívar died in 1830. A modern wing houses the Museo Bolivariano de Arte Contemporáneo.

Young guides will offer to take you around the complex for about COP$2,000, but you're probably better off on your own. The house is set in a manicured botanical garden. There is a small snack bar and gift shop on the grounds.

Recreation

DIVING

Santa Marta Dive Center

Calle 17 No. 2-41; tel. 311/694-8300; https://santamartadivecenter.com

There are some terrific diving spots nearby, and reputable Santa Marta Dive Center offers dive tours and courses, some with English-speaking instructors. Dive sites are off the coast of Parque Nacional Natural Tayrona, at two shipwrecks near Santa Marta, and offshore from the town of Taganga. A three-day course costs COP$950,000, a half-day course COP$250,000, and a diving excursion for certified divers COP$220,000.

Food

Most of Santa Marta's finest restaurants can be found in the Centro Histórico or on the waterfront around the malecón. For delightful ambience, seek out restaurants on pedestrianized streets such as Carretera 3 between Calles 15 and 16 (Callejón del Correo), Calle 19 between Carreteras 3 and 5, and on Parque de los Novios. The Rodadero area is known for its seafood joints, but many are overpriced.

★ Ikaro Café

Calle 19 No. 3-60; tel. 310/407-8533; www.ikarocafe.com; 8am-9pm daily; COP$12,000-35,000

With lush living walls, comfy daybeds, and outdoor seating on bustling pedestrian-only Calle 19, Ikaro Café is easily the coolest and coziest café in the Centro Histórico. It serves organic coffee produced on its own farm in the Sierra Nevada, Thai-Colombian fusion plates, and great raw chocolate tarts, as well as the full line of artisanal beers from Minca's Cervecería Nevada.

Maharaja

Carrera 4 No. 14-34; tel. 315/246-1905; 11am-9pm Mon.-Sat.; COP$16,000-38,000

Curry lovers will celebrate the offerings at the Rajasthani chef-run Maharaja. One of the most authentic Indian joints in the country, its veggie and meat set lunches are a great deal. The full dinner menu includes a fiery vindaloo.

Ouzo

Carrera 3 No. 19-29; tel. 5/423-0658; www.ouzosantamarta.com; noon-10:30pm Mon.-Thurs., noon-11pm Fri.-Sat.; COP$40,000-75,000

Ouzo is run by New York City-trained chef Michael McMurdo and consistently ranks as one of the top fine-dining restaurants in Santa Marta. Specializing in Mediterranean fare, Ouzo has brought some serious class to the adjacent Parque de los Novios. Order a plate of sizzling seafood or pasta accompanied by a glass of white wine. **Little Ouzo** (same hours) serves tapas and pizza on the rooftop terrace. It's one of the best spots in Santa Marta for sundown.

CARNAVAL DE BARRANQUILLA

For most Colombians, Barranquilla is synonymous with Carnaval, and they boast that the city's celebration is the world's biggest after that held in Rio (although folks from New Orleans or Trinidad and Tobago may balk at this claim). During the four days prior to Ash Wednesday, in late February or early March, the **Carnaval de Barranquilla** (www.carnavaldebarranquilla.org) is full of Costeño pageantry, with costumes, music, dancing, parades, and drinking.

Designated a World Masterpiece of the Oral and Intangible Heritage of Humanity by UNESCO, the Carnaval actually began in Cartagena, but when Barranquilla took over as the coast's most economically important city, Carnaval went with it.

THE FESTIVITIES

The Saturday before Ash Wednesday is when things kick off with the **Batalla de las Flores** (Battle of the Flowers) parade. Floats carrying beauty queens, dancers, and the general public in comparsas (groups) in elaborate costumes make their way down Calle 40 under the sizzling Barranquilla sun. This event dates to 1903, when it began as a celebration of the end of the Guerra de los Mil Días (Thousand Days' War).

On Sunday, during the **Gran Parada de Tradición y Folclor,** groups of dancers perform on Calle 40 to the hypnotic music of Carnaval, a mix of African, Indigenous, and European sounds. On Monday is another parade, the **Gran Parada de Comparsas.** Starting in the late afternoon, a massive concert attracts more than 30 musical groups that compete for the award of Congo del Oro.

On Tuesday, after four days of music and dancing, things wind down with the parade **Joselito Se Va con las Cenizas** (Carrera 54 and Calle 59). This is when Joselito, a fictitious Barranquillero, "dies" after four days of rumba, and his "body" is carried through the streets as bystanders weep. Joselito is sometimes played by an actor and other times is a mannequin.

As fun as the processions are to watch during the day, the real participatory action of Carnaval happens at night. On Friday-Sunday nights before Ash Wednesday, the **Baila la Calle** (dance the streets) brings hordes of people, including many still-costumed dancers from the processions, into the historic streets of Barrio Abajo for all-night dance parties. Different corner tiendas (stores) become de facto bars, and the pavement outside makes for impromptu dance floors, creating a raucous fiesta that just might be a highlight of the festival. After all, the ancient roots of Carnaval were about different classes mixing it up in revelry rather than sitting and watching from the bleachers.

GETTING THERE

Barranquilla is 2.5 hours from Cartagena by bus, but during Carnaval the roads become congested and may take much longer. Staying the night in Barranquilla is a much better choice. If you are planning on attending, book your hotel far in advance.

Carnaval de Barranquilla dancer

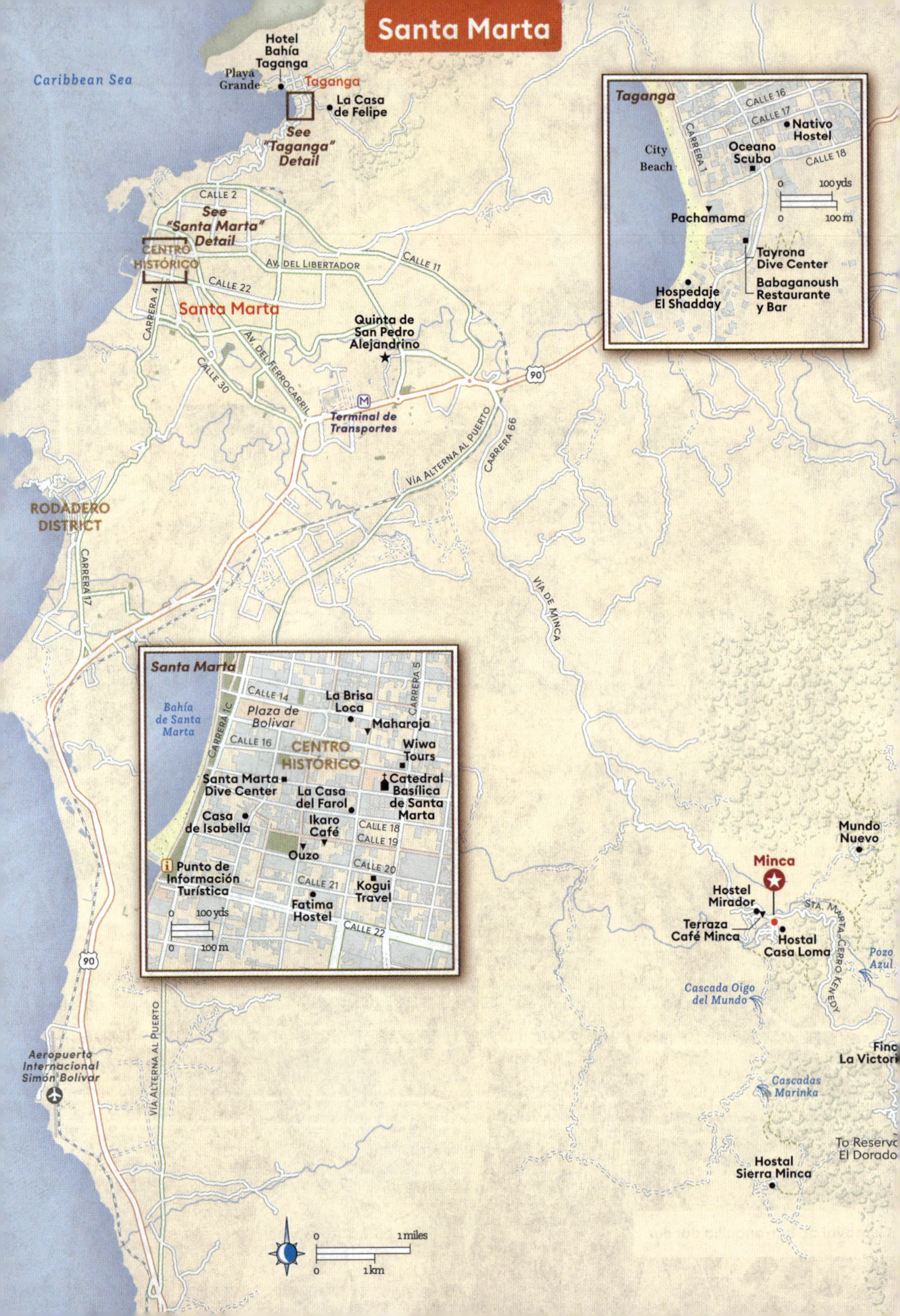
Santa Marta
Caribbean Sea
Hotel Bahía Taganga
Playa Grande
Taganga
La Casa de Felipe
See "Taganga" Detail
Calle 2
See "Santa Marta" Detail
Centro Histórico
Av. del Libertador
Calle 11
Calle 22
Santa Marta
Carrera 4
Quinta de San Pedro Alejandrino
Av. del Ferrocarril
Calle 30
Terminal de Transportes
90
Vía Alterna al Puerto
Carrera 66
Rodadero District
Carrera 17
Vía de Minca
Taganga
Calle 16
Calle 17
Nativo Hostel
Carrera 1
City Beach
Oceano Scuba
Calle 18
0 100 yds
0 100 m
Pachamama
Tayrona Dive Center
Babaganoush Restaurante y Bar
Hospedaje El Shadday
Santa Marta
Bahía de Santa Marta
Calle 14
Carrera 1C
Plaza de Bolívar
La Brisa Loca
Carrera 5
Maharaja
Calle 16
Centro Histórico
Wiwa Tours
Santa Marta Dive Center
Catedral Basílica de Santa Marta
La Casa del Farol
Casa de Isabella
Ikaro Café
Calle 18
Calle 19
Ouzo
Calle 20
Punto de Información Turística
Calle 21
Kogui Travel
Fatima Hostel
Calle 22
0 100 yds
0 100 m
Mundo Nuevo
Minca
Hostel Mirador
Terraza Café Minca
Hostal Casa Loma
Sta. Marta-Cerro Kenedy
Pozo Azul
Cascada Oigo del Mundo
Aeropuerto Internacional Simón Bolívar
Vía Alterna al Puerto
90
Cascadas Marinka
To Reserva El Dorado
Hostal Sierra Minca
0 1 miles
0 1 km

Accommodations

The Centro Histórico offers everything from comfortable hostels to posh boutique hotels, making it a great base. Rodadero is packed with high-rise hotels, many of which are all-inclusive and mostly catering to vacationing Colombian families.

Some travelers prefer to stay in the relaxed beach village of Taganga just north of town and visit Santa Marta for its restaurants in the evenings.

Fatima Hostel

Calle 21 No. 3-40; tel. 321/755-9049; www.fatimahostels.com; COP$35,000 dorm, COP$90,000 d

Just off Parque de los Novios, Fatima Hostel is the beach outpost of a popular Colombian-run landmark hostel in Bogotá; it has the same street-art aesthetic but in tropical hues. Fatima gives guests a free drink voucher on check-in; redeem it in the spacious hammock-lined rooftop bar, which also boasts a hot tub.

★ La Brisa Loca

Calle 14 No. 3-58, Centro Histórico; tel. 5/431-6121; www.labrisaloca.com; COP$45,000 dorm, COP$180,000 d

While many hostels in Santa Marta vie for the title of party hostel, La Brisa Loca occupies the top spot and has no serious competition. This revamped colonial mansion has a small pool in the main courtyard surrounded by three floors of private rooms and large mixed dorms with 6-10 beds. On the 2nd floor is a bar with balconies over the street that, thanks to daily drink specials, gets jammed with backpackers and locals alike, especially on weekends. Take your cocktail upstairs to the swank rooftop lounge and enjoy la

view from the roof of La Casa del Farol

brisa loca (the crazy breeze) along with music from a DJ.

★ Casa de Isabella

Callejón del Río, Carrera 2 No. 19-20, Centro Histórico; tel. 5/431-2082 or 301/466-5656; www.casaisabella.com; COP$378,000 d

The 10-room Casa de Isabella is a tastefully revamped republican-era house with nods to both colonial and republican styles. It surrounds a tamarind tree that's over 200 years old. The top-floor suites have fantastic private terraces and hot tubs.

La Casa del Farol

Calle 18 No. 3-115, Centro Histórico; tel. 5/423-1572; www.lacasadelfarol.com; COP$433,000 d

La Casa del Farol was one of the first boutique hotels in the city. It's in an 18th-century house and has six rooms named for different world cities. The tiny wading pool on the rooftop affords a nice view of Santa Marta.

Information and Services

In addition to a stand at the airport, there is a **PIT** (Punto de Información Turística; Carrera 1 No. 10A-12; tel. 5/438-2587; 9am-noon and 2pm-6pm Mon.-Fri., 9am-1pm Sat.) tourist information booth along the waterfront.

Transportation

Santa Marta is easily accessed by land and air from major cities in Colombia.

There is hourly bus service to Cartagena (5 hours; COP$35,000), Barranquilla (2 hours; COP$16,000), and Riohacha (3 hours; COP$26,000) from downtown Santa Marta (along Carrera 5). Many buses to nearby destinations like Minca leave from the market area (Carrera 11 and Calle 11) in the Centro Histórico. Long-haul buses for destinations such as Bogotá, Medellín, and Bucaramanga depart from the **Terminal de Transportes** (Calle 41 No. 31-17; tel. 5/430-2040) outside town (Taxi COP$18,000).

Taxis to Taganga cost around COP$15,000 and colectivo buses are around COP$2,600. These can be found on the waterfront near Parque Simón Bolívar, along Carrera 5, or at the market at Carrera 11 and Calle 11.

The **Aeropuerto Internacional Simón Bolívar** (SMR; Km 16.5, Troncal del Caribe) is 16 km (10 mi) west of the Centro Histórico. Taxis to the Centro Histórico from the airport cost around COP$20,000. Domestic carriers **Avianca** (www.avianca.com), **LATAM** (www.latam.com), and **Clic Air** (https://clicair.co) connect Santa Marta with the major cities of Colombia. **Copa** (www.copaair.com) has nonstop flights from its hub in Panama City, Panama.

★ Ciudad Perdida Trek

A highlight for many visitors to Colombia is the 4-6-day, 52-km (32-mi) round-trip trek to Ciudad Perdida (Lost City) in the Sierra Nevada. Ciudad Perdida is within Parque Nacional Natural Sierra Nevada de Santa Marta.

Ciudad Perdida, called Teyuna by local Indigenous people and Buritaca 200 by archaeologists, was a settlement of the Tayrona, forebears of the people who inhabit the Sierra Nevada today. It was probably built starting around 700 CE, at least 600 years before Machu Picchu. There is some disagreement as to when it was abandoned, although there is evidence of human settlement until the 16th century. The discovery of the site in 1976 marked one of the most important archaeological events of recent years. Archaeologists from the Colombian National Institute of

Ciudad Perdida

History and Anthropology painstakingly restored the site 1976-1982.

Spread over 35 ha (87 acres), the settlement comprises 169 circular terraces atop a mountain in the middle of dense cloud forest. Archaeologists believe this sophisticated terrace system was created in part to control the flow of water in this area, which receives torrential rainfall much of the year.

Plazas, temples, and dwellings for leaders were built on the terraces in addition to an estimated 1,000 bohíos (traditional thatched-roof huts), which housed 1,400-3,000 people. Surrounding Ciudad Perdida were farms of coca, tobacco, pumpkins, and fruit trees. The city was connected to other settlements by an intricate system of mostly stone paths.

PLANNING TIPS

The somewhat challenging hike to the Ciudad Perdida requires no special preparation. Booking your tour a few weeks in advance is necessary if you're planning to travel mid-December-mid-January, during Semana Santa, or in June-July.

The trek is mostly uphill, starting at an elevation of around 150 m (490 ft) and ascending to 1,100 m (3,610 ft). The out-and-back trek takes 4-6 days. Thousands of people of all ages walk the path each year, and each group is usually 8-12 people. Numerous groups populate different parts of the trail at any one time, and campsites can get crowded at night.

There is one set fee (COP$2,600,000) for the trek. This does not change regardless of how many days you take. Choose the four-day option only if you're short on time or in very good shape and prefer to go fast; this option requires getting up early and six hours of hiking per day, with daily hiking distances ranging 7.5-15 km (4.7-9 mi).

The tour companies that lead Ciudad Perdida treks are all similar, and trips can be booked in Santa Marta and at most hostels in Palomino and Taganga. Exceptional companies are **Wiwa Tours** (Carrera 3 No. 18-49, Santa Marta; tel. 5/420-3413; www.wiwatour.com) and **Kogui Travel** (tel. 314/680 9334; https://koguitravel.com), which both employ Indigenous guides.

Frequent rain means the trail can be muddy, and the weather is extremely humid. There are numerous river crossings, some more thrilling than others, but all manageable. To reach the spectacular terraces of Ciudad Perdida, you climb about 1,200 often slippery stone steps. In case of an emergency on the mountain, for a fee a burro or helicopter will be sent to retrieve hikers in distress.

SEASONS AND CLIMATE

In high season, mid-December-mid-January, you'll have plenty of company on the way to Ciudad Perdida. Other busy seasons are Semana Santa and when schools are on summer break in June-July. The wettest times are April-May and September-November. Expect a daily downpour and sometimes treacherous river crossings. Rainy weather makes the trek more challenging. On the plus side, there are usually fewer crowds on the mountain at that time.

WHAT TO PACK

Bring a small-medium backpack to carry a few days of clothes; good hiking boots with strong ankle support; sandals for stream crossings; long pants; mosquito repellent; sunscreen; a small towel; toilet paper; hand sanitizer; a flashlight (preferably a headlamp); sealable bags to keep things dry;

a light rain jacket; and a water container. Assume that everything in your backpack will get wet, but bring extra plastic bags to minimize damage.

THE TREK

On the first morning, you will rendezvous with your tour operator either in Santa Marta, Taganga, or Palomino, meet your fellow trekkers and guides, and take a minibus ride to the villages of Mamey and Machete, at the edge of the park, where a generous lunch at a small restaurant is served before you set off.

The first day of hiking, 3-4 hours, takes you through cleared farmland, not rainforest, so be prepared for extensive sun exposure. You take a break along the way at a coffee and fruit stall. At your campsite, you have the opportunity to plunge into a natural cool and crystalline swimming hole.

The second day of the trek is the longest, and most groups aim for an early start. Under the canopy of the Sierra Nevada, the trail hugs the Río Buritaca much of the time. There are multiple river crossings, including a swinging bridge. Before arrival at camp, you pass by the thatched roofs of the Kogi Indigenous settlement Mutanyí. Your guide will instruct you on photography etiquette. Kogi children may ask you for dulces (candy), but otherwise interaction with the people that live here is unlikely. You arrive at camp after noon, and the rest of the day includes lots of downtime.

On the third day, the various groups on the trail jockey to be the first to arrive at Ciudad Perdida. A 5:30am start is worth it to experience a sense of discovery as you climb the steps to the ancient terraces. Mosquitoes may be out in full force, so apply insect repellent. Leave your pack at camp; just carry your camera, walking stick, and water. The sun can be quite potent at the ruins, so bring sunscreen as well. After a final water crossing, the famed 1,200 stone steps dramatically appear, a silent invitation to this sacred lost city.

Take your time going up the steps. At the first series of grassy circular terraces, all that remains of the community's commercial center, your guide gives an introduction to the site. From here, climb the Queen's Path to the main site. Colombian soldiers guard the site and are always glad to chat with visitors. Take care descending the steps on your way back as they can become slippery.

Taganga

Taganga is a beachfront village tucked into a picturesque cove-like bay along the curving mountainous coastline just north of Santa Marta. In the 1970s this sleepy fishing town was discovered by hippies looking for an escape from urban life, and it soon became a backpacker haven. After gaining an infamous reputation for excessive partying in the mid-2010s, Taganga has chilled out a bit—the hard-core party scene has moved to Palomino—and is now one of the most relaxing places on the coast to spend a couple of days or weeks. On any given day you'll brush shoulders with Colombian families, beach bum expats, diving fanatics, traveling musicians, fishers, and sunseekers of all ages and nationalities.

BEACHES

Partially lined by a boardwalk packed with restaurants, Taganga's **city beach** is a long crescent of golden sand in a picturesque mountainous cove. Fishing boats dock off the northern side of the beach, but a large section of the sand on the southern side is reserved for swimmers and attracts an eclectic mix of visitors day and night. It's a magical place to take in the sunset, and people lounge around talking, drinking, and mingling late into the night.

Playa Grande

Playa Grande is just north of town around the next cove. It has a more natural setting and is also quite spectacular at sunset, which bathes the mountainous cliffs in orange. It costs COP$16,000 round-trip to get there by boat from the boardwalk; there are always boats waiting, or you can walk a pretty little mountain path to the beach in about 20 minutes. The trail is clearly marked on the northern end of the city beach and passes several detours to tiny cove beaches tucked into the rocky coastline, where more solitude can be found than at the town beach or at Playa Grande.

Playa Concha

COP$80,000 round-trip

Boats from Taganga's beach can also take you to some of the nearby beaches within **Parque Nacional Natural Tayrona,** northeast of town, although note that park staff prefer travelers visit the park by land. During the windy months of December-February, boat transportation can be rough, bordering on dangerous. The closest of the park's beaches is pretty Playa Concha, within the large Bahía Concha and offering calm clear water to splash in.

Playa Cristal

COP$110,000 round-trip

Just around the next bend in the coastline is Playa Cristal, under a rainforest-covered arm of the mountainside. This expansive wilderness beach is also called Playa del Muerto (Beach of the Dead) because it was an important ceremonial center to the ancient Tayrona people. Although visitors to the park are supposed to pay an entrance fee, these beaches are exempt most of the time; whether this is official or not is still in question.

DIVING AND SNORKELING

The warm 24-28°C (75-82°F) water off Taganga provides good diving and snorkeling opportunities. Diving excursions take you northeast off Parque Nacional Natural Tayrona, to Isla Morro off the coast of Santa Marta, or to a shipwreck near the beaches of Rodadero. The best months for diving are July-September.

Tayrona Dive Center

Carrera 1C No. 18A-22; tel. 5/421-5349 or 318/305-9589; www.tayronadivecenter.com; 8am-noon and 2pm-6pm daily

Tayrona Dive Center is an organized agency that offers PADI certification courses (COP$950,000) over three days with six dives each day, a one-day minicourse (COP$230,000), and diving excursions for those with experience. It also has a hotel (COP$120,000 d) at the same location with six rooms, five with views of the water. Rooms have a safe and big fridges. The hotel is exclusively for divers during high seasons (mid-Dec.-mid-Jan., Semana Santa, and mid-June-mid-July).

Oceano Scuba

Carrera 2 No. 17-46; tel. 5/421-9004 or 316/534-1834; www.oceanoscuba.com.co; 8am-noon and 2pm-6pm daily

Oceano Scuba offers an array of diving activities, from a one-day beginner's course (COP$255,000) to an open-water PADI certification course (COP$980,000) that lasts three days. Night dives (COP$130,000)—during which you might come across eels—and snorkeling (COP$75,000) are also on offer.

fishermen in Taganga

Playa Grande in Taganga

FOOD

One of the pleasures of even just a day visit to Taganga is eating freshly caught fish. Try the delectable cojinoa at one of the family-run open-air seafood restaurants that line the beach. Set lunch, which includes soup, a fish plate, and a lemonade, runs COP$22,000-30,000.

★ Babaganoush Restaurante y Bar

Carrera 1C No. 18-22, 3rd Fl., above Taganga Dive Center; tel. 318/868-1476; 1pm-11:30pm Wed.-Mon.; COP$22,000-48,000

Babaganoush Restaurante y Bar is an excellent Dutch-run restaurant and bar with amazing views. It's a true crowd-pleaser, with a diverse menu of falafel, seafood, steak, and even a shout-out to Southeast Asia. Go in the evening for the atmosphere and drinks. Happy hour (5pm-7pm daily) converges with sunset and is hard to pass up.

Pachamama

Calle 16 No. 1C-18; tel. 5/421-9486 or 318/393-9291; noon-11pm daily; COP$20,000-48,000

Tucked away on a side street a block or two from the beach, Pachamama has a sophisticated menu that includes Argentinian steaks, ceviche, pasta, and refreshing cocktails, all skillfully prepared by the French chef. Live music often accompanies dinner.

ACCOMMODATIONS

Nativo Hostel

Calle 17 No. 2-42; tel. 304/384-7800; COP$45,000 s, COP$60,000 d

For a local vibe, check into Nativo Hostel, where a local family rents out inexpensive rooms and serves great fresh fish lunches (COP$16,000) on a sidewalk patio.

★ La Casa de Felipe

Carrera 5A No. 19-13; tel. 5/421-9120; www.lacasadefelipe.com; COP$55,000 dorm, COP$143,000 d

A 15-minute walk up the hill from the beach, La Casa de Felipe is a spacious and comfortable hostel with extensive gardens strung with hammocks, a swimming pool, and an on-site restaurant that serves nice crepes and salads.

★ Hospedaje El Shadday

Carrera 1 No. 18-161; tel. 5/421-9232; COP$208,000 d

On the southern end of the beach, Hospedaje El Shadday is a locally owned boutique hotel with five floors of pleasant private rooms, many with large French windows opening onto panoramic views of the bay. There's also a communal rooftop terrace and snorkeling gear, kayaks, and beach chairs are available for rent.

Hotel Bahía Taganga

Calle 8 No. 1B-35; tel. 5/421-0653 or 310/216-9120; www.hotelbahiataganga.com; COP$282,000 d

Probably the most luxurious option in Taganga is the 32-room Hotel Bahía Taganga, on the northern side of the bay. Head to the terrace pool in the late afternoon and watch the sun slip behind the mountains.

TRANSPORTATION

Taganga is easily reached from Santa Marta and points east, such as Parque Nacional Natural Tayrona and Palomino. Minibuses and buses ply both routes daily.

From Santa Marta's Centro Histórico, you can take a colectivo minibus to Taganga for about COP$2,400. Taxis from the center of Santa Marta cost around COP$15,000, more from the bus terminal or the airport.

The ride from Santa Marta to Taganga takes about 20 minutes. Once in Taganga, you can walk everywhere. Note that the last bus back from Taganga to Santa Marta, and vice versa, leaves around 8pm.

★ Minca

Minca offers a change of pace, and altitude, from the beaches and seductive Caribbean cities that typify most of the coastline. At an elevation of 660 m (2,170 ft) partway up the Sierra Nevada, forest-covered mountains surround this small town. Hiking to waterfalls and vista points, bird-watching, and local high-quality coffee and chocolate are the highlights of a visit to Minca, all with a bird's-eye view of Santa Marta, just 45 minutes away. The bohemian vibe of the town is addictive, and travelers often end up staying longer than planned. Many accommodations are dispersed around the mountains in unique locations. You may want to stay at several before leaving.

There are no safety issues in and around Minca, and you can hike up the mountain on your own without a guide. Mototaxis also make travel from one destination to another relatively easy.

SIGHTS

Finca La Victoria

Vereda la Compana; tel. 324/240-1129; 9am-4pm daily; COP$25,000

The Sierra Nevada de Santa Marta is a renowned coffee-growing region, and Finca La Victoria is a historic family-run coffee farm between Pozo Azul and Los Pinos. It's a moderate 1.5-hour walk south of town, or take a 10-minute mototaxi ride (COP$10,000). The farm uses an astonishing hydroelectric system and machinery dating back over 100 years. After the tour, try the house-made chocolate banana bread with a coffee at the small on-site café. Grab some of Minca's homebrewed beer here, including Happy Coca, macerated in coca leaves to give you a small lift, made by **Cervecería Nevada** at Finca La Victoria and run by one of the family members. The working brewery isn't open to visitors, but you can take a six-pack with you.

WATERFALLS

Tranquil mountain roads lead to several spectacular waterfalls with swimming holes of either freezing-cold or wonderfully refreshing water, depending on the thickness of your skin. Three popular waterfalls are within easy walking distance of Minca along the main road: **Cascada Oigo del Mundo** (25 minutes), **Pozo Azul** (45 minutes), and **Cascadas Marinka** (1.5 hours), which has an on-site restaurant and café. All are clearly signed from town and can also be reached by mototaxi

Cascadas Marinka

(COP$5,000-15,000). Maps of the Minca area are also available at most hotels and cafés; pick one up before you set out on a walk.

BIRD-WATCHING

Reserva El Dorado

www.proaves.org

High in the Sierra Nevada, two hours from Minca at an elevation of around 2,400 m (7,870 ft), the Reserva El Dorado is one of the finest bird-watching reserves in the country. The area is home to 19 endemic species, including the Santa Marta antpitta, Santa Marta parakeet, Santa Marta bush tyrant, blossom crown, and screech owl.

To stay at the reserve (from COP$110,000), book with the **Conservation Alliance** (tel. 322/209-0501; https://conservation.co), which manages several high-caliber nature reserves across the country. There are 10 rooms and 5 huts modeled after traditional Kogi houses along with great food, and, crucially, hot showers.

Jungle Joe

tel. 317/308-5270; www.junglejoeminca.com; 6am daily; COP$50,000

Join a group tour with Jungle Joe for 3-4 hours of bird-watching in the immediate area around Minca. Binoculars and a guidebook are included. Jungle Joe Ortiz, originally from Barranquilla, also runs coffee, rafting, and other specialized tours from his office in the center of Minca, across from the police station. Tours meet at his office.

FOOD

There are some good eateries in Minca, including more vegetarian restaurants per capita than possibly anywhere else in Colombia.

La Miga Panadería

Calle 5A, next to Caja Mágica Internet; tel. 313/537-2218; 8am-6pm daily; COP$5,000

There is currently a showdown happening for the best bakery in Minca. La Miga Panadería, with its sidewalk patio, freshly brewed local organic coffee, and house-made pan de chocolate, is a sure bet.

★ Terraza Café Minca

diagonal from the police station; tel. 312/638-5353; 8:30am-8pm daily; COP$12,000-25,000

Terraza Café Minca serves pastries, breakfast, lunch, coffee, beer, and wine. The informal visitor center of Minca, it's a good place to find out what's going on in town, with tacked-up notices about local events. Run by a friendly family, it has a store stocked with locally grown coffee beans, dark chocolate, and health products as well as works by local artists. The café has a nice wraparound balcony facing the street and occasionally hosts live music on weekends.

Lazy Cat

across from Tienda Julimar; tel. 313/506-5227; noon-9pm daily; COP$18,000-25,000

Lazy Cat offers a filling meal of pasta or burgers, plus fruit smoothies and beers from Cervecería Nevada, on a back patio and a street-front bar area. It's in the center of town on the main street.

★ Arabesca Minca

Calle 3A at Carrera 5A; tel. 315/322-0964; www.arabesca-minca.business.site; 11am-10pm daily; COP$22,000-40,000

The excellent Middle Eastern food at Arabesca Minca is crafted by a Lebanese chef and served on a spacious mural-lined garden patio. The falafel is delightful, and the menu features a vegan-vegetarian section.

ACCOMMODATIONS

Hostel Mirador

200 m (660 ft) from town entrance; tel. 311/671-3456 or 318/368-1611; https://miradorminca.wordpress.com; COP$35,000 dorm, COP$90,000 d

Hostel Mirador is an enchanting hostel with a great view, warm hosts, and delicious meals. The hostel has two private rooms and a dorm room with three beds as well as a lush and art-filled garden with chairs and hammocks set up for watching the sunset. The lovely dining area is open-air and open to nonguests nightly; meals cost around COP$25,000.

★ Hostal Casa Loma

50 m (165 ft) uphill from a small church; tel. 313/808-6134; www.casalomaminca.com; COP$60,000 dorm, COP$112,000 d

Hostal Casa Loma is on a hilltop just outside of town with an impressive vantage over Santa Marta. It's a friendly place where delicious food, often vegetarian, is served, and you can mingle with other travelers. Cabins, including Casa Selva and Casa Luna farther up the hillside, are quieter than the rooms near the main social area, providing the ultimate rainforest experience. Camping (COP$30,000) is also available. To get to Hostal Casa Loma, climb a winding path just behind the church.

★ Hostal Sierra Minca

tel. 313/587-7677; COP$60,000 dorm, COP$210,000 d

Hostal Sierra Minca has a fantastic mountain location with an outdoor pool boasting views over the Minca area. Several hammocks that hold up to 10 people are built into the mountainside, suspending you over the lush valley below. A poolside bar serves the classics, while an on-site restaurant serves dinner by reservation. From the hostel, you can hike 30 minutes up to Los Pinos, with views into the interior of the Sierra Nevada and to Barranquilla to the west. You can get to the hostel on a three-hour uphill hike, but most people hire a mototaxi from Minca (COP$26,000).

Mundo Nuevo

tel. 300/360-4212; www.mundonuevo.com.co; COP$60,000 dorm, COP$320,000 d

Permaculture farm and ecolodge Mundo Nuevo is up a steep mountain road northwest of Minca, a COP$30,000 mototaxi ride, and sports dizzying views. The farm produces coffee, chocolate, and honey as well as produce that makes its way into the vegetarian meals served at the lodge. Mundo Nuevo has opened its land to the local Indigenous Wiwa people, who have built a handful of huts as rest points as they travel up and down the Sierra Nevada on foot. From Mundo Nuevo you can hike down to Pozo Azul (1.5 hours).

INFORMATION AND SERVICES

Bring plenty of cash with you to Minca: There are no ATMs here, but there is a Banco de Bogotá cash transfer office at **The Embassy Center** (10am-8pm daily) in the center of town, next to the Caja Mágica Internet.

TRANSPORTATION

Minca is easily reached from Santa Marta. Colectivos depart from Santa Marta on a regular basis from the market (Carrera 11 and Calle 11) and cost COP$12,000; the ride takes about 45 minutes. Private taxis from the airport cost around COP$80,000, and taxis from Santa Marta's Centro Histórico to Minca cost COP$75,000.

★ Parque Nacional Natural Tayrona

Troncal del Caribe highway, 34 km (21 mi) northeast of Santa Marta; tel. 5/421-1732; www.aviaturecoturismo.com, www.parquesnacionales.gov.co; 8am-5pm daily; COP$73,500

An epic meeting of mountains and sea, Parque Nacional Natural Tayrona is the best-known national park in Colombia and home to gorgeous beaches, rainforests, and archaeological sites.

The park covers 12,000 ha (30,000 acres) from the edge of Taganga in the southwest to the Río Piedras in the east. The southern border of the park is the Troncal del Caribe highway, and to the north the Caribbean Sea. To the east and south of the park is the much larger Parque Nacional Natural Sierra Nevada de Santa Marta, encompassing the peaks of the highest coastal mountain range in the world.

The frequently tempestuous sea of Tayrona provide dramatic scenery, with palms growing atop massive island boulders and waves crashing against them. More than 30 golden-sand beaches are set dramatically against a seemingly vertical

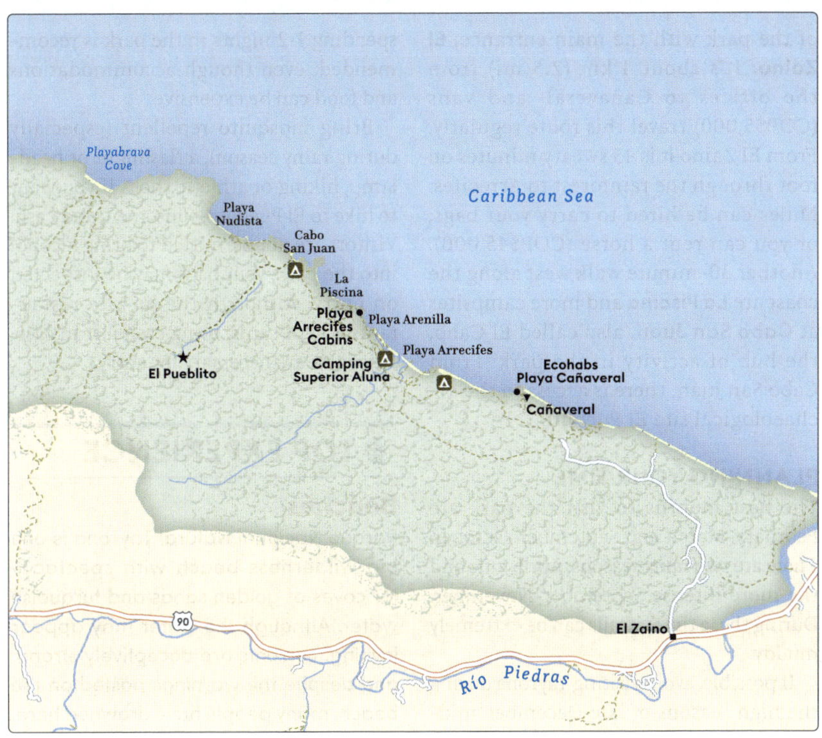

wall of rainforest. Although you can't see them from the park, the snow-covered peaks of the Sierra Nevada de Santa Marta are only 42 km (26 mi) from the coast.

The park includes significant tracts of critically endangered dry tropical forests, mostly in its western section. These forests are much less dense than humid tropical forests. At higher elevations you will see magnificent cloud forests. In addition to beaches, the coast is home to marine estuaries and mangroves. The park is laced with streams fed by chilly water that flows from high in the Sierra. In the western part of the park, many of these run dry during the dry season, while in the eastern sector they have water year-round.

Some 1,300 plant, 396 bird, and 99 mammal species have been identified in Tayrona. Four species of monkeys can often be spotted. The five species of wild cats are the margay, jaguar, ocelot, panther, and jaguarundi. Their numbers are few, and these great cats are expert at hiding in the forest, so don't count on seeing them. Other mammals include sloths, anteaters, armadillos, deer, and 40 types of bats. Birds include migratory and resident species, such as the rare el paujíl (blue-billed curassow), a threatened bird that lives in the cloud forest, as well as toucans, guacamayas (macaws), and many hummingbirds.

ORIENTATION

The majority of overnight visitors see just the extreme northeastern section of the park with the main entrance, **El Zaino.** It's about 4 km (2.5 mi) from the offices to Cañaveral, and vans (COP$5,000) travel this route regularly. From El Zaino it is 45 sweaty minutes on foot through the rainforest to Arrecifes. Mules can be hired to carry your bags, or you can rent a horse (COP$45,000). Another 30-minute walk west along the coast are **La Piscina** and more campsites at **Cabo San Juan,** also called El Cabo, the hub of activity in the park. From Cabo San Juan, there is access to the archaeological site El Pueblito.

PLANNING YOUR TIME

The best months to visit the park are February-March and September-October. There are two rainy seasons, April-June and the more intense September-November. During these times, trails can be extremely muddy.

If possible, avoid visiting Tayrona during the high seasons of late December-mid-January, Semana Santa, and to a lesser extent school holidays in mid-June-mid-July. During these times the park is swarmed with visitors. Puentes (long holiday weekends) are also busy; a weekday visit is by far the best.

Recently the Indigenous Kogi people, who still inhabit parts of the park, have begun closing the park to tourism for a month or so every year to protect the natural landscape from damage and to give wildlife a rest from human visitation. This often occurs in January-February during the height of tourist season. Check the park website (www.parquesnacionales.gov.co) in advance for the most up-to-date information on closures.

While many people visit the park on day trips from Santa Marta or Taganga, spending 1-2 nights in the park is recommended, even though accommodations and food can be expensive.

Bring mosquito repellent (especially during rainy season), a flashlight or headlamp, hiking or athletic shoes if you want to hike to El Pueblito, sunscreen, and cash. Visitors are not permitted to bring alcohol into the park; your bags may be inspected on entry. Although the on-site restaurants accept cards, bring cash just in case. Passports are necessary for entry.

 **TOP EXPERIENCE**

Beaches

Parque Nacional Natural Tayrona is one big wilderness beach with spectacular coves of golden sands and turquoise water. Although the water may appear inviting, currents are deceptively strong, and despite the warnings posted on the beach, many people have drowned here. Of the park's 34 beaches, only 6 allow swimming. There are no lifeguards on duty and no specific hours for swimming.

Playa Cañaveral

The first beach that visitors arrive at after entering the park, Playa Cañaveral invites with turquoise water and golden sand. The EcoHab lodgings are here as well as the trailhead north into the park and to more beaches, the cabañas, and campgrounds.

Playa Arrecifes

This long stretch of sand, about 45 minutes' walk from Cañaveral, is gorgeous and usually empty, as both swimming and sunbathing are prohibited due to the dangerous undertow.

Playa Arenilla

About 15 minutes' walk west from Arrecifes is Playa Arenilla. This postcard-perfect small cove sports clear still water that's perfect for taking a cooling dip.

La Piscina

Protected by rock barriers, La Piscina lives up to its name: The pool-like water is so transparent you have nearly perfect visibility. It's about five minutes west of Playa Arenilla.

Cabo San Juan

Home to the park's largest campground, the gorgeous beaches here are usually packed with people. At night bonfires and music bring the sand to life. Cabo San Juan is 20 minutes' walk from La Piscina, west along the coast.

Playa Nudista

Tayrona's famous nude beach, the only one officially sanctioned in the entire country, is a 45-minute walk west of Cabo San Juan. The water can be rough, and swimming is not advised.

Playa Brava

Those up for an adventure can hike 2-3 hours west along the wilderness coastline to Playa Brava, a secluded cove beach that feels lost in time.

Hiking

El Pueblito

Distance: 3 km (2 mi)
Duration: 1.5 hours one-way
Elevation gain: 500 m (1,640 ft)
Difficulty: Moderate
Trailhead: Cabo San Juan

A highlight of any visit to Tayrona is the hike up to El Pueblito, ruins of what was an important Tayrona settlement. The site contains well-preserved remnants of terraces, and a small Kogi community still lives nearby. The challenging path through the tropical rainforest is steep, and the stone steps can be slippery, but it's well worth it. Hikers can go to El Pueblito without a guide, but inquire when you enter the park if you'd like to hire one.

Food and Accommodations

There are three large open-air full-service restaurants in the park with similar offerings. One is in **Cañaveral,** close to the EcoHabs; one is in **Arrecifes,** near the cabañas; and one is in **El Cabo,** overlooking the campsites. All are open 7am-9pm daily, and the specialty is fresh seafood. Expect to pay around COP$45,000 for a lunch or dinner main. All three restaurants accept credit cards.

There are also some snack bars in the park, concentrated around the popular beaches, trails, and campsites and serving fried fish, empanadas, ice cream, and fresh fruit. The snack bars are usually open daylight hours (9am-6pm daily).

There are numerous lodging options in the national park for every budget: high-end EcoHabs, mid-level cabañas, and camping. Neither the EcoHabs nor the cabañas are a bargain, but the EcoHabs, where you wake to beautiful views of the sea, are indeed special and worth 1-2 nights. The cabañas are set back from the beach but are quite comfortable. Safes are included in all rooms and can be provided to campers as well. Some visitors prefer to leave a bag or valuables at a trusted hotel in Santa Marta.

Six beaches at Parque Nacional Natural Tayrona allow swimming.

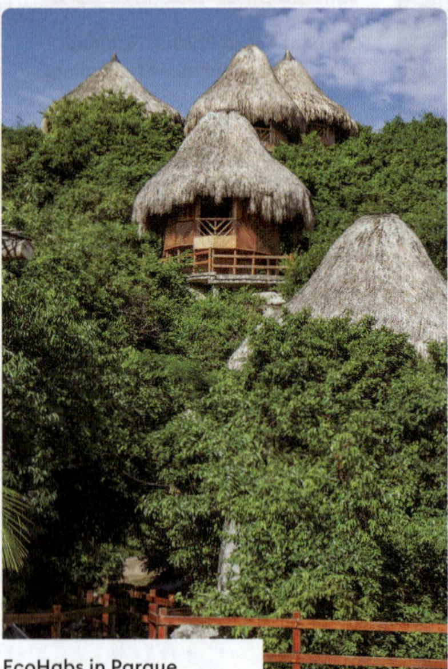
EcoHabs in Parque Nacional Natural Tayrona

EcoHabs

https://ecohabsparquetayrona.com; COP$900,000 d with breakfast

The EcoHabs, in the Cañaveral sector, consist of 14 private bohíos (thatched-roof cabins) that sleep 2-4 people. From a distance they look like giant nests amid the trees, but in reality they are modeled on the thatched-roof houses of the Tayrona people. There are two floors to the EcoHabs: the ground floor comprises the bath and an open-air social area, and upstairs is the bedroom. A flashlight is necessary if you need to go to the bathroom in the dark, as you have to go outside and downstairs. This is inconvenient for some. Vans from the park entrance at El Zaino run regularly.

Cabañas

https://ecohabsparquetayrona.com; COP$744,000 d with breakfast

In nearby Arrecifes, there are six two-story cabañas that sleep four each. These are like rainforest duplexes, with the two units divided by thin walls. You must hike in about 45 minutes.

Glamping

https://ecohabsparquetayrona.com; COP$620,000 d with breakfast

Arrecifes also offers visitors the chance to semi-rough it in yurt-style tents called Alunas, which come equipped with queen beds and Wi-Fi.

Camping

Arrecifes

https://ecohabsparquetayrona.com; COP$187,000 d with breakfast

The more peaceful of the two camping options, tents at Arrecifes come with blow-up mattresses and bedding and allow guests full use of the facilities. Limited hammock spaces here go for COP$40,000 per person.

Cabo San Juan

COP$70,000 d

Camping at Cabo San Juan is a bit of a free-for-all but also allows you to pitch a tent right off the beach. It tends to get very crowded during long weekends and holidays. Hammock spaces (COP$40,000 pp) in a round thatch-roofed open-air building right over the water are also available.

Transportation

From Santa Marta you can take any bus eastbound along the Troncal del Caribe to the park's main entrance at El Zaino. Colectivo buses can be caught at the market, at the intersection of Carrera 11 and Calle 11 in Santa Marta. The trip takes about an hour and costs around COP$10,000. You can also take a cab for about COP$90,000.

THE KOGI AND THE "YOUNGER BROTHER"

Direct descendants of the Tayrona people who built Ciudad Perdida, the Kogi, which means jaguar, are one of only a handful of Indigenous groups in Colombia to fully survive the Spanish conquest, having escaped to the high Sierra Nevada, where they lived in isolation for hundreds of years.

Kogi village

In 1988 the Kogi permitted award-winning BBC journalist Alan Ereira to enter their lands so they could get a message out to the rest of the planet. The result was the documentary *From the Heart of the World: Elder Brother's Warning* (1990), in which the Kogi advise the modern world, their "younger brother": We must change or suffer environmental disaster. In 2012 Ereira was summoned back to the Sierra Nevada by the Kogi to produce *Aluna*, a renewed call to humanity to come to terms with the interconnectedness of the world. The film was screened at the United Nations Conference on Sustainable Development in Rio de Janeiro that same year.

DAY TRIPS AND TREKS TO KOGI COMMUNITIES

While most outsiders are restricted from entering the higher reaches of Kogi territory in the Sierra Nevada, visiting low-lying Kogi communities is fairly easy, especially from Palomino, where you are likely to encounter Kogi people right in town. **Tur Palomino** (main road; tel. 320/524-9992) offers day trips to Kogi communities, such as a 4WD journey to Tungueka, home to around 180 traditional Kogi households, and a hiking trek to Sewiaka, recently built in partnership with the Colombian government and consisting of about 50 traditional-style homes, built to house displaced Kogi people, circling a large ceremonial space and community library. Some hostels in Palomino also have strong relationships with some of the Kogi communities and can arrange visits.

Tours are also available from Santa Marta. **Kogui Travel** (tel. 314/680 9334; https://koguitravel.com) employs Indigenous guides who lead multiday hiking treks to Kogi communities and mountain peaks such as Nevado Dumena (3,856 m/12,652 ft) and Nevado Debungie (3,200 m/10,500 ft), passing through several isolated Kogi villages on the way. It also offers tours to Ciudad Perdida.

Trip options and prices vary, so contact the companies for itineraries and details.

Palomino

Nestled under the towering rainforest-covered Sierra Nevada and fronting the open sea, Palomino is the Caribbean coast's ultimate backpacker mecca. Unfortunately, the beach has been steadily eroding for years, and the surf is too rough for swimming. But the attraction is more than just sunbathing. Hiking and bird-watching in the mountains, tubing down the nearby Río Palomino, visiting Kogi communities, surfing, and good old hammock lazing are all popular ways to pass the day. Palomino is a crossroads of cultures, where hipsters from Bogotá, international travelers, and Indigenous Kogi people meet to chew coca and discuss cosmic politics.

ORIENTATION

Palomino extends from either side of the main highway, **Troncal del Caribe.** There are no street names; the main points of reference are the beach, the Troncal del Caribe highway, the **main road** that cuts north-south from the beach to the highway, and the gas stations Terpel and Mobil. Because of the encroaching sea, and the fact that much of the nightlife is closer to the Troncal del Caribe, many hostels have set up about 500 m (0.3 mi) from the beach along the main road. The closest thing Palomino has to a town center is a stretch of this main road on the north side of the highway where many bars and restaurants are located.

BEACHES

Recreational activities in and around Palomino include an easy 20-minute walk west to the mouth of the **Río Palomino,** where it empties into the Caribbean; between the sea and the river is a sandbar that's as close to a nice beach as you'll find in the area, and where a variety of local seafood restaurants have set up shop.

TUBING

It's possible to tube down the river as well. **Tube rentals** (COP$50,000) are available all along the main road and include transport to a starting point along the river. Floating the river usually takes about 2.5 hours and deposits you at the mouth, on the beach, from where you can walk back to town and return your tubes.

HIKING AND HORSEBACK RIDING

Chajaka

office on the south side of the coastal highway; tel. 313/583-3288; calixtoteheran@gmail.com

Chajaka offers interesting day trips or multiday hiking or horseback trips (COP$150,000 pp per day) into the Sierra Nevada. Ask for Calixto Teheran, a longtime guide with Chajaka and a friendly expert who knows the Sierra well.

FESTIVALS AND EVENTS

Festival Jaguar

www.allticketscol.com; 1st weekend of Jan.; COP$100,000

Started in 2014, Festival Jaguar has become one of Colombia's biggest outdoor music fests. The beachfront festival features up-and-coming independent bands and DJs from across the country as well as world-renowned Colombian headliners like Bomba Estéreo and Systema Solar. Hostels and hotels raise their rates and fill up during the festival; book accommodations in advance.

FOOD

Palomino has attracted both the best and the worst of the eternal nomad crowd from across Colombia and around the world. Food is either overpriced tourist fare or meticulously well-done budget gourmet eats that you won't find anywhere else in the country.

The **cluster of seafood restaurants** at the mouth of the Río Palomino are run by a community association of local villagers who consistently serve high-quality plates of fresh local fish like pargo rojo (red snapper), lebranche (mullet), and the small but meaty cojinoa (yellow jack) beachside for around COP$35,000.

★ Turcolandia

main road; tel. 304/607-1341; 10am-11pm daily; COP$20,000-30,000

You can smell the gooey goodness of pizzeria Turcolandia from blocks away. House-infused oils like thyme, passion fruit, and coconut chili spice up your selection and make your pizza even more divine.

Los 7 Mares

main road, near the beach; tel. 301/358-0807; noon-11pm daily; COP$37,000-60,000

Fusion-style seafood specials make Los 7 Mares a hip option. Its combination of local and Asian flavors, such as the pad thai with squid, get rave reviews. Both fish and veggie burgers are available, and the cocktails are just as creative as the food. There is live music on weekends.

Panadería La Sierrita

main road; tel. 316/451-2277; 7:30am-8:30pm daily

Stop by Panadería La Sierrita for freshly baked artisanal breads, locally produced coffee and chocolate, and some invigorating coca leaf kombucha.

BARS AND NIGHTLIFE

Maria Mulata

main road; tel. 320/203-1537; 9:30am-2am daily; no cover

Though it serves coffee and snacks all day, Maria Mulata really gets kicking after the sun goes down as live bands and guest DJs take over its small stage. An open-air garden setting, super-friendly staff, and Minca's Cervecería Nevada beers on ice make dancing the night away with complete strangers—who become instant amigos—the order of the evening.

La Happycleta

main road; tel. 322/755-5740; 2pm-2am daily

La Happycleta is a small and friendly bar that opens onto the main road. With owners from Bogotá, it has a craft beer and bicycle theme and is frequently packed with other capital-city refugees discussing the daily news. Bike rentals are available, and a small guesthouse just around the corner offers a handful of private rooms (COP$80,000-100,000 d).

Nomada Bar

main road; tel. 301/545-0907; 6pm-2am Mon.-Sat.; no cover

As the night winds up, crowds gather in front of Nomada Bar to dance in the street to salsa and other Latin rhythms until the lights come on at 2am. But the party never really ends in Palomino; it just moves down to the beach until the sun comes up.

ACCOMMODATIONS

The Dreamer

tel. 300/609-7229; www.thedreamerhostel.com; COP$65,000 dorm, COP$211,000 d

Palomino dethroned Taganga as the country's top Caribbean backpacker resort several years ago thanks largely to one famous hostel: The Dreamer. This is by far the most social option this side of Santa Marta. Dorm and private rooms are in malokas (cabins) surrounding an always-happening pool area and an outdoor bar and restaurant that opens onto the beach.

El Matuy (Donde Tuchi)

tel. 315/751-8456; www.elmatuy.com; COP$230,000 pp with meals

El Matuy (Donde Tuchi) is a privately owned nature reserve with 12 cabins, each with a hammock out front, set amid palm trees and with no electricity. This means candlelit evenings and no credit card machine. Staff can help organize horseback riding or other activities. Surprisingly, there's Wi-Fi available in the reception area, making it a popular place.

Casa Campestre Ameli

La Sierrita; tel. 311/232-0034; www.hostalcasacampestreameli.mas57.co; COP$35,000 campsite, COP$55,000 dorm, COP$95,000 private room

On the southern side of the highway, in a hillside area called La Sierrita, there are a number of options for those who prefer mountains to beaches. Casa Campestre Ameli is surrounded by beautiful gardens and offers budget-conscious accommodations. They are also in close contact with several Kogi communities and can arrange visits.

TRANSPORTATION

There is regular bus transportation along the Troncal del Caribe between Santa Marta and Riohacha. From Santa Marta, at the market on Carrera 11 at Calle 11, take a bus bound for Palomino. It's about a two-hour trip and costs COP$25,000. On the highway where the bus drops you off, young men on motorbikes will take you to your hotel for about COP$5,000.

La Guajira

A dazzling combination of desert and sea, the vast Guajira Peninsula has some of the most rugged, beautiful landscapes in Colombia. It is home to the matriarchal Wayúu Indigenous people, who have maintained their independent way of life through centuries. They don colorful dresses that have caught on with the local population. Though many Wayúu people now live in cities and towns, their traditional rancherías (settlements) dot the desert. Open and outgoing compared to many more insular Indigenous groups, the Wayúu are fully integrated into society in La Guajira.

Riohacha

Called Süchiimma (City of the River) in the Wayúu language, Riohacha (pop. 231,000), bordered on the east by the Río Ranchería, is La Guajira's slow-paced departmental capital. It is one of the oldest cities in Colombia, with a smattering of colonial architecture at its center and a beautiful wide city beach lined with a pleasant malecón where families stroll at night and Wayúu women sell brightly colored mochilas (shoulder bags) and intricately patterned hats made from palm fronds.

SIGHTS

Fronting the sea and parallel to Calle 1, also known as Avenida Marina, is the 0.8-km (0.5-mi) **Paseo de la Playa** malecón, where locals and visitors leisurely gather in the evenings. Along the malecón is the monument to **La Dama Wayúu** (The Wayúu Woman), a tribute to the strength and beauty of the female leaders of this ancient matriarchal culture. The 1.2-km-long (0.7-mi) **Muelle Turístico** pier extends from the midpoint of the malecón and is another favorite place for a walk, especially in the evening, with sea breezes providing relief from the heat of the day. The pier has especially good views of the rugged peaks of the Sierra Nevada in the distance.

Centro Cultural de la Guajira

Carrera 15 No. 1-40; tel. 5/727-0990; www.banrepcultural.org/riohacha; 8am-11:30am and 2pm-5:30pm Mon.-Fri., 9am-1pm Sat.; free

With its striking murals depicting Wayúu culture, it's hard to miss the large Centro Cultural de la Guajira. Inside, the cultural center has a permanent exhibition space that tells the history of the area, from Spaniard pearl harvesters to modern times when multinationals arrived to extract natural gas and coal. A good portion of the museum discusses Wayúu culture and includes an exhibit on the area's traditions for Carnaval. The content is interesting and a must-visit for anyone interested in this unusual place. There are few English-language explanations of the exhibits. The center also houses a small public library.

BEACHES

Riohacha boasts what is quite possibly the nicest **city beach** on the Caribbean coast outside San Andrés. The wide spacious beach runs along the malecón and has beachside umbrella chairs for rent and calm baby-blue water that beckons swimmers.

Playas de Mayapo

About 30 minutes northeast or Riohacha are a series of impressive wide white-sand beaches known as the Playas de Mayapo. The farthest east, **Playa Jimatsu,** is home to several charming waterfront restaurants. The wide beaches provide privacy for swimming and sunbathing. To get to the Playas de Mayapo, take a colectivo taxi (COP$8,000 pp one-way) from downtown Riohacha's market plaza (Calle 7 and Carrera 13), or hire a taxi (COP$50,000 round-trip).

FESTIVALS AND EVENTS

Carnaval

Riohacha's beachfront is the stage for one of the biggest Carnaval celebrations on the coast outside Barranquilla. Dating to the 19th century, this is also one of the oldest continuously running Carnavals in Colombia, steeped in local traditions and heavily influenced by Wayúu culture. While the pre-Carnaval season in Riohacha lasts for weeks, the biggest celebration is on the weekend and weekdays leading up to the Tuesday before Ash Wednesday.

FOOD

★ Cocteleria Caribe

10am-midnight daily; COP$15,000-30,000

At the western end of the malecón, a cluster of ceviche shacks serve fresh shrimp, conch, octopus, and whatever else is fresh that day, cocktail-style, in a variety of sizes and prices. Jaime Torres, known as "El Caribe," runs Cocteleria Caribe, undoubtedly the best of the bunch. He makes his own aphrodisiacal ceviches, including the rompe colchon (mattress breaker), as well as fresh

Wayúu mochilas on the beach

windsurfing in Cabo de la Vela

juices, accompanied by panoramic views of the sparkling Caribbean.

★ Donde Gladys

Calle 18 No. 9-2; no phone; 5pm-10pm daily; COP$20,000

Gladys Beatriz Mendoza Guerra has been running the show at Donde Gladys since the 1980s, operating out of her own house. This is the local go-to eatery for authentic creole cuisine, including the Guajira's signature friche (pan-fried goat innards). Armadillo, rabbit, and other regional specialties are also available.

Yotojoro

Calle 7 No. 15-81; tel. 315/754-0176; 11am-10pm daily; COP$25,000

The first thing to do at Yotojoro, a well-known favorite among Riohacha's upper crust, is order a limonada de coco (coconut lemonade). Next, go for either the hearty cazuela de mariscos (seafood stew) or the signature dish, the pargo monseñor (grilled red snapper stuffed with shrimp in a tomato-coconut milk sauce). Seafood is the specialty.

ACCOMMODATIONS

Most visitors stay in Riohacha only a night or two before heading onward. These options are all centrally located, within walking distance of the city's attractions.

★ Laguna Salá

Calle 3 No. 4-81; tel. 5/729-2462; COP$61,000 dorm, COP$187,000 d

Laguna Salá, just a block from the beach, offers a luxury experience on a backpacker's budget. Rooms are spotless, the 3rd-floor rooftop bar and pool features sweeping views over the city, a TV room has a cinema-size flat-screen and beanbag chairs, and full breakfast is included in the rates.

Taroa Lifestyle Hotel

Calle 1 No. 4-77; tel. 5/729-1122; www.taroahotel.com; COP$317,000 d

The 46-room Lifestyle Hotel is the swankiest option in town, a good choice if you've been out in the desert and are ready to splurge. Go for a room with views of the boardwalk and the sea, where you can swing in a hammock to your heart's content. Sip a cocktail on the top-floor terrace and enjoy the cooling breezes.

INFORMATION AND SERVICES

A smallish supermarket, **Cumana Express** (Calle 2 No. 7-46; no phone; 8am-9pm daily) is half a block from Parque Padilla, which is ringed by **ATMs.** Discount supermarket **Metro** (tel. 5/728-9670; 8am-10pm Mon.-Sat., 8am-9pm Sun.), in the modern shopping mall **Centro Comercial Suchiimma** (Calle 15 No. 8-56; 10am-9pm daily), has all the provisions you need for an extended adventure in the desert.

TRANSPORTATION

The **bus station** (Av. El Progreso and Calle 11) has frequent buses to Santa Marta and Barranquilla as well as buses to Cartagena and Bogotá. Standard buses take longer but are more comfortable; busetas are faster minivans. There are also shared taxis, which are less comfortable but much faster and take you directly to your hotel. Shared taxis to Uribia (where you can pick up trucks to Cabo de la Vela) leave from the market area (Calle 15 and Carrera 1) in town and can be called to pick you up by your hostel or hotel. A cab to the bus station from downtown Riohacha only costs about COP$10,000.

Aeropuerto Almirante Padilla (RCH; Calle 30 No. 26a-81; tel. 5/727-3854) is five minutes north of town. There is one direct daily flight from Bogotá to Riohacha on **Avianca** (www.avianca.com).

★ Cabo de la Vela

Cabo de la Vela (known as Jepira in the Wayúu language), 180 km (110 mi) north of Riohacha, is a small Wayúu fishing village spread along the Caribbean Sea. It comes as a pleasant shock to finally arrive at the Caribbean after several hours driving through the Guajira's arid landscape. The beaches are nice, the views otherworldly, and the atmosphere peaceful. Cabo de la Vela is a destination for windsurfers and kitesurfers thanks to its smooth water and ample winds that provide near-perfect conditions.

There are several excursions around Cabo, and organized package tours should include all of them in the price. One is to **El Faro,** a lighthouse on a high promontory with wide views of the surrounding ocean. Another is to the **Ojo del Agua,** a small but pleasant beach near a freshwater spring. Farther afield is the **Pilón de Azúcar,** a high hill over the sea that affords incredible views of the surrounding region. Just below is **Playa del Pilón,** a beautiful ocher-colored beach where the water is calm and bright blue. A short walk to the east is **Playa Arcoiris,** where waves crash against the rocky shore and the sea spray forms a rainbow against the sunlight about every 30 seconds—but you have to catch it before 10am or so.

Travelers not on an organized tour can grab a mototaxi to any of these sights (around COP$7,000 pp). For COP$50,000 the mototaxistas will take you to all of them on a full-day tour, including a lunch break in town; grab a mototaxi in front of An'a Waya Restaurant before 8am-9am, before it gets too hot and they're all taken by other travelers.

KITESURFING AND WINDSURFING

Cabo de la Vela is an excellent place to learn how to kitesurf or windsurf, as there's a good breeze here December-August.

Eoletto

Calle 4 No. 9-87, Riohacha; tel. 321/468-0105 or 314/851-6216; www.windsurfingcolombia.com

Eoletto is a windsurfing and kitesurfing school that also offers accommodations in hammocks (COP$40,000) in a quiet spot facing the water. An eight-hour windsurfing course costs COP$550,000; kitesurfing is COP$800,000. Rentals (COP$100,000 per hour) are available.

FOOD AND ACCOMMODATIONS

Rudimentary family-run guesthouses are plentiful in Cabo de la Vela. Freshwater is scarce in the desert so long showers are not an option. The floors are usually sandy and electricity is limited. The street in Cabo de la Vela along the sea is lined with guesthouses that are basic but put you right at the edge of the Caribbean. Being on the beach at night, looking up at the stars, and listening to the gentle waves breaking nearby is unforgettable. There are also a few lodgings outside town toward El Faro.

Ranchería Utta

300 m (0.2 mi) northwest of town, Vía al Faro; tel. 312/687-8237 or 313/817-8076; www.rancheriautta.com; COP$40,000 hammock, COP$240,000 d

The Ranchería Utta is a nice place to stay, just far enough from Cabo de la Vela that you can experience the magic of being

flamingos in La Guajira

away from civilization. Cabins are simple, with walls made from the hearts of yotojoro (cactus), a traditional form of construction in the desert. There are 11 cabañas with a total of 35 beds and plenty of inviting chinchorros (hammocks) for lazing. A pleasant restaurant at the hotel serves breakfast (COP$14,000), lunch (COP$25,000), and dinner (COP$35,000). The fare is mostly seafood (lobster is a favorite but costs extra), but vegetarians can be accommodated.

Hostal Marparaíso

200 m (0.1 mi) south of town center on the beach; tel. 300/279-5048; COP$35,000 hammock, COP$60,000 bed

Hostal Marparaíso is one of the nicer options in the row of lodgings that stretch up the beachfront. An on-site restaurant serves decently priced fare (COP$22,000) with a stunning view of the sea.

TRANSPORTATION

Shared taxis (COP$25,000) ply the hour-long route from Riohacha to Uribia. Catch one in Riohacha at the intersection of Calle 15 and Carrera 5, or have your hostel or hotel call to have you picked up. They usually drop you off just outside Uribia, where you can grab one of the **passenger trucks** (COP$30,000) from Uribia to Cabo de la Vela, which depart 8am-2pm daily. The uncomfortable ride, on a bench in the back of a truck, can take two or more hours, depending on how many stops are made, but this is a quintessential Guajira experience.

Punta Gallinas

Punta Gallinas is a settlement on a small peninsula jutting into the Caribbean at the northernmost tip of South America. It's home to about 100 Wayúu people. The landscape is a symphony of orange, ocher, and brown tones and dotted with cacti and shrubs. The peninsula is bounded to the south by Bahía Hondita, a large bay with bright aquamarine water and thin clusters of mangroves, and to the north by the deep-blue Caribbean.

Sights in and around Punta Gallinas include the faro (lighthouse), which marks the northernmost tip of South America; **Bahía Hondita,** home to flamingos and mangroves; and the remote and unspoiled beaches at **Dunas de Taroa** (Taroa Dunes), where windswept towering sand dunes drop abruptly 30 m (100 ft) into the sea, and at **Punta Aguja,** at the southwest tip of the Punta Gallinas peninsula.

Most travelers visit these sights as part of an organized tour as they can only be accessed by 4WD vehicles and roads are nearly nonexistent. If you are on your own, hotels charge around COP$30,000 per person to see the dunes (5-person minimum); COP$220,000 for a group boat ride on the Bahía Hondita to spot flamingos; and COP$35,000 per person to go to Punta Aguja (5-person minimum).

TOURS

The typical Guajira tour (COP$920,000 pp with food and lodging) lasts three days, spending a day each in Cabo de la Vela, with a stop at the abandoned salt mines of Salinas de Manaure, and Punta Gallinas. A longer option (COP$1,500,000 pp with food and lodging) adds two nights in Nazareth to visit Parque Nacional Natural Macuira. Tours operate from Riohacha and include SUV transportation.

Most tour companies are based in Riohacha, but it's also easy to book tours in Uribia and Cabe de la Vela. Many companies don't regularly accept credit cards for payment outside Riohacha; to avoid carrying a lot of cash, consider making a consignación (bank deposit), which can be done anywhere in Colombia. Get the tour company's bank account information and go in person to a branch of their bank, then make a cash deposit of the full trip amount. There are no ATMs in Cabo de la Vela or Punta Gallinas.

Mochileros People

Uribia; tel. 313/513-3538;
maikerpinto1@gmail.com

Mochileros People employs Wayúu guides who know the desert well. It runs all-inclusive tours aimed at backpackers that includes lodging in chinchorros (hammocks) and food at their beachfront lodges in Cabo de la Vela and Punto Gallinas. A three-day tour costs COP$1,340,000 per person, and a two-day tour of Cabo de la Vela costs COP$920,000. It's also possible to craft a custom private tour or a day tour from Cabo de la Vela if you're already here.

Kai Eco Travel

Av. 1A No. 4-49, Riohacha;
tel. 311/436-2830; www.kaiecotravel.com

Kai Eco Travel has a range of tours for those who don't mind a group setting (maximum 6-8 people). A quick two-day jaunt to Cabo de la Vela costs around COP$320,000, with an extra night in Punta Gallinas bumping that up to COP$500,000. A full eight-day tour of the Alta Guajira that includes the Serranía de Macuira and Parque Nacional Natural Macuira runs COP$7,500,000 per person. If you're up for the real Guajira experience of sleeping in a chinchorro, the rates decrease slightly.

Bogotá

★ Highlights

★ **La Candelaria** *(upper right):* Explore the café- and mural-lined colonial streets of Bogotá's historical core (page 132).

★ **Museo del Oro:** Learn about the ancient Muisca civilization, known for their impressive metalworking skills (page 139).

★ **Cerro de Monserrate:** Hike or take a gondola ride up the mountain to a gleaming white cathedral overlooking the city (page 141).

★ **Usaquén:** Browse the handmade offerings of one of Latin America's largest artisan markets (page 147).

★ **Jardín Botánico:** Explore the many ecosystems of Colombia, from the Amazon rainforest to the high Andean páramo, in this world-class botanical garden (page 148).

★ **Ciclovía** *(upper left):* Grab a bike and join the party through the main streets of Bogotá every Sunday, when they are closed to vehicular traffic (page 148).

★ **Laguna de Guatavita:** Visit the cloud forest-shrouded mystical lake where the legend of El Dorado began (page 179).

Look for ★ to find recommended sights, activities, dining, and lodging.

A world-class city at nearly 2,740 m (9,000 ft) above sea level, Bogotá exudes both mystical Andean charm and the frenetic energy of a modern metropolis. A cultural microcosm of the whole country, Bogotá offers endless dining, shopping, and nightlife opportunities as well as its own impressive historical and cultural sights and attractions. Known for its excellent street art, bicycle-inclusive urban planning, and LGBTQ+-friendly attitude, it's one of the most progressive cities in the Americas.

An easy-to-use public transit system and plentiful inexpensive taxis make exploring its neighborhoods relatively easy for independent travelers. Many neighborhoods are walkable, but jump on a bike to have the city at your fingertips, as Bogotá boasts one of the best bicycle path networks in the world. Rolos (people from Bogotá) are well educated and worldly; bookstores, cultural centers, and community arts institutions are plentiful. The city hosts dozens of festivals throughout the year, and several are worth planning a trip around.

The third-largest city in South America, population 10 million, is also emerging as a gastronomical hot spot and was recently ranked on par with Lima for the quality of its restaurants. Recently, several Bogotá chefs have won global awards, including top female chef in the world.

On a high-elevation plain once home to a major pre-Columbian civilization, Bogotá is surrounded by endless adventures in the mountainous wonderland of the Department of Cundinamarca. Hot springs, waterfalls, several national parks, archaeological sites, traditional pueblos, and real campesino life thrive here and make excellent day trips from the big city.

Orientation

BOGOTÁ

Bogotá covers some 1,776 sq km (686 sq mi), filling a large part of altiplano (high plateau) or savanna. Much of your time will likely be spent along the corridor that is **Carrera 7** or **Avenida 7** (called **La Séptima**). La Séptima runs along the base of the Cerros Orientales (Eastern Mountains), at the eastern edge of the city, from the Plaza de Bolívar in La Candelaria through El Centro, then north through the Centro Internacional and Chapinero, through Northen Bogotá to Usaquén and beyond. To the west the city sprawls endlessly to farmland and humedales (wetlands) before the altiplano ends and the landscape drops steeply to the Río Magdalena valley.

Bogotá street addresses are generally easy to figure out. Calles (streets) run east-west, perpendicular to the mountains, while carreras go north-south, parallel to the mountains. The higher the number of the calle, the farther north you are. Similarly, the higher the number of the carrera, the farther west you are.

The city planners also created avenidas (avenues), diagonales, and transversales. Both diagonales and transversales are streets on the diagonal. To add to the

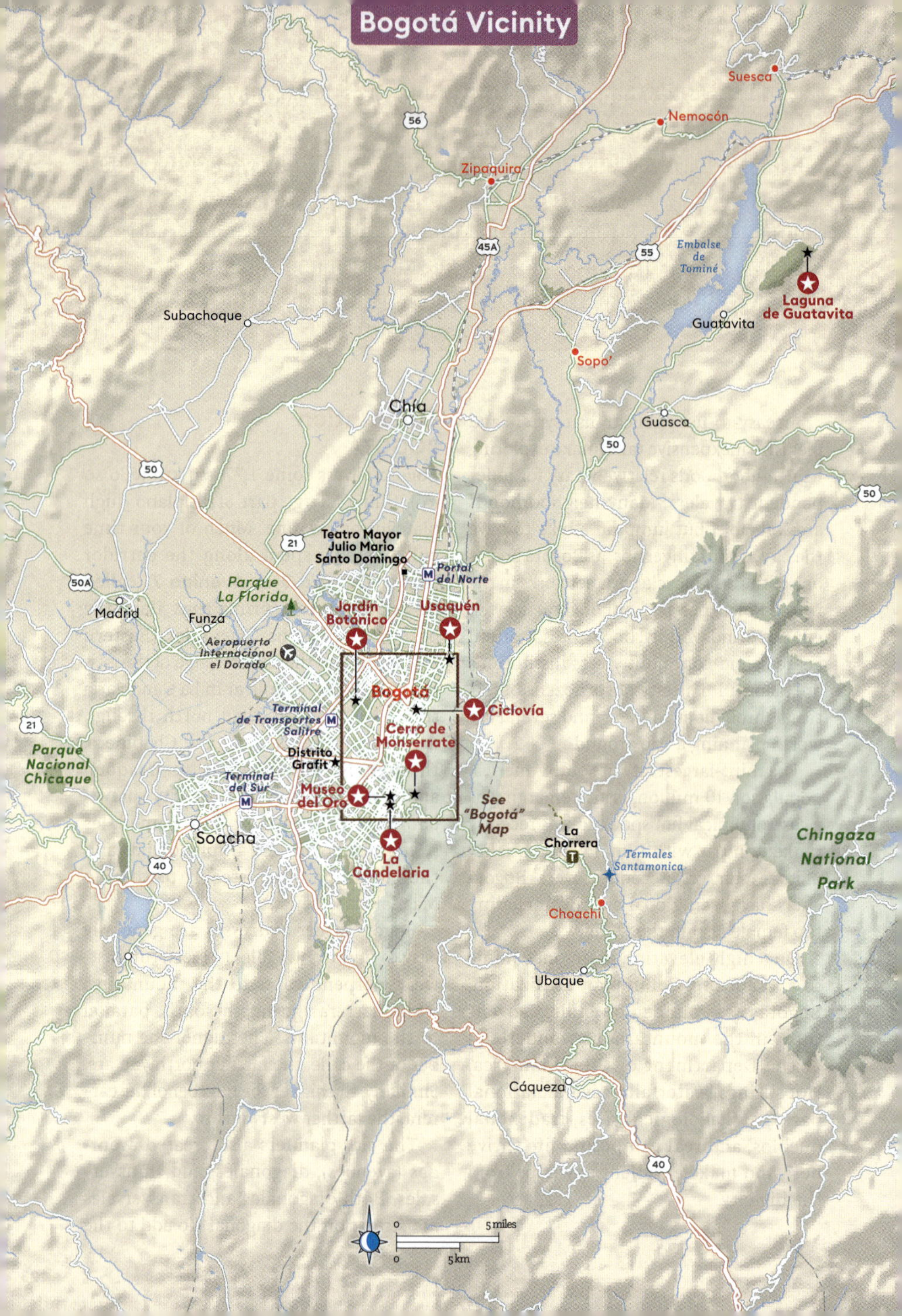
Bogotá Vicinity
Suesca
Nemocón
56
Zipaquira
45A
55
Embalse de Tominé
Laguna de Guatavita
Subachoque
Guatavita
Sopo'
Chía
Guasca
50
50
50
21
Teatro Mayor Julio Mario Santo Domingo
Portal del Norte
50A
Parque La Florida
Madrid
Funza
Jardín Botánico
Usaquén
Aeropuerto Internacional el Dorado
Bogotá
Ciclovía
21
Terminal de Transportes Salitre
Cerro de Monserrate
Parque Nacional Chicaque
Distrito Grafit
Terminal del Sur
Museo del Oro
See "Bogotá" Map
Soacha
La Candelaria
La Chorrera
Termales Santamonica
Chingaza National Park
40
Choachí
Ubaque
Cáqueza
40
0
5 miles
0
5 km

streets of La Candelaria

fun, some calles are also called avenida calles, because they are major thoroughfares, and likewise there are some called avenida carrera. Avenida Calle 26 is also known as Avenida El Dorado. Carrera 30 is also known as Avenida Quito or NQS. There are some streets that are called bis, as in Calle 70A bis or Carrera 13 bis. These are like an extra half street. Finally, addresses in the south of Bogotá have sur (south) in their address.

La Candelaria

La Candelaria is the colorful colonial center of the city, dating to the 16th century. With the Plaza de Bolívar at its heart, it is a neighborhood full of historic buildings, interesting museums, and hostels. The mural-lined streets of La Candelaria have a distinctly Bohemian vibe and bustle with students, government workers, artisanal street vendors, and international travelers. La Candelaria is bounded by Carrera 10 on the west, Calle 7 to the south, Carrera 1 to the east, and Avenida Jiménez to the north.

El Centro

The northern border of La Candelaria, Avenida Jiménez, also known as the Eje Ambiental, is a pleasant pedestrian street shared with a TransMilenio line. It follows a natural stream from the base of the mountains at Carrera 2A to Carrera 10. The area from Avenida Jiménez to Calle 25 is El Centro, Bogotá's bustling chaotic center, home to the Museo del Oro, colonial churches, Quinta de Bolívar, Cerro de Monserrate, and much of the pedestrian-only part of La Séptima.

Centro Internacional

North of El Centro, the Centro Internacional is the modern side of downtown Bogotá, home to chain hotels and restaurants as well as the Museo de Arte Moderno de Bogotá and the Museo Nacional. The historic bullfighting ring, the planetarium, and the iconic Torres del Parque complex, which rises above lush Parque de la Independencia, are also here. This neighborhood straddles La Séptima (Carrera 7) from Avenida El Dorado (Calle 26) north to Calle 36.

La Macarena

Just above Centro Internacional and north of El Centro is the artsy neighborhood of La Macarena, also known Zona M. Its quaint streets host dozens of cozy international restaurants and a handful of art galleries. To the north, La Macarena merges with the **La Perseverancia** neighborhood, a historic low-income barrio that is home to one of the city's best markets.

Teusaquillo

Just west of Centro Internacional, cool cafés and independent bookstores dot the tree-shaded streets of Teusaquillo, which runs from about Calle 26 to Calle 53 between Avenida Caracas and Carrera 30. Full of beautiful examples of 19th-century Tudor brick architecture and lush neighborhood parks, the area is home to artists, professors, and other creative types and exudes a hip alternative ambiance. The eight-block-long **Parkway,** a verdant median surrounded by restaurants and shops, is a vibrant social scene in the afternoons, while **Calle 45** has its own micro-brew-fueled nightlife district.

Chapinero

Sprawling Chapinero extends from around Calle 38 to Calle 72, although officially it continues north to Calle 100, and contains several different neighborhoods. Its western boundary is Avenida Carrera 14, also known as Avenida Caracas. Its eastern boundary pushes up against the mountains and contains mostly residential **Chapinero Alto.** To the west of La Séptima is a gritty commercial center by day and the city's most bombastic nightlife district at night. To the north, the quiet **Quinta Comacho** neighborhood gives way to the dining and cafés of the **Rosales** and **Zona G** neighborhoods, home to some of the city's top restaurants. Sights include the magnificent Basílica de Lourdes and Parque de los Hippies, an open-air party most nights of the week.

Northern Bogotá

Northern Bogotá does not have many sights, but it offers myriad options for dining, shopping, and nightlife. Calle 80 is its southern border and the neighborhood houses pockets of activity in the **Zona Rosa** (between Calles 81-85 and Carreras 11-15) and the **Parque de la 93 area** (Calles 91-94 and Carreras 11-15). In the Zona Rosa, Calle 82 and Carrera 13 form a T, hence the moniker **Zona T,** and are pedestrian streets lined with restaurants and upscale watering holes. East of La Séptima is historic **Usaquén** (Calles 116-121 and Carreras 5-7), once a small pueblo now enveloped by Bogotá. Usaquén is known for its restaurants and Sunday artisan market.

Western Bogotá

Western Bogotá (west of Av. Carrera 14) includes Parque Simón Bolívar along with the Jardín Botánico, Biblioteca Virgilio Barco, and El Dorado airport. Farther west, Avenida Carrera 30 intersects with Avenida El Dorado (Calle 26), which connects El Dorado airport with downtown.

AROUND BOGOTÁ

Surrounded by high Andean peaks and lush mountain valleys, the region around Bogotá is ripe for exploring, and much of it is off the beaten path. The must-see destinations include the sacred emerald-green Laguna de Guatavita north of the city, the waterfalls and hot springs of Choachí to the south, and Parque Natural Chicaque, a cloud forest paradise on the city's western edge.

Planning Your Time

At a minimum, give Bogotá **two days.** In that short time you can cover La Candelaria, head up to Cerro de Monserrate, discover the Museo del Oro, and enjoy a good meal in Zona G.

With **five days** you can explore neighborhoods like Teusaquillo and Chapinero, check out the botanical gardens, and make a day trip to the waterfalls in Choachí or to Laguna de Guatavita. If you're here over a Sunday, you absolutely have to head to Ciclovía and the artisan market in Usaquén.

Many museums are closed Monday or Tuesday. Museo del Oro is closed Monday and the art museums of the Manzana Cultural are closed Tuesday. Some museums have started charging foreigners in US dollars instead of Colombian pesos,

Northern Bogotá

and you will be expected to pay according to that day's exchange rate.

During the end-of-year holidays and Semana Santa, Bogotá becomes a ghost town as locals head for the countryside, the coast, or abroad. There is very little traffic at those times, but many restaurants are closed and nightspots are empty, especially around Christmas. Semana Santa is perhaps less lonely and can be a good time to visit, especially when the biennial theater festival is on. On long weekends, many Bogotanos skip town; people from the provinces come for a visit.

Bogotá is known for its cold wet weather, surprising many visitors who think that Colombia is all one big tropical beach. Because of its high elevation, temperatures are cool, and because it is close to the equator, averages vary only slightly through the year, with highs of 10-16°C (50-60°F). Drizzle is omnipresent, and March-June and November-December are particularly rainy. Bring waterproof outer layers and good socks.

Safety

Bogotá is relatively safe for a city of its size, although petty theft, especially the art of **pickpocketing,** has been perfected here. The best advice, as Colombians say, is "No dar papaya," literally, "Don't give any papayas." Don't hand someone the opportunity to take advantage of you.

While strolling in La Candelaria and El Centro, particularly along La Séptima, keep a watchful eye on cameras and smartphones. Better yet, leave your valuables—including your passport—locked in the hotel safe. Private security guards and police now regularly patrol La Candelaria at night.

Traveling by the city's TransMilenio buses is safe and comfortable, although they can get crowded at peak hours, so be aware of hands reaching for your pockets. Colectivos, the smaller privately run buses that traverse the city, are less safe, and drivers can be reckless.

Bogotá has had a serious problem with **taxi crime,** commonly known as paseo milonario, but recent technological advances have nearly eliminated these crimes. **Cabify** and **EasyTaxi** are popular free smartphone apps to request a taxi, find out the name of the driver, and have your trip tracked by a friend. Alternatively, you can use ridesharing apps like **Uber.** Avoid hailing taxis on the street, particularly when you are alone, late at night, or near nightclubs and upscale dining areas.

Elevation

At 2,580 m (8,465 ft), Bogotá is the third-highest capital city in the world after La Paz, Bolivia, and Quito, Ecuador. It is common to feel short of breath and fatigued during the first two days at this elevation. Other symptoms of altitude sickness include headache and nausea. Take it easy for the first few days in Bogotá and avoid caffeine and alcohol. If you are sensitive to high altitude, see a doctor before your trip for a prescription medication to mitigate the effects. Try coca tea to get some instant relief.

Sunburns are more common at higher elevations, as there's less atmosphere blocking out UV rays. Apply sunblock regularly, even when it's cloudy.

Itinerary Ideas

Three days is a perfect amount of time to take in the sights of Bogotá, especially if you base yourself in La Candelaria, close to all the action. Upscale restaurants, especially in Zona G, should be reserved ahead of time.

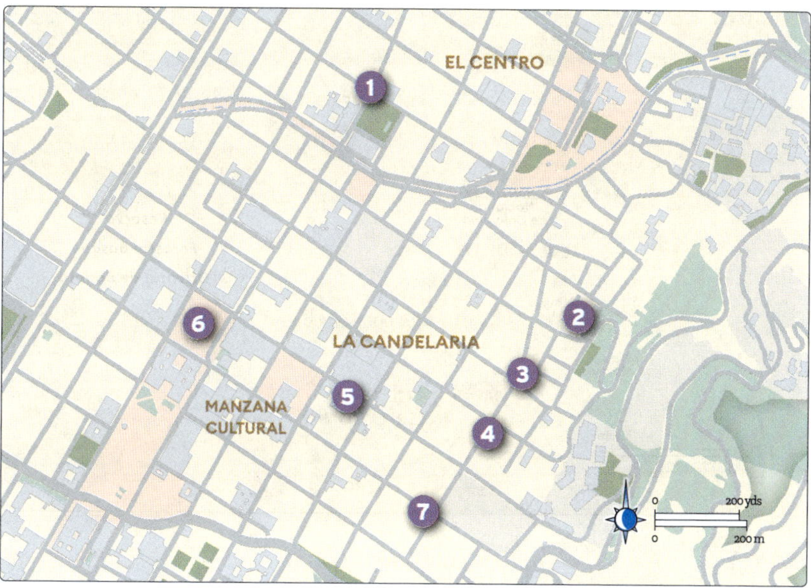

DAY 1

1. Start the day at the **Museo de Oro** and explore the complex history of Colombia's original societies, including the Muisca, who lived where modern-day Bogotá now stands.

2. Walk over to La Concordia, about five blocks, and have an ajiaco for lunch at **Recetas de Abuela.** Grab a seat on the front terrace for awesome views over the Bogotá skyline.

3. Right across the street, head up tiny Calle del Embudo, admiring the murals along the way, to **Chorro de Quevedo,** where storytellers and street performers await.

4. Crossing Chorro de Quevedo, continue down Carrera 2, stopping for a freshly roasted coffee and a house-made carrot cake at **Cafe del Mercado.**

5. Make your way to the museums of the **Manzana Cultural,** the most important Cultural Block in Colombia.

6. Finish at the **Plaza de Bolívar,** a block down Calle 11 from the Manzana, just in time to catch the sunset over the mountains.

7. When night falls, walk up pedestrian-only Calle 10 for dinner at **Chamanico.**

Itinerary Ideas

DAY 2

1. Hike or take the teleférico to the top of **Cerro de Monserrate,** with spectacular views over the city and a lush cloud forest.

2. Afterward, take a taxi to **Paloquemao,** Bogotá's massive central market, and have a mondongo (beef tripe) stew for lunch. Spend some time exploring the fruits and veggies trucked in from every department of Colombia.

3. After lunch, take a taxi to the **Jardín Botánico** and spend the afternoon checking out the native species of Colombia within temperature-controlled domes that mimic their ecosystems.

4. In the evening, take a taxi to Bogotá's Zona G and have dinner at **Restaurante Leo,** where the each of the 13 courses gives you a taste of a different region of the country.

5. If your battery is still charged, take a taxi over to **Theatrón** for the all-night LGBTQ+ friendly dance party.

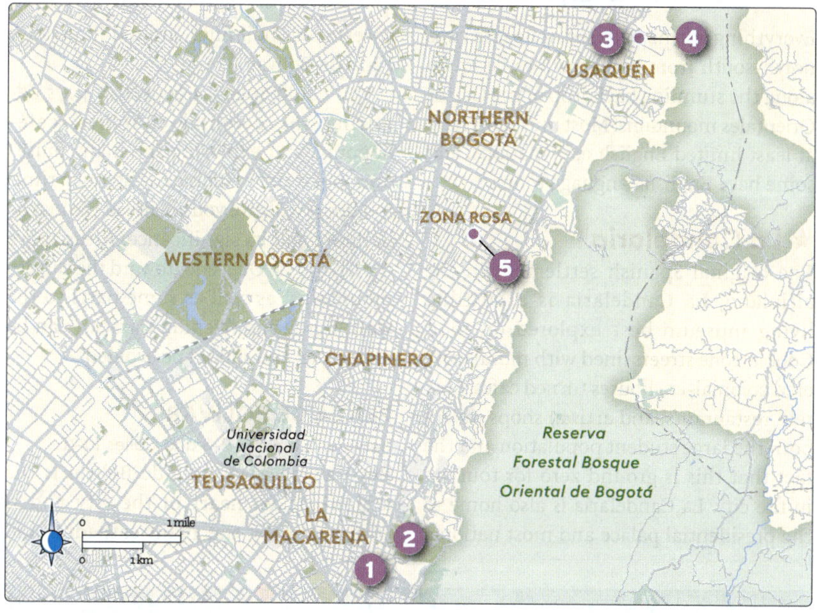

DAY 3

1 Grab a bike or bike tour and join the crowds for **Ciclovía,** where Bogotá's main thoroughfares are closed to vehicular traffic.

2 Stop at **Parque Nacional** for a massive dance class in the open air and explore the beauty of this urban forest.

3 Continue down La Séptima to **Usaquén,** about 10 km (6 mi) from Parque Nacional, where cobblestone streets are filled with art and artisan vendors, and live bands play in the main square.

4 Grab a thick Argentine steak and a glass of Mendoza red at **La Patagonia.**

5 In the evening, bike or taxi over to Zona T to refresh yourself with a cold beer at **The Pub Bogotá** and watch the well-heeled strut up and down this pedestrian mall.

Sights

Everything you need to see in Bogotá runs north-south from downtown to Usaquén along the stunning backdrop of the Cerros Orientales mountains. Most museums have at least limited English explanations, and some have English-language tours.

★ La Candelaria

The original Spanish settlement in the altiplano, La Candelaria is a bustling living museum best explored on foot. Cobblestone streets lined with mural-covered colonial-era houses turned cafés, hostels, restaurants, and artisan shops reflect both the large student population and the fact that this is ground zero for tourism in the city. La Candelaria is also home to the presidential palace and most national government buildings, around impressive Plaza de Bolívar.

You could spend a couple of days admiring the colonial churches, café-hopping, and exploring the many museums, but if you don't have that much time, 3-4 hours will give you a sense of the neighborhood and its significance. Areas above the Chorro de Quevedo (toward the eastern mountains) as well as some parts to the west, bordering Avenida Caracas, can be dangerous and should be avoided.

PLAZA DE BOLÍVAR

between Carreras 7-8 and Calles 10-11

Bogotá's massive Plaza de Bolívar is the action-packed heart of the city and is surrounded by the main cathedral and

Plaza de Bolívar

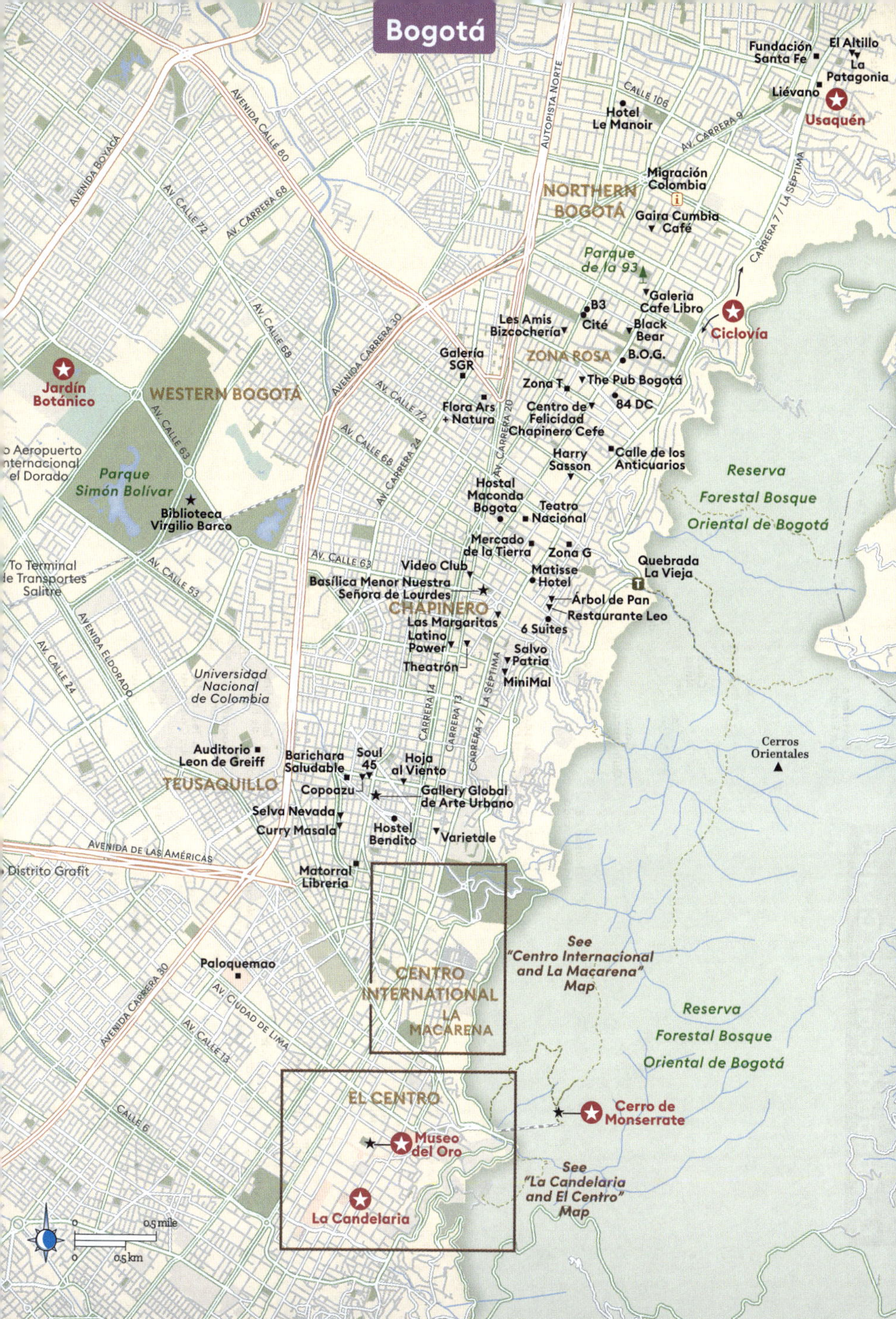
Bogotá
Fundación Santa Fe
El Altillo
La Patagonia
Liévano
Usaquén
Hotel Le Manoir
Migración Colombia
NORTHERN BOGOTÁ
Gaira Cumbia Café
Parque de la 93
Galeria Cafe Libro
B3
Cité
Les Amis Bizcochería
Black Bear
Ciclovía
ZONA ROSA
B.O.G.
Galería SGR
Zona T
The Pub Bogotá
84 DC
Flora Ars + Natura
Centro de Felicidad Chapinero Cefe
Calle de los Anticuarios
Harry Sasson
Jardín Botánico
WESTERN BOGOTÁ
To Aeropuerto Internacional el Dorado
Parque Simón Bolívar
Biblioteca Virgilio Barco
Reserva Forestal Bosque Oriental de Bogotá
Hostal Macondo Bogota
Teatro Nacional
Mercado de la Tierra
Zona G
Matisse Hotel
Quebrada La Vieja
To Terminal de Transportes Salitre
Video Club
Basílica Menor Nuestra Señora de Lourdes
CHAPINERO
Árbol de Pan
Restaurante Leo
Las Margaritas
6 Suites
Latino Power
Theatrón
Salvo Patria
MiniMal
Universidad Nacional de Colombia
Cerros Orientales
Auditorio Leon de Greiff
Barichara Saludable
Soul 45
Hoja al Viento
TEUSAQUILLO
Copoazu
Gallery Global de Arte Urbano
Selva Nevada
Curry Masala
Hostel Bendito
Varietale
Distrito Grafit
Matorral Librería
See "Centro Internacional and La Macarena" Map
Paloquemao
CENTRO INTERNATIONAL
LA MACARENA
Reserva Forestal Bosque Oriental de Bogotá
EL CENTRO
Cerro de Monserrate
Museo del Oro
See "La Candelaria and El Centro" Map
La Candelaria
0.5 mile
0.5 km
AUTOPISTA NORTE
CALLE 106
AV. CARRERA 9
AVENIDA CALLE 80
AVENIDA BOYACÁ
AV. CALLE 72
AV. CARRERA 68
CARRERA 7 / LA SÉPTIMA
AV. CALLE 68
AVENIDA CARRERA 30
AV. CALLE 72
AV. CARRERA 20
AV. CALLE 68
AV. CARRERA 24
AV. CALLE 63
AV. CALLE 63
AV. CALLE 53
AVENIDA ELDORADO
AV. CALLE 24
CARRERA 14
CARRERA 13
CARRERA 7 / LA SÉPTIMA
AVENIDA DE LAS AMÉRICAS
AVENIDA CARRERA 30
AV. CIUDAD DE LIMA
AV. CALLE 13
CALLE 6

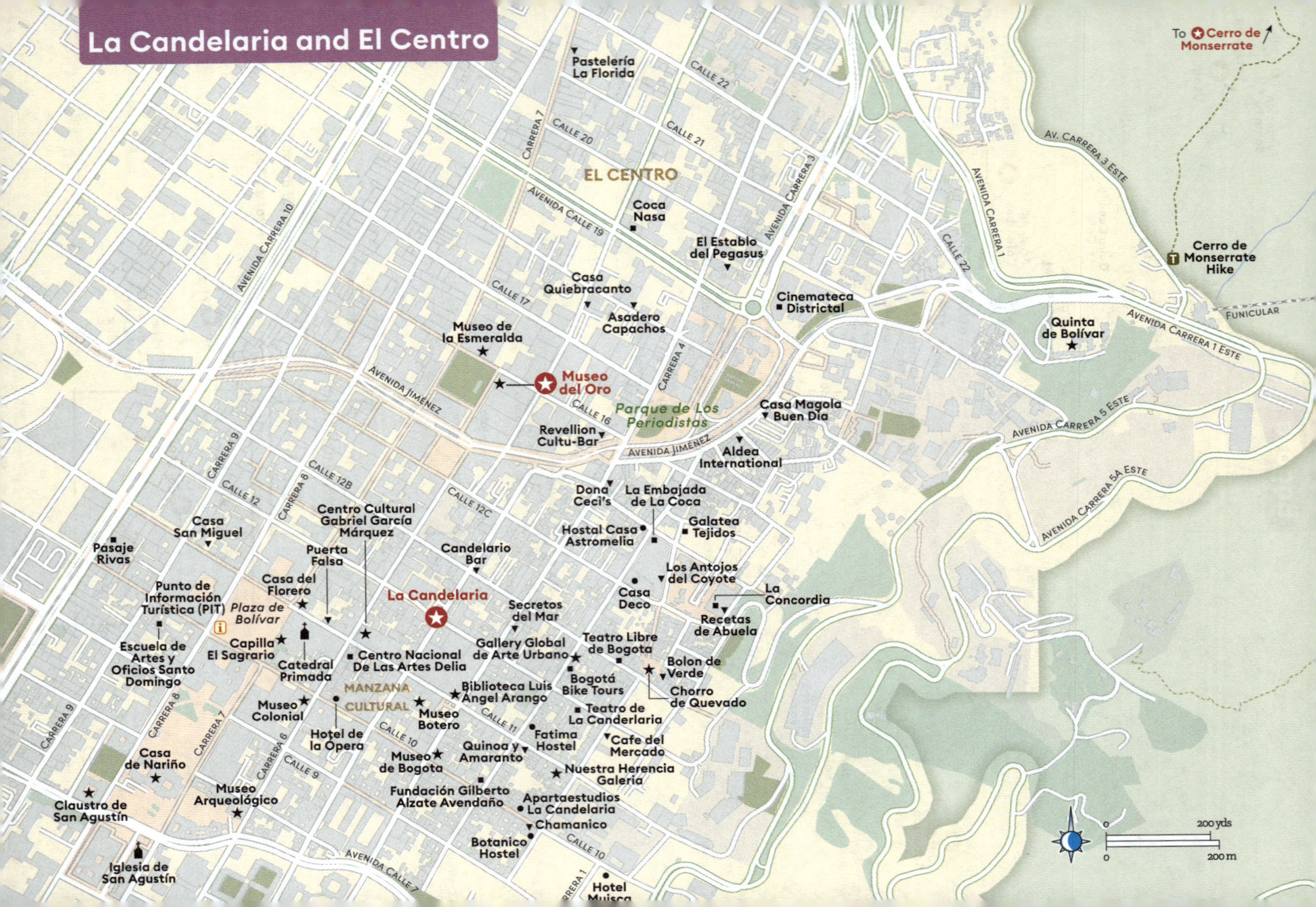
La Candelaria and El Centro
To Cerro de Monserrate
Pastelería La Florida
Calle 22
Calle 20
Calle 21
Carrera 7
El Centro
Av. Carrera 3 Este
Avenida Carrera 1
Avenida Calle 19
Coca Nasa
Avenida Carrera 3
Avenida Carrera 10
El Establo del Pegasus
Cerro de Monserrate Hike
Casa Quiebracanto
Calle 17
Asadero Capachos
Cinemateca Districtal
Funicular
Quinta de Bolívar
Avenida Carrera 1 Este
Museo de la Esmeralda
Carrera 4
Museo del Oro
Avenida Jiménez
Calle 16
Parque de Los Periodistas
Casa Magola Buen Dia
Revellion Cultu-Bar
Avenida Carrera 5 Este
Aldea International
Carrera 9
Calle 12B
Calle 12
Carrera 8
Calle 12C
Dona Ceci's
La Embajada de La Coca
Avenida Carrera 5A Este
Centro Cultural Gabriel García Márquez
Casa San Miguel
Hostal Casa Astromelia
Galatea Tejidos
Pasaje Rivas
Puerta Falsa
Candelario Bar
Los Antojos del Coyote
Punto de Información Turística (PIT)
Casa del Florero
La Candelaria
Casa Deco
La Concordia
Plaza de Bolívar
Secretos del Mar
Recetas de Abuela
Capilla El Sagrario
Escuela de Artes y Oficios Santo Domingo
Catedral Primada
Centro Nacional De Las Artes Delia
Gallery Global de Arte Urbano
Teatro Libre de Bogota
Bolon de Verde
Bogotá Bike Tours
Manzana Cultural
Biblioteca Luis Angel Arango
Chorro de Quevado
Museo Colonial
Museo Botero
Teatro de La Canderlaria
Calle 11
Hotel de la Ópera
Calle 10
Fatima Hostel
Cafe del Mercado
Quinoa y Amaranto
Casa de Nariño
Carrera 6
Museo de Bogota
Nuestra Herencia Galeria
Calle 9
Museo Arqueológico
Fundación Gilberto Alzate Avendaño
Apartaestudios La Candelaria
Claustro de San Agustín
Chamanico
Botanico Hostel
Avenida Calle 7
Iglesia de San Agustín
Hotel Muisca
0
200 yds
200 m

government buildings like the supreme court, the congress, and the neoclassical palace that houses the mayor. In colonial times the Friday market took place here. It was also the setting for executions, including that of independence heroine Policarpa Salavarrieta. Following the death of Simón Bolívar in 1846, Congress renamed the plaza in his honor. A diminutive statue of the liberator, the first of many Bolívar statues in the world, stands in the middle of the plaza.

Catedral Primada

Carrera 7 No. 11-10; 9am-4:30pm daily

The neoclassical facade of the gigantic Catedral Primada dominates the plaza. Built in 1807, the cathedral was designed by Capuchin architect Fray Domingo de Petrés. The tombs of Gonzalo Jiménez de Quesada, founder of Bogotá, and independence figure Antonio Nariño are in a side chapel on the right. No shorts, sandals, or sleeveless shirts are allowed inside.

Capilla El Sagrario

Carrera 7 No. 10-40; 8:30am-11:50am and 1pm-4pm Mon.-Fri., 8:30am-5pm Sun.

Next door to the cathedral is the Capilla El Sagrario. This chapel was built much earlier, in the 1600s. The interior is decorated with a Mudéjar (Moorish-style) vaulted wooden ceiling. Along the sides of the cross-shaped chapel are several large works depicting biblical scenes by Colombian baroque painter Gregorio Vásquez de Arce y Ceballos. A ceremony was held here to honor the army and Simón Bolívar following their decisive victory over the Spaniards at the Battle of Boyacá in 1819.

Casa del Florero

Carrera 7 No. 11-28; tel. 1/334-4150; www.museoindependencia.gov.co; 9am-5pm Tues.-Sun.; USD$10

Across Calle 10 on the northeast corner of the plaza is the Casa del Florero, also known as the **Museo del 20 de Julio** or **Museo de la Independencia.** This small house used to be a general store run by a Spaniard, José González-Llorente. The story goes that his refusal to lend a vase to a pair of creole people sparked the ire of locals, who launched a protest against Spanish rule during the busy market day. Maybe the most interesting exhibit in the museum is a room that shows the transformation of the Plaza de Bolívar over time, with raw footage of two of the most traumatic events in recent Colombian history: the Bogotazo riots following the assassination of Jorge Eliécer Gaitán in 1948 and the siege of the Palacio de Justicia following a takeover by the M-19 guerrilla group in 1985. There are some explanations in English. Tours are also available, usually in Spanish.

SOUTH OF THE PLAZA

Casa de Nariño

Carrera 8 No. 6-26; www.presidencia.gov.co

You can have your picture taken with members of the Presidential Guard (they don't mind) at the gates of the neoclassical Casa de Nariño, home to Colombia's presidents. As its name suggests, the presidential palace stands on the site of the house where Antonio Nariño, one of the early voices for independence in New Granada (the name given to the territory by the Spanish), was born. In 1906 Nariño's house was razed to make way for the first presidential palace, designed by the same French architect who designed the Palacio Liévano on Plaza de Bolívar. The palace has served as home for Colombian presidents off and on since 1886. Also on the grounds of the Casa de Nariño is the oldest **astronomical observatory** in the New

World, the initiative of famed botanist and scientist José Celestino Mutis. It was completed in 1803.

Guided tours of the Casa de Nariño (2 hours; free) require making a reservation several days in advance by filling out the form on the website. Even if you don't visit the interior of the palace, you can watch the **changing of the Presidential Guard** (2:30pm Wed. and Fri., 3pm Sun.).

Iglesia and Claustro de San Agustín

Carrera 7 No. 7-13; 9am-5pm daily

Facing the palace on the south side, the Iglesia de San Agustín was part of the first Augustinian monastery in the Spanish New World, completed in 1668. It is a three-nave temple, distinguishing it from other churches at the time. The Claustro de San Agustín (Carrera 8 No. 7-21; tel. 1/342-2340; 9am-5pm Mon.-Sat., 9am-4pm Sun.; free) didn't serve long as a seminary and was used as a garrison where Antonio Nariño was imprisoned. Today this beautiful cloister is run by Universidad Nacional, which puts on temporary art exhibits and hosts educational activities.

Museo Arqueológico (MUSA)

Carrera 6 No. 7-43; tel. 1/243-0465; www.musa.com.co; 8:30am-5pm Mon.-Fri., 9am-4pm Sat.; COP$10,000

Museo Arqueológico holds an extensive and nicely presented collection of ceramic work of pre-Columbian Indigenous peoples in a gorgeous colonial mansion. There is also a room containing colonial-era decorative arts, acknowledging the building's history as the 17th-century home of a Spanish marquess. A small café adjoins the museum.

MANZANA CULTURAL

Calle 11 No. 4-41

Just a block east of Plaza de Bolívar, the Manzana Cultural of the Banco de la República is the most important Cultural Block in Colombia. It comprises the Biblioteca Luis Ángel Arango, the library's concert hall, the Museo Botero, the Museo de Arte, the Colección de Arte del Banco de la República, El Centro Nacional de las Artes Delia Zapata Olivella, and the Casa de la Moneda. Admission is free to all institutions here.

Biblioteca Luis Ángel Arango

Calle 11 No. 4-14; tel. 1/343-1224; www.banrepcultural.org; 8am-7pm Mon.-Sat., 9am-4pm Sun.

The Biblioteca Luis Ángel Arango is one of the busiest libraries in the world, with over 5,000 visitors each day. Part of the same complex and behind the library, the **Casa Republicana** (8am-8pm Mon.-Sat., 8am-4pm Sun.; free) often hosts temporary art exhibits. There is also a stunning chamber music concert hall in the large complex. The top-level terrace has panoramic views over the city.

Museo Botero

Calle 11 No. 4-41; tel. 1/343-1316; www.banrepcultural.org; 9am-7pm Mon. and Wed.-Sat., 10am-5pm Sun.; free

In the Museo Botero are still lifes, portrayals of everyday life in Colombian pueblos, and social commentaries by Medellín-born contemporary artist Fernando Botero. In addition to paintings of corpulent Colombians, there are bronze and marble sculptures of chubby cats and bulgy birds. One side of the lovely colonial house, which surrounds a sublime courtyard, displays the artist's collection of European and American art, including works by Pablo

THE CITY IS THE CANVAS

Bogotá is world renowned for the sheer magnitude of its street-art scene. Murals are everywhere you turn, and the artistic quality of them is in a league of its own.

mural by Carlos Trilleras

Tagging hit Bogotá in the 1980s. In 2011, however, the course of the city's graffiti legacy changed forever. While spraying his tag, Felix the Cat, on the walls of an underpass, 16-year-old Diego Felipe Becerra was shot and killed by the police.

Protests erupted across the city, and due to public pressure, the city decided not only to legalize graffiti but to give it cultural heritage status. Since then, every December the government sponsors the weeklong **Festival International de Arte Urbano** that commissions dozens of new pieces across the city. This has created a viable source of income for graffiti artists and turned the metropolis into a resplendent living canvas that has gained international attention.

TOURS

- **Bogotá Graffiti Tour** (https://bogotagraffiti.com; free): A free walking tour of La Candelaria and El Centro street art.
- **Breaking Borders Social Impact Graffiti Tour** (https://impulsetravel.co; USD$60 pp): A tour guided by former gang members that visit Barrio Egipto, a historic low-income neighborhood.

SIGHTS

- **Galeria Nuestra Herencia** (Calle 11 No. 2-11; tel. 301/797-8400): A La Candelaria gallery and café run by a collective of local graffiti artists, including Carlos Trilleras, an Amazonian-born artist.
- **Gallery Global de Arte Urbano:** A gallery in La Candelaria (Carrera 3 No. 12-42) and a working studio open to the public in Teusaquillo (Calle 43 No. 18a-10).
- **Distrito Grafiti:** The city's official street-art district, home to more than 300 murals. While the area can easily be visited by TransMilenio and its own Distrito Grafiti metro stop, avoid walking around here at night.

Picasso and Salvador Dalí—all donated by the maestro so that Colombians of all backgrounds could enjoy them without paying a peso. Once the home of archbishops during the colonial era, the building was torched during the 1948 Bogotazo riots, but it has been painstakingly restored. Guided tours are offered daily.

Centro Cultural Gabriel García Márquez

Calle 11 No. 5-60; tel. 1/283-2200; www.fce.com.co; 9am-7pm Mon. and Wed.-Sat., 10:30am-5pm Sun.; free

Designed by Rogelio Salmona, the Centro Cultural Gabriel García Márquez was a gift from the Mexican government in honor of the 1982 Nobel Prize winner for literature, Colombian Gabriel García Márquez. The author lived in Mexico from the 1960s until his death in 2014. On the main level, where you can enjoy a sunset view of the cathedral, is a bookstore with an ample selection of books on Colombia. Next to the Juan Valdez Café below is an exhibition space.

Museo Colonial

Carrera 6 No. 9-77; tel. 1/341-6017; www.museocolonial.gov.co; 9am-5pm Tues.-Sat., 10am-4pm Sun.; USD$10, free Sun.

Well worth a visit, the Museo Colonial showcases a fine collection of art and religious artifacts from the colonial era, including the largest collection of works by Gregorio Vásquez de Arce y Ceballos. On the bottom floor is an exhibit that explores life in colonial times. The museum courtyard is quiet and green.

Museo de Bogotá

Carrera 4 No. 10-18; tel. 1/282-0488; 9am-5:30pm Wed.-Mon.; free

In a massive two-story colonial mansion on pedestrian-only Calle 10, the Museo de Bogotá holds a variety of exhibits relating to the architectural and urban history of the nation's capital. Particularly fascinating is a model of the city for the next 30 years showing two different outcomes—one that illustrates the increased green spaces and compact design of strong urban planning and one that shows it sprawling and doubling in size if things are left to the market.

CHORRO DE QUEVEDO

The first houses and church (the diminutive Ermita de San Miguel del Principe) in the city were built around the natural water source Chorro de Quevedo, "El Chorro," which packs with students drinking chicha in the afternoon and becomes a full-on street party in the evening. The small plaza hosts a variety of street performers, including musicians, jugglers, and theater groups, while cuenteros (storytellers) like to set up in front of the church. Most of the old houses here have been turned into cafés and bars, many offering outdoor seating on the plaza. Wander down the cobblestones of Calle del Embudo to visit traditional chicherías. El Chorro is located in the northeastern corner of La Candelaria, near the newly renovated La Concordia market.

El Centro

Avenida Jiménez used to be the Río San Francisco and the extreme northern boundary of Bogotá. In 2000, in an effort to reinvent the historic avenue, architect Rogelio Salmona created the **Eje Ambiental** (Environmental Corridor), which unearthed the river and follows it from the Universidad de los Andes campus to Avenida Caracas. Vehicular traffic is banned except for the red TransMilenio buses, and ample pedestrian space has made this a pleasant place for a stroll. Much

Chorro de Quevedo

of El Centro is dedicated to office buildings, shopping, and nightlife.

PARQUE DE LOS PERIODISTAS

Bordered by the Eje Ambiental on one side and the Las Aguas TransMilenio station on the other, Parque de los Periodistas is a large open plaza in the middle of the downtown action. A statue of Simón Bolívar graces the center of the plaza, while the eastern corner is home to an arcade of artisan vendors.

★ MUSEO DEL ORO

Carrera 6 No. 15-88; tel. 1/343-2233; www.banrepcultural.org; 9am-6pm Tues.-Sat., 10am-4pm Sun.; COP$5,000

The one must-see museum in Bogotá is the world-renowned Museo del Oro (Gold Museum). It tells the story of how and why the Indigenous peoples of Colombia created such incredibly detailed and surprisingly modern designs in gold jewelry and religious objects that the Spanish thought they had found a city of gold—El Dorado. What's on view is but a fraction of the museum's collection.

One of the highlights is the golden raft created by local Muisca people that portrays an elaborate ritual carried out at Laguna de Guatavita. Another piece to look for is the collection's first acquisition, the Quimbaya Póporo, used during religious ceremonies. English explanations are excellent throughout the museum, as is the audio tour. Just beyond the gift shop is a restaurant that specializes in Colombian and Mediterranean cuisine. There are guided tours (11am, 3pm, and 4pm daily), some of which are in English.

STREETS FOR THE PEOPLE

Bogotá has long been known for its chaotic traffic and urban pollution that still typify much of the city. To combat this, several streets in the center of the city have been completely closed to traffic in an attempt to make the area more pedestrian-friendly. More "peatonalización" projects are in the works, especially in La Candelaria.

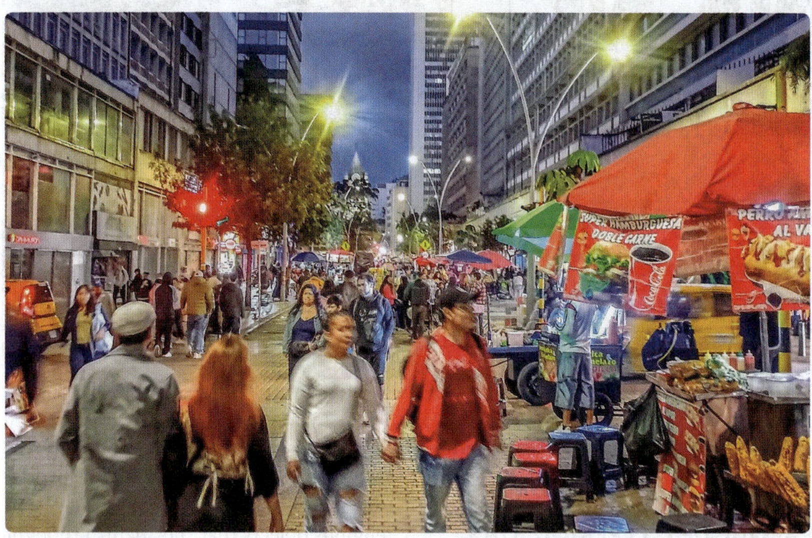

La Séptima at night

LA SÉPTIMA

Carrera Séptima, Bogotá's first real road, runs across the city south-north. In 2011 the then-mayor of Bogotá and now president of Colombia, Gustavo Petro, closed 14 blocks of La Séptima in the city's core to vehicular traffic, a move that critics said would kill businesses along this prime artery. But today crowds pack La Séptima, including street performers, food vendors, and international visitors. Connecting Plaza de Bolívar with Parque de la Independencia, La Séptima is a permanent festival and a living example of how giving streets back to the people can revitalize a downtown area.

CALLE 10

In 2016 the city also closed Calle 10, perpendicular to La Séptima, to vehicular traffic for five blocks between Carreras 7 and 2. The colonial houses on the street quickly turned into cafés and restaurants with outdoor seating where clients enjoy the historic ambience without the nuisance of car horns and exhaust. Because Calle 10 also intersects Plaza de Bolívar, it connects it to La Séptima and extends the pedestrian paradise into the heart of La Candelaria.

MUSEO DE LA ESMERALDA

Calle 16 No. 6-66; tel. 1/482-7890; www.museodelaesmeralda.com.co; 9am-5pm Mon.-Sat.; COP$6,000

On the 23rd floor of the Avianca building is the Museo de la Esmeralda, with an impressive re-creation of an emerald mine and several examples of emeralds from Colombia and elsewhere. Guides, fluent in Spanish and English, will make sure you know that the best emeralds come from Colombia, primarily from the Muzo mines in Boyacá. There is little sales pressure, but you can purchase different classes of emeralds, and the facility's jewelers can transform them into rings or earrings within a day.

QUINTA DE BOLÍVAR

Calle 21 No. 4A-30; tel. 601/342-4100; www.quintadebolivar.gov.co; 9am-5pm Tues.-Sun.; COP$10,000

Quinta de Bolívar is a lovely and leafy country estate in the heart of the city. It was presented by the vice president of the República de Gran Colombia as a gift to Simón Bolívar in 1820. Bolívar stayed here during his brief and sporadic visits to Bogotá and used the surrounding grounds to plant the many different species of he found on his travels in South America. The result is a fascinating botanical garden under walnut and cypress trees that's a pleasure to roam and relax in. Built in 1800, the estate is a beautiful example of late colonial-era architecture, furnished with period pieces and many artifacts from Bolívar's life. From Quinta de Bolívar it is just a five-minute walk uphill to Cerro de Monserrate.

★ CERRO DE MONSERRATE

Carrera 2 Este No. 21-48; tel. 1/284-5700; www.cerromonserrate.com; 6:30am-midnight Mon.-Sat., 6:30am-6:30pm Sun.

Panoramic views over Bogotá from the top of the forested mountain that towers over it makes a visit to the Cerro de Monserrate an unforgettable experience. For the easy way to the top, take either the **funicular tramway** (6:30am-10pm Mon.-Sat., 5:30am-6pm Sun.; COP$32,000 round-trip) or the ski-style gondola **teleférico** (6am-10pm Mon.-Sat., 5:30am-6pm Sun.; COP$32,000 round-trip). It's cheaper on Sunday (COP$19,000 round-trip), so expect long lines. A more challenging option involves hiking the ancient stone steps to the top.

At the top of the mountain a gleaming white church, **Santuario de Monserrate,** watches over the city from 3,152 m (10,341 ft) elevation. It is usually lit up at night. Inside the Santuario, a 17th-century sculpture of the Fallen Christ of Monserrate attracts religious pilgrims. Some climb the hill on their knees during Semana Santa, and others visit the 12 Stations of the Cross just outside. The Santuario holds mass (10am and noon Mon.-Fri., 10am, noon, and 2:30pm Sat.-Sun.) but is closed to the public outside these hours.

The views to the south are particularly spectacular, with the statue of the Virgin of Guadalupe set against the rugged peaks of the Cerros Orientales and the entire city below.

A row of artisan and souvenir vendors leads to an arcade full of traditional eateries and souvenir shops just above the Santuario. Atop the mountain there are two upscale restaurants with fantastic views but overpriced fare.

Cerro de Monserrate is most crowded on Sunday.

Centro Internacional and La Macarena

Centro Internacional

MUSEO DE ARTE MODERNO DE BOGOTÁ (MAMBO)

Calle 24 No. 6-00; tel. 1/286-0466; www.mambogota.com; 10am-6pm Tues.-Sat., noon-5pm Sun.; COP$20,000

Connected to Parque de la Independencia by the series of open-air plazas that serve as bridges over the roaring traffic of Avenida 26 is the Museo de Arte Moderno de Bogotá (Museum of Modern Art). Its large permanent collection of Colombian and Latin American creators is a fascinating dive into the continent's modern art scene, accentuated by temporary exhibits featuring emerging and established talent. The building, a creation of architect Rogelio Salmona, also features an on-site café and bookstore.

TORRE COLPATRIA OBSERVATION DECK

Carrera 7 No. 24-89; tel. 1/283-6665; 5pm-8:30pm Fri., noon-8:30pm Sat., 11am-5pm Sun.; COP$18,000

The Torre Colpatria Observation Deck offers unparalleled 360-degree views of Bogotá from the 50th floor. At night the tower goes into disco mode, displaying colorful lights.

PARQUE DE LA INDEPENDENCIA

Parque de la Independencia, long a favorite for young lovers and those seeking a pleasant stroll under the towering eucalyptus, ceiba, and wax palm trees, was created in 1910 in celebration of Colombia's 100-year anniversary of independence from Spain. The **Quiosco de la Luz** houses a **PIT** (Punto de Información Turística, a visitor information center). The park winds up the hill through lush vegetation to the La Macarena neighborhood. There's also a planetarium and bullfighting ring.

Torres del Parque

About 100 steps up from the bullfighting ring and planetarium are the iconic Torres del Parque. These three brick apartment buildings, rising parallel to the eastern mountains and twisting elegantly into the sky, were designed in the 1960s by Rogelio Salmona, the most accomplished architect from Bogotá during the late 20th century. French-born Salmona studied with the famed Le Corbusier and was awarded the Alvar Aalto Prize in 2003 for his lifetime achievements. Public space takes up three-quarters of the tower complex, and its art galleries, cafés, and bodegas are nice places to linger on a rainy day.

Planetario de Bogotá

Calle 26B No. 5-93; tel. 1/281-4150; www.planetariodebogota.gov.co; 9am-7:30pm Tues.-Sun.; COP$12,000

Within the park is a planetarium, the Planetario de Bogotá. It hosts nonstop events year-round, including astronomical talks and immersive cosmic shows in its dome-shaped movie theater.

Plaza de Toros de Santamaría

The Plaza de Toros de Santamaría, a neo-Mudéjar brick arena, was built in the 1930s by a Spanish architect and was modeled after bullfighting rings in Madrid. Bullfighting was banned in Colombia in 2024, and the ring will become an event space.

MUSEO NACIONAL

Carrera 7 No. 28-66; tel. 1/381-6470; www.museonacional.gov.co; 10am-5pm Tues.-Sun.; USD$10

The Museo Nacional was designed by English architect Thomas Reed, who also designed the Capitolio Nacional, in the late 1800s to serve as the penitentiary for

clockwise Basílica Menor Nuestra Señora de Lourdes; the bullfighting ring and Torres del Parque; Jardín Botánico

Cundinamarca, which was one of the nine states of the United States of Colombia. In the late 1940s the prison was converted into a museum. The permanent collection examines the history of Colombia from pre-Columbian cultures to the 20th century. On the top floor is a nice introduction to late-20th-century Colombian art. The museum often holds temporary exhibits on the ground floor. There are usually at least minimal English descriptions throughout. Art books and handicrafts are sold at the museum shop. A Juan Valdez Café brews coffee in the inviting interior courtyard and sculpture garden.

PARQUE NACIONAL

between Carreras 5-7 and Calles 35-39

A center of activity on weekends, Parque Nacional rambles down from the mountains all the way to La Séptima, making it the largest park in downtown Bogotá and the second oldest in the city. There are endless activities, including tennis courts, skate ramps, children's playgrounds, outdoor gymnastic equipment, and nature trails. The park is between a lovely English Tudor-style neighborhood called La Merced and, to the north, the Universidad Javeriana, founded by the Jesuits. On the northwest corner of the park is a relief scale replica of the Cordillera Oriental that contains a model of Bogotá and other nearby towns.

Chapinero

BASÍLICA MENOR NUESTRA SEÑORA DE LOURDES

Carrera 13 No. 63-27; tel. 1/756-3040; https://basilicalourdes.arquibogota.org.co; 7am-6pm daily

Bogotá's own version of Paris's Notre Dame, the impressive gothic Basílica de Lourdes rises over a bustling plaza that often hosts an artisan market on weekends. Built in 1875 by local architect Julio Garavito, it holds masses at 8am, 3pm, and 5pm daily.

Northern Bogotá

ZONA ROSA

between Calles 79-85 and Carreras 11-15

An upscale shopping and nightlife district, the Zona Rosa is where Bogotanos on the spend head to for a day of shopping and a night out. People-watching is good here, particularly in **Zona T,** a pedestrian-only T-shaped corridor that cuts through the heart of the district and is lined with brewpubs and lounges.

PARQUE DE LA 93

between Carreras 11A-13 and Calles 93A-B

Parque de la 93 is a pleasant tree-studded public square with a playground surrounded by upscale restaurants that mostly cater to the office workers in the area. It's a nice place to relax in the north part of the city and hosts a variety of public events, including soccer games on big screens for public viewing.

★ USAQUÉN

between Calles 109-121 on the east side of La Séptima

Once upon a time, charming Usaquén was its own distinct pueblo. But swallowed whole by sprawling Bogotá sometime in the early 20th century, Usaquén is now an outpost of colonial charm in the modern northern part of the city. It has become a dining and drinking hot spot, with many restaurants and bars surrounding the main square and tucked into tiny side streets. On Sundays and national holidays the neighborhood packs crowds in for the **artisan market,** one of the largest in South America. This exuberant weekly festival includes live music and dance groups in the main square, tons of independent

Colombian artists and artisans selling their wares, and streets filled with people from all walks of Bogotano life.

Western Bogotá

PARQUE SIMÓN BOLÍVAR

between Calles 53-63 and Carreras 48-68; 6am-6pm daily

When it was built in the late 1960s, Parque Simón Bolívar was in the countryside. Now in the middle of the city, the park is a welcome expanse of greenery and an excellent place for watching Bogotano families at play, especially on weekends. Numerous festivals and concerts take place here. There are more than 16 km (10 mi) of trails in the park and a large lake with boat rentals.

BIBLIOTECA VIRGILIO BARCO

Av. Carrera 60 No. 57-60; tel. 1/379-3520; www.biblored.gov.co; 8am-8pm Tues.-Sat., 10am-5pm Sun.

With the downtown skyline and mountains providing a picturesque background, the Biblioteca Virgilio Barco, designed by architect Rogelio Salmona, is one of four fantastic library-parks in the city created by former mayor Enrique Peñalosa. The purpose of these mega libraries is to provide citizens of low- and middle-income areas access to books, the internet, and cultural and educational opportunities in a peaceful environment. The well-maintained grounds are a playground for both the young and the old—and their dogs.

★ JARDÍN BOTÁNICO

Av. Calle 63 No. 68-95; tel. 1/437-7060; www.jbb.gov.co; 8am-5pm Mon.-Fri., 9am-5pm Sat.-Sun.; COP$8,000

Colombia is the most biodiverse country on the planet per square foot, and the Jardín Botánico (Botanical Garden) is a fantastic living wonderworld where you can explore all its ecosystems in one place. Besides the extensive outdoor gardens, a series of giant tropicarios (greenhouses; COP$22,000) take visitors on a tour of different climate regions in the country, from the páramos (highland moors) to cloud forests to the mighty Amazon rainforest. The Jardín Botánico also hosts a variety of cultural events, especially on Friday nights, that combine theater, music, and education with a trip to the garden.

Recreation

 **TOP EXPERIENCE**

★ Ciclovía

Over 127 km (79 mi) of Bogotá's roads are closed to vehicular traffic 7am-2pm every Sunday and on holiday Mondays so that cyclists, joggers, dog walkers, skaters, and people-watchers can claim the roadways. Ciclovía started in the 1970s as a neighborhood initiative. Today it is an institution, a take-over-the-streets celebration where people of all classes in Bogotá mix it up. On sunny days, over two million people have participated in the Ciclovía, and the initiative has sparked similar movements around the world, including in Los Angeles.

The event is most enjoyable on a bike,

Ciclovía in the Centro Internacional neighborhood

especially because you can cover a lot more of the city than on foot. Two of the most popular routes are Avenida Séptima (Av. Carrera 7) and Carrera 15. It's an excellent way to see parts of the city you might not have otherwise considered. While Ciclovía is easy to figure out and do on your own, helpful staff and volunteers are stationed along the route. Bike repair stations are located on all routes; they'll inflate flat tires and do minor adjustments for about COP$2,000.

The city's weather changes quickly, so pack a lightweight rain jacket and apply sunscreen. Vendors sell freshly squeezed orange juice and fat slices of pineapple along the way. Watch the time: At 2pm, the cars come roaring back.

Bicyclists looking for something more challenging than the mostly flat streets of Bogotá can take Carrera 3 up to the La Calera mirador over the city, where cafés, restaurants, and bars await. The turnoff is at Calle 89, just east of the Zona Rosa, and is steep, but the views are worth it.

Bike Rentals

Many hostels and hotels have bicycles available for their guests to rent. Bike tour agencies, like Bogotá Bike Tours, also have bikes to rent, but reserve one ahead of time, as Ciclovía is a big deal, and come Sunday there are usually none left.

Tembici

https://tembici.com.co

Bogotá's new public bike-sharing system Tembici is a game-changer, and you will find stations pretty much everywhere you want to go.

First you have to download the app, then purchase a single ride (COP$4,800), a monthly pass (the best deal at COP$32,000), or a yearly pass (COP$229,000). Then check out the map for the nearest bike station. Scan the QR code on the bike you want and take it for up to 60 minutes at a time, up to four times a day with the monthly or yearly pass.

Hiking

The rugged Cerros Orientales mountains that form a dramatic backdrop to the city are just too inviting to not explore. Check out the government run site **Caminos de los Cerros Orientales** (https://caminos.eeab.co) for a free downloadable map and guide to the city's many paths.

Cerro de Monserrate

Distance: 5 km (3 mi) round-trip
Duration: 2 hours round-trip
Elevation gain: 520 m (1,700 ft)
Difficulty: Moderate-strenuous
Trailhead: Carrera 2A Este No. 21-48, El Centro

The epic urban hike from the center of Bogotá up to Santuario de Monserrate, at over 3,000 m (10,000 ft) elevation, is not for the faint of heart. The trailhead begins

path up Monserrate

CITY ESCAPES: DAY TRIPS FROM BOGOTÁ

Destination	Why Go	Getting There from Bogotá	How Long to Stay
Choachí (page 177)	waterfalls, hot springs	bus, 45 minutes east	overnight
Parque Natural Chicaque (page 180)	cloud forest, waterfalls	bus, 1.5 hours west	one day
Laguna de Guatavita (page 179)	historic site, beautiful nature	bus, 1.5 hours north	one day
Nemocón	historic pueblo, salt mine	bus, 2 hours north	overnight
Chingaza National Park	high Andean páramo ecosystem	car, 1 hour east	one day
Zipaquirá	underground cathedral carved out of salt	bus, 1.5 hours north	one day
Suesca	historic pueblo, rock climbing	bus, 2 hours north	one day
Sopó	historic pueblo, hiking, paragliding	bus, 1.5 hours north	one day

just past Quinta de Bolívar next to the gondola teleférico station. Ancient stone steps zigzag up the face of the mountain, offering incredible views over the city and gorgeous vegetation, including a small cloud forest near the top, complete with darting hummingbirds. About halfway up is a small village with simple restaurants and snack stands where coffee, fruit, coca leaf tea, and restrooms can be found. The hike can be done one-way by using the gondola or the tramway for the other direction.

Cerro de Monserrate is open 5am-4pm Wednesday-Monday. Sundays are crowded.

Quebrada La Vieja

Distance: 2.6 km (1.6 mi) round-trip
Duration: 2 hours round-trip
Elevation gain: 90 m (300 ft)
Difficulty: Easy-moderate
Trailhead: Calle 71 No. 1-45, Chapinero

This pleasant trail is easier and less crowded than Cerro de Monserrate and takes you through a 200-ha (500-acre) forest reserve to a gorgeous small waterfall. Beginning in the Chapinero neighborhood, the trailhead is at the top of Diagonal 70B, where the trail winds up into a valley between the peaks of the Cerros Orientales, instead of to the top of them. You miss some of the high-altitude views but you get the feeling of the city dropping away. You must first register on the Caminos de los Cerros Orientales app before hiking this trail.

Quebrada la Vieja is open 6:30am-11am Tuesday-Friday and 6am-noon Saturday-Sunday.

GUIDES

Caminatas Ecológicas Bogotá

tel. 320/206-3523; www.caminatasecologicasbogotar.com; from COP$85,000 including transportation

Catering mostly to nature-loving locals who want to hit the trails on the weekend, Caminatas Ecológicas offers group walks, usually on Sunday, to a variety of interesting natural areas in or near the city. The group usually meets early in the morning at the Portal 80 TransMilenio Station. The price includes round-trip transportation, a guide, and a light snack and beverage.

Ecological Walks

tel. 1/377-8881; www.ambientebogota.gov.co/caminatas-ecologicas; free

The city's environmental office organizes interesting guided ecological walks throughout the city. Spaces go fast, so it's best to book ahead via the website before you arrive.

Bird-Watching

A city with one of the widest diversities of bird species in the world, bird-watching is good on the trails of the Cerros Orientales and excellent around the humedales (wetlands) on the western edge of the city.

Parque La Florida

Km 2, Autopista Medellín; no phone; 7am-5pm daily; free

The 80-ha (200-acre) Parque La Florida in western Bogotá is a world-class bird-watching destination that can be visited on a morning or afternoon trip from the center of the city. Well over 100 species have been documented in the park. Keep an eye out for two endemic species, the Bogotá rail and Apolinar's marsh wren. It is possible to get here on public transit, but that requires several bus transfers; taking a taxi is a better option.

blue-throated starfrontlet

Tours

WALKING TOURS

Beyond Colombia

tel. 322/898-8557; https://beyondcolombia.com; free

Easily recognizable by their bright-red jackets (or umbrellas, in case of rain), Beyond Colombia offers free walking tours of La Candelaria at 10am and 2pm daily. These group tours meet in front of the Museo del Oro and end at the Centro Cultural Gabriel García Márquez. While the tours are free, note that the insightful local guides live off participants' tips.

Beyond Colombia also offers gastronomical tours and can organize private tours to your specifications (from COP$300,000 pp).

Impulse Travel

tel. 601/914-3928; https://impulsetravel.co; from USD$45

Focusing on "social impact," Impulse Travel offers a variety of tours, including walking tours of La Candelaria (4.5 hours) that are more comprehensive than the free walking tours. They also offer food tours and visits to unique communities in Bogotá and around the country.

BUS TOURS

Hop On Hop Off Bogotá

tel. 314/724-9015; https://bogotacitybus.co; COP$99,000 for 3 consecutive days

This twice-daily four-hour bus tour makes 12 stops around the city on a loop between Parque de la 93 and La Candelaria. To visit any sight for more than the 10-minute stop the bus makes, take the early bus and then hop on the later bus to get home. This is a good option for those staying in the center to visit the north and vice versa.

BIKE TOURS

Bogotá Bike Tours

Carrera 3 No. 12-72; tel. 1/281-9924; www.bogotabiketours.com; from COP$55,000

Bogotá Bike Tours, run by Mike, an American who's been living in La Candelaria for decades, is a popular agency that does a variety of group bike tours around the city with English-language guidance.

EXCURSION TOURS

There are some extraordinary parques nacionales naturales (national natural parks, PNN) quite close to Bogotá, making for excellent day hiking. Visits to these parks can be difficult to organize without transportation or familiarity with the area.

Many hotels can arrange tours to attractions such as Zipaquirá and Laguna de Guatavita.

Ecoglobal Expeditions

tel. 1/579-3402; www.ecoglobalexpeditions.com; from COP$200,000

Ecoglobal Expeditions organizes excursions to destinations throughout Colombia, from hiking treks just outside of Bogotá to the famous Caño Cristales in Los Llanos. They can organize day trips to national parks such as Parque Nacional Natural Sumapaz, containing the world's largest páramo (highland moor), and Parque Nacional Natural Chingaza.

Entertainment and Events

Bogotá is one of Latin America's cultural capitals, with tons of theater, concerts, and a nonstop festival calendar that runs the gamut from poetry festivals to free rock, salsa, and jazz performances in public parks. The city is also full of nonprofit cultural centers, each with their own calendars that include events almost every night of the week.

COCA LEAF: THE PLANT OF THE FUTURE

No plant in human history has been as demonized as the coca leaf. In 1961 the UN Single Convention on Narcotic Drugs listed it as a Schedule 1 substance and targeted even traditional use of the plant as an "addiction" that needed to "phased out." But for Andean and Amazonian cultures across South America, the plant is considered a sacred medicine and is used daily both ritually and for general health.

coca tea and coca leaves

While Colombia followed the Western narrative on coca leaf for decades, even allowing the spraying of Monsanto's cancer-causing glyphosate herbicide on Indigenous and small-farm coca plantations, the national consensus has recently turned. In 2022 newly elected president Gustavo Petro suspended coca leaf eradication efforts in the country, claimed the War on Drugs was a "failure" and that coca is an "ancestral" medicine with cultural and spiritual value.

After being pushed to the fringes of Colombia society, coca leaf is now appearing in major cities as a sign of cultural pride and as a health supplement. Coca tea is served at many cafés across Bogotá, especially in La Candelaria, and will help visitors quickly adjust to the elevation. The traditional mambe consumption method, where powdered coca leaf is chewed for energy and health during the day, has taken off with the younger generation.

WHERE TO BUY IT

Note that coca-leaf products remain illegal in most countries outside the Andean region, and you should not bring them home with you.

- **La Embajada de La Coca** (Carrera 3 No. 12C-90/92; tel. 314/676-3500): In the heart of La Candelaria and run by friendly Peruvian-born Don Gerónimo Clevar, La Embajada de la Coca offers a variety of products, including pomades for pain relief and house-made cake based on ground coca leaf, that show just how versatile the plant is. It's also a neighborhood social center.
- **Coca Nasa** (CC Vía Libre, Calle 19 No. 4-85 Local 101; www.cocanasa.org): The Indigenous Nasa nation, who for decades were targeted by aerial glyphosate spraying for their traditional coca cultivations, now run their own company, compete with a retail outlet in El Centro. It offers everything from coca-infused rum and chocolate cookies to their own version of coca cola, although in this case it really is the "real thing."

Cultural Centers

LA CANDELARIA

Fundación Gilberto Alzate Avendaño

Calle 10 No. 3-16; tel. 1/282-9491; www.fgaa.gov.co; 9am-5pm Mon.-Fri.; free

The nonprofit Fundación Gilberto Alzate Avendaño is in a historic mansion in La Candelaria. It puts on theater and music performances featuring local talent and hosts art exhibits free or at low cost.

Centro Nacional de las Artes Delia

Calle 10 No. 5-23; tel. 601/381-6380; https://endelia.gov.co

Inaugurated in 2024, this world-class arts center has a robust calendar of programming that includes theater, dance, film, and several exhibition spaces.

CHAPINERO

Centro Felicidad Chapinero

Calle 82 No. 10-69; https://culturarecreacionydeporte.gov.co; 10am-7pm Tues.-Sun.

Opened in 2025, this city-run 10-story "vertical park" is an architectural wonder home to three cafés, an Olympic-size pool with stunning views over the city, a restaurant, and plenty of community rooms with classes in capoeira, tango, painting, sculpture, and more.

Centro Felicidad Chapinero

Art Galleries

Bogotá is a magnet for artists from across Colombia, and interesting galleries across the city are open to all. **Artería** (www.periodicoarteria.com) offers fantastic free walking tours of gallery districts in Bogotá. La Macarena is home to several galleries that showcase local artists, and there are an astonishing number of galleries in the San Felipe Creative District in northwestern Bogotá, between Calles 73-77 from Carreras 20a-24. In early June over 90 working artist studios in San Felipe open to the public (https://opensanfelipe.com).

LA MACARENA

Arte NC

Carrera 5 No. 26B-76; tel. 601/744-9577; https://nc-arte.com; 10am-5pm Mon.-Sat.

With an art gallery featuring some of Colombia's top modern creatives plus a next-door design studio, Arte NC is a great place to stop in for coffee at the on-site café and connect with the locals.

NORTHERN BOGOTÁ

Galería SGR

Calle 74 No. 22-28; tel. 1/631-8027; www.sgr-art.com; 10am-6pm Mon.-Fri., noon-4pm Sat.

Galería SGR highlights renowned contemporary Latin American artists. This is a great place to get your feet wet in the local art scene.

Flora Ars + Natura

Calle 77 No. 20C-48; tel. 1/675-1425; www.arteflora.org; 2pm-6pm Mon.-Fri., 10am-1pm Sat. by appointment

Nature-focused Flora Ars + Natura is a gallery, school, and community arts center well worth checking out.

Classical Music

You may not think of classical music when you think Bogotá, but the city is home to two excellent orchestras and an opera and hosts talented performers year-round. As with most concerts and events in Bogotá, purchasing tickets in advance from **Tu Boleta** (tel. 1/593-6300; www.tuboleta.com) is the most convenient option.

Orquesta Filarmónica de Bogotá

www.filarmonicabogota.gov.co;COP$30,000

The excellent Orquesta Filarmónica de Bogotá often performs on the Universidad Nacional campus at the **Auditorio León de Greiff** (Carrera 45 No. 26-85; www.divulgacion.unal.edu.co) and occasionally at other venues. The Auditorio León de Greiff is hard to miss: There is a huge stencil of iconic revolutionary Che Guevara on its exterior. There is often an international guest soloist at these concerts. Although tickets are available at the taquillas (ticket offices) at these theaters a few hours before performance time, it is recommended to purchase tickets, which are usually inexpensive, in advance at a Tu Boleta outlet.

Sinfónica Nacional de Colombia

www.sinfonica.com.co; tickets COP$90,000

The Sinfónica Nacional de Colombia often performs classical music at the spectacular **Teatro Mayor Julio Mario Santo Domingo** (Av. Calle 170 No. 67-51; tel. 1/377-9840; www.teatromayor.com) in the western localidad of Suba.

Theater

Teatro Nacional

Calle 71 No. 10-25; tel. 1/217-4577; www.teatronacional.com.co; from COP$50,000

The country's most prominent theater company, Teatro Nacional has three theaters in Bogotá and regularly puts on comedic and dramatic productions. Their main theater, Teatro Nacional Fanny Mikey, is named in honor of beloved Argentinian actor Fanny Mikey, who moved to Bogotá and started its famed theater festival.

Teatro Libre de Bogotá

Calle 12B No. 2-44; tel. 601/476-4934; www.teatrolibre.com; prices vary

This award-winning community theater group, which has performances spaces in both La Candelaria and Chapinero (Calle 62 No. 9A-65), has been providing cutting-edge and low-cost or free theater to the city for over 50 years.

Teatro de La Candelaria

Calle 12 No. 2-59; tel. 601/937-2433; https://teatrolacandelaria.com; COP$15,000-20,000

Housed in ancient colonial casona, this local troupe infuses socially relevant themes into new works and classic productions.

Film

Cinemateca Distrital

Carrera 3 No. 19-10; tel. 1/379-5750, ext. 3401; https://cinematecadebogota.gov.co; COP$6,000

In the City U complex in El Centro, the Cinemateca Distrital offers three floors, four screening rooms, and several exhibition spaces devoted to Colombian, international, and independent films. A publicly sponsored institution, ticket prices are kept low so that all can attend.

In the summer months, the open-air amphitheater known as the Media Torta hosts a free live concert series every weekend. Just above the Universidad de los Andes at the foot of the mountain, it's walking distance from La Candelaria.

Festivals and Events

YEAR-ROUND

Festivales al Parque

June-Dec.; free

Free music festivals take center stage at various parks throughout the city in the latter half of the year. The most popular outdoor music festival is **Rock al Parque** (www.rockalparque.gov.co; July), the largest free outdoor rock festival in Latin America. Other festivals include **Gospel al Parque** (Aug.), **Hip-Hop al Parque** (Oct.), **Salsa al Parque** (Nov.), **Jazz al Parque** (September), and the Colombian music showcase **Colombia al Parque** (Nov.).

SPRING

Estereo Picnic

Parque Simón Bolívar; www.festivalestereopicnic.com; Mar.; from COP$499,000

This massive four-day music festival takes over Parque Simón Bolívar and features top-name international bands as well as Colombia's hottest musical talent.

Festival Iberoamericano de Teatro

www.festivaldeteatro.com.co; Easter week in even-numbered years; free

Every even-numbered year during Semana Santa, theater and dance take over the city during the Festival Iberoamericano de Teatro. Attracting more than 100 prestigious international troupes and companies and over 170 representing Colombia, this festival is a living tribute to Fanny Mikey, an Argentinian actor who adopted Colombia as her home. She started the biennial affair in 1988. Known for her bright-red hair and distinctive smile, she died in 2008. With over 800 performances spanning two weeks, this is one of the largest such theater festivals in the world. The festival kicks off with a Saturday parade. There are always theater groups from English-speaking countries, and there are typically many circus and dance performances.

SUMMER

Gay Pride

July; free

Taking place either the last weekend of June or the first weekend of July and coinciding with a long weekend is Bogotá's gay pride celebration. The parade, called La Marcha, kicks off at noon on Sunday from the Parque Nacional and makes its disorganized but festive way down La Séptima to the Plaza de Bolívar. Anyone can join the parade. Bars and clubs host pride parties over the long weekend.

FALL

Festival Internacional de Jazz de Bogotá

Teatro Libre, Calle 62 No. 9-65; tel. 1/217-1988; Sept.; from COP$410,000

International and Colombian jazz artists perform annually at the long-running Festival Internacional de Jazz de Bogotá. Usually held in early September, tickets are available through Tu Boleta.

WINTER

ArtBo

Corferias fairground, Carrera 40 No. 22C-67; Nov.; www.artboonline.com; free

More than 50 art galleries representing

400 artists from the Americas converge on Bogotá each November during ArtBo, known more formally as the **Feria Internacional de Arte de Bogotá,** one of the top contemporary art fairs in Latin America.

Shopping

La Candelaria

The narrow streets of this neighborhood are lined with small shops specializing in Colombian artesanías (handicrafts), the quality of which ranges from trinkets to the refined. There is a whole section of independent and lower-end jewelry shops in La Candelaria, roughly between Calle 12 and Avenida Jiménez and between La Séptima and Carrera 6. They offer great deals on everything from engagement rings to family gifts.

CRAFTS

Pasaje Rivas

between Carreras 9-10 and Calles 10-11

For a fun stop while sightseeing, check out Pasaje Rivas, a bazaar that dates to the late 19th century. The passages are so narrow that it's impossible not to interact with carpenters selling furniture and women peddling handwoven baskets and curios. For high-quality hand-carved wood items and more, check out the shop of the **Escuela de Artes y Oficios Santo Domingo** (Calle 10 No. 8-73), a well-regarded school for craftspeople.

Galatea Tejidos

Carrera 2A No. 12D-16; tel. 314/356-4684; 10am-7pm Mon.-Sat.

Grab some hand-knit scarves, hats, gloves, and sweaters in a variety of creative styles that are perfect for Bogotá's weather and its bohemian fashion sense at this colorful shop in the heart of La Candelaria. All products are made on-site by Doña Blanca, the friendly owner.

Book lovers should explore the pedestrian-only Calle 15 as it branches west from La Séptima. Tons of street book dealers and several massive old-school used bookstores are in this area, the most marvelous being **Libros Merlin** (Carrera 8A No. 15-70).

Matorral Librería

Teusaquillo

BOOKSTORES

Matorral Librería

Av. Carrera 19 36-55; tel. 321/270-2921; 10am-8pm daily

A two-story tiny home packed with new books that opens onto a lush garden patio, the only place that book lovers in Bogotá will like better than Matorral's Teusaquillo location is their La Macarena outpost (Carrera 5 26C-06). Both have on-site cafés and frequent talks and events.

Northern Bogotá

JEWELRY

Bogotá's high-end jewelers specialize in locally mined gold and emeralds.

Liévano

Carrera 11 No. 82-71, Local 157; tel. 1/616-8608; https://joyerialievano.com; 10:45am-7:45pm Mon.-Sat.

Liévano, in the Zona Rosa, specializes in gold and emerald jewelry and high-end Swiss watches.

ANTIQUES

Calle de los Anticuarios

Calle 79A between Carreras 7-9

A short stroll from the Zona Rosa malls is a street dedicated almost exclusively to antiques.

Food

The traditional dish of Bogotá is **ajiaco,** a hearty potato and chicken soup seasoned with the herb guascas. But as a major cosmopolitan city, that's just the beginning of the culinary adventure to be had. With several Michelin-rated restaurants, world-renowned chefs, and even its own gastronomical zone (Zona G), Bogotá is quickly becoming a foodie destination.

La Candelaria

COLOMBIAN

★ Recetas de Abuela

Calle 12C No. 1-40; tel. 312/557-6080; 11am-4pm daily; COP$14,000-38,000

One of a half dozen traditional eateries inside La Concordia market, husband-and-wife team María and Sanders frequently win the award for the best ajiaco in the city.

Secretos del Mar

Carrera 4 No. 12-54; tel. 315/894-5928; 11am-5pm daily; COP$22,000-45,000

Pacific coastal cuisine, an African influenced affair based on fresh fish, coconut rice, and thick rich sauces, is widely considered the best food in the country by locals, although it is mostly unknown abroad. At Secretos del Mar, chef-owner Chucho, who hails from Buenaventura, does it authentically and will offer you a shot of his own house-made biche (sugarcane alcohol) as a chaser.

Puerta Falsa

Calle 11 No. 6-50; tel. 1/286-5091; 7am-10pm Mon.-Fri., 8am-8pm Sat.-Sun.; COP$30,000-55,000

The classic place for a huge tamale and a hot chocolate, Puerta Falsa claims to be one of the oldest operating restaurants in

BACK TO THE MARKET

Markets have been a central part of life for Colombians for centuries. They are the direct link between campesinos, or small family farms, and the urban consumer. But during the 1980s and 1990s, as much of the population started shopping in supermarkets and government support for market infrastructure declined, market culture in Bogotá began to wither.

In 2016 Bogotá s mayor Enrique Peñalosa started the Volver a Las Plazas Mercados (Back to the Market) campaign, which set aside funds to restore, rehabilitate, and expand the city's network of markets. Now, Bogotá's market scene is stronger than ever.

La Concordia market

BEST MARKETS

- **La Concordia** (Calle 12C No. 1-40; daily): In the heart of La Candelaria, this traditional neighborhood market was given an upscale remodeling job in 2020. Inside, fruit vendors as well as specialty gourmet shops, including the artisanal Pacific coast rainforest-grown chocolates of Late Chocó (https://latechoco.com), ply their wares, while the on the back patio a dozen restaurants serve lunch. Go for the ajiaco at Recetas de Abuela.
- **Paloquemao** (Av. Ciudad de Lima; tel. 1/742-6664; www.plazadepaloquemao.com; Sun.-Fri.): Visiting Bogotá's massive central market often leaves visitors awestruck: Mountains of fruit, trucked in from every department of Colombia, are piled sky-high. Both Beyond Colombia (https://beyondcolombia.com) and Impulse Tours (https://impulsetours.com) offer a guided experience.
- **Mercado de la Tierra** (Calle 70 No. 8-25; Sun.): A partnership between the international Slow Food movement and local organic food producers, this market takes place in the Quinta Comacho area of Chapinero every Sunday. The offerings include fresh goat milk cheeses, agraz (wild blueberry) yogurt, handcrafted chocolates, and produce of all kinds, all grown or crafted locally.
- **La Preservancia** (Carrera 5 No. 40-30a; daily): At this bustling market, a huge dining hall boasts everything from traditional Bogotano fare at Donde Esperanza to some of the city's best Pacific cuisine at La Rincón de Mary.

Bogotá, having opened in 1816. They also sell a variety of traditional sweets. Avoid the imitators that have set up shop on the same block.

★ Chamanico

Calle 10 No. 2-03; tel. 319/416-5421; noon-10pm Mon.-Sat., noon-9pm Sun.; COP$45,000-78,000

Creative takes on ancestral Indigenous foods include violet flower-infused sea bass and house-made sunbaked quinoa bread, served by the fireplace in a majestic colonial house on pedestrian-only Calle 10. Don't miss the herb-infused cocktails and shots, many based on actual traditional healing recipes.

CARIBBEAN FUSION

Casa San Miguel

Calle 11 No. 8-70; tel. 302/647-7883; 8am-10pm daily; COP$28,000-55,000

Bar, café, restaurant, bookstore, salsa club, and cannabis dispensary all rolled into one, Casa San Miguel occupies a magnificent two-story mansion with inner and outer balconies a block south of Plaza de Bolívar. Menu items like salmon over hummus with grilled mushrooms and vegetarian paella make dining here rewarding, although many just stop by for a CBD-infused cappuccino on a relaxing couch. Salsa classes on Wednesday and live bands on Saturday pack the house.

INTERNATIONAL

★ Los Antojos del Coyote

Carrera 2 No. 12c-37; tel. 322/899-0407; 11am-11:30pm daily; COP$25,000-40,000

Guadalajara-born chef Julian not only makes sure his al pastor alambres and barbacoa tacos are as authentic as possible, he also collects chili peppers from across Latin America and offers a dozen varieties to diners. The mural-covered restaurant has a nice open-air rooftop deck and is a great spot for late-night eats.

VEGETARIAN

Quinoa y Amaranto

Calle 11 No. 2-95; tel. 1/565-9982; 8am-4pm Mon., 8am-9pm Tues.-Fri., 8am-5pm Sat.; COP$22,000-38,000

Using Andean ingredients, the tiny Quinoa y Amaranto is a cozy and comfortable downtown haven for vegetarians. The three-course lunches (around COP$22,000) get bang for your buck.

CAFÉS, BAKERIES, AND QUICK BITES

Cafe del Mercado

Carrera 2 No. 11-88, 10am-7pm daily; COP$10,000

With two locations in La Candelaria, one in a two-story colonial house just a block south of Chorro de Quevedo, and one inside La Concordia market (Calle 12C No. 1-40), Cafe del Mercado serves top small-batch Colombian coffee by the cup and exquisite house-made carrot cake.

★ Casa Magola Buen Día

Carrera 3 No. 17-60; www.magolabuendia.com; 10am-9pm Mon.-Thurs., 10am-midnight Fri.-Sat., 8:30am-7pm Sun.; COP$15,000

Café, craft beer bar, ice cream parlor, bakery, and live music venue all at once, there are many reasons to visit the garden-like grounds of Casa Magola Buen Día—but the best one is their house-made dark-chocolate cake.

clockwise ajiaco; Cafe del Mercado; Chamanico restaurant

El Centro

COLOMBIAN

Asadero Capachos

Calle 18 No. 4-68; tel. 1/243-4607; www.asaderocapachos.com; 11:30am-3:30pm Tues.-Thurs., 11:30am-5pm Fri.-Sun.; COP$28,000-50,000

For a hearty meal of mamona (grilled meat), run to Asadero Capachos, an authentic llanero (cowboy) restaurant. For under COP$20,000 you get a healthy portion of tender slow-grilled meat, fried yuca, and a maduro (fried plantain), which all go down well with a beer. On weekends they have live music and dance performances. Vegetarians will have a difficult time here.

CAFÉS, BAKERIES, AND QUICK BITES

Pastelería La Florida

Carrera 7 No. 21-46; tel. 1/341-0340; 6am-9pm daily; COP$8,000-35,000

Pastelería La Florida is a local institution, a classic bakery and breakfast restaurant housed in a palatial historic edifice on La Séptima. Breakfast is big; options include tamales, eggs, waffles à la mode, and hot chocolate.

Centro Internacional

COLOMBIAN

★ Doña Elvira

Carrera 6 No. 29-08; www.restaurantedonaelvira.com; noon-4pm Mon.-Sat.; COP$35,000-50,000

Specializing in cuisine from the agricultural region of Boyacá, Doña Elvira serves hearty soups like ajiaco and lots of potatoes, corn, and beans as well as fried catfish. Tucked away amid the modern skyscrapers, this restaurant has been in the same family since 1934.

CAFÉS, BAKERIES, AND QUICK BITES

Andante Ma Non Troppo

Carrera 5 No. 26c-57; tel. 1/284-4387; 8am-8pm Mon.-Sat., 8am-3pm Sun.; COP$22,000

Andante Ma Non Troppo is a long-running café that serves breakfast, sandwiches, and salads in one of the most iconic buildings in Bogotá, the Torres del Parque. It's more atmospheric than memorable.

La Macarena

COLOMBIAN

Chibchombia

Calle 27 No. 4-29; tel. 302/288-6142; noon-9pm Mon.-Thurs., noon-10pm Fri.-Sat., noon-6pm Sun.; COP$45,000-68,000

Upscale versions of classic Colombian dishes in a cozy high-ceilinged and brick-lined dining room make Chibchombia a popular local eatery.

INTERNATIONAL

Tapas Macarena

Carrera 4A No. 26b-11; tel. 601/809-6630; www.tapasmacarena.com; noon-10pm Sun.-Thurs., noon-11:30pm Fri.-Sat.; COP$27,000-55,000

With small plates of olives, cheese, jamón serrano, and other traditional Spanish delights paired with a nice selection of imported beer and wine, Tapas Macarena draws both the after-work crowd and the weekend pre-party crowd. Open since 2005, it's the oldest tapa bar in the county.

★ La Molina

Calle 26C No. 4-43; tel. 601/801-3430; noon-10pm Mon.-Sat., noon-5pm Sun.; COP$45,000-90,000

Those craving authentic ceviche, tiradito, arroz chaufa, parihuela, and other Peruvian specialties will find their fix at this slick hole-in-the-wall. The chef hails from Lima and imports fresh ingredients for the menu, including pisco for the cocktails.

Teusaquillo

COLOMBIAN

★ Copoazú

Carrera 24 No. 39a 44; tel. 302/709-4225; 11am-3pm Mon.-Thurs., 11:30am-8pm Fri.-Sat.; COP$22,000-45,000

Run by an association of Indigenous women, this is one of the few real Amazonian restaurants in the city, despite the fact that the ecosystem makes up one-third of Colombia. A rare treat outside the rainforest, ask for the tucupi (black aji made from ants).

INTERNATIONAL

Curry Masala

Carrera 24 No. 39a 44; tel. 1/631-7062; noon-9pm Mon.-Wed., noon-10pm Thurs.-Sat., noon-4pm Sun.; COP$28,000-40,000

Those craving fully spiced Punjabi-style Indian curries should hit up Curry Masala, right across from the Parkway.

CAFÉS, BAKERIES, AND QUICK BITES

★ Selva Nevada

Carrera 24 No. 39b 52; tel. 300/623-1972; www.selvanevada.co; 11am-8pm daily; COP$8,000

This local chain of artisanal ice cream sources its ingredients directly from community producers all over the country: dark cacao from Tumaco, acai from Putumayo, and mambe (coca) from Cauca. There is also a smaller pop-up shop in La Candelaria (Carrera 6 No. 1044) in front of the Centro Cultural Gabriel García Márquez.

Varietale

Calle 41 No. 8-43; tel. 324/255-0397; www.varietale.com; 7am-8:30am Mon.-Fri., 8:30am-9pm Sat.-Sun.; COP$10,000

A wide selection of top Colombian coffees brewed how you like them is only half the attraction of Varietale. The spacious and leafy back garden and comfy indoor sitting rooms make this cavernous café a great place to relax.

GROCERIES

Barichara Saludable

Carrera 5 No. 26C-06; tel. 311/212-3932; 8am-7pm Mon.-Sat., 10am-5pm Sun.

Certified organic produce, whole grains like quinoa and brown rice, nuts and dried fruits, and a wide variety of health-conscious products await. Barichara Saludable also has a great selection of Colombian chocolates.

Chapinero

COLOMBIAN

Las Margaritas

Calle 62 No. 7-77; tel. 1/249-9468; noon-4pm Tues.-Fri., 8am-5pm Sat.-Sun.; COP$15,000-38,000

Las Margaritas has been around for over a century. Try the puchero, a meaty stew, on Thursday. The ajiaco is also good.

Salvo Patria

Carrera 54A No. 4-13; tel. 1/702-6367; www.salvopatria.com; noon-11pm Mon.-Sat.; COP$25,000-55,000

Salvo Patria is inventive and trendy, serving both Colombian and international cuisine. There's a variety of interesting appetizers, sandwiches, meaty main courses, and vegetarian options. You'll be tempted to try a carafe of gin lulada, a drink made with the juice of the lulo, a tangy fruit.

★ MiniMal

Carrera 4A No. 57-52; tel. 1/347-5464; www.mini-mal.org; noon-3pm and 7pm-10pm Mon.-Wed., noon-3pm and 7pm-11pm Thurs., noon-11pm Fri.-Sat.; COP$35,000-75,000

MiniMal pioneered the Colombian regional fusion movement decades ago, and their Amazonian-Pacific plates burst with exotic flavors. Try the stingray cazuela (stew) for an example. A small gift shop sells culinary items and souvenirs.

★ Restaurante Leo

Calle 65 bis No. 4-23; tel. 312/661-6866; https://restauranteleo.com; noon-2pm and 6:45pm-11pm Mon.-Sat.; COP$100,000-450,000 full flight

Named top female chef on the planet in 2022, Leonor Espinosa crafts 12-course set dinners that take you through every ecosystem of Colombia. In her Zona G kitchen she sources her ingredients directly from small-scale and sustainable community and Indigenous producers. Reservations are required.

CAFÉS, BAKERIES, AND QUICK BITES

Árbol de Pan

Calle 66 bis No. 4-63; tel. 1/481-7465; 8am-8pm Mon.-Sat.; COP$25,000

A popular Zona G hangout, Árbol de Pan is known for almond croissants, mimosas, and brunch.

Northern Bogotá

COLOMBIAN

Gaira Cumbia Café

Carrera 13 No. 96-11A; tel. 1/746-2696; www.gairacafe.com; 9am-10pm Mon.-Wed., 9am-2am Thurs., 9am-3am Fri.-Sat., 9am-6pm Sun.; COP$25,000-55,000

Welcome to Bogotá's version of Santa Marta. Gaira Cumbia Café specializes in good Caribbean cuisine that's popular with locals. Musician Guillermo Vives and his mom run the place, and Guillo often performs. He is the brother of Carlos Vives, the multiple Grammy Award-winning vallenato singer. On weekend mornings there are special activities for children, while on weekend nights, reservations are essential.

Harry Sasson

Carrera 9 No. 75-70; tel. 1/347-7155; noon-midnight Mon.-Sat., noon-5pm Sun.; COP$80,000-120,000

Harry Sasson is named for a celebrity Colombian chef. In a gorgeous house refitted with modern touches, this contemporary classic is a favorite among the city's power players (you can tell by the serious-looking bodyguards waiting outside in their SUVs). Try the chestnut prawns, and go for a Hendrick's gin and tonic, a favorite among this crowd.

INTERNATIONAL

Black Bear

Carrera 11A No. 89-06; tel. 1/644-7766; noon-11pm Mon.-Sat., noon-6pm Sun.; COP$55,000-90,000

In a fantastic setting bordering a park, Black Bear packs guests in around its boisterous bar, satisfying appetites with grilled octopus, hearty burgers, and smart cocktails. They host live jazz music on weekends.

★ La Patagonia

Calle 119B No. 5-19; tel. 1/342-3830; noon-noon daily; COP$60,000-99,000

Tiny hole-in-the-wall La Patagonia serves up huge almost sharable plates of grass-fed Argentine churrasco and bife on a back street in Usaquén. A nice list of malbecs by the bottle or glass and eclectic decor make it worth the trip.

CAFÉS, BAKERIES, AND QUICK BITES

Les Amis Bizcochería

Carrera 14 No. 86A-12; tel. 1/236-2124; 8:30am-7:30pm Mon.-Fri., 9am-6pm Sat.; COP$15,000

If you can find Les Amis Bizcochería, you'll love it. This bakery-café makes delicious French and Colombian pastries and has a couple of tables for clients. It's on the 2nd floor of an ordinary-looking apartment building.

★ El Altillo

Calle 119B No. 5-48; 8am-11pm Sun.-Wed., 8am-midnight Thurs.-Sat.

An Usaquén landmark, El Altillo serves up perfectly poured cappuccinos and hot mulled wine in a garden packed with locals and visitors. Croissant sandwiches, empanadas, salads, and other light fare are also on the menu.

Bars and Nightlife

Bogotá has a bar, club, or party for every taste. Popular nightlife hot-spot clusters are in El Centro, Chapinero, Teusaquillo, and Northern Bogotá, each with its own vibe. From tiendas (corner stores) with tables for drinking out back to classic salsa clubs to gigantic electronica temples, the Colombian capital rages at night just as hard as it works all day.

Expect to pay COP$10,000-50,000 cover at clubs unless there's a big-name DJ or band, when covers are higher. Covers can include a consumible (complimentary drink). Pay for drinks with small bills or exact change, as some wayward bar staff may attempt to keep the change, especially from travelers. Tips are not expected at bars.

All electronic music clubs are gay-friendly and become even more so as the night wears on. Bars and clubs generally stay open until 3am, with some operating until daylight, especially in Chapinero.

La Candelaria

The cobblestone streets of La Candelaria are dotted with little hole-in-the-wall bars decked out with kitsch art, graffiti, and antique furniture that are a pleasure to explore. Around the Chorro is the largest cluster, but the corner of Calle 12D and Carrera 5 is also particularly active. While these areas are relatively safe, avoid wandering empty streets at night.

BARS AND LOUNGES

Doña Ceci's

Carrera 4 No. 12D-18; tel. 1/282-2072; noon-3am Mon.-Sat., noon-midnight Sun.; no cover

Once just a hole-in-the-wall student dive bar, Doña Ceci's just kept expanding until it became the three-story labyrinth of cheap drinks and friendly conversations it is today.

DANCE CLUBS

Candelario Bar

Carrera 5 No. 12B-14; tel. 1/342-3742; 9pm-3am Fri.-Sat.; cover COP$20,000

Doña Ceci's bar in La Candelaria

Housed in a giant two-story colonial mansion, Candelario Bar pumps reggaetón and Latin beats and gets a nice mix of locals and visitors sweating it out on the dance floor.

LIVE MUSIC

Bolon de Verde

Carrera 1A No. 12B 20; tel. 316/876-3771; Instagram @bolondeverdebogota; 7pm-noon Wed.-Sat.; cover from COP$15,000

This father and son-owned jazz club features some of Bogotá's best local musical talent in an intimate bohemian setting. Right on the Chorro de Quevedo, Bolon de Verde is a great after-dinner option.

Aldea Internacional

Calle 17 No. 2-77; tel. 321/296-9558; 11am-8pm Wed.-Thurs., 11am-3am Fri.-Sat., 11am-9pm Sun.; cover from COP$10,000

Live folkloric bands from all over the country, including Andean music from Pasto and cumbia from the Caribbean, grace the stage at Aldea Internacional, a large cultural center that also features an ongoing artisan market, daily lunch specials, and music and art classes open to the public.

El Centro

LIVE MUSIC

Revellion Cultu-Bar

Calle 16 No. 4-23; tel. 321/996-7464; 5pm-11pm Wed.-Thurs., 5pm-2:30am Fri.-Sat.; cover from COP$15,000

In the basement of the historic Hotel Continental, Revellion is swanky steampunk-themed cocktail lounge that hosts live music on weekends and serves handmade craft cocktails.

El Establo del Pegasus

Carrera 4 No. 19-56; tel. 321/490-3971; 6:30pm-2:30am Wed.-Sat.; cover from COP$20,000

Local jazz, blues, salsa, and Afro-Caribbean bands play the intimate stage at El Establo del Pegasus every week. The artsy book- and chess board-adorned lounge is on the 3rd floor of the Paisaje Gourmet, a maze of cafés, bars, and nightlife venues just off Calle 19.

SALSA

Casa Quiebracanto

Carrera 5 No. 17-76; tel. 1/243-1630; www.quiebracanto.com; 6pm-3am Wed.-Sat.; cover from COP$15,000

A two-story colonial house turned popular salsa venue, Casa Quiebracanto has been attracting some of the city's best dancers for nearly 40 years. On weekends it hosts some of the country's top orchestras as well as visiting salsa stars from around Latin America.

Centro Internacional

LIVE MUSIC

La Casa de la Paz

KR 13 No. 36-37; tel. 350/591-2431; https://latrochacasadelapaz.com; 10am-10pm Mon.-Thurs., 10am-2am Fri.-Sat.; no cover

Home of La Trocha Cervecería microbrewery, a live music venue, several event spaces, and a cozy café-bar where book readings, films screenings, and other events take place, La Casa de la Paz is run by former combatants now dedicated to the peace process in Colombia.

Teusaquillo

LIVE MUSIC

Soul 45

Calle 45 No. 19-30; tel. 314/445-5700; 3pm-11pm Tues., 3pm-3am Wed.-Sat.; cover from COP$10,000

A standout option on the row of microbreweries and hip bars that line Calle 45, Soul 45 showcases local jazz, blues, and rock performers on weekends.

Hoja al Viento

Carrera 15A bis No. 45-08; tel. 300/390-0610; www.hojaalvientoescuela.com; daily 4pm-noon; cover varies

Everything from retro dance parties to top Colombian rock bands can be enjoyed at Hoja al Viento, an experimental arts school, local theater, and lounge space on two floors of a historic mansion.

Chapinero

Chapinero is where Bogotá nightlife goes full force, with several large top-notch clubs and dozens of gay and lesbian bars, especially around the Parque de los Hippies area and Basílica de Lourdes. Nightlife tends to go later in Chapinero than the rest of the city, and the area hosts many after-hours parties that frequently change location.

live music at Hoja al Viento

DANCE CLUBS

Video Club

Calle 64 No. 13-09; www.videoclub.com.co; cover COP$35,000

Video Club does electro-house music at its cool location in Chapinero. It's a good idea to wear a long-sleeved shirt because most of the action is on the top-floor terrace. The club hosts special LGBTQ+ events on Sunday.

Theatrón

Calle 58 No. 10-32; tel. 1/235-6879; www.theatrondepelicula.com; 9pm-5am Fri.-Sat.; cover COP$50,000

The largest LGBTQ+ nightclub in South America, Theatrón is four stories plus a rooftop deck of sheer party. It is divided into dozens of rooms, each with their own ambience, DJ, and bar. The Saturday-night open bar attracts as many straight as LGBTQ+ partiers and is a fiesta not to be missed.

lining up to get into Theatrón

LIVE MUSIC

Latino Power

Calle 58 No. 13-88; tel. 319/665-4299; www.latinopower.com.co; 8pm-3am Thurs.-Sat.; cover from COP$20,000

Get a taste of the cutting edge of the city's live alternative music scene at Latino Power. Inside an old warehouse and decked in graffiti, the ambience matches the music.

Northern Bogotá

BARS AND LOUNGES

The Pub Bogotá

Carrera 12A No. 83-48; tel. 1/691-8711; www.thepub.com.co; noon-close daily; no cover

Sit on the terrace and listen to rock music at always-packed The Pub Bogotá, where you're in a strategic position to watch people walking in the Zona T.

SALSA

Galería Café Libro

Carrera 11A No. 93-42; tel. 601/597-5506; www.galeriacafelibro.com.co; 4pm-3am Tues.-Thurs., 4pm-5am Fri.-Sat.; cover COP$20,000

A huge restaurant and lounge with a full-size stage devoted to live salsa bands, this is one of the best places in the country to sink into Colombia's addictive salsa scene as top acts play regularly. The food and drinks are a bit overpriced but the music is legendary. The Teusaquillo outpost (Carrera 15B No. 6-38) is more laid-back and intimate.

Accommodations

Many visitors choose to stay in the colonial center of La Candelaria, as there is a wealth of hostels along the neighborhood's narrow streets, and many of the city's top sights, restaurants, and cultural centers are within walking distance. In the last decade or so several higher-end boutique hotels have opened, making lodging options more dynamic.

Lodging is increasingly available in other parts of the city for travelers of all budgets and interests. Neighborhoods such as Teusaquillo and the Quinta Comacho area of Chapinero put you in local areas home to cool restaurants and vibrant nightlife. More upscale options are available around Parque de la 93 and Usaquén. Accommodations in Bogotá are more expensive than Medellín and other medium-size cities but cheaper than Cartagena.

La Candelaria

From backpacker hostels to restored colonial mansions turned boutique hotels, staying in La Candelaria is a rich cultural experience.

UNDER COP$70,000

Fatima Hostel

Carrera 3 No. 11-32; tel. 312/494-3030; COP$40,000 dorm, COP$110,000 d

Graffiti-covered walls and friendly staff greet visitors at Fatima. With an on-site bar in front open to nonguests, this is a great option for solo budget travelers to meet other travelers and locals. One of the co-owners, Maurício Milagros, is a local musician, and so karaoke nights here can get epic.

★ Botánico Hostel

Carrera 2 No. 9-87; tel. 1/745-7572; https://botanicohostel.com; COP$65,000 dorm, COP$150,000 d

With a roaring fireplace downstairs, a rooftop terrace with views of Cerro de Monserrate, a friendly on-site bar, and quaint rooms that circle a lush garden courtyard, the Botánico Hostel is an oasis in the heart of the city and one of the most iconic backpackers digs in La Candelaria. They frequently host parties and artistic events that open the hostel to the public.

COP$70,000-200,000

Hostal Casa Astromelia

Calle 12D No. 3-11; tel. 321/471-6907; COP$120,000 d shared bath, COP$180,000 with bath

A three-story colonial gem complete with a rooftop terrace, on-site bar and restaurant, and high-ceilinged rooms, 16-room Hostal Casa Astromelia is also perfectly located for La Candelaria exploration.

★ Apartaestudios La Candelaria

Calle 10 No. 2-40; tel. 1/281-6923; www.apartaestudioscandelaria.com; COP$200,000 d

There are 18 private apartments at Apartaestudios La Candelaria, a spacious complex of colonial houses that share common gardens and grounds.

COP$200,000-500,000

★ Casa Deco

Calle 12C No. 2-36; tel. 1/283-7032; www.hotelcasadeco.com; COP$260,000 d

Casa Deco is a nicely refurbished art deco building with 21 well-appointed and spacious rooms with nice views over the city and the streets of La Candelaria. The rooftop terrace is an excellent place for relaxing on a late afternoon.

Hotel Muisca

Calle 10 No. 0-47; tel. 300/755-4096; www.hotelmuisca.com; COP$332,000 d

Housed in a 200-year-old colonial mansion and decorated with Indigenous-themed art, 22-room Hotel Muisca is luxurious yet relaxing and cultural at the same time. It's located on a quiet side street of La Candelaria, several blocks above the hustle and bustle.

OVER COP$500,000

★ Hotel de la Ópera

Calle 10 No. 5-72; tel. 1/336-2066; www.hotelopera.com.co; COP$550,000 d

Hotel de la Ópera still reigns as *the* luxury place to stay in La Candelaria. The hotel comprises two converted homes, one republican-style and one colonial. There are two restaurants, including a rooftop spot that has one of the best views downtown. The hotel also offers a spa. Expect very professional service.

Teusaquillo

COP$70,000-200,000

★ Hostel Bendito

Carrera 16 No. 40a-36; www.benditohostels.com; COP$60,000 dorm, COP$150,000 d

Housed in a gloriously restored three-story brick Tudor mansion, Hostel Bendito is on a quiet tree-lined street within walking distance of the Parkway and all the nightlife and dining of Calle 45. An on-site café, nice outdoor garden patios, and the fact that it is right on a cicloruta (bike lane) and near a Tembici public bike station make it even dreamier. There are a dozen private rooms and several dorm rooms of different sizes.

Chapinero

UNDER COP$70,000

★ Hostal Maconda Bogotá

Calle 70 No. 11a-18; tel. 312/583-7147; www.hostalmacondobogota.com; COP$60,000 dorm, COP$150,000 d

With a perfect location within the historic and verdant Quinta Comacho area of Chapinero, steps from Zona G and near Lourdes Plaza, Hostal Maconda Bogotá is like a home away from home. Catering to international travelers and replete with common spaces for meeting up, they also offer yoga classes, bike rentals, and other activities.

COP$70,000-200,000

6 Suites

Carrera 3B No. 64A-06; tel. 1/752-9484 or 315/851-1427; www.6suiteshotel.com; COP$159,000 d

Classical music fills the air at intimate 6 Suites, which has exactly that number of rooms in a small house. Some packages include a dinner of Argentine cuisine. There is a Saturday vegetable and fruit market in a small park next to the house as well as a 24-hour police station.

Matisse Hotel

Calle 67 No. 6-55; tel. 1/212-0177 or 300/463-5053; www.matissehotel.com; COP$183,000 d

With just 10 rooms, the Matisse Hotel is a five-minute walk to Zona G and very close to busy La Séptima. Some rooms may not have windows or windows that open.

Northern Bogotá

Uptown is a good option if comfort trumps budget and you want to be close to many excellent restaurants.

COP$70,000-200,000

Hotel Le Manoir

Calle 105 No. 17A-82; tel. 1/213-3980; www.lemanoir-egina.com; COP$160,000 d

Hotel Le Manoir is a sound midrange hotel with 52 rooms in a residential neighborhood between Usaquén and the Parque de la 93 area.

COP$200,000-500,000

84 DC

Calle 84 No. 9-67; tel. 1/487-0909; www.84dc.com.co; COP$253,000 d

Cool 84 DC blends in well in this upscale neighborhood just blocks from the Zona T. It has 24 spacious modern rooms, and the breakfast area downstairs has a patio and lots of natural light.

★ B3

Carrera 15 No. 88-36; tel. 1/593-4490; www.hotelesb3.com; COP$278,000 d

B3 is one of the most striking hotels in town thanks to its wonderful wall of living plants. The lobby area is a lively place in the early evening, when guests munch on tapas and sip cocktails at the bar. Upstairs, the 128 rooms are minimalist and spacious. The hotel has a few bikes available for guests, and Ciclovía passes in front on Sunday. Joggers can hit the paths of Parque El Virrey next door.

★ Cité

Carrera 15 No. 88-10; tel. 1/646-7777; www.citehotel.com; COP$485,000 d

Right on Parque El Virrey, the location of 56-room Cité couldn't be better. The terrace of the hotel's restaurant, Le Bistro, is a popular place for Sunday brunch for guests and nonguests. There's a rooftop pool, and bikes are available for guests during Ciclovía, which passes by every Sunday and holiday.

OVER COP$500,000

B.O.G.

Carrera 11 No. 86-74; tel. 1/639-9999; www.boghotel.com; COP$2,000,000 d

At five-star B.O.G., every detail has been thought out. The smart restaurant in the lobby features Spanish touches and serves great lemonade. The rooftop pool is luxurious. A giant photograph of an emerald in the gym and spa area downstairs may inspire you to buy one.

Information and Services

Visitor Information

For information on all things Bogotá, go to a **PIT (Punto de Información Turística).** There is usually someone on staff who can speak English, provide you with a map, and answer questions. In La Candelaria there is a PIT on the southwest corner of the **Plaza de Bolívar** (tel. 1/283-7115; 8am-6pm Mon.-Sat., 8am-4pm Sun.). Other locations include the **Quiosco de la Luz** (Carrera 7 at Calle 26; tel. 1/284-2664; 9am-5pm Mon.-Sat.) in Parque de la Independencia, the international terminal of the airport (T1; no phone; 7am-10pm daily), and the bus terminals Terminal de Transportes (Diagonal 23 No. 69-60, Local 127; tel. 1/555-7692;

7am-7pm Mon.-Sat., 8am-4pm Sun.) and Terminal del Sur (Autopista Sur, Local 67; tel. 1/555-7696; 7am-1pm daily).

Emergency and Medical Services

The emergency hotline is tel. 123. Most operators don't speak English. You should provide the neighborhood you are in and a precise street number.

Bogotá has excellent physicians and hospitals. Mom-and-pop pharmacies are all over the city and can be less stringent about requiring prescriptions.

Fundación Santa Fe

Calle 119 No. 7-75; www.fsfb.org.co; tel. 1/603-0303, emergency tel. 1/629-0477

The Fundación Santa Fe clinic is located near Usaquén and is well versed in handling foreign patients. They offer a full range of medical services.

Profamilia

Calle 34 No. 14-52; tel. 1/339-0900; www.profamilia.org.co

For sexual and reproductive health, Profamilia, a member of the International Planned Parenthood Federation, offers clinical services. It is steps from the Profamilia TransMilenio station on Calle Caracas.

Farmatodo

tel. 1/743-2100; www.farmatodo.com.co

Farmatodo is a pharmacy chain with 30 locations in Bogotá; some are open 24 hours daily.

Phones

The telephone area code for Bogotá and many surrounding towns is 1. To call a cell phone from a landline, first dial 03 and then the 10-digit number. To call a landline from a cell phone, dial 03-1 (the 1 is for Bogotá). When in the city, there is no need to dial 1 before a landline number.

Prepaid cell phones or SIM cards can be purchased at any **Claro** (www.claro.com.co) or **Movistar** (www.movistar.com.co) store.

Money

ATMs are throughout the city and are the best option for getting Colombian pesos. Transaction fees vary. Some ATMs on the streets are closed at night. Be cautious when taking out money.

Money-changing outfits also line Avenida Jiménez in El Centro and are found in most malls in Northern Bogotá. They are usually closed on holidays. You'll need to show your passport to change money.

Visas and Officialdom

US citizens who have health, safety, or legal emergencies can contact the **US Embassy** (tel. 601/275-2000).

Migración Colombia

Calle 100 No. 11B-27; tel. 1/595-4331; 8am-4pm Mon.-Fri.

To stay beyond the 60 or 90 days allowed to visitors from the United States, Canada, Australia, New Zealand, and most European countries, you will need to go to Migración Colombia. It is best to go a few days before your current visa expires.

Transportation

Getting There

AIR

Aeropuerto Internacional El Dorado

BOG; Calle 26 No. 103-09; tel. 1/266-2000; www.elnuevodorado.com

Modern and user-friendly Aeropuerto Internacional El Dorado is the largest airport in the country. All international and most domestic flights now depart from **T1,** the main terminal. Airlines that serve domestic locations from T1 are Avianca, LATAM, SATENA, Wingo, and Viva Colombia. There is a wealth of services in T1, including a Crepes & Waffles restaurant that's open 24 hours. There are money-exchange offices and ATMs just outside the customs area.

The smaller **Puente Aéreo,** or **T2,** is a secondary terminal used only by Avianca for flights to smaller domestic destinations. It's less than 0.5 km (0.3 mi) from T1. All Avianca domestic flights depart from T2 except flights to Barranquilla, Cartagena, Cali, Medellín, and Pereira. If you have a connection that requires a transfer between T1 and T2, a complimentary shuttle bus is provided. Airline staff, usually from Avianca, are available around the clock to assist in transferring terminals.

Airport Transportation

Leaving the baggage claim and customs area, you will be approached insistently by taxi services, but these are not recommended. Instead, look for the official taxi queue outside the terminal. Metered taxis cost COP$35,000-50,000 to most points in the city.

TransMilenio service is also available. First purchase a Tullave transit card at the airport near the taxi services area, then board the **16-14 bus** that takes passengers to the Portal El Dorado TransMilenio station, about 0.8 km (0.5 mi) from the airport. From here, catch a red TransMilenio bus (COP$2,800) into the city, a 30-45-minute ride to the Las Aguas station at Parque de los Periodistas. If you don't have a lot of luggage, this can be an inexpensive way to get into town.

BUS

Bogotá has three bus terminals: the Terminal del Sur, the Portal del Norte, and the main bus station, the Terminal de Transportes in Salitre.

Terminal de Transportes Salitre

Diagonal 23 No. 69-60; tel. 1/423-3630; www.terminaldetransporte.gov.co

The Terminal de Transportes Salitre is Bogotá's main long-distance bus terminal. From here you can catch a ride to anywhere in the country. It is well organized and clean and divided into three modules, each generally corresponding to a different direction: Module 1 is south, Module 2 is east and west, and Module 3 is north. Module 4 is for long-distance taxi services and Module 5 is for arrivals. All the modules are in the same building. Each module has an information booth at the entrance with an attendant who can point you in the right direction.

In the arrivals module is a **PIT** tourist information office where the helpful attendants can give you a map of the city and assist you in getting to your hotel. There is also organized and safe taxi service and plenty of public transportation options available.

The Terminal de Transportes Salitre is in western Bogotá. A cab from La Candelaria to the terminal takes about 30 minutes and costs COP$35,000.

During the Christmas and Easter holidays the bus terminal is busy with crowds and packed buses. This is also true on puentes (long weekends).

Portal del Norte

Autopista Norte and Calle 174

The Portal del Norte, part of the TransMilenio station of the same name, may be more convenient if you are arriving from or heading to nearby destinations north of the city such as Tunja or Villa de Leyva. Taking the TransMilenio here and then jumping on a bus to one of those destinations, popular with weekenders, often allows you to cut an hour or two of city traffic. It is on Calle 175 in the north of the city.

Terminal del Sur

Autopista Sur and Carrera 72D

The Terminal del Sur is near the Portal Sur of TransMilenio in the far south of the city. This station serves locations in southern Cundinamarca such as Tequendama and travels farther south to Girardot, Ibagué, Neiva, Popayán, Armenia, and Cali, continuing all the way to Mocoa in Putumayo.

Getting Around

Walking, biking, buses, and taxis combine to make getting around this giant city pretty straightforward.

BUS

TransMilenio

www.transmilenio.gov.co

TransMilenio is the bus rapid transit (BRT) system that serves Bogotá. Begun in 2000, it has transformed the city and is the largest BRT system in the world. Over two million Bogotanos use the system each day. It can be a useful and inexpensive way for visitors to get around. There are more than 100 stations on 12 lines that cover much of the city.

There are three TransMilenio lines that are especially useful to visitors. First are the red hybrid TransMilenio buses on Carrera 7 (La Séptima). These are regular-looking buses, not the massive ones associated with TransMilenio. This is the **M line,** the best way to get from downtown to the north. This line has a modern terminal at the Museo Nacional. Going south toward La Candelaria, the M line morphs into the L line.

Second is the original **B line** on Avenida Caracas. This extends from downtown to the Portal del Norte bus terminal at Calle 170. An offshoot, the J line, makes a detour toward the Museo del Oro.

The third line of importance is the **K line** along Avenida El Dorado (Av. Calle 26), which serves the airport.

The system operates 5am-midnight Monday-Saturday and 6am-11pm Sunday and holidays. Paid for a with a Tullave card, a ride typically costs COP$2,800, and transfers within 75 minutes on TransMilenio or SITP cost only COP$500. View or download a map of the entire system at www.sitp.gov.co/publicaciones/402-36/mapas-transmilenio.

While riding the buses, keep your wallet in your front pocket and watch your belongings, especially during rush hour. When attempting to board or disembark TransMilenio buses, don't expect other passengers to make room for you. Call out "permiso, por favor" and move with purpose.

SITP

The SITP comprises regular buses that serve the TransMilenio stations and connect passengers with farther destinations. This can be complicated for travelers new to the city but actually works smoothly and fairly well.

Tullave Card

To ride TransMilenio or SITP buses, you must first purchase a refillable Tullave card. One card can be used by multiple passengers. Cards are available for purchase at TransMilenio stations and at papelerías (mom-and-pop stationery stores) located near TransMilenio and SITP bus routes. It's easier to purchase the cards at papelerías—look for the Tullave decal on storefronts—as lines at TransMilenio stations can be insufferably long. Buying or refilling Tullave cards is cash-only.

TAXIS

It's estimated that over a million people take a taxi each day in Bogotá. There are 50,000 taxis, mostly yellow Hyundais, circulating in the streets. If you plan on taking a taxi, use an app like Easy Taxi, Cabify, or Uber, as there have been some reports of robbery with taxis hailed on the street, especially at night.

A taxímetro calculates units that determine the price. The rates are listed on a tarjetón (large card) along with the driver's information. That card should always be visible. Expect to pay COP$15,000-20,000 for a ride from EL Centro to Chapinero or Teusaquillo and COP$30,000-40,000 to Northern Bogotá. There are surcharges for taxis ordered by phone, for nighttime rides, and for going to the airport. Taxi drivers do not expect tips, but you can always round up the fare. During end-of-year holidays, drivers may ask for a holiday tip.

public bike station in Teusaquillo

WALKING

You get a real feel for the city and its energy by walking its streets. The neighborhoods that make up downtown (La Candelaria, El Centro, Centro Internacional, and La Macarena) are accessible on foot, and walking is often the best way to get around. The same holds true for the upscale shopping and residential areas in Northern Bogotá.

BIKING

Bogotá has one of the most extensive bike path networks in Latin America, with over 608 km (378 mi) of ciclorutas (bike lanes). Bicyclists should take extra care when using the ciclorutas as vehicles may not yield for bikes. A popular, easy, and protected bike path extends along Carrera 11 between Calles 24 and 100.

Ciclovía is a weekly event on Sundays and holidays when usually traffic-filled streets are closed to vehicles and bicycles take their places. Helmets are not essential at Ciclovía but are advisable on the ciclorutas. Never leave a bike unlocked in Bogotá.

CAR RENTAL

With more than a million usually aggressive drivers on the clogged streets of Bogotá, renting a vehicle is a bad idea for visitors. However, if you are planning to travel to nearby places like Villa de Leyva or would like to take your time touring parks or villages, renting might be a solid option.

National (Carrera 7 No. 145-71; www.nationalcolombia.com), **Avis** (Av. 19 No. 123-52 Local 2; tel. 1/629-1722; www.avis.com), and **Hertz** (Av. Caracas No. 28A-17; tel. 1/327-6700; www.rentacarcolombia.co) have offices in Bogotá. Foreign driver's licenses are accepted in Colombia. It's important to find out your car's vehicle restriction days, which mean you can't drive during business hours for two predetermined days of the week, based on the last digit of your license plate (this restriction only applies in Bogotá).

Around Bogotá

Choachí

Recently named one of the Pueblos que Enamoran (villages to fall in love with) by the Colombian government, Choachí is a historic mountain town just an hour east of Bogotá. It's also about 800 m (2,600 ft) lower in elevation and has a nice springlike climate. Choachí offers one of Colombia's top hikes, to the base of the country's tallest waterfall. Many international visitors come on a day tour to do the hike, but it's worth spending the night in the pueblo, which exudes mountain country charm and gives you the opportunity to soak out the stress of the city in natural hot springs. Choachí is a favorite weekend escape for Bogotanos, and it can be packed Saturday-Sunday. Come midweek, however, you have this slice of paradise pretty much to yourself.

SIGHTS AND RECREATION

Plaza Mayor

Choachí's wide main plaza is the center of town activity. Fronting the glorious Parroquia San Miguel church, built in 1608, the plaza comes alive at night when food vendors, families, wandering musicians, and visitors mix under the stars in the fresh mountain air. Dozens of local restaurants and bars line the streets that branch off from the plaza.

La Chorrera

Distance: 5 km (3 mi)
Duration: 2 hours
Elevation gain: 500 m (1,650 ft)
Difficulty: Moderate
Trailhead: Park entrance

With a glorious 590-m (1,940-ft) waterfall set against the rugged face of the mountains, La Chorrera is not just Colombia's tallest waterfall, it's one of the world's most picturesque. Expeditions that include round-trip transportation plus a hiking guide are bookable at most hotels and hostels and also directly through **Beyond Colombia Tours** (www.beyondcolombia.com), but it's also easy to visit the falls independently.

La Chorrera waterfalls in Choachí

The entrance to La Chorrera is on the road between Bogotá and Choachí. The bus driver will let you off here in either direction if you ask. From here it's a 4-km (2.5-mi) walk along an often muddy country road to the parking lot and park entrance where the trailhead officially starts. Alternatively, and much more fun, you can pay a 4WD taxi driver (COP$60,000 each way, arranged by hotels in Choachí) to take you all the way to the trailhead and wait for you.

After registering (and paying the COP$15,000 per person fee, COP$40,000 with lunch) at the tourist office just past the parking lot, you can hit the trail. After climbing up into the foothills, the trail brings you to the Cascada El Chiflón, a small but enchanting waterfall nestled in the greenery, where lunch is served if you reserved it. From here it's about 4 km (2.5 mi) up to the awe-inspiring **Cascada La Chorrera.** Lunch is available at the tourist office, but the food is much better, and cheaper, back in town.

Termales Santa Monica

Km 2, Vereda Reguardo; tel. 310/349-4263; www.termalessantamonica.com; day pass COP$60,000

The palatial hot springs complex of Termales Santa Monica takes relaxing and unwinding to new levels. With six pools of varying temperatures of mineral-rich water, several saunas and jetted tubs, and lush flower-filled sprawling grounds, it's easy to see why Bogotanos flock here on weekends.

Visiting for a day is cheaper during the week, and there's an on-site hotel. The Termales Santa Monica are 2 km (1.2 mi) down a dirt road from the Plaza Mayor of Choachí, a pleasant walk through the countryside or a short COP$8,000 taxi ride.

FOOD AND ACCOMMODATIONS

Carrera 3, the town's main street, is lined with family-owned restaurants that serve local fare like tamales, grilled meats, and the town's signature dish, cocida chiguano (goat and pork meat smothered with local beans and tubers).

Lipari Rooftop

Carrera 3 No. 2-28; tel. 312/332-4407; noon-11pm daily; COP$26,000-40,000

Pizza, burgers, and house-made craft beer are served over sweeping views of the mountains at this upscale pub located half a block down Carrera 3 from the main plaza.

Hotel Santa Monica

Km 2, Vereda Reguardo; tel. 310/349-3426; www.termalessantamonica.com; COP$570,000 d

At the hot springs complex, 68-room Hotel Santa Monica offers accommodations that are all-inclusive, with access to all the facilities plus lunch, dinner, and breakfast at the on-site restaurant.

hot springs at Choachí

TRANSPORTATION

Buses to Choachí depart from the small bus terminal **Cootransfomeque** (Carrera 6 No. 15-28, Bogotá; 5:15am-8pm daily; COP$12,000 one-way). Buses leave the terminal as soon as they fill up, which usually doesn't take more than 20 or 30 minutes. Although this terminal is close to La Candelaria, it's in a sketchy part of central Bogotá, so taking a taxi (COP$10,000), is advised.

★ Laguna de Guatavita

tel. 315/831-1086; www.car.gov.co; 9am-4pm Tues.-Sat.; COP$28,000

A dazzling emerald-colored lagoon surrounded by thick cloud forest, the Laguna de Guatavita is where the myth of El Dorado (the lost city of gold) has its origins. The Muisca people, who occupied the altiplano where modern-day Bogotá lies as well as much of the surrounding territory, considered the lake sacred and performed elaborate rituals here, sometimes sending gold-plated rafts out onto the lake as an offering. When Europeans arrived in Guatavita they drained the lake at least three times, looking for treasure at the bottom of the lake. A giant cut in the lakeside can still be seen.

Today Laguna de Guatavita is being given the respect it deserves. An environmental agency maintains the park, and to preserve the lake, it can't be accessed directly. The lake is much better appreciated from above, on the well-maintained stone-paved path along the top of the crater. When visiting, you must join a **tour group** (included in admission) to see the lake. Tours leave every 30 minutes and last about an hour. Guides are knowledgeable and passionate about their work. Tours in English are possible, especially for larger groups, but should be reserved in advance.

While much of the 2-km (1.2-mi) path is flat, there is a fairly steep climb, making it difficult for those with physical limitations. At the end of the walk, you can walk or hop on a minibus (COP$3,000) back to the entrance of the park. Several food stands and artisan shops, many that feature locally made cheese and honey, are in the parking lot. When Monday is a holiday, the park is open Wednesday-Monday.

TRANSPORTATION

Guatavita is one of the most popular all-inclusive day tours from Bogotá and can be booked at any hotel or hostel or through **Beyond Colombia Tours** (https://beyondcolombia.com).

Getting to Laguna de Guatavita on public transportation is doable but time-consuming and can be more expensive than a group tour. At the TransMilenio Portal del Norte station in Bogotá, take a bus bound for Nueva Guatavita (COP$15,000). Upon arrival in Nueva Guatavita, hire a taxi driver to take you to the park, wait for you, and bring you back to Nueva Guatavita. Expect to pay up to COP$100,000 for this service. On weekends, there is a bus service (COP$10,000) from Nueva Guatavita directly to the park that departs at 11am and 1pm.

Parque Natural Chicaque

Km 8, Vía Soacha; tel. 318/350-6147; www.chicaque.com; 8am-4:30pm Mon.-Sun.; from COP$54,000

Laguna de Guatavita

A 300-ha (740-acre) swath of cloud forest that covers the slopes of the mountains at the western edge of the altiplano as it drops toward the Río Magdalena valley, Parque Natural Chicaque is natural paradise on the outskirts of the city. The forest contains four subsystems, including one dominated by *Quercus humboldtii*, a species of oak tree only found in Colombia and Panama. Seventeen species of endemic orchids have been spotted in the park, and it is home to over 200 species of birds, including the emerald toucanet *(Aulacorhynchus prasinus)*, which is in danger of extinction. With a well-developed trail network, it's easy to spend the entire day hiking here. Two on-site restaurants, **Arboloco** at the entrance and **El Refugio** in the middle of the park, serve a variety of lunch plates (COP$35,000-60,000) and arrange activities like bird-watching and horseback riding.

HIKING

Mariposa Trail

Distance: 8 km (5 mi)
Duration: 3 hours
Elevation gain: 600 m (1,970 ft)
Difficulty: Moderate
Trailhead: El Refugio

The densely forested Mariposa (butterfly) trail meanders through some of the most pristine parts of the park and gives you the opportunity to spot crystal-winged butterflies *(Greta oto)*.

Pico de Aguila Trail

Distance: 5 km (3 mi)
Duration: 1-2 hours
Elevation gain: 400 m (1,300 ft)
Difficulty: Moderate
Trailhead: Arboloco

The two-hour hike to the rocky outpost of Pico de Aguila offers incredible views over the Río Magdalena valley.

ACCOMMODATIONS

Although Chicaque makes a great day trip from Bogotá, it's also possible to spend a night or two in paradise. The park offers several options, including simple cabañas (COP$202,000), two houses (COP$500,000), a grand three-story hotel (from COP$99,000 d), and camping (COP$44,000 pp).

TRANSPORTATION

Day tours to Parque Natural Chicaque are offered by **Beyond Colombia** (https://beyondcolombia.com; COP$120,000) but you can also visit the park by public transit, especially if you go on a weekend when the park offers a free shuttle service from the Soacha TransMilenio station. The shuttle picks up passengers at 10am and returns to the station from the park at 4pm. From downtown Bogotá it's a 45-minute ride on TransMilenio to Soacha.

Boyacá and Santander

Highlights

★ **Villa de Leyva:** Explore the art galleries and boutique shops lining the cobblestone streets of this colonial gem, Bogotá's favorite weekend getaway (page 187).

★ **Monguí** *(upper right):* Relax in this traditional high Andean pueblo, the gateway to the Páramo de Ocetá (page 195).

★ **Lago Tota:** Explore the white-sand beaches and wetlands of this pristine high-altitude lake (page 197).

★ **Parque Nacional Natural El Cocuy:** Make your way up to Ritacuba glacier or simply admire it from below in the charming mountain villages of El Cocuy (page 203).

★ **Paragliding over Cañón del Chicamocha** *(lower right):* Soar out over the 915-m-deep (3,000-ft) canyon (page 208).

★ **Barichara** *(upper & lower left):* Head out on a church-to-church walking tour through the ancient streets of this majestic colonial town (page 211).

Look for ★ to find recommended sights, activities, dining, and lodging.

◂ Plaza Mayor, Villa de Leyva

The Andean regions of Boyacá and Santander offer endless immersions into the mountainous natural splendor of the Cordillera Oriental, the easternmost of Colombia's three Andean mountain ranges. These rugged but fertile regions are also the breadbasket of the country, with traditional farms dotting the green mountain slopes in every direction. While the highlands of Boyacá reach up to snow-capped heights, Santander has a lower elevation and a milder climate.

From chasing waterfalls to hang-gliding over stunning canyons, trekking up to pristine glaciers, and visiting the white-sand beaches of alpine lakes, nature lovers will find their fix in Boyacá and Santander. Besides the gorgeous mountain scenery, these regions are home to numerous picturesque small towns, including two of the country's most famous and majestic historic pueblos, Villa de Leyva and Barichara. Both overflow with boutiques and accommodations that keep creature comforts close at hand despite the old-school rural lifestyle of the surrounding countryside.

Boyacá and Santander are two of the safest departments in the country.

Planning Your Time

There are three main draws in Boyacá: the lovely colonial town of Villa de Leyva, the highland scenery and traditional Andean pueblos near Lago Tota, and the snow-capped wonderland of the Sierra Nevada del Cocuy. In Santander, the action-packed area around San Gil, including the legendary beauty of colonial Barichara, offer endless adventures. Give yourself at least five days to visit both regions as you will have to base yourself in each one.

Villa de Leyva can be visited in a short two-day excursion from Bogotá, but you could easily spend two more relaxing days seeing all the sights. To further explore Boyacá, extend your visit for two days to the area around Sogamoso, particularly the traditional villages of Iza and Monguí as well as Lago Tota. There are good public transportation links throughout Boyacá, and this is also a fairly easy place to drive.

Getting to the Sierra Nevada del Cocuy, 5 hours from Sogamoso and 11 hours by bus from Bogotá, is a journey in itself and requires a minimum stay of 2-3 days to make it worthwhile. This remote area has fewer public transportation options, although buses depart for the area from Tunja. Roads are mostly in good shape.

In Santander, San Gil and Barichara have a lot to offer, so plan on spending at least three days. Barichara is a more beautiful base for exploring the region, but San Gil is home to the main adventure sports operators. On holidays it can be difficult to get a seat on a bus to or from San Gil as it's also a stop between Bogotá and Bucaramanga, in the northern part of Santander.

The bus ride between Villa de Leyva and San Gil takes 4-5 hours with a change of bus in Tunja. Even though San Gil and the Sierra Nevada del Cocuy are only 75 km (47 mi) apart as the crow flies, there is no direct bus service between them. To get from

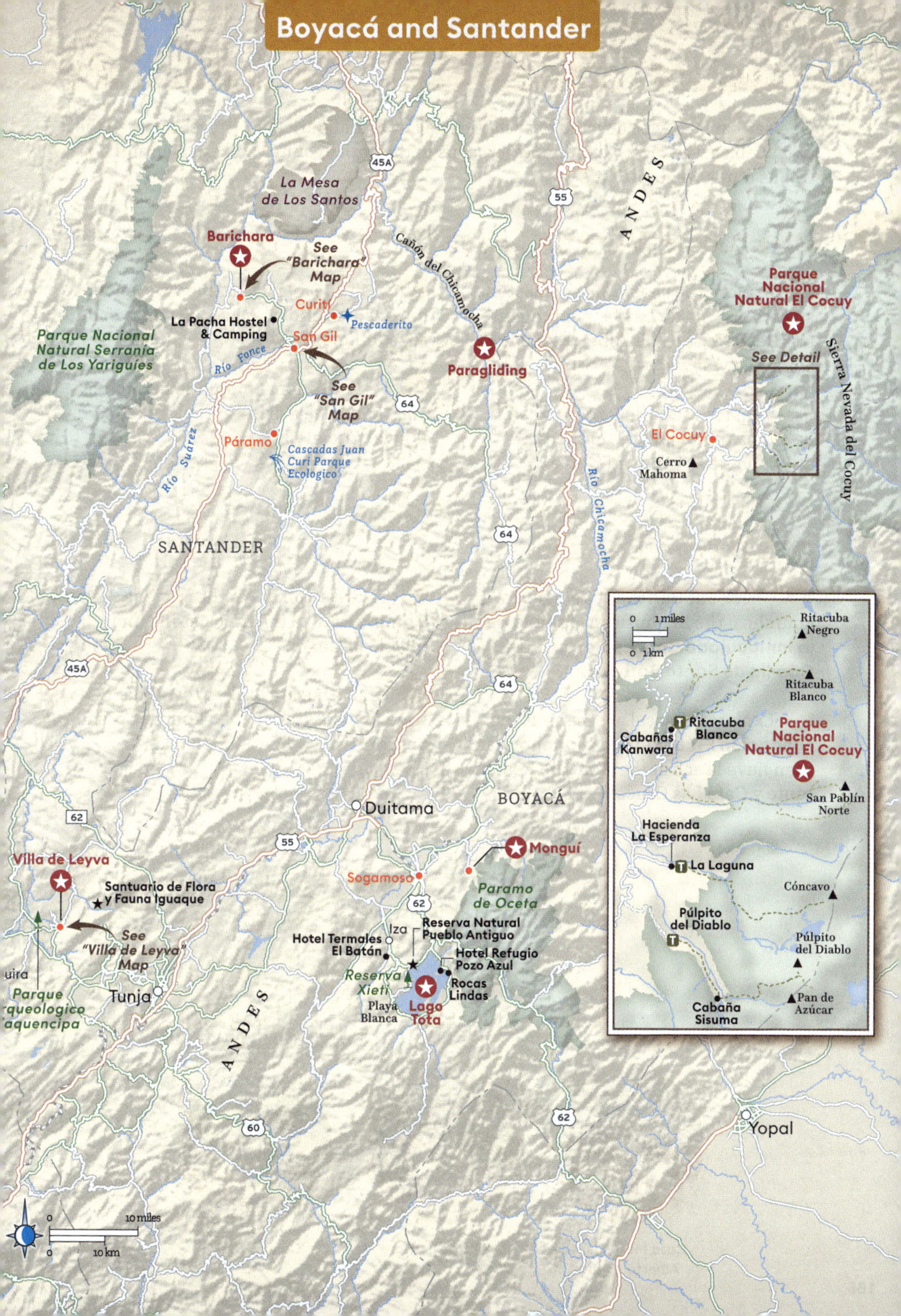

Boyacá and Santander
La Mesa de Los Santos
45A
55
ANDES
Barichara
See "Barichara" Map
Cañón del Chicamocha
Parque Nacional Natural El Cocuy
Curití
Pescaderito
La Pacha Hostel & Camping
San Gil
Parque Nacional Natural Serranía de Los Yariguíes
Río Fonce
Paragliding
See Detail
Sierra Nevada del Cocuy
See "San Gil" Map
64
Páramo
Cascadas Juan Curi Parque Ecologico
Río Suárez
El Cocuy
Cerro Mahoma
Río Chicamocha
SANTANDER
64
0 1 miles
0 1 km
Ritacuba Negro
Ritacuba Blanco
45A
64
Cabañas Kanwara
Ritacuba Blanco
Parque Nacional Natural El Cocuy
San Pablín Norte
Duitama
BOYACÁ
Hacienda La Esperanza
62
55
Monguí
La Laguna
Villa de Leyva
Sogamoso
Paramo de Oceta
Cóncavo
Santuario de Flora y Fauna Iguaque
62
Púlpito del Diablo
Iza
Reserva Natural Pueblo Antiguo
See "Villa de Leyva" Map
Hotel Termales El Batán
Púlpito del Diablo
Hotel Refugio Pozo Azul
Reserva Xieti
Rocas Lindas
Tunja
Playa Blanca
Lago Tota
Pan de Azúcar
Cabaña Sisuma
Parque Arqueologico Raquencipa
ANDES
62
60
Yopal
0 10 miles
0 10 km

Itinerary Ideas

One day can easily be devoted to each Villa de Leyva and Barichara. Travel between the two pueblos, the most famous and gorgeous in the entire country, takes an entire day by bus but is well worth it.

ONE DAY in Villa de Leyva

1. Explore the charming cobblestone streets of Villa de Leyva, popping into the **Casa Museo Luis Alberto Acuña** along the way.
2. Stop for the coffee, some fresh baked pastries, and the chilled-out atmosphere at **Sybarita Caffe.**
3. Visit the Iglesia de Nuestra Señora del Carmen and its **Museo El Carmen de Arte Religioso.**
4. Have dinner at **Mercado Municipal** and then have a drink at their on-site Bolívar Social Club.

ONE DAY in Barichara

1. Check out Barichara's gorgeous churches: the magnificent **Templo de la Inmaculada Concepción** and the **Capilla de Santa Bárbara.**
2. Explore the local art scene at the **Fundación Escuela Taller Barichara** and then have lunch at their on-site Restaurante y Café Las Cruces.
3. Take a stroll down the ancient **Camino Real** to the tiny lost-in-time pueblo of Guane.
4. Grab a buseta back to town just in time to have dinner at **La Puerta Cocina Secreta.**

Casa Museo Luis Alberto Acuña

Villa de Leyva

Camino Real

one to the other, you must change buses in Tunja, requiring more than 10 hours of travel.

Much of Boyacá is in the high Andes, so be prepared for cold nights, in the 30s F (-1-4°C). Santander has milder weather.

Boyacá

Although just a couple of hours northeast of Bogotá, the department of Boyacá feels lost in time. A mostly rural agricultural area of bucolic Andean countryside, traditional campesinos (farmers) often dressed in ruanas (wool ponchos) tend to their dairy cows and potato crops on small farms that hug the side of steep mountain slopes. Boyacenses are known for their politeness, shyness, and honesty and will often address you not with the formal *usted* but rather with the super-deferential *sumercé*, a term that is derived from the old Spanish *su merced* (literally "your mercy").

A favorite weekend getaway for Bogotanos, Villa de Leyva has the perfect combination of colonial charm, good hotels and restaurants, attractions, and fantastic weather. Boyacá is home to more picturesque pueblos than anywhere in the country, most with far less tourism than Villa de Leyva, including mountain-high Monguí and tiny Iza, the latter close to the white sand baches of Lago Tota, as well as El Cocuy up in the Sierra de Cocuy.

Don't miss trying cocido Boyacense, the region's most iconic dish, a hearty helping of slow-roasted pork covered in several types of heirloom Andean tubers and legumes all smothered in a thick tomato-herb sauce.

★ Villa de Leyva

This enchanting whitewashed colonial pueblo is set in the arid Valle de Saquencipá, which ensures it always has blue skies. Its beauty and proximity to the capital mean that the population triples on weekends, as do prices. The surrounding mountainous desert scenery, a palette of ever-changing pastels, is gorgeous as well. The typically sunny weather is never too hot nor too cool, and the town's preserved colonial mansions along ancient cobblestone streets are picturesque.

Just outside Villa de Leyva are a surprising number of activities and attractions, including archaeological sites and outdoor activities such as biking and hiking. The nearby Santuario de Flora y Fauna Iguaque is one of the most accessible national parks in the country, and you need only a decent pair of boots to hike to its sacred lakes.

SIGHTS

Plaza Mayor

Villa de Leyva's Plaza Mayor is one of the most photographed locations in Colombia. The town's main square is the largest plaza in the country at 14,000 sq m (3.5 acres) and hard to fit in one photo. In the middle of the square is a Mudéjar-style well, the Ara Sagrada, that was the source of water for the townspeople in colonial times.

Iglesia Parroquial

Carrera 9 No. 12-68; 8am-noon and 2pm-6pm Tues.-Sat., 8am-noon Sun.

On the southeastern side of the Plaza Mayor is the Iglesia Parroquial, built in the 17th century from stone, adobe, and wood. It features a large golden retablo (altarpiece).

Casa Museo Luis Alberto Acuña

Carrera 10 No. 12-83; tel. 8/732-0422; Instagram @casamuseoacuna_villadeleyva; 9am-6pm daily; COP$6,000

On the western side of the Plaza Mayor is the quirky Casa Museo Luis Alberto Acuña, dedicated to Colombian artist Luis Alberto Acuña. The house turned museum is filled with Acuña's cubist-influenced paintings of pre-Hispanic Indigenous culture along with his art collection and antiques. Acuña was instrumental in the restoration and preservation of local colonial architecture.

Museo El Carmen de Arte Religioso

Calle 14 No. 10-04; 10:30am-1pm and 2:30pm-5pm Sat.-Sun.; COP$4,000

The Museo El Carmen de Arte Religioso presents paintings, crucifixes, manuscripts, and religious figures from the colonial era. The museum is on the southwest corner of the grassy **Plazoleta de la Carmen.** The complex, which dates to around 1850, also includes a monastery and a convent.

Casa Museo Antonio Nariño

Carrera 9 No. 10-25; tel. 8/732-0342; 9am-noon and 2pm-5pm Thurs.-Tues.; free

Built in the 17th century, the Casa Museo Antonio Nariño is the house where independence figure Antonio Nariño lived and died. The museum displays some of Nariño's manuscripts as well as items from everyday life in the 19th century, such as a giant mortar used to mill corn. The small but good museum often puts on temporary art exhibits that may have a small admission fee.

Casa Museo Capitán Antonio Ricaurte

Calle 15 No. 8-17; no phone; 9am-noon and 2pm-5pm Wed.-Sun.; free

The Casa Museo Capitán Antonio Ricaurte is in the small house where independence figure Antonio Ricaurte was born in 1786. One room is filled with uniforms and memorabilia of the Colombian air force, of which Ricaurte was a part. Ricaurte died heroically, sacrificing his life by detonating a cache of gunpowder so that it would not fall into the hands of Spaniards.

Santuario de Flora y Fauna Iguaque

tel. 322/947-1031; https://parquesnacionales.gov.co

Seventeen km (11 mi) outside of Villa de Leyva lies the 7,000-ha (17,300-acre) paradise known as the Santuario de Flora y Fauna Iguaque. Nestled in a lush mountain valley, the reserve centers on the **Iguaque lagoon,** a site sacred to the Muisca people. The round-trip hike to the lagoon takes about 6 hours with 800 m (2,625 ft) of elevation gain. The trail passes through pristine cloud forest and páramo with ample opportunities to view wildlife: More than 100 species of birds have been documented here.

Visitors must be accompanied by a certified guide, which is easy to book at any hotel in Villa de Leyva. The guide's fee includes the COP$76,000 entrance fee for non-Colombians as well as a trail lunch. To preserve the fragile ecosystems of the reserve, visitors are asked not to stray off the marked trail.

HIKING

Cerro El Santo

Distance: 4 km (2.5 mi) round-trip
Duration: 2 hours
Elevation gain: 180 m (600 ft)
Difficulty: Moderate
Trailhead: To get to the path, walk east along Calle 12 to the tennis court and soccer field, north of the Hotel Duruelo. The path entrance is marked with a sign on the left.

Close to town, sporty locals regularly take a brisk morning hike up to the **Santo,** a statue on the eastern side of Villa de Leyva. It is a steep climb and hikers are rewarded with a bird's-eye view of the Plaza Mayor. It's best to make the climb early in the morning, before the midday heat envelops the valley. At times you may need both hands free to scramble over rocks.

BIKING

Renting a bike to see the sights in the valley near Villa de Leyva is a great way to spend a day and get some exercise as you huff and puff in the hilly landscape. Many hostels have bikes for rent.

Ciclotrip

Carrera 9 No. 141-101; tel. 8/732-1485 or 317/435-5202; www.ciclotrip.com

Ciclotrip can organize biking tours to many different locations in the area.

clockwise plaza in Villa de Leyva; street in Villa de Leyva; sunrise in Boyacá

FESTIVALS AND EVENTS

Festival de Astronómica de Villa de Leyva

www.festivaldeastronomia.com; Feb.; free

The crystal-clear skies above Villa de Leyva make for great stargazing. Each year the town hosts the Festival de Astronómica, when people are invited to view the stars through powerful telescopes in the Plaza Mayor.

Festival del Viento y Cometas

www.villadeleyva-boyaca.gov.co; Aug.

During the breezy days of August, hundreds of colorful kites soar above the plaza during the Festival del Viento y Cometas.

SHOPPING

For centuries, farmers and craftspeople in Villa de Leyva have specialized in woven goods. The symbol of this part of Colombia could be the ruana, a warm woolen cape worn by men and women. Woolen goods can be found on nearly every street corner in Villa de Leyva. The town is home to many creative types, and small jewelry stores, art galleries, and handicraft shops are common throughout town.

AUTHOR TIP

The Villa de Leyva area is Colombia's up-and-coming wine region. Inquire at your hotel for info on visiting wineries in the area.

Plaza de Mercado

Calles 12-13 and Carreras 5-6; 7am-3pm Thurs., 5am-4pm Sat.

There are two weekly markets at the Plaza de Mercado. The **Thursday market** is all organic fruits and vegetables, while the **Saturday market** is larger, with lots of handicrafts as well. It's held just two blocks behind the Plaza Mayor. Locals and visitors alike delight in this weekly tradition.

Alieth Tejido Artesanal

Calle 13 No. 7-89; tel. 8/732-1672; https://aliethtejidosvilladeleyva.weebly.com

Alieth Tejido Artesanal is an association of about 35 women who weave woolen sweaters, ruanas, mochilas (handwoven purses), gloves, scarves, and colorful psychedelic bags from virgin wool. A tour, the Ruta de la Lana (5 hours; COP$60,000 pp), visits nearby farms to learn about the process from sheep to sweater. Snacks and a souvenir are included. Alieth Ortíz, the head of this interesting program, requests reservations be made a few days in advance so that they can organize things with the artisans.

La Libélula

Carrera 9 No. 14-35; tel. 8/732-0040; 10am-7pm daily

La Libélula specializes in leather handbags, belts, and accessories.

FOOD

Los Kioscos de los Caciques

Carrera 9 No. 9-05; tel. 311/475-8681; noon-3pm and 6pm-8pm daily; COP$12,000-20,000

Locals tend to steer clear of the overpriced restaurants on the Plaza Mayor. Close to the Terminal de Transportes, Los Kioscos de los Caciques specializes in filling local dishes such as mazamorra chiquita (beef stew with potatoes, corn, and other vegetables)

ON MUISCA TIME

The pre-Colombian Muisca civilization, known for intricate gold-working skills and advanced agricultural practices, stretched from modern-day Bogotá to southern Santander, with Boyacá making up much of the heartland. Like other advanced American civilizations, the Muisca had a firm grasp of astronomy, and many of their most important architectural monuments reflect this in calendars and celestial observation sites. Step off the regular path and into Muisca time by checking out some of the civilization's most important ceremonial sites:

Templo del Sol replica

OBSERVATÓRIO ASTRONÓMICO DE ZAQUENZIPA (EL INFIERNITO)

7 km (4.3 mi) de Villa de Leyva; tel. 320/827-8259; 9am-noon and 2pm-5pm Tues.-Sun.; COP$12,000

Named El Infiernito (little hell) by Spanish colonizers, the Observatório Astronómico de Zaquenzipa is Colombia's own version of Stonehenge. Over 100 pink sandstone menhirs, or standing stones, are aligned with the sun and moon in rows and circular patterns to measure the seasons. Although El Infiernito was used extensively by the Muisca, studies show that many stones date back more than 2,000 years and were originally placed by earlier civilizations.

The grounds can be visited in an hour or so, and a small on-site museum, made to look like one of the ancient tombs, holds five mummified bodies that were found on the site. Getting here from Villa de Leyva by taxi costs about COP$20,000 one-way.

EL TEMPLO DEL SOL

Carrera 1A No. 9-103, El Oriente, Sogamoso; tel. 8/770-3122; 9am-noon and 2pm-5pm Mon.-Sat., 9am-3pm Sun.; COP$10,000

Although the original Temple of the Sun was burned to the ground by the Spanish, you can visit a surprisingly well-done 18-m-high (60-ft) replica of the building inside the **Museo Arqueológico Eliécer Silva.** On the winter solstice, December 22, sunlight illuminates the central pillar of the temple. The museum also displays Muisca clothing, musical instruments, and even a sculpture of the last of the Muisca rulers, Sugamuxi.

A taxi to the museum costs about COP$7,000 one-way from the bus terminal in Sogamoso.

and cuchuco con espinazo (stew with a base of pork spine and potatoes). It's an atmospheric place where you dine in thatched kiosks.

Tienda de Teresa

Calle 10 No. 8-73; tel. 316/542-0387; 8am-8pm Mon. and Wed.-Sat., 8am-5pm Sun.; COP$17,000-28,000

Popular with locals, Tienda de Teresa specializes in hearty breakfasts, including cazuela Boyacense, a milk, cheese, and egg-based soup.

★ Mercado Municipal

Carrera 8 No. 12-25; tel. 8/732-0229; 1pm-10pm daily; COP$22,000-85,000

Mercado Municipal has one of the coolest settings in Villa de Leyva, in a courtyard that was once part of a parsonage, now overflowing with herb gardens. A traditional Mexican barbecue oven is built into the ground, where a wood fire slow-cooks their famous barbecued goat, raised on their own regenerative farm. International dishes on the menu include pastas and several vegetarian offerings. It's open for breakfast on weekends, and there is a nice bakery in front. The set lunch is a good deal. For a drink and tapas, get comfortable at their adjacent swanky bar, **Bolívar Social Club,** open in the evenings.

Everywhere you go in Villa de Leyva, you see brightly painted pottery items for sale. Most of these are produced in the nearby town of **Ráquira** (40 minutes by bus), where you can visit potters in their home studios and even take a class.

★ MiCocina

Calle 13 No. 8-45; tel. 8/732-1676 or 320/488-2452; 1pm-10pm daily; COP$30,000-40,000

MiCocina has earned a name for itself as a slightly upscale restaurant serving the best of Colombian cuisine. After a calentado Bogotano, a beloved hangover cure made with fried eggs and potatoes, save room for the cheese ice cream from Paipa. They serve mostly Colombian meat-based dishes here, but there are a few vegetarian plates. There's a cooking school here as well.

★ Cervecería HISCA

Calle 14 No. 9-35; tel. 310/796-1608; www.cerverceriahisca.com; 3pm-10pm Mon.-Thurs., 1pm-midnight Fri., noon-1am Sat., noon-9pm Sun.; COP$8,000-40,000

Enjoy one of the on-site brewed craft beers in the spacious garden patio over live music at Cervecería HISCA, which also serves a pub-style food menu.

Casona Comercial La Guaca

Carrera 9 No. 13-57; tel. 320/339-6629; noon-10pm Sun.-Thurs., noon-midnight Sat.-Sun.

A handful of eateries, bars, and shops, including an outpost of **Coca Nasa,** are clustered around the lush inner courtyards of an ancient colonial mansion. On weekend nights, live music is played on the back garden stage (purchase required).

Panadería Astral

Calle 12 No. 7-56; tel. 315/817-1679; 8am-7pm Mon.-Sat.

Vegan-friendly Panadería Astral offers freshly baked bread and cakes made from masa madre (live fermented dough).

Sybarita Caffe

Carrera 9 No. 11-88; tel. 316/481-1872; 8am-8pm daily

Choose your brewing method at Sybarita Caffe, a cozy espresso bar that specializes in high-quality beans from different regions of Colombia. House-made pastries pair perfectly with the aromatic coffee.

BARS AND NIGHTLIFE

La Cava de Don Fernando

Carrera 10 No. 12-03; tel. 8/732-0073

The most popular place in the evenings on the Plaza Mayor is La Cava de Don Fernando, where live rock music gets the crowd animated and drinks keep flowing.

ACCOMMODATIONS

Villa de Leyva lives on tourism, so there are many lodging options. Rates rise on weekends and holidays like Christmas and Semana Santa, and it's a good idea to make hotel reservations in advance. During the week deep discounts are often possible, especially if you pay in cash.

Hostal Rana

Calle 10A No. 10-31; tel. 8/732-0330 or 311/464-2969; www.hostal-rana.com; COP$45,000 dorm, COP$110,000 d

A centrally located hostel option is Hostal Rana, with one dorm room and four private rooms. The rooms are clean and the beds are firm. There is a small kitchen for guest use in the back, behind a pleasant patio space.

★ Renacer

Av. Carrera 10 No. 21; tel. 8/732-1201; www.renacerhostel.com; COP$45,000 dorm, COP$120,000 d

Renacer is the best-known hostel in town and popular for good reason. Set at the foot of a mountain, it's about a 15-minute walk from town. Facilities are well-kept, and a nice common room has a fireplace and board games. There are ample open-air common spaces in the spacious garden as well as space for campers or vans. The on-site restaurant has a range of comfort food. Through **Colombian Highlands** (www.colombianhighlands.com), Renacer arranges outdoor expeditions to nearby attractions and can even assist in excursions outside Villa de Leyva. They have very good information on how to hike or bike the area solo. This is an excellent place to swap travel tips with backpackers from around the world.

Hospedería El Marqués de San Jorge

Calle 14 No. 9-20; tel. 8/732-0240; www.hospederiaelmarquesdesanjorge.com; COP$180,000 d

Just a block from the Plaza Mayor, the inviting Hospedería El Marqués de San Jorge has two interior patios filled with greenery as well as 20 clean and comfortable modern rooms, despite dating to 1972. It's a bargain compared to other luxury hotels in town.

★ Hotel Plaza Mayor

Carrera 10 No. 12-31; tel. 8/732-0425; www.hotelplazamayorvilladeleyva.com; COP$357,000 d

The location of the Hotel Plaza Mayor, with a bird's-eye view of the Plaza Mayor from its western side, is unrivaled. The hotel's terrace is a great place to watch goings-on in the plaza and to photograph the cathedral bathed in a golden light in the late afternoon. The 32 rooms are spacious, some with fireplaces, and all are tastefully decorated. Breakfast is served in the pleasant courtyard.

Hotel Plazuela de San Agustín

Calle 15 No. 8-65; tel. 8/732-3486; www.hotelplazuela.com; COP$525,000 d

Overlooking Plaza de Ricaurte, the Hotel Plazuela de San Agustín is a cozy hotel with fewer than a dozen enormous carpeted rooms. One room has four beds and a fireplace. Mornings start with breakfast served near a fountain in the lovely courtyard. The hotel is two blocks from the Plaza Mayor.

INFORMATION AND SERVICES

There are several **ATMs** in Villa de Leyva, particularly along the southern end of the Plaza Mayor.

Tourist Office

Carrera 9 and Calle 13; tel. 8/732-0232; 8am-12:30pm and 2pm-6pm Mon.-Sat., 9am-1pm and 3pm-6pm Sun.

The Villa de Leyva tourist office, located in the Centro Comercial Casa Juan de Castellanos, just a block off Plaza Mayor, has free maps and brochures.

TRANSPORTATION

Villa de Leyva is easily accessible by car or by bus from Bogotá as well as from Tunja, the largest city in Boyacá. Renting a car in Bogotá and driving to Villa de Leyva gives you a lot of flexibility to visit enchanting pueblos to your heart's content. Nearly all hotels have parking lots.

There are direct buses to Villa de Leyva (3.5 hours; COP$40,000) from both the Terminal de Transportes and the Portal del Norte in Bogotá. The bus terminal in Villa de Leyva is the **Terminal de Transportes** (Carrera 9 between Calles 11-12).

To get to Villa de Leyva from Bucaramanga or San Gil in Santander, you'll have to take a bus to Tunja (COP$45,000). The highway that extends from Bogotá to Venezuela is a busy one, and the journey can take 5-6 hours. Once in Villa de Leyva, it is easy and pleasant to walk everywhere. A few streets around the Plaza Mayor, including the main drag, Calle 13, are pedestrian-only. Even on regular streets it's hard for vehicles to zoom along.

★ Monguí

The chilly but architecturally stunning highland colonial village of Monguí was founded in 1601 and was a strategic post for the Spaniards thanks to its location between Tunja and the vast Llanos, the eastern plains. It is considered one of the most beautiful small towns in Boyacá and still bustles with authentic village life. Its narrow cobblestone streets are lined with white and green houses, and ancient stone stairways lead up to traditional neighborhoods, on to quaint small farms, and beyond to gorgeous lookout points over the Cordillera Oriental.

PÁRAMO DE OCETÁ

The most untouched and pristine páramo (highland moors) in Colombia, the massive Páramo de Ocetá lies just over the mountains behind Monguí and makes for one of the most awe-inspiring day treks in the entire country. An 18-km (11-mi) loop route,

Andean condor

old house in Monguí

Monguí

which usually takes 8-10 hours, leads from the village into the heart of this wilderness, stopping at the City of Rocks before circling a glimmering lagoon. Watch for white-tailed deer and Andean condors. Guides are required, and a full-day tour starts at COP$150,000 per person. Local guides can be found hanging out in the main square, but you can also book a guide ahead of time through **Montana Sagrada Monguí** (tel. 313/837-7213), who also offer bicycle tours of the surrounding high-elevation countryside.

FOOD AND ACCOMMODATIONS

De La Villa Pa Sumercé

Carrera 5A 5-13; tel. 321/211-3183; COP$38,000 s, COP$64,000 d

Clean, cozy, and cheap accommodations with an on-site restaurant makes De La Villa Pa Sumercé an excellent choice for budget travelers. Rooms with and without private baths are available. It's a five-minute walk to the main square.

La Casona de San Francisco de Asis

Carrera 4A No. 3-41; tel. 8/778-2498 or 311/237-9823; COP$150,000 d

La Casona de San Francisco de Asis has a view over the Río Morro canyon, and the hotel is tidy, with just six spacious rooms. The restaurant has been in service for over two decades and is one of the best in town, specializing in cocido Boyacense.

★ Calicanto Real

Carrera 3, next to Puente de Calicanto; tel. 311/811-1519; calicantoreal.hostal@gmail.com; COP$175,000 d

The Calicanto Real is a spectacular historic mansion with five rooms and spacious gardens overlooking the Puente de Calicanto, an ancient stone bridge over a rushing stream. It was once the home of a wealthy emerald miner. Rooms have views and a lot of character, but the beds are on the soft side. Within the hotel is a quirky tavern (hours vary) filled with decorations like cowboy hats, animal heads, and an homage to Monguí's most famous poet, El Indio Rómulo.

TRANSPORTATION

To visit Monguí, you must first get to the city of Sogamoso, 3.5 hours from Villa de Leyva by bus (COP$28,000) and 5 hours from Bogotá (COP$55,000). From the Sogamoso bus terminal, it's about 20 km (12 mi) to Monguí by bus (45 minutes; COP$8,000).

★ Lago Tota

Lago Tota is Colombia's largest lake and the second-largest high-altitude lake on the continent, next to Lake Titicaca in Bolivia. It covers 55 sq km (21 sq mi) and is surrounding by wetlands and traditional farming communities. The views are spectacular, with mountains, valleys, and fields in every direction. The lake itself is a biodiversity hot spot; over 110 species of birds have been spotted. A country highway circles the lake, connecting the different towns and natural attractions and

cocido Boyacense

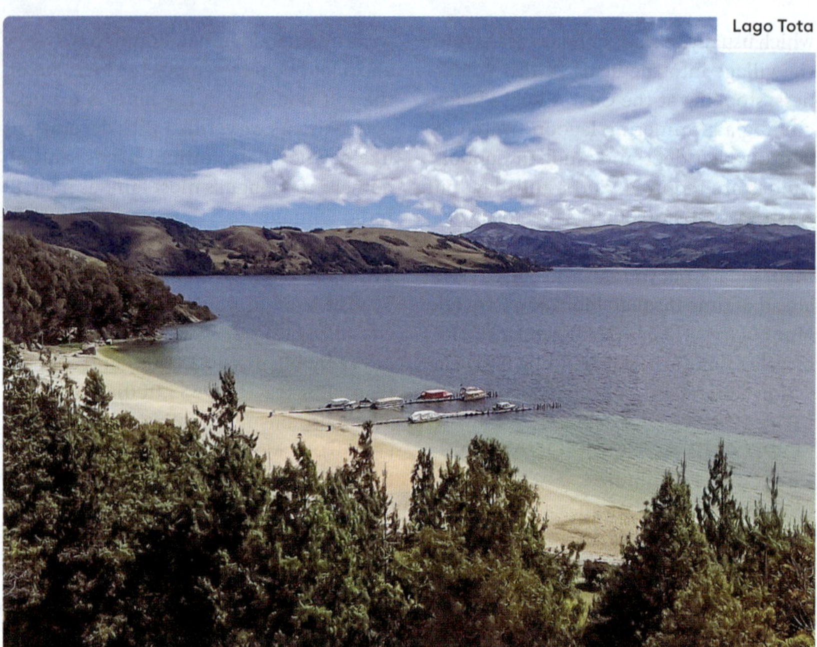
Lago Tota

converging in Aquitania, the largest town on the lake.

SIGHTS

Iza

The whitewashed colonial houses of Iza, a perfectly preserved colonial pueblo 5 km (3 mi) inland from Lago Tota, are home to several traditional textile workshops where you can pick up virgin wool scarfs, sweaters, and ruanas directly from the artisans. Iza was recently named a Pueblo que Enamoran (village to fall in love with) by the Colombian tourism authority, Fontur. Buses that run between Sogamoso and Playa Blanca stop in Iza.

BEACHES

Playa Blanca

Vereda la Puerta, Lago Tota;
entry COP$20,000

Lakeside Playa Blanca has white-sand beaches and turquoise water so translucent they almost fool you into thinking the water isn't freezing cold. Wading is possible, but swimming is not advised. At the water's edge, locals hawk boat rides on the lake. You can also arrange to camp next to the beach (COP$40,000 pp), which makes for a chilly night but a rewarding scene at dawn. Buses run directly to Playa Blanca from Sogamoso and Aquitania.

FOOD AND ACCOMMODATIONS

Along the shore of Lago Tota are many traditional hotels and glamping-style accommodations, often with spectacular views, especially between Aquitania and Playa Blanca. Bargains can be had during the week, when you will have your lodge, if not the lake, blissfully to yourself. On long weekends it's especially lively with visitors

A LAKE IS A LIVING BEING

Despite the clarity of its water and the beauty of the surrounding countryside, Lago Tota is in peril. The dumping of fertilizers and pesticides from lakeside farms has been the primary reason that this lake, which provides drinking water for hundreds of thousands of people, has been declared one of the top-five most threatened wetlands in the world by the World Wetlands Network. The wetlands themselves, which once ringed the lake, now only exist in fast disappearing patches, as there is only one publicly protected area of lakeshore—the several hectares surrounding Playa Blanca.

Lago Tota

In 2020 Lago Tota won an important court case. The judgment, one of eight such "rights of nature" rulings in the country, including one that recognizes the entire Amazon rainforest as a living being, holds the state and any private actors who do damage to the lake criminally responsible and provides mechanisms for forcing them to pay for restoration. How that will play out remains to be seen, but several local organizations have already taken action to conserve and restore the lakefront ecosystems.

RESERVA XIETI

Vereda Guáquira Km 3

The privately run Reserva Xieti (tel. 608/773-1118; www.xieti.abctota.org) is only 3.2 ha (8 acres) but demonstrates what can be done in a short time by a small number of dedicated people. Purchased in 2014 by a local nonprofit, which immediately began reforesting the area, planting native species and implementing beehives to pollinate them, the reserve now bustles with wildlife like nowhere else on the lakefront. The wetland reserve has won support from both the Colombian and Norwegian governments and is open to visitors with prior reservations. Bird-watching here is epic.

RESERVA NATURAL PUEBLO ANTIGUO

Cuitiva

Located on the site of an abandoned lakefront pueblo, the Reserva Natural Pueblo Antiguo (www.pueblitoantiguo.com; entry COP$20,000) is more like a step back in time than a pristine nature reserve, but there are several trail networks along the undeveloped shoreline and wilderness beaches. The reserve offers bird-watching and sustainability workshops as well. An antique locomotive now serves as a restaurant and cafeteria with stunning views over the lake.

from Bogotá. Most lakeside lodges offer all meals. Local buses circle the lake semi-frequently, making it an adventure in slow travel to get around.

Rocas Lindas

Aquitania; tel. 310/349-1107; www.hotelrocaslindas.wordpress.com; COP$120,000 d

Rocas Lindas, on an inlet, was built in 1953 as the first upscale hotel on the lake, and it retains its charm. You'll often see guests gathered by a circular fireplace in the lobby or relaxing at the lakefront lounge. The hotel has 15 rooms and two cabañas (COP$500,000) that sleep four and have fireplaces. The lodge can arrange a boat excursion around the lake for an additional cost. There's no Wi-Fi, and this hotel could use some upgrading.

Hotel Termales El Batán

Vereda La Vega, Cuitiva; tel. 321/242-7511; www.termaleselbatan.com; COP$331,000 d

A historic resort, the 22-room Hotel Termales El Batán was built in the 19th century to provide access to the mineral-rich hot springs that were sacred to the Muisca people. It is located outside Iza on the road to Lago Tota. A large pool, full spa services, and an on-site restaurant round out the experience. Day passes to the hot springs (COP$30,000) are available.

★ Hotel Refugio Pozo Azul

Aquitania; tel. 1/620-6257 or 320/384-1000; www.hotelrefugiopozoazul.com; COP$365,000 d

With lush gardens and spacious terraces overlooking the lake, Hotel Refugio Pozo Azul is just outside of Aquitania. The ancient main house and surrounding grounds were purchased by a US businessman in the 1970s to protect the lakefront from development. There are 14 hotel rooms in the main building and 2 cabanas tucked into the garden.

TRANSPORTATION

To get to Lago Tota, you first have to get to the city of Sogamoso, 3.5 hours from Villa de Leyva by bus (COP$28,000) and 5 hours from Bogotá (COP$55,000). To get to Playa Blanca from Sogamoso, buses take two different routes around the lake. Each takes about an hour and costs COP$8,000. One route goes through Iza, and the other takes you to Aquitania, which requires transferring to a minivan at Aquitania's market, four blocks from the town's Plaza Principal. This second leg takes 10 minutes and costs COP$1,500.

Another option is to hire a taxi or private driver in Sogamoso (about COP$45,000 one-way).

Sierra Nevada del Cocuy

The Sierra Nevada del Cocuy, the highest mountains within the Cordillera Oriental (Eastern Range) of the Andes Mountains, are 260 km (160 mi) northeast of Bogotá in northern Boyacá. The entire mountain range is contained within and protected by Parque Nacional Natural El Cocuy, the country's fifth-largest national park. With its 11 jagged snowcapped peaks, massive glacier-formed valleys, extensive páramos (highland moors) studded with exotic frailejón plants, and stunning crystalline mountain lakes, streams, and waterfalls, it is one of the most beautiful places in Colombia.

PLANNING YOUR TIME

Getting to the Sierra Nevada del Cocuy entails a long grueling trip, albeit through the beautiful verdant countryside of Boyacá. Ideally you want to spend at least **three days** here to take in the spectacular mountain landscapes. The park has three hiking trails. Each is a full-day hike to the glacier topped peaks and back before sundown. A guide is mandatory.

The gateway town of El Cocuy is a pleasant experience with friendly locals and clean mountain air. You can find basic visitor services, tour operators and guides, and stores to stock up on food.

The only time to visit the Sierra Nevada del Cocuy with dependably good weather is **December-March,** the verano (summer dry season) in the Cordillera Oriental. In other seasons there may be permanent cloud cover and much rain. High season, when Colombian visitors flock to the mountains, is mid-December-mid-January, and again during Semana Santa (late March or April).

The best available topographical maps of the Sierra Nevada de Cocuy can be viewed and downloaded online at www.nevados.org.

TRANSPORTATION

The town of El Cocuy is served from Bogotá by three bus companies. The trip takes 11 hours. The most comfortable option is **Libertadores** (COP$85,000), which operates a big bus that leaves Bogotá at 8:30pm. The return trip departs El Cocuy at 7:30pm. **Fundadores** (COP$80,000) has two buses that leave Bogotá at 5am and 4:30pm, returning from El Cocuy at 7:30am and 8:30pm.

El Cocuy

El Cocuy

El Cocuy is a charming colonial town nestled in the lower folds of the Sierra Nevada del Cocuy at an altitude of 2,750 m (9,020 ft). The town is meticulous, with whitewashed houses painted with a band of aquamarine; it was recently named a Pueblo que Enamoran (pueblo to fall in love with) by the Colombian tourism authority, Fontur. El Cocuy offers decent accommodations, a handful of restaurants and cafés, tour operators, the national park office, and some stores to stock up for a visit to the park. The clean mountain air, the friendly locals, and the pretty town make it hard to leave.

The only sight to check out is in the pleasant **Parque Principal,** where there is a large diorama of the Sierra Nevada del Cocuy. This illustrates the mountain geography with its multitude of snowcapped peaks, lakes, and valleys.

HIKING

Cerro Mahoma

Distance: 8 km (5 mi) round-trip
Duration: 6-7 hours
Elevation gain: 1,040 m (3,400 ft)
Difficulty: Strenuous
Trailhead: El Cocuy

For a spectacular panoramic view of the entire Sierra, take a hike up Cerro Mahoma (Mahoma Hill), to the west of town. The 4,000-m (13,000-ft) peak also offers a great opportunity to acclimatize before trekking in the Sierra Nevada del Cocuy. Most people hire a car and just do the last hour (1.5 km/1 mi) of the journey, in the highest altitude possible, but to do the full 6-7-hour hike you need to hire a guide, as the road splits several times and the route is not marked.

ASEGUICOC

tel. 311/557-7893, 311/236-4275, or 313/371-9735; aseguicoc@gmail.com

You must book a guide before registering at the National Park Service to get permission to enter the park. The first step is to stop by the Asociación de Prestadores de Servicios Ecoturísticos de Güicán y El Cocuy (ASEGUICOC), near the center of town, to get your guide.

FOOD AND ACCOMMODATIONS

El Cafe de Mi Tierra

Calle 8 No. 3-73; tel. 312/484-5989; 10am-1pm daily

Specializing in locally grown Boyacá coffee and with comfy sofas and lounge chairs to enjoy it in, spacious Cafe de Mi Tierra is the best place to meet up with the crew for pre-trip planning or to relax after a hike. It shares an inner courtyard with a pizzeria next door, and you can order from both businesses at the outside tables.

★ El Caminante

Carrera 4 No. 7-30; tel. 311/885-4263; COP$50,000 d

With comfy sofas surrounding a fireplace, hammocks for relaxing, a guest kitchen, and a large terrace with views over the mountains, El Caminante is the best place in town to hook up with fellow travelers and form a group to share guide costs into the park. The 15 comfy rooms are spotless, and the friendly owner, Don Alfredo, doubles as a guide and can provide you with all the local info you might need.

Hotel la Posada del Molino

Carrera 3 No. 7-51; tel. 8/789-0377; www.elcocuycasamuseo.blogspot.com; COP$50,000 d

Hotel la Posada del Molino is a friendly guesthouse with 16 rooms set around two colorful interior patios. The house has history: During the deadly feuds between the nearby conservative pueblo of Güicán and liberal El Cocuy, the famous Virgen Morenita image was taken from its shrine in Güicán and hidden away in the house where the hotel is located. You can see the room that hid this secret.

INFORMATION AND SERVICES

There is an **ATM** at the Banco Agrario (Carrera 4 and Calle 8).

Parque Nacional Natural El Cocuy Office

Calle 5 No. 4-22; tel. 8/789-0359; cocuy@parquesnacionales.gov.co; 7am-noon and 1pm-4:45pm daily

At the offices of Parque Nacional Natural El Cocuy you can obtain a park entry permit (COP$97,500) and general information.

★ Parque Nacional Natural El Cocuy

tel. 8/789-0359; cocuy@parquesnacionales.gov.co

About 20 km (12 mi) east of the towns of El Cocuy and Güicán, Parque Nacional Natural El Cocuy is 306,000 ha (756,000 acres) spanning the departments of Boyacá, Arauca, and Casanare.

Entry permits (COP$97,000) include entry fees and are required. Permits are valid for four consecutive days and can easily be obtained at the park offices in El Cocuy (Calle 5 No. 4-22; tel. 8/789-0359; cocuy@parquesnacionales.gov.co; 7am-noon and 1pm-4:45pm daily). In peak seasons, mid-December-mid-January and Semana Santa, it is better to obtain the permit several weeks in advance through the National Park Service in Bogotá; call tel. 1/353-2400 or email ecoturismo@

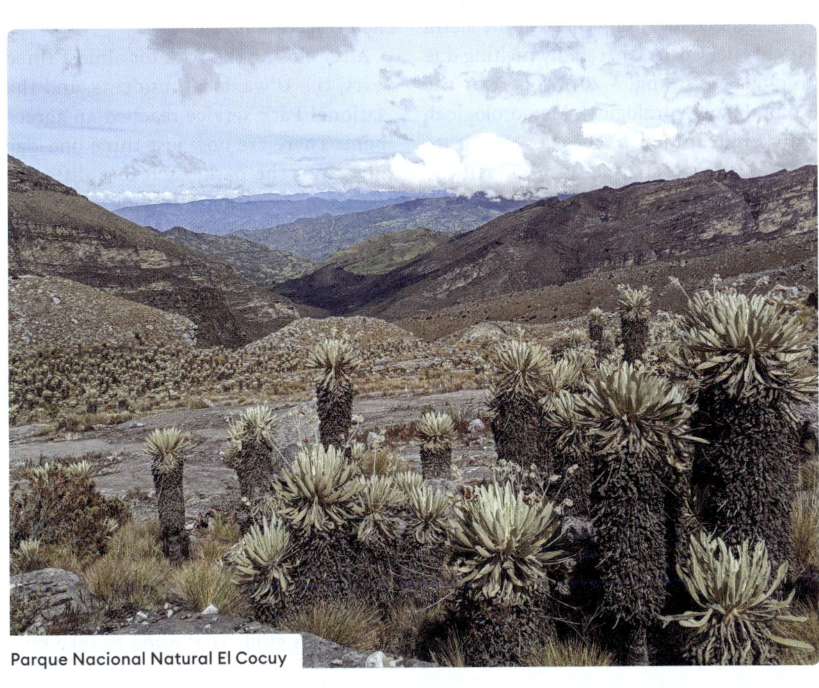

Parque Nacional Natural El Cocuy

parquesnacionales.gov.co to request a permit. You will be asked to submit the names of visitors, passport numbers, and the expected dates of arrival. The park service will provide instructions for paying and will send the permit by email.

The Sierra Nevada del Cocuy, consisting of two parallel ranges 30 km (19 mi) long with 11 peaks higher than 5,000 m (16,400 ft), is the centerpiece of the park. However, the park extends farther north and east from the Sierra and includes extensive tracts of temperate and tropical forests. It also includes 92,000 ha (227,000 acres) of U'wa Indigenous resguardos (reservations), which are not open to tourism.

The Sierra Nevada del Cocuy is home to the largest expanse of glaciers in Colombia, covering 16 sq km (6 sq mi). What are usually referred to as nevados (snowcapped mountains) are in fact glacier-capped mountains. Unfortunately, all the glaciers in Colombia, including those of the Sierra Nevada del Cocuy, are rapidly melting due to global warming. A 2013 report by the Colombian Hydrological, Meteorological, and Environmental Studies Institute (IDEAM) forecasts that, by 2030, all the glaciers in Colombia will have disappeared.

The Sierra's highest peak is **Ritacuba Blanco** (5,380 m/17,650 ft). Other notable glacier-capped peaks are **Ritacuba Negro** (5,350 m/17,550 ft), **San Pablín Norte** (5,200 m/17,060 ft), **Cóncavo** (5,200 m/17,060 ft), and **Pan de Azúcar** (5,100 m/16,730 ft). One of the most striking peaks in the Sierra Nevada del Cocuy is the **Púlpito del Diablo** (5,100 m/16,730 ft) or Devil's Pulpit, a massive flat-topped rock formation.

At the bases of the peaks are numerous glacier-formed valleys supporting páramos, unique tropical high-altitude ecosystems of the Andes. The páramos are covered with beautiful frailejones, plants that have imposing tall trunks and thick greenish-yellow leaves. Other páramo vegetation includes shrubs, grasses, and cojines (cushion plants).

Erwin Krauss, a Colombian of German descent, was the first modern explorer of the Sierra in the 1930s. In the 1960s and 1970s Colombian and European expeditions climbed most of the peaks. During the 1980s and 1990s, there was a significant presence of ELN and FARC armed insurgents and tourism all but disappeared. In the next decade, the army reestablished control of the area around the Sierra Nevada de Cocuy, and tourists began flocking to the area. In 2018 the U'wa people, for whom the Sierra de Cocuy is sacred, launched a protest against the damaging effects of unregulated tourism in the park. There were more than 30 trails into the Sierra, campers were leaving debris on the glaciers, and hikers were encroaching into their reservation.

After closing the park for almost three years, the U'wa, local residents, and the National Park Service reached an agreement. There are now just three one-day hikes into the park, each to a different spectacular location. Camping and horseback riding are prohibited, although there are lodges at the trailhead of each hike. Touching a glacier is also prohibited. The daily capacity for each hike is also strictly enforced—about 100 people each day for each trail. This means that in the high season you may need to reserve a place ahead of time.

Keep in mind that visiting the park requires a permit, a guide, and transportation to and from the park.

HIKING

Hiring a guide is mandatory to visit the park. Each guide is allowed to take only

4-5 people into the park and charges a set daily rate (around COP$220,000) per group regardless of group size. Guides are easy to find through your hotel or by visiting the ASEGUICOC office.

ASEGUICOC

tel. 311/557-7893, 311/236-4275, or 313/371-9735; aseguicoc@gmail.com

The local guide association, Asociación de Prestadores de Servicios Ecoturísticos de Güicán y El Cocuy (ASEGUICOC), oversees and manages the capacity for the three daily hikes. At their office near the center of town, they can tell you what hikes are available on any given day and get you a guide if you don't have one.

Laguna Grande

Distance: 20 km (12 mi) round-trip
Duration: 10 hours
Elevation gain: 915 m (3,000 ft)
Difficulty: Strenuous
Trailhead: Hacienda la Esperanza

The longest but least steep of the three day hikes goes up to La Laguna, a large high-altitude lake surrounded by glaciers. It leads through a lush páramo valley strewn with different types of frailejones and passes four smaller lakes. The hike reaches an elevation of 4,300 m (14,100 ft).

Púlpito del Diablo

Distance: 17 km (11 mi) round-trip
Duration: 8 hours
Elevation gain: 915 m (3,000 ft)
Difficulty: Strenuous
Trailhead: Cabaña Sisuma

This hike takes you to Púlpito del Diablo (Devil's Pulpit), an intriguing rock formation that juts out of an icy glacier. On the way you pass a nice páramo and a glacier fed lake. Lots of wildlife is seen on this route.

Ritacuba Blanco

Distance: 16 km (10 mi) round-trip
Duration: 9 hours
Elevation gain: 975 m (3,200 ft)
Difficulty: Strenuous
Trailhead: Cabañas Kanwara

The highest peak in the Sierra Nevada del Cocuy, Ritacuba Blanco offers spectacular views of the entire Sierra stretched out before you. It's the most grueling of the three treks but also the most popular. There is often no space on three-day weekends or in high season if you try to book a guide just a day or two beforehand.

ACCOMMODATIONS

While not luxurious by any means, the lodging options in and around the park are homey. They are also all located at the trailheads to the treks into the park, making getting an early start that much easier.

Cabaña Sisuma

tel. 311/236-4275 or 311/255-1034; aseguicoc@gmail.com; COP$80,000 pp with meals

The best-located lodging, near the trailhead to El Púlpito, is Cabaña Sisuma, a cozy cabin inside the park run by the local guide

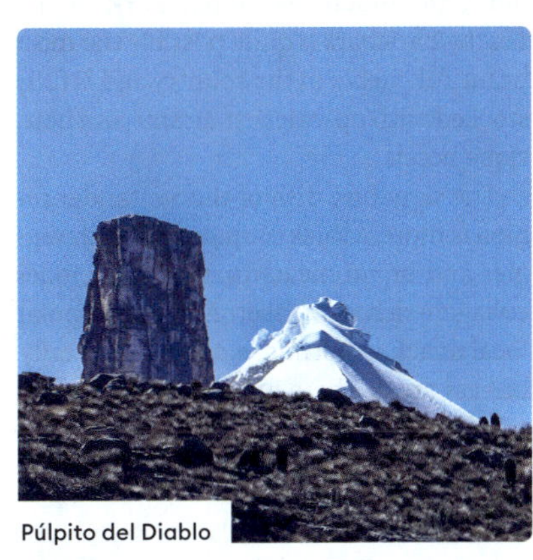

Púlpito del Diablo

association ASEGUICOC. It has six rooms, good food, and fireplaces to keep warm.

★ Hacienda La Esperanza

tel. 314/221-2473; haciendalaesperanza@gmail.com; COP$80,000 pp with meals

A working farm on the edge of the park and at the trailhead to La Laguna, Hacienda La Esperanza provides accommodations in a rustic farmhouse that oozes character. The family running the hotel is hospitable, and the host is a trained chef who enjoys pampering his guests. Nothing beats hanging out by the fireplace in the late afternoon with a warm drink after a day of mountain climbing. There are a half dozen rooms, most set up for sharing.

Cabañas Kanwara

tel. 311/231-6004 or 311/237-2260; infokanwara@gmail.com; COP$80,000 pp with meals

The most conveniently located place to stay in the Northern Sector and at the trailhead to Ritacuba Blanco is Cabañas Kanwara. This lodge of eight cute wooden A-frame houses also serves good food.

TRANSPORTATION

To get to the park you must either take a car (COP$200,000 for up to 4 people) or a motorcycle (COP$60,000). Transportation is arranged through ASEGUICOC or your tour guide.

Santander

Lush mountainous scenery, a delightful climate, well-preserved colonial pueblos, and friendly outgoing people—this is the Santander department. In northeastern Colombia, Santander is north of Boyacá and southwest of Norte de Santander. The area around San Gil is packed with outdoor adventure activities, including the Cañón del Chicamocha National Park, while nearby Barichara is quite possibly the most beautiful pueblo in the country and is fully stocked with upscale restaurants and boutique hotels.

The signature dish of the Santander region is mute, a thick soup packed with veggies and organ meats that often includes collagen-rich cow's feet. Another popular local snack is hormigas culonas (literally, big-ass ants). These jumbo-size fried ants taste like peppered peanuts and are sold on the street all over the department.

San Gil

This spry city (pop. 43,000) on the steep banks of the Río Fonce is 95 km (59 mi) southwest of Bucaramanga. Rafting, paragliding, caving, mountain biking, canyoneering, hiking, birding, and rappelling are all within reach in San Gil, Colombia's outdoor adventure capital. Even if your idea of adventurous is merely being in Colombia, the breathtaking Santander scenery of canyons, rivers, waterfalls, and mountains is more than enough reason to visit.

During the late 19th-early 20th centuries, San Gil and nearby towns built their prosperity on quinine, coffee, cocoa, and tobacco cultivation. Today, old tile-roofed hangars to dry tobacco, known as caneys, still dot the landscape.

While accommodations are plentiful and cheap here, there's no need to stay in

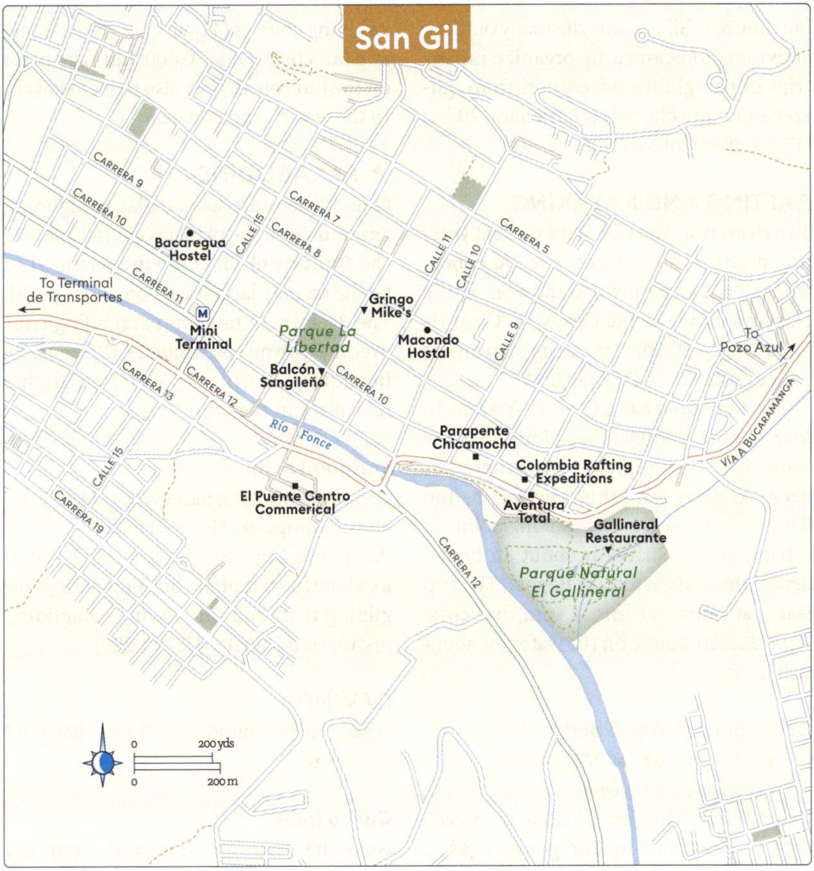

San Gil

Carrera 9
Carrera 10
Carrera 7
Carrera 8
Calle 15
Bacaregua Hostel
Carrera 11
To Terminal de Transportes
Mini Terminal
Parque La Libertad
Gringo Mike's
Macondo Hostal
Carrera 5
Calle 11
Calle 10
Calle 9
To Pozo Azul
Balcón Sangileño
Carrera 13
Carrera 12
Carrera 10
Río Fonce
Parapente Chicamocha
Colombia Rafting Expeditions
Aventura Total
Vía a Bucaramanga
Calle 15
Carrera 19
El Puente Centro Commerical
Gallineral Restaurante
Parque Natural El Gallineral
Carrera 12
0 200 yds
0 200 m

countryside in Santander

bustling San Gil to enjoy the many outdoor activities. You can easily organize rafting trips or paragliding adventures from quieter and more charming Barichara, 20 km (12 mi) north of San Gil.

RAFTING AND KAYAKING

Two rivers near San Gil offer excellent year-round rafting adventures. The **Río Fonce,** whose banks the town stands on, is the closest and one of the best, with Class II-III rafting. A 90-minute rafting trip on the Fonce costs about COP$30,000.

The **Río Suárez** is a Class IV-V river. In March-April and October-November the water levels are higher, and if there has been excessive rain, this river can be too dangerous to tackle. The starting point for rafting on the Suárez is about an hour's drive from San Gil toward Bogotá. The trip leaves at 10am, returns at 4pm, and costs COP$22,000. You're on the water for about two hours.

Colombia Rafting Expeditions

Carrera 10 No. 7-83; tel. 7/724-5800; www.colombiarafting.com

Colombia Rafting Expeditions is considered the best rafting company in town. They focus exclusively on river activities. The walls of their small office are covered with diplomas and certificates earned by their team of experienced guides. They also do kayaking trips. This company takes safety seriously and conducts safety training exercises in English. Three-day kayaking courses (4 hours per day, starting at 8am) cost COP$750,000 and take place on the Río Fonce. They also rent out kayaks to those with experience.

> Just 20 minutes by bus from San Gil, the historic colonial pueblo of **Socorro** played an important role in the history of Colombia. It was here that the first group of revolutionaries against Spanish rule, the Comuneros, were founded in 1781.

★ PARAGLIDING

One of the most spectacular paragliding adventures on the planet is gliding out over the **Cañón del Chicamocha,** claimed to be the second-largest canyon in the world. The 35-minute tandem paragliding trips over the canyon cost around COP$250,000, including transportation. These flights take place in the mornings.

Parapente Chicamocha

Carrera 10 No. 8-33; tel. 607/724-3839; https://parapentechicamocha.com

Parapente Chicamocha is a highly rated local outfit that offers both tandem paragliding trips and full 10-day paragliding instruction courses (USD$1,200).

CAVING

Several caves around San Gil make for good exploring.

Cueva Indio

Near the town of Páramo, the popular Cueva Indio is filled with bats, and you don't have to do much bending to explore it. An excursion, including equipment and a guide, costs COP$60,000, but that doesn't include transportation. Contact **Páramo Extremo** (Carrera 4 No. 4-57, Páramo; tel. 7/725-8944; www.paramosantanderextremo.com) in the town of Páramo to sign up for a visit to Cueva Indio.

Cueva Vaca

Near the town of Curití, the Cueva Vaca is the most challenging cave in the area. You will be in water and mud the entire time you are underground, and at one point you'll have to swim underwater to get through to the next cave. There are lots of stalactites and stalagmites and bats to see. It is action-packed, and there are some tight squeezes, but the adventure is worth it. An excursion costs COP$60,000 plus about COP$5,000 in bus transportation. **Colombia Rafting** (Carrera 10 No. 7-83; tel. 311/283-8647; www.colombiarafting.com) can organize a trip.

SWIMMING

On weekends and holidays, families head to the area's swimming holes. The atmosphere is joyous, and there's usually music and plenty of food and drink. It's much quieter during the week.

Pozo Azul

Km 2, Vía San Gil

Pozo Azul is a natural pool with small cascades surrounded by trees. From San Gil, Pozo Azul is just off the highway, about five minutes by bus or taxi or a 20-minute walk.

Pescaderito

Nature lovers will enjoy Pescaderito, with five different swimming holes to cool off, each a short distance from the others and all completely free. It's near the town of Curití, about a 40-minute bus ride (COP$5,000) from San Gil.

WATERFALLS

Parque Ecológico Juan Curí

Km 22, Vía San Gil-Charalá; https://parquejuancuri.com; 8am-5pm daily; COP$12,000

Home to two impressive waterfalls often used in Colombian movies, one 70 m (230 ft) in height and the other over 100 m (330 ft), this private 20-ha (49-acre) reserve also contains some pristine rainforest and offers zip-lining and rappelling under the waterfalls for an extra fee. Camping on-site (COP$22,000 pp) is possible. To get here, take a bus from San Gil that goes to Charalá and get off at Km 22 (COP$3,500). The waterfalls are a short 2-km (1.2-mi) walk through lush rainforest into the reserve.

TOURS

San Gil is packed with adventure tour agencies, but hostels can also organize activities for guests.

Aventura Total

Calle 7 No. 10-27; tel. 7/723-8888 or 316/693-9300; www.aventuratotal.com.co

Aventura Total has a good reputation and offers all-inclusive packages that include rafting, caving, and other activities as well as hotel accommodations. Aventura Total often organizes activities for large school groups.

waterfall in Parque Ecológico Juan Curí

SHOPPING

El Puente Centro Comercial

Calle 12 No. 12-123; https://elpuente.com.co; 9am-8pm daily

Just across a pedestrian bridge from San Gil's downtown, this modern mall is in what was once a train depot and retains lots of historic charm. It sports outdoor cafés and restaurants with nice views and has all the modern goods you may need to stock up on.

FOOD

Balcón Sangileño

Calle 12 No. 102; tel. 7/724-0515; 7am-10pm daily; COP$18,000-36,000

With hearty traditional breakfasts and locally caught trucha (trout) on the menu, locally priced Balcón Sangileño, with balcony seating overlooking the gorgeous Parque Principal of San Gil, is one of the best bets in town.

Gringo Mike's

Calle 12 No. 8-35; tel. 7/724-1695; 8am-11:45am and 5pm-10pm daily; COP$26,000-40,000

Tex-Mex-style Gringo Mike's is a change from the norm for those who have been on the road awhile, with guacamole and chips, barbecue burgers, black bean burgers, Philly cheesesteaks, and even breakfast burritos.

Gallineral Restaurante

Carrera 11, Parque Gallineral; tel. 300/565-2653; 8am-5pm daily; COP$35,000-55,000

The best aspect of Gallineral Restaurante is its lush setting within Parque Natural El Gallineral. They serve typical parrilla-style (grilled meat) Colombian dishes as well as pastas, salads, and other international fare.

ACCOMMODATIONS

Excellent and affordable lodging options are plentiful in San Gil, but they are geared toward international backpackers. If you're looking for fresh air, more luxury, or more privacy, consider staying in nearby Barichara.

Bacaregua Hostel

Carrera 9 No. 16-77; tel. 7/724-2241 or 320/260-6277; COP$35,000 dorm, COP$80,000 d

Bacaregua Hostel is a low-key, locally operated hostel in a familial setting with hot showers, high ceilings, and ample common space. There are a couple of dormitory rooms in addition to six private rooms.

★ Macondo Hostal

Carrera 8 No. 10-35; tel. 7/724-8001; www.macondohostel.com; COP$35,000 dorm, COP$98,000 d with bath

One of the first hostels in town to cater to international backpackers, Macondo Hostal remains an excellent and reliable choice. Their clean dorm rooms and four private rooms fill quickly, so make a reservation in advance. They have a hot tub, a small garden, and hammocks for post-adventure relaxing. What sets Macondo apart is its extremely knowledgeable, helpful, and friendly staff, who can organize outdoor activities in the region.

★ La Pacha Hostel and Camping

Km 7, Vía San Gil-Barichara; tel. 310/221-1515; www.lapachahostel.com; COP$55,000 pp

Halfway between San Gil and Barichara on a quiet farm is La Pacha Hostel and Camping, where goats roam free and guests sleep in tents, yurts, geodesic domes, and earth-built hobbit houses. They have solar-run showers, their own organic farm where they also grown their own coffee, and an on-site restaurant famous for its Indian-style curry. It's run by a friendly English-Colombian couple.

TRANSPORTATION

San Gil's main **Terminal de Transportes** (Vía al Socorro; tel. 7/724-5858) is five minutes out of town, on the south side of the Río Fonce. Buses depart for major cities such as Bucaramanga, Tunja, and Bogotá. Taxis between Terminal de Transportes and the town center cost COP$6,000. The bus to San Gil from Tunja takes 4-5 hours, and from Bogotá (COP$85,000) takes 7 hours. From Santa Marta or Medellín (COP$95,000), the bus takes about 12 hours. From Bucaramanga (COP$25,000), the trip takes 6 hours.

A smaller bus terminal for nearby towns is on Carrera 15 at Calle 11. It serves towns such as Barichara, Charalá, Curití, and Pescadero. It doesn't have an official name, but some refer to it as the **Mini Terminal.** Buses to Barichara depart every 30 minutes 6am-6:30pm.

 **TOP EXPERIENCE**

★ Barichara

In 1975, when it was declared a national monument, Barichara (pop. 8,000) was named the most beautiful pueblo in Colombia. Its popularity with weekenders and a steady stream of international visitors mean that almost all the old houses have been meticulously restored to their former glory. Add the fact that it is permanently blessed with bright blue skies and warm temperatures and you have one of the most enchanting destinations in the country. Located 20 km (12 mi) northwest of San Gil, the town is on a plateau that overlooks the Río Suárez and offers plenty of hiking opportunities. Don't skimp on your time here.

SIGHTS

All around town are structures that utilize the adobe block-making technique called tapia pisada. You'll often see a small patch of the mud interior exposed on these brilliantly white walls, purposely done to show passersby that it's authentic tapia pisada. There are a half dozen historic churches in Barichara. Most still observe Sunday mass but are open to the public during the day.

Templo de la Inmaculada Concepción

Calle 5 No. 6-71

On the serene Parque Principal is the circa-1780 Templo de la Inmaculada Concepción, with two grandiose towers that soar 22 m (72 ft). The sandstone church is particularly striking when lit up at night.

Capilla de Santa Bárbara

Calle 6 No. 12114

Up picturesque Calle 6, at the top of the hill, is the Capilla de Santa Bárbara, a Romanesque-style church that is a popular place for weddings.

Casa Aquileo Parra Gómez

Calle 6 at Carrera 2

Barichara is the birthplace of Aquileo Parra Gómez, the 11th president of the Estados Unidos de Colombia. His childhood home, Casa Aquileo Parra Gómez, has been extremely well preserved and is an excellent example of typical 19th-century Barichara architecture. The site is also a handicraft workshop (Mon.-Thurs.) for the elderly, who weave shoulder bags and other items from natural fique fiber.

Barichara was declared the most beautiful pueblo in Colombia in 1975.

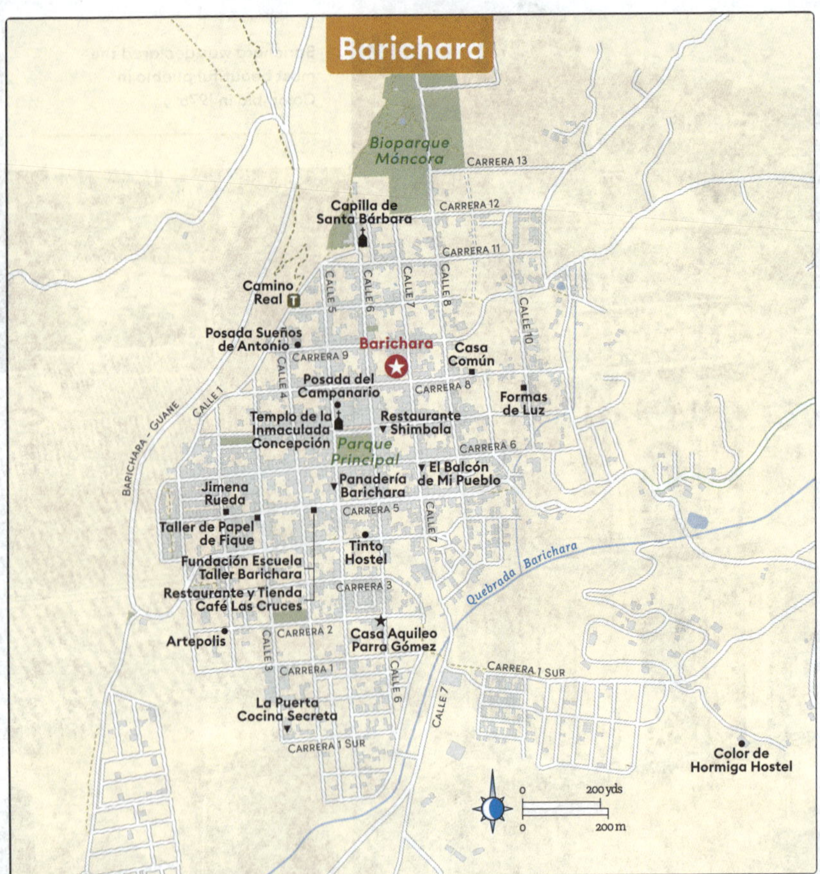

HIKING

Camino Real

Distance: 10.6 km (6.6 mi) round-trip
Duration: 3 hours
Elevation gain: none
Effort: Easy
Trailhead: Piedra de Bolívar

A must-do activity in Barichara is to take the 5.3-km (3.3-mi) Camino Real to the pueblo of **Guane.** It's a lovely ancient stone path that zigzags down from the plateau of Barichara through farmland, affording nice views of the countryside. Parts of the path are lined with centuries-old stone walls.

Before the Spanish conquest, Indigenous groups throughout what is now Colombia traded crops and goods utilizing an extensive network of footpaths. These trails meandered through the countryside of present-day Santander, Boyacá, Norte de Santander, Cundinamarca, and beyond. During Spanish rule, the paths continued to be a major means of communication between colonial towns, and the networks became known as Caminos Reales. In the late 19th century, a German, Geo von Lengerke, restored the Barichara-Guane Camino Real and built a stone bridge across the Río Suárez to improve transportation.

The hike to Guane takes two hours, and you don't need a guide. It's well marked, well-trodden, and safe. To get to the trailhead, walk west along Carrera 10 to the Piedra de Bolívar, where you'll see the stone path leading down toward the valley. If you are not up for the hike back, a bus (COP$3,500) departs from Guane to Barichara at 6:30am, 10am, noon, 3pm, and 6pm.

FESTIVALS AND EVENTS

Festival Internacional de Cine de Barichara

www.ficba.com.co; June; prices vary by event

The Festival Internacional de Cine de Barichara brings in independent filmmakers from all over the world.

Festival de Cine Verde

www.festiver.org; Sept.; prices vary by event

The Festival de Cine Verde, an environmentally themed festival, is held annually in the town's churches.

SHOPPING

Barichara has always been a magnet for artists and craftspeople, many of whom have shops in town.

Fundación Escuela Taller Barichara

Carrera 5 No. 4-26; tel. 7/726-7577; 8am-7pm Mon.-Thurs., 8am-9pm Fri.-Sat., 8am-4pm Sun.

The Fundación Escuela Taller Barichara is a gallery, museum, school, shop, and restaurant. Occasional photography and painting exhibitions are held at this lovely cultural center, traditional decorative objects from the area are always on display, ceramics and other items made by students are for sale, and anyone can take a monthlong or longer course here. They offer dozens of classes for free. The on-site **Restaurante y Café Las Cruces** is one of the finest places to eat in town.

Taller de Papel de Fique

Calle 6 No. 2-68; tel. 7/726-7234; www.tallerdepapeldebarichara.com; 8am-3pm Mon.-Thurs.

The Taller de Papel de Fique makes for an interesting stop. At this workshop, artisans make beautiful paper out of natural fique

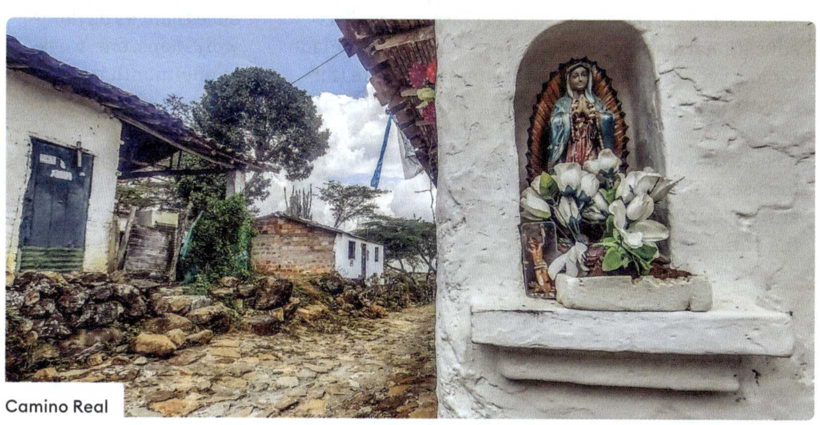

Camino Real

THINK GLOBALLY, REGENERATE LOCALLY

The tropical dry forest is Colombia's most endangered forest ecosystem, with only 3 percent of its original coverage remaining, but it is home to incredible biodiversity that includes endemic species like the aptly named beautiful woodpecker *(Melanerpes pulcher)*. Unfortunately, after decades of deforestation, much of the former dry forest around Barichara has nearly become a desert.

Enter **Regenerate Barichara** (https://regeneratebarichara.org), a local organization run by Joe Brewer, author of *The Design Pathway for Regenerating Earth* and founder of the Design School for Regenerating Earth and Bioregional Earth (https://bioregionalearth.org), a global network of on-the-ground bioregional regeneration projects.

Over the years Barichara has attracted many ecologically minded people, and one of the goals of Regenerate Barichara is to unite them to create a critical mass for rapid change. Within town, a locally based economy is already beginning to change the dynamic of Barichara's social and economic fabric, and there are over 30 different regenerative projects taking place in the area.

Regenerate Barichara oversees or is involved in nearly a dozen local projects, including:

- **Bioparque Móncora:** A community-owned 2.4-ha (6-acre) native tree forest on the edge of town above the Capilla de Santa Bárbara, the Bioparque is open to visitors and serves as an educational classroom for local youth. In 2018 a syntropic agroforestry food forest project, designed to strengthen food security in Barichara, was integrated into the park.
- **Casa Común:** This community center and store is in the heart of Barichara (Carrera 8 No. 8-61). Find fresh produce, prepared foods, and artisanal products from local farms as well as fresh-baked bread made from masa madre (fermented living dough). Casa Común also hosts classes throughout the week in everything from food processing to yoga.
- **Suna Barichara** (https://sunabarichara.org) is a learning platform that connects the different regenerative projects in Barichara and allows visitors to experience them as daylong workshops, one-week to one-month intensive courses, or long-term volunteer positions. Options include working on a regenerative farm, native bird sketching, dry stone building techniques, and tai chi.

fiber. On sale in this small store are cards, stationery, and handicrafts, all produced from fique. They also experiment with paper made from pineapple leaves. Short tours explaining the papermaking process are given for a small fee.

Jimena Rueda

Carrera 5 No. 2-01; tel. 314/400-5071; 10am-6pm Mon.-Sat.

One of the best-known ceramic artists in town is Jimena Rueda. In addition to browsing her work, you can ask Señora Jimena if she has any pieces of the famous rustic handmade pottery of the Guane Indigenous people. There is only one person who knows and uses this technique: **Ana Felisa Alquichire.** Doña Ana Felisa has been declared a living national cultural treasure by the Colombian presidency; her plates and bowls are sold in a few different shops in Barichara and Guane.

Formas de Luz

Calle 10 No. 7-20; tel. 7/726-7279 or 317/438-4042; www.formasdeluz.com; 8am-noon and 2pm-6pm Mon.-Sat., 9:30am-1:30pm Sun.

Formas de Luz is the workshop of talented furniture designer Muriel Garderet. Her lamps and other objects integrate fique fiber in unique ways.

FOOD

Restaurants in Barichara gear up for the weekend crowd, but opening hours may vary during the week.

El Balcón de Mi Pueblo

Calle 7 No. 5-62; tel. 318/280-2980; noon-5pm daily; COP$18,000-45,000

Locals flock to El Balcón de Mi Pueblo for good meaty Colombian fare like cabro (grilled goat), carne oreada (sun-dried steak), and churrasco (steak). It's a cute place up on the 2nd floor.

Restaurante Shimbala

Carrera 7 No. 6-22; tel. 318/391-3124; COP$30,000-50,000

Restaurante Shimbala serves Asian-inspired dishes including big stir-fries, both vegetarian and nonvegetarian, as well as salads and fresh juices.

★ Restaurante y Tienda Café Las Cruces

Carrera 5 No. 4-26; tel. 7/726-7577; www.tallerdeoficiosbarichara.com; 9am-4pm Tues.-Thurs., 9am-8pm Fri.-Sat., noon-4pm Sun.; COP$40,000-60,000

Restaurante y Café Las Cruces is considered the top restaurant in Barichara for its ambience and creative dishes. It's in the beautiful patio of the Fundación Escuela Taller Barichara. Look for signature dishes such as pernil de cabro (barbecued goat leg) with an ant sauce or costillitas de tamarindo (tamarind ribs).

La Puerta Cocina Secreta

Calle 3 No. 1 sur 58; tel. 312/364-7238; noon-9pm Tues.-Sun.; COP$62,000-120,000

La Puerta is a beautiful place, with candlelit tables at night under the stars in a private garden patio. They serve tasty pastas and use local organic ingredients when possible. Reservations are mandatory.

Panadería Barichara

Calle 5 No. 5-33; tel. 7/726-7688; www.panaderiabarichara.com; 7am-1pm and 2pm-8pm daily

For a coffee or the popular galletas de cuajada (cheese cookies), head to Panadería Barichara. They've been around since 1954.

ACCOMMODATIONS

With Barichara's growth in popularity, lodging options to fit all budgets and styles have popped up in town. Weeknight rates are lower.

★ Color de Hormiga Hostel

Calle 6 No. 5-35; tel. 315/297-1621; COP$35,000 dorm, COP$65,000 d

The Color de Hormiga Hostel used to house teachers from a neighboring school. It's decorated with institutional furniture that was left behind, and it still has its original groovy tiled floors. There are seven small rooms for one or two people, each with its own private bath. The kitchen is open for guest use.

Tinto Hostel

Carrera 4 No. 5-39; tel. 7/726-7725; www.tintohostel.com; COP$40,000 dorm, COP$120,000 d

At Tinto Hostel there's a ton of open green space, a pool, and perfectly fine rooms, making it a backpacker favorite. Dorm rooms have four or six beds.

Artepolis

Carrera 2 No. 2-2; tel. 300/203-4531; www.artepolis.info; COP$130,000 d

On the edge of town, peaceful Artepolis has eight minimalist rooms overlooking the countryside. Artist workshops are held occasionally. An on-site French bakery serves freshly baked goods and coffee (8am-noon daily).

Posada Sueños de Antonio

Carrera 9 No. 4-25; tel. 7/726-7793; www.suenosdeantonio.com.co; COP$180,000 d

The peaceful Posada Sueños de Antonio has five spacious rooms surrounding an interior patio that attracts birds every morning.

★ Posada del Campanario

Calle 5 No. 7-49; tel. 7/726-7261; www.posada-campanario.com; COP$440,000 d

The wonderful Posada del Campanario, one of the first hotels in Barichara, has seven rooms that are comfortable but not overly luxurious. It's surrounded by gardens and has an open-air dining area as well as a divine mirador (lookout) with a view of the Templo de la Inmaculada Concepción. Church bells may awaken you early in the morning.

TRANSPORTATION

Most visitors to Barichara arrive either in their own vehicle or by bus. To get to Barichara from Bogotá, head to Bogotá's Portal del Norte bus terminal. The journey to Barichara (COP$80,000) takes six hours or more and you have to transfer in San Gil.

Busetas leave San Gil every half hour starting at 5am daily from the Terminal de Transportes, with the last bus departing at 6:45pm. The 20-km (12-mi) journey to Barichara (COP$7,000) takes 45 minutes. Buses drop passengers a block below the main square.

Medellín
and the
Coffee Region
COLOMBIA

Medellín and the Coffee Region

★ Highlights

★ **Museo de Antioquia:** Explore the country's top fine-art museum, situated in a former palace (page 228).

★ **Guatapé** *(lower right):* Climb the stairs to the top of Piedra del Peñol for amazing views of the lake-dotted countryside (page 251).

★ **Jardín** *(upper right):* Relax to the max in this peaceful pueblo after bird-watching in the lush cloud forests (page 255).

★ **Parque Nacional Natural Los Nevados:** Hike up to the rim of snow-capped volcanos and to lost-in-time lagoons (page 268).

★ **Coffee Farm-Stays** *(lower left):* Immerse yourself in Colombia's coffee culture on a tour or an overnight stay (page 270).

★ **Salento** *(upper left):* Visit coffee farms and trek through a pristine valley dotted with towering wax palms (page 274).

★ **Bahía Solano:** Whale-watch and explore the super biodiverse Pacific coastal rainforest (page 283).

Look for ★ to find recommended sights, activities, dining, and lodging.

◂ Medellín's Metro

Medellín is not just Colombia's second city—it actively vies with Bogotá as the true capital of the country. One of the most modern metropolises on the continent, it boasts a dynamic and highly efficient public transportation system, extensive park networks, well-planned public spaces, a vast network of public libraries, and other urban features that put it in a league of its own. World-class museums, a dynamic arts and entertainment scene, and fascinating local barrios entice visitors into making the city their base while in Colombia.

Outside Medellín, the green mountains of Antioquia and the coffee region still move at a more traditional pace, and there are beautiful little pueblos and glorious natural parks and preserves to explore. The region is famous for its eternally springlike weather, making slow travel simply irresistible, as there are endless treasures to discover. Medellín and the surrounding coffee region is a nation within a nation, with the most powerful economy in the country and a sense of Paisa nationalism that sometimes feels over-the-top, even if it's well deserved.

Heading west, the biodiverse rainforests of the Chocó region are home to Afro-descendant communities and some of the most famous beaches on the Colombian Pacific coast.

Orientation

MEDELLÍN

Medellín is in the verdant Valle de Aburrá, with the trickling and polluted Río Medellín dividing the city into east and west. Both Metro Línea A and Avenida Regional (Autopista Sur), a busy expressway, run south-north, parallel to the river. Metro Línea B runs east-west, connecting Centro to neighborhoods like Laureles and Comuna 13.

Centro

The heart of Centro is the **Plaza Botero** and **Parque Berrío Metro station** area, home to many plazas, ancient churches, and pedestrian-only streets that bustle by day but turn empty and often dangerous at night. Across Carrera 46 (Av. Oriental), however, the **La Playa** area is filled with cultural centers, independent theaters, hip nightlife, and an up-and-coming dining scene and makes for a great base. It is also two blocks from the Pabellón del Agua Tranvía stop, which connects to the entire public transit system.

El Poblado

If you arrive in Medellín from the Rionegro airport, you will descend the hill into the valley and land more or less in El Poblado. The upscale neighborhood is packed with overpriced restaurants, bars, hostels, hotels, and shopping malls. Parque Lleras is the center of the **Provenza** neighborhood, a small, leafy, and very trendy part of El Poblado on the eastern side of Avenida El Poblado. To the west, down Calle 10, is

Medellín and the Coffee Region
Cascadas Cocacola
See "Chocó" Map
Bahía Solano
El Valle
Estación Septiembre Sea Turtle Hatchery & Release Program
ANTIOQUIA
CHOCÓ BIOGEOGRÁFICO
CHOCÓ
PACIFIC OCEAN
60
13
50
13
0
10 miles
0
10 km
ANDES
VALLE DEL CAUCA

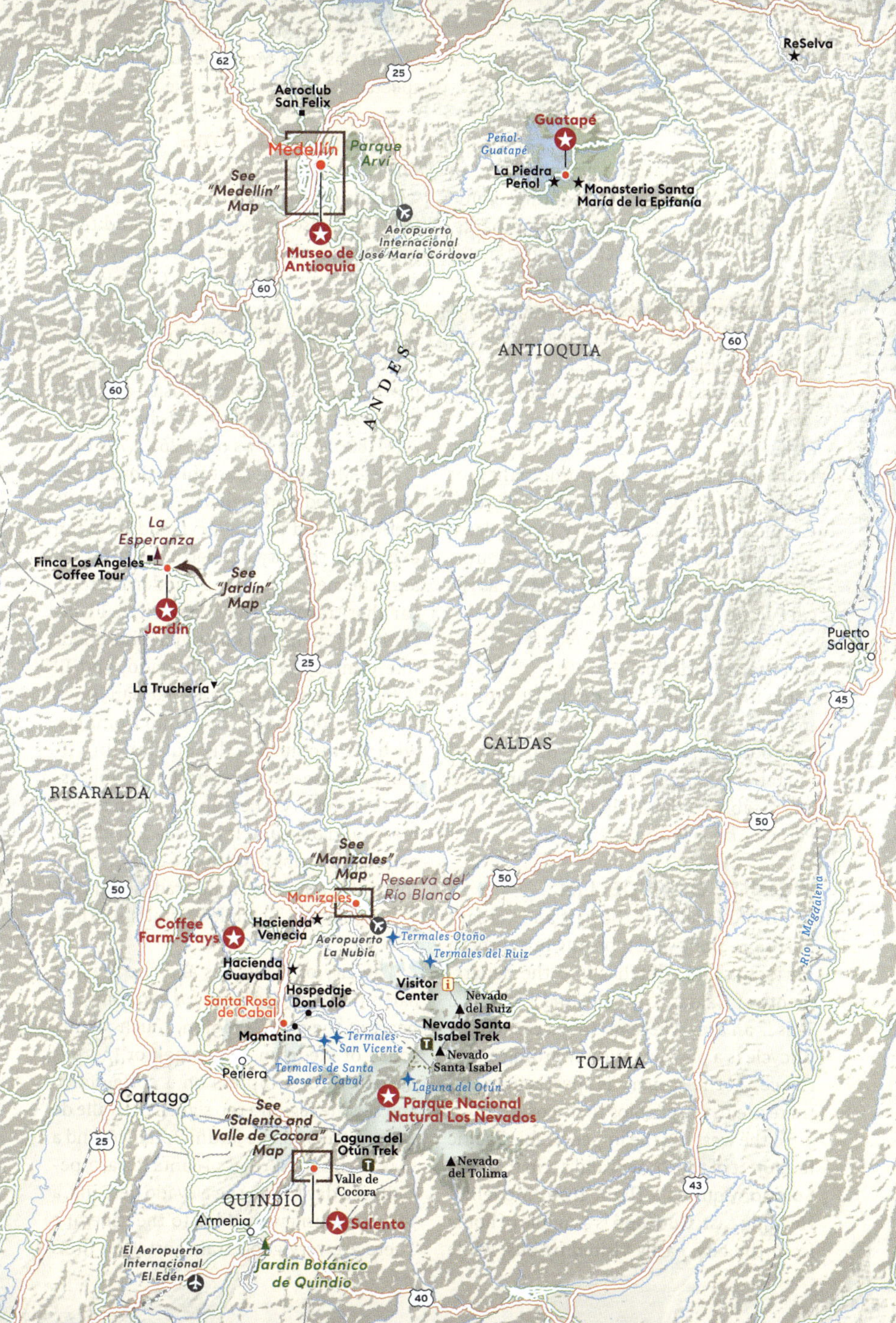
ReSelva
Aeroclub San Felix
Guatapé
Medellín
Parque Arví
Peñol-Guatapé
La Piedra Peñol
Monasterio Santa María de la Epifanía
See "Medellín" Map
Aeropuerto Internacional José María Córdova
Museo de Antioquia
ANTIOQUIA
ANDES
La Esperanza
Finca Los Ángeles Coffee Tour
See "Jardín" Map
Jardín
La Truchería
Puerto Salgar
CALDAS
RISARALDA
See "Manizales" Map
Reserva del Río Blanco
Manizales
Coffee Farm-Stays
Hacienda Venecia
Aeropuerto La Nubia
Termales Otoño
Termales del Ruiz
Río Magdalena
Hacienda Guayabal
Hospedaje Don Lolo
Visitor Center
Nevado del Ruiz
Santa Rosa de Cabal
Mamatina
Termales San Vicente
Nevado Santa Isabel Trek
Nevado Santa Isabel
TOLIMA
Periera
Termales de Santa Rosa de Cabal
Laguna del Otún
Cartago
Parque Nacional Natural Los Nevados
See "Salento and Valle de Cocora" Map
Laguna del Otún Trek
Nevado del Tolima
Valle de Cocora
QUINDÍO
Armenia
Salento
El Aeropuerto Internacional El Edén
Jardín Botánico de Quindío
62
25
60
45
50
43
40

Parque de El Poblado, and a few blocks farther is the Poblado Metro station.

Laureles

The upper-middle-class neighborhood of Laureles, just south of the stadium, is home to peaceful tree-lined streets and parks, lots of restaurants and cafés, and some of the city's best nightlife. Recently the area has become full of hostels as travelers flee the price gouging and gaudy nightlife scene of the El Poblado area. The Metro Línea B Estadio stop connects the area with Centro.

Envigado

In the far south, the municipality of Envigado feels like a pueblo within the city. Parque Principal is the busy main plaza, and there are some important museums and cultural centers as well as the paradisical Parque El Salado.

Northern Medellín

Sprawling northern Medellín is a mishmash of middle- and low-income neighborhoods that are mostly off visitors' radar but hold some hidden treasures. The Metrocable to the Biblioteca España and Parque Arví is located here.

VICINITY OF MEDELLÍN

South of Medellín is the vast and verdant **coffee region,** which begins in southern Antioquia and stretches into the departments of Caldas, Quindío, and Risaralda. This is an area where renting a car or motorcycle is a pleasant and rewarding experience, as the scenery is spectacular and there are many pueblos to discover.

To the west lies the impenetrable Pacific rainforest of the **Chocó,** and a trip to **Bahía Solano** requires a flight from Medellín. Heading east, **Guatapé** is a couple of hours from the city, easily visited by bus, while farther east, the **Magdalena Valley** holds spectacular natural areas like Río Claro.

Planning Your Time

The City of Eternal Spring can be enjoyed any time of year, and the surrounding coffee region also has ideal year-round temperatures, with average highs rarely above 30°C (86°F) and lows of 16-21°C (60s F). The Pacific coast, however, is one of the rainiest places on earth, and during the winter, October-December, it can be a nonstop downpour that dampens a visit—although it's always warm, with average highs of 27-32°C (80s F) and lows of 21-26°C (70s F).

Give Medellín at least **three days** to experience landmark sights like the Museo de Antioquia and Parque Arví, and have fun exploring the city by Metro, Metrocable, and the new Tranvía, a modern streetcar that traverses the city's original trolley line. Getting to know neighborhoods like Centro, Laureles, Envigado, and El Poblado—as well as barrios like San Javier, home to Comuna 13, and Santo Domingo, with its architecturally outstanding library—are some of the most enjoyable aspects of the city. The transit system makes it easy and pleasant. If you stay a week, you can add day trips to **Guatapé** or overnights to Jardín, an enchanting traditional coffee pueblo just a couple of hours south of the city.

The city of Manizales and the town of Salento make good bases for exploring the heart of the **coffee region,** much farther south of Medellín. **One week** or more is needed to decompress on a coffee farm and see the region's top sights: the Valle de Cocora, Salento, the Jardín Botánico, and a soak in the hot springs of Santa Rosa, especially if a day trip to the Nevado del Ruiz, a 14-hour journey, is added to the itinerary. There are very good transportation links

Itinerary Ideas

Medellín is many travelers' favorite city in Colombia, and it's easy to spend a week or more enjoying the tropical yet modern city vibes. But with only three days, you can follow this itinerary with a base in El Poblado, Laureles, or La Playa, as it visits all three and relies on the Metro to get around.

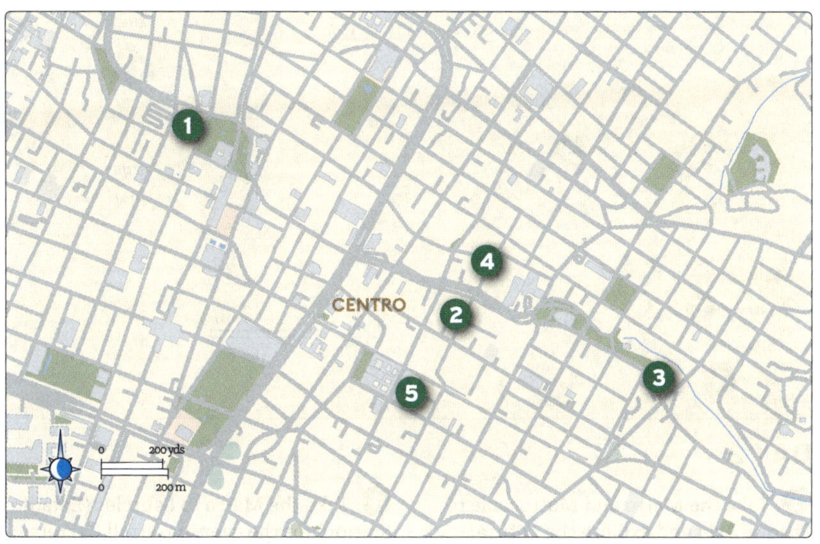

DAY 1

1. Visit the stunning **Museo de Antioquia** and the surrounding Plaza de Botero.

2. Walk over to the La Playa area and have lunch at **La Antigua.**

3. Afterward, check out the **Museo Casa de la Memoria.**

4. Have dinner at **Salón Centro** in La Playa to get a taste of the local food scene. Try the ceviche sabanero.

5. Check out the nightlife on Calle de Cervantes. Stop by **Ubuntu** for friendly conversation and live music.

Itinerary Ideas

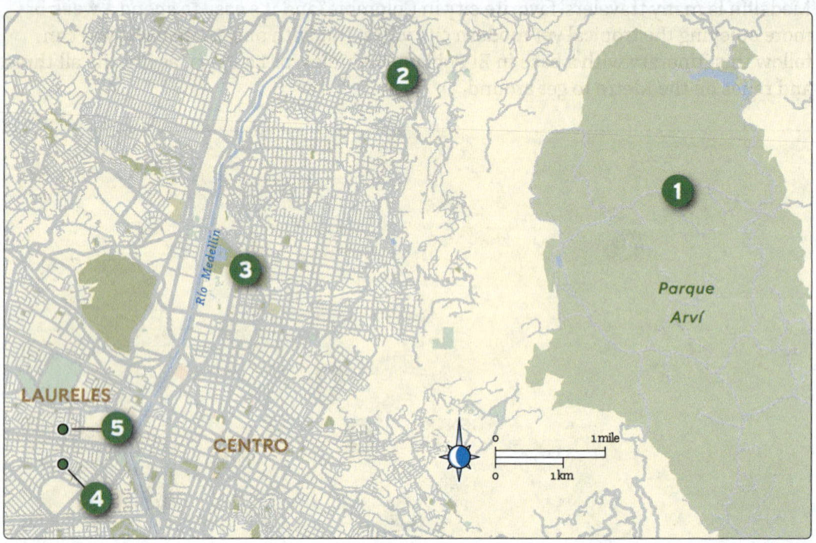

DAY 2

1 Take the Metro and Metrocable to **Parque Arví** and explore the natural areas.

2 On the way back, stop to check out the **Biblioteca España** and the views over the city.

3 In the afternoon, take the Metro to the **Jardín Botánico de Medellín** (Universidades Station). The on-site restaurant does a nice lunch.

4 Take the Metro to Laureles (Estadio Station) for the evening, stroll Carrera 70, and then grab dinner at **La Tienda.**

5 At night, its back to Carrera 70 to get your salsa on at local favorite **El Tíbiri.**

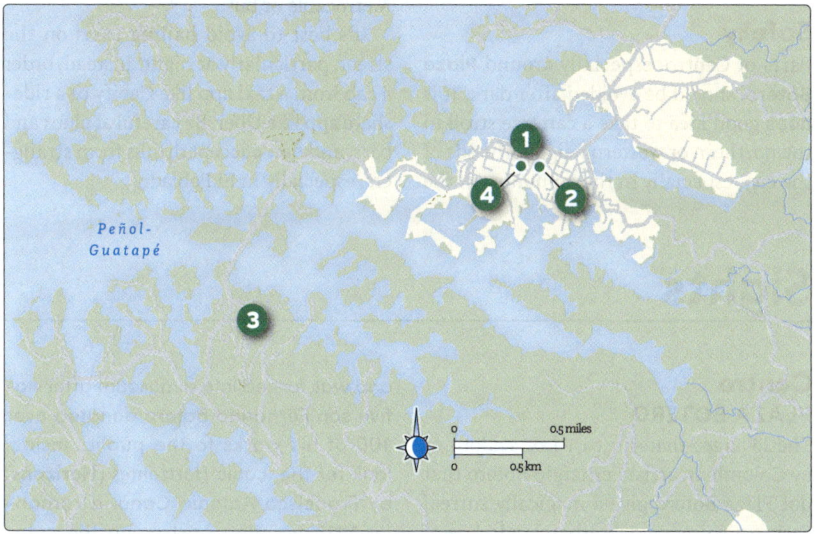

DAY 3

1 Take an early morning bus to **Guatapé** and spend the rest of the morning exploring the picture-perfect lakeside village.

2 Grab a hearty late breakfast at **Montano** to fuel up for the day.

3 Take a mototaxi over to **La Piedra Peñol** and climb to the top. Sunsets from here are spectacular.

4 At night, visit the picturesque **Calle del Recuerdo** and hang out in the main square of Guatapé.

Guatapé reservoir

La Piedra Peñol

Guatapé

between Salento and the major cities, and roads are generally excellent.

Safety

Parts of Centro, especially around **Plaza Botero,** should be avoided after dark. It is not a good idea to take a carefree stroll in the northern or western neighborhoods of the city, especially in the **comunas** on the surrounding hills—but the specific sights described can be visited easily and safely by Metrocable or bus.

It's best to avoid hailing taxis on the street, particularly at night. Instead, order a cab from a taxi app like Cabify or a ride-share app like Uber. Be careful at clubs and bars, and don't accept drinks from strangers, especially in El Poblado.

Sights

Centro

PLAZA BOTERO

The 23 larger-than-life cast-iron sculptures by Colombian artist Fernando Botero that dot Plaza Botero give a magically surreal cast to an already rich urban landscape of sex workers, local businesspeople, and travelers meandering in the shadow of former palaces and decaying early-20th-century hotels. Grab a coffee and sit for a while before checking out the Museo de Antioquia and other sights. Plaza Botero is adjacent to the Parque Berrio Metro station.

TOP EXPERIENCE

★ MUSEO DE ANTIOQUIA

Carrera 52 No. 52-43; tel. 4/251-3636; www.museodeantioquia.org.co; 10am-5pm Mon.-Sat., 10am-4:30pm Sun.; COP$40,000

In Plaza Botero, the Museo de Antioquia is one of the top art museums in Latin America, with an extensive permanent collection of works from Colombian artists from the 19th century to modern times. The building is an architectural gem, an art deco structure from the 1930s that originally served as the Palacio Municipal and was turned into a museum after native son Fernando Botero donated over 100 of his works to the public. Inside, look for the iconic *Horizontes* (**Horizons**) by Francisco Antonio Cano, a romantic 1913 painting portraying the colonización antioqueña, the period when families from Antioquia headed south to settle in what is now known as the coffee region. In the contemporary art rooms, you'll see *Horizontes* by Carlos Uribe. This 1997 painting presents the same bucolic scene, except in the background a plane sprays pesticides over the countryside to eradicate coca and marijuana crops.

PALACIO DE LA CULTURA RAFAEL URIBE

Carrera 51 No. 52 01; 8am-5:30pm Mon.-Sat.; free

An impressive example of Gothic-revival architecture that towers over the western edge of Parque Botero, the Palacio de la Cultura Rafael Uribe was built by a Belgian architect in 1920 to serve as the headquarters of the government of Antioquia. Turned into a cultural center and later designated a national landmark, the palace hosts art and history exhibits, a permanent

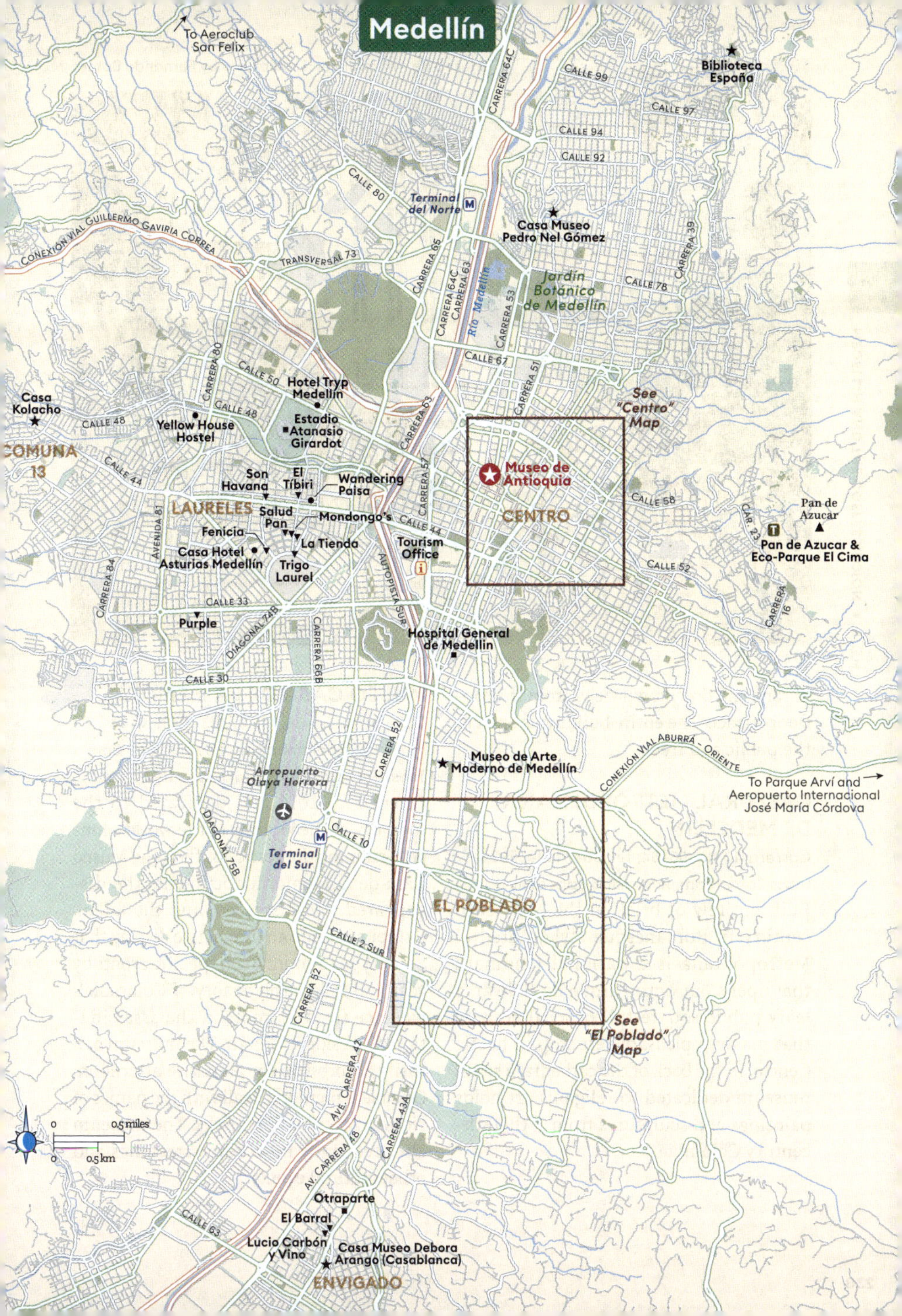
Medellín
To Aeroclub San Felix
Biblioteca España
Calle 99
Calle 97
Calle 94
Calle 92
Carrera 64C
Calle 80
Terminal del Norte
Casa Museo Pedro Nel Gómez
Conexión Vial Guillermo Gaviria Correa
Transversal 73
Carrera 65
Carrera 64C
Carrera 63
Río Medellín
Carrera 53
Jardín Botánico de Medellín
Calle 78
Carrera 39
Calle 67
Carrera 80
Calle 50
Hotel Tryp Medellín
Carrera 51
See "Centro" Map
Casa Kolacho
Calle 48
Calle 48
Yellow House Hostel
Estadio Atanasio Girardot
Carrera 63
Comuna 13
Calle 44
Son Havana
El Tíbiri
Wandering Paisa
Carrera 57
Museo de Antioquia
Calle 58
Pan de Azucar
Laureles
Salud Pan
Mondongo's
Calle 44
Centro
Car. 23
Avenida 81
Fenicia
La Tienda
Tourism Office
Pan de Azucar & Eco-Parque El Cima
Casa Hotel Asturias Medellín
Trigo Laurel
Autopista Sur
Calle 52
Carrera 84
Calle 33
Carrera 16
Purple
Diagonal 74B
Carrera 66B
Hospital General de Medellín
Calle 30
Carrera 52
Museo de Arte Moderno de Medellín
Conexión Vial Aburrá - Oriente
To Parque Arví and Aeropuerto Internacional José María Córdova
Aeropuerto Olaya Herrera
Calle 10
Diagonal 75B
Terminal del Sur
El Poblado
Calle 2 Sur
Carrera 52
See "El Poblado" Map
Ave. Carrera 42
Carrera 43A
0 0.5 miles
0 0.5 km
Av. Carrera 48
Otraparte
El Barral
Calle 63
Lucio Carbón y Vino
Casa Museo Debora Arango (Casablanca)
Envigado

Museo de Antioquia and sculptures by Fernando Botero

library, and downtown views from the top-floor terrace. The entire building is open to the public and free.

CATEDRAL METROPOLITANA DE MEDELLÍN

Carrera 48 No. 56-64; tel. 604/423-8592; mass 7am, 10am, noon, and 6pm daily

Built entirely of brick in the early 20th century in Romanesque style, Catedral Metropolitana is a national landmark that opens out onto Parque de Bolívar, a leafy public square full of local activity that makes a pleasant rest stop in hectic Centro. In the back of the cathedral a small museum dedicated to religious art holds paintings and sculptures from 17th-18th-century Colombia.

MUSEO CASA DE LA MEMORIA

Calle 51 No. 36-66; tel. 4/383-4001; www.museocasadelamemoria.gov.co; 9am-6pm Tues.-Fri., 10am-4pm Sat.-Sun.; free

Opened in 2016 and dedicated to the memory of the victims of the world's longest-running domestic conflict, the Museo Casa de la Memoria documents the disappeared, the displaced, and the fallen. Exhibits include an interactive display that allows you to zoom in on specific events by year and follow the history of Colombia's violence from its roots in the assassination of President Gaitán. The museum can easily absorb you for an entire afternoon. Outside is memorial wall with the names of victims inscribed on bricks. The museum also frequently hosts film screenings and other cultural events.

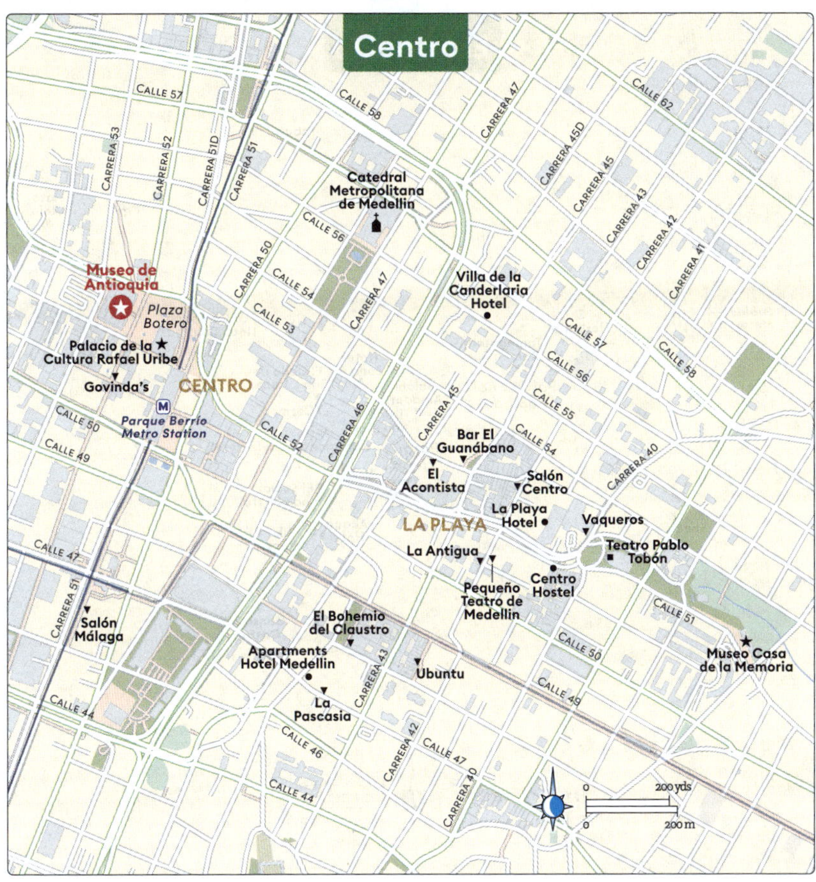

El Poblado

MUSEO DE ARTE MODERNO DE MEDELLÍN (MAMM)

Carrera 44 No. 19a-100; tel. 604/444-2622; www.elmamm.org; 11am-7pm Tues.-Fri., 11am-6pm Sat.-Sun.; COP$24,000

An artistic marvel in its own right, the stacked-cube architecture of the Medellín Museum of Modern Art was designed to pay homage to the jumbled houses of the low income comunas that cling to the hills of the city. The five-story structure holds permanent exhibitions of top Colombian artists, including Débora Arango, as well as temporary exhibitions that have featured rocker Patti Smith and Indigenous artists from across the country. To get here, take the Metro Línea A to the Industriales station and walk three blocks south.

Northern Medellín

BIBLIOTECA ESPAÑA

Carrera 33B No. 107A-100; tel. 4/528-9495; www.reddebibliotecas.org.co; 8am-7pm Mon.-Sat., 11am-5pm Sun.

When this public library was opened in

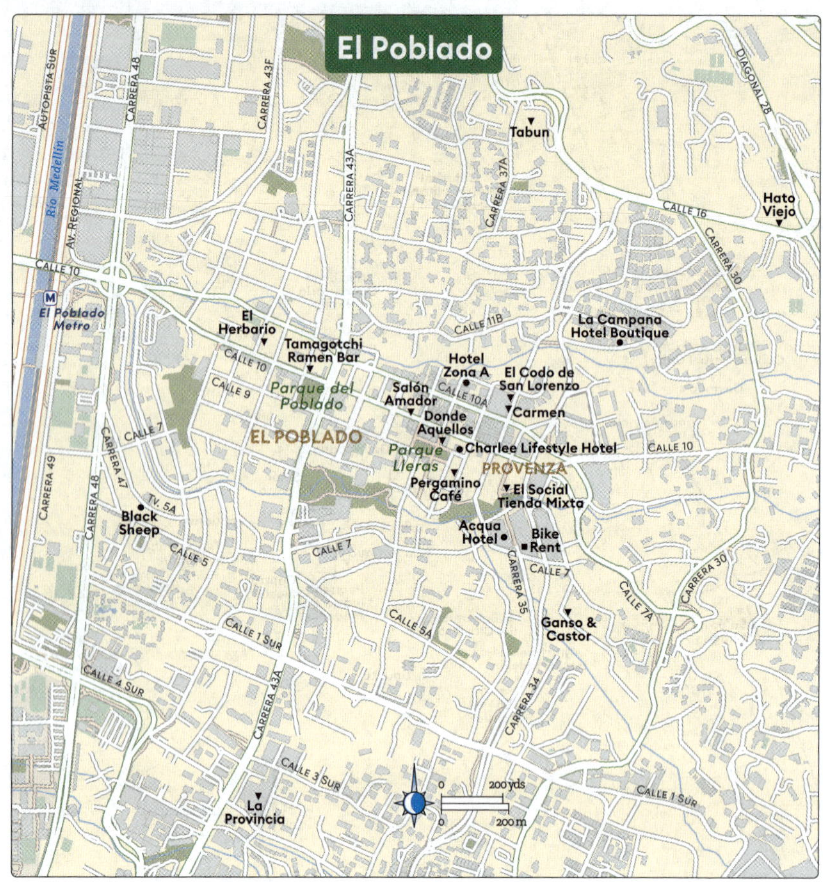

the low-income neighborhood of Santo Domingo, King Juan Carlos came from Madrid for the ceremony. As the facility's name implies, the Spanish government helped fund the project. It's one of many newly created **biblioteca parques** (public library parks) in Medellín. More than a place for books, library parks have become community centers and sources of pride in neighborhoods that continue to struggle with poverty and violence. Biblioteca España boasts one of the most daring designs: It resembles giant boulders clinging to the edge of the mountainside. It was designed by architect and Barranquilla native Giancarlo Mazzanti, who won a prize for this work at the Bienal Iberoamericana de Arquitectura y Urbanismo in Lisbon in 2008.

Getting to Santo Domingo is an attraction itself. The neighborhood is connected to the metropolis by the Metrocable cable car system. When the Metrocable Línea K opened in 2004 it was the first of its kind: a gondola-like public transport system with a socioeconomic purpose to connect

Another palace almost identical to the Palacio de la Cultura Rafael Uribe is a few blocks away on bustling pedestrian-only **Carrera Carabobo** near Calle 49. Now a shopping center, the first few floors are packed with cheap clothing shops and cell phone dealers, but the top floor and rooftop feature room after room of local art and several cafés with outdoor seating and views of the city.

low-income residents to the Metro. Take the Metro toward Niquía and transfer to the Metrocable at Acevedo station. Get off the Metrocable at the Santo Domingo stop. Many visitors are content to view the library from the Metrocable gondola as they continue onward to Parque Arví.

PARQUE ARVÍ

Vía a Piedras Blancas, Santa Elena; tel. 4/444-2979; www.parquearvi.org; 9am-5pm Tues.-Sun.; COP$60,000

For some fresh air, a visit to Parque Arví's 16,000 ha (40,000 acres) of nature hits the spot. Many visitors enjoy the trip to the park on the Metrocable as much as the park itself. To get here from the city, take the Metro to Acevedo station, on Línea A toward Niquía. At Acevedo station, transfer to the Metrocable Línea K to the Santo Domingo station. From Santo Domingo station, you must transfer to Línea L, an additional COP$16,850 one-way.

Unfortunately, the park is not well organized, and several different entities control different sections, each charging different admission rates. This makes visiting by yourself confusing. At the Parque Arví Metrocable stop, a ticket booth run by the Parque Arví Corporation charges COP$60,000 for entrance to a small 3-km (2-mi) trail that, while pleasant, offers few stand out features and is simply not worth the price.

Booking a guide in advance through the website (https://parquearvi.org) will get you a guided tour for an additional COP$30,000. Bird-watching tours are also available (COP$230,000 pp). To visit other areas of the extensive park, you need to take a taxi, which wait behind the Parque Arví Corporation building, and negotiate fares and entrance fees.

JARDÍN BOTÁNICO DE MEDELLÍN

Calle 73 No. 51d-14; tel. 604/444-5500; www.botanicomedellin.org; 9am-4pm Thurs.-Tues.; free

Take a walk through an Andean cloud forest, learn about Colombia's 4,200 species of orchids, and take part in an urban gardening class all free of charge at the Medellín Botanical Garden, a 6-ha (14-acre) oasis of greenery near the Universidad de Antioquia. It is full of families on the weekend but peaceful during the week. The on-site restaurant, **INSITU** (COP$45,000-60,000), is overpriced but makes for a great place to enjoy an afternoon cocktail.

SMALL ART MUSEUMS IN MEDELLÍN

Fernando Botero's massive profile in the modern art world often overshadows the many other high-caliber visual artists from Medellín. For example, the city also produced Débora Arango and Pedro Nel Gómez, who both garnered international acclaim and grappled with social issues head on. Visiting the homes of these artists, now both public museums, is a fascinating and rewarding firsthand way to immerse yourself into Colombian art, history, and culture.

bust of Débora Arango

CASA MUSEO PEDRO NEL GÓMEZ

Carrera 51B No. 85-24, Barrio Aranjuez; tel. 4/444-2633, ext. 102; 9am-5pm Mon.-Sat.; COP$17,200

In the barrio of Aranjuez this delightful museum houses an extensive collection of the painter's works, including several of the murals for which he is best known. His paintings can be found all over the city, with a particularly large and intricate mural by Gómez outside the Parque Berrio Metro station. Much of his work portrays the plight of campesinos (rural peasants), workers, and Indigenous people.

The house, now the museum, was designed by Gómez. In the back an extensive garden has become a neighborhood community farm. Guided tours (COP$130,000 for up to 30 people) are available. The museum is not easy to get to on public transportation, and it is in a rough part of town, so take a taxi.

CASA MUSEO DÉBORA ARANGO

Carrera 43 No. 32a

Débora Arango (1907-2005) was a Medellín-born painter, sculptor, and ceramic artist who faced harsh criticism during her lifetime but is now regarded as one of Colombia's most important visual artists and social critics. By the end of her career Arango racked up dozens of national and international awards, including the Order of Boyacá, the highest distinction in Colombia. In 2016 the government added her profile to the 2,000-peso bill.

While Arango donated most of her work to the Museo de Arte Moderno de Medellín, her home and work studio for the last four decades of her life, Casablanca, is now a museum devoted to her life. It holds several of her works. The museum offers free guided tours (2pm Tues. and Thurs.; free) that focus on the life and legacy of Colombia's most prominent female visual artist. There is no sign on the museum; ring the bell next to the garden gate to be let in to the compound.

Recreation

Biking

CICLOVÍA

8am-1pm Sun.

On Sundays and holidays Medellín closes several main streets and residents mount their bikes and don blades for Ciclovía. There are several routes, including along Avenida El Poblado and Río Medellín. On Tuesday and Thursday evenings **Ciclovía Nocturna** (8pm-10pm) has two routes, one along the river and the other around the stadium.

OUTFITTERS

Encicla

www.encicla.gov.co

Encicla is Medellín's free bike-sharing program. Visitors can check out a bike, though it will take a week to get permission, which can be obtained online. Some nice bike paths are along Carreras 65 and 70 and around the universities, connecting the Estadio and Universidad Metro stations.

Parque Arví Metrocable

Bike Rent

Calle 10 No. 52-18; tel. 310/448-3731; www.bikerent.com.co; 9am-7pm Mon., Wed., and Fri.-Sat., 9am-10pm Tues. and Thurs., 8am-1pm Sun.; half day COP$35,000, full day COP$55,000

Bike Rent has good bikes to rent out cheaply, and prices decrease for longer rentals. It also has information on routes at this convenient Provenza location.

Paragliding

Aeroclub San Felix

Km 6, Vía San Pedro de los Milagros; tel. 4/388-1077; www.parapenteencolombia.com; 20-minute flight COP$25,000, complete course COP$3,200,000

For incredible views of both the verdant Antioquia countryside and the metropolis in the distance, check out a paragliding adventure organized by the Aeroclub San Felix. Bus transportation toward the town of San Felix is available from the Portal del Norte bus station, and buses can drop you at the Estadero El Voladero.

Hiking

Surrounded by green mountains, Medellín offers urban hiking opportunities in every direction. Many trails begin at or pass by low-income comunas, however, so leave your valuables at home.

Pan de Azucar and Eco-Parque El Cima

Distance: 2 km (1.2 mi) round-trip
Duration: 1.5 hours round-trip
Elevation gain: 150 m (500 ft)
Difficulty: Moderate
Trailhead: Trece de Noviembre Metro station

For gorgeous views over downtown Medellín and the Aburrá valley, the short but vigorous jaunt up to the top of Pan de Azucar is a morning well spent. To get to the trailhead, take the Tranvía to Miraflores station, then transfer to the Metrocable Línea M and get off at the last stop, Trece de Noviembre. From the station, the entrance to the Eco-Parque El Cima is three blocks down Calle 18C.

From here it's a steep 500-m (0.3-mi) climb to the statue of the Virgin Mary at the top of the rocky outcrop of Pan de Azucar, but the trail is well maintained and mostly consists of stone stairways. Below the peak, the Eco-Parque El Cima offers a network of trails along the forested hillside that follow ancient Indigenous trading routes and connects all the way to Parque Arví. Over 200 species of birds have been spotted here, the most common being the white-collared swift *(Streptoprocne zonaris)*.

Spectator Sports

SOCCER

Medellín has several professional teams that play at the **Estadio Atanasio Girardot** (Calle 48 No. 73-10; www.inder.gov.co). Tickets can be purchased at **Ticket Factory Express** (tel. 4/444-4446; www.ticketexpress.com.co).

Atlético Nacional

www.atlnacional.com.co

By far the most famous team, with rabid followers across the country, is Atlético Nacional, wearing the green and white of the Antioquian flag and playing since 1947. It's one of the most successful teams in Colombia and has won the top division 11 times. Nacional is wildly popular with young men and boys in Medellín, Antioquia, and beyond. The cheap seats at Nacional games are always packed with kids from the barrios. It's an intense affair.

Tours

BUS TOURS

Turibus

www.turibuscolombia.com; 9am-7:40pm daily; COP$69,000

Turibus operates a hop-on, hop-off service that begins in El Poblado and has seven stops, including Plaza Botero and Cerro de Nutibara-Pueblito Paisa. It also offers tours to other parts of the Antioquia department, including Jericó and Guatapé.

El Dorado Trips

tel. 321/874-3440; www.eldoradotrips.com; from COP$109,000 pp

El Dorado Trips offers more conventional day tours to coffee farms, Guatapé, and Río Claro as well as to Hacienda Nápoles, the former home of Pablo Escobar.

WALKING TOURS

Beyond Colombia

tel. 322/898-8557; www.beyondcolombia.com; free

Locally-owned Beyond Colombia offers three donation-based walking tours of Medellín daily. A historical tour of the city center visits churches and historic buildings. The Violence and Post-Conflict Tour traverses Centro, visiting sights that include Parque San Antonio, where a bomb damaged one of Fernando Botero's public

KEEPING IT REAL IN COMUNA 13

It's an interesting paradox in a city renowned for its urban design and elevated arts scene that a ghetto, Comuna 13, gets twice the number of visitors as Parque Arví, the city's second-most-visited sight.

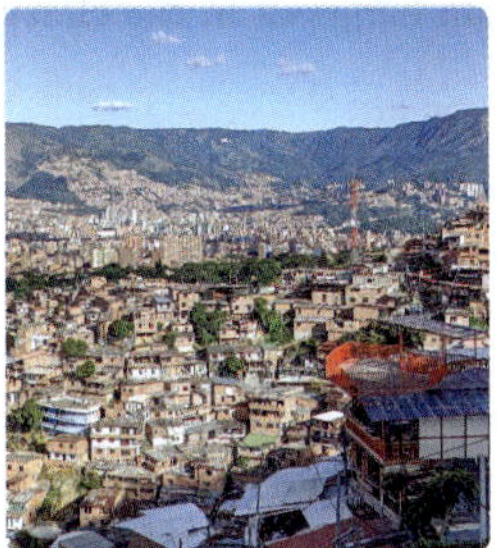
Comuna 13

In the 1970s-1980s the vast hillside area originally settled by displaced rural campesinos became a hotbed of violence as revolutionary guerrilla groups and later Pablo Escobar's narco-trafficking organization used its strategic location as a base. In 2002 the Colombian military, along with right-wing paramilitary groups, launched a full-scale invasion of Comuna 13, known as Operation Orion, which left several dead, dozens wounded, and hundreds simply "disappeared."

In 2006, as a way to apologize, Medellín built a Metrocable line connecting Comuna 13 to the rest of the city. In 2011 the city built a 400-m (1,300-ft) electric elevator, the first of its kind in the world. It began to draw residents from across the city simply to ride it up and down, and a new tourism industry was born.

Residents of Comuna 13 quickly opened up restaurants, cafés, and bars to serve the visitors. Graffiti artists started painting on canvas and opened up impromptu galleries. Hip-hop artists organized street performances, and the rest is history. Comuna 13 is packed with visitors and is a full-on street party every weekend. The fact that the neighborhood sports epic views of the city is icing on the cake.

LOCAL TOUR OPERATORS

Success always brings complications. Residents of Comuna 13 say that outside tour companies come between them and the economic contributions of visitors and also often misrepresent the culture of the neighborhood. While visiting Comuna 13 independently is easy, a tour from a locally owned operator is highly recommended:

- **Casa Kolacho** (Carrera 100B No. 45-5; tel. 311/347-3131): A cultural center managed by a collective of hip-hop and graffiti artists from Comuna 13, Casa Kolacho runs annual festivals, weekly events, and daily tours (COP$49,000) that focus on street art and the gritty daily life of the residents.
- **Culturizzarte** (tel. 312/326-7445): Lifelong Comuna 13 resident Malu Medina runs this local tour company that focuses on the history and culture of Comuna 13. Tours (2-3 hours; COP$50,000) include lunch at a local restaurant and visits to neighborhood cultural centers and art galleries.

statues, leading the artist to rename it *El Pájaro Herido* (The Wounded Bird), and ends at the Museo Casa de la Memoria. The third tour is of El Poblado. You must reserve your spot for all tours ahead of time on the website.

Entertainment and Events

Cultural Centers

La Pascasia

Calle 47 No. 43 88; www.comunycorriente.org; noon-7pm Mon.-Tues., noon-midnight Wed.-Thurs., noon-2am Fri.-Sat.

The largest and most famous of the half dozen or so cultural centers in the La Playa area, La Pascasia is a two-story café, bookstore, art gallery, bar, live music venue, and even a vinyl shop under one roof. Local bands play every weekend, and they serve a decent set lunch special during the week (COP$22,000). For art and music lovers, this is a home away from home.

Otraparte

Carrera 43A No. 27AS-11, Envigado; tel. 4/448-2404; www.otraparte.org; 8am-8pm Mon.-Fri., 9am-10pm Sat.-Sun.

Otraparte is a cultural center built around the house of writer Fernando González that offers a dynamic program of free concerts, films, book launches, and even free yoga classes. In back of the historic house, a café-restaurant serves food and cocktails in a sprawling garden setting.

Theater

Teatro Pablo Tobón

Carrera 40 No. 51-24; tel. 4/239-7500; www.teatropablotobon.com

A large public theater with 1960s flair right on La Playa, Teatro Pablo Tobón offers a full range of cultural events that include concerts, theater, yoga, lectures, parties, chess, and more. Even when there isn't anything going on, you can hang out in the classy lobby café.

Pequeño Teatro de Medellín

Carrera 42 No. 50A-12; tel. 604/480-7740; www.pequenoteatro.com

With over 40 years of nightly live theater on a pay-what-you-wish model, the Pequeño Teatro de Medellín pioneered the theater scene in the La Playa area, which now has over a dozen local community-run theater venues. The award-winning theater has a full year-round calendar of works by top Colombian playwrights. It's in a gorgeous historical mansion and has an on-site bar open on Friday-Saturday nights.

Festivals and Events

SUMMER

Festival Internacional de Tango

June

The Festival Internacional de Tango and the perseverance of tango culture in Medellín is largely due to one man's passion and efforts: Argentine Leonardo Nieto visited Medellín in the 1960s, primarily to get to know the place where tango icon Gardel died in an airplane crash. He fell in love with the city, stayed, and created the Festival Internacional de Tango. During this festival, tango concerts and events take place across the city, the culmination of which is the World Tango Championship, held at the

Teatro Pablo Tobón (Carrera 40 No. 51-24; www.teatropablotobon.com).

Festival Internacional de Poesía de Medellín

www.festivaldepoesiademedellin.org; mid-July; free

Since 1991 Medellín has hosted the impressive Festival Internacional de Poesía de Medellín, which routinely attracts poets from dozens of countries; they share their work in more than 100 venues across the city.

Colombiamoda

www.inexmoda.org.co; July

As the leading textile manufacturing center in Colombia, Medellín is the obvious choice for the most important fashion event in the country: Colombiamoda. It attracts designers and fashionistas from across the globe, and during this week the Plaza Mayor becomes a fabulous model-fest. Colombiamoda often coincides with the Feria de las Flores.

Feria de las Flores

www.feriadelasfloresmedellin.gov.co; Aug.

The Feria de las Flores is the most important festival of the year in Medellín, when the city is at its most colorful. It's a weeklong celebration of Paisa culture, with horseback parades, concerts, and the highlight, the Desfile de los Silleteros, when flower farmers from Santa Elena show off incredibly elaborate flower arrangements in a parade through the streets. The festival includes a staggering number of events, mostly free of charge, and takes over the city for three weeks.

WINTER

Alumbrado Navideño

On December 7, the Alumbrado Navideño, the city's Christmas light display, begins. The Cerro de Nutibara and the Río Medellín, along with other city sites, are illuminated with 14.5 million multicolored lights. Sponsored by the electric company, it's quite a sight to behold.

Food

The signature dish of Medellín and the coffee region is **bandeja Paisa,** a massive heap of red beans and rice smothered with pork rinds, ground beef, sausage, and egg. Thankfully, Medellín has plenty of other options. Twice a year, typically in April and September, around 75 of the city's top restaurants participate in **Medellín Gourmet** (www.medellingourmet.com), when they offer special prix-fixe menus.

Centro

COLOMBIAN

La Antigua

Carrera 42 No. 49-71; tel. 505/335-9993, 11am-4pm daily; set lunch COP$22,000

A downtown tradition for more than 30 years, La Antigua serves set lunches that including soup, desert, a beverage, and classic mains like grilled liver and chicken in mushroom sauce in the spacious rooms of a massive colonial mansion. Unfortunately they are only open for lunch.

★ Salón Centro

Calle 53 No. 42-13; tel. 301/734-3219; www.saloncentro.co; 10am-9pm Mon.-Sat.; COP$35,000-45,000

Market-fresh ingredients go into creative takes on regional Colombian plates at Salón Centro, in lovingly restored 2nd-floor colonial digs in La Playa. Besides dishes like Pacific prawns in coconut rice, the restaurant is known for their eclectic selection of fruit-infused chicha (a traditional Andean corn fermented drink) and handmade desserts.

CARIBBEAN FUSION

El Acontista

Calle 53 No. 43-81; tel. 4/512-3052; noon-10pm Mon.-Thurs., noon-midnight Fri.-Sat.; COP$20,000-28,000

El Acontista is a café and restaurant by day and a jazz club at night. It has a great bookstore on the 2nd floor and live music on Monday and Saturday evenings. They serve a set lunch (COP$20,000) daily and do an excellent selection of wood-fired pizzas plus salads at night. Sharable plates like marinated tomatoes with cheese and olives go quite well with their wine list.

VEGETARIAN

Govinda's

Calle 51 No. 52-17; tel. 4/293-2000; www.govindas.co; 11am-3pm Mon.-Sat.; COP$18,000

Govinda's is a Hare Krishna restaurant located on Plaza Botero, on the 2nd floor and easy to miss. It serves delicious vegan Indian curry-based lunches, with a salad bar included, at one of the best prices in the city. A tranquil outdoor terrace offers views of the chaos below.

CAFÉS, BAKERIES, AND QUICK BITES

★ El Bohemio del Claustro

Carrera 44 No. 48-18; tel. 314/712-0180; 7am-9pm Mon.-Sat., 9am-4pm Sun.

At the 19th-century temple of San Ignacio and opening onto Parque San Ignacio, which bustles with chess players and an open-air library and is home to magnificent old trees that keep it shady and cool, El Bohemio del Claustro is a great place to grab a coffee and a slice of dark-chocolate cake after a day of exploring Centro. The cavernous café is lined with books and hosts live musical acts on weekends.

El Poblado

COLOMBIAN

Hato Viejo

Calle 16 No. 28-60, Av. Las Plamas; tel. 4/268-5412 or 4/268-6811; www.hatoviejo.com; noon-11pm daily; COP$35,000-50,000

Along Avenida Las Palmas above El Poblado are several large famous grilled meat and **comida típica** restaurants. They are especially popular on weekend afternoons. Under a giant thatched roof in the open air is Hato Viejo, popular for weekend lunch with the gang. On Friday nights they have live music.

CARIBBEAN FUSION

El Herbario

Carrera 43D No. 10-30; tel. 4/311-2537; www.elherbario.com; noon-3pm and 7pm-11pm daily; COP$28,000-40,000

El Herbario has an inventive menu with items such as lemongrass tuna, turmeric prawns, and artichoke risotto. Rooftop seating makes it even more enjoyable. The attached store sells exotic jams, chutneys, and the like.

clockwise arepa de queso; buñuelos, a savory fried bread; Tamagotchi Ramen Bar

La Provincia

Carrera 42 No. 3 Sur-81; tel. 4/322-0192; www.laprovinciarestaurante.com; noon-3pm and 7pm-midnight Mon.-Sat.; COP$65,000-80,000

La Provincia is a Medellín classic, always ranked at the top of the city's restaurant list. It is a fusion of Mediterranean cuisine, with lots of seafood, and Colombian flair. Try for a table on the romantic patio out back. Choose the exotic grilled fish fillet in peanut sauce with green papaya strips. Reservations are advised.

Carmen

Carrera 36 No. 10A-27; tel. 4/311-9625; www.carmenrestaurante.com.co; noon-2:30pm Tues.-Fri., 7pm-10:30pm Mon.-Sat.; COP$85,000-120,000

Rated among the top 50 restaurants in Latin America, Carmen has a fantastic location within an intimate homelike setting, where the backyard is part of the dining room, on the fringes of El Poblado. Reservations are required. The open kitchen allows you to observe the attention to detail while the chefs prepare dishes like roasted duck and spare ribs.

INTERNATIONAL

Ganso & Castor

Carrera 36 No. 7-46; tel. 4/268-9572; 8am-7:30pm Mon.-Sat., 8am-1pm Sun.; COP$16,000-40,000

Stylish French bistro Ganso & Castor serves breakfast anytime and has menu items such as croque monsieur, quiche, steak tartare, and escargot. There are two tables outside. It has a second location at the Museo de Arte Moderno.

★ Tamagotchi Ramen Bar

Calle 10 No. 12; tel. 311/389-3220; noon-10pm daily; COP$26,000-35,000

It's almost worth the trip to El Poblado from the other side of town to experience this authentic Japanese ramen bar, hidden on the unmarked 2nd floor of a corner building across the street from Parque de El Poblado. Decked out with anime and classic Japanese cinema paraphernalia, Tamagotchi is the real thing—the fully spiced soba and udon bowls will not disappoint.

Tabun

Carrera 33 No. 7-99; tel. 4/311-8209; www.eltabun.com; noon-10pm Mon.-Wed., noon-11pm Thurs.-Sat., noon-5:30pm Sun.; COP$35,000

A local favorite since 2008, Tabun serves standard Middle Eastern fare like falafel plates and grilled lamb in generous portions. They also have a few Indian dishes. Belly dancers perform on weekends.

CAFÉS, BAKERIES, AND QUICK BITES

Pergamino Café

Carrera 37 No. 8A-37; tel. 4/268-6444; 10am-9pm Mon.-Fri., 11am-9pm Sat.

If you're feeling decadent, as in you'd like your latte in an actual coffee cup and served to you at a table, try Pergamino Café. It's on a relatively quiet street in the Provenza area.

El Codo de San Lorenzo

Carrera 36 No. 10A-71; tel. 4/580-4022; noon-8pm Mon.-Tues., noon-9pm Wed., noon-11:30pm Thurs., noon-1:30am Fri.-Sat.

They serve food at El Codo de San Lorenzo, but the café's terrace may be nicer for a beer or two on a pleasant spring evening.

Laureles

COLOMBIAN

La Tienda

Carrera 70 Circular 3-28; tel. 4/260-6783; 10am-2am daily; COP$25,000-40,000

A popular place on the Carrera 70 strip is La Tienda. It's a festive restaurant that morphs into a late-night drinking place as the Medellín evenings wear on. Their **bandeja Paisa** is famous.

Mondongo's

Carrera 70 No. C3-43; tel. 4/411-3434; www.mondongos.com.co; 11:30am-9:30pm daily; COP$32,000-50,000

Mondongo's is a well-known popular place for typical Colombian food and drinks with friends. Mondongo is tripe stew, a Colombian comfort food. In addition to the Carrera 70 location is Mondongo's on busy Calle 10 in El Poblado (Calle 10 No. 38-38; tel. 4/312-2346) that is a popular drinking spot. They even have a location in Miami.

INTERNATIONAL

★ Fenicia

Carrera 73 No. C2-41, Av. Jardín; tel. 4/413-8566; www.feniciacomidaarabe.com; noon-8pm Mon.-Thurs., noon-9pm Fri.-Sat., noon-4pm Sun.; COP$20,000-35,000

Fenicia is an authentic Lebanese restaurant run by a family who immigrated to Colombia years ago. **Pastel cartageneros** (rice tamale) are served only on weekends, while delicious desserts like date pastries and fig flan with coconut await after a delicious meal.

VEGETARIAN

★ Salud Pan

Circular 4N 70-84; tel. 604/322-2299; 8am-8pm Mon.-Sat.; COP$22,000-35,000

A restaurant, bakery, and grocery store in one, Salud Pan is a health food lover's dream come true. Besides a variety of set lunches, including a raw food option, the cakes are divine. The market is a great place to stock up on things like cacao, coconut oil, and natural hygiene products.

CAFÉS, BAKERIES, AND QUICK BITES

Trigo Laurel

Circular 1A No. 70-06; tel. 4/250-4943; 24 hours daily

Four in the morning and you've got the munchies? Join the legion of taxi drivers, college kids, and miscellaneous night owls at Trigo Laurel, where it never closes. They specialize in baked goods but also serve cheap lunches. It's on a quiet corner of Carrera 70.

Envigado

INTERNATIONAL

★ Lucio Carbón y Vino

Carrera 44A No. 30S-40; tel. 4/334-4003; noon-midnight Mon.-Sat.; COP$32,000-55,000

With Colombian newspapers plastered on the walls displaying headlines of yesteryear, and tango playing on the stereo, the Argentinian steak house Lucio Carbón y Vino is the right place to enjoy a grilled churrasco-style steak smothered in house-made chimichurri and paired with a nice malbec.

El Barral

Calle 30 Sur No. 43A-38; tel. 4/276-1212; noon-10pm Mon.-Sat.; COP$38,000-55,000

Cozy and chic Spanish restaurant El Barral specializes in paella, tapas, and sangria and does them well in sophisticated surroundings.

Bars and Nightlife

Medellín has many different nightlife districts scattered across the city, but in general the big three are **El Poblado,** where flashy clubs cater to travelers and the upper crust; **Laureles,** which draws the university crowd and has a strip of discos and bars along Avenida 70; and **Centro,** where old school tango bars and artistic live music venues attract a bohemian crowd. Most clubs and live music venues have a cover charge—expect to pay US prices in El Poblado.

LGBTQ-friendly hot spots are in all three of these areas, especially around Parque del Periodista in Centro. The online guide **Guia Gay Colombia** (www.guiagaycolombia.com) has a complete listing of bars.

Centro

BARS AND LOUNGES

Bar El Guanábano

Parque del Periodista, Carrera 43 No. 53-54; tel. 4/216-3742

Working-class locals, intelligentsia, and students converge on the bar-lined Parque del Periodista in the La Playa area to meet friends over a few beers and listen to music. Bar El Guanábano is a faithful and funky friend at the center of it all. Rock like David Bowie plays on the sound system in this dark and cozy hangout, the centerpiece of which is the sacrilegious yet good-natured depiction of the Divino Niño made from the guanábana fruit.

Ubuntu

Calle de Cervantes, Carrera 42A No. 48-39; no phone

A string of bars and hip cafés spill out onto outside tables along the pedestrian-only Calle de Cervantes, each with its own vibe. Ubuntu, which means "I exist because you exist," serves Afro-Pacific food and cocktails, including a borojo fruit-flavored beer, over live music and even livelier conversations. It's good place to meet local amigos.

SALSA, TANGO, AND JAZZ

Salón Málaga

Carrera 51 No. 45-80; tel. 4/231-2658; www.salonmalaga.com; 9am-11pm daily; no cover

The downtown Salón Málaga has plenty of character. It's filled with old jukeboxes and memorabilia and has clientele who come in for a tinto (coffee) or beer during the day. The Saturday tango show (5:30pm) and oldies event on Sunday afternoon are especially popular with locals and travelers, but a stop here is a fine idea anytime.

LGBTQ+

The La Playa area is not only LGBTQ-friendly in general, it's home to a cluster of gay- and queer-oriented dive bars, particularly near Parque del Periodista and toward the Catedral Metropolitana.

Vaqueros

Carrera 40 No. 52-41; tel. 323/332-1909; www.vaqueros.com.co; 6pm-2am daily; no cover

Grab your cowboy hat and chaps and hit the dance floor at this country-themed gay bar right on La Playa. Busy every night of the week, Vaqueros is also big on karaoke. A male-only sauna is located upstairs.

El Poblado

BARS AND LOUNGES

El Social Tienda Mixta

Carrera 35 No. 8A-8; tel. 4/311-5567

Since 1969, El Social Tienda Mixta has been selling basics like soap, sugar, and coffee to neighborhood residents; it's only a recent phenomenon that at night it is converted into bar that provides a breath of authenticity in trendy Provenza. It's so popular on weekend evenings that you can forget about finding a vacant plastic chair.

DANCE CLUBS

Salón Amador

Carrera 36 No. 10-38; www.salonamador.com; cover COP$50,000

Those looking for an all-night electronic music party will find plenty of overpriced and underwhelming options in El Poblado. Fortunately, the folks at Salón Amador, which has been a local favorite for over a decade, flies in international DJs from around the world and is certain to give you the night you have been searching for.

LGBTQ+

Donde Aquellos

Carrera 38 No. 9A-26; tel. 4/312-2041 or 313/624-1485; 4:30pm-2am daily

There is a lively and youthful gay nightlife scene in El Poblado, and Donde Aquellos is an easygoing kind of place near Parque Lleras, with a rooftop terrace where you can mix and mingle as well as watch all the action down below.

Laureles

Dozens of crossover clubs, where the music is a mix of reggaetón, merengue, bachata, and salsa, line Carrera 70 in Laureles. All are good local fun, and the area has a couple of standout options for true salsa purists.

outside Ubuntu on Calle de Cervantes

SALSA, TANGO, AND JAZZ

Son Havana

Carrera 73 No. 44-56; tel. 4/586-9082; www.sonhavana.com; 8pm-3am Wed.-Sat.; cover COP$20,000 weekends

Swanky and hip, mural-covered Son Havana features live local salsa bands on weekend nights and friendly social dancing during the week. Ask about lessons if you are new to the game.

El Tíbiri

Carrera 70 No. 44B-01; tel. 310/849-5461; hours vary Wed.-Sat.; no cover

Unpretentious and friendly, El Tíbiri is a basement salsa and Afro-Colombian music joint on Carrera 70 that is hugely popular on weekends. They say the walls sweat, as after 10pm it gets packed, especially on Friday nights. There is no sign on the door: Look for the stairway heading down and the walls covered with vintage posters.

LGBTQ+

Purple

Calle 10A No. 36-29; www.eslacarta.com/purpleclub; cover COP$30,000

A massive LGBTQ+ electronic music venue, Purple is where people go to dance the night away in an open-minded atmosphere that welcomes everyone.

Accommodations

Lodging to fit every budget and taste is plentiful in Medellín. El Poblado has the most options, with luxury hotels along Avenida El Poblado and hostels and boutiques in the walkable Provenza area, close to a smorgasbord of restaurants and bars and close to the El Poblado Metro station. Laureles is a quiet green residential area with a growing number of options to escape the crowds. Note that Centro is an area that feels unsafe at night. Room rates drop on weekends and vacancies increase.

Medellín is a top destination on the international backpacker trail, and hostels geared to that market have sprung up throughout the city. Hostels have distinct vibes, with chill places clustered in Laureles and the wild places close to the action near Parque Lleras in El Poblado.

Centro

UNDER COP$70,000

★ Centro Hostel

Calle 51 No. 40-65; tel. 314/812-0739; COP$38,000 dorm, COP$120,000 d

With two hammock-strewn balconies overlooking La Playa, a stylish living room, comfy capsule-style dorms, and a fat gourmet breakfast included in the rates, Centro Hostel is one of the best backpackers digs in town. Several cool bars and cafés are right outside, and Teatro Pablo Tobón is half a block away.

Villa de la Candelaria Hotel

Carrera 42 No. 50a-34; tel. 4/239-1172; COP$65,000 d

Simple and straightforward, Villa de la Candelaria offers good deals on 24 well-kept rooms in a good location. It just added a rooftop restaurant to the mix.

COP$70,000-200,000

★ La Playa Hotel

Calle 52 No. 40-122; tel. 300/230-4239; https://laplayahotel.co; COP$110,000 d

Christian, the friendly owner of La Playa Hotel, worked as a waiter in the area for 20 years before opening his dream boutique hotel. The love shows in this restored art deco building's eight rooms, individually decorated with art, live plants, and buddha statues. One in the back has a private garden patio and outdoor fireplace. It's one of the best deals in town.

Apartments Hotel Medellín

Carrera 44 No. 47-02; tel. 301/779-0117; https://appartments.com.co; COP$150,000 d

Twenty-two fully furnished studio apartments, complete with kitchens and some with balconies, make Apartments Hotel Medellín a good choice if you plan to stay in town for a while. The rooftop pool is a refreshing place to cool off and offers spectacular views of the eastern mountains.

El Poblado

Rates in El Poblado are at least double what you find in the rest of the city, often approaching US and European costs.

COP$70,000-200,000

Black Sheep

Transversal 5A No. 45-133; tel. 317/518-1369; www.blacksheepmedellin.com; COP$70,000 dorm, COP$200,000 d

Just minutes from the El Poblado Metro station and sporting a lovely avocado tree-studded backyard patio, Black Sheep has been a backpacker's crash in Medellín for over two decades. A large shared kitchen, a comfy sofa-strewn TV room, and a newly designated coworking space round out the draws.

COP$200,000-500,000

Hotel Zona A

Calle 10B No. 37-69; tel. 4/580-3800; COP$285,000 d

Hotel Zona A is a cute little hotel with 19 small rooms and a nice outdoor terrace where you can have breakfast. The location is perfect, in a surprisingly woodsy area of El Poblado, but there is traffic noise.

★ La Campana Hotel Boutique

Calle 11A No. 31A-70; tel. 4/312-2525; COP$234,000 d

A touch of rustic charm in happening El Poblado is on offer at La Campana Hotel Boutique, a house with 13 rooms and pleasant common areas.

Acqua Hotel

Carrera 35 No. 7-47; tel. 4/448-0482 or 320/788-4424; www.hotelacqua.com; COP$458,000 d

Acqua Hotel is a fairly good value, especially if you want to be in the heart of Provenza. The 43 spotless rooms have nice street views. Staff can arrange tours and other services, including private drivers.

OVER COP$500,000

★ Charlee Lifestyle Hotel

Calle 9A No. 37-16; tel. 4/444-4968; www.thecharlee.com; COP$704,000

Yes, the 40-room Charlee Lifestyle Hotel is awesome: hot tubs on room balconies with a view of Parque Lleras, a massive minibar, a pool on the terrace, a spectacular gym, good food, and a disco.

Laureles

UNDER COP$70,000

Wandering Paisa

Calle 44 A No. 68A-76; www.wanderingpaisahostel.com;

tel. 320/749-2073 or 4/436-6759; COP$35,000 dorm, COP$90,000 d

Wandering Paisa has a social vibe, with the on-site Paisa Bar and frequent events like karaoke. It's close to the Estadio Metro station. There are four dorm rooms, two with eight beds and two with four beds; it's more comfortable to be in a room with four.

★ Yellow House Hostel

Carrera 81A No. 47A-48; tel. 4/411-2873; www.yellowhouse.com.co; COP$55,000 dorm, COP$140,000 d

Between a bed-and-breakfast and a hostel, Yellow House Hostel is a laid-back option on a quiet residential street in Floresta, a 10-minute walk to the Metro station. There are five private rooms, four of them with en suite baths, and one dorm room with six beds. Besides the relaxing and welcoming environs, guests love the breakfast and the fluffy canine residents.

COP$70,000-200,000

Casa Hotel Asturias Medellín

Circular 4 No. 73-124; tel. 4/260-2872; COP$183,000 d

The Casa Hotel Asturias Medellín is a small quiet hotel on a delightful corner of the tree-lined Laureles neighborhood. The 15 rooms are modern and comfortable but not large. It's a good deal for the area.

COP$200,000-500,000

Hotel Tryp Medellín

Calle 50 No. 70-24; tel. 4/604-0686; www.tryphotels.com; COP$350,000 d

Across from the Estadio Atanasio Girardot sports complex, the Hotel Tryp Medellín has 140 large, comfortable, Spartan rooms and an excellent rooftop terrace with a whirlpool tub and a steam room. Guests have access to an on-site gym. Restaurants are nonexistent in this area, except for street food, and hotel room service is iffy. The area revs up when Atlético Nacional is playing.

Information and Services

Visitor Information

Medellín produces the most comprehensive visitor information of any city in Colombia. In addition to information booths at the bus terminals and airports, there is a large office at the **Plaza Mayor** (Calle 41 No. 55-80; tel. 4/261-7277; 8am-noon and 2pm-6pm Mon.-Sat.). The tourism office website (www.medellin.travel) maintains up-to-date information on what's going on in the city.

Emergency and Medical Services

Hospital General de Medellín

Carrera 48 No. 32-102; tel. 604/384-7300; www.hgm.gov.co; 24 hours daily

This giant public hospital offers all medical services, including 24-hour urgent and emergency care. It's so big it even has its own Metro station.

Transportation

Getting There

AIR

Aeropuerto Internacional José María Córdova

MDE; Vereda Sajonia, Rionegro; tel. 4/402-5110 or 4/562-2885

There are two airports serving Medellín, and the main one, with several international flights, is Aeropuerto Internacional José María Córdova in the town of Rionegro, 35 km (22 mi) from the city. Avianca, LATAM, and Clic Air operate domestic flights here.

Taxis cost around COP$100,000 and take 45 minutes between the city and the airport. To go to the airport, call the special **Rionegro airport taxi service** (tel. 4/261-1616 or 313/744-0680; https://acoataxiaeropuerto.com). These white cabs have a blue stripe on them.

There are also busetas (small buses) leaving the airport for the San Diego neighborhood, which is convenient to El Poblado. These can be found to the right as you exit the terminal. Traveling to the airport from Medellín, there are buses (Conbuses; tel. 4/231-9681) that depart from a side street just behind the **Hotel Nutibara** (Calle 52A No. 50-46; tel. 4/511-5111) in Centro. These depart about 4:30am-8:30pm daily, and the trip costs COP$12,000. The buses are hard to miss: They're green and white with the word "aeropuerto" printed in all caps on the front window.

Aeropuerto Olaya Herrera

EOH; Carrera 65A No. 13-157; tel. 4/403-6781; www.aeropuertoolayaherrera.gov.co

Aeropuerto Olaya Herrera is the very convenient in-town airport. It's especially useful for traveling to the Pacific coast and other Colombian cities. From this airport, **SATENA** serves Bogotá, Quibdó, Apartadó, Bahía Solano, and Nuquí; **Clic Air** connects the city with Bahía Solano, Acandí, and Capurganá. The terminal was built in the 1930s and is an architectural gem—you'll love it.

Aeropuerto Olaya Herrera is about 1 km (0.6 mi) from the Poblado Metro stop—it's a safe walk but also an easy and cheap taxi or rideshare trip. Several bus lines serve the airport from different parts of the city.

Getting Around

INTERCITY BUSES

Medellín has two bus terminals: the Sur and the Norte.

Terminal del Sur

Carrera 65 No. 8B-91; tel. 4/444-8020 or 4/361-1186

The Terminal del Sur is across from Aeropuerto Olaya Herrera and serves destinations in southern Antioquia and the coffee region.

Terminal del Norte

Carrera 64C No. 78-580; tel. 4/444-8020 or 4/230-9595

The Terminal del Norte is connected to the Caribe Metro station. It serves Santa Fe de Antioquia and Guatapé, the Caribbean coast, and Bogotá.

METRO

tel. 4/444-9598; www.metrodemedellin.gov.co

Medellín's Metro is the only urban train system in the country. It's a safe and clean system of two lines: Línea A, which runs from Niquía in the north to La Estrella in the south, and Línea B, from San Antonio in Centro west to San Javier. Línea A is useful for traveling between Centro, El Poblado, and Envigado. Línea B has a stop at the stadium, next to the Laureles neighborhood. The current Metro fare is COP$3,200, but if you use the Metro, Metrocable, Tranvía, and Metroplús system on a regular basis, consider purchasing a refillable Tarjeta Cívica card valid on all three. The cost per ride with the Tarjeta Cívica drops to COP$2,800. The card can be purchased at Metro ticket booths.

METROCABLE

The Metrocable public transportation system, consisting of six gondola **(teleférico)** lines, was inaugurated in 2004. It has been internationally lauded as an innovative approach to solving the unique transportation needs of the isolated and poor comunas on the city's mountainsides. The six Metrocable lines are: Línea J from the San Javier Metro station to La Aurora in the west, Línea K from the Acevedo Metro station in the north to Santo Domingo, Línea L from Santo Domingo to Parque Arví, Línea M from the Miraflores Tranvía station to Trece de Noviembre, Línea H from the Oriente Tranvía station to Villa Sierra, and Línea P from Acevedo to El Progresso. The Metrocable runs 9am-10pm daily. Línea L from Santo Domingo to Parque Arví operates 9am-6pm Tuesday-Sunday. When Monday is a holiday, Línea L runs that day and does not operate the next day, Tuesday.

TRANVÍA

Inaugurated in 2015, the Tranvía is a streetcar that runs from the San Antonio Metro station, through the La Playa area, and up the eastern hills to Oriente station. This route was once served by a trolley car system built in the 1940s, but like many cities around the world, it was taken out when cars took over in the 1950s. Its construction has helped to revitalize the historic La Playa and Buenos Aires areas.

Tranvía streetcar

METROPLÚS RAPID BUS

www.metroplus.gov.co

The first line of the Metroplús rapid bus system, with dedicated bus stops similar to those of the TransMilenio in Bogotá, debuted in 2013. There are two Metroplús lines: Línea 1 and Línea 2. Línea 1 connects the working-class neighborhood of Aranjuez in the north with the Universidad de Medellín in the southwest. Línea 2 connects the same two sectors but passes through the Centro and Plaza Mayor area. To access the system, you must use the Tarjeta Cívica, which can be purchased at any Metro station.

TAXIS AND RIDESHARE APPS

Taxis are plentiful in Medellín. You can order them over the phone (tel. 4/444-4444) or use an app like **Easy Taxi, Tappsi,** or **Uber.**

Around Medellín

★ Guatapé

The stone monolith La Piedra dominates the landscape, but the Guatapé area is more than just a big rock: It's a historical pueblo full of recreational activities that keep the crowds from Medellín busy. While Guatapé is doable as a day trip, the charming pueblo is romantic at night, with packed bars and cafés surrounding the main plaza leading to colorful winding streets, and it makes a good getaway.

SIGHTS

Guatapé is a resort town. Aside from La Piedra, it's known for its zócalos, the colorful hand-carved and painted friezes on the lower levels of the town's houses. Many of these honor local traditions such as farming and fishing; others have sheep or other animals; and still others are hot rods or the occasional Pink Panther. A particularly colorful street is the **Calle del Recuerdo** near Parque Principal.

La Piedra Peñol

8am-6pm daily; COP$25,000

Known simply as La Piedra, La Piedra Peñol is a giant rock monolith that soars 200 m (660 ft) from the scenic Embalse Peñol-Guatapé, a reservoir covering 64 sq km (25 sq mi) that is an important source of hydroelectric energy. In front of La Piedra is a statue of Luis Villegas López, the man who first climbed the monolith in 1954. Inspired by a priest, López and two friends took five days to slowly climb up cracks in the rock. They had to deal with a beehive and a rainstorm along the way, adding to the challenge.

Today the rock is one of the top attractions in Antioquia. La Piedra can be visited several ways. You can walk from Guatapé, which takes 45 minutes (sunscreen and water are essential). You can bike it, although the road that winds up to the rock entrance is quite steep. You can take a mototaxi from your hotel (COP$12,000), or you can hop on a Jeep from the Parque Principal (between Carreras 28-29 and Calles 31-32) in Guatapé. Visit in the early morning or late in the afternoon.

Once you're at the bottom of the rock, look up and notice the hundreds of bromeliads growing along the sides of it, then head to the top. The 360-degree views over the reservoir and the countryside are worth the toil of climbing the 700 steps of the ramshackle brick-and-concrete stairwell that is stuck to the rock. To celebrate your feat, you can have a drink at one of the snack bars at the top.

Monasterio Santa María de la Epifanía

www.monjesbenedictinosguatape.org

On a serene mountainside near Guatapé, beyond El Encuentro hostel on the same

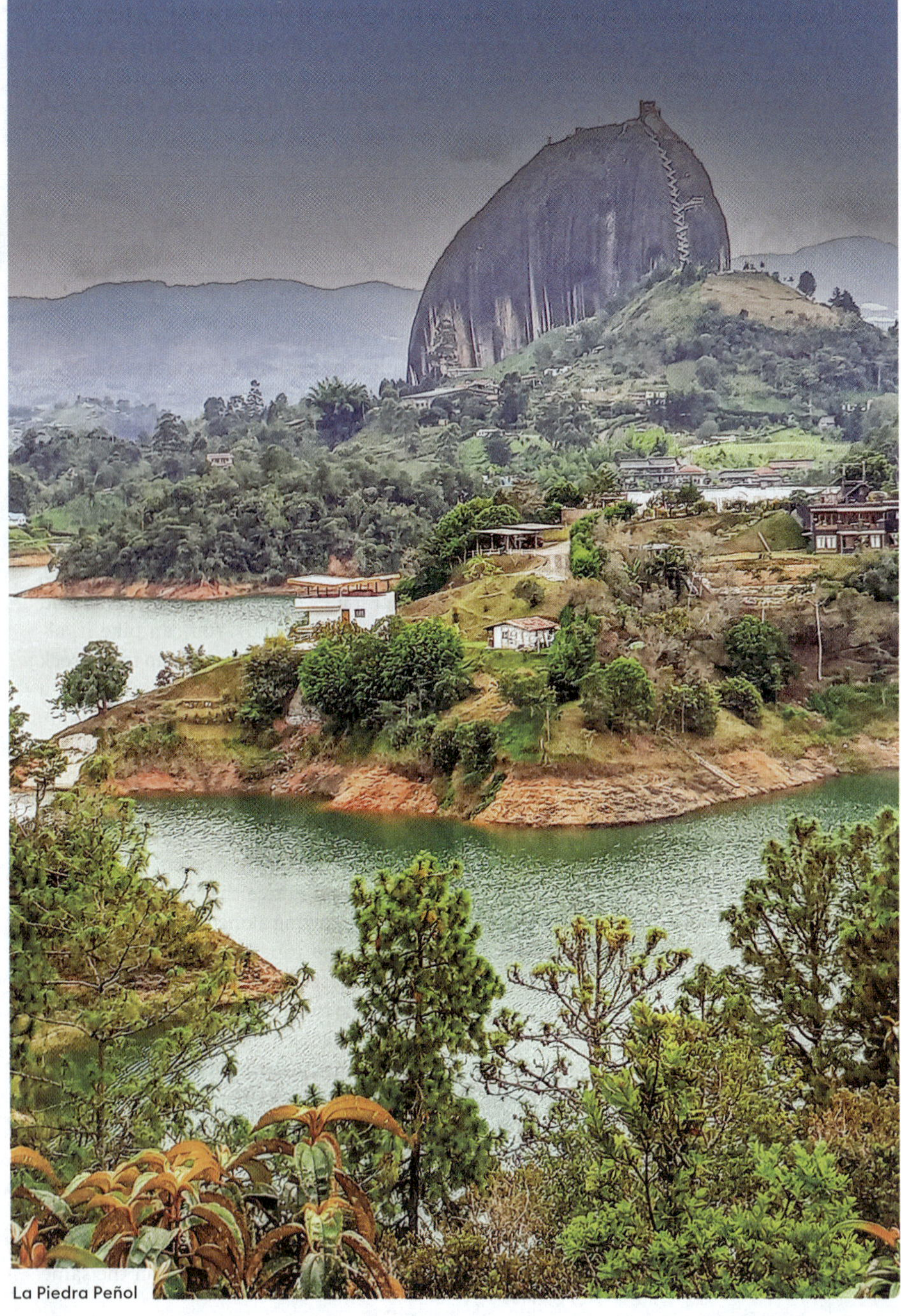

La Piedra Peñol

road, is the Monasterio Santa María de la Epifanía, home to around 30 Benedictine monks. Up to eight guests can stay at the monastery. At the 5:15pm daily **vísperas** (vespers) service, the public is invited to hear the monks sing Gregorian chants.

TOURS

A popular excursion is a **boat tour** of the reservoir (book through Hotel Las Araucarias; tel. 313/646-7946). A standard stop on the tour is above the submerged town of Viejo Peñol. It was flooded during the construction of the reservoir and nearby dam in 1978, and today the only visible remnant of the town is a large cross rising out of the water. A small historical museum displays old photos and historical memorabilia from the town. These tours typically last 45-90 minutes and cost around COP$50,000.

Guatapé Motos

Calle 32 No. 22-09; tel. 313/788-9332; www.guatapemotos.com

Guatapé Motos does fun 1-3-day motorcycle and scooter tours with activities such as visits to the old farms of Pablo Escobar, Hacienda Nápoles and Finca Manuela; tubing; and people-watching at a refreshing waterfall. They can even throw in a paragliding adventure. Guatapé Motos also rents scooters (COP$140,000 per day), perfect for zipping around town and beyond.

FOOD

★ Montano

Carrera 27A No. 30-71; tel. 314/883-6730; 9am-5pm daily; COP$20,000-35,000

Famous for their house-made Greek yogurt-smothered granola-and-fresh-fruit bowl, Montano is the place to fill up on

Guatapé reservoir

real country food before or after climbing La Piedra Peñol.

La Fogata

Carrera 30 No. 31-32; tel. 4/861-1040 or 314/740-7282; 8am-8pm daily; COP$35,000-50,000

Fish such as massive tilapia and trout from the reservoir are the specialty in Guatapé. Of the dozens of restaurants that line the waterfront, La Fogata stands out for its quality and service.

Dulces de Guatapé

Calle 29 No. 23C-32, Barrio Villa del Carmen; tel. 4/861-0724; 7am-6pm daily

Sometimes exceptional hospitality can give you a sugar headache. That's what happens at Gloria Elena's generous candy tastings at Dulces de Guatapé. At this small candy factory, they make all kinds of sweets, many with arequipe (caramel) and some with fruits like the tart uchuva and guava. There are also some chocolate bonbons that have peanuts and almonds.

ACCOMMODATIONS

During the week, rates drop significantly at most hotels, especially if you pay in cash.

Lake View Hostel

Carrera 22 No. 29B-29; tel. 321/493-7060; www.lakeviewhostel.com; COP$40,000 dorm, COP$180,000 d

Nice views from the 4th-floor sun deck and authentic Thai eats at the on-site bar and restaurant make the Lake View Hostel a top choice. The on-site tour agency can also arrange everything from mountain bike tours to fishing trips on the lake.

Hotel El Paisaje

Calle 31 No. 29-12; tel. 304/657-5706; COP$95,000 d

A rooftop café with hot coffee in the morning and live music at night makes staying at Hotel El Paisaje a fun option. The dozen rooms are basic and clean, but the location, one block from the main plaza and just down the street from the Plazoleta de Los Zócalos, can't be beat.

TRANSPORTATION

There is frequent bus service from Medellín's Terminal del Norte to Guatapé. The trip takes about two hours with no traffic and costs COP$20,000. Buses depart Guatapé at a waterfront bus terminal, one block from the main plaza. Buses returning to Medellín often fill quickly on Sunday, especially during holidays. If you are relying on public transportation, book your return bus trip early. The last bus for Medellín departs at 6:30pm.

The Coffee Region

Colombia's coffee region, known as the Eje Cafetero, is a meticulously manicured tropical countryside dotted with beautiful haciendas and towns against a backdrop of massive snowcapped mountains. Nature here is a thousand colors: bright-green bamboo groves, emerald-colored forests with patches of silvery-white yarumo trees, dark-green coffee groves, and green-blue mountains in the distance punctuated by brightly colored flowers and polychromatic butterflies and birds.

And then there is coffee. Coffee grown in some parts of the country, including Cauca and Huila, is considered superior to this region's, but here more than anywhere, coffee is an inseparable part of Paisa identity. The numbers are impressive: The department of Caldas contains 87,000 ha (200,000 acres) of coffee production, Risaralda 54,000 ha (128,000 acres), and Quindío 31,000 ha (74,000 acres), while Antioquia devotes over 110,000 ha (272,000 acres) to coffee, mostly in the south. Visit a coffee farm to understand the laborious production process, or even better, stay overnight.

PLANNING YOUR TIME

It's hard to go wrong as a visitor in the coffee region. No matter your starting point or base, immersion in coffee culture is easy, nearby, and rewarding. If you can, plan to spend about **five days** in this most pleasant part of Colombia to stay at a coffee hacienda, visit a natural park, and tour a picture-perfect pueblo.

If time is short, a quick visit can be rewarding. With easy transportation to major cities and excellent tourism infrastructure for all budgets, **Salento** has the trifecta of coffee region attractions: It's a cute pueblo, coffee farms are within minutes of the main plaza, and epic hikes through tropical forest to the **Valle de Cocora** are easy to organize. The town gets packed with visitors on weekends and holidays, resulting in a more festive atmosphere, but that also means traffic jams.

Day trips to natural parks, including **Parque Nacional Natural Los Nevados,** are easily organized. Los Nevados is home to páramos (highland moors), lunar landscapes, and snowcapped volcanoes. It can be accessed from Salento or Manizales.

> The coffee region is an ideal place for a road trip, stopping at pretty Paisa towns and lush coffee farms along the way. The area between Manizales and Jardín holds hidden jewels like majestic **Salamina,** the lost-in-time former capital of the Caldas department, and **Jericó,** sometimes called the new Jardín.

★ Jardín

Sometimes place-names fit perfectly, as with the picture-perfect Antioquian town of Jardín. The main park is lush year-round with trees and flowers in bloom, and even the streets are corridors of color, lined with brightly painted houses.

The word is out about Jardín. Even so, if you arrive during the week, you'll feel like you've stumbled on something special. On weekends and especially holidays, the atmosphere is festive and the Plaza Principal buzzes with activity. The colorful town is an attraction in itself, especially for shutterbugs, but the cloud forests nearby—with caves, waterfalls, and birds

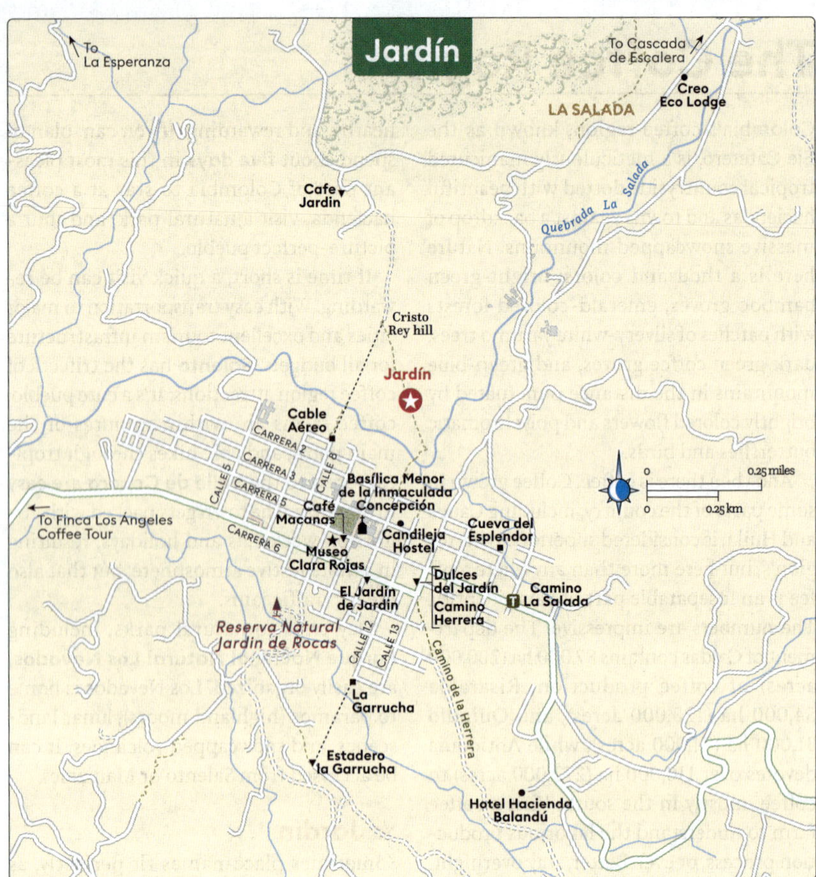

aplenty—provide reasons to lace up those hiking boots.

SIGHTS

Parque Principal

Parque Principal is the center of life in Jardín. It's full of colorful wooden chairs, flower gardens, tall trees that provide welcome shade, and an endless cast of characters passing through, hanging out, or sipping coffee. Prominent on the east side of the park is the neo-Gothic cathedral **Basílica Menor de la Inmaculada Concepción** (Carrera 3 No. 10-71; mass 11am daily), a 20th-century construction with a striking interior painted in shades of turquoise.

Museo Clara Rojas

Carrera 5 No. 9-31; tel. 6/845-5652; http://mcrpjardin.blogspot.com; 8am-noon and 2pm-6pm daily; COP$3,000

The Museo Clara Rojas has 19th-century period furniture and relics from the colonización antioqueña as well as a small collection of religious art, including a painting of

Jesus as a child surrounded by lambs with medals hanging around their necks. The town's tourism office is behind the facility, operating the same hours as the museum.

HIKING

There's almost no better Jardín plan than taking a morning walk. You'll be enchanted by the scenery, reinvigorated by the fresh air, and perhaps get your heart rate up a little as you explore the countryside. There are two fairly easy walks that can be done in a couple of hours and are manageable without a guide; if you get lost, there's always a kind local to point you in the right direction.

Camino Herrera

Distance: 5 km (3 mi) round-trip
Duration: 2 hours round-trip
Elevation gain: 500 m (1,640 ft)
Difficulty: Easy
Trailhead: Dulces del Jardín, Calle 13 No. 5-47

Beginning at the sweets shop Dulces del Jardín, this easy but scenic trail begins on a stone pathway and leads to the Cascada del Amor waterfall and the Charco del Amor swimming hole. The trail then winds up the hillside past gorgeous country houses and small farms to the **Estadero la Garrucha,** a restaurant-café with panoramic views over Jardín that puts out feeders to attract swarms of hummingbirds. From here the trail winds back town to town, ending at the Reserva Natural Jardín de Rocas.

Camino La Salada

Distance: 8 km (5 mi) round-trip
Duration: 3 hours round-trip
Elevation gain: 800 m (2,600 ft)
Difficulty: Easy
Trailhead: Liceo San Antonio, Calle 16 and Carrera 5

The Camino La Salada is a nice loop hike along a country road to the 55-m (175-ft) Cascada Escalera waterfall and back to **Cafe Jardín,** a coffee shop with views galore, and then to Cristo Rey hill, where you can take the cable car back down to town if you wish.

CHAIRLIFTS

Jardín has two mini chairlifts in town. Although they are popular with visitors, they were built so that rural farmers would have an easier way to bring their coffee and other crops to market.

Cable Aéreo

8am-6pm daily; COP$10,000 round-trip

The Cable Aéreo goes from Calle 8 on the eastern edge of town up to the Cristo Rey hill, where you can get off and admire the views and drink a coffee.

La Garrucha

8am-6pm daily; COP$10,000

The rustic La Garrucha goes from the southwest side of town up into the coffee finca-dotted mountains. There is a pleasant restaurant at the turnaround where you can have lunch.

BIRD-WATCHING

La Esperanza

tel. 312/837-0782; USD$120 pp, meals included

La Esperanza is a 30-ha (74-acre) nonprofit nature reserve dedicated to habitat preservation, education, and research. It's on a mountain ridge 15 minutes from town. Sunrises, with a view to Jardín, and sunsets, looking toward the mountains of Los Farallones de Citará, cannot be beat. Of the 400 bird species estimated to live in the Jardín area, this site has registered 175. Also present are numerous mammals: the newly

El Nevado

Plaza Principal in Jardín is the heart of this picture-perfect Antioquian town.

discovered olinguito (a big deal), tayras, two-toed tree sloths, aquatic opossums, northern tamanduas (a tree anteater), and western night monkeys. Nightly rates include all meals.

Reserva Natural Jardín de Rocas

Calle 9 No. 7-184 7-320; tel. 312/756-2650; entry COP$12,000

Just five blocks north of Parque Principal, the Reserva Natural Jardín de Rocas is where you can go to observe the gallina de rocas (Andean cock-of-the-rock, *Rupicola peruvianus*). Flocks of 5-25 of these gorgeous birds, native to the cloud forest, can be seen every morning and evening at this roosting site, where males lek, competing for the attention of females by prancing around and cawing.

TOURS

Cueva del Esplendor

Vereda La Linda; entry COP$7,000, tour COP$95,000 including entry and lunch

One of the most popular excursions in the area is to the Cueva del Esplendor, a cave where water cascades into a chilly natural pool. Groups typically meet in Parque Principal around 8am and take a Jeep Willy 20 minutes to the Alto de la Rosa farm, where the trail begins. There are a couple of river crossings, so rubber boots are needed (ask the tour provider about this). A country lunch is provided, and you may visit a farm where they make panela (brown sugar loaf). To organize a tour, contact **Jardín Eco-Tours** (Calle 9 No. 5-09; tel. 311/373-0631; www.jardinecotours.com), which also offers bird-watching tours and visits to apiaries and coffee farms in the area.

Finca Los Ángeles Coffee Tour

Vereda La Casiana; tel. 300/774-9395; COP$40,000 pp

For a taste of campesino life, take the Finca Los Ángeles Coffee Tour. At this family farm outside town, you take part in a standard coffee tour and then sit together for a delicious home-cooked meal. To participate you must reserve at least 24 hours beforehand.

FOOD

★ El Jardín de Jardín

Calle 11 No. 604; tel. 301/783-0855; 11am-9pm Thurs.-Mon.; COP$18,000-35,000

Tucked away down a side street, El Jardín de Jardín specializes in "green cuisine" in an even greener setting—the restaurant is in what used to be a plant nursery and retains much of the ambiance. From trout smothered in mushrooms to the house-made cacao cake, you will enjoy the food and atmosphere.

La Truchería

Km 5, Vía Riosucio; tel. 4/845-5159; noon-6pm daily; COP$29,000

It's a weekend ritual in Jardín: Spend the afternoon with family and friends at one of the trucheras (trout farms). One of the largest and best-known is La Truchería. Trout is served infinite ways here: a la mostaza (mustard), with fine herbs, and stuffed with vegetables, to name a few.

Café Macanas

Carrera 5 No. 9-43; tel. 313/657-5979; 7am-9pm daily

Café Macanas wins with its massive 2nd-floor terrace overlooking Parque Principal and its dedication to high-quality local coffee. It also has great pastries and light meals.

★ Dulces del Jardín

Calle 13 No. 5-47; tel. 4/845-6584; 8am-6pm Mon.-Sat.

Dulces del Jardín is the candymaker in town. In addition to arequipe (caramel) sweets, they make all-natural jams and fruit spreads (COP$6,000) from pineapple, coconut, and papaya. Enjoying them in the garden patio with a fresh coffee is truly heaven on earth.

ACCOMMODATIONS

If you are planning to visit Jardín on a puente (long weekend) or during holidays, you need to reserve a hotel well in advance. During the week, the town is yours, and rates drop substantially, especially if you plan to pay in cash.

★ Candileja Hostel

Carrera 3 No. 11-50 primer piso; tel. 322/681-8994; COP$40,000 dorm, COP$120,000 d

Run by a young couple from Medellín, Candileja Hostel has everything you need to make your stay in Jardín comfortable. They even printed maps of the surrounding trails so you can explore the area independently. Spacious and spotless dorms, comfy private rooms, plus a shared kitchen, a back patio complete with hammocks, and fresh complimentary coffee all day make it hard to say no.

Creo Eco Lodge

La Salada; tel. 302/442-8024; https://creoecolodgejardin.com; COP$52,000 dorm, COP$145,000 d, breakfast included

Nature lovers will find peace at Creo Eco Lodge, a family-run hostel with comfy dorms and eclectic private rooms just minutes from the **Cascada de Escalera** in the forested hills outside town in the La Salada area. Daily yoga classes are just before the fruit-based breakfast, much of it grown on-site.

Hotel Hacienda Balandú

Km 1, Vía Jardín Riosucio; tel. 4/845-5561; COP$300,000 d

A comfortable choice is the Hotel Hacienda Balandú, on a historic coffee farm with 24 rooms and all the extras: a restaurant, a sauna, and a heated swimming pool. It's a tranquil 15-20-minute walk from town and has a couple of resident peacocks wandering around.

TRANSPORTATION

The bus company **Transportes Suroeste Antioqueño** (tel. 4/352-9049; COP$18,000) leaves Medellín each day bound for Jardín, leaving from the Terminal de Transportes Sur. Jardín's bus companies are two blocks east of Parque Principal.

There is also one bus that departs Jardín for Manizales at 6:30am daily. This route goes south through the town of Riosucio. From there you can board a chiva (rural

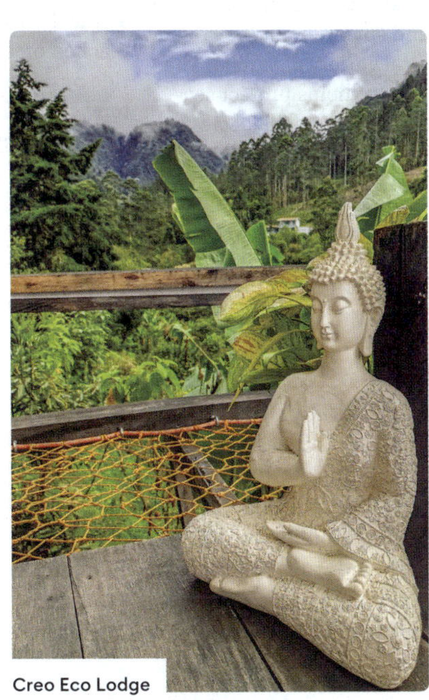

Creo Eco Lodge

CHOCOLATE FOR THE PLANET

Everyone loves chocolate: The global chocolate trade is a USD$300 billion industry, and consumption grew over 20 percent worldwide between 2020 and 2024 alone. But according to the National Wildlife Federation, cacao plantations are a major driver of deforestation on the planet.

In 2018 Colombia became the first country to commit to deforestation-free chocolate production, and since then has become a major producer of sustainable cacao and chocolate products, many of which actually contribute to reforestation and ecosystem revitalization.

RESELVA

Vereda 71, Caracoli; tel. 312/212-8969

A great example is ReSelva, a 1.2-ha (3-acre) cacao cultivation where 1,200 cacao trees grow in the shade of a tropical wet forest that also produces a variety of other fruits and spices, including a local variety of vanilla. The reserve helps protect several endangered species, including the white-footed tamarin *(Saguinus leucopus)*, a gregarious monkey that scampers through the trees in large families.

Overnight stays at the farm (COP$320,000) include a tour of the grounds, an introduction to chocolate making, and all meals. The farm is reached on a 20-minute ride on a jerry-rigged motorcycle hooked to train tracks through the lush Antioquia countryside. The family can arrange to pick you up at your hotel in Medellín or at the airport.

ReSelva's tree-to-bar chocolates are also on sale in many outlets in Medellín, including the gift shop of the Museo de Arte Moderno de Medellín, the Jardín Botánico, and local health food shops like Salud Pan.

bus) bound for Jardín (8am and 3pm Sun.-Fri., noon Sat.). It's a bumpy three-hour journey from Riosucio to Manizales.

Manizales

The capital of the Caldas department, pleasant and easygoing Manizales (pop. 393,200) is a mini city atop meandering mountain ridges. Its location means that getting around involves climbing hills on foot, enduring roller coaster-like bus or taxi rides along curvy roads, or the scenic route on the city's expanding Cable Aéreo gondola network.

Perched above lush coffee farms at an elevation of 2,160 m (7,085 ft), spectacular views abound in Manizales—but only when the sky is despejado (clear). On those days, you might see the peaks of Parque Nacional Natural Los Nevados in the distance. It's easy to visit that park and other sights with Manizales as a base.

SIGHTS

The two main roads in Manizales, Avenida Santander (Carrera 23) and the Paralela (Carrera 25), take you to where you want to go in town. They connect the Zona Rosa-

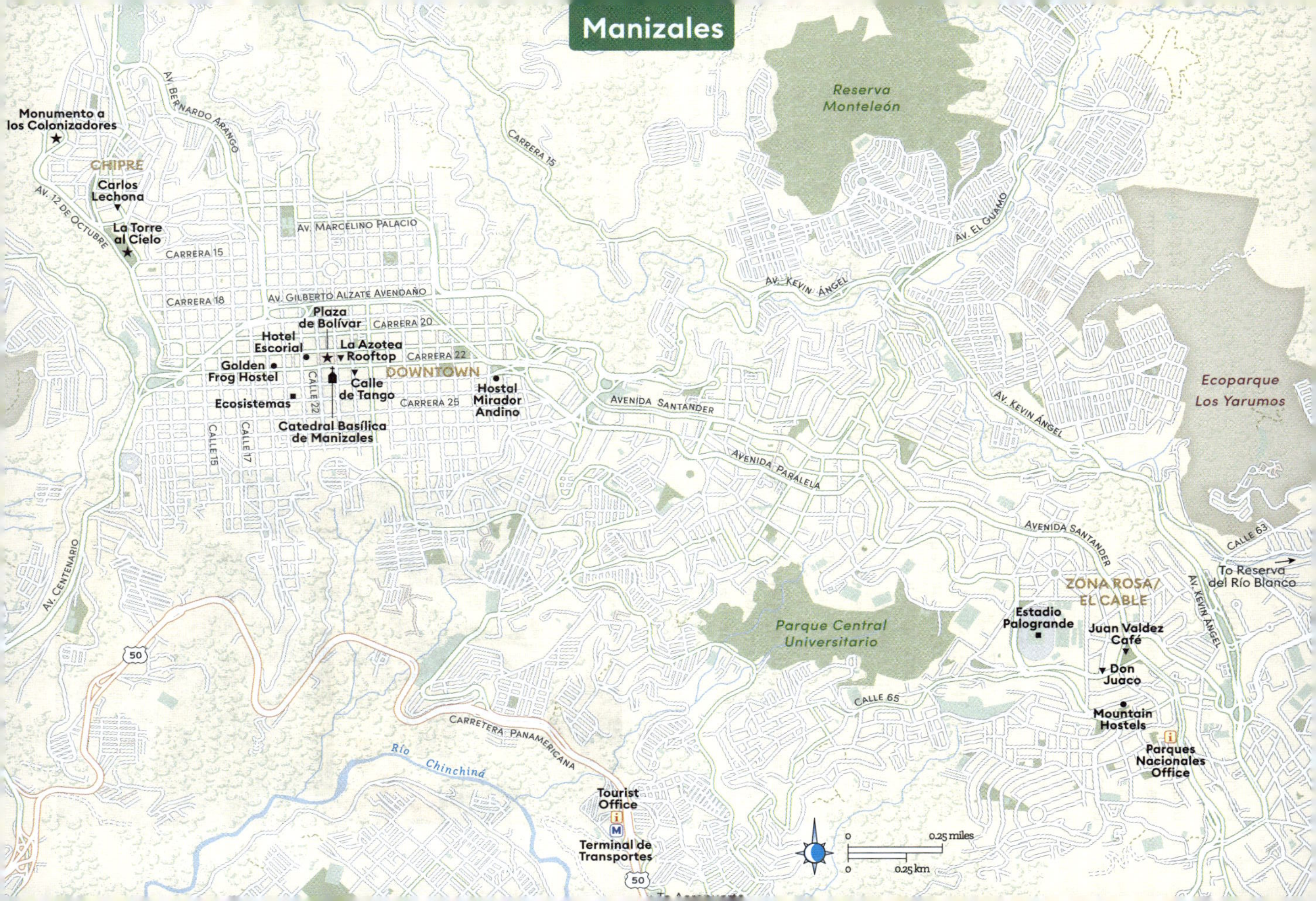
Manizales
Monumento a los Colonizadores
CHIPRE
Carlos Lechona
La Torre al Cielo
Av. 12 de Octubre
Av. Bernardo Arango
Carrera 15
Av. Marcelino Palacio
Carrera 18
Av. Gilberto Alzate Avendaño
Plaza de Bolívar
Carrera 20
Hotel Escorial
La Azotea Rooftop
Carrera 22
Golden Frog Hostel
Calle de Tango
DOWNTOWN
Hostal Mirador Andino
Ecosistemas
Calle 22
Carrera 25
Catedral Basílica de Manizales
Calle 15
Calle 17
Av. Centenario
Reserva Monteleón
Av. El Guamo
Av. Kevin Ángel
Avenida Santander
Avenida Paralela
Ecoparque Los Yarumos
Calle 63
To Reserva del Río Blanco
ZONA ROSA/ EL CABLE
Estadio Palogrande
Juan Valdez Café
Don Juaco
Mountain Hostels
Parques Nacionales Office
Parque Central Universitario
Calle 65
Carretera Panamericana
Río Chinchiná
Tourist Office
Terminal de Transportes
50
0 0.25 miles
0 0.25 km

El Cable area with downtown and Avenida 12 de Octubre, which leads to Chipre and the Monumento a los Colonizadores. A handy Cable Aéreo system connects downtown with the main bus terminal below (COP$2,300).

Downtown Manizales is compact, historic, and bustles with activity day and night. Republican-period architecture, some noteworthy churches, dynamic nightlife that includes old-school tango bars, and tons of traditional cafés give it an authentic Paisa vibe.

Plaza de Bolívar

Carreras 21-22 and Calles 22-23

Plaza de Bolívar holds an odd sculpture to honor Simón Bolívar created by Antioqueño Rodrigo Arenas Betancourt. It's known as the **Condor-Bolívar,** portraying the liberator with the body of a condor, the national bird. On the north side of the plaza is a **tourist office.** It's a great place to grab a coffee and enjoy some people-watching.

Catedral Basílica de Manizales

Carrera 22 No. 22-15; tel. 6/883-1880; until 6:30pm daily

On the south side of the plaza, the neo-Gothic Catedral Basílica de Manizales is imposing. Construction began in the late 1920s and was completed in 1936, replacing the previous cathedral on the same site that had been damaged by earthquakes and had to be demolished. For 360-degree views of Manizales and beyond, climb the 500 steps of the spiral Corredor Polaco (Polish corridor) in Colombia's tallest church tower (9am-noon and 2pm-5pm Thurs.-Sun.). To climb the tower, a guide is required (COP$12,000), although it's hard to imagine getting lost inside.

tango dancers in Manizales

Calle de Tango

Calle 24 between Carreras 22-23

While tango is popular all over the coffee region, and Medellín has an annual tango festival, nowhere is the dance as alive as in Manizales. The Calle de Tango is a solid block of tango salons packed with dancers of all ages almost every night of the week. Several offer nightly groups dance classes before the party starts (usually around 6pm), while the upstairs **Mr. Tango** (Calle 24 No. 22-38; tel. 312/727-6293) can arrange private classes during the day.

Chipre

This neighborhood west of downtown hovers over a dramatic drop to the valley below and is known for its views and sunsets. Manizaleños boast how Chilean poet Pablo Neruda, when strolling on the promenade in Chipre along Avenida 12 de

sculpture in Chipre by Luis Alberto Reyes

Octubre, marveled at this "sunset factory." You're guaranteed a nice view from atop the futuristic lookout tower **La Torre al Cielo** (8am-8pm daily; COP$3,000), which hosts a restaurant as well.

At the far end of the promenade is the **Monumento a los Colonizadores** (Av. 12 de Octubre and Carrera 9; tel. 6/872-0420, ext. 22; 10am-6pm daily; free) designed by Luis Guillermo Vallejo. To get to this part of the city, look for a bus with a "Chipre" sign along Avenida Santander (Carrera 23).

Reserva del Río Blanco

Vereda Las Palomas; tel. 6/887-9770 or 311/775-5159; reservarioblanco@aguasdemanizales.com.co; 6am-6pm daily; COP$20,000

Nearly 400 species of birds have been spotted at the Reserva del Río Blanco, only 3 km (2 mi) outside Manizales. August-March the area receives many migratory birds from North America. This 5,000-ha (12,400-acre) reserve is a must-do for serious birders.

Most visitors ask front-desk staff at hostels or hotels to set things up for them, but you can also reserve your trip ahead of time online (www.reservarioblanco.co). A half-day guided hike costs COP$91,000 per person; some guides speak English. To see birds at their most active, consider staying overnight in one of the park's two guesthouses (COP$206,000 pp), with eight rooms and meals included. Hummingbird feeders dangle along the deck, and there are nearly always customers to be seen. Taxi transportation to the reserve entrance costs COP$35,000 each way from downtown Manizales.

Ecoparque Los Yarumos

Calle 61B No. 15A-01, Barrio Toscana; tel. 6/872-0420, ext. 22; 9am-6pm Tues.-Sun.; free

On undisturbed mountainsides throughout Colombia, you have undoubtedly noticed the silvery-white leaves of the yarumo blanco tree. Should you get a closer look, you'll see that the leaves of this tree are actually green, with a fuzzy outer layer that makes them appear white. Ecoparque Los Yarumos is named for those tricky trees. A few yarumos can be seen in the more than 50 ha (124 acres) of cloud forest and green space of this park. Geared toward families, the park has nature paths, a lookout tower, and activities such as forest zip lines. Get here by taking a bus from the Manizales city center bound for Minitas. It's a 7-10-minute walk from the bus stop to the entrance.

HOT SPRINGS

Near Manizales, on the road to Parque Nacional Natural Los Nevados, are several termales (hot springs). Bring your own towel and sandals and visit on a weekday to avoid the crowds.

Termales Otoño

Km 5, Vía Antigua El Nevado del Ruiz; tel. 6/874-0280; www.termaleselotono.com; 7am-midnight daily; day pass COP$45,000, rooms COP$140,000-380,000 d

Termales Otoño is a large hot springs and hotel complex a 25-minute taxi ride (COP$22,000) southeast of the city. Four pools are divided by islands of leafy trees, although two of the pools are for hotel guests only.

Termales del Ruiz

35 km (22 mi) south of Manizales; tel. 310/455-3588; www.termalesdelruiz.com; day pass COP$18,000

One of the area's old mountain lodges has been given a much-needed facelift. Termales del Ruiz is the most picturesque of the region's hot springs, at 3,500 m (11,500 ft) elevation on the edge of Parque Nacional Natural Los Nevados, 35 km (22 mi) from Manizales and 10 km (6 mi) from its source, the Nevado del Ruiz volcano. There is one large thermal pool as well as a nature path and many bird species on the mountain slopes. Rooms at the hotel (COP$545,000 d) have been completely revamped and are luxurious. The restaurant is good too. There is no public transportation, but you can hire a taxi from Manizales (about COP$200,000) or have your hotel arrange for a hired car (about COP$175,000).

BIKING

Ciclovía

8am-noon Sun., 7pm-10pm last Thurs. of the month

The Ciclovía in Manizales takes place along Avenida Santander (Carrera 23) and other main streets. A **Ciclovía Nocturna** is held the last Thursday evening of each month.

SPECTATOR SPORTS

Once Caldas

www.oncecaldas.com.co

Once Caldas is the Manizales soccer club, and their stadium, the **Estadio Palogrande** (Carrera 25 No. 65-00), is in the Zona Rosa, within walking distance of many hostels and hotels. Tickets can be purchased at the Cable Plaza Mall (Carrera 23 No. 65-11; tel. 6/875-6595; 9am-9pm daily).

FESTIVALS AND EVENTS

Feria de Manizales

www.feriademanizales.gov.co; Jan.

The Plaza de Toros (Carrera 27 10A-07; tel. 6/883-8124; www.cormanizales.com), or bullfighting ring, is the heart of the action during Manizales's biggest annual bacchanal, the citywide Feria de Manizales. The festivities include concerts, the Festival de Trova (ballad festival), and a Miss Coffee beauty pageant.

Colombo Jazz Festival

June

Each year jazz takes center stage at the Universidad de Caldas, the main university in town, during the Colombo Jazz Festival. Quartets from universities in the United States are often invited to perform in this event sponsored by the

Centro Colombo Americano and the US Embassy.

Festival Internacional de Teatro de Manizales

www.festivaldemanizales.com; Sept.

One of the country's top theater festivals is the Festival Internacional de Teatro de Manizales. Theater troupes from Manizales and around Colombia, the Americas, and beyond perform in theaters throughout the city, and free performances are given in the Plaza de Bolívar, El Cable, and other public spaces.

FOOD

Don Juaco

Calle 65 No. 23A-44; tel. 6/885-0610 or 310/830-2218; noon-10pm daily; COP$18,000-24,000

For excellent down-home regional cuisine, head to Don Juaco, serving contented diners for decades. Try the Paisa hamburger, a burger sandwiched between two arepas (cornmeal cakes). Enjoy it or the popular set-lunch meals on the pleasant terrace.

Carlos Lechona

Calle 10 No. 12-04; tel. 315/470-7394; 11:30am-8:30pm Thurs.-Sat.; COP$26,000-40,000

Lechona is a Colombian dish where and entire pig is cooked, the meat is scooped out and stir-fried with rice and peas, and then stuffed back into the skin and served in slices. Crispy and addictive, it's a great hunger crusher for those that have just hiked up to Chipre to enjoy the view. Carlos Lechona knows how to do it to perfection.

★ La Azotea Rooftop

Calle 23 No. 21-45, piso 5; tel. 322/306-8358; www.laazotearooftop.com; noon-10pm Mon.-Sat., noon-6pm Sun.

With 360-degree views over the Manizales skyline, live music on weekends, and a roaring outdoor fireplace, La Azotea Rooftop attracts the hip downtown set to its 5th-floor terrace dining area. The fusion menu includes Peruvian ceviche, pad thai, and lots of Colombian-style meat dishes.

Juan Valdez Café

Carrera 23B No. 64-55; tel. 6/885-9172; 10am-9pm daily

A fantastic place for a late-afternoon cappuccino and snack is the El Cable-area Juan Valdez Café. Yes, it's a chain, and there's one in any self-respecting mall in Colombia. But this one is different: Locals proudly boast that it is the largest Juan Valdez on the planet. What truly sets this one apart is its great location, under the shadow of the huge wooden tower that once supported the coffee cable-car line that ran from Manizales to Mariquita.

ACCOMMODATIONS

Downtown is the most happening place to stay in Manizales. It is historic, walkable, and full of cafés and bars. The El Cable area also draws international visitors looking for something more upscale and suburban.

★ Golden Frog Hostel

Carrera 22 No. 19-11; tel. 315/437-1521; COP$38,000 dorm, COP$100,000 d

On the top floor of a historic republican-style building, this spacious backpacker place has several rooms of stacked-to-the-roof dorms, a handful of comfy doubles, and a large central living space complete with couches and a ping-pong table. The rooftop terrace throws frequent barbecues and social events. It's a great place to trade travel info before setting off into the coffee region.

Mountain Hostels

Calle 66 No. 23B-91; tel. 6/887-4736 or 300/521-6120; www.mountainhostels.com.co; COP$45,000 dorm, COP$120,000 d

One of the long-standing budget accommodations geared toward international travelers in Manizales is Mountain Hostels. Spread over two houses, it has both dorms and private rooms plus a small restaurant where you can order a healthy breakfast. It's also a fantastic source of information.

Hotel Escorial

Calle 21 No. 21-11; tel. 304/142-1807; COP$100,000 d

A four-story 1936 art deco masterpiece in the center of downtown, Hotel Escorial offers nicely remodeled rooms, a swanky on-site café, and a rooftop deck with views of the cathedral.

★ Hostal Mirador Andino

Carrera 23 No. 32 20; tel. 310/609-8141; COP$220,000 d

Hosting 15 rooms decked out with antique furniture and sporting a rooftop terrace bar-restaurant with incredible views, Hostal Mirador Andino is run by a friendly local family who like to make visitors feel at home. It's a perfect location, next to the Cable Aéreo stop and on **Parque Fundadores,** where you can catch a bus to just about anywhere in the city.

INFORMATION AND SERVICES

A **PIT** (Punto de Información Turística; Carrera 22 at Calle 31; tel. 6/873-3901; 7am-7pm daily) can be of assistance in organizing excursions to parks and coffee farms throughout Caldas. A small **tourist office** is in the main hall of the Terminal de Transportes (Carrera 43 No. 65-100).

In case of an emergency, Manizales has a single emergency line: tel. 123.

TRANSPORTATION

Avianca and **Clic Air** serve **Aeropuerto La Nubia** (MZL; Calle 95D No. 36-3; tel. 6/874-5451), about 10 km (6 mi) southeast of downtown. The runway is often shrouded in clouds; because of this the airport is closed 35 percent of the daytime and is always closed at night.

The **Terminal de Transportes** (Carrera 43 No. 65-100; tel. 6/878-5641; www.terminaldemanizales.com) is spacious, orderly, and clean. It is a 15-minute taxi ride to the Zona Rosa. The terminal adjoins the **Cable Aéreo** station, and the cable-car route transports passengers from the terminal (Estación Cámbulos) to the Fundadores station (Carrera 23 between Calles 31-32) in Centro. Buses to Cali and Medellín cost around COP$55,000 and take five hours to either city. Buses to Bogotá cost COP$80,000 and take about nine hours.

Local buses can get you where you want to go in Manizales, but you'll likely have to ask a local which one to take and where to flag it down. To get downtown from the Zona Rosa, take a bus bound for Chipre.

★ Parque Nacional Natural Los Nevados

www.parquesnacionales.gov.co

This national park covers 583 sq km (225 sq mi) of rugged terrain along the Cordillera Central between the cities of Manizales to the north, Ibagué to the southeast, and Pereira to the northwest. A visit to Parque Nacional Natural Los Nevados allows you to enjoy firsthand the stark beauty and intriguing flora and fauna of the upper reaches of the Andes, far above the tree line. Within the park are three snow-capped volcanoes: **Nevado del Ruiz** (5,325 m/17,471 ft), **Nevado del Tolima** (5,215 m/17,110 ft), and **Nevado de Santa Isabel**

(4,950 m/16,241 ft), as well as myriad lakes, such as **Laguna del Otún.**

Most of the park consists of páramo, a unique tropical high-altitude ecosystem, and super páramo, rocky terrain above the páramo and below the snow line. Páramo thrives where UV radiation is higher, oxygen is scarcer, and temperatures vary considerably from day to night and fall below freezing. It is the kingdom of the eerily beautiful frailejones, plants with tall statuesque trunks and thick greenish-yellow leaves. The black-and-white Andean condor, *Vultur gryphus,* with its wingspan up to 3 m (10 ft), can sometimes be spotted gliding along the high cliffs in the park. While it is estimated that there are over 10,000 of the birds on the continent, mostly in Argentina, few remain in Colombia. The population of the endangered birds in Los Nevados ranges 8-15. Other fauna includes oso de anteojos (spectacled bears), tapirs, weasels, squirrels, bats, and many species of birds.

Parques Nacionales has an office in Manizales (Calle 69 No. 24-69; tel. 6/887-1611 or 6/887-2273; 8:30am-4pm Mon.-Fri.). It provides updated information on park conditions.

ORIENTATION

The **northern sector** of the park includes Nevado del Ruiz, with its three craters (Arenales, La Piraña, and La Olleta), and extends south to the extinct Cisne volcano and Laguna Verde. This area is usually accessed from Manizales.

The **southern sector** includes everything from the Nevado de Santa Isabel south to Nevado del Quindío, as well as Nevado del Tolima and the famous Laguna del Otún. Most people access this area from Salento or Pereira.

VISITOR CENTER

turnoff to Las Brisas entry point at Km 43, Vía Manizales-Honda; tel. 6/887-1611; www.parquesnacionales.gov.co; 8am-2pm daily; COP$38,000

Just outside Manizales, a small area from **Las Brisas entry station** to the beautiful and eerie landscape of the **Valle de las Tumbas** (also known as Valle del Silencio) is open to visitors on tours and private vehicles. For current conditions at the Nevado del Ruiz volcano, check the Colombian Geological Service website (www.sgc.gov.co/Manizales.aspx). The cost is COP$61,000 plus COP$20,000 per group for an obligatory guided tour, COP$9,500 if you are in your own vehicle.

HIKING

Nevado de Santa Isabel Trek

Distance: 11 km (7 mi) round-trip
Duration: 6 hours round-trip
Elevation gain: 750 m (2,460 ft)
Difficulty: Strenuous
Trailhead: Conejeras

A spectacular day trek from Manizales is up to the snow line of Nevado de Santa Isabel. It is a long day trip, starting with a bumpy 50-km (30-mi) drive to the border of the park at Conejeras and then a three-hour, 5.5-km (3.4-mi) hike up the canyon of the Río Campo Alegre and then to the snow line. This hike requires good physical condition; it takes you from an elevation of 4,000 m (13,100 ft) up to 4,750 m (15,600 ft) through páramo and super páramo.

While often offered as a day hike, more serious mountaineers can extend the trek to the summit of the Nevado de Santa Isabel (4,950 m/16,241 ft) by camping past Conejeras and doing an early-morning ascent to the top. At sunrise, views of the surrounding high mountain landscape, with Nevado del Ruiz and Nevado del Tolima

TOP EXPERIENCE

 COFFEE FARM-STAYS

There is no better way to enjoy Colombia's coffee culture than completely immersing yourself in it. Hacienda Venecia and Hacienda Guayabal are two of the most highly recommended for coffee tours as well as overnight stays. Both are near Chinchiná, a 30-minute drive from Manizales.

HACIENDA VENECIA

Vereda El Rosario, Vía a Chinchiná; tel. 320/636-5719; www.haciendavenecia.com; coffee tour COP$90,000

Run by Juan Pablo Echeverry, this large working coffee plantation has been in his family for four generations, and the coffee was the first in Colombia to receive UTZ certification for sustainable farming.

The 2.5-hour tour is at 9:30am daily, and a delicious lunch (COP$22,000) is offered at the end. A farm tour by Jeep and private tours can also be arranged if requested in advance.

There are lodging options for all budgets at Venecia. The hostel (COP$54,000 dorm) is in the former quarters of the coffee pickers. In the Casa de Huéspedes (COP$429,000 d) are seven basic rooms, some with private baths. The Casa Principal (COP$600,000 d) has six rooms, some with private baths, along with lovely common areas.

For those staying overnight, other activities at the farm include horseback riding (for an additional fee) and a self-guided birding walk. More than 117 species have been documented here. Guests are permitted to wander at their leisure on six trails.

Getting There

From Manizales, take any bus heading west on the Autopista del Café and get off at Restaurant La Palma (25 minutes; COP$6,000). From there, call the Hacienda, and they will pick you up.

HACIENDA GUAYABAL

Km 3, Vía Chinchiná-Pereira; tel. 314/772-4856 or 315/540-7639; www.haciendaguayabal.com; tour COP$60,000

Hacienda Guayabal has a jaw-dropping setting, with mountains and valleys covered in coffee crops and guadua (bamboo) enveloping the hacienda. It has been in Doña María Teresa's family for over 50 years. Tours (COP$60,000) around the finca take about two hours. You can hike up to a spectacular lookout on a mountainside for breathtaking views.

Accommodations in a handful of rooms (COP$85,000 pp) are simple and comfy, and Guayabal is known for its delicious meals. Near the guesthouse, just past the pool, is a small coffee bar made from guadua and recycled floor tiles. Guayabal occasionally hosts meditation retreats.

Getting There

To get to Guayabal, take an Autolujo bus (COP$5,000) or a shared taxi from Manizales to Chinchiná. From Chinchiná it's about COP$12,000 for a taxi to the hacienda. Regular cabs from Manizales are also an option.

a coffee farm in the coffee region

in the background, are magnificent. The ascent to the top requires specialized gear.

Asdeguias (Calle 25 No. 20-25; tel. 6/884-4525 or 314/507-4735; www.asdeguiascaldas.org) and **Ecosistemas** (Carrera 24 No. 20-29; tel. 6/880-8300 or 312/705-7007; www.ecosistemastravel.com.co) both offer the Nevado de Santa Isabel tour from Manizales for around COP$300,000, with all meals and equipment included. You'll have to get up with the chickens, though: You'll be leaving town at 4am.

Laguna del Otún Trek

Distance: 20 km (12 mi) round-trip
Duration: 3 days round-trip
Elevation gain: 2,300 m (7,550 ft)
Difficulty: Moderate
Trailhead: Salento

A popular three-day trek from Salento is to Laguna del Otún. This hike first passes through the famous Valle de Cocora before reaching the entrance to Parque Nacional Natural Los Nevados. The next day is spent exploring the páramo around the lagoon, often shrouded in thick cloud cover, giving the area a mystical feel. The third day is the return hike to Salento. Numerous agencies offer this trek, including **Salento Trekking** (Calle 5 No. 3-61; tel. 313/654-1619; https://salentotrekking.co), and the average cost is around USD$100.

Santa Rosa de Cabal

Ready to soak up some atmosphere? Do as the Colombians do and head to the hot springs of Santa Rosa de Cabal. Start at **Parque las Araucarias** (between Carreras 14-15 and Calles 12-13), the main square, where there are juices to be drunk, chorizo santarosano sausages to be devoured (a specialty here), handicrafts to be bought, and people to be watched.

SIGHTS

Monumento al Machete

Parque Gonzalo Echeverry, Carrera 16N No. 12-77; www.monumentoalmachete.blogspot.com.co

The Monumento al Machete is a small plaza with what are assumed to be the largest machetes in the world at 4.5 m (15 ft) long. There's food, beer, and souvenir stalls at this quirky homage to Paisa masculinity.

HOT SPRINGS

There are two termales (hot springs) near Santa Rosa de Cabal: Termales de Santa Rosa de Cabal and Termales San Vicente. Both can get packed with Colombian families on weekends and holidays. Go during the workweek, when it's less a scene and prices drop.

Termales de Santa Rosa de Cabal

Km 9, Vía Termales; tel. 6/364-5500; www.termales.com.co; 9am-11:30pm daily; COP$55,000 Feb., Sept., and weekdays, COP$75,000 weekends and high season

Built in 1945, the hot springs of Termales de Santa Rosa de Cabal is just outside Santa Rosa de Cabal. A taxi should cost no more than COP$15,000. The complex is at the base of some spectacular cool mountain waterfalls, the tallest dropping 175 m (575 ft). You can stay the night at three on-site hotels (COP$620,000 d, including 3 meals). The advantage is that you can use the pools from 6am, before the day-trip crowd begins arriving at 9am; the drawback is that the rooms are not luxurious, and the food doesn't receive raves either. There are additional activities, such as a guided nature walk (COP$22,000) to some waterfalls. Wear shoes with traction, as the path is slippery. Spa treatments are available, including massages (30 minutes; COP$75,000).

THE LAND OF BUTTERFLIES

With 3,672 registered species, Colombia is home to more species of butterflies than any other country. To put this in perspective, all of Europe has around 400 species, while the continent of Africa lists 4,000.

Over 200 of Colombia's butterfly species are endemic, meaning they are only found within the country, usually only within a particular eco-system. With several of Colombia's ecosystems in danger, including the tropical dry forest, home to nearly 700 species of butterflies, biologists warn that the country must take action now to prevent the permanent loss of unique butterflies, some of which are important pollinators.

Ioruhama eyemark

JARDÍN BOTÁNICO DE QUINDÍO

Km 3, Vía al Valle, Calarcá; tel. 6/742-7254 or 310/404-5223; www.jardinbotanicoquindio.org; 9am-4pm daily; tour in English COP$47,000

Action is being taken. Shaped like a huge butterfly and used to breed over 1,500 species of the winged marvels, including all the endemic ones, the mariposario (butterfly farm) at Jardín Botánico de Quindío is the largest and most important in the country.

After breeding the butterflies, the mariposario releases them into the wild in the hope that they will breed again in their natural habitat and help strengthen numbers throughout the country. The botanical garden is home to a 12-ha (30-acre) rainforest, part of it containing old-growth trees and all of it bursting with flowers, which give the butterflies a nice place to get used to being free. A five-story lookout tower in the garden allows you to see the butterflies and the many bird species that live here as they dance around the forest canopy.

Call in advance to inquire about English-speaking tours. It's easy to get to the park using public transportation from Salento or Manizales. First take a bus to Armenia, and then from the terminal, take a bus to the pueblo of Calarcá (20 minutes; COP$3,000).

Termales San Vicente

18 km (11 mi) east of Santa Rosa de Cabal; tel. 6/333-3433; www.sanvicente.com.co; 8am-midnight daily; COP$85,000 including transportation

Termales San Vicente are remote hot springs, but the scenery of rolling hills, distant mountains, and farms is enchanting. Particularly scenic are the pozos de amor, small natural pools the size of whirlpools that fit two. Several plans can include lunch, massage treatments, and visits to a nearby river hot spring. On-site luxury cabins for up to four people run COP$500,000. Taxis from Santa Rosa de Cabal cost COP$30,000-40,000.

FOOD AND ACCOMMODATIONS

The bucolic countryside outside Santa Rosa de Cabal is home to many roadside family-style restaurants and lodging options.

Mamatina

Km 1, Vía Termales, La Leona; tel. 311/762-7624 or 314/767-2519; www.mamatinahotel.com; 9am-10pm daily; COP$35,000

On the road toward Termales de Santa Rosa de Cabal, Mamatina specializes in trout covered with sausage, sancocho (a meaty stew), grilled meats, and beans and rice. Adjoining the restaurant is a hotel of the same name, with clean comfortable rooms ranging COP$65,000 per person to COP$195,000 for the suite with a hot tub. Horseback riding and walks through the countryside can be arranged.

★ Hospedaje Don Lolo

Km 5, Vía Termales San Vicente; tel. 316/698-6797; COP$50,000 pp d

The Hospedaje Don Lolo is on a farm with cows, pigs, fish, horses, and dogs. If you're interested, you can lend a hand milking a cow or two. Some walks through the countryside are options, such as to an old Indigenous cemetery, to a big waterfall, and through the rainforest to see birds and butterflies. There are six rooms with private baths that open onto a lush patio and an on-site restaurant that serves regional fare, including **bandeja Paisa** (COP$35,000).

TRANSPORTATION

To get to Santa Rosa de Cabal from Salento, first take a bus to Pereira (1 hour; COP$8,000), then take the buseta from the Pereira terminal to Santa Rosa de Cabal (20 minutes; COP$4,000).

★ Salento

On the western edge of Parque Nacional Natural Los Nevados, Salento (pop. 7,000) is a one-stop town for a quintessential coffee region experience. An enchanting pueblo home to coffee growers and cowboys, Salento is adorned with the typical colorful balconies and facades of Paisa architecture. It was one of the first settlements in the region during the 19th-century colonización antioqueña. In the nearby countryside, coffee farms dominate the landscape, and you can do a coffee tour in which you harvest coffee beans, learn about the bean-to-bag process, and sip the freshest coffee you've ever tasted.

Within minutes east of town is the Valle de Cocora, with forests of palma de cera (wax palm, Colombia's national tree), the skyscrapers of the palm family. Some reach 60 m (200 ft) tall. For a more challenging hike, continue to the Reserva Acaime, a private nature reserve of tropical forest, babbling brooks, and not a few hummingbirds. From here adventurers can ascend into the páramo and eventually the snow-capped peaks of Parque Nacional Natural Los Nevados.

Salento is loaded with hostels, hotels, and restaurants catering to visitors. For fewer crowds, go during the week. During high seasons around New Year and Semana Santa, it can be a nightmare, with long traffic jams on the road into town. At times authorities close the roads, not allowing any visitors into town.

SIGHTS

Calle Real

between Calles 1-5

Parque de Bolívar, or **Plaza Principal,** is the center of town and the center of activity. The festive pedestrian Calle Real, lined by restaurants and shops painted

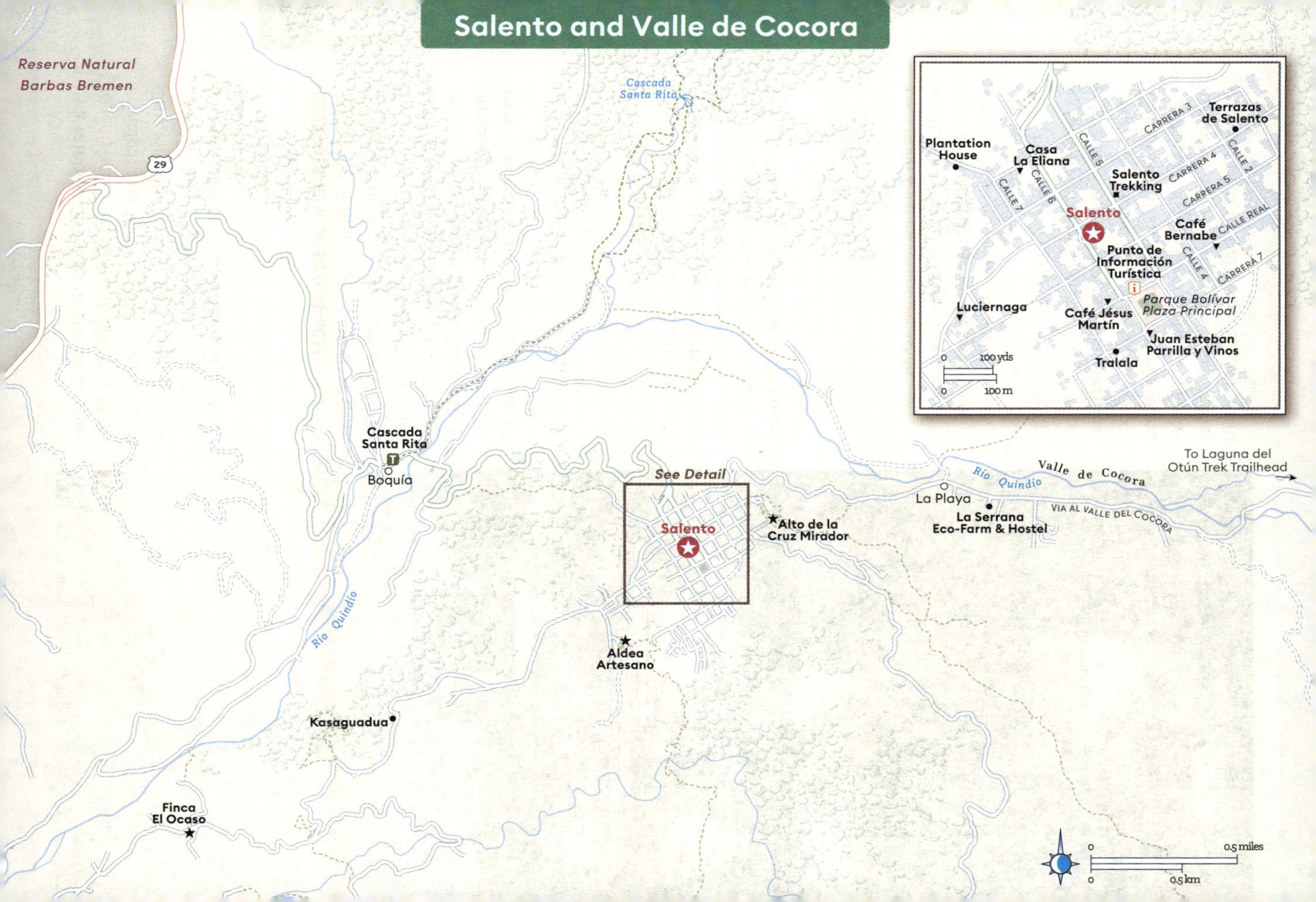

Salento and Valle de Cocora
Reserva Natural
Barbas Bremen
29
Cascada
Santa Rita
Cascada
Santa Rita
Boquía
Río Quindío
See Detail
Salento
Alto de la
Cruz Mirador
Aldea
Artesano
Kasaguadua
Finca
El Ocaso
La Playa
La Serrana
Eco-Farm & Hostel
Río Quindío
Valle de Cocora
VIA AL VALLE DEL COCORA
To Laguna del
Otún Trek Trailhead
Plantation
House
Casa
La Eliana
Terrazas
de Salento
Salento
Trekking
Café
Bernabe
Punto de
Información
Turística
Parque Bolívar
Plaza Principal
Luciernaga
Café Jésus
Martín
Juan Esteban
Parrilla y Vinos
Tralala
CARRERA 3
CARRERA 4
CARRERA 5
CARRERA 7
CALLE 2
CALLE 4
CALLE 5
CALLE 6
CALLE 7
CALLE REAL
0
100 yds
0
100 m
0
0.5 miles
0
0.5 km

in a rainbow of colors, is the most photogenic street in town. It starts at Plaza Principal and leads up to the **Alto de la Cruz Mirador,** a scenic lookout with a nice view of Salento. Farther on is another lookout with views of the surrounding forests and valleys.

Aldea de Artesano

tel. 315/436-6850 or 312/868-8633

About a 10-minute walk southwest from the town center, near the cemetery, is the Aldea de Artesano, a funky artists commune where jewelers, weavers, painters, and musicians live and work. Browse their workshops and participate in a class. The artists enjoy sharing their craftsmanship with visitors. Aldea de Artesano is in a peaceful setting, with a short nature path and a community garden.

COFFEE TOURS

On the outskirts of Salento are two very popular coffee tours. Your experience may vary depending on your guide and their English abilities (or your adeptness in Spanish). Tours typically last 1-1.5 hours. Tack on an hour or so if you plan to walk from Salento.

Finca El Ocaso

Km 3.8, Vía Salento-Vereda Palestina; tel. 310/451-7329; cafeelocaso@hotmail.com; www.fincaelocasosalento.com; tours in English 9am, 11am, 1pm, and 4pm daily; COP$50,000

Finca El Ocaso is a family-run farm with 12 ha (30 acres) of coffee crops that produces coffee with several international certifications, such as the European UTZ and the Rainforest Alliance. Elevation is around 1,780 m (5,800 ft), a good altitude for growing coffee. If you're doing the tour as a day trip and plan to walk, you can do a full

loop, starting from the Puente Amarillo in Salento and returning along a river to Boquía, then taking a bus back to Salento. Visitors can also spend the night in one of four cozy rooms (COP$317,000 d).

Finca Don Eduardo Coffee Tour

Calle 7 No. 1-04; tel. 316/285-2603; www.theplantationhousesalento.com; tours in English 9:30am and 2:30pm Mon.-Sat.; COP$40,000

The Finca Don Eduardo coffee tour is run by the owners of the Plantation House hostel, Tim and his Colombian partner, Cristina. This gorgeous land has been a working coffee farm for over 80 years. The farm grows four subvarieties of arabica coffee and has a nice open-air kitchen where you can stay for lunch or dinner after a tour. There are waterfalls to visit nearby. The tour leaves from Plantation House.

HORSEBACK RIDING

Don Álvaro

tel. 311/375-1534; 3-hour trip COP$50,000 pp

For the real Paisa experience, horseback riding is a good way to enjoy the fresh air and birdsong of the hilly back roads near Salento and Boquía. In Parque de Bolívar there are usually horses at the ready, especially on weekends. Don Álvaro treats his horses well and is considered the best guide for this activity.

BIKING

Most hostels and hotels can arrange bike rentals. The dirt roads around Salento, which lead to coffee farms, waterfalls, and scenic lookout points, make for endless two-wheeled exploration.

Caution: The winding paved road leading into town from the Valle de Cocora does not have a shoulder for bikes. Vehicles tend to speed along this road, making this a dangerous stretch for cyclists and pedestrians.

HIKING

Cascada Santa Rita

Distance: 4.5 km (2.8 mi) round-trip
Duration: 3-4 hours round-trip
Difficulty: Moderate
Trailhead: Monteroca campground

A popular day hike takes you to Cascada Santa Rita, a 15-m (50-ft) waterfall and swimming hole in the tropical forest north of Salento. The starting point is near the Monteroca campground in Boquía. There's a small fee to visit the waterfalls, as they are on the Santa Rita farm property. It's best to contract an experienced local guide such as **Salentour** (tel. 312/288-0579; www.salentourcafetero.com), which is run by Ananda and Andriego, a local couple who focus on the ancestral history of the area. The cost of this guided day hike is COP$102,000.

Valle de Cocora

The main attraction for many visitors to Salento is seeing the palmas de cera (wax palms) that shoot skyward in the Valle de Cocora. These are some of the tallest palms in the world, reaching 50-60 m (160-200 ft), and they can live over 100 years. They have beautiful, smooth, cylindrical trunks with dark rings. In 1985 the species was declared the national tree of Colombia. **Día del Arbol Nacional** (National Tree Day) is celebrated on September 16 with gusto, including seed planting and other events.

Valle de Cocora is a 15-km (9-mi) section of the lower Río Quindío valley. The starting point for the loop is the blue gate after the last building in the Vereda de Cocora. There may be a sign for Acaime,

a street in Salento

which is what you want. After walking about 4 km (2.5 mi) through pasture, you'll enter the dense cloud forest. After 3 km (2 mi) you reach **Reserva Acaime** (tel. 321/636-2818 or 320/788-1981; COP$8,000), a private cloud forest reserve. With the entrance fee you can enjoy a complimentary cup of hot chocolate, agua de panela (a hot sugary drink), or coffee and watch the throngs of hummingbirds.

After energizing and warming up a little at Acaime, backtrack 1 km (0.6 mi) and then climb a steep path to **La Montaña** (elevation 3,000 m/9,800 ft), where a nice lookout awaits. From La Montaña you descend back to Vereda del Cocora through hills and valleys adorned with towering wax palm trees. It's a cinematic experience. From Valle de Cocora, there are many longer hikes into the mountains and even into Parque Nacional Natural Los Nevados, including the three-day Laguna del Otún trek. You will need a guide for these trips, and luckily, Salento is fully stocked with them.

To get to Vereda del Cocora from Salento, take the 20-minute Jeep Willy ride (COP$5,800), which leaves Parque de Bolívar at 6:10am, 7:30am, 9:30am, 11:30am, 2pm, and 4pm daily. On weekends there can be a massive line for the Willys, so plan accordingly. The last Willy back to town departs at about 5pm.

Salento Trekking (Calle 4 between Carreras 6-7; tel. 313/654-1619; www.salentotrekking.co) may be the most professional trekking outfit around, as the multilingual owners lead every hike. The company offers 2-5-day hiking trips for all fitness levels and takes care of everything. A three-day trek is COP$650,000

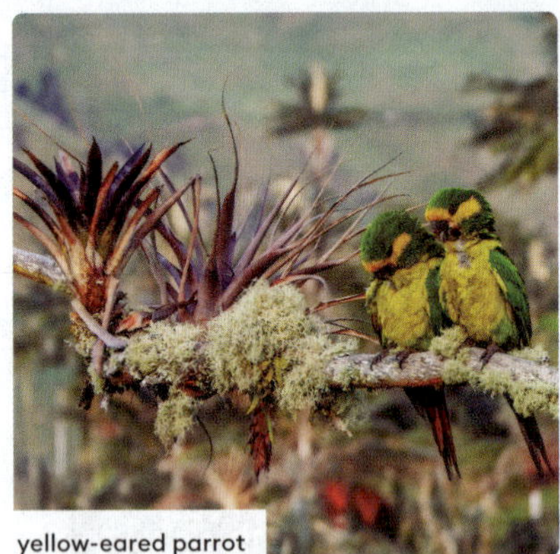

yellow-eared parrot

per person. **Páramo Trek** (tel. 311/745-3761; www.paramotrek.com) is also recommended. They have a four-day trek from Salento all the way to Manizales, crossing the entire Parque Nacional Natural Los Nevados in the process.

FOOD

★ Casa La Eliana

Carrera 2 No. 6-45; tel. 314/660-5987; 10am-9pm daily; COP$26,000-55,000

It's a treat to discover a restaurant like Casa La Eliana, where great service, a cozy atmosphere, and fantastic food are the norm. This Spanish-run spot a few blocks from the center of town is the only local place where you can find both Indian and Thai curry dishes and gourmet pizzas on the menu. Try as they might, the friendly cocker spaniels aren't allowed to mingle with diners.

Juan Esteban Parrilla y Vinos

Carrera 7 No. 5-45; tel. 315/410-1059; 9am-10pm daily; COP$35,000-58,000

With a fantastic location on Parque de Bolívar, Juan Esteban Parrilla y Vinos is a popular place, with beautiful photographs

Valle de Cocora

of local scenery on the walls and a big menu of traditional Colombian dishes. It's a grilled meat place but it happily accommodates vegetarians.

Café Bernabe

Carrera 6, Calle Real No. 3-29; tel. 318/393-3278, 3pm-9pm daily; COP$40,000-60,000

On a quiet side street, Café Bernabe is the gourmet address in Salento, serving delicious coffee and desserts along with interesting main dishes like filet mignon with blackberry and coffee sauce. The outdoor terrace is perfect for a sunny Salento afternoon.

Luciernaga

Carrera 3 No. 9-19; tel. 310/425-0197; 7am-11:30pm daily

Luciernaga is swanky, with great views from the 2nd-floor balcony, and offers fine drinks and comfort food. Friday-Saturday nights have live music. This is the best place in Salento for a sundown cocktail.

★ Café Jesús Martín

Carrera 6 No. 6-14; tel. 6/759-3282; www.cafejesusmartin.com; 8am-8pm daily

Hands down, the finest and fanciest café in this coffee-region pueblo is Café Jesús Martín, a family-run coffee producer. It runs on-site tastings and excellent coffee tours, with transportation included, to the Finca Santana near the town of Quimbaya.

ACCOMMODATIONS

La Serrana Eco-farm and Hostel

Km 1.5, Vía Palestina Finca; tel. 316/296-1890; www.laserrana.com.co; COP$22,000 dorm, COP$55,000 d

La Serrana Eco-farm and Hostel is on a bluff with lovely views of coffee farms in every direction. Nine rooms of various types and sizes are comfortable, and there is a women-only dorm. Camping is available (COP$12,000). It's a peaceful place where you can enjoy sunrises and sunsets, walk into town, or just hang out. La Serrana is best known for its delicious and nutritious family-style dinners and other meals. Vegetarians always have options, and the cooks make an effort to buy local fresh food.

★ Tralala

Carrera 7 No. 6-45; tel. 314/850-5543; www.hostaltralalasalento.com; COP$38,000 dorm, COP$120,000 d

One of the best hostels in the area is Tralala. It's hard to miss this in-town option: It's a two-story white house with bright-orange wooden trim. The owner, Hemer, has been in town for over two decades and hails from the Netherlands. Staff are friendly and knowledgeable, and the kitchen is a pleasant area to hang out and chat with others. There's a sundeck and garden area in case relaxation is needed.

Plantation House

Alto de Coronel, Calle 7 No. 1-04; tel. 316/285-2603; www.theplantationhousesalento.com; COP$58,000 dorm, COP$95,000 d

Londoner Tim's Plantation House, with 24 rooms, remains one of the top places to get to know Salento and the surrounding areas. Catering to international visitors, this hostel has two houses, one of them over 100 years old. Plantation House can organize bike excursions, horseback riding, hikes to Valle de Cocora, and more. Making life easier, it can also take care of airport transfers to Armenia and Pereira.

It is an environmentally friendly hostel: Solar panels enable hot showers, and a rainwater collection system provides water. Tim also runs the coffee farm **Finca Don Eduardo.**

★ Kasaguadua

2.5 km (1.6 mi) south of town; tel. 313/889-8273; www.kasaguaduanaturalreserve.org; COP$150,000 d

Kasaguadua is a 12-ha (30-acre) Andean rainforest nature reserve outside town. Several of the trails can be visited by nonguests for interesting guided walks. The true Kasaguadua experience is to stay a few nights in one of the half dozen geodesic pods, called EcoHabs, that owners Nick and Carlos built themselves out of guadua, a local variety of bamboo. Meals are communal with staff and fellow travelers. The very popular tours (COP$20,000-50,000) generally last 3-3.5 hours and begin promptly at 9am. At least 82 species of birds inhabit the area, and birders will want to rise early to spot them. A Jeep Willy to Kasaguadua from Parque de Bolívar in Salento costs about COP$12,000.

MOON

AUTHOR TIP

Love Salento but hate the crowds? Check out its smaller and far less popular twin, Filandia, just 30 minutes by taxi from Salento or 45 minutes by bus from Armenia.

Terrazas de Salento

Carrera 4 No. 1-30; tel. 317/430-4637; COP$465,000 d

Terrazas de Salento has seven rooms in gorgeous understated Scandinavian style, a beautiful backyard garden area, and views of the pueblo. It's quiet, with tons of natural light, and furnishings are made of natural materials.

INFORMATION AND SERVICES

Hostels usually provide the best visitor information, and most have maps, but there is also a good city-run tourist kiosk, the **PIT** (Punto de Información Turística; 10am-5pm Wed.-Mon.), in front of the alcaldía (city offices) in Parque de Bolívar.

TRANSPORTATION

To get to Salento from Manizales, first take a bus to Armenia (1.5 hours; COP$12,000). From Armenia there are buses (COP$8,000) every 20 minutes to Salento, with the last COTRACIR bus at 9pm. Bus service is more frequent on weekends. Buses to Armenia (every 20 minutes 6am-9pm daily; COP$8,000) depart from Parque de Bolívar. **Flota Occidental** (tel. 321/848-4158 to reserve) buses to Medellín (COP$75,000) depart at 9:30am and 4pm.

Armenia is also home to **El Aeropuerto Internacional El Edén** (AXM; Calle 23 No. 22-08; tel. 6/747-9400), served by most national carriers and with daily direct flights from Fort Lauderdale, Florida, on Spirit Airlines (www.spirit.com).

Chocó

You fly into the department of Chocó over green mountains, part of the Cordillera Occidental, punctuated by orderly Antioquian pueblos and pastureland. But then the rainforest begins: thick tropical forest in a thousand shades of green. This lowland tropical forest, second only in biodiversity to the Amazon, begins to rise with the hills as you pass over the smaller Serranía del Baudó mountain range, one of the rainiest places on Earth. If you look down you will notice the tops of these low mountains shrouded in clouds. Every once in a while a chocolate-brown river meanders westward through the forest, and tiny Afro-Colombian and Emberá communities of thatched or zinc roofs appear alongside it. Here rivers are the only means of transportation, as it has been for centuries. Just after the captain announces the initial descent, you'll find yourself above the turquoise coastal water of the Pacific.

Don't expect wireless internet, regular cell phone service, or 24-hour electricity at your hotel along the coast. There are internet cafés in the towns, such as Bahía Net in Bahía Solano, but connection speeds are slow.

A recommended tour agency, affiliated with the Humpback Turtle hostel in El Valle, is **Pacífico Tours** (www.pacificotours.com). This outfit prides itself on its commitment to the environment and community and specializes in surfing (COP$1,300,000 pp), fishing, and rainforest adventures (COP$350,000 pp). **Xawak Travel** (tel. 315/613-2625; https://xawak.co) specializes in cultural immersion travel and offers several all-inclusive tours to the Chocó region each year, particularly during whale-watching season.

★ Bahía Solano

Many visitors arrive at the tiny Bahía Solano airport and go straight to the village of El Valle, about 22 km (14 mi) away, or the hotels on the beaches of Playa El Almejal. But Ciudad Mutis, as Bahía Solano is officially named, after a famed botanist, is actually a good base for your visit. Excellent diving and whale-watching excursions can be arranged from here. Although it's the largest town on the Chocó Pacific coast, Bahía Solano is small, and everywhere is accessible on foot.

Nice rainforest walks to swimming holes fed by crystalline freshwater waterfalls are within walking distance of town, and depending on the tide, you can walk to the beaches of **Punta Huína** and **Playa Mecana.** These can also easily be reached by boat. During low tide, the bay becomes a soccer field; when the tide comes in, it's a place to cool off.

WHALE-WATCHING

July-October the Pacific just off Bahía Solano is a major migratory route for humpback whales, and they are easy to spot just a mile or two from the coast. It's estimated that over 2,000 adults pass by, often with their offspring. The season is a major economic driver, and many local fisherfolk offer whale-watching tours on their craft. Most last 2-3 hours and cost COP$50,000-80,000. Alternatively, you can book an all-inclusive 4-6-day whale-watching expedition from **Eco-Global Expeditions** (tel. 310/823-3974; https://ecoglobalexpeditions.com) that includes lodging and food at the award-winning El Almejal Eco-Lodge and a trained marine biologist guide.

Chocó
Choibaná Casa
Punta Huína
Jardin Botanico de Pacifico
Playa Mecana
PACIFIC OCEAN
Quebrada Mecana
Bahía Solano
Bahía Solano
La Marea
CALLE 2
Posada Turística Rocas de Cabo Marzo
CRA. 3
Virgen de la Loma
CRA. 2
CALLE 2
Posada Turística Hostal del Mar
Hospital
CRA. 1
0 100 yds
0 100 m
See "Bahía Solano" Detail
Bahía Solano
Cascada del Aeropuerto
Aeropuerto José Celestino Mutis
Río Chadó
CHOCÓ
Playa El Almejal
To Cascada El Tigre
Humpback Turtle
El Mirador
Playa El Almejal
El Almejal
PACIFIC OCEAN
Posada Don Ai
0 50 yds
0 50 m
To El Valle
Cascada El Tigre
PACIFIC OCEAN
See "Playa El Almejal" Detail
Río Valle
Río Valle
Doña Rosalía
El Nativo
El Valle
0 1 mile
0 1 km

BIODIVERSITY IN CHOCÓ

howler monkey

One of the most biodiverse regions in the world, the **Chocó Biogeográfico** comprises a wide swath of rainforest from Panama to Ecuador, bordered by the Pacific Ocean to the west and the Andes to the east. The Colombian part of this region includes an amazing 8,000 plant species, of which 2,000 are endemic. In comparison, all of Canada, which is hundreds of times larger, has 3,270 plant species, of which 140 are endemic. In addition there are 838 species of birds, 261 amphibians, 188 reptiles, and 180 mammals.

Some creatures that call the region home include leatherback turtles, colorful poison dart frogs, red-capped manakin birds (the moonwalking birds), and basilisk lizards, called the Jesus lizard for its impressive running-on-water skill. The relative isolation of this region has resulted in a high level of endemism of about 25 percent. It is one of the wettest places on Earth, with annual rainfall of 10,000 mm (390 in), with some places registering up to 20,000 mm (790 in). Due to the high rainfall, this biodiversity hot spot boasts one of the densest river networks in the world, with dozens of major arteries, including the Baudó, San Juan, and Patía.

To see as much of this incredible biodiversity in one place as possible, visit the **Jardín Botánico de Pacífico** (Playa Mecana; tel. 320/686-9523; www.jbdp.org; COP$60,000 including a guided tour). This 163-ha (403-acre) rainforest preserve is on the beach and has its own on-site hotel (COP$320,000).

HIKING

There are three easy walks around Bahía Solano. These paths are maintained by a group of community members with the help of high school students who have posted signs to point the way.

Punta Huína, Playa Mecana, and the **Cascadas Cocacola** can also be reached on foot from town in under two hours. You may want to go with a guide—hotels can arrange one—at least the first time, and find out the day's tide information before heading out. If the tide comes in, you have to take a boat back to town.

Cascada Chocólatal

Distance: 2.2 km (1.4 mi) round-trip
Duration: 1 hour round-trip
Elevation gain: Negligible
Difficulty: Easy
Trailhead: West side of Bahía Solano

On the west side of town is the trail to Cascada Chocólatal, which leads along a river to a roaring 5-m (16-ft) waterfall. This hike doesn't require a local guide, but hiring someone with trained eyes may be helpful to point out the occasional colorful frog, lizard, bird, or humongous spider.

Virgen de la Loma

Distance: 2 km (1.2 mi) round-trip
Duration: 1 hour round-trip
Elevation gain: 200 m (660 ft)
Difficulty: Easy
Trailhead: Hostal del Mar

The Virgen de la Loma path is a climb through lush vegetation to the top of a hill with a nice view of the bay. The entrance to the trail is well marked, 20 m (66 ft) from Hostal del Mar. For this hike you'll need no guide.

Cascada del Aeropuerto

Distance: 2 km (1.2 mi) round-trip
Duration: 1 hour round-trip
Elevation gain: Negligible
Difficulty: Easy
Trailhead: Across the street from the airport

This hike leads to a towering rainforest waterfall. You won't need a guide, but it is not impossible to become lost. Follow the stream and note that it eventually veers to the left.

DIVING

Morena (moray eel), mero (grouper), tiburón (shark), tiburón ballena (whale

Playa El Almejal in Bahía Solano

shark), pargo (snapper), and pompano are some of the species divers may view off the Pacific coast. You'll likely spot larger species than the colorful tropical fish observed in the Caribbean. A popular trip is to the shipwrecked Colombian navy vessel *Sebastián de Belalcázar,* northeast of Bahía Solano. Note that diving in the Pacific may be more expensive than elsewhere due to the higher price of gasoline. Most hotels and hostels in town, particularly expert diver-run **Posada Turística Hostal del Mar,** can organize diving expeditions.

FOOD AND ACCOMMODATIONS

Most hotels in Bahía Solano have on-site restaurants, and there are also tons of informal fish shacks along the beach. Freshly caught snapper, tuna, and swordfish are all specialties.

La Marea

Bahía Solano; tel. 312/793-3787; COP$40,000-80,000

A standout option for fresh seafood, including steaming house cazuela de mariscos that will keep you full for days, this family-run eatery is on the waterfront on the west side of town.

★ Posada Turística Hostal del Mar

Carrera 3 and Calle 1; tel. 4/682-7415 or 314/630-6723; hostaldelmarbahiasolano@yahoo.com; COP$70,000 d

There are a handful of good lodging options near the bay, each of which can organize whale-watching, diving, and other excursions. Posada Turística Hostal del Mar is run by Rodrigo Fajardo and Estrella Rojas. They are pioneers in the area in terms of community organizing and ecotourism. The property has four comfortable cabins amid gardens filled with orchids, chickens, and a lazy cat named Julia. Meals, often served with homemade ají (hot sauce), are on a picnic table in this miniature tropical paradise.

Rodrigo is a certified diving instructor, and you can learn that sport in the Pacific with him or arrange a diving trip if you already know what you're doing. A nearby shipwreck is a popular place for underwater exploration. Both he and Estrella know the area exceptionally well and can coordinate day trips and can give you pointers to make the most of your stay. Estrella has a small tienda in the arrivals area of the airport, where she sells handicrafts made by locals.

Posada Turística Rocas de Cabo Marzo

Carrera 1 and Calle 2; tel. 4/682-7525 or 313/681-4001; bahiatebada@hotmail.com; 3 nights COP$280,000 pp d with meals and activities

Posada Turística Rocas de Cabo Marzo is a cozy lodge-like guesthouse with five rooms. Rates include airport pickup and drop-off, all meals, and excursions such as rainforest hikes and walks to nearby beaches. The small hotel restaurant might be the only place in the forest where you'll find homemade pizza. It's open daily but only for guests.

In addition to fishing and diving expeditions, Rocas de Cabo Marzo organizes visits to the Estación Septiembre sea turtle hatchery (COP$80,000), a walk to the Playa and Río Mecana (COP$120,000 for 2 people) with the return by boat, and a specialized expedition to see poisonous frogs as well as howler monkeys and sloths in the rainforest with an Indigenous Emberá guide. A day trip with two dives costs COP$250,000, while a day of catch-and-release sportfishing costs COP$1,500,000, including all equipment.

Choibaná Casa

Playa Huína; tel. 310/878-1214 or 312/548-2969; www.choibana.com; COP$160,000 d with breakfast

Choibaná Casa is a cute colorfully painted wooden house on the beach 2 km (1.2 mi) from lively Punta Huína. Five rooms include one spectacular hut set majestically atop a rock. It's a 20-minute boat ride from Bahía Solano, and the property can take care of airport pickup (COP$50,000).

INFORMATION AND SERVICES

There is an **ATM** at the **Banco Agrario.** You can access the internet at **Bahía Net,** but the connection is very slow.

There is a small **hospital** (Calle 3 near Carrera 1; tel. 314/812-8476) in Bahía Solano as well as a **pharmacy.**

TRANSPORTATION

The only way to get to Bahía Solano is by plane. Military-owned **SATENA** has flights between the convenient Aeropuerto Olaya Herrera in Medellín and Bahía Solano's airport, **Aeropuerto José Celestino Mutis** (BSC), about 3 km (2 mi) southwest of town. **Clic Air** (www.clicolombia.com) offers flights to Bahía Solano from Aeropuerto Olaya Herrera as well. Two small charter airlines also serve the region: **TAC** (tel. 4/361-0945 or 1/413-5819; www.taccolombia.com) and **Selvazul** (tel. 4/362-2590 or 4/352-8560; www.selvazul.net) both fly from Aeropuerto Olaya Herrera in Medellín. For information and reservations on the charters, you'll need to call.

If you have a reservation, most hotels will pick you up at the airport. This is the worry-free recommended way to go. Otherwise it costs COP$5,000 by mototaxi to get to Bahía Solano from the airport, only 2 km (1.2 mi) from the town.

El Valle

This fishing community south of Bahía Solano is authentic, if grubby, with wooden houses lining unpaved and often muddy streets. Just outside town, a 15-minute walk north, is **Playa El Almejal,** a broad beach with hotels set against the forest. The beach is home to thousands of cangrejos fantasmas (ghost crabs) scurrying about at a speed of up to 20 km/h (12 mph). The gray-sand beaches are often covered with driftwood, but during the spectacular sunsets, the pastel sky is perfectly reflected on the wet sand. The water is great for jumping in the waves, bodysurfing, and surfing.

SIGHTS

Estación Septiembre Sea Turtle Hatchery and Release Program

Playa La Cuevita, 5 km (3 mi) south of El Valle, contact Fundación Natura in Bogotá; tel. 1/245-5700; csolano@natura.org.co or sgalan@natura.org.co

August-December, female olive ridley sea turtles return to local beaches, to the same spot where they were born, to lay up to 80 eggs. Around 40-60 days later the eggs hatch. At Estación Septiembre Sea Turtle Hatchery and Release Program, turtle eggs are collected from the beaches and protected from stray dogs, birds, and humans. They remain protected in the sand until the turtles are born, after which the baby turtles are released into the ocean. Witnessing one of these releases, most common in September, can be the highlight of a visit to the Pacific coast. Run by the Fundación Natura, the program is administered by the community-based **Fundación Caguama** (*caguama* means sea turtle in the Emberá language).

Estación Septiembre can be visited for the day at any time of year, but it's best to contact them in advance so they can coordinate your visit. A small donation may be requested. You can also stay in one of the three simple rooms at the Estación Septiembre (contact Fundación Natura, Bogotá; tel. 1/245-5700; csolano@natura.org.co or sgalan@natura.org.co; COP$50,000 pp, meals additional COP$50,000 pp).

To get to the Estación Septiembre, take a mototaxi along the beach (COP$8,000) from El Valle. There is also a fairly well-marked path that takes 1.5-2 hours to walk from El Valle to Parque Nacional Natural Utría. Estación Septiembre is at Km 4 of the path.

Cascada El Tigre

There are some pleasant excursions near Playa El Almejal. Cascada El Tigre can be reached by boat (COP$85,000, including a guide), and the fall of cool water in secluded cove makes for an unforgettable shower massage. Local fisherfolk moonlight as tour guides, meaning prices can be negotiated.

BARS AND NIGHTLIFE

El Mirador

Playa El Almejal

Shops in El Valle sell snacks and usually have seating if you want a cold drink or beer among the locals. Besides these, the best option by far is El Mirador. Hard to miss, it's the only multicolored bar on a boulder on the beach. It's between Humpback Turtle and El Almejal, and only open Sunday afternoon, when it gets packed with mostly locals. Visitors are more than welcome.

FOOD AND ACCOMMODATIONS

At most guesthouses in the region, don't expect hot showers or air conditioning, except perhaps at higher-end places.

Doña Rosalía

El Valle, past the internet café; no phone; COP$25,000

Home-cooked meals are on offer in the small but immaculate casa of Doña Rosalía. If you can't find it, just ask around; everybody knows Rosalía. If you have a special request—lentils or beans instead of fish, for instance—let her know by dropping by beforehand.

★ Humpback Turtle

Playa El Almejal; tel. 314/766-8708 or 312/756-3439; thehumpbackturtle@gmail.com; www.humpbackturtle.com; camping or hammock COP$20,000 pp, COP$65,000 dorm, COP$175,000 d

When you first walk up from the beach, you pass through several enormous boulders, and then the Humpback Turtle suddenly appears. Nestled at the edge of the forest, this colorful beachside hostel, started by an American, has a dorm room with six beds and four private rooms as well as a campsite. With an organic garden, composting, water conservation measures such as dry toilets, and reuse of plastic water bottles as construction material, this is by far the most environmentally minded option in the area. It's also a fun place to hang out. Staff have many ideas on adventurous excursions and can assist with arrangements. Options include trips to the Cascada El Tigre waterfall (COP$85,000), rivers (COP$60,000), and Indigenous Emberá communities. Sportfishing (COP$150,000) trips and, of course, outings to observe humpback whales, one of the main draws to the region, can also be arranged.

El Nativo

Playa El Almejal; tel. 311/639-1015; nativo58@hotmail.com; COP$80,000 d with meals

Between Playa El Almejal and the town of El Valle, El Nativo has two simple cabins with four rooms total made from natural materials such as guadua (bamboo) and palm leaves. Run by locals, they can organize day-trip excursions.

Posada Don Ai

Playa El Almejal; tel. 314/651-1160 or 320/662-7014; COP$135,000 pp with meals

On Playa El Almejal, Posada Don Ai is a relaxed place with nine small cabins, each with a porch and a hammock. Meals, usually fried fish, patacones, rice, and salad, are included in the room rates and served under a breezy thatched-roof dining area overlooking the Pacific. It's quite good value. Even if you are not staying here, you can stop by for a meal.

★ El Almejal

tel. 4/412-5050; www.almejal.com.co; COP$350,000 pp with meals

Just beyond Posada Don Ai on the beach is El Almejal. This eco-conscious award-winning lodge and nature reserve, with airy tastefully done cabins, is a consistent favorite for a little more comfort. One of the pioneers of ecotourism in the region, El Almejal has been around since the 1980s. Today there are 10 cabins, plus 2 in the forest along a bird-watching trail. Organized early-morning bird-watching walks are available.

El Almejal has its own organic garden, and the restaurant is probably the best in the area. Electricity is available 24 hours a day and some cabins have hot water. Staff can arrange many excursions and activities for guests. This lodge is also the best place to stay for birders as staff are knowledgeable and can organize bird-watching itineraries. Some of the 800 species in the area include the rare harpy eagle, snowy cotingas, endangered and endemic Baudó oropendolas, toucans, and tanagers. May-June is dolphin time, and El Almejal can take guests to spot them frolicking in the Pacific.

INFORMATION AND SERVICES

There is no ATM in El Valle. There is a **pharmacy** in El Valle.

TRANSPORTATION

To get to El Valle and Playa El Almejal on your own from the Bahía Solano airport, take a mototaxi or truck (from COP$26,000 pp). Much of the road to El Valle through the forest has been paved. The 18-km (11-mi) trip takes about 45 minutes.

Cali and Southwest Colombia

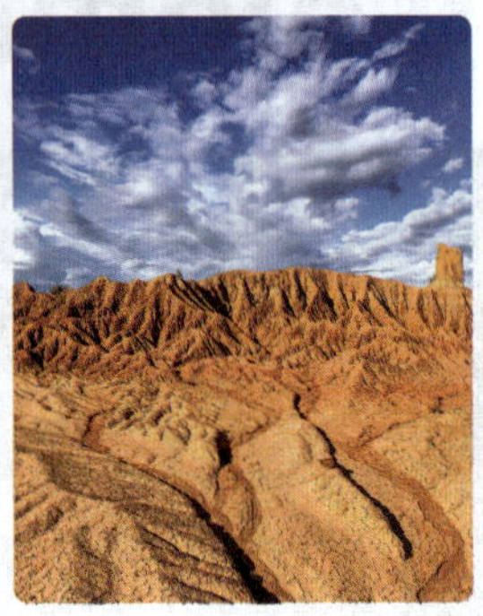

★ Highlights

★ **Salsa in Cali** *(upper right):* Dance the night away in the famous salsa clubs of Colombia's Afro-Latin capital (page 308).

★ **Parque Nacional Natural Farallones de Cali** *(upper left):* Spot an incredible number of bird species amid rainforest-covered peaks (page 317).

★ **San Cipriano:** Take the "brujita" to pristine rivers and waterfalls of this lost-in-the-forest paradise (page 320).

★ **Popayán's Centro Histórico** *(lower left):* Explore the impressive cathedrals and churches of the White City (page 325).

★ **Desierto de Tatacoa** *(lower right):* Pitch a tent under the star-filled sky in the high desert (page 333).

★ **San Agustín:** Visit the mysterious pre-Columbian stone statues of this magical coffee town (page 335).

Look for ★ to find recommended sights, activities, dining, and lodging.

◂ view from Parque Artesanal Loma de la Cruz

Things move at a slower pace in Cali and the southwest, at least during the daytime. Colombia's third-largest city is dubbed the Salsa Capital of the World because of its legendary nightlife. Balmy Cali also has some museums and historic neighborhoods worth checking out and an impressive culinary scene heavily influenced by the Pacific coast, connected by highway.

Along the way, small rainforest towns sit on the banks of crystalline rivers. North of the port city of Buenaventura, several beach resorts and small seaside fishing villages cater to vacationing Caleños and are attracting a growing number of international visitors.

South of Cali the elevation climbs and the culture becomes more Indigenous, reminiscent of Ecuador and Peru. This area is also home to some of the country's most important archaeological sites, including San Agustín and Tierradentro, as well as incredible national parks and gorgeous historic towns like Popayán, the "White City." Naturally, southern Colombia is a super biodiverse wonderland that contains Pacific rainforests, the high Andes, lush river valleys, and the Tatacoa desert, one of the few arid regions in the country.

Orientation

CALI

Nearly all the city's attractions are in **El Centro** in three areas: **La Merced, La Ermita,** and **Plaza de Cayzedo-Iglesia San Francisco.** You can visit these areas on foot in one day. El Centro is brimming with activity on weekdays. Avoid the midday heat by visiting in morning or late afternoon. At night El Centro is also the center of nightlife.

Inviting neighborhoods such as historic **San Antonio,** upscale **Granada,** and classy **El Peñón** are a delight, and because they are just a short walk or cab ride from El Centro, they also make good bases.

SOUTHERN COLOMBIA

Cali is in the fertile Valle de Cauca backed by the Farallones de Cali mountain range. On the other side of this range is the Pacific coast, and south of Cali the three Andean cordilleras of Colombia come together to form the Macizo Colombiano. This mountainous wonderland was home to some of the country's most advanced pre-Columbian civilizations and still hides many lost-in-time treasures.

Planning Your Time

Three days is just enough time to get a feel for the Cali way of life. Visit over part of the weekend so that you can go to a salsoteca (salsa club) or simply enjoy the street party on the Bulevar and La Calle del Sabor.

It's an easy trip between Cali and Popayán, about three hours by minivan on a good road. To check out sights near Popayán, such as the Guambiano Indigenous town of Silvia, or to hike to the Puracé volcano, plan for at least 3-4 days in the capital of Cauca. A circuit tour

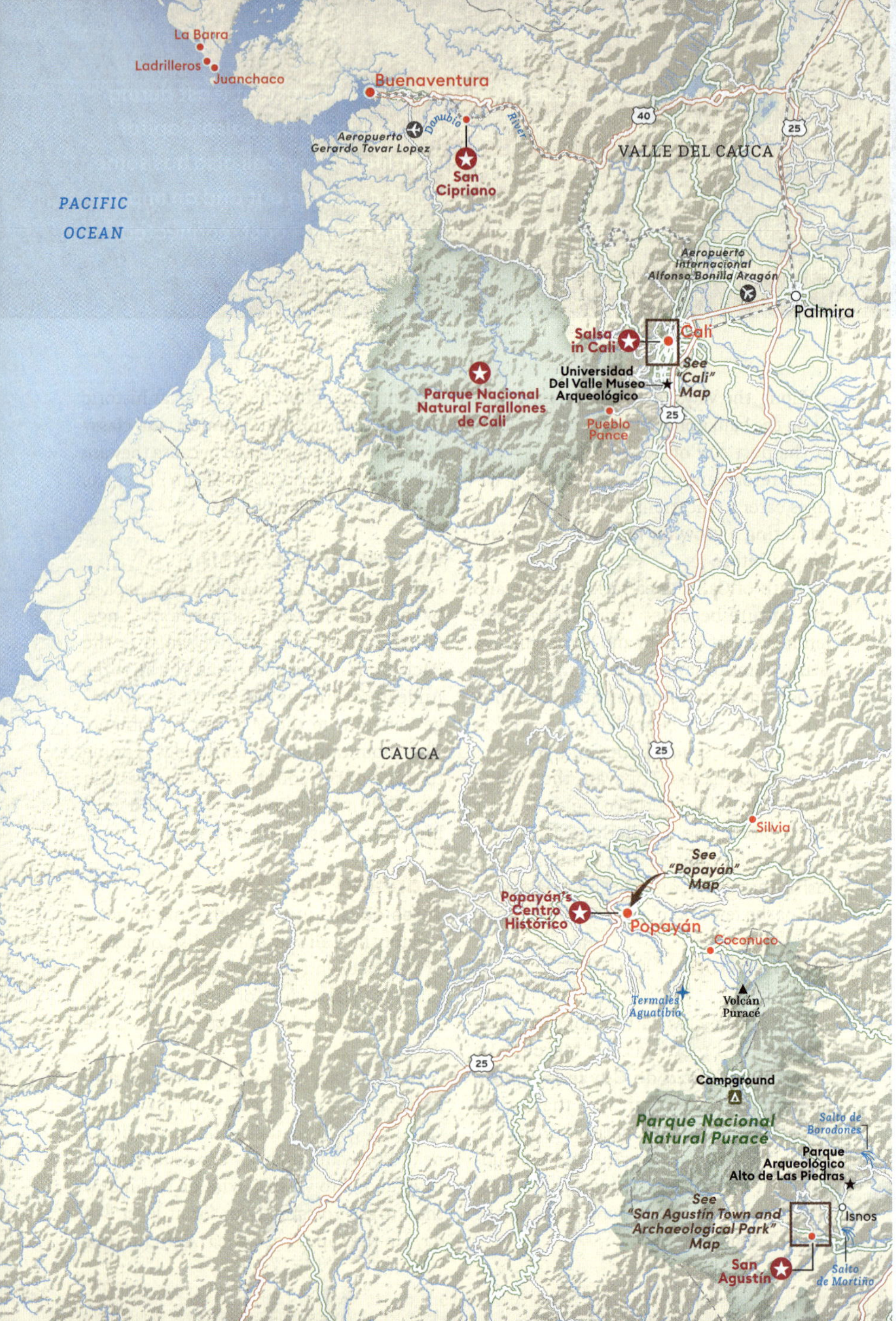
La Barra
Ladrilleros
Juanchaco
Buenaventura
Danubio River
Aeropuerto Gerardo Tovar Lopez
San Cipriano
40
25
VALLE DEL CAUCA
PACIFIC OCEAN
Aeropuerto Internacional Alfonso Bonilla Aragón
Palmira
Salsa in Cali
Cali
See "Cali" Map
Universidad Del Valle Museo Arqueológico
Parque Nacional Natural Farallones de Cali
Pueblo Pance
CAUCA
Silvia
See "Popayán" Map
Popayán's Centro Histórico
Popayán
Coconuco
Termales Aguatibia
Volcán Puracé
Campground
Parque Nacional Natural Puracé
Salto de Bordones
Parque Arqueológico Alto de Las Piedras
See "San Agustín Town and Archaeological Park" Map
Isnos
San Agustín
Salto de Mortiño

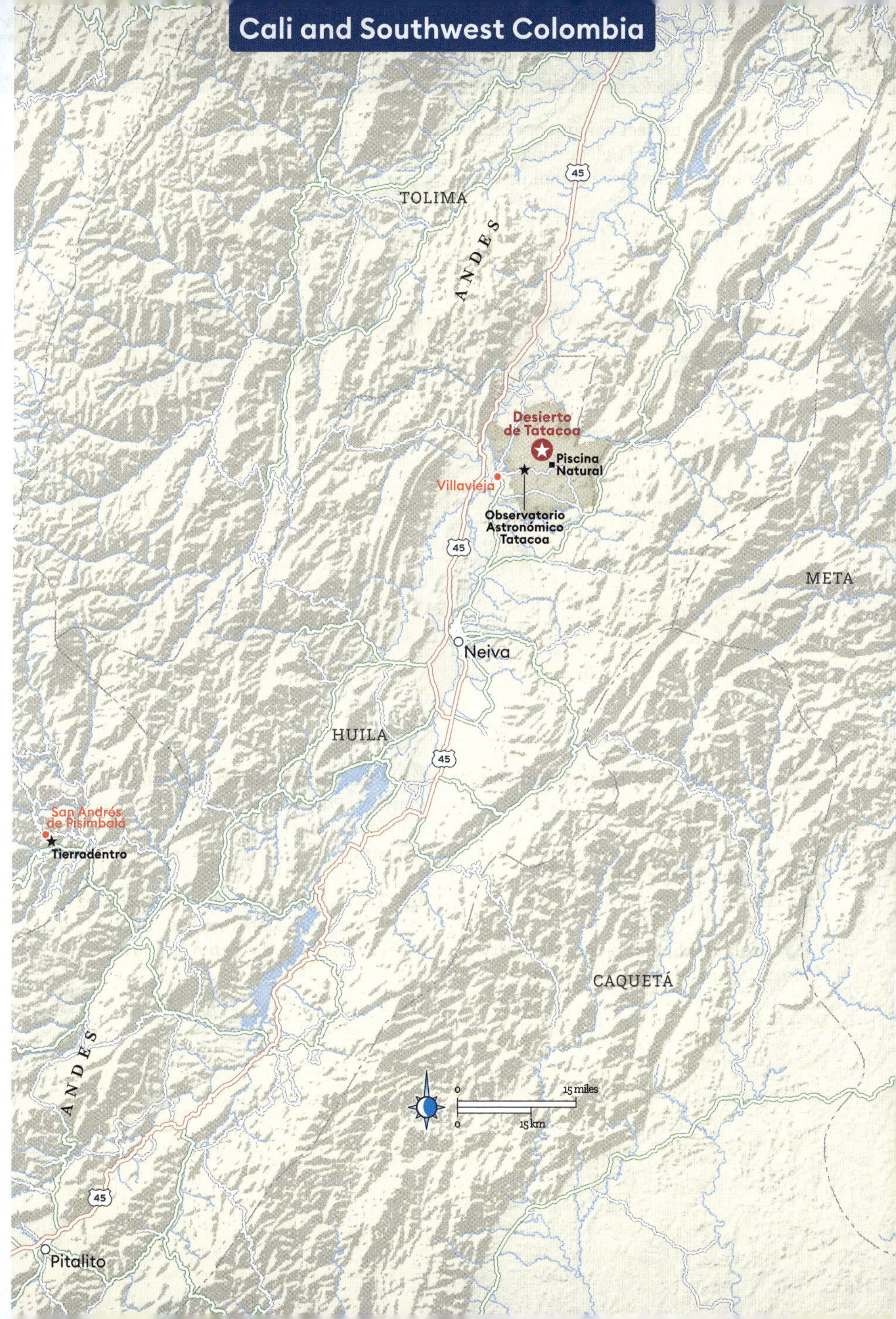
Cali and Southwest Colombia
45
TOLIMA
ANDES
Desierto de Tatacoa
Piscina Natural
Villavieja
Observatorio Astronómico Tatacoa
45
META
Neiva
HUILA
45
San Andrés de Pisimbalá
Tierradentro
CAQUETÁ
ANDES
0
15 miles
0
15 km
45
Pitalito

Itinerary Ideas

Three days is a perfect amount of time to get a sampling of the soulful music and sumptuous cuisine of Cali and make an excursion into the lush Farallones de Cali. The only problem is that just a sampling will leave you wanting more.

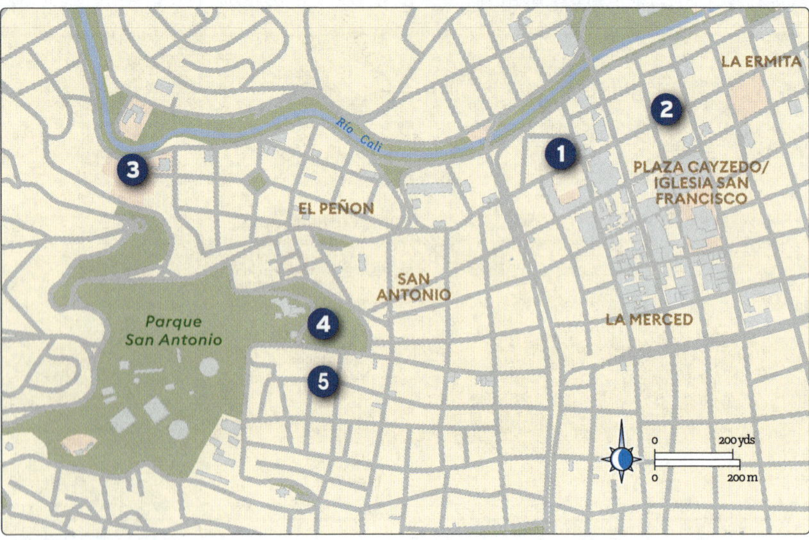

DAY 1

1. Spend the morning exploring the downtown area and its sights, starting at **Iglesia La Merced.**

2. For lunch try the local fare at **Da'Gusto.**

3. After lunch, take a taxi to the city's top museum, **Museo La Tertulia.**

4. Afterward, walk up through El Peñón to **Parque San Antonio** for sunset views over the city and music in the park.

5. Try the gourmet arepas at **Zea Maiz** for dinner before heading back to your hotel or hostel in the San Antonio area.

DAY 2

❶ Wake up early to climb **El Cerro de las Tres Cruces** and look west for spectacular views over the Farallon mountains.

❷ After working up an appetite on the mountain, take a taxi to the Plaza Alameda market and get a fresh fish lunch at **Pedro Junior.** Spend some time exploring the market after lunch.

❸ In the early evening, head to **Parque Artesanal Loma de la Cruz** for some live entertainment and check out the artisan stands.

❹ Afterward, check out the salsa scene at **La Topa Tolondra** on La Quinta (Calle 5).

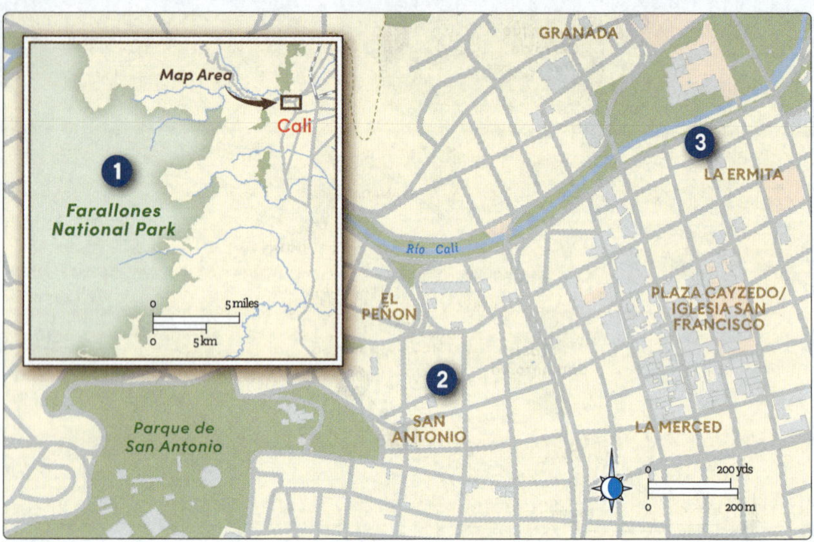

DAY 3

1. Take a bird-watching tour in the city or into **Parque Nacional Natural Farallones de Cali.**

2. Book a table at **Domingo** so that when you get back after a long day in paradise you can refuel on local fusion cuisine.

3. At night, walk over to the Bulevar to mingle with the locals and check out the salsa street party on **La Calle del Sabor.** If you want more, pop into nearby Malamaña.

statue in San Agustín

of the sights of Tierradentro, the Tatacoa desert, and San Agustín can be done from Popayán. For that you'll need five days. Relaxing San Agustín itself easily seduces travelers into spending more time than planned.

Some of the big goings-on in the region are the Semana Santa processions in Popayán the week before Easter, the Carnaval de Negros y Blancos in Pasto in January, and the Feria de Cali in late December.

The average temperature in Cali is about 24°C (75°F), and the average daily high is a sizzling 30°C (86°F). But 4:30pm-6:30pm, as the sun begins its descent over the Farallones into the Pacific, the temperature drops to around 19°C (66°F), and a gentle breeze combines to make the weather absolutely delicioso. During this most pleasant time of day, head to Parque San Antonio or Parque Artesanal Loma de la Cruz, or stroll on the Bulevar.

Safety

Cali has one of the highest crime rates in the country, but much of it is concentrated in low-income areas far from the center and touristed neighborhoods. Caution should always be exercised when walking in Cali, especially at night and on streets with little foot traffic. Hostels provide useful maps with go and no-go areas. As in most Colombian cities, there are Centros de Atención Inmediata (CAI, community police stations) in every neighborhood and often in parks such as Parque San Antonio.

Follow the general precautions of any large Colombian city, especially regarding the use of taxis and night spots. The national toll-free hotline for any emergency is tel. 123. The police have an additional number, tel. 112.

Southern Colombia is also where much of the country's narco activity takes place. Here more than anywhere it's a good idea to do some research and talk to locals before exploring off the beaten trail. All the destinations covered in this section are safe.

Cali

Salsa and choke (a mix of salsa and hip-hop) rhythms pervade this tropicool city of 2.8 million, which has the second highest Afro-Latin population on the continent next to Salvador, Brazil. Far more relaxed than Bogotá or Medellín, Cali is a leafy metropolis at the base of the Farallones de Cali mountain range, a highly biodiverse wilderness that separates the city from the Pacific coast. The sultry city, at about 1,000 m (3,280 ft) elevation in the Valle de Cauca, a region known for sugarcane production, is so seductive that the rest of the world seems to fade away. Here in the Valle locals like to say, "Cali es Cali y lo demás es loma" (Cali is Cali and everywhere else is just hills).

In 2011 the city tore out a freeway that cut through the center and replaced it with a wide pedestrian walkway that follows the course of the river. The Bulevar del Río Cali turned around the destiny of the center of Cali, which was once desolate and dangerous after 7pm. It's now packed with after-work office folks, local families, and visitors almost every evening, and many restaurants and nightlife venues have

Cali
San Antonio
El Encuentro
Carrera 4
Carrera 3
La Colina Tertuliadero
Calle 2
Calle 3
Ensifera Nature
Domingo
Macondo Postres y Café
SAN ANTONIO
Carrera 5
Azul
Carrera 4C
Valle Pacífico
Iglesia de San Antonio
San Antonio Hotel Boutique
Salsa Pura
Carrera 9
Carrera 10
Ruta Sur
Magic Garden House
Antigua Contemporánea
Zea Maiz
Carrera 12
Ecoparque Cerro de las Tres Cruces
El Cerro de las Tres Cruces
Chipichape
Av. 6A Norte
Av. 2B Norte
Panadería Kuty
Martyn's
Terminal de Transportes
Av. 3 Norte
Av. 6A Norte
Zaperoco Bar
Av. 15 Oeste
Av. 9A Norte
Hotel Portón Granada
NOW Hotel
Carrera 1
GRANADA
Av. 2 Norte
Donde Fabio
Carrera 5
Calle 23
Barakha Panadería Ancestral
Iglesia La Ermita
Salsa in Cali
Platillos Voladores
LA ERMITA
See "El Centro" Detail
Carrera 8
Av. 4 Oeste
Parque de los Gatos
Av. 2 Norte
Río Cali
PLAZA CAYZEDO/ IGLESIA SAN FRANCISCO
Carrera 2
EL PEÑÓN
Museo La Tertulia
Hotel Peñón
Hotel Foresto 365
Zoológico de Cali
Carrera 10
La Matraca
Av. 2 Oeste
Parque San Antonio
SAN ANTONIO
LA MERCED
CENTRO
Espacio 10-60
See "San Antonio" Detail
La Topa Tolondra
Carrera 15
LiberTienda
La Caldera del Diablo
El Tertuliadero Finisteria
Parque Artesanal Loma de la Cruz
Calle 11
Calle 13
Calle 9E
Calle 10
Calle 8
Calle 9
Calle 15
El Cerro de Cristo Rey
Cra 24
Pedro Junior
Positivo
Plaza Alameda
Calle 5
Calle 6
Calle 7
Calle 10 Oeste
0.25 miles
0.25 km
Centro Médico Imbanaco
Carrera 39
Calle 5
Calle 6
To Universidad Del Valle Museo Arqueológico
El Centro
Calle 8
Calle del Sabor
Salsa in Cali
LA ERMITA
Palacio Nacional
Bulevar
Carrera 3
Calle 10
Carrera 4
Plaza Cayzedo
Bocados
Da'Gusto
Malamaña
Museo Arqueológico La Merced
Museo de Arte Religioso La Merced
PLAZA CAYZEDO/ IGLESIA SAN FRANCISCO
Iglesia La Merced
Carrera 5
Punto de Información Turístico de Cali
Carrera 6
Iglesia San Francisco
Centro Cultural de Cali
Museo del Oro Calima
Carrera 6
Calle 9
La Vaina
100 yds
100 m

opened. More plans to pedestrianize Cali are in the works.

Sights

The easily walkable main points of interest in El Centro are clustered near Iglesia La Merced and Plaza de Cayzedo and along the Río Cali. You'll need just a few hours to see everything.

Beyond Colombia (https://beyondcolombia.com) offers **walking tours** of the downtown area, focused on history or street art and activism, as well as a food tour of the Plaza Alameda market (10am daily). Tours are in English and free but tips are expected.

EL CENTRO

There are a few historical sights and museums in Cali's center that are worth exploring, particularly in the morning before the heat kicks in. The heart of the area is the La Merced complex, home to the city's first church and convent, which hosts two small museums.

Iglesia La Merced

Carrera 4 at Calle 7; tel. 2/889-2309; 6:30am-10am and 4pm-7pm daily, mass 7am and 6pm Mon.-Sat., 9am and 6pm Sun.

On June 25, 1536, the city of Santiago de Cali was founded by Sebastián de Belalcázar. He changed his mind about the location and moved the city shortly thereafter to its present location, and a mass was held to celebrate the foundation of the city. It was on this site that the Iglesia La Merced was built sometime around 1545. The oldest church in Cali, it is a lovely example of colonial construction, with thick whitewashed walls. The church, in the shape of a cross, has a single nave with red wooden beams. The only extravagance is the golden baroque altar with a statue of La Virgen de las Mercedes, patron saint of Cali.

Museo Arqueológico La Merced (MUSA)

Carrera 4 No. 6-59; tel. 2/889-3434; 9am-6pm Mon.-Sat.; www.museoarqueologicomusa.com; COP$6,000

This small but interesting museum holds a collection of pre-Colombian artifacts, including funeral urns, vases and other earthenware from a variety of civilizations that occupied southern Colombia. In the garden is a replica of one of the underground tombs of Tierradentro.

Museo de Arte Religioso La Merced

Carrera 4 No. 56; no phone; 9am-noon and 2pm-5pm Mon.-Sat.; COP$6,000

While this small but well curated museum focuses on religious artifacts, history buffs will find a fascinating array of items from Colombia's colonial period that provide interesting perspectives on what life was like 400-500 years ago.

Museo del Oro Calima

Calle 7 No. 4-69; tel. 2/684-7754; www.banrepcultural.org/cali; 9am-5pm Tues.-Fri., 10am-5pm Sat.; free

Within the Banco de la República building across the street from Iglesia La Merced is the excellent Museo del Oro Calima. Cali's gold museum has a collection of more than 600 ornamental gold and utilitarian ceramics, attributed to the ancient Calima people, that have been unearthed northwest of present-day Cali.

Centro Cultural de Cali

Carrera 5 No. 6-05; tel. 2/885-8859, ext. 109; www.cali.gov.co/cultura, www.funhi.org; 8am-noon and 2pm-5pm Mon.-Fri.; free

There are always art exhibitions on in the

Iglesia La Ermita

Bulevar del Río Cali

Museo La Tertulia

basement galleries of the Centro Cultural de Cali, a building that also houses the visitor information offices.

Iglesia La Ermita

Carrera 13 at Calle 1; no phone; mass 7am and 5pm Mon.-Fri., 10am and 5pm Sat.-Sun.

At the eastern end of the Bulevar is one of the city's most iconic landmarks: the miniature neo-Gothic Iglesia La Ermita. Originally built in the 16th century, the church was nearly destroyed by earthquakes in 1787 and 1925. Not much was left after the 18th-century tremor, except for the painting of the *Señor de la Caña* (Lord of the Sugarcane). Its survival was attributed to a miracle. The current building was completed in the 1940s. The three-nave church has an Italian marble altar and many stained-glass windows. A small park dedicated to local poets sits outside the church.

Plaza de Cayzedo

Carreras 4-5 between Calles 11-12

The dozens of majestic wax palms in the Plaza de Cayzedo create a green oasis in the middle of gritty downtown Cali. Plaza de Cayzedo was known as the Plaza Mayor during the colonial era, but in 1913 it was renamed to honor the most famous independence figure from Cali, Joaquín de Cayzedo y Cuero. When passing through the park on the brick walkways, you'll encounter a colorful cross-section of Caleños, from university students to shoe shiners to dapper older men watching the world go by from the comfort of a park bench.

The most stunning building on the plaza is the French neoclassical gem the **Palacio Nacional** (Carrera 4 No. 12-04), also known as the Palacio de Justicia. Completed in the early 1930s, it houses various judicial bodies of the Valle de Cauca departmental government. The Palacio Nacional is not open to the public.

Iglesia San Francisco

Calle 10 No. 6-00; tel. 2/884-2457; mass 7am and 5pm Mon.-Sat., 9am and 6pm Sun.

The distinctive redbrick church complex of Iglesia San Francisco includes the

Capilla de la Inmaculada, the **Convento de San Joaquín,** and the **Torre Mudéjar,** all built in the 17th-19th centuries by Franciscans. The architectural star is the Torre Mudéjar, a four-story, 23-m-high (75-ft) bell tower. It is divided into four brick sections with each level displaying a different geometric design. It is considered a good example of neo-Mudéjar design in the New World. The architect of the tower was supposedly a Moor who had fled Spanish authorities, seeking refuge in the convent. In return for shelter, he designed the bell tower.

EL PEÑÓN

Museo La Tertulia

Av. Colombia No. 5 Oeste-105; tel. 2/893-2939; www.museolatertulia.com; 10am-6pm Tues.-Sat., 2pm-6pm Sun.; COP$20,000

One of the best art museums in the country is Cali's Museo La Tertulia. Museum galleries highlight contemporary Colombian artists such as Beatriz González, Hugo Zapata, Ómar Rayo, and others. Built in the 1960s, Museo La Tertulia is perhaps the most important cultural center in Cali. The word *tertulia* refers to a social gathering for talking and sharing ideas about culture, art, and other themes. The cinemateca shows art films in the evenings almost every day and hosts festivals such as EuroCine. A concert hall offers chamber music concerts and poetry readings, and the lush grounds house an amphitheater as well as yoga on Wednesday evenings. A deli-café on the terrace is a popular meeting place in the evenings.

Zoológico de Cali

Carrera 2 Oeste and Calle 14; tel. 2/488-0888; 9am-4:30pm daily; COP$18,000

The Zoológico de Cali is considered the best zoo in the country, which has as much to do with its lush setting as its collection of Colombian species. Straddling the Río Cali and full of trees and flowers, this is a pleasant place to spend a weekday afternoon. The zoo is accessible by MIO by taking the A02 bus from the San Bosco station.

Parque de los Gatos

Calle 3 Oeste 2-3

Artists from all over Colombia were asked to paint the several dozen cat sculptures in this small but verdant park on the banks of the Río Cali. It's a fun and relaxing place to spend an hour or two in the late afternoon when the mountain breeze swirls through the city.

SAN ANTONIO

Parque and Iglesia de San Antonio

Calle 1 Oeste at Carrera 10; tel. 2/893-7185

A lush green space with panoramic views of downtown Cali, Parque San Antonio is the place to experience San Antonio life. You'll see a vibrant mix of Caleños and their canine companions, especially in the early evening and on weekends. Lining one side of the sloping park are fast-food joints, bars, and ice cream shops.

At the top of the park, the small white Iglesia de San Antonio is beautiful in its

Parque de los Gatos

simplicity, with whitewashed adobe walls and wooden beams. It was built in the 18th century and is often used by locals for wedding photos.

Parque Artesanal Loma de la Cruz

Calle 5 between Carreras 14-16; 9am-10pm daily

While technically it's an artesanías (handicrafts) market, Parque Artesanal Loma de la Cruz has such a pleasant atmosphere, especially in the early evening, that it's worth a visit even if you're not in the mood for shopping. Handicrafts such as mochilas (shoulder bags) created by Indigenous weavers as well as leather goods are for sale. Frequent musical events take place, including the weekly Andean dancing that packs the "loma" every Thursday night. The surrounding area is full of local restaurants and bars.

SOUTHERN CALI

El Cerro de Cristo Rey

south of Cerro de las Tres Cruces, Los Andes neighborhood

The statue of Christ on El Cerro de Cristo Rey stands 26 m (85 ft) tall. It was created by an Italian sculptor to celebrate 50 years of peace following the Guerra de Mil Días (Thousand Days' War) at the turn of the 20th century that claimed 100,000 lives in Colombia and Panama. You can take a taxi to the top (COP$45,000), but in 2025 a 6-km-long (4-mi) elevated pedestrian walkway was installed that allows you to walk there from La Quinta (Calle 5) from several access points. Along the way you can check out the sculpture on the side of the mountain called *El Lamento de la Pacha Mama,* a tribute to Indigenous peoples, and munch on an empanada at a roadside stall. Don't make this excursion after dark.

Universidad del Valle Museo Arqueológico

Calle 13 No. 100-00, Universidad de Valle, under the Biblioteca Mario Carvajal; tel. 2/321-2975; museo.arqueologico@correounivalle.edu.co; 9am-noon and 2pm-5pm Mon.-Fri., 10am-1pm Sat.; free

The dynamic Museo Arqueológico has a massive archaeological collection and changing exhibits. It is a great place to warm up before visiting the sites of San Agustín and Tierradentro. It's located in the south of the city in one of the main libraries on the expansive grounds of the Universidad del Valle, one of Colombia's largest campuses. The campus itself is interesting to visit, as it won a national architectural prize when it was built in the early 1970s. With around 30,000 students, it makes an important contribution to the city's cultural fabric.

Recreation

HIKING

El Cerro de las Tres Cruces

Distance: 8 km (5 mi) round-trip
Duration: 2-3 hours
Elevation gain: 245 m (800 ft)
Difficulty: Moderate
Trailhead: Av. 10 Norte No. 15a-5, Barrio Santa Monica

A weekend ritual for many Caleños is to hike up El Cerro de las Tres Cruces (Three Crosses Hill), west of the Santa Monica neighborhood and not far from Granada and El Centro. The climb will get your blood pumping, and you'll have good views of Cali and the jagged peaks of the Farallones de Cali, especially early in the day. The ascent takes about an hour. At the top, you can work out in the outdoor gym next to the hill's crosses. Bring some cash to enjoy a freshly squeezed orange or carrot juice.

Festival Petronio Álvarez

BIKING

Ciclovida

8am-1pm Sun.

On Sundays and holidays many streets are closed to traffic and open only to cyclists, joggers, and pedestrians during the Ciclovida. The main route extends from Calle 9 at Carretera 66 Sur, near the Canchas Panamericanas sports complex, to Calle 70 at Carretera 1 Norte. If you can't find a bike, you can always jog or walk the route, plus there are free open-air Zumba classes at various points in the city, such as along the river near downtown. Many hostels rent bicycles.

BIRD-WATCHING

Ensifera Nature

Carrera 5 No. 3-76, San Antonio; tel. 314/818-2811; https://ensiferanature.com; 10am-7pm daily

A small shop in San Antonio that also sells binoculars, birding manuals, and everything else you need to spot birds, Ensifera offers bird-watching tours (6am daily; COP$40,000) along the Río Cali right in the city limits. The tours leave from the shop.

Colombia Bird Fair

www.colombiabirdfair.org; Mar.

The Colombia Bird Fair is an annual birding event held at the Cali Country Club in March, when there are a number of birding excursions, all open to the public.

Entertainment and Events

CULTURAL CENTERS

Teatro de Presagio

Av. 9A Norte No. 10N-50; tel. 2/487-6432 or 301/485-8228; www.teatrodelpresagio.com

Teatro de Presagio often has theater or dance performances on the weekends in

TOP EXPERIENCE

★ THE WORLD CAPITAL OF SALSA

Caribbean music hit Cali in the 1940s through vinyl brought in at the port city of Buenaventura. Finding the son, charanga, and early salsa songs too slow, Afro-descendant Caleños started playing them at 45 RPM instead of the 33 RPM speed they were recorded on. Creating dance moves to keep up with this accelerated beat is how Cali-style salsa was born. Cali bands like Grupo Niche and Guayacán are now considered some of the best in the world, and Cali's distinctive style of dancing, with its emphasis on lightning-fast footwork, is catching on in international salsa dance competitions.

SALSOTECAS

On weekend nights a section of El Centro next to the Bulevar, **La Calle del Sabor** (Calle 10), becomes an outdoor salsa party. But also visit the city's classic salsotecas and immerse yourself in the rumba.

- **Malamaña** (Carrera 4 No. 9-59; tel. 323/594-4747; 7pm-3am Thurs.-Sat.; cover COP$15,000) is a low-lit mural-covered speakeasy-style basement salsa club in El Centro.
- **Zaperoco Bar** (Av. 5N No. 16-46; tel. 2/661-2040; www.zaperocobar.com; 8pm-3am Thurs.-Sat.; cover COP$20,000) is a classic templo de la salsa that packs a regular and older crowd.
- **La Topa Tolondra** (Calle 5 No. 13-27; tel. 314/664-1470; 6pm-1am Wed.-Thurs., 6pm-3am Fri.-Sat.; cover COP$15,000) has become the tourist hot spot of salsa in Cali.
- **La Caldera del Diablo** (Calle 5 No. 14-35; tel. 312/639-9316; 10pm-3am Wed.-Sat.; cover COP$15,000) attracts a hip and alternative crowd. It is across La Quinta (Calle 5) from Parque Artesanal Loma de la Cruz.
- **Donde Fabio** (Calle 20 No. 3-14; tel. 318/438-2862; 8pm-6am Thurs.-Sat.; cover COP$20,000) attracts the after-hours crowd that just can't stop dancing.

FESTIVAL MUNDIAL DE SALSA

www.cali.gov.co, tickets www.colboletos.com; mid-Sept.

The Festival Mundial de Salsa began in 2006. It is a fiercely competitive dance contest, attracting thousands of salsa dancers from around the world.

SALSA CLASSES

Most hostels and hotels can hook you up with private salsa teachers of good reputation. **Salsa Pura** (Calle 4 No. 6-61; tel. 602/484-2769; www.salsapura.com; group class COP$20,000) in San Antonio has group classes in both Salsa Caleña and Salsa en Linea (LA Style).

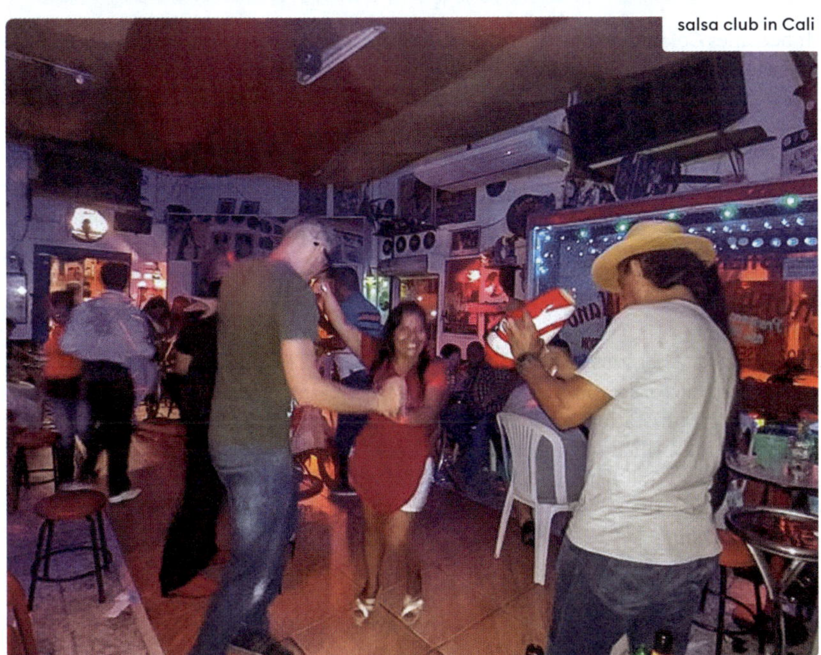
salsa club in Cali

its Granada space. Tuesday evening is free art house cinema night.

FESTIVALS AND EVENTS

Festival Petronio Álvarez

www.festivalpetronioalvarez.com; mid-Aug.; free

A celebration of Afro-Colombian Pacific coast culture, the Festival Petronio Álvarez is a weeklong flurry of outdoor concerts mostly held at the Canchas Panamericanas sports complex. It's fast becoming Cali's premier and most beloved annual event. Besides the vibrations of the drums and marimbas, the home-cooked Pacific-style meals and local herb-spiked viche-based cocktails at this annual festival are delightful.

> In Cali dancing is not just for the young ones: The city is home to dozens of **viejotecas,** where the 50-and-over crowd gets together to get their rumba on. Several classic viejotecas are around Parque de Alameda near the Plaza Alameda market as well as in Barrio Obrero, on the eastern edge of El Centro.

Cali International Film Festival

www.festivaldecinecali.gov.co; mid-Nov.; from COP$10,000

The Cali International Film Festival is held for several weeks with screenings at various theaters in the city, including at the Chipichape mall.

Feria de Cali

www.feriadecali.com; Dec.; free

During the last week of the year, when other Colombian cities become virtual ghost towns, the opposite occurs in Cali.

It becomes Colombia's party central with parades, concerts, beauty pageants, and plenty of drinking and dancing during the beloved Feria de Cali. Between Christmas and New Year's, the feria is a celebration that crosses barriers of class and age, with everyone dancing salsa in the streets.

Shopping

Chipichape

Calle 38N 6N-35; tel. 2/659-2199; www.chipichape.com.co; 9am-midnight daily

A historic train station turned outdoor shopping mall filled with chain stores, Chipichape is a Cali landmark worth visiting if just for the architecture and the people-watching.

LiberTienda

Carrera 16 No. 2A-47; tel. 318/643-5286; 4pm-10pm Tues.-Sun.

With room after room of an ancient colonial house packed with used books plus a banana leaf-shaded back patio, LiberTienda is a local gem in San Cayetano. Well-done espresso drinks, cold beer, and light snacks are served.

Food

Cali lacks the international cuisine options of Bogotá, but a regionally driven local food scene, especially in San Antonio, is far more exciting. Visitors must try the Pacific cuisine, a blend of African flavors and fresh seafood that is hands down Colombia's most delicious culinary tradition. **Plaza Alameda,** a market 20 minutes' walk or 5 minutes' taxi ride from San Antonio, is surrounded by traditional Pacific restaurants where what's on your plate for lunch was still in the sea that morning.

Street food in Cali is also delectable, with Pacific coast specialties like chontaduro (peach palm served with salt and honey) and cocadas (shredded coconut with raw sugar) found on nearly every corner of El Centro. Nothing beats the afternoon heat like a cool lulada drink, made from lulo, a tangy fruit in the tomato family.

EL CENTRO

Da'Gusto

Carrera 4 No. 9-49; tel. 2/881-8697; 6am-5pm daily; COP$18,000-25,000

Despite its location in a parking lot, Da'Gusto serves reasonably priced traditional fare and packs in the crowds at lunchtime. Sancocho, a meaty stew, is a favorite, as is bagre al cocado (catfish in coconut sauce).

Bocados

Calle 7 No. 1-08; tel. 2/881-1666; 7am-7pm Mon.-Wed., 7am-8:30pm Thurs.-Sat.; COP$20,000-30,000

For healthy brunches (think granola and fresh fruit) and light meals, head to Bocados, a refreshing addition to the Bulevar.

GRANADA

Panadería Kuty

Av. 6 Norte No. 27N-03; tel. 2/661-1465; www.panaderiakuty.com; 6am-9pm daily; COP$10,000-25,000

A top contender for the best pandebono, a delicious pastry made of yuca flour and cheese, is Panadería Kuty. Kuty also serves breakfast all day long and is popular with the after-party crowd.

Platillos Voladores

Av. 3 Norte No. 7-19; tel. 2/668-7750; www.platillosvoladores.com; noon-3pm and 7pm-11pm Mon.-Sat.; from COP$55,000

Platillos Voladores is consistently rated as one of Cali's top restaurants. Fusion is the watchword: Thai, Lebanese, Italian, French, and Colombian Pacific cuisine all make appearances on the menu. Reservations are advised.

EL PEÑÓN

Barakha Panadería Ancestral

Carrera 1 Oeste No. 1-109, 2nd Fl.; tel. 2/892-0135; 8am-9pm Mon.-Sat.; COP$12,000-25,000

In addition to whole-grain bread and baked goods made from masa madre (live dough), Barakha Panadería Ancestral is a place to spend a leisurely afternoon enjoying sandwiches, salads, desserts, and coffee.

SAN ANTONIO

★ Zea Maiz

Carrera 12 No. 1-27; tel. 311/846-2774; 5:30pm-10:30pm Tues.-Sun.; COP$14,000-25,000

Heirloom corn arepas stuffed with several dozen options, including pesto and baba ghanoush, make Zea Maiz a favorite local spot. Iced jamaica (hibiscus) tea and creative desserts round out the experience. It's hidden in a basement with no outside sign a block behind Parque San Antonio.

Azul

Carrera 9A No. 4-02; tel. 2/893-6057; noon-3pm and 6pm-11pm Mon.-Fri., 6pm-11pm Sat.; COP$45,000-55,000

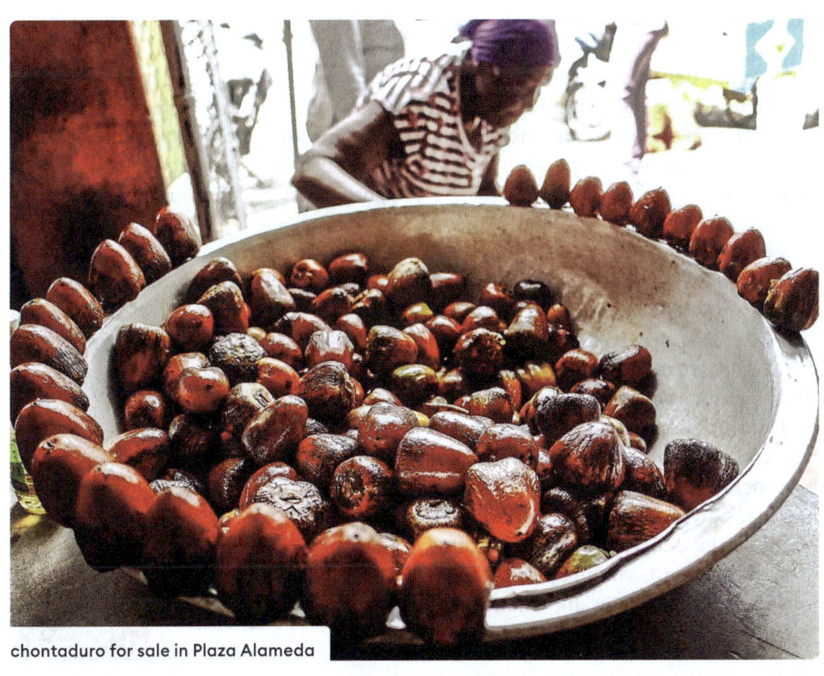

chontaduro for sale in Plaza Alameda

Azul is a fusion-style restaurant with Mediterranean, Colombian, Middle Eastern, and Asian flavors. Ask for the clandestinos—dishes that don't appear on the menu.

Valle Pacífico

Calle 2 No. 4-52; tel. 300/245-2827; restaurantevallepacifico@hotmail.com; 12:30pm-3pm and 6:30pm-10pm Mon.-Sat.; COP$45,000-66,000

Coconut milk is a regular ingredient in the seafood dishes at Valle Pacífico, which features food from the Guapi area on the Cauca coast.

Antigua Contemporánea

Calle 2 No. 9-08B; tel. 2/893-6809 or 2/893-6813; noon-11pm Mon.-Sat.; COP$50,000-65,000

An upscale addition to the San Antonio culinary scene is Antigua Contemporánea, with items such as seafood pasta and Vietnamese curry in an elegant antiques and interior design store. Ample outdoor seating under the stars with live music on weekends makes this a favorite for a night out. Try the uchuva (cape gooseberry) margarita.

★ Domingo

Carrera 5 No. 2-97; tel. 313/790-2109; 10am-10pm Mon.-Wed., 10am-11pm Thurs.-Fri., 9am-11pm Sat., 9am-5pm Sun.; COP$55,000-70,000

Chef Catalina Vélez spent years forging relationships with small-scale sustainable farmers and producers in the region before opening Domingo in a restored colonial mansion in the heart of San Antonio. Many of the ecosystem-to-table items used in the award-winning plates—think mussel-stuffed tamales and chontaduro hummus—can also be purchased in the on-site market. Reservations are necessary for dining.

★ Macondo Postres y Café

Carrera 6 No. 3-03; tel. 2/893-1570; www.macondocafe.blogspot.com; 11am-11pm Mon.-Thurs., 11am-midnight Fri.-Sat., 4:30pm-11pm Sun.

Weary travelers and San Antonians alike flock to Macondo Postres y Café at all hours of the day. It's one of the best places to hang out in San Antonio and is known for its sandwiches, coffee, and beer as well as its busy calendar of cultural events, such as nightly free film screenings and Friday jazz evenings.

PLAZA ALAMEDA

★ Pedro Junior

Calle 8 No. 23A-67; tel. 317/665-5375; 8am-9pm daily; COP$18,000-30,000

The best of the many Pacific restaurants surrounding the market, Pedro Junior serves hefty and well-seasoned set lunches that revolve around fresh fish, coconut rice, plantains, and borojó (a dark-purple Pacific fruit) juice. The shrimp ceviche is also delightful—ask for a free sample.

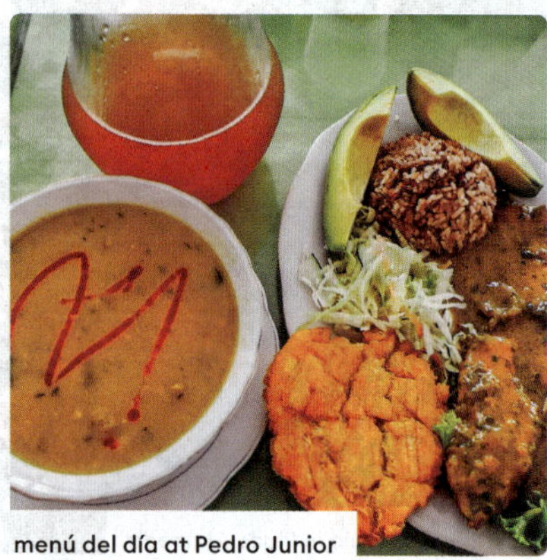

menú del día at Pedro Junior

Positivo

Carrera 25 No. 7-57; tel. 321/775-3202; 10am-6pm daily; COP$30,000-50,000

The love child of singer Nidia Góngora, who hails from the Pacific coast village of Timbiquí and has racked up multiple awards, including best folkloric album, Positivo serves well-done seafood dishes with a shot of house-made viche (sugarcane liquor).

Bars and Nightlife

BARS AND LOUNGES

★ La Colina Tertuliadero

Calle 1 No. 4-83B; no phone; 5pm-2am daily

La Colina is an old-school San Antonio tienda recently renovated and expanded to include patio and terrace seating where the local creative class gathers at night. It's been around for over seven decades and is a perfect spot to start the evening.

Martyn's

Av. 6A Norte No. 24N-22; tel. 2/667-3296; 8pm-3am Wed.-Sat.

Martyn's in Granada is a rock-and-roll institution in Cali. For over 30 years Martyn, originally from Wales, has been serving tequila shots and playing rock classics to a devoted clientele.

El Tertuliadero Finisteria

Carrera 16 No. 3-40; tel. 317/718-2829; 5pm-2am daily

Next to Parque Artesanal Loma de La Cruz, El Tertuliadero Finisteria is a friendly neighborhood bar and local live music venue that also has some nice sidewalk seating.

DANCE CLUBS

Although Cali itself is packed with nightlife, because local laws require most establishments to close at 3am, a whole nightlife district located outside city limits, called **Menga,** rages till dawn. The area is packed with dance clubs of different varieties, from vallenato to techno to salsa and reggaetón. Menga is a 15-20 minute taxi ride from El Centro.

★ Espacio 10-60

Carrera 10 No. 10-60; tel. 316/740-5607; 8pm-3pm Wed.-Sat.; cover COP$20,000-30,000

With an open-air dance floor on the rooftop of a downtown music recording studio, Espacio 10-60 attracts a hip, artistic, and open-minded crowd that is very LGBTQ-friendly. DJs play electronic and world music, usually pausing for a salsa set or two at least every hour.

TANGO

La Matraca

Carrera 11 No. 22-80; tel. 2/668-6783; www.lamatracacali.com; 6pm-2:30am Fri.-Sat., 3pm-11pm Sun.

Tango lovers may feel outnumbered in this salsa town, but not at La Matraca, a Cali institution for over 50 years. On Parque del Obrero, La Matraca used to be a corner shop where you could buy staples like rice and potatoes and hear tango from the owner's collection. It tends to be happening after 3pm Sunday.

Accommodations

Cali has no shortage of sound lodging options for all types of travelers. San Antonio, with its charming colonial houses turned restaurants, cafés, and hotels and its proximity to the center is unbeatable, but Granada, El Peñón, and San Cayetano are also good options. These areas are safe, walkable, and offer diverse dining options.

EL CENTRO

★ La Vaina

Carrera 5 No. 6-32; tel. 314/315-3297; www.lavaina.co; COP$40,000 dorm, COP$120,000 d

With a swimming pool and hammocks in the lush garden courtyard of a restored colonial mansion, La Vaina is more like a backpacker's resort than a run-of-the-mill hostel. Yoga and salsa classes are offered, and the location, just two blocks from San Antonio and two blocks from the Bulevar, is sweeter than panela.

GRANADA

Granada is close to the center and full of rowdy nightlife and high-end dining.

Hotel Portón Granada

Av. 9 Norte No. 13-19; tel. 2/379-9595 or 318/696-6117; www.hotelportondegranada.com.co; COP$183,000 d

With just eight rooms, Hotel Portón Granada, in an old converted home with high ceilings, offers what few others do in trendy Granada: a dose of charm.

★ NOW Hotel

Av. 9A Norte No. 10N-74; tel. 2/488-9797; www.nowhotel.com.co; COP$399,000 d

A dose of Miami's South Beach in the middle of Granada, NOW Hotel has 19 industrial-chic high-tech rooms with balconies and satellite TV. There are two restaurants and for sunset a rooftop terrace bar, sometimes host to weekend parties.

EL PEÑÓN

This upscale neighborhood, with Parque del Peñón as its main landmark, hugs the Río Cali and is home to restaurants and hotels. Despite its proximity to San Antonio and El Centro, its tree-lined streets are an oasis of calm.

Hotel Peñón

Calle 1 Oeste No. 2-61; tel. 2/893-3625; www.hotelelpenon.com; COP$179,000 d

Hotel Peñón has 28 large rooms near the river in El Peñón. Much of this hotel, built in the 1980s, has been given a needed facelift.

Hotel Foresto 365

Calle 3 Oeste. No. 3-65; tel. 318/517-1238; COP$441,000 d

On Parque del Peñón and a stone's throw from dozens of restaurants, Hotel Foresto 365 is a boutique hotel with six floors of rooms and suites, many with balconies and some with jetted tubs. The on-site terrace café has nice views.

SAN ANTONIO

Cali's oldest residential neighborhood is a magical maze of crooked streets and colonial architecture that centers on verdant Parque San Antonio, the best place in the city to catch sunset. The neighborhood is full of restaurants, cafés, and cultural centers, but local laws prohibit bars and late-night venues.

El Encuentro

Calle 2 Oeste 4-16; tel. 2/890-2464; www.hostalencuentro.com; COP$45,000 dorm, COP$90,000 d with shared bath

El Encuentro is surrounded by greenery and flowers, has a terrace with views of downtown, and is in one of the most peaceful corners of San Antonio.

★ Ruta Sur

Carrera 9 No. 2-41; tel. 2/893-6946; www.hostalrutasur.com; COP$140,000 d

In a lovingly restored colonial home covered in flowering passion fruit vines, comfy Ruta Sur has 10 rooms—including some with three beds—that each have their own

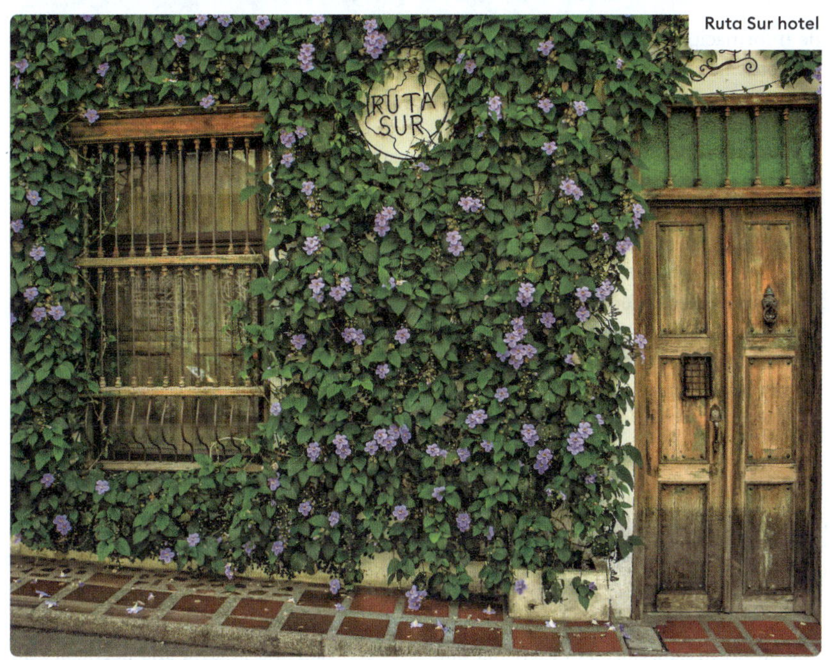

Ruta Sur hotel

private bath, fan, and TV. Local coffee is served in the lush central courtyard. Owner Claudia Martínez, who opened one of the first hostels in the area, is a wealth of local information and history.

★ Magic Garden House

Carrera 10 No. 1-83 Oeste; tel. 311/629-3156; COP$168,000 d

With a fruit tree-filled back garden strung with hammocks to relax in and fronting Parque San Antonio, Magic Garden House lives up to its name. Communal breakfast is served on the terrace, where sweeping views over the city and fresh mountain breezes make for a relaxing start to the day. The 12 rooms are individually decked out with artistic and historical touches.

San Antonio Hotel Boutique

Carrera 6 No. 2-51; tel. 2/524-6364 or 317/404-6647; www.hotelboutiquesanantonio.com; COP$270,000 d

San Antonio Hotel Boutique is a high-end choice if personalized attention and comfort are your priorities. Two of the hotel's 10 rooms have their own terrace, but anyone can enjoy the rooftop patio. Rooms have air-conditioning, comfortable beds, and satellite TV.

Information and Services

VISITOR INFORMATION

Punto de Información Turístico de Cali

Carrera 4 No. 6-05, Oficina 102; tel. 2/885-8855, ext. 122; 8am-noon and 2pm-5pm Mon.-Fri., 10am-2pm Sat.

If you are downtown, stop by the Punto

de Información Turístico de Cali for maps and brochures on Cali and the surrounding region.

EMERGENCY AND MEDICAL SERVICES

Centro Médico Imbanaco

Carrera 38A No. 5A-100; tel. 2/682-1000; appointments tel. 2/685-1000; www.imbanaco.com; 8am-9pm daily

The Centro Médico Imbanaco is one of the top hospitals in the country. It is close to El Centro and offers emergency care.

MONEY

ATMs are not as easy to come by in San Antonio compared to other neighborhoods, but in a bind there is an ATM at the nearby Dann Hotel casino.

To receive a wire transfer, **Western Union** (www.westernunion.com) has several offices in Cali. Currency exchange outfits proliferate in El Centro.

INTERNET AND TELEPHONE

Wireless internet is more the norm than the exception at restaurants, cafés, and big shopping malls. Small internet cafés, open until about 8pm, are also plentiful.

To report any emergency, dial tel. 123. The area code for Cali is 2, but you only need to use it if you're calling Cali from a different part of the country or from abroad. It's generally easy to find people selling use of their cell phones, called minutos (minutes), for cheap on the street downtown and in tiendas elsewhere. Cell phone numbers are dialed with all 10 digits.

Transportation

GETTING THERE

Air

Cali's airport, **Aeropuerto Internacional Alfonso Bonilla Aragón** (CLO; tel. 2/280-1515; www.aerocali.com.co) is 20 km (12 mi) northeast of El Centro, less than an hour's drive. A taxi ride from the airport to the San Antonio neighborhood costs around COP$50,000. Minibuses from the airport to the city are usually waiting just outside the departure hall. They cost about COP$12,000 and take you to the main bus station, the **Terminal de Transportes** (Calle 30 Norte 2AN-29). From here, the most convenient way to get to San Antonio or Granada is a taxi (about COP$15,000) from the official taxi area.

All major Colombian airlines and some international carriers serve Cali. **Avianca** (Calle 38 No. 6AN-35; tel. 2/398-2000; www.avianca.com; 9am-9pm Mon.-Fri., 9am-8pm Sat., 9am-7pm Sun.) flies to Cali from Bogotá, Medellín, Cartagena, Barranquilla, Pasto, and Tumaco. Internationally, Avianca flies nonstop between Cali and Madrid and between Cali and Miami. **LATAM** (Calle 25N No. 6 Bis-36; tel. 1/745-2020; www.latam.com; 8am-6pm Mon.-Fri., 9am-1pm Sat.) flies nonstop from Bogotá, Medellín, San Andrés, and Quito, Ecuador. **Copa Airlines** (tel. 1/800-011-2600; www.copaair.com) flies to Cali from Panama City, Panama.

American Airlines (Carrera 1 No. 2-72; tel. 2/892-7256; www.aa.com; 9am-6pm Mon.-Fri.) is the only US-based airline with service to Cali, from Miami.

Bus

Cali's organized and bustling **Terminal de Transportes** (Calle 30 Norte No. 2AN-29; tel. 2/668-3655; www.terminalcali.com) is a 15-minute taxi ride (COP$15,000) from El Centro. A small **information booth** is in the center of the terminal, and attendants will be able to give you a rough idea of bus fares and provide bus company suggestions. There is an efficient taxi stand at the main entrance (Puerta 3). Food options are dismal at the bus station.

Getting to Cali from Buga costs COP$12,000 and takes 1 hour. From Popayán it's COP$28,000 and 3 hours, and from Medellín COP$85,000 and 9 hours. From faraway Bogotá the ride will set you back COP$95,000 and 12 hours.

If you are taking a MIO bus to the terminal, the nearest station is Las Américas, about two blocks away.

GETTING AROUND

Taxi

Yellow taxis are plentiful in Cali, and you will need to travel by taxi often to get around, especially at night. It's always advisable to order a taxi from a company like **Taxi Express** (tel. 2/555-5555) over the phone or by using the apps Cabify or Easy Taxi or a rideshare service like Uber. From Granada, expect to pay about COP$15,000 to get to the bus terminal and COP$8,000 to get to San Antonio.

Bus

The **MIO** (Masivo Integrado de Occidente; www.mio.com.co) is Cali's public transport system, comprising several dedicated bus rapid transit lanes with stations, as well as alimentadores—feeder buses that connect with the articulated MIO buses at various points. MIO is mildly useful if you are staying in or near Granada and plan to visit El Centro or sights in the south. The bright-blue buses are immaculately maintained and considered safe. Note that to ride one of the alimentadores, you must present a MIO card on board. Those must be purchased at MIO stations such as Versailles (Av. 3 and Calle 21) or Cayzedo (Calle 13 and Carrera 4). MIO runs 5am-11pm Monday-Saturday, 6am-10pm Sunday and holidays. The fare for a single trip is COP$2,300.

Car or Motorcycle

The roads in the Valle de Cauca region are generally of high quality and the terrain is flat. Renting a car or motorcycle may be a good option for excursions outside Cali to the valley's haciendas, Buga, Lago Calima, and Roldanillo. Driving to Popayán or to Pasto along the Pan-American Highway is more taxing because of its winding two-lane roadway.

Hertz (Av. Colombia No. 1-14, El Peñón; tel. 2/892-0437; www.rentacarcolombia.co; 8am-noon and 2pm-6pm Mon.-Fri., 8am-3pm Sat.; airport tel. 2/666-3283; 7am-5pm Mon.-Sat.) has two offices in Cali.

★ Parque Nacional Natural Farallones de Cali

Clear Cali mornings often make visitors gasp in awe at the sight of the jagged peaks that tower over the city to the west. The Farallones de Cali rise from the Valle de Cauca to over 4,000 m (13,100 ft) before descending again on the other side to the Pacific coast. A nature lover's dream come true, Parque Nacional Natural Farallones de Cali is a 200,000-ha (49,400-acre) reserve that contains an extraordinarily high level of natural diversity, including more bird species than anywhere else in the world: Nearly half of all Colombian bird species can be found here. Luckily, it's easy to get to and enjoy, even on a day trip, as it's just outside Cali.

TRANSPORTATION

The main access point to Parque Nacional Natural Farallones de Cali is **Pueblo Pance,** a small village at the upper reaches of the Río Pance, whose lower reaches are a favorite bathing spot for Caleños on weekends. To get to Pueblo Pance, first take the MIO 20 minutes to Unicentro Mall in the south of the city. From there, several local

Parque Nacional Natural Farallones de Cali

buses (COP$2,300) on the A line go to the lower part of Río Pance and the various swimming holes before stopping in the town of La Voragine after about an hour. From La Voragine, Jeep-style colectivos go up the curvy mountain road (45 minutes; COP$6,000) to Pueblo Pance. On the weekends, Anahuac, a private bus company, also runs a direct recreational bus from central Cali (Calle 24 No. 2e-N35; 1.5 hours; 4:30am, 6am, and 8:30am Sat.-Sun.) directly to Pueblo Pance.

HIKING AND BIRD-WATCHING

Walking and bird-watching go hand to hand in Parque Nacional Natural Farallones de Cali, home to over 600 species, including the multicolored tanager *(Chlorocrysa nitidissima)*, which looks like a tie-dyed sparrow and is in danger of extinction. Because the Farallones climb from tropical dry forest on the Cali side up into Andean cloud forest and then down into Pacific rainforest, species from all three ecosystems can be spotted in the park.

Easy day hikes can be done from Pueblo Pance, including **Charco Burbajas** (2 km/1.2 mi round-trip), a nice swimming hole surrounded by lush forest, but to really explore the national park, a guide is needed. **Parques Nacionales de Colombia** recently published a gorgeous full-color guide to the birds of the Farallones, "Entre Cielos y Bosques" (Between the Sky and Forest), available at Ensifera in San Antonio as well as local bookstores.

black-and-chestnut eagle

GUIDES

Fundación Pico Pance

tel. 318/574-7956; interpretespance@gmail.com

Fundación Pico Pance is a nonprofit comprising local guides that specialize in ecological and bird-watching hikes into the interior of Parque Nacional Natural Farallones de Cali. The most popular option is the 7-9-hour trek to the top of Pico de Loro, a sharp peak visible from the center of Cali. The group trek (COP$43,000 pp) leaves at 6am Saturday-Sunday from the Finca Ecoturística Super Cheers. It can also be booked during the week for a higher price that depends on how many people are in your group. Other hikes, like the 4-6-hour trek to Esmerelda Falls, are also available.

ACCOMMODATIONS

Pueblo Pance offers a handful of rustic country inns and eco-hotels.

★ Reserva Natural Anahuac

Pueblo Pance-Vía al Pato Km, Carrera 1; tel. 316/524-4891; www.reservanaturalanahuac.com; tent rental COP$53,000, COP$85,000 d

At the entrance to Parque Nacional Natural Farallones de Cali, this pleasant 6-ha (15-acre) private reserve offers cabañas, lodge rooms, and camping under the stars and serves three meals a day in the on-site restaurant for an additional charge. With 65 species present, bird-watching begins your first morning.

Finca Ecoturística Super Cheers

Vereda el Topacio; tel. 315/705-0258; https://supercheers.wixsite.com; tent rental COP$80,000 d, with meals COP$182,000 d

About a 15-minute walk from Pueblo Pance, this pleasant ranch centers on an artificial lake and has an on-site restaurant for guests. They offer about a dozen private rooms in private cabanas sprinkled around the property. There is a nice swimming hole nearby.

South Pacific Coast

The beaches of the southern Pacific coast of Colombia in and around the port of Buenaventura have not been on the radar of many international visitors, but they offer chances to enjoy the culture and nature of Colombia's Afro-descendant homeland. Juanchaco and Ladrilleros offers beach access and full amenities, while La Barra is an authentic fishing village with a fun local music scene and fresh-caught cuisine.

★ San Cipriano

A tiny village in the Pacific rainforest along the banks the glassy iridescent green Río Danubio, San Cipriano draws visitors to its natural beauty and for the fun way you must arrive—on a jerry-rigged motorcycle attached to railroad tracks. Locals called these contraptions brujitas (little witches), as they often emit screaming and screeching sounds as they barrel through the dense rainforest.

The town is like a trip back in time, with the Afro-descendent population still living largely off the bounty of the rainforest and the river. The area around San Cipriano has been turned into a protected reserve. It's a fascinating place brimming with culture and natural splendor that makes for a perfect stopover between Cali and the Pacific coast. Many hostels and hotels in Cali offer guided day trips to San Cipriano, which includes lunch and a river tube, but it's also worth spending a night or two, as the friendly locals, who love to party, are welcoming.

TRANSPORTATION

Take the Cali-Buenaventura bus (COP$25,000) from the Terminal de Transportes and get off in the town of Córdoba (about 2 hours). It's a 30-minute journey from Córdoba to San Cipriano on a brujita (COP$9,000). From Buenaventura,

the Río Danubio in San Cipriano

Córdoba is less than 30 minutes by bus (COP$6,000).

HIKING

Several mesmerizing hikes into the rainforest, many that end at waterfalls and crystal-clear swimming holes, are available in San Cipriano. Guides are essential and can be booked at your hotel. Prices must be negotiated.

La Cascada del Amor

Distance: 5 km (3 mi) round-trip
Duration: 2-3 hours
Elevation gain: 200 m (660 ft)
Difficulty: Easy
Trailhead: San Cipriano

One of the most popular hikes is the short trail through lush rainforest to La Cascada del Amor (Waterfall of Love). Although the trailhead and the trail are clearly marked, visitors should not attempt to do this hike alone and should hire a guide (COP$50,000 pp).

RAFTING

Floating down the Río Danubio under the dense rainforest canopy with tooth-billed hummingbirds *(Androdon aequatorialis)* darting about is one of the most fun ways to spend a day in San Cipriano. A tube rental for the day from any hotel costs COP$20,000-30,000. Hiring a guide to take you to remote areas of the river and pick you up at the end of a long run costs COP$50,000.

FOOD AND ACCOMMODATIONS

Accommodations in San Cipriano are basic and local-style, but that's part of the charm. Simple wooden shacks in the rainforest, some with decks overlooking the river, are economical and feel like homestays.

Sazón Doña Noemi

San Cipriano; tel. 320/844-9211; COP$28,000-40,000

Home-cooked meals based on freshly caught fish and river prawns, spiced with wild rainforest herbs and simmering in coconut curry, are always a crowd-pleaser. Doña Noemi is one of a handful of locals who serve these delicacies out of their house. Call ahead to reserve lunch or dinner.

Hotel Rio-Mar

San Cipriano; tel. 311/762-9039; COP$50,000 dorm, COP$90,000 d

This rather institutional-feeling concrete-block hotel is about the closest thing San Cipriano has to city-style lodging. The 26 private rooms are Spartan, and dorms are cramped, but the staff is friendly and good local cuisine is served at the on-site restaurant. The riverfront location is a draw.

★ Mama Yeya Raices

San Cipriano; tel. 310/840-6026; COP$150,000 d

A family-run hotel near the riverbank and a short walk to the center of town, Mama Yeya Raices offers six private rooms and cabañas, most with private balconies overlooking the rainforest. The family also offers guests home-cooked Pacific-style fare, including rich coconut cazuelas (stews) packed with local river prawns.

Experienced divers should inquire about visiting **Isla de Malpelo,** 500 km (310 mi) off the southern Pacific coast. The barren rocks are surrounded by deep water and coral reefs home to hundreds of hammerhead and silky sharks. Tours (from USD$450 pp) leave from Buenaventura.

Buenaventura

Buenaventura is the largest city on the Pacific coast, with a population over 300,000. It is Colombia's busiest port and home to one of the most vibrant Afro-Colombian communities. Most visitors pass through Buenaventura on their way to the coastal communities of Juanchaco, Ladrilleros, and La Barra.

The area around the **Muelle Turístico,** the tourist port, hums with activity and is safe to meander day and night. Hotels in the port area are also safe.

SAFETY

Buenaventura has been severely affected by turf battles involving rival drug-trafficking gangs in recent years. The beaches north of the city, however, are secluded and safe, and visitors are welcomed with open arms. But avoid the interior of the city. Buses drop you right at the port.

FOOD

La Escuela

Calle 2 No. 1A-07; tel. 2/297-8948; lunch 10am-3pm Mon.-Sat.; COP$18,000-40,000

La Escuela is a restaurant in the old train station that has been beautifully refurbished. It is run by the Escuela Taller de Buenaventura, a local culinary school that specializes in regional cuisine, particularly seafood. They also serve cocktails made with Pacific ingredients and herbs.

TRANSPORTATION

Most travelers get to Buenaventura by land from Cali. It's a four-hour trip to Buenaventura from Cali's Terminal de Transportes (COP$28,000).

SATENA (tel. 1/605-2222; www.satena.gov.co) offers a daily flight from Bogotá to Buenaventura's **Aeropuerto Gerardo Tovar López** (BUN), about 4 km (2.5 mi) south of town.

Juanchaco and Ladrilleros

From Buenaventura's Muelle Turístico, you can catch a boat to the nearby gray-sand beaches of Juanchaco and Ladrilleros, which have their charm. The surf is often up in Ladrilleros. From the beachside bluffs, during whale-watching season (June-Nov.), you can spot humpbacks frolicking in the water. These resort towns mostly serve beach-seeking Caleños on the weekend and have great deals on rooms during the week.

ACCOMMODATIONS

★ Pacífico Hostel

Despensa, Juanchaco; tel. 312/241-5490; www.pacificohostel.com; COP$70,000 dorm, COP$170,000 d

In a lush rainforest reserve right on the outskirts of Juanchaco, this popular backpacker meetup offers dorms in cabañas, private rooms in the main house, and luxury private cabañas overlooking the sea (COP$300,000). Access to the beach adds to the appeal, and there's a full on-site travel agency that can help with tours, whale-watching, surf lessons, kayak rentals, and more.

Reserva Aguamarina

Playa de Ladrilleros; tel. 2/246-0285; tel. 311/728-3213 or 321/768-0539; www.reservaaguamarina.com; COP$438,000 d including meals

A popular hotel on a cliff in Ladrilleros, with a spectacular view of the infinite Pacific, is the Reserva Aguamarina, which has 18 traditional hotel rooms as well as 2 cabañas. The pool is a popular gathering place, and there is a lot of green space.

TRANSPORTATION

Asturías

Muelle Turístico Local No. 2; tel. 2/240-4048; www.buceaencolombia.com

Lanchas (boats) make the trip to Juanchaco from the Muelle Turístico in Buenaventura several times a day. Asturías is one company that provides this service, with boats at 10am, 1pm, and 4pm daily. Round-trip fares are around COP$85,000. It's a 45-minute ride to Juanchaco. Ladrilleros is a 30-minute walk from Juanchaco, but on weekends a 4WD bus (about COP$8,000) makes the run.

La Barra

A traditional Pacific fishing village bordering a mangrove forest, La Barra was the set for the famous Colombian movie *El Vuelco de Congrejo*. A wide sandy beach, friendly locals, and trips up the river and into the rainforest often keep visitors here longer than anticipated, as it is an opportunity to live in a real Afro-Colombian village and help support community-based tourism. Bonfires and live music on the beach, fueled by locally made viche, are part of the plan. Many hotels and restaurants are informal in La Barra, often run from people's homes, and thus do not have internet listings.

TRANSPORTATION

La Barra is a 20-minute walk down the open beach from Ladrilleros. Alternatively, locals with dirt bikes will take you there for about COP$8,000.

RIVER AND RAINFOREST TRIPS

At the north end of La Barra, a small river winds through a mangrove forest into the deep interior of the Pacific rainforest, the

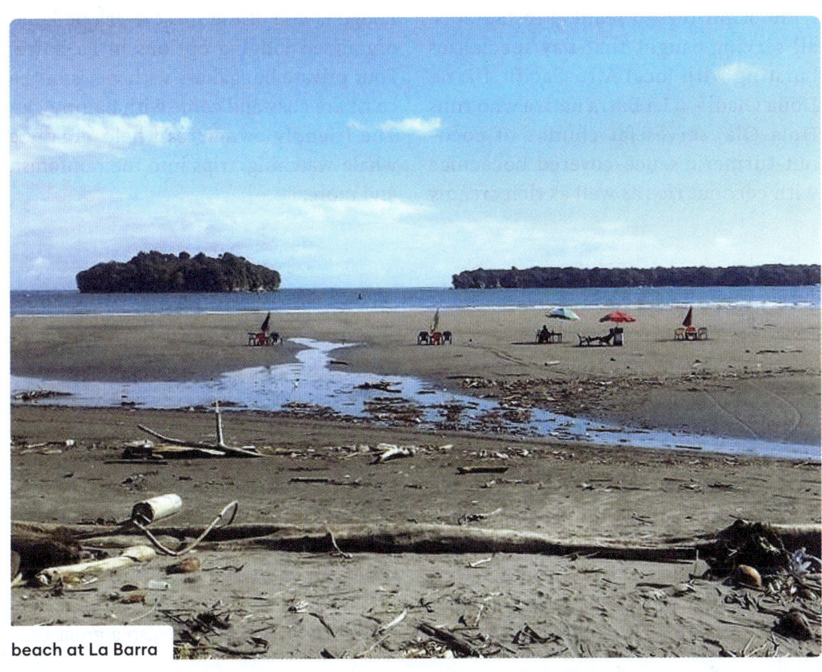

beach at La Barra

second most biodiverse place on earth next to the mighty Amazon. Several different trips into this magical world by canoe (2-3 hours; COP$60,000) can be organized by locals (ask at your hotel or hostel), including hunting for pinguas, a kind of mussel that lives in the root systems of mangroves and is delicious when roasted over an open fire. Visits to a waterfall and a swimming hole surrounded by dense rainforest (2-3 hours; COP$60,000 pp) are also possible. Deeper into the rainforest, Indigenous communities live mostly untouched by outside civilization, but the nearby Bonan reservation is often open to visits (full day; COP$130,000 pp).

FOOD AND ACCOMMODATIONS

Hola-Ola

Playa La Barra; 10am-6pm daily; COP$25,000-40,000

The main beach of La Barra is lined with locally owned seafood restaurants, all serving caught-that-day specialties bursting with local Afro-Pacific flavor. Doña Oladia, a La Barra native who runs Hola-Ola, serves fat chunks of coconut-turmeric sauce-covered bocachica with coconut rice as well as rich creamy jaiba (local crab) stews that will keep you coming back for more.

★ Hostal Doña Elisa

Playa La Barra; tel. 318/518-8788; COP$40,000 dorm, COP$80,000 d

A family-run guesthouse in the village of La Barra, just north of the beach, Hostal Doña Elisa offers homestyle lodging and food served around a huge communal table that often attracts other locals who want to stop by and meet visitors. Doña Elisa is famous for her homemade aborajjados (fried plantains stuffed with cheese and guava sauce), which can become quite addictive.

Selva Luna Eco-Lodge

tel. 315/045-5554; https://selvalunahostal.co; COP$200,000 d

Up a short 1,000-m (0.6-mi) trail from the beach on a forested bluff overlooking the sea just south of town, Selva Luna Eco-Lodge is one of the most developed and organized lodging options in La Barra. Four private bungalows with views of the coast are cozy and come with hammocks. The friendly owners can help organize whale-watching, trips into the rainforest, and more.

Popayán

The temperate capital of the Cauca department, Popayán is known as the White City. It is on the banks of the Río Cauca between the Cordillera Central and Cordillera Occidental mountain ranges and is known for its perfectly preserved colonial architecture that has miraculously survived several major earthquakes. It's full of gorgeous churches and cathedrals and is a major pilgrimage site for Colombian Catholics. During the annual Semana Santa celebrations, the entire city takes part in solemn processions through the streets. The city also has a lively student population, interesting Andean-influenced cuisine, and fun nightlife. Lingering in Parque Caldas on a sunny afternoon or strolling the lonely streets on a Sunday evening are delightful.

Although most city sights can be seen in a day or two, Popayán is also a great base

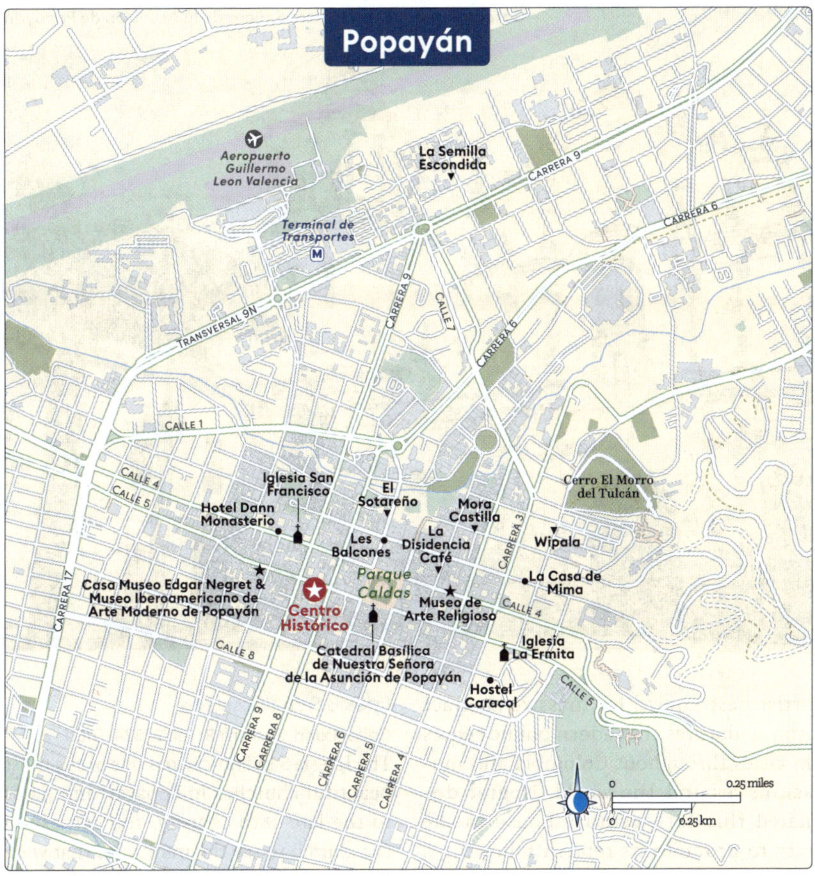

to explore nearby. Just outside town is the Misak Indigenous town of Silvia, famous for its colorful Tuesday market. In Coconuco you can take a dip in the hot springs, and in nearby Parque Nacional Natural Puracé you can hike to the rim of Volcán Puracé.

Sights

★ CENTRO HISTÓRICO

Parque Caldas (between Calles 4-5 and Carreras 6-7) in the center of Popayán is a shade-filled pedestrian square and the city's main point of reference. It contains several towering palms and an ancient oak tree and makes a fantastic place to have a coffee or just hang out, day or night.

Casa Museo Edgar Negret and Museo Iberoamericano de Arte Moderno de Popayán

Calle 5 No. 10-23; tel. 2/824-4546; 8am-noon and 2pm-6pm Wed.-Mon.; COP$4,000

The Casa Museo Edgar Negret and Museo Iberoamericano de Arte Moderno de Popayán (MIAMP) are two museums in the home of Edgar Negret, a Colombian

Catedral Basílica de Nuestra Señora de la Asunción de Popayán

artist best known for massive abstract iron sculptures that adorn public spaces in cities throughout Colombia and museums around the world. Negret donated this 18th-century house to the city to promote its rebirth following a devastating earthquake in 1983. MIAMP is the city's modern art museum. It has four galleries that feature southern Colombia's top visual artists.

Museo de Arte Religioso

Calle 4 No. 4-56; tel. 2/824-2759; 8am-noon and 2pm-6pm Mon.-Fri., 9am-2pm Sat.; COP$6,000

The Museo de Arte Religioso has 10 rooms of religious art from the colonial era in an 18th-century neoclassical house covering Quiteño, Popayán, and Spanish styles. You'll probably be guided through by a friendly police cadet.

Iglesia San Francisco

Calle 4 and Carrera 9; tel. 2/824-0160

The Iglesia San Francisco is one of the most beautiful churches in Popayán and dates to the late 18th century. You can ask at the church to see the mummies that were found here following the 1983 earthquake.

Iglesia La Ermita

Calle 5 and Carrera 2; tel. 2/820-9725

The Iglesia La Ermita dates to the 16th century. A small church, it has a photogenic location, and the interior has some fine woodcarvings and paintings.

Catedral Basílica de Nuestra Señora de la Asunción de Popayán

Calle 5 and Carrera 6; tel. 2/824-1710

The neoclassical cathedral on Parque Caldas was completed in the early 20th century. The cathedral's official name is

Catedral Basílica de Nuestra Señora de la Asunción de Popayán, but it is always referred to as "la catedral."

CERRO EL MORRO DEL TULCÁN

For a quick early-morning or afternoon walk and some nice views of the city, check out Cerro El Morro del Tulcán, a hill northeast of the historic center of Popayán. A statue of the city's founder, Sebastián de Belalcázar, stands on horseback on top of the hill. It is thought that this hill is actually a pyramid built by pre-Columbian peoples. Don't take any valuables with you if you make this walk, as there have been some isolated cases of theft.

Recreation

WALKING TOURS

Get Up and Go Colombia

tel. 316/461-3893; https://getupandgocolombia.org

Get Up and Go Colombia is a locally run nonprofit that offers donation-based daily walking tours of the historic center and hikes to the nearby Cerro las Tres Cruces. A special peace and art tour (COP$60,000) is led by victims of conflict and focuses on the Cauca region's history as told through murals and public art in the city. Get Up and Go can also organize Spanish classes and homestays with local families.

Festivals and Events

Semana Santa

the week before Easter; free

The most important religious site in Colombia during Semana Santa is Popayán. Solemn processions take place on the streets of the center, a tradition fulfilled every year since 1566. This is also the only time of the year that the mummies discovered in Iglesia San Francisco are displayed.

Festival de Música Religiosa de Popayán

the week before Easter; www.fespo.co; free

The Festival de Música Religiosa de Popayán has been running since 1964 and takes place during Semana Santa, with mostly classical and religious music performed each day. Many of the performances are in stunning settings, including cathedrals and parks, and most are free to attend.

Food

COLOMBIAN

Mora Castilla

Calle 2 No. 4-44; tel. 2/824-1513; www.moracastilla.com; 10am-7pm Mon.-Sat., 3pm-8pm Sun.; COP$15,000-25,000

Mora Castilla packs a punch with local specialties such as the famous empanada de pipián, an empanada filled with mashed potatoes and veggies and served with a spicy peanut sauce.

La Semilla Escondida

Calle 9 Norte No. 10-29; tel. 310/823-0313; noon-3pm and 6pm-10pm Mon.-Sat.; COP$22,000-30,000

La Semilla Escondida serves healthy meat and vegetarian lunches, many with Andean grains like quinoa. Go for the crepes, as the French owner does them with zeal.

CAFÉS, BAKERIES, AND QUICK BITES

La Disidencia Café

Carrera 5 No. 3-48; tel. 311/367-0457; 8:30am-10pm Mon.-Sat.; COP$10,000

La Disidencia Café is a hip coffee shop and art gallery that caters to university students. In addition to light bites and drinks it is also hosts live music events.

Bars and Nightlife

El Sotareño

Carrera 6 No. 8-05; no phone; 8pm-midnight daily

For unsurpassed old-school atmosphere, El Sotareño can't be beat. It's a cozy mom-and-pop place where the pop plays lots of tango on old vinyl from his collection and patrons of all ages settle into the comfortable booths.

Wipala

Carrera 2 No. 2-38; tel. 2/823-3141; 3pm-9pm daily; COP$15,000-25,000

Casa Cultural Wipala is a live music venue, gallery, and restaurant surrounding a verdant patio. In the evenings it's a cool place to visit and mingle with locals as well as visitors and expats. Wipala serves unique juices, some with coca leaf, and also serves light meals.

Accommodations

UNDER COP$70,000

There are many low-priced hotels in gorgeous, if in need of repair, colonial buildings in the city center. Most do not have internet listings.

Les Balcones

Carrera 7 No. 2-75; tel. 2/824-2030; COP$35,000 dorm, COP$65,000 d

In a two-story former mansion and offering private rooms with balconies, true to its name, overlooking the bustling market area below, Les Balcones is clean and safe, if basic, for travelers on a budget. Dorm rooms are stark but cozy. A kitchen for guest use, comfy sofas for hanging out, and a ping-pong table make it homey.

COP$70,000-200,000

★ Hostel Caracol

Calle 4 No. 2-21; tel. 2/820-7335; www.hostelcaracol.com; COP$80,000 d shared bath, COP$120,000 studio apartment

"Relaxed" is the best word to describe the Hostel Caracol, housed is a massive restored colonial mansion with multiple garden patios and terraces. Mingling with other travelers or locals is easy in the small on-site café. Hostel Caracol can also arrange outings, such as a wildly popular day trip to the Coconuco hot springs with an exhilarating bike ride back (USD$35); a multiday trip to Parque Nacional Natural Puracé (USD$270 pp, 4-person minimum); or a trip to the market at Silvia.

La Casa de Mima

Calle 3 No. 2-37; tel. 310/494-4082; www.lacasademima.com; COP$180,000 d

La Casa de Mima is a quiet and cozy bed-and-breakfast a few blocks from Parque Caldas. Seven rooms overlook three courtyards. The owner, Doña Olga, lives here and will make you feel right at home.

COP$200,000-500,000

★ Hotel Dann Monasterio

Calle 4 No. 10-14; tel. 2/824-2191; www.hotelesdann.com; COP$323,000 d

The finest option in town, although falling short of five stars, is the classic Hotel Dann Monasterio. It's 47 rooms are in an old monastery overlooking a serene interior courtyard where you can have a coffee. It has a pool amid spacious well-kept grounds.

Transportation

The **Aeropuerto Guillermo León Valencia** (PPN) is just 1 km (0.6 mi) north of the Centro Histórico. The airport is served by

Avianca (Carrera 5 No. 3-85; tel. 2/824-4505; www.avianca.com; 8am-noon and 2pm-6pm Mon.-Fri., 9am-1pm Sat.) and offers several daily flights from Bogotá.

There are frequent buses from Cali (3-4 hours; COP$32,000) and Pasto (5 hours; COP$55,000), arriving at the **Terminal de Transportes** (Transversal 9 No. 4N-125, Oficina 201; tel. 2/823-1817; www.terminalpopayan.com), a modern bus station within walking distance of the airport. It's a 15-minute walk south to downtown.

Vicinity of Popayán

The Cauca Region surrounding Popayán is picturesque and pastoral. Small farms dot the rolling hills and extensive Indigenous territories are found here. Unfortunately, the area has suffered greatly from violence by national armed groups and the US-backed war on drugs, as Cauca is a traditional coca-leaf growing area and has been targeted for aerial spraying. Since the Covid-19 pandemic, armed groups again are vying for power in the region, and some rural areas are currently not safe to visit. The areas listed here are safe for travelers.

With the exception of Tierradentro, most of these places can be visited as day trips from Popayán.

Market at Silvia

town of Silvia; 5am-2pm Tues.

A popular day trip from Popayán is the market at Silvia, 60 km (37 mi) north of the city. Silvia can also be visited on the way from Cali. On market days, starting at dawn, Misak Indigenous people converge on the market from nearby communities to buy and sell fruit, vegetables, and textiles. There are few handicrafts to purchase. With their azure-blue shawls and handmade top hats, the people are photogenic, but if you want to take photos, request permission first.

To get to the market, take a bus bound for Silvia from Popayán's Terminal de Transportes (COP$9,000). They leave every 20 minutes or so, and the trip takes about an hour.

Termales de Coconuco

For a dip in termales (hot springs), there are two possibilities near the town of Coconuco and Parque Nacional Natural Puracé, about 50 minutes from Popayán.

TERMALES AGUATIBIA

Km 4, Vía Coconuco; tel. 310/543-7172; www.termalesaguatibia.com; 8am-6pm daily; COP$30,000

Termales Aguatibia is nestled among the hills, with six pools that vary 27-40°C (80-104°F). There is also a waterslide, making it a popular destination for families on weekends.

TERMALES AGUA HIRVIENDO

Vía Comfandi; tel. 321/934-1746; COP$18,000

Termales Agua Hirviendo, 3 km (2 mi) from the town of Coconuco, is another option. Although the pools are basic, the water is piping hot and has one of the highest mineral contents recorded in the country. Locals come from far and wide claiming that the water here cures various ills. These springs are run by a local Coconuco Indigenous community and offer basic cabañas (COP$80,000 d) where you can spend the night, as well as an on-site restaurant that serves traditional fare.

TRANSPORTATION

To get to these hot springs, take a taxi from Popayán, but expect to pay around COP$80,000 each way. Alternatively, buses depart from Popayán's **Terminal de Transportes** (Transversal 9 No. 4N-125) to the town of Coconuco, about 30 km (19 mi) away. This trip takes about an hour and costs COP$7,000. From Coconuco, you can either walk about 4 km (2.5 mi) along a well-marked road to the springs or take a mototaxi (COP$4,000). The last bus from Coconuco to Popayán departs at 6pm.

Tierradentro

The area of Tierradentro was settled 500-900 CE by an agricultural society that dug magnificent decorated underground tombs, produced large stone statues, and built oval buildings on artificial terraces. These people, related to and sharing cultural practices with the inhabitants of San Agustín, disappeared, and we don't even know what they called themselves. By the time of the Spanish conquest, the area was inhabited by the Nasa-Páez, a Chibcha-speaking people who still inhabit the area and who are organized in cabildos (Indigenous ruling bodies) that are recognized by the Colombian government.

Tierradentro is the site of a major Indigenous necropolis that includes monumental funeral statues and hypogea (underground burial chambers). These chambers, some 12 m (39 ft) wide, are

market at Silvia

decorated with intricate red and black anthropomorphic and zoomorphic geometric designs, some of which are in relief. They were first excavated and studied in the 1930s. This archaeological park was declared a UNESCO World Heritage Site in 1995.

PARQUE ARQUEOLÓGICO NACIONAL DE TIERRADENTRO

91 km (57 mi) east of Popayán; www.icanh.gov.co; 8am-4pm daily; COP$20,000

Parque Arqueológico Nacional de Tierradentro comprises five sites spread across four hills, straddling Vía San Andrés de Pisimbalá-El Crucero.

It's possible to visit all the archaeological sites in one circuit for a total of about 14 km (9 mi) in one long day. Many people visit the museums and the three sites on the eastern side of Vía San Andrés de Pisimbalá-El Crucero, take a break for lunch in San Andrés de Pisimbalá, then continue onward to the two sites on the western side of the road. It's also possible to go at a slower pace, as your admission ticket is good for two consecutive days. If you are in a hurry, prioritize a visit to Alto de Segovia, the first stop on the circuit and the easiest to access. Expect to spend 15-20 minutes at each site.

Begin your visit at the two small museums, located at the park entrance and at the start of the circuit. Across the street from one another, they provide a good introduction to the park. On the western side of the road is the **archaeological museum,** featuring artifacts found in Tierradentro's tombs. On the opposite side of the road, across from the ticket booth, is the **ethnographic museum,** which focuses on the Páez Indigenous communities who live in the area. Plan to spend 15-20 minutes in each museum.

ACCOMMODATIONS

Basic accommodations are plentiful near the official park entrance and museums, and all are on the same main road to San Andrés de Pisimbalá.

El Refugio

tel. 2/825-2904; hotelalbergueelrefugio@gmail.com; COP$60,000 d

El Refugio is a large and somewhat luxurious hotel run by a local Indigenous organization. It has 20 tastefully decorated rooms, a pool, and an on-site restaurant.

★ La Portada

tel. 311/601-7884; laportadatierradentro@hotmail.com; www.laportadahotel.com; COP$100,000 d with private bath, COP$60,000 d shared bath

La Portada offers five rooms in a handcrafted structure made from guadua, a type of bamboo. Leonardo, the owner, is friendly and full of good information. His wife is an excellent cook. Nonguests can dine at the restaurant. La Portada is close to the center of San Andrés de Pisimbalá.

TRANSPORTATION

The 100-km (60-mi) trip to Tierradentro from Popayán will take you through gorgeous countryside of farms, villages, and gentle mountains shrouded in mist. One bus a day leaves from Popayán directly to San Andrés de Pisimbalá, the closest town to the park. It leaves at 10:30am, takes 4-5 hours, and costs around COP$45,000. From San Andrés de Pisimbalá back to Popayán, there is one direct bus that departs at 6am daily.

Public transportation between San Agustín and Tierradentro requires multiple transfers. From San Agustín you can take the 6am bus bound for Bogotá, then transfer in Garzón (COP$18,000) to the bus toward La Plata (COP$9,000). From there you can take the 10:30am bus to San Andrés de Pisimbalá. That trip takes about three hours and costs COP$16,000. To return to San Agustín, you can take a bus at 6am. It arrives in the early afternoon.

Parque Nacional Natural Puracé

main ranger station 44 km (27 mi) east of Popayán; COP$36,000

Parque Nacional Natural Puracé is a national park covering some 83,000 ha (205,000 acres) that include important mountainous formations within the Cordillera Central, the Serranía de los Coconucos. Spanning the Macizo Colombiano between Cauca and Huila, it is a region of immense environmental importance and was declared a UNESCO Biosphere Reserve in 1979.

The Serranía de los Coconucos is a 6-km (4-mi) chain of 11 volcanoes, including the snow-covered Pan de Azúcar (5,000 m/16,400 ft), Coconuco (4,600 m/15,100 ft), Volcán Puracé (4,580 m/15,000 ft), and Volcán Sotará (4,400 m/14,400 ft). Puracé and Sotará are currently active. The Macizo Colombiano is a tight knot of mountains where all three Colombian cordilleras come together. Four major Colombian rivers originate here: the Río Magdalena and Río Cauca, which flow into the Caribbean Sea; the Río Patía, which flows into the Pacific Ocean; and the Río Caquetá, a major tributary of the Amazon.

The park includes more than 50 mountain lakes, including Laguna Magdalena, the source of the Río Magdalena. Most of the park lies at greater than 2,600 m (8,500 ft) elevation. Because of the high volcanic activity, sulfur-rich hot springs dot the area.

PRACTICALITIES

High season in the park is mid-December-mid-January as well as during Semana Santa and school vacations, mid-June-mid-July.

The main ranger station and main entrance is called **Pilimbalá,** 44 km (27 mi) east of Popayán. Entrance to the park costs COP$36,000.

Near Pilimbalá, the park has three **cabins** (COP$35,500-45,000 pp high season), and **camping** (COP$20,000 pp) is also available. To make a reservation, contact the Pilimbalá ranger station (tel. 8/521-2578, 8/521-2579, or 313/680-0051). A **restaurant** at Pilimbalá serves three meals a day (under COP$15,000).

Note that most of the park is under the jurisdiction of the Yanacona and Paeces Indigenous communities, and their leaders have the final word on whether visitors will be permitted into the park and to which locations. Certain areas of the park, especially the peaks themselves, are frequently closed to visitors. The main hikes are also often closed due to volcanic activity.

VOLCANO TREK

The primary attraction at this park is the fairly strenuous 7-km (4.3-mi) climb to the summit of **Volcán Puracé** in the northern part of the park. The trek requires about five hours up and three hours down. It takes you through high mountain tropical rainforest and then páramo, a unique high-elevation Andean ecosystem.

It's imperative to hire a guide for this trek. Contact the Popayán branch of Parques Nacionales (Carrera 9 No. 25N-6; tel. 2/823-1279; purace@parquesnacionales.gov.co) or the **Pilimbalá ranger station** (tel. 8/521-2578 or 8/521-2579) in advance to arrange for a guide. Guides usually charge around COP$55,000 pp for the hike up to the crater. The highly recommended outfitter **Popayán Tours** (www.popayantours.com), run by Hostal Caracol, works with the community and offers both hiking and biking tours to Puracé (USD$270 pp). Transportation, food, and a guide are included.

TRANSPORTATION

The main entrance of the park, Pilimbalá, is 45 km (28 mi) east of Popayán. From Popayán, buses depart the **Terminal de Transportes** bound for the community of La Plata (COP$9,000). The company Sotracauca runs buses (COP$11,000) that leave at 4:30am and 6:45am daily, but there are often delays. The trip takes approximately 1.5 hours. Get off at the Cruce de la Mina, also known as El Crucero, and from there walk about 800 m (0.5 mi) to the left to the Pilimbalá ranger station. There are return buses to Popayán until around 5:30pm. You can find a return bus at Cruce de la Mina-El Crucero.

★ Desierto de Tatacoa

The 330-sq-km (127-sq-mi) Tatacoa desert makes an enchanting overnight or two on the way to San Agustín from Bogotá. It's not technically a desert but rather a semi-arid zone with dry tropical forest. It feels and looks like a desert, with red rock outcrops on one side and a dry white rocky landscape dotted with towering cacti on the other. Temperatures regularly soar above 32°C (90°F) here. At night the sky is ablaze with stars, and the milky way traces a dazzling river across the sky. Camping in Desierto de Tatacoa is a great way to experience one of Colombia's most unique ecosystems.

Desierto de Tatacoa

SIGHTS

A visit to Tatacoa includes a stop at the historic town of **Villavieja,** with its 17th-century **Capilla de Santa Bárbara** (Plaza Principal Villavieja), a church founded by the Jesuits in honor of the Indigenous cacique Tocaya, who was killed by the Spaniards.

Museo Paleontológico

Calle 3 No. 3-05; 7:30am-1pm Mon.-Fri., 7am-6pm Sat.-Sun.; COP$5,000

The Museo Paleontológico provides a sample of the many fossils, dating from 3.8 million years ago, that have been found in the Desierto de Tatacoa.

Observatorio Astronómico Tatacoa

Vereda El Cuzco; tel. 8/879-7584 or 310/465-6765; www.tatacoa-astronomia.com; COP$5,000

The Observatorio Astronómico Tatacoa, near Villavieja, provides telescopes for visitors to scan the sky in the evening hours. Entrance to the observatory includes free educational talks by Javier Fernando Rúa Restrepo, the house astronomer, at around 6:30pm. After the talks, and everyone's basic astronomy skills are leveled up, a sky-watching party begins that often lasts till at least midnight.

Piscina Natural

Las Yeguas, Tatacoa; COP$8,000

The clear turquoise water of the Piscina Natural—really a swimming pool carved into the white rocks of the desert—makes for cooling off on hot afternoons. The picturesque place often gets swamped on weekends.

ACCOMMODATIONS

Camping is available in the red-rock desert between the park's entrance and the observatory. If you bring a tent the cost is a meager COP$25,000, while tents and spaces together go for COP$55,000. There are plenty of local restaurants to grab grub; the local specialty is grilled goat.

La Casona

Calle 3 No. 3-60; tel. 8/879-7636 or 320/243-9705; http://hotellacasonavillavieja.blogspot.com; COP$80,000 d

In Villavieja, La Casona is a small hotel in an old house on Parque Principal, overseen by friendly owners. Simón Bolívar is said to have stayed here.

Hostal Noches de Saturno

400 m (0.2 mi) past the observatory; tel. 313/305-5898 or 314/288-3337; moisestatacoa@yahoo.es; COP$110,000 d

Hostal Noches de Saturno has five rooms, a pool, and an on-site bar and restaurant that attracts a lot of people most nights of the week. It's a fun social place to visit even if you are camping down the road.

TRANSPORTATION

To get to Desierto de Tatacoa from Bogotá is a 5-6-hour bus ride (COP$65,000) to Neiva. From Popayán, it's an 8-hour bus ride that costs around COP$75,000 to Neiva. From Neiva it's a 1-hour, COP$6,000 bus ride to Villavieja, a charming historic town on the outskirts of the desert.

From Villavieja, mototaxis regularly transport visitors to the Desierto de Tatacoa. These cost about COP$22,000 per person. This is the best way to go as the scenery and desert light are gorgeous.

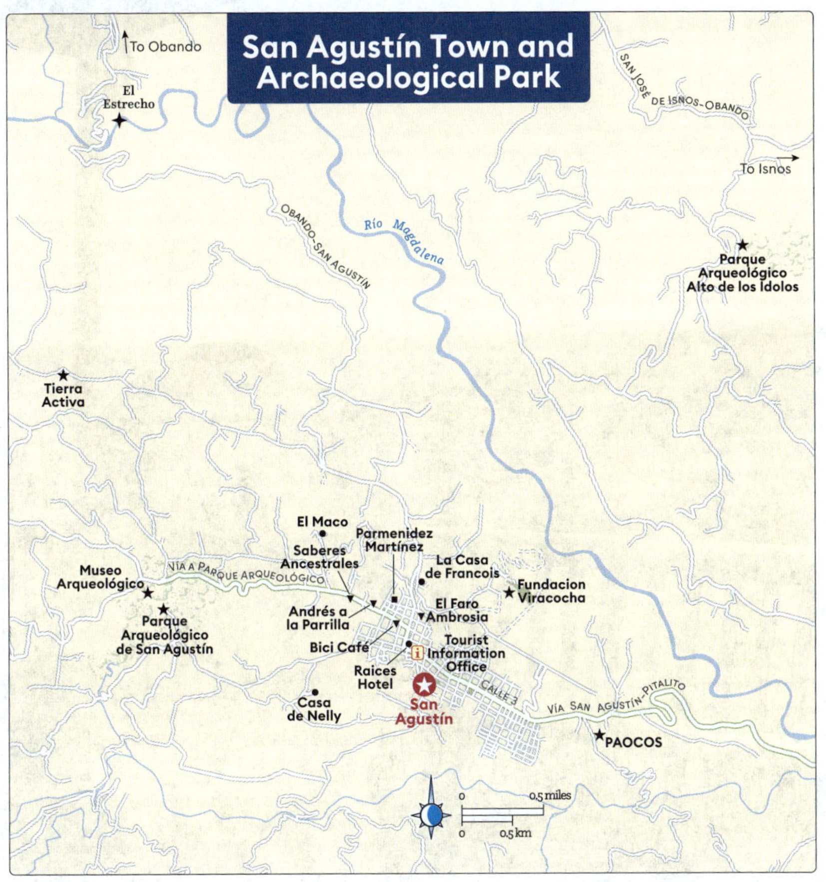

TOP EXPERIENCE

★ San Agustín

The quaint colonial coffee town of San Agustín, nestled within the folds of the Macizo Colombiano and perched over the Río Magdalena gorge, is an attractive destination. At an elevation of 1,800 m (5,900 ft), its setting has enormous natural beauty and wonderful springlike weather. Its fame stems from its location near the largest pre-Columbian archaeological site between Central America and Peru. Approximately 100-800 CE this region was home to an Indigenous culture that produced spectacular monumental funeral statues hewn from volcanic rock. Researchers do not know what these people called themselves and so labeled them the San Agustín Culture. In 1995 UNESCO gave the site World Heritage designation.

To visit the main archaeological sites near San Agustín, you need at least two days. Don't rush your stay, however, as it is a relaxed and peaceful place to visit, with options for hiking to waterfalls and

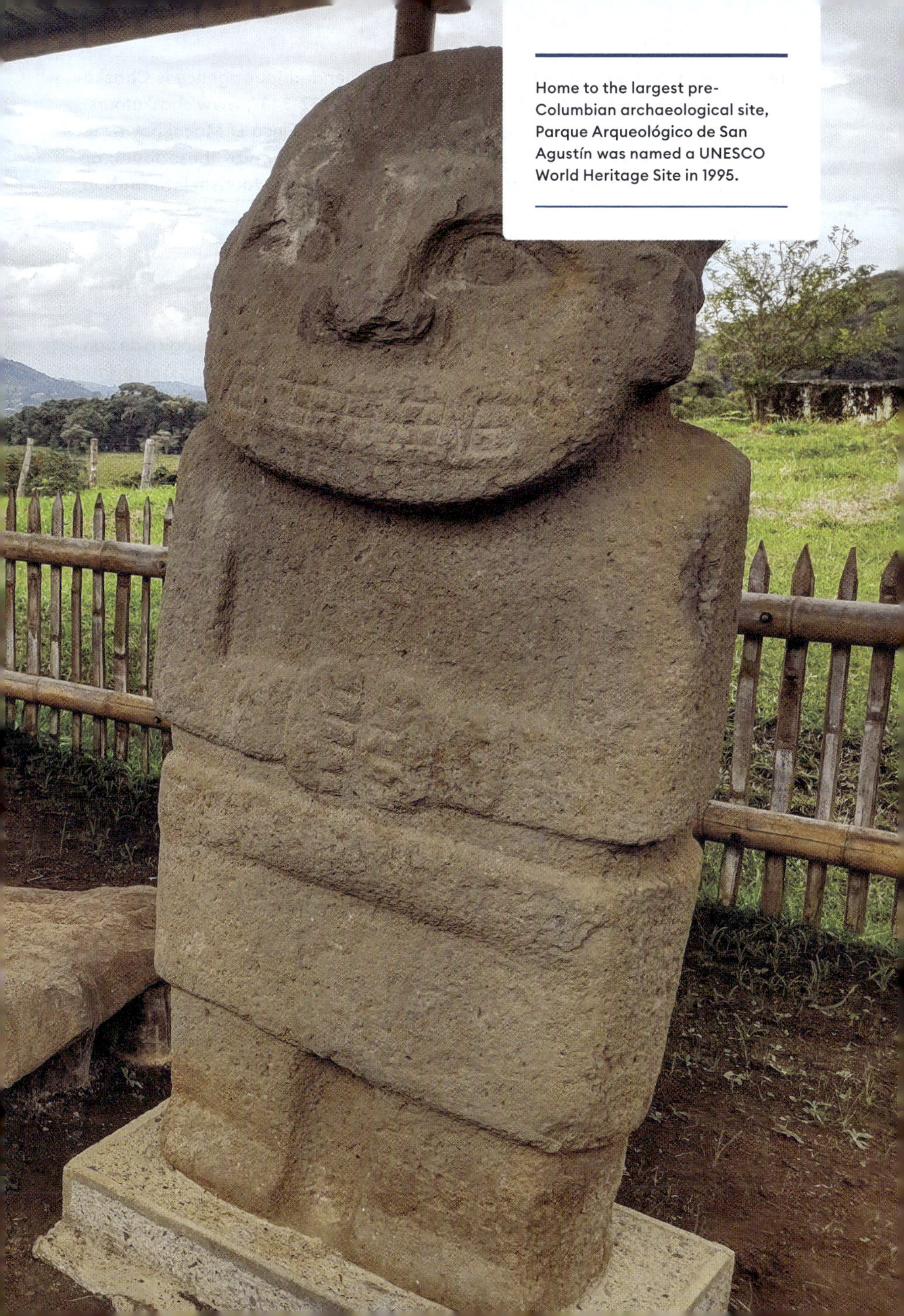

Home to the largest pre-Columbian archaeological site, Parque Arqueológico de San Agustín was named a UNESCO World Heritage Site in 1995.

rafting amid spectacular mountain landscapes. This little town has attracted an eclectic community from across Colombia and abroad and offers surprisingly good restaurants, cafés, and accommodations.

HISTORY

The area around San Agustín was occupied as early as 3300 BCE. Starting in the 1st century CE, the people of San Agustín created hundreds of monumental funeral stone statues set on large platforms. Very little is known about these people except that they were agrarian and formed compact settlements. By 800 CE this society had mysteriously vanished, and other Indigenous peoples from the Amazon basin occupied the area. Today the inhabitants are predominantly mestizo campesinos.

PRACTICALITIES

Horseback Tours

While the main archaeological park is easy to visit on foot, there are many sites scattered around the mountains that make for great half-day or full-day **horseback tours.** It usually costs about COP$65,000 for a horse and a guide; a local guide is **Parménidez Martínez** (Carrera 7 No. 17-50; tel. 312/477-7878). The **tourism information office** can also assist with booking horseback tours, or you can ask your hotel to recommend a guide.

Jeep Tours

Visiting the sights near the town of Isnos (the other archaeological parks, El Estrecho, and the waterfalls) by public transportation can be difficult; most people opt for daylong Jeep tours that cover Parque Arqueológico Alto de los Ídolos, Parque Arqueológico Alto de Las Piedras, El Estrecho, and several waterfalls. A recommended tour agency is **Chaska Tours** (tel. 8/837-3437; www.chaskatours.net), run out of Finca El Maco; however, any hotel can organize these tours, or you can stop by the **tourism information office.**

SIGHTS

Parque Arqueológico de San Agustín

8am-4pm daily; COP$65,000

The excellent Parque Arqueológico de San Agustín covers 80 ha (200 acres) of an important ritual area of the San Agustín culture. Some 130 km (80 mi) southeast of Popayán, it was established in 1937 and declared a UNESCO World Heritage Site in 1995. The park contains over 130 statues with striking human and animal-like features as well as carved tombs and monumental stone tables, or dolmens. The park is easy to navigate: Plan on a couple of hours to stroll it at leisure and absorb the beauty. The park is 2 km (1.2 mi) west of the town of San Agustín and can be reached on foot or by bus. The admission ticket is also valid at Parque Arqueológico Alto de los Ídolos.

Near the entrance to the park is the highly recommended **Museo Arqueológico** (free). It contains pottery, tools, jewelry, and some smaller-scale statues. It's a good educational stop to learn more about the San Agustín culture before visiting the sites themselves.

As you enter the park, you'll walk along the lovely 800-m (0.5-mi) Bosque de las Estatuas, a meandering shady path lined with statues. Many of these were recovered from other locations in the region. Most of the park's monumental stone objects are concentrated on four funerary hills, designated Mesitas A, B, C, and D. The first stops in the park are Mesitas B and A. **Mesita B,** atop a hill, has some of

THE AGROECOLOGICAL REVOLUTION

San Agustín, a bastion of back-to-the-earth farmers and traditional campesinos, is pioneering a cure for the harmful effects of industrial agriculture, including pesticides and mono-crop cultivation: the agroecological revolution. Agroecology is an umbrella term for a variety of sustainable food-producing methods that include permaculture, regenerative agriculture, agroforestry, and more. San Agustín is set to become Colombia's first "transition town," or community that completely moves from the toxic practices of industrial agriculture to the nature-based agroecological ones of the future.

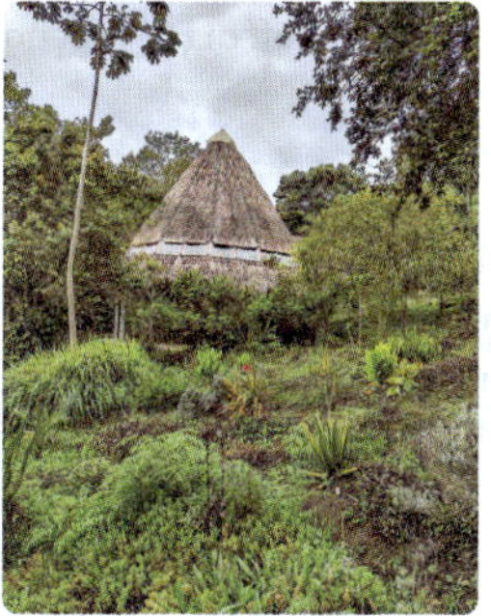

Fundación Viracocha

TIERRA ACTIVA

Vereda Puratal; tel. 312/476-2181; www.tierractiva.com

At the forefront of the movement is Yilema Muñoz, who cultivates over 100 edible species on a 1-ha (2.5-acre) parcel that buzzes with bees and hummingbirds in the hills above San Agustín. Amazonian rainforest foods like sacha inchi wind through the branches of the coffee plants, while the herbs ward off pests. Day tours (COP$35,000), culinary and gardening classes, and homestays for up to a week are available.

FUNDACIÓN VIRACOCHA

Finca Viracocha, Carrera 11-Vereda La Antigua; tel. 312/346-6789; https://fundacionviracocha.org

A paradisical 18-ha (45-acre) permaculture complex dotted with buildings made of guadua (local bamboo) and other natural materials awaits visitors. Steffen and Lina, the German-Colombian couple behind the school, have been here for 30 years and offer both apprenticeship and volunteer opportunities as well as one-day Regeneration Experience tours that include lunch at the on-site restaurant, with food all grown on the grounds. The center also operates **La Antigua** (COP$80,000 d), a small hotel next door.

PAOCOS

Vereda La Florida; tel. 314/268-6209; https://organicospaocos.wixsite.com

Formed over 30 years ago after their 7-year-old son developed cancer from exposure to the agrochemicals used in traditional coffee production, PAOCOS is a family-run sustainable coffee farm. They have successfully helped over 100 local farmers transition away from industrial production to their model organic practices. With lush coffee plants thriving under towering fruit and nut trees, the 16-ha (40-acre) grounds are a glimpse into the future of ecological coffee farming. Guided two-hour tours (COP$20,000) are offered daily.

the best-known statues. **Mesita A** was the first area open to the public and holds some of the largest funerary mounds ever excavated, 30 m (100 ft) in diameter and 4 m (13 ft) high. **Mesita C** has one burial mound with 15 statues and 49 simple tombs. Statues here tend to be more abstract with less detail.

The unusual **Fuente de Lavapiés** contains bas-reliefs of human and animal figures sculpted on the rocky bed of a stream. This is the only non-funerary site in the park. Behind the Fuente, on a hill at the highest point of the park, excavations at the **Alto de Lavapiés** have shown human presence dating back to 3300 BCE.

Parque Arqueológico Alto de los Ídolos

8am-5pm daily; COP$20,000

On the other side of the Río Magdalena, 5 km (3 mi) southwest of the town of Isnos and about 25 km (16 mi) northeast of the town of San Agustín, Parque Arqueológico Alto de los Ídolos is the second-largest archaeological park. It includes an anthropomorphic statue that measures 4.3 m (14 ft) along with large sarcophagi. The admission ticket is also valid for Parque Arqueológico Nacional de San Agustín. To get here from San Agustín, take a public bus toward Isnos (COP$3,500) or call a cab (COP$22,000).

Parque Arqueológico Alto de Las Piedras

8am-5pm daily; admission included with Parque Arqueológico de San Agustín

The much smaller Parque Arqueológico Alto de Las Piedras is 6 km (3.7 mi) north of Isnos on the road to Salto de Bordones waterfall. It has statues and tombs with original pigments, including the Doble Yo—a statue that is half man, half animal. It's not easy to get here by public transportation, so take a cab from San Agustín (COP$22,000).

El Estrecho

While the entire upper gorge of the Río Magdalena is majestic, about 15 km (9 mi) north of San Agustín, at El Estrecho, the river rushes through a 2.2-m (7-ft) rocky funnel. This is where the bridge crossing the river is located, and several restaurants and tons of souvenir vendors are at the entrance. Take a bus toward Obando and ask to be let off at El Estrecho (COP$8,000).

La Chaquira

La Chaquira is the name of a unique petroglyph that seems to be standing guard over the Río Magdalena gorge. A nice lookout platform has been built just below the rock carving with stunning views of several waterfalls and the gorgeous mountain scenery. La Chaquira is a frequent destination for horseback tours but is also easy to get to on foot. It makes for a nice 45-minute walk through the countryside from the center of town that passes by the El Tablón archaeological site, where several stone statues await. There is no entrance fee for La Chaquira or El Tablón.

WATERFALLS

Less than 10 km (6 mi) north of the town of Isnos are two waterfalls, the 400-m (1,300-ft) **Salto de Bordones** and 200-m (650-ft) **Salto del Mortiño.** To get here, take a bus to Isnos (COP$6,000), then a mototaxi (COP$5,000) to the waterfalls.

cakes at Saberes Ancestrales

RAFTING

About an hour from the town of San Agustín, the upper Río Magdalena offers some of the best white-water river rafting in Colombia, set in spectacular mountain landscapes.

Magdalena Rafting

tel. 311/271-5333;
www.magdalenarafting.com

Magdalena Rafting offers rafting, rappelling, and hiking tours for people of all abilities, ranging from 90-minute excursions to daylong trips that pass through the white water of the El Estrecho (COP$150,000 pp).

FOOD

There is a surprisingly wide variety of excellent food options in San Agustín, as the area is in a fertile agricultural region that produces some of the best coffee beans in the world as well as a diverse array of fresh produce. Lunch at the main market (from COP$12,000) is always a good option.

★ Saberes Ancestrales

Calle 5A No. 18-287; tel. 311/858-4451;
2pm-10pm daily; COP$20,000-30,000

Chef Paola Pinzón uses native species like chachafruto (a bean-producing tree) to create heaping plates of vegan food

Río Magdalena valley

The Macizo Colombiano outside San Agustín is full of magical outdoor adventure opportunities, and you will see many multiday treks and horseback rides advertised in town. By far the most enchanting of these is **Laguna Magdalena,** a mist-shrouded high-altitude lake where three of Colombia's most important rivers are all born: Río Magdalena and Río Cauca, which both flow to the Caribbean Sea, and Río Caquetá, a major tributary of the Amazon.

packed with nutritional value at her cozy restaurant-café. Her cakes, based on flour ground from bore root and served with house-made kombucha or organic dark hot chocolate, are the ultimate afternoon pickup.

Andrés a la Parrilla

Calle 5 No. 15-67; tel. 311/858-4451; 11am-9pm daily; COP$35,000-45,000

On the road to the archaeological park, Andrés a la Parrilla is known for asado huilenese, a plate of tender pork slow-cooked in banana leaves, as well as other traditional fare like conejo (rabbit).

El Faro Ambrosia

Carrera 13 No. 6-70; tel. 311/287-6696; 5pm-midnight Tues.-Sun.; COP$35,000-45,000

Wood oven-fired pizzas and live local bands on the garden patio make El Faro one of the most popular places in town. Local cervecería Laboyano, which makes craft beer flavors like cholupa (a local passion fruit variety) and coffee, is on tap.

Bici Cafe

Calle 2 No. 13-17; tel. 314/661-6337; 8:30am-8pm daily

For a top-end cup of coffee produced, roasted, and ground in San Agustín, head to Bici Cafe, which also has a book lending library and offers well done set lunches daily (COP$16,000).

ACCOMMODATIONS

There are a surprising number of cozy and friendly lodging options in San Agustín, many run by expats who settled here decades ago. Staff at these spots can provide expert advice on the area, arrange recreational activities such as horseback riding and rafting, and assist with travel needs.

La Casa de Francois

tel. 8/837-3847 or 314/358-2930; www.lacasadefrancois.com; COP$35,000 dorm, COP$80,000 d

La Casa de Francois offers cabins, two dorm rooms with 10 beds in total, and lots of hammocks to laze in after a hard day's archaeological exploration. The on-site restaurant is quite good and reasonably priced, and they bake their own bread. Its garden-like setting, perched on a hilltop just a 10-minute walk north of town, is ideal.

★ Casa de Nelly

Vía Vereda La Estrella; tel. 310/215-9067 or 311/535-0412; www.hotelcasadenelly.co; COP$35,000 dorm, COP$110,000 d

Bursting with flowers and vegetation, Casa de Nelly is on the mountainside 2 km (1.2 mi) from town and sports sweeping views over the valley. The lush gardens and cozy living room, complete with a raging

CARNAVAL DE NEGROS Y BLANCOS

Every January the population of sleepy **Pasto** explodes as over 350,000 visitors from Colombia and beyond converge on the city during the Carnaval de Negros y Blancos (www.carnavaldepasto.org; Jan. 2-6), recognized as a world heritage tradition by UNESCO. It's a unique Carnaval that mixes Indigenous, African, and Catholic traditions and celebrates the rich diversity of southern Colombia with an emphasis on racial equality.

Carnaval de Negros y Blancos

PRE-CARNAVAL

The festivities start **December 28,** Día de los Inocentes (Day of the Holy Innocents), a day of purification and celebration of the natural beauty of the area; many hop on their bikes, cruising down the main parade route. On **December 31** a parade pokes fun at politicians and other unpopular figures from the previous year, and sometimes effigies of them are burned.

FESTIVITIES

Parades take place all week long, culminating on **January 5,** the day of the negros, when revelers paint themselves or others black. The Carnaval actually has its roots in a rebellion of enslaved people in the 17th century that resulted in the king giving the enslaved population one day to do as they pleased. Free for 24 hours, they went around painting everyone's face black and inviting them to join in dancing through the streets.

On **January 6,** the festival concludes with the day of the blancos, when fantastic floats slowly make their way along city streets and hundreds of thousands of onlookers pelt each other with white powder. Historians say the Spanish colonizers were so envious of the fun the enslaved people were having, they needed to have their own party day. Eventually, everyone just painted their faces white and joined in the fun.

MUSIC

In addition to the parades, there are nonstop concerts featuring Andean and Pacific music, and presentations by elaborately costumed stilt walkers and dancers fill the streets and parks.

GETTING THERE

Airlines add dozens of flights to Pasto during this time, but it's still best to make plans several months in advance if you want to be a part of the fun, as hotels tend to book up fast. From Popayán, it's a five-hour bus ride (COP$35,000) to Pasto.

fireplace, board games, and books, are great for meeting other travelers.

★ Finca El Maco

tel. 8/837-3437; tel. 311/271-4802; www.elmaco.ch; COP$50,000 pp dorm, COP$85,000 d

A perennial favorite of international travelers is Swiss-run Finca El Maco, nestled in the hills about a 20-minute walk from town. Accommodations are small cabins, a tepee, a chalet, and an Indigenous-style maloca (cabin) distributed among pleasant gardens home to dogs and chickens. Live Andean music bands play on weekends, which brings folks in from the hills.

Raices Hotel

Carrera 13 No. 3-36; tel. 310/437-4768; COP$50,000 d

Locally run Raices Hotel is in a massive colonial mansion half a block from the main square of San Agustín. Twelve well-kept yet simple rooms, a sunny backyard garden complete with hammocks, and a traditional breakfast included in the price all make the experience hard to beat.

INFORMATION AND SERVICES

Tourist Information Office

Calle 3 and Carrera 12; tel. 320/486-3896; 8am-noon and 2pm-6pm Mon.-Fri.

The tourist information office, just half a block from the main plaza, can assist with transportation and activities in the area.

TRANSPORTATION

From Bogotá

Direct buses from Bogotá (COP$112,000) leave Terminal de Transportes in Salitre at 7am and 11am daily and take about 10.5 hours. Alternatively, take any southbound bus to Pitalito (hourly; COP$90,000). From Pitalito it's a 45-minute ride in colectivo truck ($9,000) to San Agustín.

From Popayán

From Popayán four buses per day head to Pitalito (5 hours; COP$45,000). This journey takes you through the spectacular scenery of Parque Nacional Natural Puracé. It's often slow going.

San Andrés and Providencia

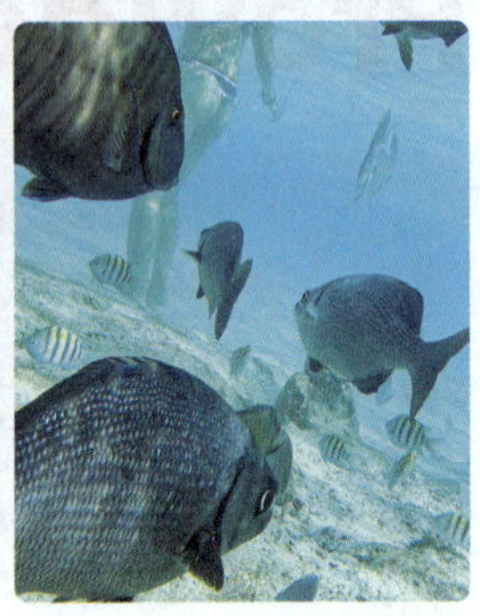

★ Highlights

★ **Jardín Botánico:** Learn about the unique fruits, medicinal plants, and exotic species of San Andrés (page 353).

★ **Johnny Cay** *(upper left & right):* Relax on the perfect white-sand beaches of this tiny Caribbean island (page 355).

★ **Seaflower Biosphere Reserve** *(lower right):* Enjoy world-class diving among the living reefs of this UNESCO Biosphere Reserve (page 358).

★ **Parque Nacional Natural Old Providence McBean Lagoon** *(lower left):* Watch for birds in the dense mangrove forests of this national park (page 367).

★ **The Peak:** Hike to the highest point on Providencia for excellent views over the turquoise sea (page 370).

Look for ★ to find recommended sights, activities, dining, and lodging.

◂ Johnny Cay

The idyllic Caribbean islands of San Andrés and Providencia are a piece of Caribbean paradise far offshore from mainland Colombia and feel more like Jamaica or Belize, partly because English is the main language. A popular vacation destination for middle- and upper-class Colombians and well as international visitors, there are of lots of inexpensive domestic flights from major cities to San Andrés, but in general prices are higher here on everything from food to hotels.

The white-sand beaches and perfect turquoise water are legendary, the food is freshly caught, and the reggae-infused nightlife is tons of fun and markedly different to the rest of the country. Nature lovers will find gorgeous areas to explore, and scuba and snorkeling aficionados will be in heaven on earth. The islands are great extra stop on any Colombian vacation and add another cultural dimension, not to mention some quality beach time.

The Landscape

The Archipelago of San Andrés, Providencia and Santa Catalina covers 280,000 sq km (174,000 sq mi) of marine area. It includes three major islands, seven atolls, and some well-preserved coral reefs, particularly the barrier reef surrounding Providencia and Santa Catalina, home to more than 80 species of coral and 200 species of fish. The three islands and much of the surrounding Caribbean Sea were designated the Seaflower Biosphere Reserve by UNESCO in 2000 in recognition of the region's status as a biodiversity hot spot.

The islands were once covered by forest. Much of it has been cleared, especially in San Andrés, but significant tracts remain, with cedars, cotton trees, stinking toes, birch gums, and other indigenous species. The abundance of fruit-bearing trees and plants includes breadfruit, tamarind, mango, coconut, and guava. There are several large well-preserved mangrove lagoons, notably the McBean Lagoon in Providencia and Old Point Mangrove Regional Park in San Andrés.

The islands support a wide range of reptiles, including snakes, iguanas, geckos, and lizards. Other land animals include crabs, especially the black and shankey crabs, which migrate to and from the sea to spawn, protected by army personnel who block traffic on Providencia's roads during the migration. Four species of protected sea turtles nest here, and 100 bird species have been identified, but only 18 are resident. The island's only nonhuman land mammals are bats. Dolphins and whales are sighted occasionally.

Despite environmental degradation, especially in San Andrés, the archipelago remains one of the best-preserved corners of the Caribbean.

Planning Your Time

San Andrés is a possible long-weekend getaway from mainland Colombia. Visiting the islands can be accomplished in **five nights,** although a full week allows for a more relaxed pace, especially if you want to

San Andrés and Providencia

Caribbean Sea

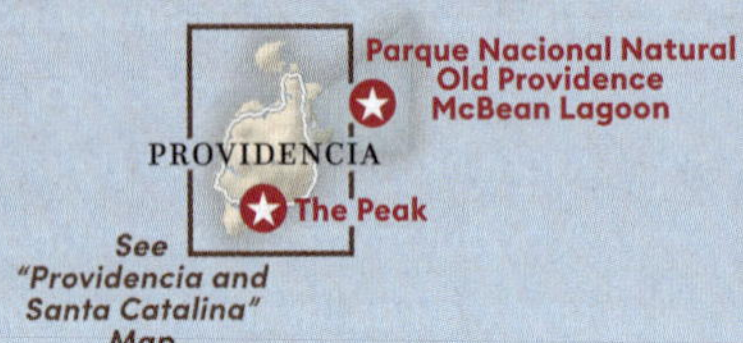

Seaflower Biosphere Reserve

Caribbean Sea

Seaflower Biosphere Reserve

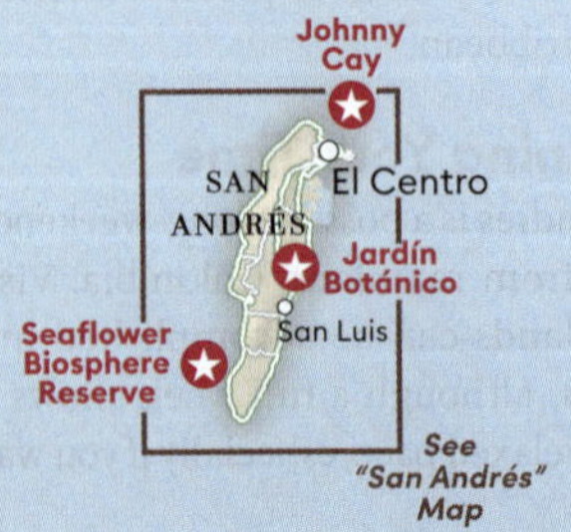

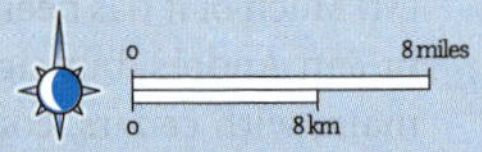

do some serious diving. Wait 24 hours after diving to get in an airplane due to pressurization concerns.

A visit to Providencia from San Andrés can be a budget buster, but it is worth the expense if you're interested in getting away from it all. Getting to Providencia and Santa Catalina involves an extra flight or catamaran ride, and hotels and restaurants are generally more expensive than in San Andrés, which itself is more expensive than the mainland.

High seasons on the islands are during Christmas and New Year's. It may be hard to find a hotel mid-December-mid-January, when throngs of Colombian families and a growing number of Brazilians and Argentinians take over San Andrés. Also popular are Semana Santa as well as school vacations mid-June-August. May-September are quiet. Because it's more difficult to reach, Providencia rarely feels crowded.

The average daily temperature is 27°C (81°F). During the dry season (Jan.-Apr.), water rationing can be necessary, especially in Providencia, where it rains as little as five days per month. The rainy season is June-November, when it can rain 20-24 days per month. October is the rainiest month and is also when hurricanes occasionally churn up the warm Caribbean. March-April are the best months for snorkeling and diving because the water is calm. December-January are windy, making snorkeling and diving challenging. Strong winds can prompt airlines to cancel flights in and out of Providencia.

Johnny Cay

Itinerary Ideas

If you only have two days to enjoy San Andrés, pack in as much beach time and sightseeing as possible. Here is the best way to do it.

DAY 1

1. In the morning, join an all-day tour that gets you to **Johnny Cay** in time for lunch, then enjoy the afternoon on the sand.
2. In the evening, walk along the **Spratt Bight Pathway,** enjoying the festive atmosphere.
3. After the walk, enjoy the high-quality seafood and open-air dining at **La Regatta.**
4. Before hitting the hay, pop into **Bocca de Oro** for some live music and cocktails.

DAY 2

1. Enjoy a morning walk around the **Jardín Botánico.**
2. Head down to San Luis for a beachside lunch at **Donde Francesca.**
3. After lunch, clock in some quality beach time at **San Luis Beach.**
4. Around sunset, join the locals at **Madguana Beach** for a cocktail over reggae music.

Johnny Cay

San Andrés

ceviche at San Luis

San Andrés

Surrounded by a large barrier reef, San Andrés is a Caribbean island playground for a growing number of domestic and international travelers. The water is seven shades of blue, the sandy beaches are white, and a coco loco, the official island cocktail, is always available. Days here are spent sun-worshipping, island-hopping, snorkeling and diving, partying on the beach, and enjoying fresh seafood. For many Colombians the deals at the many duty-free stores are too good to pass up and one reason for a visit to the island.

San Andrés has a population of about 75,000, about two-thirds of mainland Colombian origin. The rest are English- and creole-speaking native islanders, known as Raizals or nativos, whose ancestors were enslaved and brought to the islands; they're related to the inhabitants of the nearby Corn Islands of Nicaragua and the Miskito coast region of Central America. There is also a community of "Turcos" or "Arabes," whose roots can be traced mostly to Lebanon and Syria. Their presence on the island is not insignificant, as demonstrated by a modern brilliant-white mosque that stands prominently in the commercial center.

ORIENTATION

The island of San Andrés resembles a seahorse floating gently eastward in the western Caribbean Sea. It's only 13 km (8 mi) long from top to bottom and 3 km (2 mi) wide and has a total area of 26 sq km (10 sq mi). The Circunvalar ring road more or less circles the entire island.

The "town" of San Andrés is usually called **El Centro.** It's in the northeast, in the snout of the seahorse. This is the center of activity and home to the majority of the island's restaurants, hotels, and shops, nearly all of which are owned and operated by mainland Colombians. The center of action here is the paseo peatonal, or malecón, along Avenida Colombia, known in English as the Spratt Bight Pathway. This delightful 1.6-km (1-mi) pedestrian promenade along Spratt Bight Beach is lined with hotels and restaurants and stays bustling late into the night.

The town of **San Luis** extends along the southeastern edge of the island. It has a much more local feel and is more laid-back than El Centro. This area has some hotels, restaurants, and waterfront reggae bars, mostly along a series of beaches, including **San Luis Beach** and **Rocky Cay Beach,** named after a small offshore island just east.

The west side of the island is quieter, with a handful of points of interest, hotels, and restaurants. The coastline on the west side is all coral, with no beaches.

The middle part of the island is home to the town of **La Loma** (The Hill), the highest point on the island. The main point of reference is the stately white First Baptist Church. This area is home to the largest community of native Raizal islanders and is an interesting place to immerse yourself in local life.

Sights

EL CENTRO

Banco de Colombia Cultural Center

Av. Colón No. 2-74, El Centro; 8:30am-6pm Mon.-Fri., 9am-1pm Sat.; free

Home to permanent interactive exhibits on the music of San Andrés as well as a salon where elder Raizals have orally recorded

San Andrés

Tourist Information Kiosk
Hotel Tiuna
Calle 3
Hotel Casablanca
Spratt Bight Pathway & Beach
El Centro
Banco de Colombia Cultural Center
Club Kitesurf San Andres
Beer Station
Coco Loco
Av. Colombia
Carrera 5
Gourmet Shop
Calle 2
El Viajero
Bocca de Oro
Miss Celia
Parque de la Barracuda
Banda Dive
Carrera 2
Carrera 1
La Regatta
Bicycle Rental Shop
0 100 yds
0 100 m

Johnny Cay
Renta de Motos T.T. 9
Fisherman's Place
See Detail
Vía Circunvalar de San Andrés
Casa Harb
Aeropuerto Gustavo Rojas Pinillas
El Centro
Summer House Inn
Posada Nativa
Lizard House
Av. La Loma Barrack
Vía Circunvalar de San Andrés
Seaflower Biosphere Reserve
First Baptist Church
San Andrés Island
Caribbean Sea
El Acuario
Vía Loma Cove
La Loma
Coconut Paradise Lodge
Cocoplum Hotel
Madguana Beach
San Luis Beach
Donde Franz
Vía Duppy Gully
Breeze View & Culture
Jardín Botánico
Restaurante Lydia
Paradise Farm
San Luis
La Piscinita
Sound Bay Rd
Arnol's Place
El Paraiso
Donde Francesca
Sea Pride Dive Center
Vía Tom Hooker
Caribbean Sea
Seaflower Biosphere Reserve
Vía Circunvalar de San Andrés
Vía Elsy Bar / Vía Tana
Vía Velodia
Seaflower Biosphere Reserve
Hoyo Soplador
0 1 miles
0 1 km

A mini road trip by motorcycle or scooter to circumnavigate the entire island is loads of fun. Of particular interest is the less inhabited southern part of the island, where you will find wilderness beaches and the **Hoyo Soplador,** a hole in the rocky coastline that creates a geyser-like blowhole effect when the waves come in.

their memories for future generations, the Banca de Colombia Cultural Center makes a fascinating stop for the cultural history of San Andrés and Providencia. A rooftop terrace provides spectacular views over the sea.

LA LOMA

★ Jardín Botánico

Vía Harmony Hill, in front of Hotel Sol Caribe Campo; tel. 8/513-3390; 9am-5pm Mon.-Sat., 10am-5pm Sun.; COP$10,000

Extending over 8 ha (20 acres) of wilderness, the Jardín Botánico is easily the most peaceful place on San Andrés. In this lovely botanical garden, run by the Universidad Nacional, you can stroll several paths to view the trees and plants, including San Andrés natives. Of particular interest are the many fruit trees, like the ever-present and abundant breadfruit, as well as mango, mamey, tamarind, and more.

There is also an impressive section on medicinal plants used by the locals including yarumo, used for asthma, and herbs like oregano and achiote, used in cooking but also with medicinal properties. Several species of native animals live in the garden, including blue lizards, iguanas, and the chincherry *(Vireo caribaeus)*, a bright yellow bird that darts among the foliage.

From a five-story lookout tower you can take in impressive views of the eastern coast and the barrier reefs. Guided tours, included in admission, are available but not required and take about an hour.

First Baptist Church

Calle 4 No. 18134-18-2a, La Loma

Built in Mobile, Alabama, in the mid-19th century, then deconstructed and shipped through New York City to San Andrés, the First Baptist Church is the island's most important architectural and cultural structure. Considered the mother church for the heavily Protestant population of the islands, full gospel-style services, often accompanied by calypso beats, are held at 9am Sunday and several nights a week. The church also holds the birth records of most island Raizal families in books that date back to the era of enslavement. If the church is open and not holding a service, you can climb the steeple and enjoy views over the island.

Recreation

BEACHES

Spratt Bight Pathway and Beach

Always packed, Spratt Bight Pathway and Beach is the center of the action in El Centro. The pedestrian walkway is lined with restaurants, hotels, and souvenir shops on one side and the beach on the other. Spratt Bight Beach is wide and pleasant and boasts the clearest water and whitest sand on the island. Offshore coral reefs break the tide and create a swimming pool effect, making the water safe for swimming for all ages. Because the duty-free shops sell cerveza and bottled liquor absurdly cheap (the only things that are inexpensive in San Andrés), the walkway and beach are also party central until late into the night. Expect champeta dance shows and impromptu salsa parties at night.

First Baptist Church

boat at Johnny Cay

★ Johnny Cay

entry COP$15,000

You'll find San Andrés's best beaches on Johnny Cay, which boasts postcard-quality white sand and gleaming sapphire water as well as restaurants and bars overlooking the Caribbean. Located just 1.6 km (1 mi) off the northern tip of the island and visible from the sands of Spratt Bight Beach, it's a perfect palm-fringed nature reserve home to some iguanas.

The 4-ha (10-acre) island is easy to reach with a 15-minute lancha ride (COP$55,000 round-trip) from Sunrise Park, next to the ferry terminal on Avenida Colombia in El Centro. These are organized as group tours and leave at 9am daily, returning around 4pm. Lunch is not included.

San Luis Beach

Several miles south of El Centro is San Luis Beach, a long stretch of golden sand adjacent to the town of San Luis. The beach is dotted with some of the island's top local eateries as well as reggae bars. Relaxing in the Caribbean breeze backed by tropical tunes makes you feel a world away. San Luis beaches are much more laid-back than Spratt Bight or Johnny Cay, though the water quality isn't quite as clear, and there is stronger surf.

SNORKELING

El Acuario

Snorkeling is spectacular off of **Rose Cay,** aptly known as El Acuario (The Aquarium) for its great visibility. It is usually visited on a day tour along with Johnny Cay. Locals will rent you snorkeling gear for around COP$20,000.

La Piscinita

A popular snorkeling spot is La Piscinita, on the western side of the island. A rocky cove creates a natural swimming pool effect. Snorkeling gear is available for around COP$20,000, but bringing your own gear is a better idea.

KITESURFING

Balmy but strong breezes around San Andrés mean there are ample opportunities to kitesurf.

Club Kitesurf San Andrés

Calle 1 No. 1B-24; tel. 312/280-6283; www.kitesurfsanandresschool.com

In El Centro and running a tent on Spratt Bight Beach, Club Kitesurf San Andrés offers basic skill classes (2 hours; COP$500,000 pp), rentals, and sales for experienced kitesurfers.

Kitesurf Rocky Cay

Cocoplum Hotel; tel. 317/462-6763; www.kiterockycay.com; 9am-5pm Mon.-Fri.

In San Luis, Kitesurf Rocky Cay offers personalized one-on-one classes with local instructor Eliu Silvera (COP$150,000 per hour) plus sales and rentals.

TOURS

A popular way to take in the sights of San Andrés is a day tour that includes a stop at **El Acuario** for snorkeling, a trip out to see the "sea of seven colors" and some shipwrecks, plus several hours on **Johnny Cay.** Most day tours can be booked through your hotel, and you can also negotiate directly with the boat owners at Sunrise Park, where most of the tours leave from. Tours usually leave at 9am, return at 2pm, and cost around COP$60,000.

Festivals and Events

San Andrés is host to several lively cultural fairs and festivals throughout the year, some worth planning a trip around. These island-wide events are free and open to the public.

Green Moon Festival

Sept.; free

Around the first weekend in September, the Green Moon Festival is an explosion of reggae music and cultural activities that bring visiting musicians and artists from other Caribbean countries to public stages around the island.

Ethnic Roots International Theatre Festival

Sept.; free

The last weekend in September is the Ethnic Roots International Theatre Festival, which aims to preserve native cultures of Colombia through theater. Besides performances by local Raizal theater groups exploring their unique history, the festival also hosts groups from the Colombian mainland and showcases, for example, Afro-Colombian performances from the Pacific coast and Indigenous presentations from Guajira. Most performances are in Sunrise Park in El Centro.

Fiestas Patronales de San Andrés

Nov.; free

Parades and concerts for the Fiestas Patronales de San Andrés fill the island for the entire month of November to celebrate the island's patron, Saint Andrew. The colorful festival concludes with a coconut carnival and the crowing of a coconut queen.

Food

Seafood is on every menu in every restaurant in San Andrés. Fish, **langosta** (lobster), **cangrejo** (crab), and **caracol** (conch) are likely to come from the

kitesurfing on the Caribbean

water off of San Andrés and Providencia. A Caribbean specialty you'll likely find only on San Andrés, Providencia, and Jamaica is **rondón** (rundown). This filling stew has fish or conch, pig's tail, dumplings, yuca, and other ingredients slow-cooked in coconut milk.

All restaurants are beach casual, and most of the larger ones accept credit cards. Service is often laid-back. Inexpensive local dishes such as caracol stew, lobster and crab empanadas, banana bread, and coconut and lime pies are sold by local women in the afternoon and evening along **Spratt Bight Pathway** and also at the **entrance to the beach in San Luis** at the intersection of Sound Bay Road.

EL CENTRO

Fisherman's Place

Carrera 4 No. 2-37, Spratt Bight; tel. 8/512-2774; 11:30am-4pm daily; COP$25,000-48,000

Near the north end of Spratt Bight Beach, the blue-collar Fisherman's Place is a restaurant run by a cooperative of local fishers. Overlooking the water, it's close to the airport runway. Try the rondón or the lobster.

Miss Celia

Av. Newball and Av. Raizal; tel. 8/512-6495; restaurantemisscelia@gmail.com; noon-10pm daily; COP$30,000-55,000

Although the namesake Miss Celia died, the restaurant continues. In front of the Club Náutico, Miss Celia is surrounded by flower gardens with local music adding to the atmosphere. Lobster is the house specialty, and there are various rice dishes, some with shrimp, some vegetarian. For dessert there's homemade ice cream.

Gourmet Shop

Av. Newball, in front of Parque de la Barracuda; tel. 8/512-9843 or 315/770-0140; noon-11pm Mon.-Sat., 6pm-11pm Sun.; COP$35,000-50,000

Gourmet Shop is an excellent choice for a break from seafood (although it also makes an excellent grilled octopus). The salads, pasta, and other dishes are good, and on every table is a big bottle of imported spicy chili sauce. A wide variety of wine is for sale along the walls, and thousands of empty wine bottles decorate the ceiling.

★ La Regatta

Av. Newball and Carrera 1, next to Club Náutico; tel. 8/512-0437; www.restaurantelaregatta.com; noon-11pm daily; COP$60,000-100,000

Ask anyone in town to recommend the best seafood place on the island and a solid majority will mention La Regatta, an open-air restaurant that juts onto the water. For a sampling of the finest San Andrés seafood, try their Fiesta Náutica, which includes lobster tails, prawns, and crab, or go for the tesoros del mar, a filling seafood stew. The restaurant is festively decorated. Reservations are advised.

SAN LUIS

El Paraíso

Sound Bay No. 69-87; tel. 8/513-3881; 9am-5pm daily; COP$30,000-45,000

Right on the beach is El Paraíso, a no-nonsense seafood restaurant where thick fillets of freshly caught pargo are served with sides of breadfruit and coconut rice for decent prices. A variety of chairs and loungers are available to guests for after-lunch lounging on the sand and cocktailing the afternoon away.

MOON

TOP EXPERIENCE

★ DIVING THE SEAFLOWER BIOSPHERE RESERVE

Part of UNESCO's Seaflower Biosphere Reserve, San Andrés is surrounded by a well-preserved coral reef teeming with marine life, making it a diving and snorkeling paradise. On the eastern edge is the windward barrier, 15 km (9 mi) long and 60-80 m (200-260 ft) wide, with significant live coral communities. Beyond the reef, the shelf ends abruptly in a vertical wall that drops hundreds of meters. In all, the sea surrounding San Andrés includes more than 40 species of corals and 131 species of fish. It's common to see large schools of brightly colored jacks, tangs, grunts, and snappers as well as barracudas, groupers, and parrot fish. Other marine creatures include turtles, stingrays, moray eels, octopuses, squid, and lobsters.

Because it is within the reserve, a unique feature of San Andrés is that dives are close to shore, which means at most a 10-30-minute boat ride. The water is warm and has excellent visibility year-round. The best conditions for diving are January-May, with stronger winds in June-July. Popular dive sites are **The Pyramids,** a shallow 4-m (13-ft) dive with striking anemones and fish; **Nirvana,** a reef at about 15 m (50 ft) that teems with marine life; **Trampa Tortuga,** a reef at about 15 m (50 ft) with great visibility; and **Blue Wall,** on the eastern edge of the windward barrier, which starts at 6 m (20 ft) and drops to 60 m (200 ft). It contains magnificent corals and large tube sponges.

BANDA DIVE

Calle 2 No. 1-14, Local 9, El Centro; tel. 8/513-1080; www.bandadiveshop.com

Banda Dive, where friendly owner Gloria will help with everything, offers both single-day diving excursions into the Seaflower Biosphere Reserve for those with experience and courses for those who need to prep first. A beginner's dive is COP$225,000, and an open-water course COP$1,600,000.

SEA PRIDE DIVE CENTER

Circunvalar Km 11 Metro 800; tel. 316/249-9901; www.escueladebuceoseapride.com

On the south end of the island near La Piscinita, a natural pool where beginners can train, Sea Pride offers a variety of excursions into the Seaflower Biosphere Reserve for experienced divers and everything you need to get ready for them. A beginner's dive is COP$190,000, and an open-water course COP$1,700,000.

sea turtle off Providencia

fresh fish lunch

Donde Francesca

El Pirata Beach; tel. 8/513-0163 or 318/616-8547; restaurantedondefrancesca@gmail.com; 11am-6pm daily; COP$30,000-65,000

Tables on the sand and hip tropical decor make Donde Francesca an atmospheric spot to try the island's gourmet fare. The acclaimed and varied menu includes langosta tempura (tempura lobster) and pulpo reducción al balsámico (balsamic octopus). The gin cocktails and margaritas are good too, made from nonbottled ingredients. It's easy to understand why folks arrive for lunch at 11am and don't leave until sundown.

★ Restaurante Lydia

Ground Rd. No. 64-65; tel. 8/513-2192; COP$33,000-55,000

In-the-know locals make a weekly visit to Restaurante Lydia a ritual. It's open only for lunch, 11am-5pm Saturday-Sunday and holiday Mondays. It gets great reviews from foodies and is considered one of the top places to try an authentic rondón; expect to be full for the rest of the day. Lydia's crab empanadas are also recommended.

Bars and Nightlife

The **coco loco,** a coconut filled with rum, is the island's cocktail of choice, and the mix of coconut water and liquor is quite delicious.

EL CENTRO

The nightlife scene in El Centro mostly caters to visitors from mainland Colombia and abroad, and venues feel tourist-oriented rather than local. Clubs are generally open Thursday-Saturday during the

RAIZAL FOOD AND CULTURE

The Raizal population of San Andrés has lived on the island since the 17th century, when their enslaved ancestors were brought from Africa by the British to work the sugarcane fields, even though the islands were officially the territory of Spain. This is why English is the main language and Protestant sects still predominate. Besides these Anglo influences, Raizal culture is deeply African at its core, from the music to the food, and especially the community-based way of life.

breadfruit, a Raizal staple

Run by local singer and farmer Job Saas, **Paradise Farm** (Circunvalar Km 10; tel. 315/770-3904; hours vary daily) keeps the Raizal agricultural traditions of San Andrés alive. Not only does he cultivate species like the breadfruit, once a staple of enslaved people, he has scoured the island collecting seeds of native fruit-bearing trees and edible plants and grows them to make sure they do not go extinct as the island develops. On weekends local families show up to work the gardens, share seeds, and learn techniques for their own plots.

Also president of the Raizal Indigenous Musician Movement (RIMM), Sass has built a performance stage on the property and hosts concerts by local musicians Thursday-Saturday nights. Stop by for a tour of the grounds, which include a refreshing glass of cold sugarcane juice, and then stick around for the local music and food. It just might be the highlight of a trip to the islands. The farm is on the western side of the island. Taxis from El Centro will run around COP$25,000 each way.

off-season and every night in high season. Cover charges range free-COP$20,000 at most clubs, depending on the season and the night of the week. Things get cranking around 10pm.

Coco Loco

Av. Colombia; tel. 8/513-1047; cover COP$20,000

The most iconic disco in El Centro is Coco Loco, where a mix of Latin and electronic beats keep the party going till the wee hours just about every night.

Bocca de Oro

Carrera 1 No. 2252; tel. 316/426-2690

Over at Bocca de Oro, which serves cocktails on a large outdoor patio, top local bands perform live on weekends.

Beer Station

Av. Colombia No. 55A1; tel. 316/471-7872; https://beerstation.com.co; noon-1am daily

If you're not into the club scene, a good place to go is the Beer Station. With a sports bar theme indoors and a terrace overlooking Spratt Bight Beach outdoors, it's a popular option for cold craft beer, cocktails, or a light meal.

Street Parties

Another fun alternative is to join the impromptu street parties that happen along the Spratt Bight Pathway, fueled by cheap alcohol from the duty-free shops. The area around **Hotel Tiuna** is especially rambunctious as revelers flow in and out of the hotel's top-floor Discoteca Coco's. An outdoor stage on Carrera 2, about three blocks in from Spratt Bight Beach, hosts live calypso and reggae bands around 8pm most evenings that are free and put on by the local government.

SAN LUIS

In San Luis, nightlife moves at a completely different pace than in El Centro. Sipping on a cold beer as reggae music pumps from a loudspeaker accompanied by the sounds of the Caribbean as it laps the shore is the perfect way to end a day on the island. Several locally owned beachfront bars have turned this style of bar into an art form.

Arnol's Place

San Luis Beach; no phone; hours vary

At Arnol's Place, family and friends come together for fresh fish barbecues on weekends and stay for the after-party, which consists of enjoying rum drinks on the sand at sunset as reggae plays in the background. It's as friendly and local as it gets.

Donde Franz

San Luis Beach; no phone; hours vary

At the north end of San Luis Beach is another great place for sunset, Donde Franz. It serves cocktails, including a tasty coco loco, and fresh seafood appetizers both

Arnol's Place

beachfront and upstairs in its rooftop dining room.

Madguana Beach

Rocky Cay Beach; no phone; hours vary; no cover

Madguana Beach is a beachfront bar that makes a great spot for a night swim to the soothing sounds of reggae. It has a small stage for local and visiting musicians to perform should the mood strike, and it keeps the party going until about midnight on weekends. On weekdays it typically closes about an hour after sunset—unless someone cranks up the dancehall.

Accommodations

On this island where tourism is king, lodging options are plentiful, except during high seasons: mid-December-mid-January, Semana Santa, and to a lesser extent during school vacations in June-July. Mid-upper-range all-inclusive hotels are popular with Colombian families and couples, but there is also an extensive network of **posadas nativas** (native guesthouses), owned and operated by locals, many with deep roots on the island. Staying at a posada nativa is the best way to get to know the local culture.

Most visitors stay in El Centro, where beaches, restaurants, nightlife, and services are in walking distance, but more local-style San Luis is also a pleasant option. There are several options in the inland village of La Loma, home to the largest Raizal population on the island for an immersion into local life. Staying in La Loma may require mastering public transportation or taking cabs if you want to go downtown, but renting a motor scooter, golf cart, or bicycle is also relatively easy.

The western side of the island has coral coastline instead of beaches, and the few hotels here cater mostly to divers, so this side feels more isolated.

UNDER COP$70,000

★ Posada Nativa Lizard House

Av. 20 de Julio No. 189, El Centro; tel. 8/512-5400; COP$55,000 dorm, COP$135,000 d

Just outside El Centro in a residential area, Posada Nativa Lizard House offers eight cozy private rooms and one six-bed dorm around a small but lush tropical patio. Ernesto, the owner, offers a wealth of information on the history of the islands and will direct you to authentic eateries in town.

El Viajero

Av. 20 de Julio No. 3A-122, El Centro; tel. 8/512-7497; www.elviajerohostels.com; COP$70,000 dorm, COP$264,000 d

The small hotels in the busy downtown are far more reasonably priced than those with a view of the sea and are just a few blocks away. The most popular choice for backpackers is the five-floor El Viajero, part of a Uruguayan chain. It has several air-conditioned gender-separated dorms as well as private rooms. The top-floor bar serves cold beer and assorted rum drinks, and there are several common areas with wireless internet and computers. A small breakfast is included, and a kitchen is provided for guest use.

COP$70,000-200,000

Coconut Paradise Lodge

Vía La Loma-Claymount No. 50-05, La Loma; tel. 8/513-2926 or 301/543-2344; oldm26@hotmail.com; COP$120,000 d

In the village of La Loma, Coconut Paradise Lodge is a beautiful turn-of-the-20th-century wooden home with just four rooms. It's close to the botanical gardens and the

San Luis beaches. Try for the top-floor room, which has great views and a refreshing breeze.

★ Breeze View and Culture

Av. Loma Barrack, San Luis;
tel. 315/518-3258; COP$140,000 d

Breeze View and Culture is a comfortable posada nativa across the street from the sea and just down the hill from the Jardín Botánico. The five rooms, including one with water views, are sparsely but comfortably decorated by Greg, who inherited the house from his mother. His front-porch eatery, Greg's Place, has some of the best-priced fresh-fish lunch specials (COP$25,000) on the island.

COP$200,000-500,000

Summer House Inn

Av. 20 De Julio No. 10-22; tel. 313/310-5181; www.summerhousesanandres.com; COP$442,000 d

An oversized jetted tub in the garden makes up for the fact that Summer House Inn is not on the beach, but that's what brings the price down too. The 14 nicely appointed rooms and friendly staff make the place feel homey despite being in the chaotic heart of El Centro.

OVER COP$500,000

★ Cocoplum Hotel

Vía San Luis No. 43-49; tel. 8/513-2121; www.cocoplumhotel.com; COP$665,000 d

Brightly colored Cocoplum Hotel in the San Luis area has the most important feature for a beach hotel: Its 41 rooms are on the beach, steps from the water. Rooms are colorful but basic, and many have balconies. The included breakfast is decent.

Hotel Casablanca

Av. Colombia No. 3-59; tel. 8/512-4115; www.hotelcasablancasanandres.com; COP$780,000 d with breakfast

Blindingly white Hotel Casablanca faces the Spratt Bight Pathway and overlooks the sea. Of its 91 rooms, 10 are cabañas. There is a small pool and, more importantly, a pool bar, Coco's. The hotel has three on-site restaurants. Casablanca gets mixed reviews, but it is one of the better options along Spratt Bight.

Hotel Tiuna

Av. Colombia No. 4-31; tel. 8/513-1351; www.tiuna.com; COP$875,000 d with breakfast and dinner

The party-hearty set will enjoy Hotel Tiuna. On Spratt Bight Pathway across from the beach, this 158-room hotel has a classic Miami Beach vibe. The top-floor Discoteca Coco's draws crowds most nights, and the two on-site restaurants, swimming pool, café, and movie theater make this more a resort than a hotel. In addition to a basic plan that includes breakfast and dinner, there's also the Super Tiuna Plan that includes all meals and drinks 11am-11pm, plus entry to the disco and a trip to Johnny Cay, but this option requires a minimum four-night stay.

★ Casa Harb

Calle 11 No. 10-83; tel. 8/512-6348; www.casaharb.com; COP$990,000 d

Boutique hotel Casa Harb is by far the most luxurious place to stay in San Andrés. The six suites, lobby, dining area, and spa are thoughtfully decorated with fantastic art and furniture from Morocco to Malaysia, personally chosen by owner Jak Harb. The fabulous on-site restaurant is open to nonguests (but call first). It's on the waterfront in El Centro and close to Spratt Bight Beach.

Information and Services

Tourist Office

Av. Newball; tel. 8/513-0801; 8am-noon and 2pm-6pm daily

A tourist office is located downtown across from Club Náutico.

Tourist Information Kiosk

Av. Colombia and Av. 20 de Julio; 8am-7pm daily

Tourism bureau staff are on hand at an information kiosk on Spratt Bight Beach.

Transportation

San Andrés's **Aeropuerto Gustavo Rojas Pinillas** (ADZ) is about 2 km (1.2 mi) northwest of El Centro and very close to many hotels. Taxis to and from the airport cost COP$15,000. San Andrés is served by all the major Colombian airlines, with most flights from Bogotá and Medellín. There are nonstop flights from Cartagena on **Avianca** (Avianca.com) and **Copa** (www.copaair.com); Copa also offers nonstop flights from Barranquilla and Panama City, Panama, with connections from major Latin American cities, including Lima, São Paulo, Santiago, and Mexico City.

Public buses serve the entire island; rides cost about COP$3,000 one-way. To get to San Luis, flag down a bus from Parque de la Barracuda just south of El Centro.

At **Renta de Motos T.T. 9** (Av. Boyacá, Calle las Proveedoras; tel. 315/749-8325), you can rent a motor scooter starting at COP$90,000 for the day.

Rent a bike at the **Bicycle Rental Shop** (Carrera 1B, Sector Punta Hansa, in front of Edificio Hansa Reef, El Centro; tel. 318/328-1790 or 321/242-9328; 8am-6pm daily; COP$45,000 per day).

Both taxis and mototaxis ply the main thoroughfares of El Centro as well as the road between San Luis and El Centro. Within El Centro, you shouldn't pay more than COP$12,000 for a taxi or COP$6,000 for a mototaxi. Expect to pay around COP$25,000 for a taxi between El Centro and San Luis or around COP$9,000 for a mototaxi.

Providencia and Santa Catalina

Of volcanic origin, Providencia and Santa Catalina islands are older and more mountainous than San Andrés. But they are much smaller in area and population, about 18 sq km (7 sq mi) and 5,000 residents. Only 300 people live on minuscule Santa Catalina, known as the Island of Treasures and once home to an English fort. Located 90 km (56 mi) north of San Andrés, these islands are the easygoing cousins of hyperactive San Andrés. Secluded palm-lined beaches, gorgeous turquoise Caribbean water, mellow locals, fresh seafood, and rum drinks make it easy to become smitten with Providencia. Tiny Santa Catalina is home to historic Fort Warwick and a beautiful waterfront promenade.

ORIENTATION

The islands of Providencia and Santa Catalina combined are about 7 km (4 mi) long and 4 km (2.5 mi) wide. A ring road encircles the entire island of Providencia. The harbor and downtown area of Providencia

Providencia and Santa Catalina
SANTA CATALINA
Seaflower Biosphere Reserve
Morgan's Head
Posada Sunshine Paradise
Tourist Office
Hotel Old Providence
Santa Isabel
Garet Bay
Caribbean Sea
VÍA CIRCUNVALAR DE PROVIDENCIA
Crab Cay (Cangrejo Ca
Maracaibo
Old Town Bay
Maracaibo Bay
Old Providence Taste
Almond Bay
Parque Nacional Natura Old Providence McBean Lagoon
Parque Nacional Natural Old Providence McBean Lagoon
Aeropuerto el Embrujo
Iron Wood Hill
PROVIDENCIA
Caribbean Place
Hotel Posada del Mar
Freshwater Bay
Morgan's Market
Miss Elma
Freshwater Bay Beach
Felipe Diving
The Peak Regional Park
The Peak
Lighthouse Providencia
Richard's Place
Café Studio
Cabañas Miss Mary
Restaurante Arturo
Southwest Bay
The Peak
Windy View Guesthouse
Smoothwater Bay
Seaflower Biosphere Reserve
Bottom House
Discover Old Providence
Roland Roots Bar
Manchineel Bay
Playa Manzanillo
0
0.5 miles
0.5 km

is called **Santa Isabel** and is the center of island activity. Connected to the northwest corner of Providencia by a 200-m (660-ft) pedestrian bridge is **Santa Catalina,** a tiny island with no motorized vehicles.

Other settlements on Providencia are usually referred to by the names of their beaches or bays. The main ones are on the western side of the island: **Bahía Manzanillo (Manchineel Bay),** on the southern end, which has some excellent beaches; **Bahía Suroeste (Southwest Bay);** and **Bahía Aguadulce (Freshwater Bay),** home to most of the island's hotels and restaurants. **Bahía Aguamansa (Smoothwater Bay),** on the southeastern edge of the island, is more remote and its town, **Casa Baja (Bottom House),** feels lost in time. In the middle of the island is its highest point, **The Peak.**

★ Parque Nacional Natural Old Providence McBean Lagoon

office Jones Point, east of the airport; tel. 8/514-8885 or 8/514-9003; oldprovidence@parquesnacionales.gov.co, www.parquesnacionales.gov.co; 9am-5pm daily; COP$21,000

Parque Nacional Natural Old Providence McBean Lagoon is a small national park on the northeast coast of the island and occupies 1,485 ha (3,670 acres); of that, 1,390 ha (3,435 acres) is sea. You can observe five ecosystems: coral reefs, seagrass beds, mangroves, dry tropical forests, and volcanic cays.

Just offshore, **Cayo Cangrejo (Crab Cay)** is one of the main attractions of the park, a spot for splashing in the incredibly clear warm water. This is a great place for easy snorkeling. In addition to tropical fish, you may see manta rays and sea turtles. A short five-minute nature path takes you to the top of the island. A snack bar on Crab Cay, open until around 1pm daily, sells water and snacks such as ceviche.

HIKING

Iron Wood Hill Trail

Distance: 3 km (2 mi) round-trip
Duration: 1 hour
Elevation gain: None
Difficulty: Easy
Trailhead: Park office

The park's Iron Wood Hill Trail is a 3-km (2-mi) round-trip nature trail to explore the tropical dry forest landscape and see different types of lizards, birds, and flora. There are nice views of the coastline. This path is less popular than the hike to The Peak, but many find it more beautiful. Visitors are encouraged to go with a local guide arranged by the **park office** (Jones Point, east of the airport; tel. 8/514-8885 or 8/514-9003; www.parquesnacionales.gov.co; 8am-12:30pm and 2pm-6pm daily; COP$30,000 pp plus park entry fee). Be sure to pay the park entry fee before leaving.

Sights

LIGHTHOUSE PROVIDENCIA

Hoy's Hill; tel. 313/380-5866 or 318/758-1804; www.lighthouseprovidencia.com; 5pm-9pm Mon.-Sat.

Lighthouse Providencia is a cultural center and café that's worth a stop. It hosts a range of cultural activities, including art exhibitions and film showings, all with an environmental bent, including a film on the famous black crab migration that brings the island to a virtual standstill. The lighthouse is on the western side of the island near Freshwater Bay. Try to come for sunset, as the café terrace has spectacular views over the Caribbean.

MORGAN'S HEAD

English colonists and privateers once ruled from atop Santa Catalina, watchful for potential enemies, usually the Spanish Armada or competing Dutch pirates. Today you can see remains of 17th-century English rule at **Fort Warwick,** adjacent to a big rock known as Morgan's Head. If you squint, it resembles the head of Henry Morgan, the notorious Welsh pirate and admiral of the Royal Navy who marauded the Spanish New World colonies during the mid-17th century. Morgan captured Santa Catalina from the Spaniards in 1670. Morgan's Head is next to **Morgan's Cave,** where the pirate supposedly hid his loot. You can go snorkeling inside the cave, where you may encounter the occasional harmless shark. To get here, take the colorful pedestrian bridge that connects Providencia with Santa Catalina in the Santa Isabel area. When crossing the bridge, particularly in the evening, you may be able to spot graceful manta rays in the water. Once on Santa Catalina, take a left and follow the path.

Recreation

BEACHES

The best beaches on Providencia are generally on the western side of the island. From Bahía Manzanillo (Manchineel Bay) on the southern end to Almond Bay, also called Allan Bay, in the northwest, they are each worth exploring: The water is calm, the sand golden, and there's always a refreshing breeze.

Playa Manzanillo

Playa Manzanillo, also called Manchineel Bay, home to Roland Roots Bar, is a gorgeous but remote 300-m (0.2-mi) beach on the southern tip of the island. It has crystal-clear water where you can relax in the shade of a palm tree (be careful of falling coconuts).

Freshwater Bay

Freshwater Bay, the most tourist-oriented part of the island, is on the western coast. The 150-m (0.1-mi) beach is lined with hotels and restaurants.

Maracaibo Bay

On the northeast side of the island, near the bridge to Santa Catalina, this wilderness beach sports glassy green water and views out to Cayo Cangrejo.

Almond Bay

North of Freshwater Bay on the west coast of the island, Almond Bay, also called Allan Bay, is a wilderness beach with turquoise water and white sand, marked by a large octopus sculpture on the side of the road. You can't miss it. The beach area is a public park, and there is a snack bar and a stand where you can purchase handicrafts.

SNORKELING AND DIVING

Providencia, part of the **Seaflower Biosphere Reserve** and surrounded by a 32-km-long (20-mi) barrier reef, is a fantastic place to dive or learn to dive. The water is always warm, and visibility is usually 25-35 m (80-115 ft). The best time of year to dive is June-October. In January the water can be particularly rough.

Popular diving sites are **Felipe's Place,** comprising several ledges with significant coral and marine life; **Turtle Rock,** a large rock at 20 m (66 ft) covered with black coral; **Tete's Place,** teeming with fish; **Confusion,** with corals and sponges at 20-40 m (66-130 ft); and **Nick's Place,** a deep crack in the island's shelf that starts at 18 m (60 ft) and drops to 40 m (130 ft). Good snorkeling can be had near **Cayo**

clockwise Morgan's Head; bridge to Santa Catalina; emerald sea in Providencia

Cangrejo, at the small islands of **Basalt** and **Palm Cays,** and around **Morgan's Head** in Santa Catalina, among other places.

Snorkeling is a popular activity frequently offered on tours of Providencia and Santa Catalina, but it can also be done independently near **Morgan's Head** in Santa Catalina and **Freshwater Bay.** Bring your own gear or rent it from Felipe Diving.

Felipe Diving

Freshwater Bay; tel. 316/628-6664 or 317/805-8684; www.felipediveshop.com

Felipe Diving is a professional diving outfit at Freshwater Bay. They offer guided day dives, a three day open-water course (COP$1,200,000), and also rent diving and snorkeling gear.

KAYAKING

Israel Livingston Archbold

tel. 318/587-7898

For kayak rentals and mangrove tours, contact guide Israel Livingston Archbold. A two-hour tour for two costs COP$150,000. Israel's tours depart from Posada Coco Bay in Maracaibo Bay.

HIKING

★ The Peak

Distance: 7 km (4 mi) round-trip
Duration: 2-3 hours
Elevation gain: 110 m (360 ft)
Difficulty: Moderate
Trailhead: Manchineel Bay

The Peak (El Pico) is the highest point on Providencia at 360 m (1,180 ft), and the 360-degree views from this mountaintop are impressive. This hike takes about 1.5 hours to the top and less than 1 hour down. The path begins in the middle of the island and meanders along relatively well-marked trails through tropical rainforest and tropical dry forest. You'll likely come across lizards, cotton trees, and maybe a friendly dog who will follow you to the top and back.

From the top you can see the barrier reef that extends 32 km (20 mi) off of the east coast of the island, the second longest in the Caribbean and part of Parque Nacional Natural Old Providence McBean Lagoon.

To get to the trailhead, go to the Casa Baja (Bottom House) neighborhood in the southeastern corner of the island, just to the east of Bahía Manzanillo (Manchineel Bay). Although you may come across a sign pointing toward the Peak, roads are not well marked. Ask at your hotel for directions to the starting point.

During rainy seasons, the path can become muddy and slippery. Make sure to bring a bottle of water with you. Guides are not necessary for this walk, but it's not impossible to get lost. All hotels can contract a guide for you; this usually costs around COP$60,000.

TOURS

Boat tours, organized by all hotels and dive shops, motor around the coast of Providencia, stopping at beaches and at Cayo Cangrejo (Crab Cay) for snorkeling or swimming. These tours depart the hotels around 9am daily and cost about COP$65,000 per person. Once you

> In 2020 Providencia was hit by Category 5 **Hurricane Iota,** which severely damaged many of the island's ecosystems, including the mangrove forests. Experts say it will take more than a decade to fully recover from this damage. Visitors should be extra careful about their environmental impact while visiting this recovering paradise.

disembark at Crab Cay, you pay the park entry fee (COP$21,000). Following the stop at Crab Cay, the boats go to Bahía Suroeste (Southwest Bay) for a seafood lunch, not included in the price of the tour. Otherwise, you can hire a boat yourself for around COP$350,000 total. On arrival at the island, you're required to pay the park entry fee. All hotels can arrange this more exclusive option.

Paradise Tours

Freshwater Bay; tel. 8/514-8283 or 311/605-0750; paradisetourscontact@gmail.com

Paradise Tours is a one-stop shop for tours around the island and snorkeling, diving, and fishing excursions. A popular option is the Reefs and Snorkeling Tour (3-4 hours; COP$85,000; 4 people minimum), during which you boat to coral reefs around the island, exploring the underwater cities that exist just below the surface. Snorkeling equipment costs extra. A full-day trip to idyllic **El Faro Island** and reef, 9 km (6 mi) off Providencia, costs COP$160,000. It's an excellent place for snorkeling in warm crystalline water.

On land, Paradise Tours offers several guided hiking options, including the Peak, where you can see coral reefs in the distance; Manchineel Hill, where you might see wild orchids on the way; and Iron Wood Hill in Parque Nacional Natural Old Providence McBean Lagoon. These hikes cost COP$95,000.

Discover Old Providence

Bottom House; tel. 318/587-7898 or 316/761-5770; enjoyprovidence.pespo@gmail.com; COP$120,000 pp

Discover Old Providence offers fishing, hiking, and kayak tours in and around Providencia.

Bernardo "Big Boy" Henry

tel. 313/811-0121 or 311/853-5166; bbernardhenry@gmail.com

A recommended guide who can assist with transportation on the island is Bernardo "Big Boy" Henry. It generally costs about COP$35,000 to get from one part of the island to the other.

Festivals and Events

Black Crab Migration

The black crab migration happens April-August. This species of crab lives in the mountainous interior of the island most of the year, but when the rainy season begins in April or May, thousands of females, carrying up to 120,000 eggs each, make an arduous journey to the sea to deposit their eggs. The migration peaks during nighttime hours, so watch your step. More crabs can be seen on the western side of the island. A second migration occurs a few weeks later, when the young crabs make their trip from the sea up to the mountain. During both migrations, the main road on the island may be closed, enforced by military personnel, as a means of protecting the crabs from vehicles.

Festival del Chub

tel. 8/514-8885 or 8/514-9003; Dec.

In early December, usually on a Saturday, Parque Nacional Natural Old Providence McBean Lagoon organizes the colorful Festival del Chub. Chub is a plentiful fish but is not very popular due to its strong aroma. The purpose of the festival is to encourage fishers and consumers to choose chub instead of red snapper, the stocks of which have been depleted throughout the Caribbean. The festival is held at Punta Rocosa (Rocky Point), where chub is widely eaten. In addition to the food component, which features dishes like chub burgers and chub ceviche, there is also a sailing race from Southwest Bay to Manzanillo.

Food

Providencia is synonymous with fresh Caribbean seafood. Many restaurants in Providencia do not accept credit cards. Hotel restaurants are open daily while others often close on Sunday.

BAHÍA AGUADULCE (FRESHWATER BAY)

★ Caribbean Place

across from the beach on the ring road; tel. 8/514-8698; noon-3pm and 6pm-10pm Mon.-Sat.; COP$40,000-80,000

Caribbean Place, also known as Donde Martín, is one of the best seafood spots in Providencia. Try the fish in ginger-butter sauce or the coconut shrimp, and for dessert, the coconut pie. Cheerfully decorated, it's a great choice for lunch and dinner.

Morgan's Market

ring road; 8am-noon and 3pm-8pm Mon.-Fri., 9am-noon and 4pm-8pm Sat.-Sun.

Morgan's Market is one of the main grocery stores on the island. It's hard to miss this hub of activity. There's a sandwich and juice stand inside.

BAHÍA SUROESTE (SOUTHWEST BAY)

Restaurante Arturo

on the beach; tel. 317/620-0814; 11am-5pm daily; COP$30,000-45,000

Right on the sand is Restaurante Arturo, where the specialty is rondón. It's open-air and has a relaxed atmosphere.

★ Café Studio

ring road; tel. 8/514-9076; 11am-10pm Mon.-Sat.; COP$30,000-75,000

Café Studio, on the side of the road near Southwest Bay, is a favorite among visitors, and not just because of its trademark cappuccino pie. Everything is good here, it's open for lunch and dinner, and it's the island's best spot for afternoon coffee and dessert. Café Studio has a varied menu with pastas, interesting seafood dishes, and salads. An awesome blues soundtrack plays in the background. It's run by a local and his Canadian wife.

SANTA ISABEL AND SANTA CATALINA

Old Providence Taste

Old Town Bay, west of Santa Isabel; tel. 8/514-9028 or 311/264-6789; 11:30am-3pm Mon.-Sat.; COP$28,000-55,000

Old Providence Taste, on the beach west of Santa Isabel, is run by a local sustainable seafood and farming co-op. Each day they offer a menu based on what fishers and farmers bring in. It's the best deal on the island. They can also organize visits to farms and excursions with local fishers.

Bars and Nightlife

Roland Roots Bar

Manchineel Bay; tel. 8/514-8417; hours vary Sat.-Sun.

Bob Marley never seems to fall out of fashion at Roland Roots Bar. This spot beneath the coconut palms is perfect to spend a lazy sunny day in Providencia. Or go at night, when you can order a rum drink to go and walk to the beach to stargaze, or hang out by a bonfire. On Sunday afternoon it's a popular spot for locals.

Richard's Place

Southwest Bay; hours vary Sat.-Sun.

Roland's competition is Richard's Place on the beach in Southwest Bay. You can broaden your Caribbean music horizons here with reggae roots, rocksteady, ska calypso, ragamuffin, and soca dub—but more often than not, it's Marley on the sound system.

Accommodations

Providencia and Santa Catalina offer an array of interesting and comfortable accommodations. Most options are in Freshwater Bay, but each area on this enchanting island has its charms. Note that internet service is unreliable, and it's best to communicate with hotels by phone or text message rather than email for reservations and inquiries.

BAHÍA AGUADULCE (FRESHWATER BAY)

Hotel Posada del Mar

Freshwater Bay; tel. 8/514-8052; www.posadadelmarprovidencia.com; COP$385,000 d

Hotel Posada del Mar is a 24-room hotel with air-conditioning and a pool. Instead of a beach, a grassy lawn overlooks the water.

★ Miss Elma

Freshwater Bay; tel. 8/514-8229, 8/514-8854, 310/566-3773; COP$500,000 d

Miss Elma is simple but elegant, with just six rooms, all of which overlook the sea, and a restaurant on the beach.

BAHÍA SUROESTE (SOUTHWEST BAY)

Cabañas Miss Mary

tel. 8/514-8454; hotelmissmary@yahoo.com; COP$250,000 d

Cabañas Miss Mary is just steps from the beach in the southwest part of the island. It has eight rooms, five of which have beach views. A large pool lends to mingling.

BAHÍA AGUAMANSA (SMOOTHWATER BAY)

★ Windy View Guesthouse

Bottom House; tel. 8/514-8750 or tel. 310/589-4888; www.windyviewprovidence.blogspot.com; COP$280,000 d

English writer Sam Cuming, author of *A Short History of Providence and San Andrés*, owns Windy View Guesthouse. They offer two fully appointed apartments with a nautical feel that are brimming with books.

SANTA ISABEL AND SANTA CATALINA

Hotel Old Providence

Santa Isabel; tel. 8/514-8691 or 8/514-8094; COP$185,000 d

Hotel Old Providence is the only option in the "town" area of Providencia. It's close to Santa Catalina and offers 15 basic comfortable rooms with air-conditioning.

★ Posada Sunshine Paradise

Santa Catalina; tel. 8/514-8208 or tel. 311/227-0333; COP$280,000 d

Posada Sunshine Paradise is a charming guesthouse with four clean rooms surrounded by flower gardens. A major selling point is the warm hospitality of the owner, Francisca.

Information and Services

In case of emergency the police can be reached at tel. 112 or tel. 8/514-8000. For medical emergencies, call tel. 125. The town has a bank, an ATM, and an internet café.

Many hotels on the island sell *A Short History of Providence and San Andrés* (COP$30,000) by resident author Sam Cuming. It's a good read about the mostly forgotten history of these tiny islands.

Tourist Office

Santa Isabel; tel. 8/514-8054, ext. 12; www.providencia.gov.co; 8am-noon and 2pm-6pm Mon.-Fri.

There is a tourist office in town area near the port. It may be able to assist with accommodations, including posadas nativas, and give you some maps.

Transportation

There are two ways to travel to Providencia: by plane or by fast catamaran from San Andrés.

SATENA (Centro Comercial New Point, Local 206, San Andrés; tel. 8/512-1403 or 8/514-9257; www.satena.com) offers two daily flights, one in the early morning and one in the late afternoon, to Providencia's **Aeropuerto El Embrujo** (PVA), near Parque Nacional Natural Old Providence McBean Lagoon. Charter flights are usually organized by **Decameron** (tel. 1/800-051-0765; www.decameron.co) from San Andrés to Providencia. All flights are on small propeller planes, and there are strict weight limits: Passengers are allowed 10 kg (22 lbs) in their checked baggage, and each passenger is required to be weighed at check-in along with their carry-on bag, which makes for an amusing photo op. The average weight per passenger cannot exceed 80 kg (176 lbs), including luggage. The flight takes about 35 minutes.

The **Catamaran Sensation** (tel. 8/512-3675 or 318/347-2336; www.conocemosnavegando.com; COP$220,000 one-way, COP$400,000 round-trip) provides **fast boat service** between San Andrés and Providencia. The trip takes four hours from San Andrés to Providencia and three hours in the other direction. It provides service Sunday-Monday and Wednesday-Friday during low season and greater frequency during high season. Boats leave San Andrés at 8am from the Muelle Toninos and depart Providencia from the docks in Santa Isabel at 2:30pm.

Taxis are expensive in Providencia, costing around COP$25,000 no matter where you go. Mototaxis are much cheaper and can be found almost anywhere. You can rent mulas (gasoline-powered golf carts; COP$150,000 per day) and motorbikes (COP$100,000 per day) in Providencia. All hotels can arrange these rentals. Reputable rental agencies include **Renta Car y Motos Old Providence** (Santa Isabel; tel. 8/514-8369 or 313/450-4833; 9am-6pm Mon.-Sat.) and **B&Q Providence Center Hans Bush Felipe** (tel. 311/561-1537; hours vary).

The Amazon

Highlights

★ **Amazon River Tours** *(upper & lower right):* From Leticia, take a boat cruise up the Amazon, the largest river in the world (page 385).

★ **Parque Nacional Natural Amacayacu** *(upper left):* Spot monkeys and other wildlife in the unspoiled Amazon rainforest (page 396).

★ **Puerto Nariño** *(lower left):* Unwind in a car-free, Indigenous-run eco-village (page 398).

★ **Lago Tarapoto:** Visit the breeding grounds of the Amazon's endangered pink dolphins (page 399).

★ **Río Javari:** Stay in an ecolodge in the heart of a rainforest preserve (page 402).

Look for ★ to find recommended sights, activities, dining, and lodging.

◂ the Amazon River

The Amazon region covers over 40 percent of the surface of Colombia, yet this vast territory has a small population and most of it is nearly inaccessible. Leticia, however, on the Amazon River and bordering Brazil to the east and Peru across the river, is easy to get to by plane and boat. Luckily for visitors, it's one of the most charming towns in the Amazon region and offers a handful of highly rewarding natural and cultural attractions.

Covering an expanse of 8.2 million sq km (3.2 million sq mi), the Amazon rainforest is the largest humid tropical forest in the world. Home to one-tenth of all species on Earth, even though it occupies only 1.6 percent of the world's surface, it's also the world's most biodiverse ecosystem. It holds more than 40,000 species of plants, 3,000 of fish, 1,300 birds, 428 mammals, and 380 reptiles. By contrast, all of Canada, which occupies an area larger than the Amazon rainforest, has 3,270 species of plants, 1,100 fish, 838 birds, 188 reptiles, and 180 mammals. Rainforests are also important as the world's lungs, pulling in vast amounts of carbon dioxide through photosynthesis.

Río Amazonas, the Amazon River, is about 6,400 km (4,000 mi) long and fed by more than 1,000 tributaries. This system is home to more species of fish than the entire Atlantic Ocean. Colombia only has 180 km (112 mi) on the Río Amazonas, but several major tributaries originate and flow through the Colombian Amazon region, including the Putumayo and the Caquetá. It is estimated that one-fifth of all the water that runs off the Earth's surface flows through this basin. The gradient is very slight: Leticia, more than 2,000 km (1,200 mi) from the mouth of the river, is at an elevation of 96 m (315 ft). During the annual flood, November-April, the river can rise as much as 16 m (53 ft), submerging large sections of the rainforest.

A trip to the Amazon is a highlight of any visit to Colombia and a highlight in most people's lives. The survival of this vast ecosystem, the preservation of which is by no means assured, is of great importance. It is fascinating to learn about its variety of plants and animals, how it stabilizes the world's climate, how Indigenous people managed to make a home there for thousands of years without disturbing its balance, and how modern civilization is threatening to destroy it. Long after an introduction to Amazonia, you might find yourself reflecting on its significance for all of humanity.

Planning Your Time

To visit the Amazon, at least **3-5 days** are required, and more if you want to spend time in a nature reserve in the rainforest. The Leticia area is often used as a stopover when traveling between Peru or Brazil and Colombia, but the region is worth spending some time in.

From Leticia to the southeast are rainforest lodges in Brazil along the Río Javari, and toward the northwest are many

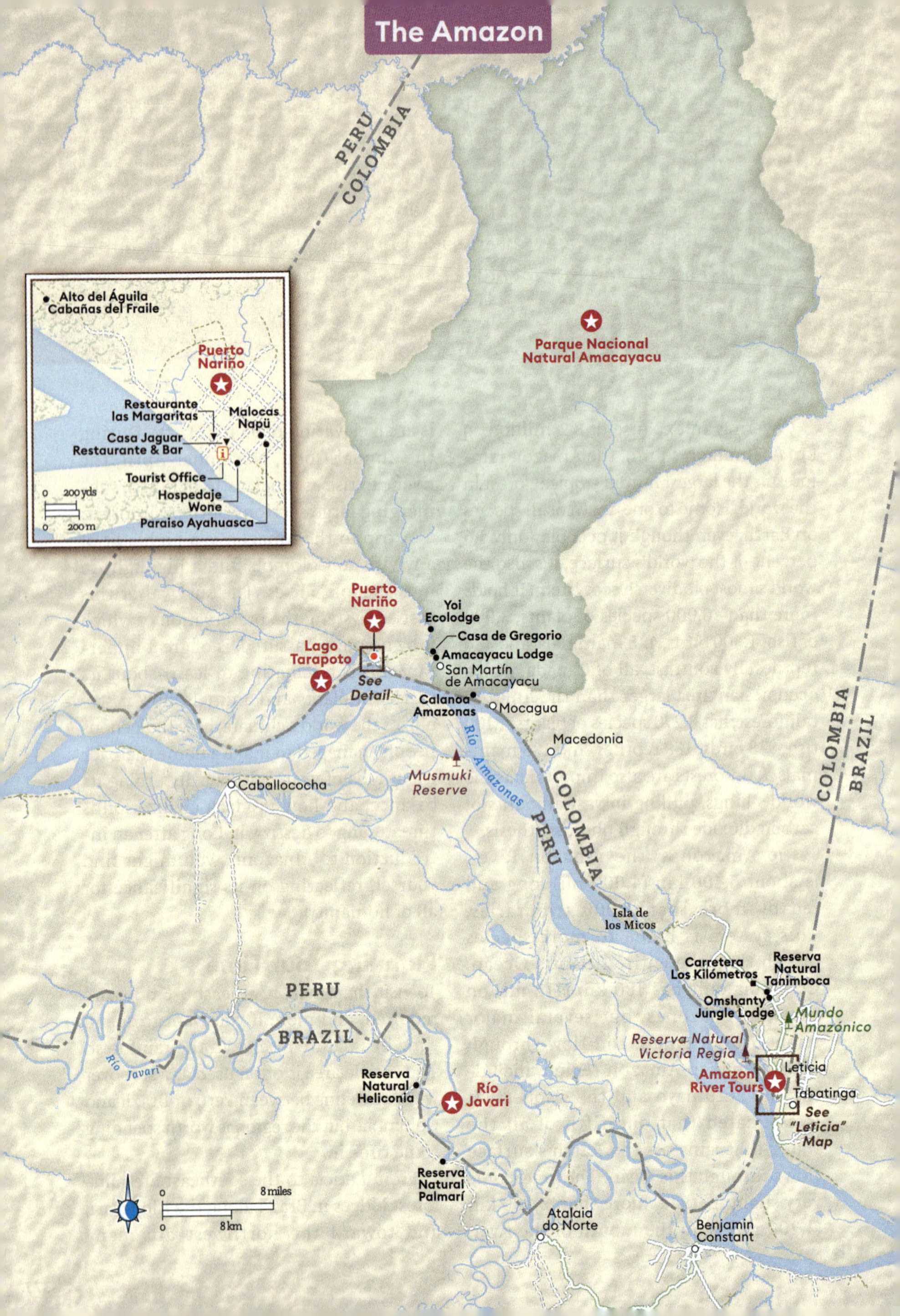
The Amazon
PERU
COLOMBIA
Parque Nacional
Natural Amacayacu
Alto del Águila
Cabañas del Fraile
Puerto
Nariño
Restaurante
las Margaritas
Malocas
Napü
Casa Jaguar
Restaurante & Bar
Tourist Office
Hospedaje
Wone
Paraiso Ayahuasca
0 200 yds
0 200 m
Puerto
Nariño
Yoi
Ecolodge
Casa de Gregorio
Amacayacu Lodge
San Martín
de Amacayacu
Lago
Tarapoto
See
Detail
Calanoa
Amazonas
Mocagua
Macedonia
Río Amazonas
Musmuki
Reserve
Caballococha
COLOMBIA
PERU
COLOMBIA
BRAZIL
Isla de
los Micos
Carretera
Los Kilómetros
Reserva
Natural
Tanimboca
Omshanty
Jungle Lodge
Mundo
Amazónico
Reserva Natural
Victoria Regia
Amazon
River Tours
Leticia
Tabatinga
See
"Leticia"
Map
PERU
BRAZIL
Río Javari
Reserva
Natural
Heliconia
Río
Javari
Reserva
Natural
Palmarí
0 8 miles
0 8 km
Atalaia
do Norte
Benjamin
Constant

easy-to-access points of interest up to the town of Puerto Nariño.

Colombian health authorities recommend **yellow fever vaccination** at least 10 days before arriving in the area. Malaria is very rare, but some visitors opt to take antimalarial pills before arrival and for four weeks after leaving the region. These can be purchased in pharmacies across Colombia without a prescription. Wear light-colored, long-sleeved shirts, pants, and socks, especially during dawn and dusk, to prevent mosquito bites, and insist on mosquito nets if you are staying in the rainforest.

It is always muggy in the Amazon, and rarely is there a breeze to provide relief from the heat. The border town of Leticia reports an average 85 percent humidity year-round with an average temperature of 25.8°C (78.4°F). The region has one dry season that used to run June-August; due to climate change, it now extends into September or even October. The rainy season is January-May. In August it can rain as little as 10 days per month. During the dry season, rivers shrink, creating beaches, and trees and shrubs appear in parts of the rainforest that during the rainy season are hidden underwater.

During the rainy season, water falls from the sky and pours down from the Andes into the mighty river. Canoes become the only means of travel in the rainforest. You can glide through the treetops in a canoe, an unforgettable experience. Ponchos, rubber boots, and insect repellent are especially critical during the rainy season.

Safety

While some parts of the Colombian Amazon, including the departments of Caquetá and Putumayo, still suffer from violence and are partially controlled by armed groups, the Leticia area is perfectly safe. Visitors should check for info about mosquito-borne illness outbreaks like dengue, Zika, malaria, and yellow fever before traveling to the Amazon regions.

Environmental Threats

Unfortunately, the Amazon rainforest is under severe threat. Over the past 40 years, 20 percent of this extremely biodiverse ecosystem has been destroyed. If strong measures are not taken, half of what remains could be destroyed within the next few decades. The main causes of the destruction, in order of importance, are oil drilling, cattle ranching, agriculture, dams, and both legal and illegal mining. The main means of destruction are roads. Without these, human encroachment is limited to the borders of navigable rivers. Because of its proximity to major roads and cities, significant deforestation has occurred along the Andes piedmont, especially in the headwaters of the Caquetá and Putumayo rivers in Colombia, where illegal coca cultivation has been one of the main culprits.

There is alarming evidence that, as deforestation progresses, the Amazon ecosystem is breaking down and will be unable to sustain itself. With deforestation comes lower evaporation and rainfall. As the forest dries up, it becomes more prone to fires, changing the overall dynamics. The Amazon has not yet reached that scary tipping point after which it cannot sustain itself, but vastly reduced measured rainfall points in that direction.

The Colombian section of the Amazon rainforest represents only 10 percent of the total region, but it is the best preserved due to a dearth of roads, and it's the most likely to be preserved thanks to enlightened policies. From 1986 to 1990 President Virgilio Barco transferred 163,000 sq km (63,000 sq

Itinerary Ideas

Three days is the bare minimum for exploring the Leticia area. Here is how to make the most of it.

DAY 1

1 Check out the **Museo Etnográfico de Leticia** and its botanical gardens to learn about the natural and cultural history of the Amazon.

2 Head over to the **Mercado Municipal** to try some freshly caught fish for lunch.

3 In the afternoon, visit the **Tienda Solidaria Leticia** and stock up on some locally made products.

4 Make your way to **Parque Santander** to watch the parrots roost at sunset.

5 At night, grab some pirarucú ceviche at **Sazón 100% Peruano.**

DAY 2

1 Take a tour or the express boat to **Puerto Nariño.**

2 After checking into your hotel, grab lunch on the waterfront before booking a locally run tour to **Lago Tarapoto** to see the pink dolphins.

3 After working up an appetite, relax with a meal and a copoazú cocktail at **Casa Jaguar.**

Puerto Nariño

Lago Tarapoto

tree frog

DAY 3

1 Hire a local guide or join a group tour into **Parque Nacional Natural Amacayacu** to do some wildlife watching and experience the deep rainforest.

2 Lunch is included in the tour or can be purchased in the village of **San Martín de Amacayacu.**

3 Take the afternoon boat back to Leticia and have dinner at **Tierras Amazónicas.**

capuchin monkey

mi), twice the area of Austria and 15 percent of Colombia, to national parks and Indigenous resguardos (land collectively owned by Indigenous groups) and protected areas. Predio Putumayo, the largest resguardo, measures 59,000 sq km (23,000 sq mi), the size of Costa Rica. Subsequent governments have continued to expand the protected areas, and now at least 65 percent of the Colombian Amazon is protected, either as national parks or resguardos.

The 1991 constitution enshrined significant rights for Colombia's Indigenous peoples, adding further protections. In 2013 the Colombian government took a positive step by more than doubling the size of its Parque Nacional Natural Sierra de Chiribiquete, in the Amazon departments of Caquetá and Guaviare, to over 28,000 sq km (11,000 sq mi). It is the largest national park in Colombia.

In 2018, the Colombian Supreme Court ruled that the Amazon Rainforest was subject to the same rights as a living being, meaning that damage to the ecosystem is now considered equal to violence against a person. The case was brought by 25 Colombian youths who argued that threats to the rainforest put their own futures in jeopardy.

When President Gustavo Petro was elected in 2022, he immediately implemented the Salvemos la Selva (Save the Rainforest) campaign, which directs funds to combat deforestation in the eight Amazonian departments and calls for an end to oil drilling in the region. Although the threat of illegal logging and mining is ever present, these protective actions seem successful.

The Amazon is also home to large deposits of the rare-earth minerals needed for much of the so-called green energy transition around the world. In the lush rainforest-covered mountains just outside of Mocoa, capital of the Putumayo department, for example, the largest copper ore deposit on the continent was recently found, and a Canadian mining company immediately bought the rights to it. Petro has vowed to block all mining projects that threaten a water source, and Mocoa, which means "where the rivers run" in Quechua, are where the mighty Río Putumayo, one of the largest tributaries of the Amazon, begins. As of early 2025, plans to mine the area were still approved.

Leticia

Leticia, the capital city of the Amazonas department, is the southernmost city in Colombia, on the northern side of the Río Amazonas where Colombia borders Brazil and Peru. This is commonly known as the tres fronteras (three borders) region. It is 1,100 km (700 mi) southeast of Bogotá. The closest Colombian town of any size is Puerto Nariño, 87 km (54 mi) northwest.

Visitors come to Leticia to experience the rainforest, and the town itself is quite charming. Ecotourism is the future for Leticia, and more Colombians and visitors from abroad are discovering the area.

A handful of sights in town and along Carretera Los Kilómetros will keep you occupied for a couple of days, and there are comfortable lodging options. Best of all, the rainforest is at Leticia's doorstep, and the Río Amazonas—a busy waterway serving

Leticia
Tienda Solidaria Leticia
Tarapoto Amazonas Jungle Tours
Calle 8
Carrera 11
Carrera 10
Museo Uirapuru
Fondo de Promoción Ecoturística del Amazonas
Hotel Anaconda
Parque Orellanas
El Abuelo
Calle 7
Parque Orellana
0 50 yds
0 50 m
Vía Los Lagos
Migración Colombia
Aeropuerto Internacional General Alfredo Vásquez Cobo
Carrera 10
Reserva Natural Heliconia Office
Fundación Entropika
Transversal 16
Calle 17
La Casa del Kurupira
Colombia
Brazil
Peru
Selvaventura
Hospital San Rafael
Carrera 6
Carrera 5
Peruvian Consulate
Sazón 100% Peruano
Policía Nacional
Cra. 10
Amazon B&B
Calle 11
Hippielandia Hostel
Tanimboca
Leticia
Parque Santander
Brazilian Consulate
Río Amazonas
Museo Etnográfico de Leticia
Calle 10
Mercado Municipal
Tierras Amazónicas
Calle 8
Calle 7
Parque Orellanas
Carrera 6
Calle 6
Perimetral Norte Dois
Carrera 9
Amazon River Tours
See Detail
Muelle Turístico
Carrera 11
Calle 5
Calle 3
Rua Marechal Rondon
Santa Rosa de Yavari
Rua Marechal Mallet
Transtur
Golfinho
Rua Pedro Teixeira
Isla de Santa Rosa
Rua Santos Dumont
Tabatinga
Av. da Amizade
Rua Duarte Coelho
0 400 yds
0 400 m
Rua Aires da Cunha
Polícia Federal

hamlets, rainforest lodges, Indigenous reservations, and rough-and-tumble towns—is always at the ready.

ORIENTATION

Leticia borders the Brazilian town of Tabatinga to the east. Isla de Santa Rosa, Peru, is an island in the Río Amazonas to Leticia's south.

Leticia is laid out on a grid that is easy to figure out. The airport is north of town on Avenida Vásquez Cobo, which turns into Carrera 10, one of the main drags in town. Carreras run north-south, and calles go east-west. The malecón, also known as the **Muelle Turístico,** from where all boats depart, is on the eastern side of town at the end of Calle 8. **Carretera Los Kilómetros,** also called Vía a Tarapacá, leads to the nature preserves of Mundo Amazónico, Tanimboca, and Cerca Viva and well as some rainforest lodging options close to town. There are some Huitoto settlements close to those attractions, and then the road abruptly stops, surrendering to the rainforest.

Sights

PARQUE SANTANDER

Carrera 10

Like most small towns in Latin America, Leticia centers on a leafy town square. But Parque Santander offers a daily spectacle that visitors should not miss: Every late afternoon just before sunset, thousands of bright-green parrots circle over the park, eventually diving into the ancient trees and roosting for the night. This awe-inspiring event is entirely free, although many vendors sell everything from ice cream to arepas to help you enjoy it.

Leticia at sunset

MUSEO ETNOGRÁFICO DE LETICIA

Carrera 11 No. 9-43; tel. 8/592-7783; www.banrepcultural.org/leticia; 8:30am-6pm Mon.-Fri., 9am-1pm Sat.; free

Occupying the bright pink **Banco de la República** building, the Museo Etnográfico de Leticia provides a good introduction to the ways of life of some of the primary Indigenous groups that inhabit the Colombian Amazon region, including the Ticuna, Huitoto, and Yukuna peoples. Colorful feather crowns made of guacamaya (macaw) feathers and descriptions of chagras (islands of small vegetable plots in the middle of the rainforest) and malocas (community houses) are part of the exhibit. Explanations are provided in Spanish and English. Art exhibits and other events are sometimes held in the building. Make sure to check out the small but informative **botanical garden.** A small **public library** is also in the building, and it is a quiet place to work, read, or check email; it operates the same hours as the museum. Guided tours are available for a donation.

MUNDO AMAZÓNICO

Km 7, Vía a Tarapacá/Carretera Los Kilómetros; tel. 8/592-6087 or 321/472-4346; www.mundoamazonico.com; 8am-3pm daily; COP$90,000-200,000

To learn about some of the medicinal plants, fruits, and trees you will see in the Amazon, a visit to the Mundo Amazónico is a must. In the park you can take a walk among exotic fruit trees found in the area, including the copoazú; learn about Indigenous farming techniques; see medicinal plants found in the rainforest; and observe unusual fish, reptiles, and amphibians in the aquarium and terrarium. There are several "plans" available for visiting the park, each with its own price, including a simple day visit and a nighttime rainforest walk.

Taking public transportation to the park is easy. Look for a green Kilom 11 bus (not headed toward Lagos) departing from Parque Orellana (Carrera 11 between Calles 7-8). Tell the bus driver you'd like to be dropped off at Mundo Amazónico. From where the bus lets you off, it's a 10-15-minute walk to the park entrance. The ride costs COP$2,600 by bus; by mototaxi is COP$22,000.

TOP EXPERIENCE

★ Amazon River Tours

The Río Amazonas is home to more than 1,500 species of fish, including the endangered pirarucú, one of the largest freshwater fish on Earth, and the notorious meat-eating piranha. Also here are dolphins, both gray and pink, a magical species only found in the Amazon and its tributaries. Other aquatic mammals include manatees and nutrias (otters). There are dozens of species of turtles, alligators, lizards, snakes, and frogs. Land mammals include deer, anteaters, armadillos, tapirs, jaguars, ocelots, and pumas, although sightings of these large cats are rare. The trees support sloths, squirrels, and many species of monkeys and bats. With more than 3,000 species of birds, the Amazon is truly a bird-watcher's paradise. A variety of birds, including herons, kingfishers, ducks, woodpeckers, oropendolas, kiskadees, hawks, and harpy eagles all also make their home here. Finally, there are innumerable insects, including giant leaf-cutting ants, as well as centipedes and scorpions.

To truly get a sense of the place, you need to get into the rainforest, either on a trek or canoe rides on the river and flooded rainforest. The small details that make up this wonderland will come into focus: a ray of sun shining through the canopy; a massive 40-m-tall (130-ft) ceiba tree; a vine that has wound itself around a tree like a boa constrictor; an orange mushroom popping up from a fallen tree, accelerating its final stage of decay; a single bright-blue butterfly that crosses your path momentarily and then flutters away; a leaf as big as your head floating to the ground; a whimsical song from a bird somewhere above in the canopy.

Tanimboca

Carrera 10 No. 11-69; tel. 8/592-7679; www.tanimboca.org

Tanimboca is affiliated with the Reserva Natural Tanimboca in the rainforest just outside Leticia. Package tours with Tanimboca include rainforest walks, a couple of nights in its fabulous treehouses or tree tents at the reserve, and overnight visits to Puerto Nariño and Reserva Natural Marashá in Peru. Tanimboca offers mostly private or small-group tours. For a stay of five days and four nights, including activities, expect to pay around COP$1,800,000 per person. Tanimboca can also arrange private one-day tours on the river. This is a highly recommended and reputable agency.

Tarapoto Amazonas Jungle Tours

Carrera 10 No. 8-40; tel. 312/490-9600; www.tarapotoamazonasjungletours.com

The family behind Hippielandia, who also run a hostel and cultural center by that name in the center of town, have been doing Río Amazonas and rainforest tours for over a decade and have made strong connections with local Indigenous communities. They offer several three-day rainforest expeditions (USD$250 pp) every month that include wildlife watching, cultural exchanges, deep rainforest treks, and river excursions.

Selvaventura

Calle 14 No. 9-06; tel. 8/592-3977 or 311/287-1307; www.selvaventura.org

Selvaventura is a reputable tour operator that offers several excursions, all highlighted on its website, including a three-night trip through the rainforest that visits an Indigenous village by kayak through the rainforest (COP$1,900,000 pp). You'll sleep on a platform in a tree, in a tent in the rainforest, and in an Indigenous maloca. Selvaventura is affiliated with the hostel La Casa del Kurupira and shouldn't be confused with Selva Tours, from the Colombian all-inclusive megahotel On Vacation.

Festivals and Events

Festival de Confraternidad Amazónica

Leticia; usually July 15-20

The Festival de Confraternidad Amazónica has been going strong since 1987 and is a celebration of Amazonian culture and friendship among neighboring Colombia, Brazil, and Peru.

Festival Pirarucú de Oro

Leticia; end of Nov.-early Dec.

Named in honor of the enormous pirarucú river fish, the Festival Pirarucú de Oro takes place over three days, with numerous musical and dance performances at the amphitheater in Parque Orellana (Carrera 11 between Calles 7-8) in Leticia.

Shopping

Mercado Municipal

Calle 8 at Carrera 12; 7am-3pm daily

The Mercado Municipal has many food stalls perfect for lunch and has several fascinating handicraft stalls. It is also a great place to learn about the different fish of the Río Amazonas, as they are on display and for sale.

Museo Uirapuru

Calle 8 No. 10-35; tel. 8/592-7056; 9am-noon and 3pm-7pm Mon.-Sat., 9am-noon Sun.

The Museo Uirapuru is more handicraft store than museum, although you can look at various river creatures in aquariums in the back. Traditional medicines are also sold here.

Food

Leticia is the place to sample some unusual Amazonian dishes. The standard Amazon meal includes fried fish, cassava, rice, patacones (fried plantains), and perhaps a small salad. Pirarucú is the king of fish around here. It is one of the largest in the world, reaching up to 3 m (10 ft) and weighing 350 kg (770 lbs). This fish is threatened, and regional governments have banned its catch and consumption November-March. Another not-for-the-shy is mojojoy, a fat grub worm that looks like a giant maggot but tastes like fried butter. A popular dish here is the patarasca, which is two types of fish, usually dorado and pintado, grilled with herbs and vegetables in banana leaves. This is accompanied by a juice such as copoazú, acai, or the ever-popular camu camu.

At night, head to **Parque Orellanas,** just east of Mercado Municipal and in front of Hotel Anaconda, for fresh fish cooked in front of you by street vendors on the open grill.

El Abuelo

Carrera 11 at Calle 7; no phone; set lunch COP$16,000-20,000

El Abuelo is a popular place with locals and those on a budget. There is usually a buffet offering a variety of dishes. The upstairs turns into a rocking watering hole at night.

★ Sazón 100% Peruano

Carrera 10 No. 13-9; tel. 310/786-0820; 10am-9pm daily; COP$22,000-55,000

It's common for visitors to cross the Río Amazonas just to have lunch on the Peruvian side, but you really don't have to leave Leticia to get your ceviche fix on. Sazón 100% Peruano is as authentic as its name promises it to be, serving up giant sized cusquena beers alongside its heaping arroz de mariscos and chicharrón de pirarucú.

★ Tierras Amazónicas

Calle 8 No. 7-50; no phone; hours vary Tues.-Sun.; COP$28,000-55,000

With dusty Amazonian handicrafts adorning its walls, Tierras Amazónicas is a required stop for most hungry travelers. Some of the unusual dishes you can order include chicharrón de pirarucú, which are sort of like fish nuggets, and pirarucú steamed in banana leaf. Big lemonades to complement the big food portions hit the spot.

Accommodations

Very good lodging options for all budgets are available in and around Leticia. Staff are generally helpful and can suggest and sometimes organize a rainforest adventure. Many travelers arrive in Leticia and leave a

THE AMAZONIAN BIOECONOMY

copoazú fruit

Just as the Amazon rainforest is slipping toward a point of no return, a promising solution has emerged: the Amazonian Bioeconomy. Literally a "life" economy, a bioeconomy is based on products that an ecosystem naturally produces instead of ones that requires exploitation and destruction.

A 2023 study by the World Resources Institute showed that a standing Amazon rainforest could produce a USD$8 billion bioeconomy based on sustainably harvested edible and medicinal products. That's more than is currently being made from oil, gas, timber, and cattle combined. The Amazonian Bioeconomy is also more equitable, with the profits going to local communities instead of transnational corporations. Both president Lula of Brazil and Colombia's Petro have promised to invest heavily in the Amazonian Bioeconomy, the latter proposing significant changes to the country's agricultural infrastructure to promote the production and commercialization of Amazonian products.

To get a taste of the many different products that can be produced sustainably from the Amazon rainforest, visit the **Tienda Solidaria Leticia** (Carrera 10 No. 8-63, Leticia; tel. 312/585-4306; 9am-noon and 3pm-8pm Mon.-Sat.). Here you will find coconut oil soaps, traditional Indigenous baskets, locally brewed beer infused with acai, and endless chocolates. Medicinal herbs from the Amazon, like copaiba resin and guayusa leaf tea, are also available.

The nonprofit **Hábitat Sur** (https://habitatsuramazonas.org) runs the tienda plus two local community centers, one in Leticia and one in Puerto Nariño, as well as a 214-ha (529-acre) rainforest reserve 16 km (10 mi) outside Leticia. The preservation of traditional culinary and artisanal skills, which are pillars of the bioeconomy, are focal points of the cultural centers, while at the reserve, guests can stay in a treehouse (USD$140 pp) or a geodesic dome (USD$120 pp), both constructed from local natural materials. Rates include all food, based on locally sourced native Amazonian species and traditional recipes, and day and night guided walks.

pirarucú ceviche

bag with the hotel in order to lighten their load as they explore the region, picking it up before leaving Leticia. Staff can also assist with making reservations for river travel, from the express boat to Puerto Nariño to longer journeys such as the famous slow-boat trip to Manaus.

La Casa del Kurupira

Carrera 9 No. 6-100, 2nd Fl.; tel. 311/287-1307; https://casakurupira.wixsite.com; COP$35,000 dorm, COP$80,000 d

Run by the same folks as tour operator Selvaventura, La Casa del Kurupira is a hostel that offers clean and comfortable private and spacious dorm rooms for budget travelers. It's a laid-back place right in the center of town.

A must-try in the Amazon region is **tucupi,** an ají (hot sauce) made from black chili peppers and rainforest ants. It's served as a side with just about everything, especially fish. Ask for it specifically, as locals often assume that visitors will not like it.

★ Hippielandia Hostel

Carrera 10 No. 8-40; tel. 312/490-9600; https://hipilandia.com; COP$45,000 dorm, COP$90,000 d

In the center of town and home to a pub and cultural center where local bands play on the weekends, Hippielandia is the best place in town to meet other travelers. Run by a father-and-son team, it also offers a variety of local tour options, including bike rides to Brazil and three-day rainforest excursions. Private rooms and shared dorms are sparsely furnished, but an on-site library and arts space, where you can get involved with community initiatives, make the experience homey.

Omshanty Jungle Lodge

Km 11, Vía a Tarapacá/Carretera Los Kilómetros; tel. 311/489-8985; COP$55,000 dorm, COP$184,000 d

The Omshanty Jungle Lodge offers budget travelers the chance to stay in the rainforest. Located 11 km (7 mi) north of Leticia, five rustic thatched roof cabañas, one of them with six dorm-style beds, are available. A locally run restaurant and traditional handicraft store, Las Aranas, is across the street and sells interesting and authentic crafts made from chambira and chambecua, typical natural fibers. You can get here by bus from the center of Leticia.

Hotel Anaconda

Carrera 11 No. 7-34; tel. 8/218-0125; www.hotelanaconda.com.co; COP$292,000 d

Hotel Anaconda is a large standard hotel on Parque Orellano. The 50 air-conditioned rooms are spacious, there is wireless internet in the lobby, and a restaurant is onsite. It also has a big pool and a poolside bar. If you're not staying here and want to cool off at the pool, you can get a day pass (COP$15,000).

Amazon B&B

Calle 12 No. 9-30; tel. 8/592-4981; www.theamazonbb.com; COP$370,000 d

An excellent choice in Leticia is the friendly and sustainably run Amazon B&B. It's on a quiet street away from the bustle of the city but still within an easy walk to restaurants and services. There's no air-conditioning in the six cabañas, but they have fans and are modern and tastefully decorated. A good breakfast is included. The bed-and-breakfast also offers Spanish classes and can arrange all sorts of excursions.

★ Reserva Natural Tanimboca

Km 11, Vía a Tarapacá/Carretera Los Kilómetros, office Carrera 10 No. 11-69; tel. 8/592-7679; www.tanimboca.com; COP$500,000 d

At the Reserva Natural Tanimboca, 11 km (7 mi) north of town, you can spend the night in a treehouse 12 m (40 ft) up in the canopy, where it's just you and thousands of chatty rainforest creatures. There are also a variety of thatched-roof bungalow-style houses dispersed in the forest. These houses are comfortable and come equipped with a toilet. Local cuisine, mostly grilled fish, is served at the restaurant. The reserve also does a variety of 3-7-day packages that come with tours into the rainforest, river excursions, and educational walks, including a nocturnal one.

Information and Services

TOURIST INFORMATION

Fondo de Promoción Ecoturística del Amazonas

Calle 8 No. 9-75; tel. 8/592-4162; www.fondodepromocionamazonas.com; 8am-noon and 2pm-5pm Mon.-Fri., 8am-1pm Sat.

The Fondo de Promoción Ecoturística del Amazonas is the tourism office. It may be of help, especially with recommendations for certified guides.

EMERGENCY AND MEDICAL SERVICES

Hospital San Rafael

Carrera 10 No. 13-78; tel. 8/592-7074

The hospital in town is the Hospital San Rafael.

Policía Nacional

Carrera 12-30; emergency tel. 112 or tel. 8/892-5060

Report emergencies to the local Policía Nacional.

INTERNET ACCESS

Internet cafés can be found around town, and you will have no problem with access at hotels and hostels in Leticia, but don't expect to find internet access in lodges outside of town. In Leticia and throughout the region, smartphones seem to operate more slowly than simple cell phones. It may be difficult to get in touch with hotels or guides in the region, especially in the rainforest communities along the river. Often the best means of communication is WhatsApp, a commonly used smartphone messaging app.

MONEY

There are several Colombian banks in Leticia with **ATMs,** especially on Carrera 10 between Calles 7-10. This is the best, if not only, place in the region to get cash. Farther from Leticia, credit cards are rarely accepted and ATMs are nonexistent. Colombian currency is accepted in the entire Amazon region near Leticia, including in Brazil and Peru.

VISAS AND OFFICIALDOM

Migración Colombia

3 km (2 mi) north of Leticia; tel. 8/592-4562

To travel to Tabatinga, Brazil; Isla de Santa Rosa, Peru; or for stops at Peruvian villages on the way to Puerto Nariño, there is no need for immigration formalities, but carry your passport just in case. If traveling to destinations in the interior of Brazil or Peru from Leticia, you must obtain an exit stamp at Migración Colombia at the airport.

Crossing to Brazil or Peru

650 Av. da Amizade, Tabatinga; 7am-noon and 2pm-6pm Mon.-Fri.

Once you get your passport stamped at the airport, if you're continuing to Manaus, Brazil, you must present your papers at the **Brazilian Policía Federal,** near the Tabatinga hospital. If continuing to Peru, get your Peruvian entry stamp at the **Peruvian police office** in Isla de Santa Rosa, which is on the main path through town.

Brazilian Consulate

Carrera 10 No. 10-10; tel. 8/592-7530; 8am-noon Mon.-Fri.

At the Brazilian Consulate, you can obtain a visa for Brazil, which is necessary for US and Canadian citizens planning an overnight stay in that country. You must present a yellow fever vaccination card and an onward airline ticket. Processing time is 2-3 days. For US citizens, the visa costs around USD$160. It may be easier to obtain the visa at the consulate in Bogotá (Calle 93 No. 14-20, 8th Fl.; tel. 1/635-1694; 9am-noon Mon.-Fri.).

Peruvian Consulate

Calle 11 No. 5-32; tel. 8/592-3947; 8am-2pm Mon.-Fri.

The Peruvian Consulate in Leticia can assist with entry information.

Transportation

GETTING THERE

Air

The Leticia airport is **Aeropuerto Internacional General Alfredo Vásquez Cobo** (LET; Carrera 10 No. 15-2003 a 15-1503), 3 km (2 mi) north of Leticia. **Avianca** (tel. 1/401-3434; www.avianca.com) and **LATAM** (tel. 1/745-2020; www.latam.com) fly here from Bogotá. **SATENA** (tel. 1/605-2222; www.satena.gov.co) offers limited flights from Leticia to Amazonian locations La Chorrera, La Pedrera, and Tarapacá. A decent restaurant is in the small airport.

On arrival in Leticia, you are required to pay a tourism fee (around COP$35,000), for which you should receive a receipt. Taxis between town and the airport should cost about COP$12,000.

Boat

The **slow boats** to and from **Manaus,** Brazil, depart from the main port in **Tabatinga,** Brazil, around 8am Tuesday and 2pm Saturday. The journey takes three days and costs COP$380,000 for a hammock that you must purchase in town beforehand, or COP$1,800,000 for a two-person cabin with air-conditioning. These fares include food on board. If you plan to sleep in a hammock, try to board early to stake out a good place. Stock up on snacks and water, as the food is basic—think meat and rice. The reverse journey upstream, from Manaus to Leticia, can also be made, but it takes six days. Weekly **fast boats** (30 hours) depart on Tuesday and Friday and cost COP$620,000. Be sure to obtain a departure stamp at the Leticia airport.

For travel to Iquitos, Peru, the boat operators **Transtur** (Rua Marechal Mallet No. 349, Tabatinga; tel. 97/8113-5239; iquitostours@hotmail.com; www.transtursa.com; 9am-noon and 2pm-6pm Mon.-Fri., 9am-1pm Sat.) and **Golfinho** (Av. Marechal Mallet No. 306, Tabatinga; tel. 97/3412-3186; 8:30am-12:30pm and 2:30pm-5:30pm Mon.-Fri., 10am-1pm Sat.) have offices in Tabatinga. Boats leave six days a week from the Peruvian town of Isla de Santa Rosa, across from Leticia, where you must get stamped into Peru before embarking. The trip to Iquitos takes nine hours and costs COP$160,000. Departure time is 3:30am or 5:30am, depending on the boat company.

The Brazilian town of **Tabatinga** is not much to look at, but there are at least two reasons to walk or mototaxi over. The first is great deals on Havaianas flip-flops, and the second is the live **samba** shows 2pm-10pm every Saturday-Sunday at the Mirador de la Camara, overlooking the Río Amazonas.

GETTING AROUND

Leticia is a small town; you can walk everywhere you'd like to go. Some hotels have rental bikes to explore the town and beyond. Mototaxis and tuk-tuks (three-wheeled mototaxis) are plentiful.

Sights along Vía a Tarapacá (Carretera Los Kilómetros) can be reached by public buses (COP$3,300) that depart from Parque Orellana (Carrera 11 and Calle 7).

Along the Río Amazonas

Most visitors to the Colombian Amazon region travel on the great river northwest from Leticia, stopping at Indigenous communities or nature reserves along the way, with Puerto Nariño being the final destination. About 84 percent of the Amazonas department consists of resguardos indígenas (Indigenous reservations); these reservations have been in existence since the colonial era, though it wasn't until the latter half of the 20th century that they would be formally recognized by Colombia. Along the Río Amazonas are several Indigenous communities, with the Ticuna group predominant.

PRACTICALITIES

All travel agencies in Leticia can organize river excursions as a day trip or multiday guided adventure, but you can also travel on your own if you have minimal Spanish skills and some patience. This usually means taking the **Expreso boat** (2.5 hours; 8am, 10am, and 2pm daily; COP$35,000 pp) between Leticia and Puerto Nariño three times daily. Buy tickets at the Malecón Plaza Local 101, a shopping corridor facing the port, also known as the Muelle Turístico. There are three agencies with offices here that take turns providing the Expreso service: **Transportes Amazónicos** (tel. 8/592-5999 or 313/347-8091), **Líneas Amazonas II** (tel. 8/592-6711 or 311/532-0633), and **Expreso Unidos Tres Fronteras** (tel. 8/592-4687 or 311/452-6809). It's best to go in person to the offices the day before your trip.

Day tours, which begin in Leticia, hit most of the sights below, stop for lunch and a wander around Puerto Nariño, and then head back at 9am daily (COP$180,000). Tours include meals. Book the day ahead through your hotel or at the port.

The river is more scenic during the **rainy season** (Nov.-Mar.), as water levels climb to the tops of some trees, though in the **dry months** (Apr.-Oct.) you'll be astonished to see islands of beaches appear under blue skies in the middle of the Río Amazonas. Keep your eyes peeled for dolphins, both gray and pink, usually spotted in the early morning or late afternoon. Every once in a while, you'll pass a fisher in a peque-peque (a type of dugout canoe) loaded with bananas.

Reserva Natural Victoria Regia

COP$8,000

Seven km (4 mi) and a 15-minute boat ride west from Leticia, Reserva Natural Victoria Regia is a private reserve that is usually the first stop on the river. You can view large circular *Victoria amazonica* lily pads and their lovely white lotus flowers floating on the water. These are some of the largest water plants in the world, with leaves up to 1.5 m (5 ft) across, with roots extending 7 m (23 ft) below the water's surface. It's said that these plants are so strong they can support the weight of a small child (but don't test this theory out on your offspring). You can also marvel at a magnificent old ceiba tree farther along on the park walkway.

Isla de los Micos

COP$40,000

Isla de los Micos (Monkey Island) is the most popular attraction on the river. It's about 40 km (25 mi) west of Leticia. At this island, owned by the Colombian hotel

Amazon River

chain Decameron, elevated walkways meander through the rainforest, and with just a morsel of fruit in your hand, you'll make the monkeys go bananas. They'll proceed to climb all over you in hopes of a snack. The monkeys are not native to the island; they were brought here by controversial hotel owner and entrepreneur Mike Tsalickis in the 1970s. Up to 12,000 monkeys supposedly lived here at one point. It is a tourist trap, but it's hard to deny that kids love it.

Macedonia

entry COP$3,000

The Ticuna village of Macedonia, one hour up the river from Leticia, is a regular stop for tourist boats. As each boatload of visitors arrive, they are invited in to the maloca (community house), where a ceremonial dance is performed. Visitors are led onto the middle of the dance floor to the beat of a turtle-shell drum. Around the maloca you can peruse an array of handicrafts at stalls set up by local women. A specialty is palo de sangre (bloodwood) carvings. Although touristy, it is nice that the community manages all the activities here, and all the income goes directly to them.

Calanoa Amazonas

tel. 311/842-4392; www.calanoaamazonas.com; 3-night package COP$2,230,000 pp

It's possible to find local-style lodging along the Río Amazonas, especially in the Ticuna communities of Macedonia and Mocagua, but there is also one of the top-rated ecolodges in the entire Amazon rainforest. Calanoa Amazonas, just over an hour and 60 km (37 mi) upriver from Leticia, offers understated Amazonian luxury at its finest. Guests stay in one of a

COMMUNITY-RUN TOURISM IN THE AMAZON

Indigenous Amazonian communities are on the frontline of rainforest conservation. In fact, studies show that territories inhabited by Indigenous people show even less deforestation than those designated as protected areas, including national parks. Yet most Indigenous communities are not rewarded for the important conservation work they do, even though it benefits countless species and the entire planet.

One way to help support Indigenous communities is through participating in community-run tourism, where all proceeds go directly to the communities involved instead of a tour agency or other middleman. One of the best organized community tourism projects in the Amazon is **Fundación Entropika** (Calle 18 No. 7B-23, Leticia; tel. 302/397-9484; https://entropika.org), which works with local Ticuna communities, many of which were previously involved in the illegal wildlife trade, to develop sustainable community tourism initiatives based around wildlife conservation.

The nonprofit offers visitors the chance to live in the Ticuna village of **Mocagua,** next to Parque Nacional Natural Amacayacu, 60 km (37 mi) from Leticia. The community is known for their protection of the woolly monkey *(Lagothrix lagotricha),* and visitors will have ample opportunities to view these beauties in their native habitat around the village and visit a locally run foundation that rehabilitates those that were rescued from the wildlife trade. Just across the Río Amazonas from Mocagua lies the **Musmuki Reserve,** a community-run wildlife preserve that offers rainforest hikes, canoe rides, and chances to see even more Amazonian primates, including the nocturnal owl monkey *(Aotus nancymaae),* after which the reserve is named.

Three-day and two-night experiences, which include stays in Mocagua and visits to the Musmuki Reserve plus all food, guides, and transportation to and from Leticia, run around COP$1,800,000 per person, but prices go down when there are more people in the group.

handful of gorgeous cabins amid the trees with views to the water and are served delicious food in the dining room. Activities include day and nighttime canoe trips, bird- and dolphin-watching, and visits to local communities. The on-site restaurant is one of the pioneers of high-end gourmet Amazonian cuisine and frequently hosts culinary courses that draw some of the country's top chefs. The reserve also offers wildlife photography courses with cofounder Diego Samper, a multimedia artist who has also produced a musical album that samples the sounds of the rainforest.

The lodge can arrange transportation, but the express boat between Leticia and Puerto Nariño will also drop you here if you request it.

★ Parque Nacional Natural Amacayacu

70 km (43 mi) west of Leticia; tel. 1/353-2400; www.parquesnacionales.gov.co

The prime unspoiled land known as Parque Nacional Natural Amacayacu covers 300,000 ha (740,000 acres). Its southern border is on the banks of the Amazon between the Río Amacayacu (River of Hammocks) and the Quebrada Matamata stream and extends north to the Río Cotuhé. It was declared a national park in 1975. The park is characterized by rainforest-covered undulating hills and swamps and an intricate network of streams. The highest point in the park reaches 200 m (660 ft) elevation. It is estimated to contain more than 5,000 species of plants, 150 of mammals, including pink dolphins, tapirs, jaguars, manatees, and numerous primates, 500 birds, about 100 fish. Resident animals such as squirrel monkeys, sloths, wild boars, and jaguars are hard to spot in the park and in the rainforest in general.

If you are traveling by boat up the spectacular and serpentine Río Amacayacu, ask the captain to completely cut the engine at least once or twice during the journey so that you can enjoy the incredible sounds of the rainforest. When you float along in silence, hearing nothing but the calls of distant monkeys, shrieks of birds, or the constant hum of legions of frogs and insects, it is a magical experience.

San Martín de Amacayacu

70 km (43 mi) northeast of Leticia; COP$5,000

Just 15 minutes up the Río Amacayacu, within Parque Nacional Natural Amacayacu, is the Ticuna community of San Martín de Amacayacu. The community has organized itself to receive visitors and offers rainforest walks, canoe rides, and other activities such as handicrafts workshops. The entrance fee is used to pay for a kindergarten and other services. One of over 20 Indigenous communities in and around Puerto Nariño, San Martín is considered one of the most traditional, and community members are committed to preserving their cultural identity.

Activities in San Martín include a visit to a chagra (traditional farm), visits with local artisans to observe how they make ceramics and woven handicrafts, and a rainforest walk. Contact community elder Victor Ángel Pereira (tel. 310/911-9725) for assistance with accommodations, food, and activities. To get to San Martín directly, take the Expreso boat service from Leticia or Puerto Nariño to the Bocana Amacayacu settlement.

ACCOMMODATIONS

Amacayacu Lodge

tel. 311/251-3841 or 320/481-5817; COP$45,000 pp

A more economical option in the community of San Martín is the Amacayacu Lodge. It's a basic rainforest house with about five rooms for rent run by a friendly local family that can also help you connect with locals willing to give you walking tours into the National Park. Its restaurant is open to all.

Casa de Gregorio

tel. 310/279-8147 or 311/201-8222; casagregorio@outlook.com; COP$400,000 pp

The Casa de Gregorio is a lodge in the village of San Martín run by a Ticuna-Dutch couple, Heike and José Gregorio. Heike arrived in San Martín as a doctoral student in agriculture sciences in 2004, and José is a Ticuna community leader. They cook food for you with many ingredients from the on-site garden as well as the surrounding

Yoi Ecolodge

village. They offer three basic yet comfortable rooms and a deluxe cabin, with all meals and activities, including tours, included in the package. Even if you are coming to the park on a day trip from Puerto Nariño, this is a great place to stop for a snack and get connected with a local guide.

★ Yoi Ecolodge

tel. 320/372-2806; www.yoiecotours.com; 2 nights all-inclusive COP$2,775,000 pp

Run by local Ticuna couple Agusto Morán and María Ayla Angel, the Yoi Ecolodge gives you the option of staying in a luxury ecolodge within the park itself. Accommodations are in private cabins amid pristine rainforest splendor. Rates are all-inclusive and give you options like bird-watching, canoe trips, and even lessons in blow-gun hunting as well as all food. It's about 30 minutes up the Río San Martín from the village by boat, and the friendly couple will arrange for a local to take you.

★ Puerto Nariño

On arriving at the village of Puerto Nariño, atop a sloping hill overlooking the Río Loretoyacú, you'll wonder: Where are the motorbikes? Here in idyllic Puerto Nariño, there are no roads and no motorized vehicles. An environmentally minded town council decided years ago that they wanted Puerto Nariño to chart a different path than other towns in Colombia, and for their efforts, this town was named the first tourism-sustainable town in the country by the national government. Roads here are palm-lined sidewalks that connect the neighborhoods. Puerto Nariño is so peaceful that you'll probably want to linger awhile.

Festivals and Events

Festival Autóctono de Danza, Murga y Cuento

end of Dec.-early Jan.

The Festival Autóctono de Danza, Murga y Cuento is a celebration of Indigenous culture and identity. Each night the town gathers around the basketball court for evenings of storytelling, dance, and the requisite beauty pageant. Interestingly, an important component of the pageant is a demonstration of the girls' knowledge of their native tongue.

Food and Accommodations

Restaurant options in Puerto Nariño are mostly clustered along the riverbank and along Calle 6, often swamped with visitors from day tours during lunch hours.

★ Casa Jaguar Restaurante and Bar

Carrera 6A; tel. 310/279-8147; COP$20,000-45,000

With a nice garden patio and a central location, Casa Jaguar is a good place to try some cassaba (tapioca) crepes stuffed with different toppings and smothered in tucupi (ant sauce). They also serve the local Amazónico craft beer by the bottle.

Restaurante Las Margaritas

Calle 6 No. 6-80; hours and days vary; COP$20,000-50,000

Restaurante Las Margaritas specializes in the usual freshly caught Amazonian fish dishes and can also whip up vegetarian fare. The large open-air dining room is near the port, making it a great place to catch a last-minute meal before heading back to Leticia.

Hospedaje Wone

Carrera 1 No. 4-14; tel. 314/266-5496 or 320/878-5785; COP$40,000 d

Hospedaje Wone is a pleasant and inexpensive local-style hotel, with potted plants and flowers throughout, and has just three rooms. It's near the port. A bath is outside in back, meaning there's no indoor plumbing.

Paraiso Ayahuasca

Calle 4 No. 2-45; tel. 320/244-0187; COP$55,000 dorm, COP$140,000 d

Tangled vines of the sacred ayahuasca plant cover the exterior of Paraiso Ayahuasca, a three-story lodge located on a hill with nice views of town just a few blocks from the riverfront. The friendly owner, who hails from Medellín but married a local over two decades ago, built the structure himself and has been studying with local ayahuasceros. He can point you to a good ceremony in the area.

Malocas Napü

Calle 4 No. 5-72; tel. 314/437-6075 or 315/607-4044; www.malocanapu.com; COP$68,000 dorm, COP$151,000 d

Set amid a garden of fruit trees higher up in Puerto Nariño is Malocas Napü, a popular choice among international travelers. There are eight rooms, some with private baths, in two traditional thatched-roof rainforest houses. In addition to a trip to Lago Tarapoto, the staff can organize several lesser-known excursions in the area, such as a walk to a nearby Indigenous community and visits to a fishpond and a small refuge for alligators.

★ Alto del Águila Cabañas del Fraile

tel. 311/502-8592; altodelaguila@hotmail.com; COP$55,000 pp private bath, COP$180,000 d

To get away from the bustle of Puerto Nariño but still be within walking distance, the Alto del Águila Cabañas del Fraile is your best bet. The home of a Franciscan friar turned bird-watcher, it's perched on a bluff overlooking the Río Amazonas and has several tame macaws that have become permanent residents. Cabins are clean and cheerful, the kitchen area is a comfortable place to hang out, and you can take a kayak out on the river for free. To get here, you have to walk about 20 minutes from town and cut across the boarding school grounds.

Information and Services

There are no ATMs in Puerto Nariño. There are a couple of internet cafés, but the connections are very slow.

Tourist Office

Carrera 1 at Calle 5, Palacio Municipal; no phone; 7am-noon and 2pm-5:45pm Mon.-Fri.

The tourist office can assist you with finding official tour guides.

Transportation

All river transportation to Puerto Nariño departs from the **Muelle Turístico,** the port in Leticia. There are boats to Puerto Nariño at 8am, 10am, and 2pm daily. The trip takes about 2.5 hours and costs COP$35,000 per person. Tickets can be obtained at the port in the Malecón Plaza Local 101, a shopping corridor facing the port. Three agencies have offices there and take turns providing the Expreso boat service to Puerto Nariño: **Transportes Amazónicos** (tel. 8/592-5999 or 313/347-8091), **Líneas Amazonas II** (tel. 8/592-6711 or 311/532-0633), and **Expreso Unidos Tres Fronteras** (tel. 8/592-4687 or 311/452-6809). It's best to go in person to the offices the day before your trip. Alternatively, your hotel can make a reservation for you by phone or purchase the tickets on your behalf.

When leaving Puerto Nariño for Leticia, make sure you reserve your spot a day or more in advance. You can do this at the office along the walkway to the docks. Boats leave Puerto Nariño at 7:30am, 11am, 2pm, and 4pm daily.

★ Lago Tarapoto

Just 3 km (2 mi) northwest of Puerto Nariño, Lago Tarapoto, at 37 sq km (14 sq mi), is much larger than the adjacent **Lago El Correo,** next to town. The tranquil water of both, which are really lagoons that feed into the Río Amazonas and not lakes, are prime wildlife-watching areas and can be

The village of Puerto Nariño has no roads and no motorized vehicles.

visited with a 20-minute boat ride from Puerto Nariño.

Known as a breeding ground for pink dolphins, Lago Tarapoto offers the opportunity to see these magical mammals up close. They often swim right up to the boat to check you out. Bird-watching is also spectacular here, with elegant white herons roosting in trees and powerful mama viejas (black-collared hawks) swooping down to pluck fish out of the water. There are several spots where you can see renacos, also known as el arbol que camina (the tree that walks), a tree with a jumble of aboveground roots.

To get to the lake, you have to go with a guide. The tourist office in Puerto Nariño or any hotel can help organize a visit to these lakes and surrounding flooded rainforests. This excursion, pleasant to make in the late afternoon, costs around COP$60,000 per person.

★ Río Javari

The Río Javari (Río Yavarí in Spanish) begins in Peru and serves as a border between Brazil and Peru. It flows some 1,050 km (650 mi) before meeting the Amazon in Brazil. About a six-hour journey from Leticia by boat (three hours when the rainforest is flooded), this part of the Amazon basin is unspoiled, isolated, and home to two excellent private natural reserves where you will be immersed in the rainforest. Spend at least three days or up to a week at one of the Javari nature reserves (both are excellent) to gain a real appreciation for rainforest life. The longer you stay, the more wildlife you are apt to see: pink dolphins, alligators, snakes, and dozens of birds. Although this region is technically in Brazil, it very well may be one of the highlights of your trip to the Colombian Amazon.

Reserva Natural Palmarí

office Carrera 10 No. 93-72, Apt. 602, Bogotá; tel. 1/610-3514; www.palmari.org; 3-night minimum, meals included, hammock COP$400,000 pp, COP$600,000 pp d

Located on a bluff overlooking the Río Javari about 110 km (70 mi) southeast of Leticia, Reserva Natural Palmarí is a pioneer in ecotourism in this part of the Amazon. Once you arrive, you are paired with a guide who accompanies you throughout your stay. You won't be grouped with others. Activities include rainforest walks, including at night, as well as treks, canopying, kayaking, canoe rides, and visits to nearby Indigenous communities. Near Reserva Natural Palmarí you can admire massive ceiba trees, also called lupuna trees. These noble giants reach up to 70 m (230 ft) tall and have witnessed a lot in their 400-year lifespan. The Indigenous Ticuna people believe these trees are what started life and created the river.

The reserve, first and foremost, has a strong commitment to the environment and community. The rooftops are made from durable recycled material imported from Canada because of the growing scarcity of the native palm trees. Palmarí works with local communities on sustainable agriculture and ecotourism projects as well as environmental education, and has been instrumental in the construction of schools in several villages. Much credit is due to gregarious Axel, the German-Colombian owner of the reserve, for being a forward-thinking eco-example. Some of the proceeds from Palmarí go toward a conservation nonprofit it set up, the Instituto De Desenvolvimento Socioambiental Do Vale Do Javari (www.idsavj.org).

Palmarí has a range of accommodations, and if you are traveling in a group, this is an excellent choice. You can sleep in a hammock, in a communal lodge, or in private rooms. Food is delicious and varied and is included in the rates. You can also get online, although this might be the perfect time for an internet diet. There are two great places at Palmarí to spend the late-afternoon hours as you watch the sun go down: the lookout tower and the swing set. Although it is possible (and adventurous) to get to Palmarí on your own, they will arrange your transportation directly from Leticia.

Reserva Natural Heliconia

office Calle 19 No. 4b-17, Leticia; tel. 8/592-5773 or 311/508-5666; www.amazonheliconia.com; 3 nights COP$2,700,000 pp d, including transportation

In Brazil, 109 km (68 mi) southeast of Leticia, the Reserva Natural Heliconia is a fantastic lodge and nature reserve hidden in the dense Amazonian rainforest on a tributary of the Río Javari, which flows into the Río Amazonas. Like a bird of paradise flower (for which it is named) growing in the middle of a sea of green in the rainforest, it's truly an escape from the rest of the world—there is no phone or internet

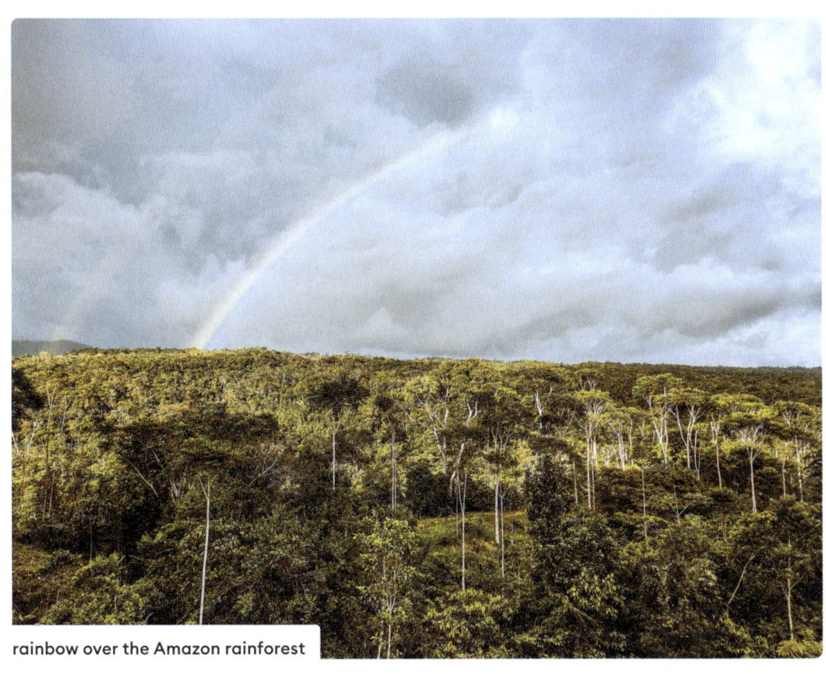

rainbow over the Amazon rainforest

service. Ideally, plan on spending at least three nights, as anything less than that will feel rushed.

Activities are included in the rates, except for canopying, and include nature walks, bird-watching, pink dolphin-watching, canoeing above the inundated forest, and fishing. You'll usually have two outings each day, and sometimes you can explore the rainforest at night, panning the darkness with your flashlight as you look for the red eyes of rainforest beasts looking back at you. Another nocturnal activity is a canoe ride in search of alligators, or if there are none, simply enjoying the sounds of the rainforest and the millions of stars above.

The comfortable cabins at this reserve are made of all-natural materials. Cabins come in different sizes, for two guests or for families, and they have an area for larger groups. At night you don't even realize there are others around, such is the privacy. The reserve will arrange to pick you up in Leticia.

Background

THE LANDSCAPE

Colombia covers a land area of 1.14 million sq km (440,000 sq mi), roughly the size of Texas and California combined, making it the fourth-largest South American country in area after Brazil, Argentina, and Peru. It is located in the northwest corner of South America, with coasts on both the Pacific and the Atlantic, and it borders Venezuela, Brazil, Peru, Ecuador, and Panama. The Amazonian departments of Putumayo, Caquetá, Amazonas, and Vaupés in the south straddle the equator.

For a country of its size, Colombia has an astonishing variety of landscapes, including the dense rainforests of the Amazon and the Pacific coast, the vast grassland plains of Los Llanos, the lofty Andes Mountains, and the Caribbean islands of San Andrés and Providencia. Colombia's mountainous regions themselves hold a succession of vertically layered landscapes: tropical rainforests at their base, followed by cloud forests at higher elevations, topped by the unique tropical high mountain páramo (highland moor) above 3,500 m (11,500 ft). The country boasts several peaks higher than 5,000 m (16,400 ft), including Nevado del Ruiz (5,325 m/17,470 ft) and Pico Cristóbal Colón (5,775 m/18,950 ft).

Geography

REGIÓN ANDINA

This central part of Colombia is dominated by the Andes Mountain Range. Referred to as the Región Andina or simply el interior (the interior), this region is the heartland of the country. It covers roughly 25 percent of the country's area and is home to 60 percent of its population.

The Andes Mountain Range, 8,000 km (5,000 mi) long, runs the length of South America. Relatively young mountains and the second highest in the world after the Himalayas, the Andes resulted from the collision of the westward-moving South American plate with the Nazca and Antarctic plates starting 145 million years ago. The heavier Nazca and Antarctic plates to the west subducted under the lighter and more rigid South American plate, propelling it upward to form the Andes. In Colombia, as a result of a complex pattern of tectonic collisions, three parallel ranges were formed. At the Macizo Colombiano (Colombian Massif), a mountain range 175 km (110 mi) north of the border with Ecuador, the Andes split into the Cordillera Occidental (Western Range), Cordillera Central (Central Range), and Cordillera Oriental (Eastern Range).

The Cordillera Occidental is the lowest and least populated of the three ranges. It runs roughly 750 km (465 mi) parallel to the Pacific coast and ends 150 km (90 mi) from the Caribbean Sea. Its highest point is the Cerro de Tatamá (4,250 m/13,945 ft). Of Colombia's three ranges, it has the least human intervention and is home to some of the world's only pristine high mountain páramo ecosystems, notably that covering the Cerro de Tatamá.

The Central Cordillera is the highest of the three ranges and is the continuation in Colombia of the main Andes range. It runs roughly 800 km (500 mi) and tapers off in the northern Caribbean plains, 200 km (120 mi) from the Caribbean coast. Like the Andes in Ecuador, it is dotted with volcanoes. North of the Macizo Colombiano is the Serranía de los Coconucos (Coconucos

◀ plaza in Guatapé

Range), a range of 15 volcanoes including Volcán del Puracé (4,580 m/15,025 ft). North of the Coconucos, the Cordillera Central reaches its maximum elevation at the massive Nevado del Huila (5,750 m/15,585 ft). Farther north is a large complex formed by the Nevado del Tolima (5,215 m/17,110 ft), Nevado de Santa Isabel (4,950 m/16,240 ft), and Nevado del Ruiz (5,325 m/17,470 ft). In its northern part, the Cordillera Central broadens to form the uneven highland that is the mountainous heartland of Antioquia with Medellín as its capital.

Several of the volcanoes of the Cordillera Central have seen recent activity, notably Volcán Galeras (4,276 m/14,030 ft), near the southern city of Pasto, which last erupted in 2005, forcing evacuation of nearby settlements. Volcán Galeras is currently closed to visitors because of the threat of volcanic activity. In 1985 the Nevado del Ruiz erupted unexpectedly, creating a landslide that engulfed the town of Armero, killing more than 20,000 people. Since 2012, the Nevado del Ruiz has seen some activity, which has restricted access to the northern part of Parque Nacional Natural Los Nevados.

Like the Cordillera Occidental, the Cordillera Oriental is not volcanic. It extends more than 1,100 km (680 mi) to the border with Venezuela. The range broadens to form a broad high plateau called the Altiplano Cundiboyacense, which extends 200 km (120 mi) north of Bogotá. This is an area of broad valleys with the extremely rich soil of sedimentary deposits. The Sábana de Bogotá, or Bogotá High Plateau, where Bogotá is located, is a particularly broad valley. North of the altiplano is the soaring Sierra Nevada del Cocuy, a mountain range with 11 glacier-covered peaks, including Ritacuba Blanco (5,380 m/17,650 ft). North of El Cocuy, the Cordillera Oriental loses elevation and splits in two: A smaller western segment forms the Serranía del Perijá on the border of Colombia and Venezuela, and a larger branch continues into Venezuela to form the Venezuelan Andes.

The 1,500-km-long (930-mi) Río Magdalena flows along a broad valley that separates the Cordillera Central and the Cordillera Oriental, making it the main commercial waterway of Colombia. Due to heavy sedimentation, it is now only navigable when the water rises during the rainy seasons in the central part of the country (Apr.-May and Oct.-Nov.). The Río Cauca, which flows parallel to the Magdalena along the much narrower valley between the Cordillera Central and the Cordillera Occidental, is the main tributary of the Magdalena. They join in northern Colombia and flow into the Caribbean.

Andean Colombia is a seismically volatile area, and the country has suffered some major earthquakes in the past. The deadliest, with a magnitude of 7.5, occurred in Cúcuta in 1875. It killed 10,000 and completely destroyed the city. In recent years, around 600 were killed in the Pacific port city of Tumaco during a quake and tsunami in 1979; in the 1983 Holy Week earthquake in Popayán, 300 perished; and over 1,100 died in the Armenia quake of 1999.

CARIBE

Colombia's Caribbean coast runs 1,760 km (1,100 mi) from the border of Panama to Venezuela, slightly longer than the California coast. The term Caribe or Región Caribe refers to more than the coast; it encompasses all of Colombia north of the Andes, including vast plains. This region covers 15 percent of the area of Colombia and is home to 20 percent of the population.

The terrain is mostly low-lying and undulating. Near the border with Panama, the land is covered by dense tropical forests, similar to those on the Pacific coast. Farther east is the Golfo de Urabá, a large shallow bay. Between the Golfo de Urabá and Cartagena is the Golfo de Morrosquillo, a broad inlet 50 km (30 mi) wide. Off the shore of the Golfo de Morrosquillo are two small archipelagoes, the Islas de San Bernardo and the Islas del Rosario, with beautiful coral reefs. Inland to the south is a large savanna in the departments of Córdoba and Sucre, largely devoted to cattle ranching. This area was once covered by dry tropical forests and have largely been felled.

Bahía de Cartagena, farther east, is a magnificent deep bay that caught the attention of the early Spanish explorers. To the southeast of Cartagena is the lower valley of the Magdalena and Cauca rivers, a vast expanse of low-lying lagoons and land prone to seasonal flooding. Río Magdalena flows into the Caribbean east of Cartagena at the port city of Barranquilla. Farther east along the coast is a major mountain range, the Sierra Nevada de Santa Marta. It was formed by the collision of the South American plate and the Caribbean plate to the north and is entirely independent of the Andes. This range is home to Colombia's two highest peaks, the twin Pico Cristóbal Colón and Pico Bolívar (5,776 m/18,950 ft), and is considered the highest coastal mountain range in the world. The Sierra Nevada de Santa Marta contains the same range of vertically layered landscapes as the Andes, from low-lying tropical forest through cloud forest, Andean forests, páramo, and glaciers. There are eight peaks with elevations greater than 5,000 m (16,400 ft).

Northeast of the Sierra Nevada de Santa Marta is La Guajira, an arid peninsula jutting into the Caribbean. Punta Gallinas, at the tip of La Guajira, is the northernmost point in South America. There are a few low-lying mountain ranges in La Guajira, such as the Serranía de Macuira (864 m/2,835 ft), which is covered with rainforest. The Sierra Nevada de Santa Marta and Serranía de Macuira are biological islands, and their upper reaches are home to numerous endemic species that evolved in isolation.

PACÍFICO

The Pacific coast of Colombia extends 1,329 km (825 mi) from Ecuador to Panama, about the same length as the coast of California. The term Pacífico, as it relates to Colombia, designates all the land—rainforest, to be accurate—that lies between the Pacific Ocean and the Cordillera Occidental. This region covers 6 percent of Colombia and is home to about 2 percent of the population.

The topography of this region is mostly flat, with the low-lying coastal Serranía del Baudó (1,810 m/5,940 ft) providing a mountainous backdrop to the coastal plain and forming an inland basin that is drained by the mighty Río Atrato, which flows north into the Caribbean Sea. The coast has a number of bays and inlets, notably the Ensenada de Utría (Utría Inlet), visited by humpback whales traveling every winter from the Antarctic Sea to give birth in the warm Colombian Pacific. South of Buenaventura, the coast has extensive mangroves, much of them well-preserved. Offshore are two islands: Isla Gorgona is 35 km (22 mi) off the coast on the continental shelf, and tiny Isla de Malpelo is 490 km

(305 mi) off the coast. Both of these islands are likely of volcanic origin.

The Colombian Pacific region is one of the wettest places on Earth, with average annual rainfall of 10,000 mm (400 in). Due to the enormous amount of precipitation, the region has a dense river network with dozens of major arteries, such as the Río Baudó, Río San Juan, and Río Patía.

AMAZON

The Amazon region of Colombia comprises 400,000 sq km (154,000 sq mi), or roughly 35 percent of Colombia's territory, including all the territory east of the Andes and south of the Río Guaviare. The Colombian portion covers only 10 percent of the Amazon basin. Total population in the Amazon region is 1.1 million, or 2 percent of the country's total. It is the most sparsely populated part of the country.

Like Los Llanos, the Amazon has an undulating terrain, interrupted occasionally with ancient low-lying mountainous formations of the Guyana Shield, such as the Serranía de Chiribiquete, a series of highly eroded tabletop mountains. The Amazon consists of two distinct but intermingled areas: terra firme, the undulated lands above the highest flood point, and varzea, floodplains along the main rivers, which can extend 50 km (30 mi) from the river.

There are two types of rivers in the Amazon: the predominant white rivers that carry sediments down from the Andes, and the black rivers that originate in the rainforest in the Guyana Shield formations that were long ago denuded of soil due to erosion. As the water travels though the flooded forest, it picks up pigments that give it the characteristic black color. Igapo is the name given to rainforests flooded by black-water rivers. Most of the rivers of the Colombian Amazon are white, such as the massive Río Putumayo, Río Caquetá, Río Apaporis, and Río Vaupés, all of which are more than 1,000 km (600 mi) long. The main black river in Colombia is the Río Guainía. It actually originates in the Andes and is the headwater of the largest black river of the Amazon, the Río Negro, which flows into the milky Amazon at Manaus, Brazil.

LOS LLANOS

Los Llanos, Colombia's vast eastern plains, cover 250,000 sq km (97,000 sq mi), roughly 25 percent of Colombia's territory. Bordered to the west by the Cordillera Oriental and to the south by the Amazon rainforest, the plains extend far into Venezuela. The transition between the Amazon and Los Llanos is gradual, but the Río Guaviare, which flows west-east roughly midway between the northern and southern tips of Colombia, is considered the demarcation between the two. Los Llanos are home to about 1.5 million people, about 3 percent of the population, making it the region with the second-lowest population density after the Amazon.

After the genesis of the Andes, water flowing eastward down the mountains accumulated in a vast freshwater lake that was confined on the east by old mountainous formations, now the Guyana and Brazilian highlands. Large amounts of sediments were deposited, forming the basis for Los Llanos's undulating topography. Near the Andes, elevations can reach 300 m (980 ft) and, moving east, slowly decrease until they reach the north-flowing Río Orinoco, which forms the border between Colombia and Venezuela.

The only significant mountain range in Los Llanos is the Serranía de la Macarena, a 120-km-long (75-mi), 30-km-wide (19-mi) range that is 45 km (28 mi) east of the

Andes just north of the Río Guayabero, a tributary of the Río Guaviare. This range is part of the Guyana Shield complex of ancient, highly eroded remnants of mountains that existed long before the formation of the Andes.

Los Llanos are drained by a multitude of large rivers, such as the Río Guaviare, Río Vichada, and Río Meta, which meander east from the Andes. All the rivers of Los Llanos are tributaries of the Orinoco. For this reason, the region is often called La Orinoquía.

Climate

Colombia has a typically tropical climate, with no change of seasons. Climate is related primarily to elevation, and there are defined annual precipitation patterns.

In the mountainous areas, temperature decreases approximately 6 degrees Celsius per 1,000 m of elevation (3 degrees Fahrenheit per 1,000 ft). The common designations for the altitudinal zones are: tierra caliente (hot lands) is anywhere below 1,000 m (3,280 ft) elevation; tierra templada (temperate lands) is 1,000-2,000 m (3,280-6,560 ft); and tierra fría (cold land) is above 2,000 m (6,560 ft). Roughly 80 percent of the country is tierra caliente, 10 percent is tierra templada, and 7 percent is tierra fría.

Cartagena, at sea level, has an average temperature of 27.5°C (82°F); Medellín, at 1,600 m (5,250 ft), averages 22°C (72°F); and the capital city, Bogotá, at 2,625 m (8,610 ft), averages 13.5°C (56°F).

Precipitation patterns vary throughout the country. In the Andean region, there are generally two periods of verano (dry season, literally "summer"), December-March and June-September, and two periods of invierno (rainy season, literally "winter"), in April-May and October-November. On the Caribbean coast, the dry period is December-April and the rainy season is May-November. In the Pacific it rains almost the entire year, but there is a slight dry spell December-March. In Los Llanos, there are two marked seasons: a very dry verano November-March and a very wet invierno April-October. In the Amazon it rains almost the entire year, but there is a slight dry spell August-October.

Extreme weather in Colombia is rare, but the country is susceptible to weather phenomena such as El Niño and La Niña, when temperatures in the Pacific Ocean rise or fall. In 2015-2016, the country was affected by a strong El Niño, which brought prolonged drought.

August-October, San Andrés and Providencia are occasionally, and the Caribbean mainland of Colombia rarely, in the path of Atlantic hurricanes. The last storm of significance was Hurricane Beta in 2005. It caused considerable damage in Providencia.

COLOMBIA'S NATIONAL PARKS

With undisturbed coral reefs, the Amazonian rainforest, and snow-covered mountain ranges, Colombia's national park system is a treasure. The country's natural parks and protected areas cover more than 14 million ha (35 million acres), around 13.4 percent of the land. It includes 43 parques nacionales naturales (national natural parks), areas of major ecological interest that have remained largely untouched by human intervention, and 12 santuarios de flora y fauna (flora and fauna sanctuaries), areas that are devoted to the preservation of specific ecosystems. Of the 43 parks, 24 are open to visitors. The rest are officially off-limits due to the lack of infrastructure, security concerns, or in order to respect the territory of Indigenous peoples.

In 1960, Parque Nacional Natural Cueva de los Guácharos, in the southwest, was the first to be established. The number of parks steadily increased, especially 1986-1990, when President Virgilio Barco doubled the park holdings. In 2013 President Juan Manuel Santos doubled the size of Parque Nacional Natural Sierra de Chiribiquete to its present 2.8 million ha (7 million acres), or three times the size of Yellowstone National Park.

Entry permits and fees are only required in a handful of highly visited parks, such as Parque Nacional Natural Tayrona, Parque Nacional Natural Gorgona, Parque Nacional Natural El Cocuy, and Parque Nacional Natural Los Nevados. At these, you will automatically be charged if you book lodging in advance, or if not, when you arrive. If you want to be meticulous, you can obtain the entry permit and pay the fees in advance by contacting **Parques Nacionales** (tel. 1/353-2400; www.parquesnacionales.gov.co) in Bogotá.

The national parks covered in this book are:

- **Parque Nacional Natural Tayrona:** A true coastal wilderness (page 104)
- **Parque Natural Chicaque:** Waterfall-chasing in the cloud forest outside Bogotá (page 180)
- **Parque Nacional Natural El Cocuy:** Glacier-capped Andean splendor (page 203)
- **Parque Nacional Natural Los Nevados:** Mighty peaks and lush valleys (page 268)
- **Parque Nacional Natural Farallones de Cali:** Epic bird-watching in the lush mountains outside Cali (page 317)
- **Parque Nacional Natural Puracé:** Remote alpine adventures and thermal baths (page 332)
- **Parque Nacional Natural Old Providence McBean Lagoon:** Deep mangrove swamps in a Caribbean paradise (page 367)
- **Parque Nacional Natural Amacayacu:** A pristine swath of Amazonian rainforest (page 396)

PLANTS AND ANIMALS

When it comes to biodiversity, Colombia is a place of superlatives. Though representing only 0.2 percent of the planet's surface, it is home to about 10 percent of all the species in the world. The country has an estimated 55,000 plant species, including 3,500 species of orchids. Only Brazil, with seven times the land surface, has as many. Colombia is the country with the greatest number of bird species: about 1,800. It's also home to about 3,200 fish species, 750 amphibians, 500 reptiles, and 450 mammals. No wonder Colombia was designated as one of 17 megadiverse countries, a select group that is home to an outsized proportion of the world's biodiversity. Other megadiverse countries include Australia, Brazil, China, Democratic Republic of Congo, Indonesia, Madagascar, Mexico, the United States, and South Africa.

This enormous biodiversity is the result of Colombia's location in the tropics, where year-round sunlight and high precipitation are conducive to plant growth, plus the country's mountainous topography with numerous climatic zones and microclimates that have created biological islands where species have evolved in relative isolation. Furthermore, the most recent ice ages were not as severe in this part of the world, and as a result many ancient species were preserved. Finally, Colombia's location at the crossroads of Central and South America has further enriched its biodiversity.

Rainforest

Rainforests are among the most complex ecosystems on Earth. They have a layered structure with towering trees that soar 30-40 m high (100-130 ft) to form the forest's canopy. Some of the most common rainforest trees are the ceiba, mahogany, myrtle, laurel, acacia, and rubber trees. Occasionally, particularly tall trees known as emergentes pierce the canopy, reaching up to 60 m (200 ft). Below the canopy is the sotobosque, a middle layer of smaller trees and palms that vie for the sunlight filtering in through the canopy. In the canopy and sotobosque are many epiphytes (plants such as orchids and bromeliads) that have adapted to live on top of trees to get more sunlight. Near the ground live plants that require little sunlight, including ferns, grasses, and many types of fungi. The two main rainforests in Colombia, the Amazon and the Chocó, have the same layered structure, though they have some differences in their flora and fauna.

The Amazon rainforest is home to an impressive array of vertebrates. Over millennia a large number of canopy-dwelling species evolved. Monkeys, such as the large and extremely agile spider monkey, the woolly monkey, and the howler monkey, evolved prehensile tails that allow them to move easily from branch to branch. Anteaters, such as the tamandua, the oso mielero (giant anteater), and the incredibly cute kinkajú (kinkajou), also developed prehensile tails. Other inhabitants of the canopy include sloths, such as the adorable three-toed sloth, whose strategy is not agility but passivity: It eats tree vegetation and is covered with algae that gradually turns the animal green to allow for good camouflage. The canopy is also home to myriad bats and many birds, including exotic eagles, curassows, toucans, woodpeckers, cotingas, and macaws.

Notable is the majestic harpy eagle, with

COLOMBIAN FRUITS

Colombia is a land bursting with exotic fruit. Sold from the back of pickup trucks by farmers on the roadside, overflowing at stalls in colorful markets in every town and village, lined up in neat rows in the produce section at fancy grocery stores and at juice stands—just about anywhere you go, delicious fruit is in reach.

You know pineapple, papaya, mangoes, and bananas, but be sure to try these tropical delights that you may not have encountered outside Colombia.

- **pitahaya (dragon fruit):** Pitahayas look like a yellow grenade and have sweet white meat inside.
- **guanábana (soursop):** By far the strangest-looking fruit, guanábanas resemble prehistoric dinosaur eggs. Inside the large green spiky fruit is milky and slimy flesh. Guanábana is great in juices and desserts.
- **granadilla:** Crack open this orange-yellow fruit and slurp down the slimy gray contents, seeds and all. It's delicious.
- **higo (prickly pear):** This green fruit comes from cactus plants and has sweet, if tough, orange-colored meat.
- **chirimoya (cherimoya):** This green fruit that resembles a smooth artichoke is covered with a smooth silky skin and filled with delectable sweet pulp.
- **níspero (sapodilla):** A fruit with a deep brown color that tastes like a prepared sweet.
- **mangostino (mangosteen):** Crack open a deep-purple mangosteen and enjoy the sweet segments inside. They're full of antioxidants.
- **uchuva (Cape gooseberry):** Known in English as Cape gooseberries, these tart yellow berries are a cousin of the tomato and are tasty on their own or in salads but are often used in jams and sweets.
- **mamoncillo:** Tough-skinned grapes (don't eat the skin), mamoncillos are usually only sold on the street.

powerful claws and the ability to fly unencumbered through the canopy. It preys on monkeys and sloths, which it kills with the force of its claws. The tigrillo (tiger cat) is a small and extremely endangered species. It has a long tail that helps with its balance as it moves from tree to tree.

On the ground, large vertebrates include the extremely endangered tapir, an ancient mammal species that can grow 2 m (6 ft) long and weigh 300 kg (660 lbs). It is equally at ease on land as in the water. Other land mammals include the giant armadillo, giant anteater, deer, and boars, such as the saíno and pecarí. Smaller mammals include the guatín and borugo, both rodents. These animals are often prey to the puma and jaguar, both of which inhabit the Amazon but are difficult to observe in the wild.

The rivers of the Amazon are home to more than 1,500 species of fish, including endangered pirarucú, one of the largest freshwater fish on Earth. There are also dolphins, both pink and gray. Pink dolphins evolved separately from the oceangoing dolphins when the Amazon was an inland sea. The Amazonian gray dolphins are sea dolphins that adapted to living in freshwater. Other aquatic mammals include the highly endangered manatee and otters.

The Chocó rainforest is particularly rich in palms, of which 120 species have been identified. Chocó is sometimes referred to as the "Land of the Palms." The forest also abounds in cycads, ancient plants that have a stout trunk and crowns of hard, stiff leaves. Chocó is also notable for more than 40 species of brightly colored poisonous frogs, known locally as ranas kokois. These small frogs are covered with a deadly poison and have evolved stunning coloration, from bright orange to red, gold, and blue. They are active in the day and therefore relatively easy to spot. Of Colombia's 1,800 species of birds, more than 1,000 have been identified in the Chocó, including a large number of hummingbirds.

Offshore, the Pacific Ocean sees the annual migration of Antarctic humpback whales. The beaches of the Pacific coast are popular nesting areas for sea turtles, in particular the tortuga golfina (olive ridley) and tortuga carey (hawksbill) sea turtles.

Cloud Forest

Rainforests that grow at higher altitudes on the flanks of the Andes are known as montane rainforests or cloud forests because they are often enveloped in mist that results from the condensation of warm air against chillier mountain currents. Unlike the lowland rainforest, cloud forests only have two layers, the canopy and the ground layer. Generally, the vegetation is less dense than that in the lowland rainforest. However, it is home to many palms, ferns, and epiphytes, particularly orchids.

The type of cloud forest vegetation is dictated by altitude. Selva subandina (sub-Andean forest) vegetation grows at 1,000-2,300 m (3,280-7,550 ft) elevation, where temperature ranges 16-23°C (61-73°F). Plant species include the distinctive Seussian white yarumo with its oversize leaves as well as cedar, oak, and mahogany trees. Many palms grow, including the svelte wax palm and tagua, which produces a nut that resembles ivory. Ferns include the striking palma boba or tree fern. Colombia's premier crop, coffee, is grown at this elevation.

At elevations of 2,300-3,600 m (7,550-11,800 ft), the vegetation is described as selva Andina (Andean forest). This vegetation is even less dense, and at higher elevations, the trees are smaller. Selva Andina includes many oak, encenillo, sietecuero (glory bush), and pine trees.

Mammals include the spectacled or Andean bear, the only species of bear in South America, the mountain or woolly tapir, anteaters, armadillos, sloths, boars, foxes, and olingos, small arboreal carnivores of the raccoon family. In 2013, the olinguito (small olingo), an incredibly cute animal, was declared a new species. Other unusual animals include the slow-moving guagua loba and guatín, both rodents. In addition, numerous species of monkeys inhabit the cloud forest, including noisy troops of howler monkeys. Birds include many types of barranqueros (motmots), including the spectacular blue-crowned motmot. Other common birds include tángaras (tanagers), woodpeckers, warblers, parrots, owls, and ducks, including the beautiful white-and-black torrent duck.

Páramo

Páramos are unique tropical highland ecosystems that thrive above 3,500 m (11,500 ft), where UV radiation is higher, oxygen is scarcer, and temperatures range

–2-10°C (28-50°F). Due to frequent mist and precipitation, páramos are often saturated with water and have many lakes. They are true "water factories" that provide water to many of Colombia's cities, notably Bogotá. Though páramos exist throughout the New World tropics, most are located in Colombia. Parque Nacional Natural Sumapaz, south of Bogotá, is the world's largest páramo.

Páramo vegetation includes more than 50 species of frailejón (genus *Espeletia*), eerily beautiful plants that have imposing tall trunks and thick yellow-greenish leaves. Other páramo vegetation includes shrubs, grasses, and cojines (cushion plants). Mammals include the spectacled bear, páramo tapir, weasels, squirrels, and bats. The páramo is the realm of the majestic black-and-white Andean condor, which has a wingspan of up to 3 m (10 ft). The condor, whose numbers had declined almost to the point of extinction, is found in the national parks of the Sierra Nevada de Santa Marta, Sierra Nevada del Cocuy, and Los Nevados. The páramo lakes welcome many types of ducks, including the Andean duck, as well as smaller birds.

Tropical Dry Forests

Tropical dry forests exist in areas where there is a prolonged dry season. The vegetation includes deciduous trees that lose their leaves during the dry season, allowing them to conserve water. Trees on moister sites and those with access to groundwater tend to be evergreen. Before Columbus, this ecosystem covered much of the Colombian Caribbean coast. Much of it has since been cut down for cattle ranching. Pockets still exist east of the Golfo de Morrosquillo and at the base of the Sierra Nevada de Santa Marta. Tropical dry forests are the most endangered tropical ecosystem in the world.

Though less biologically diverse than rainforests, tropical dry forests are home to a wide variety of wildlife. They were once the stomping ground of the now highly endangered marimonda, or white-fronted spider monkey.

Tropical Grasslands

Los Llanos (The Plains) of Colombia are covered with lush tropical grasslands. Vegetation includes long-stemmed and carpet grasses in the drier areas and swamp grasses in low-lying humid areas. There are also thick patches of forest throughout the plains and along the rivers (known as gallery forests). These plains are teeming with wildlife, including deer, anteaters, armadillos, tapirs, otters, jaguars, pumas, and chigüiros (also known as capybaras), the world's largest rodent. Los Llanos are also home to the giant anaconda and to one of the most endangered species on Earth, the Orinoco crocodile, which reaches up to 7 m (23 ft) long.

HISTORY

Before Columbus

At the juncture of Central and South America, what is now Colombia was a necessary transit point for the migration of people who settled South America. Because these peoples left few physical traces of their passage, little is known of them. The oldest human objects found in Colombia, utensils discovered near Bogotá, date to 12,000 BCE. With the expansion of agriculture and sedentary life throughout the territory of present-day Colombia around 1000 BCE, various Indigenous cultures started producing stunning ceramic and gold work as well as some monumental remains that provide rich material evidence of their development. Nonetheless, there are significant gaps in the understanding of the history of these early peoples.

From around 700 BCE, the area of San Agustín, near the origin of the Río Magdalena in southern Colombia, was settled by people who practiced agriculture and produced pottery. Starting in the 1st century CE, the people of San Agustín created hundreds of monumental stone statues set on large platforms, the largest extant pre-Columbian archaeological site between Mesoamerica and Peru. By 800 CE, this society had disappeared.

On the northwestern plains of Colombia, south of present-day Cartagena, starting in the 1st century CE, the Sinú people constructed a large complex of mounds in the shape of fish bones. These mounds regulated flooding, allowing cultivation in both rainy and dry seasons. During rainy seasons, the water flooded the lower cavities, allowing for cultivation on the mounds; during dry season, cultivation took place in the cavities that had been enriched by the floodwater. These monumental formations are still visible from overhead. By the time of the Spanish conquest, these people no longer inhabited the area.

In 500-900 CE, the area of Tierradentro, west of San Agustín, was settled by an agricultural society that dug magnificent decorated underground tombs, produced large stone statues, and built oval-shaped buildings on artificial terraces. As in the case of the San Agustín and Sinú peoples, it is not known what happened to these people.

At the time of the conquest, present-day Colombia was populated by a large number of distinct agricultural societies that often maintained peaceful trading relations among themselves. The two largest groups were the Muisca people, who lived in the altiplano of the Cordillera Oriental, and the Tayrona people, who lived on the slopes of the Sierra Nevada de Santa Marta. Other groups included the Quimbaya people, who settled the area of the present-day

Historical Timeline

12,000 BCE

Human remains have been found in the area of Tequendama, now part of southeastern Bogotá. The area is inhabited by hunter-gatherer groups.

10,000 BCE

The petroglyphs of El Abra, an archaeological site located in Zipaquirá, about an hour outside modern Bogotá, are the oldest evidence of human artistic activity in Colombia.

6500-1500 BCE

Ceramic arts develop across Colombia. The archaeological site of El Infiernito in Boyacá is built near the end of this period, around 1500 BCE.

coffee region; the Calima people, in present-day Valle de Cauca; and the Nariño people, in the mountainous areas of southwest Colombia.

These Indigenous societies were mostly organized at the village level with loose association with other villages. Only the Muisca and the Tayrona had a more developed political organization. Although these were agricultural societies, they also engaged in hunting, fishing, and mining and produced sophisticated ceramics and goldwork. Each group specialized in what their environment had to offer and engaged in overland trade. For example, the Muisca produced textiles and salt, which they traded for gold, cotton, tobacco, and shells from other groups.

The Muisca, a Chibcha-speaking people, were the largest group, with an estimated 600,000 inhabitants at the time of the Spanish conquest. They settled the Cordillera Oriental in 300 CE and occupied a large territory that comprises most of the highland areas of the present-day departments of Cundinamarca and Boyacá. At the time of the conquest, they were organized into two large confederations: one in the south headed by the Zipa, whose capital was Bacatá, near present-day Bogotá, and another headed by the Zaque, whose capital was at Hunza, the location of present-day Tunja. The Muisca had a highly homogeneous culture and were skilled in weaving, ceramics, and goldwork. Their cosmography placed significant importance on high Andean lakes, several of which were sacred, including Guatavita, Siecha, and Iguaque.

The Tayrona, who settled the slopes of the Sierra Nevada de Santa Marta, were also a Chibcha-speaking people. They had a more urban society, with towns that included temples and ceremonial plazas built on stone terraces, and practiced farming on terraces carved from the mountains. There are an estimated 200 Tayrona sites, of which Ciudad Perdida, at 1,100 m (3,600 ft) elevation in the Sierra Nevada de Santa Marta, is the largest and best known. Many of these towns, including El Pueblito in Parque Nacional Natural Tayrona, were occupied at the time of the Spanish conquest. The Kogi, Arhuaco, Kankuamo, and Wiwa, current inhabitants of the Sierra Nevada, are their descendants and consider many places in the Sierra Nevada sacred.

Spanish Conquest (1499-1550)

As elsewhere in the New World, the arrival of Europeans was an unmitigated disaster for the Native American societies. Although there were pockets of resistance, on the whole the Indigenous people were unable to push back the small number of armed Spanish conquistadores. Harsh conditions after the conquest and the spread of European diseases, such as measles and smallpox, that Indigenous people

1000 BCE

The Formative Stage begins, where hunter-gatherer groups begin to practice agriculture, setting the stage for advanced civilizations to emerge.

800 BCE

The early Tayrona civilization forms in the Sierra Nevada de Santa Marta. Ciudad Perdida is evidence of this period.

200 BCE

The mysterious San Agustín culture spreads across southern Colombia, leaving the magnificent stone sculptures now contained in the UNESCO designated Parque Arqueológico Nacional de Tierradentro.

had no immunity to, killed off millions of Indigenous people. The Spanish conquest of present-day Colombia took about 50 years and was largely completed by the 1550s.

In 1499, the first European set foot in present-day Colombia in the northern Guajira Peninsula. In 1510, a first unsuccessful colony was established in the Golfo de Urabá near the current border with Panama. In 1526 the Spanish established Santa Marta, their first permanent foothold, from where they tried, unsuccessfully, to subdue the Tayrona. In 1533 they established Cartagena, which became a major colonial port.

In 1536 Gonzalo Jiménez de Quesada set off south from Santa Marta to conquer the fabled lands of El Dorado in the Andean heartland. After a year of grueling travel up the swampy Río Magdalena valley, 200 surviving members of Jiménez de Quesada's 800 original troops arrived in the Muisca lands near present-day Bogotá. After a short interlude of courteous relations, the Spaniards' greed led them to obliterate the Muisca towns and temples. They found significant amounts of gold, especially in the town of Hunza, but they were, by and large, disappointed. In 1538 Jiménez de Quesada founded Santa Fe de Bogotá as the capital of this new territory, which he called Nueva Granada (New Granada) after his birthplace.

Sebastián de Belalcázar, a lieutenant of Francisco Pizarro, led a second major expedition that arrived in the Muisca lands from the south. Having conquered the Inca city of Quito, Belalcázar and his army traveled north, conquering a vast swath of land from present-day Ecuador to the Sábana de Bogotá. Along the way, he founded several cities, including Popayán and Cali in 1536. He arrived shortly after Quesada had founded Bogotá. Incredibly, a third conquistador, the German Nikolaus Federmann, arrived in Bogotá at the same time, having traveled from Venezuela via Los Llanos. Rather than fight for supremacy, the three conquistadores decided to take their rival claims to arbitration at the Spanish court. In an unexpected turn of events, none of the three obtained title to the Muisca lands: When Bogotá became the administrative capital of Nueva Granada, they came under the sway of the Spanish crown. Other expeditions swept across the Caribbean coast, through current-day Antioquia and Santander.

Colonial Nueva Granada (1550-1810)

For most of its colonial history, Nueva Granada, as colonial Colombia was called, was an appendage of the Viceroyalty of Peru. In 1717 Spain decided to establish a viceroyalty in Nueva Granada but changed its mind six years later because the benefits did not justify the cost. In 1739 the viceroyalty was reestablished, with Santa

200 BCE-400 CE	600-1600 CE	1499	1525
The Calima civilization rises in the fertile Valle de Cauca near present-day Cali.	The Muisca civilization rises and evolves into the Muisca federation, a wide-ranging culture known for their expert goldsmithing skills.	The Spanish first set foot in Colombia at Cabo de la Vela in La Guajira.	The city of Santa Marta, the first European city in Colombia, is founded.

Fe de Bogotá as its capital. It was an unwieldy territory, encompassing present-day Colombia, Venezuela, Ecuador, and Panama. To make it more manageable, Venezuela and Panama were ruled by captain-generals and Ecuador by a president. At the local level, the viceroyalty was divided into provincias (provinces), each with a local assembly called a cabildo.

Settlement in Nueva Granada occurred primarily in three areas: where there were significant Indigenous populations to exploit, as in the case of Tunja in the former Muisca territory; where there were gold deposits, as in Cauca, Antioquia, and Santander; and along trade routes, for example at Honda and Mompox on the Río Magdalena. Cartagena was the main port for the biennial convoys of gold and silver sent to Spain. Bogotá lived off the official bureaucracy and sustained a fair number of artisans. Present-day Antioquia and Santander supported small-scale farming to provide provisions to the gold mining camps. Nueva Granada was one of the least economically dynamic of Spain's New World possessions. The mountainous topography and high transportation costs meant that agricultural production was primarily for local consumption, and gold was the only significant export.

Colonial society comprised a small Spanish and creole (descendants of Spanish settlers) elite class that governed a large mestizo (mixed Indigenous and Spanish) population. The Spanish had initially preserved Indigenous communal lands known as resguardos, but the demographic collapse of the Indigenous population and intermarriage meant that, unlike in Peru or Mexico, there were relatively few people who were fully Indigenous. There were also enslaved Africans who were forced mostly to work in the mines and haciendas (plantations). Society was overwhelmingly Roman Catholic and Spanish-speaking.

Culturally, Nueva Granada was also somewhat of a backwater. There was a modest flourishing of the arts, but Bogotá could not compete with the magnificent architectural and artistic production of Quito, Lima, or Mexico City. The only truly notable event of learning that took place was the late 18th-century Expedición Botánica (Botanical Expedition), headed by Spanish naturalist José Celestino Mutis, the personal doctor to one of the viceroys. The aim of the expedition was to survey all the species of Nueva Granada—a rather tall order given that Colombia is home to 10 percent of the world's species. However, the expedition did some remarkable research and produced beautiful prints of the fauna and flora.

The late colonial period saw unrest in Nueva Granada. Starting in 1781, a revolt known as the Rebelión de los Comuneros took place in the province of Socorro, north of Bogotá in present-day Santander, as a result of an attempt by colonial authorities to

1536-1538

The Spanish begin the conquest of the Muisca civilization. The settlement of Santa Fe de Bogotá is founded in 1538.

1718

Bogotá is named the capital of the Spanish viceroyalty of Nueva Granada, which includes Ecuador and Venezuela.

1819-1830

Simón Bolívar wins a decisive battle against the Spanish and founds Gran Colombia—a state that included present-day Ecuador, Panama, and Venezuela. It dissolves 10 years later.

1899-1902

The Thousand Days' War between Colombia's conservative and liberal parties leaves over 100,000 dead and results in Panama breaking off to form its own country.

levy higher taxes. It was not an antiroyalist movement, however, as its slogan indicates: ¡Viva el Rey; Muera el Mal Gobierno! (Long live the king; down with bad government!). Rather it was a protest against unfair taxes, not much different from the Boston Tea Party. However, it gave the Spanish government a fright. A rebel army, led by José Antonio Galán, marched on Bogotá. Negotiations put an end to the assault, and later the authorities ruthlessly persecuted the leaders of the revolt.

Struggle for Independence (1810-1821)

Although there was some ill feeling against the colonial government, as the Rebelión de los Comuneros attests, as well as rivalry between the Spanish- and American-born elites, it was an external event, the Napoleonic invasion of Spain, that set off the chain of events that led to independence of Nueva Granada and the rest of the Spanish dominion in the New World.

In 1808 Napoleon invaded Spain, took King Ferdinand VII prisoner, and tried to impose his own brother, Joseph, as king of Spain. The Spaniards revolted, establishing a Central Junta in Seville to govern during the king's temporary absence from power. Faced with the issue of whether to recognize the new Central Junta in Spain, the colonial elites decided to take matters in their own hands and establish juntas of their own. The first such junta in Nueva Granada was established in Caracas in April 1810. Cartagena followed suit in May and Bogotá on July 20, 1810. According to popular myth, the revolt in Bogotá was the result of the failure of a prominent Spaniard merchant to lend a flower vase to a pair of creoles.

Although they pledged alliance to Ferdinand VII, once the local elites had tasted power, there was no going back. Spanish authorities were expelled, and in 1811 a government of sorts, under the loose mantle of the Provincias Unidas de la Nueva Granada (United Provinces of New Granada), was established, with its capital at Tunja. Bogotá and the adjoining province of Cundinamarca stayed aloof from the confederation, arguing that it was too weak to resist the Spanish. Subsequently, various provinces of Nueva Granada declared outright independence, starting with Venezuela and Cartagena in 1811 and Cundinamarca in 1813.

Several cities remained loyal to the crown, namely Santa Marta and deeply conservative Pasto in the south. There was a senseless civil war 1812-1814 between the Provincias Unidas and Cundinamarca, and this period is called the Patria Boba (Foolish Fatherland). Ultimately, the Provincias Unidas prevailed with the help of a young Venezuelan captain by the name of Simón Bolívar.

After the restoration of Ferdinand VII, Spain attempted to retake its wayward

1948

Presidential frontrunner Jorge Eliécer Gaitán, a hero of the working class, is assassinated. This leads to a massive riot that leaves much of Bogotá in rubble.

1964-1982

The country is gripped by the Guerrilla Wars. The Revolutionary Armed Forces of Colombia (FARC) is formed in 1966.

1984-2002

The US-funded War on Drugs militarizes Colombia's police force to try to stamp out guerrilla forces, many of which turn to cocaine cultivation to support themselves.

1998-2016

A series of peace talks implemented by different presidents tries to find ways to stop the violence and reach agreements with the dissident guerrilla groups.

colonies, with a military expedition and reign of terror known as the Reconquista (Reconquest). Spanish forces took Cartagena by siege in 1815 and took control of Bogotá in May 1816. However, in 1819, a revolutionary army composed of Venezuelans, Nueva Granadans, and European mercenaries headed by Bolívar arrived across Los Llanos from Venezuela and decisively defeated the Spanish army in the Batalla del Puente de Boyacá (Battle of the Boyacá Bridge) near Tunja on August 7. The rest of the country fell quickly to the revolutionary army. With support from Nueva Granada, Bolívar defeated the Spanish in Venezuela in 1821. Panama, which had remained under Spanish control, declared independence in 1821. Finally, Bolívar dispatched Antonio José de Sucre to take Quito in 1822, bringing an end to the Spanish rule of Nueva Granada.

Gran Colombia: A Flawed Union (1821-1830)

Shortly after the Battle of Boyacá, the Congress of Angostura, a city on the Río Orinoco in Venezuela, proclaimed the union of Nueva Granada, Venezuela, and Ecuador under the name of the República de Colombia. Historians refer to this entity as Gran Colombia. In 1821, while the fight for independence was still raging in parts of Venezuela and Ecuador, a constitutional congress met in Cúcuta. An ongoing debate about whether a centralist or federalist scheme was preferable resulted in a curious compromise: República de Colombia assumed a highly centralist form, considered necessary to finish the battle for independence, but left the issue of federalism open to review after 10 years. The document was generally liberal, enshrining individual liberties and providing for the manumission of enslaved people, meaning that the children of enslaved people were born free.

Bolívar, who was born in Venezuela, was named president. Francisco de Paula Santander, who was born near Cúcuta in Nueva Granada, was named vice president. Santander had fought alongside Bolívar in the battles for independence of Nueva Granada and was seen as an able administrator. While Bolívar continued south to liberate Ecuador and Peru, Santander assumed the reins of power in Bogotá. He charted a generally liberal course, instituting public education and a curriculum that included avant-garde thinkers such as Jeremy Bentham. However, the highly centralist structure was unsavory to elites in Venezuela and Ecuador, who disliked rule from Bogotá. Shortly after the Congress of Cúcuta, revolt broke out in Venezuela and Ecuador. In 1826, Bolívar returned from Bolivia and Peru, hoping for the adoption in Gran Colombia of the Bolivian Constitution, an unusual document he drafted that called for a presidency for life.

There had been a growing distance between Bolívar and Santander: Bolívar saw

2016

A peace deal between the Colombian government and FARC is signed. President Santos is awarded the Nobel Peace Prize for his role in the negotiations.

2022

The first progressive president in nearly a century, Gustavo Petro, is elected. He implements a series of land reforms.

Santander as an overzealous liberal reformer while Santander disliked Bolívar's authoritarian tendencies. In 1828, after a failed constitutional congress that met in Ocaña in eastern Colombia, Bolívar assumed dictatorial powers. He rolled back many of Santander's liberal reforms. In September 1828 there was an attempt on Bolívar's life in Bogotá. This was famously foiled by his companion, Manuela Sáenz. The last years of Gran Colombia were marked by revolts in various parts of the country and a war with Peru. In 1830 a further constitutional assembly was convened in Bogotá, but by that point Gran Colombia had ceased to exist: Venezuela and Ecuador had seceded. In March 1830 a physically ill Bolívar decided to leave for voluntary exile in Europe and died on the way in Santa Marta.

Civil Wars and Constitutions (1830-1902)

After the separation of Venezuela and Ecuador, what is now Colombia adopted the name República de Nueva Granada. In 1832 it adopted a new constitution that corrected many of the errors of the excessively centralist constitution of Gran Colombia. There was a semblance of stability with the orderly succession of elected presidents. The elimination of some monasteries in Pasto sparked a short civil conflict known as the Guerra de los Supremos in 1839-1842. During this war, conservative and liberal factions coalesced for the first time, establishing the foundation of Colombia's two-party system. Generally, the Conservative Party supported the Catholic Church, favored centralization, and followed the ideas of Bolívar. The Liberal Party supported federalism and free trade and identified with the ideas of Santander.

The country's rugged topography meant that Nueva Granada was not very integrated into the world economy. Gold, extracted mostly in Antioquia, was the main export. Most of the country eked out its subsistence from agriculture, with trade restricted within regions. This period saw some economic development, such as steam navigation on the Magdalena and Cauca rivers, and a contract for the construction of the transisthmian railroad in Panama, which had yet to secede.

Mid-century saw the rise of a new class of leaders who had grown up wholly under republican governments. They ushered in a period of liberal reform. In 1851, the congress abolished slavery. In 1853, a new constitution established universal male suffrage, religious tolerance, and direct election of provincial governors. The government reduced tariffs, and Nueva Granada experienced a short export-oriented tobacco boom.

Conflicts among radical reformers within the Liberal Party, moderates, and Conservatives led to unrest in various provinces. In 1859 discontented Liberals under Tomás Cipriano de Mosquera revolted, leading to generalized civil war in which the Liberals were ultimately victorious. Once in power, they pushed radical reform. Mosquera expropriated all nonreligious church property, partly in vengeance for church support of the Conservatives in the previous civil war.

The 1863 constitution was one of the world's most audacious federalist experiments. The country was renamed the Estados Unidos de Colombia (United States of Colombia), comprising nine states. The president had a two-year term and was not immediately reelectable. All powers that were not explicitly assigned to the central government were the responsibility of the states. Many of the states engaged in true progressive policies, such as establishing public education and promoting the construction of railroads. This period coincided with agricultural booms in quinine, cotton, and indigo that, for the first time, brought limited prosperity. This period saw the establishment of the Universidad Nacional (National University) and the country's first bank.

In 1880 and then in 1884, a coalition of Conservatives and moderate Liberals, who were dissatisfied with radical policies, elected Rafael Núñez as president. Núñez tried to strengthen the power of the central government, sparking a Liberal revolt. The Conservatives were ultimately victorious and, in 1886, enacted a new centralist constitution that lasted through most of the 20th century. The country was rechristened República de Colombia, the name it has conserved since then. During 1886-1904, a period known as the Regeneración, the Conservative Party held sway, rolling back many of the previous reforms, especially anticlerical measures and unrestricted male suffrage. The Liberal Party, excluded from power, revolted in 1899. The ensuing Guerra de los Mil Días (Thousand Days' War), which raged through 1902, was a terribly bloody conflict. It is not clear how many died in the war, but some historians put the figure as high as 100,000, an incredible 2.5 percent of the country's population of 4 million at the time.

One year after the end of the war, Panama seceded. During the late 19th century, there had been resentment in Panama about the distribution of revenues from the transit trade that were mostly sent to Bogotá. However, in 1902 the local Panamanian elites had become alarmed at the lackadaisical attitude of the government in Bogotá regarding the construction of an interoceanic canal. After the failure of the French to build a canal, Colombia had entered into negotiations with the United States. In the closing days of the Guerra de los Mil Días, Colombia and the United States signed the Hay-Terran Treaty, which called for the construction of the canal, surrendering control over a strip of land on either side of the canal to the United States. The Americans threatened that if the treaty were not ratified, they would dig the canal in Nicaragua. Arguing that the treaty undermined Colombian sovereignty, the congress in Bogotá unanimously rejected it in August 1903. That was a big mistake: A few months later, Panama seceded with the support of the United States.

Peace and Reform (1902-1946)

Under the leadership of moderate Conservative Rafael Reyes, who was president 1904-1909, Colombia entered a period of peace and stability. Reyes focused on creating a professional, nonpartisan army. He gave representation to Liberals in government, enacted a protective tariff to spur domestic industry, and pushed public works. During his administration, Bogotá was finally connected by railroad to the Río Magdalena. He reestablished relations with the United States, signing a treaty that provided Colombia with an indemnity for the loss of Panama. During the 1920s-1930s, Colombia was governed by a succession of Conservative Party presidents. Though there was often electoral fraud, constitutional reform that guaranteed minority representation ensured peace.

Expanding world demand for coffee spurred production across Colombia, especially in southern Antioquia and what is now known as the coffee region, creating a new class of independent farmers.

Improved transportation, especially the completion of the railroads from Cali to Buenaventura on the Pacific coast and from Medellín to the Río Magdalena, was key to the growth of coffee exports. In the Magdalena Medio region and in Norte de Santander, US companies explored and started producing petroleum. Medellín became a center of textile manufacturing. With the country's broken geography, air transportation developed rapidly. The Sociedad Colombo Alemana de Transportes Aéreos (Colombian German Air Transportation Society) or SCADTA, the predecessor of Avianca, was founded in Barranquilla in 1919, and is reputedly the second-oldest commercial aviation company in the world after KLM.

In 1930 a split Conservative ticket allowed the Liberals to win the elections. After being out of power for 50 years, the Liberal Party was happy to regain control of the state apparatus. This led to strife with Conservatives long accustomed to power, presaging the intense interparty violence that was to erupt 14 years later.

From 1932 to 1933, Colombia and Peru fought a brief war in the Amazon over control of the port city of Leticia. The League of Nations brokered a truce, the first time that this body, a precursor to the United Nations, actively intervened in a dispute between two countries.

Starting in 1934, Liberal president Alfonso López Pumarejo undertook major social and labor reforms, with some similarities to Roosevelt's New Deal. His policies included agrarian reform, encouragement and protection of labor unions, and increased spending on education. He reduced the Catholic Church's sway over education and eliminated the literacy requirement for male voters. Many of these reforms simply returned the country to policies that had been enacted by Liberals 80 years prior in the 1850s. In opposition to these policies, a new radical right, with a confrontational style and strains of fascism and anti-Semitism, arose under the leadership of Laureano Gómez.

During World War II, Colombia closely allied itself with the United States and eventually declared war on the Axis powers in retaliation for German attacks on Colombian merchant ships in the Caribbean Sea. The government concentrated those of German descent in a hotel in Fusagasugá near Bogotá and removed all German influence from SCADTA.

La Violencia (1946-1953)

In the 1946 elections, the Liberal Party split its ticket between establishment-backed Gabriel Turbay and newcomer Jorge Eliécer Gaitán. Gaitán was a self-made man who had scaled the ladders of power within the Liberal Party despite the opposition of the traditional Liberal elite. He had a vaguely populist platform and much charisma. The moderate Conservative Mariano Ospina won a plurality of votes and was elected to the presidency. As in 1930 the transfer of power from Liberals to Conservatives and bureaucratic reaccommodation led to outbursts of violence.

On April 9, 1948, a deranged youth killed former presidential candidate Gaitán as he left his office in downtown Bogotá. His assassination sparked riots and bloodshed throughout the country, with severe destruction in the capital. The disturbance in Bogotá, known as El Bogotazo, occurred during the 9th Inter-American Conference, which had brought together leaders from all over the hemisphere. Young Fidel Castro happened to be in Bogotá that day, though he had no part in the upheaval.

The assassination of Gaitán further

incited the violence that had started in 1946. Over the course of 10 years, an estimated 100,000-200,000 people died in what was laconically labeled La Violencia (The Violence). This conflict was comparable in destruction of human life with the Guerra de los Mil Días, the last civil war of the 19th century. The killing took place throughout the country, often in small towns and rural areas. Mostly it involved loyalists of the predominant party settling scores or intimidating members of the opposite party in order to extract land or secure economic gain. In some cases, the violence was sheer banditry. Numerous horrific mass murders took place. The police often took sides with the Conservatives or simply turned a blind eye. In response, some Liberals resorted to armed resistance, giving birth to Colombia's first guerrilla armies. The Liberal Party boycotted the 1950 elections, and radical Conservative Laureano Gómez was elected president. His government pursued authoritarian and highly partisan policies, further exacerbating the violence.

Dictatorship (1953-1957)

In 1953, with the purported aim of bringing an end to fighting between Liberals and Conservatives, the Colombian army, under the command of General Gustavo Rojas Pinilla, staged a coup. Rojas was able to reduce, but not halt, the violence by curtailing police support of the Conservatives and by negotiating an amnesty with Liberal guerrillas. In 1954 Rojas was elected for a four-term period by a handpicked assembly. Incidentally, it was this nondemocratically elected assembly that finally got around to extending suffrage to women, making Colombia one of the last countries in Latin America to do so. Rojas tried to build a populist regime with the support of organized labor, modeled after Perón in Argentina. His daughter, María Eugenia Rojas, though no Evita, was put in charge of social welfare programs. Though a majority of Colombians supported Rojas at first, his repressive policies and press censorship ended up alienating the political elites.

The National Front (1957-1974)

In May 1957, under the leadership of a coalition of Liberals and Conservatives, the country went on an extended general strike to oppose the dictatorship. Remarkably, Rojas voluntarily surrendered power and went into exile in Spain. As a way to put an end to La Violencia, Liberal and Conservative Party leaders proposed alternating presidential power for four consecutive terms while divvying up the bureaucracy on a 50-50 basis. The proposal, labeled the National Front, was ratified by a nationwide referendum and was in effect 1958-1974.

The National Front dramatically reduced the level of violence. After years of fighting, both factions were ready to give up their arms. During this period, thanks to competent economic management, the economy prospered and incomes rose. The government adopted import substitution policies that gave rise to a number of new industries, including automobiles.

By institutionalizing the power of the two traditional parties, the National Front had the unintended consequence of squeezing out other political movements, especially from the left. As a result, during the 1960s a number of leftist guerrilla groups appeared. Some were simply the continuation, under a new name, of the guerrilla groups formed during La Violencia. The Fuerzas Armadas Revolucionarias de Colombia (FARC) was a rural peasant-based group espousing Soviet Marxism. The Ejército de Liberación Nacional (ELN) was a smaller group inspired by the Cuban revolution. The even smaller Ejército Popular de Liberación (EPL) was a Maoist-inspired group. The Movimiento 19 de Abril (M-19) was a more urban group formed by middle-class intellectuals after alleged electoral fraud deprived the populist ANAPO Party (Alianza Nacional Popular, created by ex-dictator Rojas) of power. During the 1970s-1980s, M-19 staged flashy coups, such as stealing Bolívar's sword in 1974 and promising to return it once the revolution had been achieved, and seizing control of the embassy of the Dominican Republic in Bogotá in 1980.

Under Siege (1974-1991)

THE DRUG TRADE AND THE RISE OF ILLEGAL ARMED GROUPS

Due to its relative proximity to the United States, treacherous geography, and weak government institutions, Colombia has been an ideal place for cultivation, production, and shipment of illegal drugs, primarily to the United States. During the 1970s Colombia experienced a short-lived marijuana boom centered on the Sierra Nevada de Santa Marta. Eradication efforts by Colombian authorities and competition from homegrown marijuana produced in the United States quickly brought this boom to an end.

During the late 1970s, cocaine replaced marijuana as the main illegal drug. Most coca cultivation at the time was in Peru and Bolivia, but Colombian drug dealers based in Medellín started the business of picking up coca paste in Peru and Bolivia, processing it into cocaine in Colombia, and exporting the drug to the United States, where they even controlled some distribution at the local level. At its heyday in the mid-1980s, Pablo Escobar's Medellín Cartel controlled 80 percent of the world's cocaine trade. The rival Cali Cartel, controlled by the Rodríguez brothers, emerged in the 1980s and started to contest the supremacy of the Medellín Cartel, leading to a bloody feud.

During the 1980s-1990s coca cultivation shifted from Peru and Bolivia to Colombia, mainly to the Amazon regions of Putumayo, Caquetá, Meta, and Guaviare. Initially, leftist guerrillas such as the FARC protected the fields from the authorities in return for payment from the cartels. Eventually they started processing and trafficking the drugs themselves. The guerrillas had other sources of income, such as kidnapping and extortion, especially of oil companies operating in Los Llanos, but the drug trade was a key factor in their growth. With these sources of income, they no longer needed popular support and morphed into criminal organizations. By the mid-1980s the FARC had grown into a 4,000-person-strong army that controlled large territories, especially in the south of the country.

During the 1980s-1990s the price of land was depressed as a result of the threat posed by the guerrillas. Using their vast wealth and power of intimidation, drug traffickers purchased vast swaths of land, mostly along the Caribbean coast of Colombia, at bargain prices. To defend their properties from extortion, they allied themselves with traditional landowners to create paramilitary groups. These groups often operated with the direct or tacit support of the army.

Colombian campesinos (small farmers), caught in the middle of the conflict between guerrillas and paramilitaries, suffered disproportionately. They were accused by both guerrillas and paramilitaries of sympathizing with the enemy, and the government was not there to protect them. The paramilitaries were particularly ruthless, often ordering entire villages to abandon their lands or massacring the population. The conflict between guerrillas and paramilitaries is at the source of the mass displacement of people in Colombia. According to the Office of the United Nations High Commissioner for Refugees, the number of displaced people in Colombia ranges 3.9-5.3 million, making it the country with the most internal refugees.

PEACE NEGOTIATIONS WITH THE FARC AND M-19

In 1982 President Belisario Betancur was elected with the promise of negotiating peace with the guerrillas. The negotiations with the guerrillas got nowhere, but the FARC did establish a political party, the Unión Patriótica (UP), which successfully participated in the 1986 presidential elections and 1988 local elections, managing to win some mayoralties. The paramilitaries and local elites did not want the political arm of the FARC to wield local power. As a result, the UP was subjected to a brutal persecution by the paramilitaries, who killed more than 1,000 party members. In the midst of this violence, Colombia suffered one of its worst natural disasters: the eruption of the Nevado del Ruiz in November 1985, which produced a massive mudslide that engulfed the town of Armero, killing more than 20,000 people.

In 1985, the M-19 brazenly seized the Palacio de Justicia in Bogotá. The Colombian army responded with a heavy hand, and in the ensuing battle, half of Colombia's Supreme Court justices were killed. Many people, including many cafeteria employees, disappeared in the army takeover, and there is speculation that they were executed and buried in a mass grave in the south of Bogotá. Weakened by this fiasco, leaders of the M-19 took up President Virgilio Barco's offer to negotiate peace. The government set down clear rules, including a cease-fire on the part of the M-19, before talks could proceed. Unlike the FARC, the M-19 was still an ideological movement. The leaders of the M-19 saw that by participating in civil life they could probably gain more than by fighting. And they were right: In 2011 the people of Bogotá elected Gustavo Petro, a former M-19 guerrilla, as their mayor. On March 19, 1990, Barco and the M-19's young leader, Carlos Pizarro, signed a peace agreement, the only major successful peace agreement to date between the authorities and a major guerrilla group.

THE RISE AND FALL OF THE MEDELLÍN CARTEL

Initially, the Colombian establishment turned a blind eye to the rise of the drug cartels and even took a favorable view of the paramilitaries, who were seen as an antidote to the scourge of the guerrillas. For a time, Escobar was active in politics and cultivated a Robin Hood image, funding public works such as parks and housing projects. Rather than stick to his business, as the Cali Cartel did, Escobar started to threaten any official who tried to check his power. In 1984 he had Rodrigo Lara Bonilla, the minister of justice, assassinated. When the government subsequently cracked down, Escobar declared outright war. He assassinated judges and political leaders, set off car bombs to intimidate public opinion, and paid a reward for every police officer that was murdered in Medellín—a total of 657. To take out an enemy, he planted a bomb in an Avianca flight from Bogotá to Cali, killing all the passengers on board. The Medellín Cartel planted dozens of massive bombs in Bogotá and throughout the country, terrorizing the population. The cartel is allegedly responsible for the assassination of three presidential candidates in 1990: Luis Carlos Galán, the staunchly anti-mafia candidate of the Liberal Party; Carlos Pizarro, the candidate of the newly demobilized M-19; and Bernardo Jaramillo, candidate of the Unión Patriótica.

There was really only one thing that Escobar feared—extradition to the United States. Through bribery and intimidation, he managed to get extradition outlawed, and he negotiated a lopsided deal with the government of César Gaviria: In return for his surrender, he was allowed to control the jail where he was locked up. From the luxurious confines of La Catedral, as the prison was named, he continued to run his empire. In 1992 there was an outcry when it became known that he had interrogated and executed enemies within the jail. When he got wind that the government planned to transfer him to another prison, he fled. In December 1993, government intelligence intercepted a phone call he made to his family, located him in Medellín, and killed him on a rooftop as he attempted to flee. It is widely believed that the Cali Cartel actively aided the authorities in the manhunt.

A NEW CONSTITUTION

The 1990s started on a positive footing with the enactment of a new constitution in 1991. The Constitutional Assembly that drafted the charter was drawn from all segments of the political spectrum, including the recently demobilized M-19. The new constitution was very progressive, devolving considerable power to local communities and recognizing the rights of Indigenous and Afro-Colombian communities to govern their communities and ancestral lands. The charter created a powerful new Constitutional Court, which has become a stalwart defender of basic rights, as well as an independent accusatory justice system, headed by a powerful attorney general, which was created to reduce impunity.

Colombia on the Brink (1992-2002)

NEW CARTELS, PARAMILITARIES, AND GUERRILLAS

Drug cultivation and production increased significantly during the 1990s. The overall land dedicated to coca cultivation rose from 60,000 ha (148,300 acres) in 1992 to 165,000 ha (407,700 acres) in 2002. As a result of the government's successful crackdown first on the Medellín Cartel and then on the Cali Cartel, drug production split into smaller, more nimble criminal organizations. During the 1990s the paramilitaries became stand-alone organizations that engaged in drug trafficking, expanding to more than 30,000 members in 2002. They created a national structure called the Autodefensas Unidas de Colombia (AUC) under the leadership of Carlos Castaño. AUC coordinated activities with local military commanders and committed atrocious crimes, often massacring scores of so-called sympathizers of guerrillas.

At the same time, the guerrillas expanded significantly during the 1990s. Strengthened by hefty revenues from kidnapping, extortion, and drug trafficking, they grew to more than 50,000 mostly peasant fighters in 2002. Their strategy was dictated primarily by military and economic considerations and they had little to no public support. At their heyday

FARC covered the entire country, attacking military garrisons and even threatening major urban centers such as Cali. They performed increasingly large operations, such as attacking Mitú, the capital of the department of Vaupés, in 1998 and kidnapping 12 members of the Assembly of Valle del Cauca in Cali in 2002. FARC commanders moved around the countryside unchecked. In the territories they controlled, they ruled over civilians, often committing heinous crimes. In 2002 they attacked a church in the town of Bojayá in Chocó, killing more than 100 unarmed civilians, including many children, who had sought refuge there.

PLAN COLOMBIA

The increasing growth of drug exports from Colombia to the United States in the 1990s became a source of concern for the US government. The United States was reluctant to provide support to Colombia 1994-1998 because the president at the time, Ernesto Samper, was tainted by accusations of having received campaign money from drug traffickers and because of evidence about human rights abuses by the Colombian army. When Andrés Pastrana was elected president in 1998, the Colombian and US administrations designed a strategy called Plan Colombia to curb drug production and counteract the insurgency. This strategy had both military and social components and was to be financed jointly by the United States and Colombia. Ultimately, the United States provided Colombia, which was becoming one of its strongest and most loyal allies in Latin America, with more than USD$7 billion, heavily weighted toward military aid, especially for training and for providing aerial mobility to Colombian troops. While the impact of Plan Colombia was not immediately visible, over time it changed the balance of power in favor of the government, allowing the Colombian army to regain the upper hand in the following years.

FLAWED PEACE NEGOTIATIONS WITH THE FARC

President Pastrana embarked on what is now widely believed to have been an ill-conceived, hurried peace process with the FARC. He had met Manuel Marulanda, the head of the FARC, before his inauguration in 1998 and was convinced that he could bring about a quick peace. Without a clear framework, in November 1998 he acceded to the FARC's request to grant them a demilitarized zone the size of Switzerland in the eastern departments of Meta and Caquetá. In hindsight, it seems clear that the FARC had no interest or need to negotiate as they were at the peak of their military power. Rather, the FARC commanders saw the grant of the demilitarized zone as an opportunity to strengthen their organization.

From the beginning it became clear that the FARC did not take the peace process seriously. Marulanda failed to show up at the inaugural ceremony of the peace process, leaving a forlorn Pastrana sitting alone on the stage next to a now famous silla vacilla (empty seat). They ran the demilitarized zone as a mini-state, nicknamed Farclandia, using it to smuggle arms, hold kidnapped prisoners, and process cocaine. During the peace negotiations, the FARC continued their attacks on the military and civilians. In February 2002, after the FARC kidnapped Eduardo Gechem, senator and president of the Senate Peace Commission, Pastrana declared the end of this ill-advised demilitarized zone and sent in the Colombian army.

A FAILED STATE?

In 2002 the Colombian army was battling more than 50,000 guerrillas and 30,000 paramilitaries with an estimated 6,000 child soldiers among the groups. The insurgents controlled approximately 75 percent of the country's territory. An estimated 100,000 antipersonnel mines covered 30 of 32 departments. More than 2.5 million people had been internally displaced 1985-2003, with 300,000 people displaced in 2002 alone. Not surprisingly, prestigious publications such as *Foreign Policy* described Colombia at the time as failed state.

Regaining Its Footing (2002-2016)

ÁLVARO URIBE'S ASSAULT ON THE GUERRILLAS

In the 2002 elections, fed-up Colombians overwhelmingly elected Álvaro Uribe, a former governor of Antioquia who promised to take the fight to the guerrillas. Uribe had a real grudge against the FARC, who had assassinated his father. The FARC were not fans of his either. In a brazen show of defiance, during Uribe's inauguration ceremony in Bogotá on August 7, 2002, the guerrilla group fired various rockets aimed at the presidential palace during a post-swearing-in reception. Several rockets struck the exterior of the palace, causing minor damage, although attendees were unaware of the attack, but many more fell on the humble dwellings in barrios nearby, killing 21.

During his first term, Uribe embarked on a policy of Seguridad Democrática (Democratic Security), based on strengthening the army, eradicating illicit crops to deprive the guerrillas of revenues, and creating a controversial network of civilian collaborators who were paid for providing tips that led to successful operations against the insurgents. The government increased military expenditure and decreed taxes on the rich totaling USD$4 billion to finance the cost of the war. Colombian military personnel grew from 300,000 in 2002 to 400,000 in 2007.

In 2002-2003, the army evicted the FARC from the central part of the country around Bogotá and Medellín, although that did not prevent them from causing terror in those cities. In February 2003 a car bomb attributed to the FARC exploded in the parking lot of the exclusive social club El Nogal, killing more than 30 people, mostly employees. In 2004-2006 the army pressed the FARC in its stronghold in the southern part of the country. Aerial spraying of coca crops brought down cultivated areas from 165,000 ha (407,700 acres) in 2002 to 76,000 ha (187,800 acres) in 2006.

In 2006 Uribe was reelected by a landslide after the congress amended the constitution to allow for immediate presidential reelection. There is clear evidence that the government effectively bribed two congressmen whose votes were necessary for passage of the measure. Uribe interpreted the election results as a mandate to continue single-mindedly pursuing the guerrillas. The FARC came under severe stress, with thousands of guerrillas deserting, and for the first time the FARC was subjected to effective strikes against top commanders. No longer safe in their traditional forest strongholds in Colombia, many FARC operatives crossed the border into Venezuela and Ecuador, causing tension between Colombia and the governments of those countries.

In early 2008 the Colombian military bombed and killed leading FARC commander Raúl Reyes in a camp in Ecuador, causing a diplomatic crisis with that country. Later that year the military executed Operación Jaque (Operation Checkmate), a dramatic rescue operation in which they duped the FARC into handing over their most important hostages. The hostages released included three US defense contractors and Ingrid Betancur, a French-Colombian independent presidential candidate who was kidnapped by the FARC during the 2002 presidential election as she proceeded by land, against the advice of the military, toward the capital of the former FARC demilitarized zone. In 2008, Manuel Marulanda, founder of the FARC, died a natural death. At that time it was estimated that the FARC forces had plummeted to about 9,000 fighters, half of what they had been eight years before.

The Colombian army has been implicated in serious human rights abuses. Pressure from top brass to show results in the war against the guerrillas and the possibility of obtaining extended vacation time led several garrisons to execute civilians and present them as guerrillas killed in combat. In 2008 it was discovered that numerous young poor men from the city of Soacha, duped by false promises of work, had been taken to rural areas, assassinated by the army, and presented as guerrillas killed in anti-insurgency operations. This macabre episode—referred to as the scandal of falsos positivos (false positives)—was done under the watch of Minister of Defense Juan Manuel Santos, who was later elected president of Colombia.

PEACE PROCESS WITH AUC

In 2003-2008 the Uribe government pursued a controversial peace process with the right-wing paramilitaries, the Autodefensas Unidas de Colombia. As part of that process, an estimated 28,000 paramilitary fighters demobilized, including most of the high-level commanders. In 2005 the Colombian Congress passed the Justice and Peace Law to provide a legal framework for the process. Unlike previous peace laws that simply granted amnesty to the insurgents, this law provided for reduced sentences for paramilitaries who had committed serious crimes in exchange for full confessions and reparations to victims. Domestic and international observers were extremely skeptical about the process, worrying that the paramilitaries would use their power to pressure for lenient terms. These misgivings were justified by evidence that they used their power of coercion to influence the results of the 2006 parliamentary elections, a scandal referred to as parapolítica. Many congressmembers, including a first cousin of Uribe, ended up in prison.

It soon became clear that the paramilitary commanders were not sincere in their commitment to peace. Many refused to confess crimes and transferred their assets to front men. Covertly, they continued their drug-trafficking operations. The government placed scant importance on the truth and reparation elements of the Justice and Peace Law, severely underfunding the effort to redress crimes committed against more than 150,000 victims who had signed up as part of the process. Through 2008 the paramilitaries had confessed to a mere 2,700 crimes, a fraction of the estimated total, and refused to hand over assets. Fed up with their lack of cooperation, in 2008 Uribe extradited 14 top-ranking paramilitary commanders to the United States, where they were likely to face long sentences. However, the extradition severely hampered the effort to obtain truth and reparation for the victims of their crimes.

The difficulty in redressing the crimes

against victims has been further troubled by the growth of the dozens of small bacrim (bandas criminales, illegal armed groups) who have taken territorial control of former paramilitary areas, intimidating victims who have returned to their rightful lands under the peace process. Many of these bacrim inherited the structures of the former AUC groups and employed former paramilitaries.

SOCIAL AND ECONOMIC TRANSFORMATION

During the past decades, Colombia has made some remarkable strides in improving social and economic conditions. Due to improved security conditions, both domestic and international investment has boomed, totaling almost USD$80 billion in 2003-2012. Economic growth averaged 4.8 percent 2010-2014, a significant increase over the prior decades. The number of people living in poverty, as measured by the ability to buy a wide basket of basic goods and services, declined from 59.7 percent in 2002 to 27.8 percent in 2015. In Colombia's 13 largest cities, which represent 45 percent of the population, poverty has fallen to 18.9 percent. In terms of basic needs, most urban areas are well served in terms of education, health, electricity, water, and sewage. However, there is a wide gap between the cities and rural areas, where 30 percent of the country's population lives. The Covid-19 pandemic sent Colombia's economy into a downward spiral, and despite economic growth, inflation rose to 9 percent in 2023 and 2024. As of 2025 both economic growth and inflation have stabilized, hovering at around three percent each. Though income inequality has been slowly falling, Colombia still has one of the most unequal distributions of income in the world.

PEACE WITH THE FARC

In the 2010 elections, Uribe's former minister of defense, Juan Manuel Santos, was elected president by a large majority. Santos continued to pursue an aggressive strategy against the FARC. Army operations killed Alfonso Cano, the new leader of the FARC, as well as Víctor Julio Suárez Rojas, the guerrillas' military strategist. As evidenced in the diary of Dutch FARC member Tanya Nijmeijer, found by the Colombian army after an attack on a rebel camp, morale within the FARC had sunk to an all-time low.

At the same time, Santos recognized the need to address nonmilitary facets of the violence. In 2011, the congress passed the comprehensive Victims and Land Restitutions Law, meant to rectify Uribe's Justice and Peace Law. This law provides a framework to redress the crimes committed against all victims of violence since 1985.

After a year of secret negotiations, Santos announced the start of peace dialogues with the FARC in October 2012, first in Oslo, Norway, and then in Havana, Cuba. These have proceeded at a slow pace and have covered a large number of topics, including agrarian development and drug trafficking. Former president Uribe and his allies are against this initiative, claiming that a military defeat of the FARC is the best path forward.

In 2016, after four years of arduous negotiations, the government and the FARC agreed to comprehensive terms that covered rural development, political participation, illegal drugs, justice for victims, and ending the armed conflict, among other topics. On September 26, 2016, the government and the FARC signed the agreement, only to have it rejected by a slim majority in a national vote. The government and the guerrillas renegotiated the agreement, which was ratified by the congress on November 30, 2016. Demobilization began in December 2016 and the guerrillas handed over their weapons to the UN during the first half of 2017. President Juan Manuel Santos won the 2016 Nobel Peace Prize for his efforts.

A NEW DAWN (2016-PRESENT)

In 2022 President Gustavo Petro and Vice President Francia Márquez became the first progressive administration Colombia has seen in over a century. Márquez, a lifelong community leader and environmental activist from the Pacific coast, is also the first Afro-Colombian to hold the office. The dynamic duo have promised to radically reshape Colombian society through a series of initiatives aimed at protecting the country's rural campesinos, Indigenous populations, and Afro-Colombian communities and putting an end to extractive industries like fracking and mining.

Soon after taking office, Petro announced a land reform plan that will redistribute over 1 million ha (2.5 million acres) of land to landless peasants, many of them displaced from their traditional territories during the decades of violence that rocked the country. In 2024 Petro also announced that he was putting a permanent end to the War on Drugs and instead would seek to follow Bolivia's example by legalizing the coca leaf and declaring it a national heritage. In 2025 the country broke away from several key free-trade agreements with the United States and began the application process to join BRICS, a Global South-oriented economic alliance named after key members Brazil, Russia, India, China, and South Africa.

GOVERNMENT AND ECONOMY

Under the 1991 constitution, Colombia is organized as a republic, with three branches of power: the executive, the legislative, and the judicial. The country is divided into 32 departamentos (departments or provinces) and the Distrito Capital (Capital District), where Bogotá is located. The departments are in turn divided into municipios (municipalities). These municipios include towns and rural areas.

The president of the republic, who is both head of state and head of government, is elected for a four-year term. With the exception of the military dictatorship of General Gustavo Rojas Pinilla 1953-1957, presidents have been elected by the people since 1914. In 2005 then-president Álvaro Uribe succeeded in changing the constitution to allow for one immediate presidential reelection. In 2009 he attempted to get the constitution changed once more to allow for a second reelection but was thwarted by the powerful Constitutional Court, which decreed that this change would break the necessary checks and balances of the constitutional framework.

Presidential elections are held every four years in May. If no candidate receives more than 50 percent of the votes, there is a runoff election. Inauguration of the president takes place on August 7, the anniversary of the Batalla del Puente de Boyacá, which sealed Colombia's independence from Spain.

The legislative branch is made up of a bicameral legislature: the Senado (102 members) and the Cámara de Representantes

(162 members). These representatives are elected every four years. Senators are voted for on a nationwide basis, while representatives are chosen for each department and the Distrito Capital. In addition, two seats in the Senado are reserved for Indigenous representation. In the Cámara de Representantes, there are seats reserved for Indigenous and Afro-Colombian communities as well as for Colombians who live abroad. As negotiated in 2016, until 2022 FARC was assured 10 seats in congress: 5 in the Senado and 5 in the Cámara de Representantes.

All Colombians over age 18, with the exception of active-duty military and police as well as those who are incarcerated, have the right to vote in all elections. Women only gained the right to vote in 1954.

Political Parties

Historically Colombia has had a two-party system: the Conservative Party and the Liberal Party. The Conservative Party has traditionally been aligned with the Catholic Church and has favored a more centralized government, following the ideas of Simón Bolívar. The Liberal Party favored a federal system of governing, has opposed church intervention in government affairs, and was aligned with the ideas of General Francisco de Paula Santander.

The hegemony of the two largest political parties came to a halt in the 2002 presidential election of rightist candidate Álvaro Uribe, who registered his own independent movement and then established a new party called El Partido de la Unidad. Since then, traditional parties have lost some influence. A third party, the Polo Democrático, became a relatively strong force in the early 2000s, capturing the mayorship of Bogotá, but has since faded, leaving no clear representative of the left.

Political parties today have become personality-oriented, and many candidates have been known to shop around for a party, or create their own, rather than adhere to the traditional parties. In 2014 President Juan Manuel Santos won a second term representing the Partido de la Unidad, known as La U, defeating a candidate allied with the founder of La U, former president Álvaro Uribe.

Economy

Colombia has a thriving market economy based primarily on oil, mining, agriculture, and manufacturing. The country's GDP in 2015 was USD$274 billion and per capita GDP was USD$5,800, placing it as a middle-income country. Growth over the past decade has been a robust 3.3 percent. Inflation has averaged 3.8 percent in the past five years and unemployment has hovered around 10 percent.

During the colonial period and until the early 20th century, small-scale gold mining and subsistence agriculture were the mainstays of Colombia's economy. Starting in the 1920s, coffee production spread throughout the country and rapidly became Colombia's major export. Coffee production is of the mild arabica variety and is produced at elevations of 1,000-1,900 m (3,200-6,200 ft), mostly by small farmers. During most of the 20th century, Colombia emphasized increasing the volume of production, using the Café de Colombia name and mythical coffee farmer Juan Valdez and his donkey Paquita to brand it. A severe global slump in coffee prices in recent decades has led to a reassessment of this strategy and an increasing focus on specialty coffees. Today, coffee represents only 3 percent of all Colombian exports.

Colombia's wide range of climates, from hot on the coast to temperate in the mountains, means that the country produces a wide range of products. Until recently, sugarcane production, fresh flowers, and bananas were the only major export-driven agribusiness. However, improvements in security in recent years have resulted in a boom in large-scale agricultural projects in palm oil, rubber, and soy. Cattle ranching occupies an estimated 25 percent of the country's land. Commercial forestry is relatively underdeveloped, though there is considerable illegal logging, especially on the Pacific coast.

In recent decades, oil production and mining have become major economic activities. The main center of oil production is Los Llanos, the eastern plains of Colombia, with oil pipelines extending over the Cordillera Oriental to Caribbean ports. Oil currently represents roughly half of all Colombian exports. There are also significant natural gas deposits, mostly dedicated to residential use. Large-scale mining has been focused on coal and nickel, with large deposits in the Caribbean coastal region. With the improvement of security conditions in the past decade, many international firms such as AngloGold Ashanti and Libero Copper have requested concessions for large-scale gold and copper mining, often with opposition from local communities.

During the postwar period Colombia pursued an import substitution policy, fostering the growth of domestic industries such as automobiles, appliances, and petrochemical goods. In the early 1990s the government opened the economy to foreign competition and tore down tariffs, signing free-trade agreements with the United States and the European Union. The post-pandemic era is ushering in every more change as Colombia breaks free of some of those exploitative agreements with Western powers and joins other nations in the Global South to create more just trade treaties. Today, the country has a fairly diversified industrial sector. The country is self-sufficient in energy, with hydropower supplying the bulk of electricity needs.

Until recently, tourism was minimal because of widespread insecurity and a negative image. Things started to change in the mid-2000s, and the annual number of international visitors increased from 600,000 in 2000 to 2.3 million in 2015. The Covid-19 pandemic caused several years of downturn, but in 2024 the country welcomed nearly 7 million visitors. Clearly, the word is out.

While Bogotá, Medellín plus the coffee region, and Cartagena and the Caribbean coast still receive the bulk of visitors, almost the entire country has opened up for tourism, although there are still pockets of no-go zones. This boom in tourism has fostered a growth of community and ecotourism options, often with support from government. The network of posadas nativas (guesthouses owned and operated by locals) is one initiative to foment tourism at the community level, particularly among Afro-Colombians. In recent years, Parques Nacionales has transferred local operation of ecotourism facilities in the parks to community-based associations.

PEOPLE AND CULTURE

Demography

Colombia was estimated to have had a population of 52.3 million in 2023 and has the third-largest population in Latin America after Brazil and Mexico. Around 5 million Colombians live outside Colombia, mostly in the United States, Venezuela, Spain, and Ecuador. The population growth rate has fallen significantly in the past two decades and was estimated at 1 percent in 2023. The population is relatively young, with a median age of 29.3 years. Average life expectancy is 73.7 years.

Sixty percent of the Colombian population lives in the highland Andean interior of the country, where the largest metropolitan areas are located: Bogotá (11.7 million), Medellín (4.6 million), and Cali (2.9 million). On the Caribbean coast, Barranquilla is the largest metropolitan area (2.3 million), followed by Cartagena (1.3 million).

It is increasingly an urban country, with around 80 percent of the population living in urban areas. This trend began during La Violencia and accelerated in the 1970s-1980s. At least 4 million people have been internally displaced due to armed conflict, leaving their homes in rural areas and seeking safety and economic opportunity in large cities.

Most of the population, over 84 percent, is either mestizo (having both Amerindian and European ancestry) or white. People of African (10.6 percent) and Indigenous or Amerindian (4.4 percent) origin make up the rest of the Colombian population. There is a tiny Roma population of under 1 percent, but nonetheless they are a protected group according to the constitution.

There are more than 80 Indigenous groups, with some of the largest being the Wayúu people, who make up the majority in La Guajira department; the Nasa, from Cauca; the Emberá, who live in the isolated rainforests of the Chocó department; and the Pastos in Nariño. Departments in the Amazon region have the highest percentages of Indigenous residents. In Vaupés, for example, 66 percent of the population is of Indigenous background. Many Indigenous people live on resguardos, areas that are collectively owned and administered by the communities.

Afro-Colombians, descendants of enslaved people who arrived primarily through Spanish slave-trade centers in the Caribbean, mostly live along both Pacific and Caribbean coasts and in the San Andrés Archipelago. Chocó has the highest percentage of Afro-Colombians (83 percent), followed by San Andrés and Providencia (57 percent), Bolívar (28 percent), Valle del Cauca (22 percent), and Cauca (22 percent). Cali, Cartagena, and Buenaventura have particularly large Afro-Colombian populations. In the Americas, Colombia has the third-largest number of citizens of African origin, behind Brazil and the United States.

While Colombia has not attracted large numbers of immigrants, there have been periods in which the country opened its doors to newcomers. In the early 20th century, immigrants from the Middle East, specifically from Lebanon, Syria, and Palestine, arrived, settling mostly along the Caribbean coast, especially in the cities of Barranquilla, Santa Marta, Cartagena, and Maicao in La Guajira. A sizable number of Sephardic and Ashkenazi Jews immigrated to Colombia 1920-1950. Colombia has not had substantial immigration from Asia,

HAPPY MONDAY!

Colombians enjoy a long list of over 20 national holidays. With a few exceptions, such as the independence celebrations on July 20 and August 7, Christmas, and New Year's Day, holidays are celebrated on the following Monday, creating a puente (literally a bridge, meaning a three-day weekend).

During Semana Santa and between Christmas Day and New Year's, interior cities such as Bogotá and Medellín become ghost towns as locals head to the nearest beach or to the countryside. Conversely, beach resorts, nature reserves, parks, and pueblos fill up. Along with that, room rates and airfare can increase substantially.

The following is a list of Colombian holidays, but be sure to check a calendar for precise dates. Holidays marked with an asterisk are always celebrated on the Monday following the date of the holiday.

- Año Nuevo (New Year's Day): January 1
- Día de los Reyes Magos (Epiphany): January 6*
- Día de San José (St. Joseph's Day): March 19*
- Jueves Santo (Holy Thursday): Thursday before Easter Sunday
- Viernes Santo (Good Friday): Friday before Easter Sunday
- Día de Trabajo (International Workers Day): May 1
- Ascensión (Ascension): 6 weeks and one day after Easter Sunday
- Corpus Christi: 9 weeks and one day after Easter Sunday
- Sagrado Corazón (Sacred Heart): 10 weeks and one day after Easter Sunday
- San Pedro y San Pablo (St. Peter and St. Paul): June 29*
- Día de la Independencia (Independence Day): July 20
- Batalla de Boyacá (Battle of Boyacá): August 7
- La Asunción (Assumption of Mary): August 15*
- Día de la Raza (equivalent of Columbus Day): October 12*
- Todos Los Santos (All Saints Day): November 1*
- Día de la Independencia de Cartagena (Cartagena Independence Day): November 11*
- Inmaculada Concepción (Immaculate Conception): December 8
- Navidad (Christmas): December 25

although in the early 20th century there was a small immigration of Japanese people to the Cali area.

Religion

Over 90 percent of Colombians identify as Roman Catholics, and it has been the dominant religion since the arrival of the Spaniards. The number of evangelical Christians, called simply cristianos, continues to grow, and there are other Christian congregations, including Latter-Day Saints and Jehovah's Witnesses, but their numbers are small. In San Andrés and Providencia, the native Raizal population, of African descent, is mostly Baptist.

The Jewish community, estimated at around 5,000 families, is concentrated in

GAY RIGHTS IN COLOMBIA

In a country still struggling with armed conflict and basic human rights, it might come as a surprise that gay and lesbian rights have not been pushed aside. Colombia has some of the most progressive laws regarding the rights of LGBTQ+ people in the western hemisphere. Since 2007 same-sex partners have enjoyed civil union rights with a wide range of benefits, such as immigration, inheritance, and social security rights.

However, when it comes to marriage, it's a little more complicated. In 2016 the top judicial body, the Colombian Constitutional Court, legalized marriage and adoption by same-sex couples. These rulings created a backlash with conservative politicians, who have vowed to hold a referendum to block the marriage and adoption rights. But in 2018, then-president Juan Manuel Santos passed a law prohibiting discrimination against the LGBTQ+ population in the workplace and social sector, including health, housing, education, sports, and culture. Currently, under its first real progressive administration since the mid-20th century, Colombia is expanding both protection and rights for the LGBTQ+ population.

the large cities, such as Bogotá, Medellín, Cali, and Barranquilla. There are significant Muslim communities, especially along the Caribbean coast, and there are mosques in Barranquilla, Santa Marta, Valledupar, Maicao (La Guajira), San Andrés, and Bogotá.

Semana Santa (Holy Week), the week leading up to Easter, is the most important religious festival in the country, and Catholics in every village, town, and city commemorate the week with a series of processions and masses. The colonial cities of Popayán, Mompox, Tunja, and Pamplona are known for their elaborate Semana Santa processions. Popayán and Mompox in particular attract pilgrims and travelers from Colombia and beyond. In the cities there are multitudinous processions to mountaintop religious sites, including Cerro de Monserrate in Bogotá, El Cerro de Cristo Rey in Cali, and Convento Nuestra Señora de la Candelaria in Cartagena.

Language

Spanish is the official language in Colombia. In the San Andrés Archipelago, English is still spoken by native islanders who arrived from former English colonies after the abolition of slavery, but Spanish has gained prominence.

According to the Ministry of Culture, there are at least 68 native languages spoken by around 850,000 people. These include 65 Indigenous languages, two Afro-Colombian languages, and Romany, spoken by the small Roma population.

Three Indigenous languages have over 50,000 speakers: Wayúu, primarily spoken in La Guajira; Páez, primarily spoken in Cauca; and Emberá, primarily spoken in Chocó.

Essentials

GETTING THERE

Air

Most visitors to Colombia arrive by air at the **Aeropuerto Internacional El Dorado** in Bogotá, with some carrying on from there to other destinations in the country. There are also nonstop international flights to the **Aeropuerto Internacional José María Córdova** in Medellín and to airports in Cali and Cartagena.

FROM NORTH AMERICA

Avianca (www.avianca.com) has nonstop flights to Bogotá from Miami, Fort Lauderdale, and Orlando in Florida as well as Washington DC, Los Angeles, and New York's JFK. From Miami there are also nonstops to Medellín, Cali, Barranquilla, and Cartagena.

American (www.american.com) flies from Miami and Dallas to Bogotá, and Miami to Medellín and Cali. **Delta** (www.delta.com) flies from Atlanta and New York's JFK to Bogotá. They also fly from Atlanta to Cartagena. **United** (www.united.com) has flights from Newark and Houston to Bogotá.

Spirit (www.spirit.com) has flights from Fort Lauderdale, Florida, to Bogotá, Medellín, Cartagena, and Armenia (near Salento in the coffee region).

Air Canada (www.aircanada.com) operates nonstop flights from Toronto to Bogotá. **Air Transat** (www.airtransat.com) provides seasonal (Nov.-Apr.) flights to Cartagena and San Andrés from Montreal.

FROM EUROPE

Avianca (www.avianca.com) has service to Bogotá and Medellín from Madrid and Barcelona, and to Bogotá from London. **Air France** (www.airfrance.com) flies from Paris to Bogotá. **Iberia** (www.iberia.com) serves Bogotá from Madrid, as does **Air Europa** (www.aireuropa.com). **Lufthansa** (www.lufthansa.com) offers flights to Bogotá from Frankfurt. **Turkish Airlines** (www.turkishairlines.com) flies to Bogotá from Istanbul. **KLM** (www.klm.com) flies from Amsterdam to Bogotá with a stopover in Cali.

FROM LATIN AMERICA

Avianca (www.avianca.com) flies to Bogotá from Buenos Aires, São Paulo, and Rio de Janeiro in Brazil, Valencia and Caracas in Venezuela, and Lima, Santiago, and La Paz. Flights to Bogotá from Central America include Guatemala City, Cancún, Mexico City, San José, San Juan, San Salvador, and Panama City, and from the Caribbean, Havana, Santo Domingo, Punta Cana, Aruba, and Curaçao. Other airlines with connections to Colombia include Aerolíneas Argentinas, Avianca Ecuador, Aeroméxico, Conviasa, Copa, Cubana, LATAM, and Gol.

Car or Motorcycle

A growing number of travelers drive into Colombia in their own car or with a rented vehicle. The most common point of entry is at the city of Ipiales on the Pan-American Highway, the site of the Rumichaca border crossing with Ecuador at Ipiales (Tulcán on the Ecuador side). This entry point is open 5am-10pm daily.

For those taking the Pan-American Highway southbound, note that you will run out of pavement in Panama. In the Darién Gap, the road is interrupted by the

◀ river in the mangrove forest near La Barra

Darién mountain range. The road picks up again in the town of Turbo on the Golfo de Urabá. Many travelers ship their vehicle from Panama City to Cartagena, which is not difficult to arrange, and will set you back about USD$1,000. It takes about 10 days to be able to retrieve your vehicle in Cartagena.

Border crossings with Venezuela are currently closed.

Bus

Frequent buses depart Quito bound for Cali (20 hours) or Bogotá (30 hours). You can also take a taxi from the town of Tulcán to the border at Ipiales and from there take an onward bus to Popayán, Cali, or beyond. In Quito contact **Líneas de los Andes** (www.lineasdelosandes.com.co).

Boat

It is possible to enter Colombia from Panama, usually through the San Blas Islands. **Blue Sailing** (US tel. 203/660-8654; www.bluesailing.net) offers sailboat trips between various points in Panama to Cartagena. The trip usually takes about 45 hours and costs around USD$850. Sometimes, particularly during the windy season November-March, boats stop in Sapzurro, Colombia, near the border. From here you can take a boat to the town of Turbo.

GETTING AROUND

Air

Air travel is an excellent, quick, and, thanks to discount airlines such as Wingo and Clic Air, economical way to travel within Colombia. Flying is the best option for those looking to avoid spending double-digit hours in a bus or for those with a short amount of time; sometimes it's cheaper than taking a bus. Airlines have excellent track records and maintain modern fleets. For Leticia in the Amazon, the Pacific coast destinations of Bahía Solano, and San Andrés and Providencia in the Caribbean, the only viable way to get there is by air.

Bogotá is the major hub in the country, with the majority of domestic **Avianca** (tel. 1/401-3434; www.avianca.com) flights departing from the **Puente Aéreo** terminal (not the main terminal of the adjacent international airport). Other domestic carriers **LATAM Airlines** (tel. 1/800-094-9490; www.latam.com), **Wingo** (tel. 601/307-8133; www.wingo.com), **Clic Air** (tel. 601/307-8133; https://clicair.co) **SATENA** (tel. 1/800-091-2034; www.satena.com), and **Copa** (tel. 1/800-011-0808; www.copaair.com) fly out of the new domestic wing of the international airport.

If you plan to fly to Caribbean destinations such as Cartagena, San Andrés, Providencia, and Santa Marta during high season, be sure to purchase your ticket well in advance as seats quickly sell out and fares go through the roof. If your destination is Cartagena or Santa Marta, be sure to check fares to Barranquilla. These may be less expensive, and that city is only about an hour away. Similarly, if you plan to go to the Carnaval de Barranquilla in February, check fares to both Cartagena and Santa Marta. If you are flying to the coffee region, inquire about flights to Pereira, Armenia, and Manizales, as the distances between these cities are short. The Manizales airport, however, is often closed due to inclement weather.

Medellín has two airports: **Aeropuerto Internacional José María Córdova** (in Rionegro) and **Aeropuerto Olaya Herrera.** All international flights and most large-airplane flights depart from Rionegro, a town about an hour away from Medellín. The airport is simply referred to as Rionegro. **SATENA** (tel. 1/800-091-2034; www.satena.com) uses the Olaya Herrera airport, which is conveniently located in town. This is a hub for flights to remote communities in the western and Pacific region, including Bahia Solano.

There are strict weight restrictions for flights to Providencia from San Andrés, which generally use small planes such as those used by the military-owned SATENA airline. These island flights sell out fast.

Long-Distance Bus

In order to thoroughly cover the country, you will have to hop on a bus at some point, just like the vast majority of Colombians. This is the money-saving choice and often the only option for getting to smaller communities. There are different types of buses, from large coaches for long-distance travel to colectivos (minivans) for shorter distances. Colectivos are often much quicker, although you won't have much legroom. There are also shared taxis that run between towns, a cramped but quick option. During major holidays, purchase bus tickets in advance if you can, as buses can quickly fill up.

Be alert and aware of your surroundings and of your possessions when you arrive at bus stations, are waiting in the bus terminal, and are on board buses. Try to avoid flashing expensive gadgets and cameras while on board. If you check luggage, request a receipt. During pit stops along the way, be sure to keep your valuables with you at all times.

Buses may be stopped by police, and you may be required to show or temporarily hand over your passport; keep it handy. Sometimes passengers may be asked to disembark from the bus so that the police can search it for illegal drugs or other contraband. Young males may be given a pat-down. Even if it annoys you, it is always best to keep cool and remain courteous with police officers, who are just doing their job.

Public Transportation

For visitors, public transportation networks are most useful in Bogotá, Medellín, and Cali. Many cities, such as Medellín, Cali, Barranquilla, and Cartagena, have adopted the Bogotá rapid bus system (BRT) model of the TransMilenio.

Buses such as the SITP bus network in Bogotá are clean, safe, and only pick up passengers at designated stops. In large cities, you will need to purchase an electronic refillable bus card. These can be purchased at papelerías (stationery shops), which are often close to bus stops and stations.

The free app **Moovit** provides route information for public transportation options in many Colombian cities.

Car, Motorcycle, or Bicycle

Driving in Colombia can be a good idea for international visitors. In the more developed regions, roads are well maintained and signage is plentiful, but be ready for more adventure in remote areas.

There are car rental offices at the major airports in the country. **Hertz** (tel. 1/756-0600; www.rentacarcolombia.co) and the national **Colombia Car Rental** (US tel. 913/368-0091; www.colombiacarsrental.com) are two with offices nationwide.

Touring Colombia on motorcycle is an increasingly popular option. One of the best motorcycle travel agencies in the country is **Motolombia** (tel. 2/665-9548; www.motolombia.com), based in Cali. A growing number of travelers are motoring the Pan-American Highway, shipping their bikes from Panama or the United States to Cartagena, or vice versa.

Bicyclists will not get much respect on Colombian roads, and there are rarely any significant bike lanes. In Santander and in Boyacá the scenery is absolutely spectacular, but it is often quite mountainous. In Valle del Cauca the roads are good and flat. Staff at **Colombian Bike Junkies** (San Gil tel. 316/327-6101, Medellín tel. 318/808-6769; www.colombianbikejunkies.com), based in San Gil, are experts on biking throughout the country, with an emphasis on mountain biking. Another outfitter is **Colombia en Bicicleta** (www.colombiaenbicicleta.com), catering mostly to enthusiasts living in Bogotá.

Every Sunday in cities across Colombia thousands of cyclists along with joggers, skaters, and dog walkers head to the city streets for some fresh air and exercise. This is **Ciclovía,** an initiative that began in Bogotá, where city streets are closed to traffic. Except in Bogotá, it may be difficult to find a bike rental place, but you can still head out for a jog. Ciclorutas (bike paths) are being built in the major cities, and Bogotá has an extensive cicloruta network. Again, cyclists don't get much respect from motorists, so be careful!

Boat

In some remote locations in Colombia the most common way to get around is by lancha (boat). Many of the isolated villages and beaches and Parque Nacional Natural Utría along the Pacific coast are accessed only by boat from Bahía Solano.

In the Amazon region, the only way to get from Leticia to attractions nearby, including Puerto Nariño and the ecolodges on the Río Javari, is by a boat on the Amazon, which is a memorable experience. All boats leave from the malecón (wharf) in Leticia.

The fabulous beaches of Islas del Rosario, off the coast of Cartagena, are accessed only by boat from the Muelle Turístico or from the docks in Manga. The same goes for Barú, although you can technically drive there.

VISAS AND OFFICIALDOM

Passports and Visas

US and Canadian citizens do not need a visa for visits to Colombia of less than 90 days. You may be asked to show a return ticket.

To renew a tourist visa, you must go to an office of **Migración Colombia** (www.migracioncolombia.gov.co) to request an extension of another 90 days.

Customs

On arrival in Colombia, bags will be spot-checked by customs authorities. Duty-free items up to a value of USD$1,500 can be brought into Colombia. Firearms are not allowed into the country, and many animal and vegetable products are not allowed. If you are carrying over USD$10,000 in cash, you must declare it.

Departing Colombia, expect a pat-down by police, perhaps looking for illegal drugs, at the airport. In addition, luggage may be screened for drugs, art, and exotic animals.

Embassies and Consulates

The **United States Embassy** (Calle 24 Bis No. 48-50; tel. 1/275-2000; https://co.usembassy.gov) is in Bogotá, near the airport. In case of emergency, contact the **US Citizen Services Hotline** (business hours tel. 1/275-2000, after-hours and weekends tel. 1/275-4021). Nonemergency calls are answered at the US Citizen Services Section 2pm-4pm Monday-Thursday. To be informed of security developments or emergencies during your visit, you can enroll in the Smart Traveler Enrollment Program (STEP) on the US Embassy website. In Barranquilla, there is a **Consular Agency Office** (Calle 77B No. 57-141, Suite 511; tel. 5/353-2001 or 5/353-2182), but its hours and services are limited.

The **Canadian Embassy** (Carrera 7 No. 114-33, Piso 14; tel. 1/657-9800) is in Bogotá. There is a **Canadian Consular Office** (Bocagrande Edificio Centro Ejecutivo Oficina 1103, Carrera 3, No. 8-129; tel. 5/665-5838) in Cartagena. For emergencies, Canadian citizens can call the **emergency hotline** (Canada tel. 613/996-8885) in Canada collect.

ACCOMMODATIONS AND FOOD

Most hotels include free wireless internet and some include breakfast, although the food quality will vary. While upscale hotels and backpacker places have English-speaking staff, at least at the front desk, smaller hotels may not. Room rates sometimes depend on the number of occupants, not the size of the room. Except for some international chains and high-end hotels, most will not have heating or air-conditioning in the rooms.

Note that moteles are always, residencias are usually, and hospedajes are sometimes Colombian love hotels.

Hotels

Midrange hotels are often harder to find, and their quality can be unpredictable. Beds can be uncomfortable, rooms may be small, views might be unappealing, and service hit-or-miss. Spanish is the most prevalent language spoken at these types of accommodations.

High-end hotels, including international brands, are in all large cities. In tourism centers such as Cartagena and Santa Marta, boutique hotels are good options for those seeking charm. Expect courteous service and comfort. The only place to expect international television channels and access for travelers with disabilities are at high-end international hotels.

Hostels

Hostels catering to backpackers are found just about everywhere, and more are offering private rooms for those not interested in sharing a dorm with strangers. Young people are drawn to hostels, but an increasing number of older travelers opt for hostels, as these are the best places for information on activities, in addition to offering budget accommodations. Most hostel staff speak English. Hostels generally maintain updated information on their Facebook pages.

Food and Drink

In all major cities, and Bogotá especially, Colombian foodie culture is alive and well, and visitors will have a wealth of excellent dining options, if you don't mind the occasional upscale prices. In the major cities, a 10 percent tip is usually included in the price of a meal, but it is a requirement for the server to ask to include it. You can say no, but that would be considered harsh. If you are truly impressed with the service, you can always leave a little more on the table.

While seafood, especially pescado frito (fried fish), is de rigueur in the Caribbean and along the Pacific, in the interior, beef and chicken rule. In the Medellín area the famed and hearty bandeja paisa is a dish made of red beans cooked with pork, white rice, ground meat, chicharrón (fried pork rinds), fried egg, plantains (patacones), chorizo, hogao sauce, morcilla (black pudding), avocado, and lemon. In Bogotá the dish for cool evenings is ajiaco, a chicken and potato soup. In rural areas the typical lunchtime meal includes soup and a main dish (seco) such as arroz con pollo (chicken with rice). Eat what you can, but foreigners are forgiven if they can't finish a plate.

Vegetarians have decent options available, especially in Bogotá and tourist centers. A can of lentils can be a helpful travel companion in rural areas. In coastal areas it will be hard to avoid eating fish.

Be sure to try the many unusual fruits and juices in Colombia. Juice is either served in water or in milk, and sometimes has a lot of sugar. The same goes for freshly squeezed lemonade. Ask for bajo azucar to lighten the load.

Tinto (percolated coffee), served on the street from thermoses, can be downright dismal: watery and overly sweet. For a good cup of coffee outside major cities and tourist areas, where indie cafés abound, look for national brand like Juan Valdez or Oma. Non-coffee drinkers will enjoy aromatica, herbal tea that is typically served after dinner.

Colombia is a major chocolate producer and has some award-winning local brands, such as ReSelva; Late Chocó, sold in the La Concordia market in Bogotá; and Cacao Hunter's Chocolate, which works with small farmers in different regions, including the Sierra Nevada and near Tumaco.

Breakfast almost universally consists of eggs, bread or arepas, juice, and coffee. Fresh fruit is not that common at breakfast. Arepas are important in Colombia: Every region has its own take on these starchy corn cakes. Arepas in Medellín are large, thin, and bland, while arepas in other parts of the country can be cheese-filled.

RECREATION

A natural playground of incredibly proportions, Colombia offers nearly endless opportunities for outdoor recreation. Diving, hiking, river-rafting, hang-gliding, rock-climbing, wind-surfing, and much more are available to travelers. But visitors to Colombia should be aware that there are sometimes conflicts between the way that modern society, including both international travelers and urban Colombians, see natural areas and the way they are viewed by their original inhabitants, the Indigenous peoples of the region. Several popular natural areas, including both Tayrona and Cocuy national parks, have regulations implemented by Indigenous communities that control visitation, and in the case of Tayrona, often close them off completely to the public for periods of time.

When visiting natural recreation areas in Colombia, keep in mind that features of the land, including waterfalls, rock formations, and mountain tops, are often sacred sites to Indigenous people, and treat them as such. We all depend on the resources provided by the natural world. In this book, nature-appreciating activities like bird-watching, hiking, and even direct participation in ecological projects are prioritized over extreme sports.

TRAVEL TIPS

Access for Travelers with Disabilities

Only international and some national hotel chains offer rooms, usually just one or two, that are wheelchair-accessible. Hostels and small hotels in secondary cities or towns do not. Airport and airline staff will usually bend over backward to help those with disabilities if you ask.

Getting around cities and towns is complicated, as good sidewalks and ramps are the exception, not the rule. Motorists may not stop, or even slow down, for pedestrians.

Women Traveling Alone

Along the Caribbean and Pacific coasts especially, women traveling alone should expect to be on the receiving end of flirting and various friendly offers by men and curiosity from everyone. Women should be extra cautious in taxis and buses. Always order taxis by phone and avoid taking them alone at night. While assaults are unlikely, it is not a good idea to go out for a jog, a walk on a remote beach, or a hike through the rainforest on your own. Walking around small towns alone at night may elicit looks or comments. Don't reveal personal information, where you are staying, or where you are going to inquisitive strangers. In the past there have been assaults on single women travelers in remote areas of La Guajira.

LGBTQ+ Travelers

Colombia has some of the western hemisphere's most progressive laws regarding the rights of LGBTQ+ people. The Constitutional Court legalized same-sex marriage and adoption in 2016 after a torturous decades-long struggle marked by court victories, legislative defeats, and much debate.

Colombia is a fairly tolerant country, especially in its large cities. Bogotá is one of the most gay-friendly cities on the continent, with a large gay nightlife scene and city-supported LGBTQ+ community centers. In many neighborhoods, passersby don't blink an eye when they see a gay couple holding hands on the sidewalk.

The Caribbean region is generally less open to LGBTQ+ people, and this is especially true in rural areas. Nevertheless, the main cities of the region—Cartagena, Barranquilla, and Santa Marta—have gay clubs and are home to active LGBTQ+ communities. All bars and clubs, while catering to men, are welcoming to all. In the San Andrés Archipelago, homophobia is the norm among the native islanders, although violence against gay travelers is unheard of. The online guide **Guia GAY Colombia** (www.guiagaycolombia.com) has a listing of meeting places for LGBTQ+ people throughout the country.

Discrimination, especially against transgender people and even more so against trans sex workers, continues to be a problem in many cities and towns, in particular in Cali and the Caribbean. The award-winning nonprofit group **Colombia Diversa** (www.colombiadiversa.org) is the main advocate for LGBTQ+ rights in the country, with **Caribe Afirmativo** (www.caribeafirmativo.lgbt) focusing its efforts on the Caribbean region.

Gay men in particular should be cautious using dating apps, keep an eye on drinks at nightclubs, and avoid cabs on the street when departing clubs.

Same-sex couples should not hesitate to insist on matrimonial (double) beds at hotels. Most hotels in cities and even in smaller towns and rural areas are becoming more clued in on this. At guesthouses, hostels, and some midsize hotels, front desk staff may charge if you invite a guest to the room. At large international hotels and at apartments for rent, this is never the case.

Travelers of Color

Colombia is not just the most naturally biodiverse country in the world, it's also very racially and culturally diverse. This means that travelers of color, particularly those of African ancestry, are often warmly greeted and welcomed with open arms, especially in the Caribbean and Pacific areas. That being said, racism is a problem in Colombia, and a deeply entrenched class system, where wealth and privilege have been concentrated in a small, mostly white, social group, does exist. This is most apparent in major cities, where the rich live worlds apart from the poor.

Racially motivated crimes are rare, however, and travelers of color do not need to worry about their safety while traveling in Colombia. Antiracist and anti-discriminatory laws and regulations have been passed in Colombia, but you can still expect to see examples of social prejudice against Colombians of Indigenous and African ancestry in some parts of the country. If you feel you have been discriminated against due to your race, cultural heritage, skin color, or ancestry, report the incident to local police and post about the business, organization, or person online.

Conduct and Customs

Colombians are generally friendly to visitors and are often inquisitive about where you are from and how you like Colombia so far. This is most often the case in rural areas. Colombians are also quite proud of their country, after emerging from decades of armed conflict.

With acquaintances and strangers alike, it is customary to ask how someone is doing before moving on to other business. You're even expected to issue a blanket buenos días (Good morning) in the elevator. When greeting an acquaintance, it's customary to shake hands (between men) or give an air kiss on the cheek (for women), although this is mostly the case in urban areas, especially with the upper crust.

Colombians are comfortable with noise: expect the TV to always be on and music blasting almost everywhere. Many Colombians you meet will ask about your family. Family ties are very important to Colombians. Sundays often mean lunch in the countryside with nuclear and extended family members.

While tourists get a pass on appearance, it's preferred that men avoid wearing shorts, especially at restaurants, except on the Caribbean coast. Dress up, like the locals do, when going out on the town.

Indigenous cultures are much more conservative, and women are expected to refrain from showing much skin.

Language Schools

The Spanish spoken in Bogotá is considered neutral and clear, making the city an excellent place to study Spanish. The best schools are operated by the major universities in town and offer a variety of options, including one-on-one tutoring and larger classroom environments.

BOGOTÁ

Universidad Externado

Centro de Español para Extranjeros/CEPEX, Carrera 1A No. 12-53; tel. 1/282-6066, ext. 1221; www.uexternado.edu.co/cepex; summer Spanish intensive COP$777,000

Perched on the mountainside overlooking La Candelaria, the Universidad Externado is known for its top-notch and progressive educational programs. They offer summer Spanish intensives for foreigners every year.

Universidad Javeriana Centro Latinoamericano

Transversal 4 No. 42-00, 6th Fl.; tel. 1/320-8320; www.javeriana.edu.co

Located in Chapinero, the Universidad Javeriana Centro Latinoamericano is the country's top Catholic University. They offer six different levels of Spanish instruction that fits into their semester curriculum, meaning students can apply for a long-term student visa and stay in Colombia for years.

Spanish World Institute

Carrera 4A No. 56-56; tel. 1/248-3399; www.spanishworldinstitute.com; from USD$225 per week

Spanish World Institute is a private language school in La Candelaria with a variety of options, including business Spanish, Spanish intensives, and one-on-one conversation practice.

CARTAGENA

Cartagena offers many opportunities to take group and individual Spanish classes. Many hostels have local Spanish tutors or can recommend a school or private teacher. You may want to try out a class before committing to several days' instruction.

Nueva Lengua

Callejon Ancho No. 10B-52, Getsemaní; tel. 5/660-1736; USD$190 for a 20-hour week

Nueva Lengua has a solid track record, with locations in various cities. They offer several different packages that combine language with different cultural activities like dancing or history.

Centro Catalina

Calle Siete Infantes No. 9-21, San Diego; tel. 310/761-2157; www.centrocatalina.com; USD$239 for a 20-hour week

Centro Catalina offers small-group classes in a nice historic house in the San Diego district. They can also arrange homestays with local Colombian families for a more immersive experience.

MEDELLÍN

Medellín hosts many private schools that cater to international students of Spanish, but the best option may be the city's massive public university.

Universidad de Antioquia
Calle 67 No. 53-108, Aranjuez; tel. 604/219-8332; www.udea.edu.co; 3-week course COP$1,200,000

The Universidad de Antioquia (U de A for short) offers an immersive three-week, 110-hour Spanish course aimed at beginners several times throughout the year. The course is also designed to teach students key facets of Colombian culture, music, and cuisine along the way.

HEALTH AND SAFETY

Vaccinations

There are no vaccination requirements for travel to Colombia. At present, proof of vaccination is no longer required in the national parks (specifically Parque Nacional Natural Tayrona). However, having proof of vaccination may make life easier, especially if you plan to travel onward to Brazil or other countries.

The US Centers for Disease Control recommends that travelers to Colombia get up-to-date on the following vaccines: measles-mumps-rubella (MMR), diphtheria-tetanus-pertussis, varicella (chicken pox), polio, and the yearly flu shot.

Diseases and Illnesses

MALARIA, ZIKA, CHIKUNGUNYA, AND DENGUE FEVER

In low-lying tropical areas of Colombia, mosquito-borne illnesses such as malaria, dengue fever, chikungunya, and Zika are common. It is best to assume that there is a risk, albeit quite small, in all areas of the country.

Malaria is a concern in the entire Amazon region and in the lowland departments of Antioquia, Chocó, Córdoba, Nariño, and Bolívar. There is low to no malarial risk in Cartagena and in areas above 1,600 m (5,200 ft) elevation. The Colombian Ministry of Health estimates that there are around 63,000 annual cases of malaria in the country, 20 of which result in death. Most at risk are children under age 15. Malaria symptoms include fever, headache, chills, vomiting, fatigue, and difficulty breathing. Treatment involves the administration of various antimalarial drugs. If you plan on spending a lot of time outdoors in lowland tropical areas, consider taking prophylactic antimalarial drugs.

The number of cases of **dengue fever** in Colombia has grown from 5.2 cases per 100,000 residents in the 1990s to around 18.1 cases in the 2000s. It is another mosquito-borne illness. The most common symptoms of dengue fever are fever; headaches; muscle, bone, and joint pain; and pain behind the eyes. It is fatal in less than 1 percent of cases. Treatment usually involves rest and hydration and the administration of pain relievers for headache and muscle pain. **Chikungunya virus** has similar symptoms to dengue, and an infection, involving painful aches, can last for several months. It is spread, like dengue, by the *Aedes aegypti* mosquito, often during daytime.

Zika virus is the latest scare to grip South America and is a concern to pregnant women as there is a link between the virus and birth defects. Pregnant women should avoid traveling to low-lying areas (under 2,000 m/6,500 ft elevation), where Zika is present. This includes much of Colombia. Symptoms include fever, rash, joint pains, and conjunctivitis.

The US Centers for Disease Control (www.cdc.gov) remains the best resource on health concerns for worldwide travel.

Prevention

Use mosquito nets over beds when visiting tropical areas of Colombia. Examine them well before use, and if you notice large holes in the nets, request replacements. Mosquitoes tend to be at their worst at dawn, dusk, and in the evenings. Wear lightweight, long-sleeved, and light-colored shirts, long pants, and socks, and keep some insect repellent handy.

DEET is considered effective in preventing mosquito bites, but there are other less-toxic alternatives, most available from online retailers.

If you go to the Amazon region, especially during rainy seasons, take a prophylactic antimalarial drug starting 15 days before arrival and continuing 15 days after departing the region. According to the CDC, the recommended medication for visitors to malarial regions of Colombia is atovaquone-proguanil, doxycycline, or mefloquine. These drugs are available at most pharmacies in Colombia with no prescription necessary.

ALTITUDE SICKNESS

The high elevations of the Andes, including in Bogotá, at 2,625 m (8,610 ft), can be a problem for some. If arriving directly in Bogotá, or if you are embarking on treks in the Sierra Nevada del Cocuy or in Los Nevados, where the highest peaks reach 5,300 m (17,400 ft), for the first couple of days take it easy and avoid drinking alcohol. Make mountain ascents gradually if possible. You can also take the drug acetazolamide to help speed up your acclimatization. Drinking coca tea or chewing on coca leaves may help prevent soroche, as altitude sickness is called in Colombia.

TRAVELER'S DIARRHEA

Stomach flu or traveler's diarrhea is a common malady when traveling through Colombia. These are usually caused by food contamination resulting from the presence of *E. coli* bacteria. Street foods, including undercooked meat, raw vegetables, dairy products, and ice, are some of the main culprits. If you get a case of traveler's diarrhea, be sure to drink lots of clear liquids, avoid caffeine, and take an oral rehydration solution of salt, sugar, and water.

TAP WATER

Tap water is fine to drink in Colombia's major cities, but you should drink bottled, purified, or boiled water in the Amazon, the Pacific coast, the Darién Gap, La Guajira, and San Andrés and Providencia. As an alternative to buying plastic bottles, look for bolsitas (bags) of water. They come in a variety of sizes and use less plastic.

Medical Services

Colombia has excellent hospitals in its major cities. Over 20 hospitals in Bogotá, Medellín, Bucaramanga, and Cali have appeared on the *América Economía* magazine listing of the top 40 hospitals of Latin America. Four hospitals were in the top 10. Those were the **Fundación Santa Fe de Bogotá** (www.fsfb.org.co), the **Fundación Valle del Lili** (www.valledellili.org) in Cali, the **Fundación Cardioinfantil** (https://fundacion.cardioinfantil.org) in Bogotá, and the **Fundación Cardiovascular de Colombia** (www.fcv.org) in Floridablanca, near Bucaramanga. For sexual and reproductive health issues, **Profamilia** (www.profamilia.org.co) has a large network of clinics that provide walk-in and low-cost services throughout the country.

Aerosanidad SAS (tel. 1/439-7080, 1/266-2247, or 1/439-7080; www.aerosanidadsas.com) provides transportation services for ill or injured people in remote locations of Colombia to medical facilities in the large cities.

It is a good idea to purchase travel insurance before arriving in Colombia, especially if you plan on doing a lot of outdoor adventures. Visas longer than a tourism visa require that you purchase basic travelers' medical insurance. Before taking a paragliding ride or white-water rafting trip, inquire whether insurance is included in the price of the trip; it should be.

Crime

Colombia is safe to visit, and the majority of visitors have a wonderful experience. For international travelers there is little to worry about when it comes to illegal armed groups today. The threat of kidnapping of civilians and visitors has been almost completely eliminated.

Even in the worst of times, places like Cartagena and Bogotá have always been less affected by violence from the armed conflict plaguing the rest of the country. Now, with implementation of a peace deal between FARC guerrillas and the Colombian government, the outlook is brighter than ever. However, uncertainty remains and bacrim, smaller groups of former paramilitaries and guerrillas, operate in some cities and towns, while drug lords and dangerous gangs rule marginalized urban areas.

There are still places to avoid, even along the peaceful Caribbean coast. In the northwest, avoid the rainforest and rural areas in and around Parque Nacional Natural Los Katios in the Darién region, as well as Parque Nacional Natural Paramillo in Córdoba. On the eastern side of the country, the Catatumbo region, along the Venezuelan border, remains volatile. In the rest of the country, hot spots include much of the Amazonian rainforest, with the notable exception of Leticia and Puerto Nariño. Rural areas of Cauca are to be avoided, although Popayán and Tierradentro are fine. Avoid rural areas near Tumaco and Buenaventura on the Pacific coast, and much of the Chocó rainforest, except the tourist areas of Bahía Solano.

For updated travel advisories, check the website of the **US Embassy** (www.co.usembassy.gov) in Bogotá. The embassy always errs on the side of caution.

STREET CRIME

Cell phone theft continues to plague much of the country. Keep wallets in front pockets, be aware of your surroundings, and keep shopping bags and backpacks near you at all times. Muggings in major cities are not unheard of but are quite rare. Be alert to your surroundings late at night.

TAXI CRIME

Bogotá has had a serious problem with taxi crime, commonly known as paseo milonario. This crime involves a pirate taxi that picks up a fare off the street, usually in high-income areas, and then kidnaps them in order to rob them or demand a ransom from their families. While this type of crime has been heavily prosecuted and has drastically reduced in frequency, visitors should be cautious while hailing a taxi on the street. It is wiser to simply use an app.

POLICE

From just about anywhere in the country, the police can be reached by dialing tel. 123 on any phone. Otherwise, many parks are home to neighborhood police stations, called CAI (Centros de Atención Inmediata). Authorities may not be able to do much about petty theft, however.

RECREATIONAL DRUGS

In Colombia, the legal status of the use, transport, and possession of recreational drugs can be best described as murky. A 1994 high court decision legalized a "personal dose" of recreational drugs for adults. The sale of drugs is prohibited. An attempt by President Uribe to criminalize recreational drugs failed in 2005. In practice, police may harass those caught with drugs in addition to confiscating the drugs, and they may solicit bribes.

Medical use of marijuana was legalized in 2015, and dispensary-type outlets where a wide variety of cannabis products can be purchased legally, without any special medical permission, exist in all major cities.

INFORMATION AND SERVICES

Money

CURRENCY

Colombia's official currency is the peso, which is abbreviated as COP. Prices in Colombia are marked with a dollar sign, but remember that you're seeing the price in Colombian pesos. COP$1,000,000 isn't enough to buy a house in Colombia, but it will usually cover a few nights in a nice hotel!

Bills in Colombia are in denominations of $1,000, $2,000, $5,000, $10,000, $20,000, $50,000, and $100,000. Coins in Colombia are in denominations of $50, $100, $200, $500, and $1,000. The equivalent of cents in Colombian Spanish is centavos.

The Colombian peso has devalued to record levels, making the country a bargain for international visitors. In 2025 one US dollar was the equivalent of COP$4,000.

Most banks in Colombia do not exchange currency. For that, you'll have to go to an exchange bank, located in all major cities. There are money changers on the streets of Cartagena, but this is not the place for safe and honest transactions.

Traveler's checks are not worth the hassle, as they are hard to cash. US dollars are sometimes accepted in Cartagena and other major tourist destinations. To have cash wired to you from abroad, look for a Western Union office. These are located only in major cities.

Counterfeit bills are a problem in Colombia, and unsuspecting international visitors are often the recipients. Bar staff, taxi drivers, and street vendors are the most common culprits. It's good to keep a stash of small bills to avoid getting large bills back as change. Tattered and torn bills will also be passed off to you, which could pose a problem. Try not to accept those.

CONSIGNACIONES

Consignaciones (bank transfers) are a common way to pay for hotel reservations, especially in areas such as Providencia and remote resorts, as well as tour packages, guides, and entry to national parks. It's often a pain to make these deposits in person, as the world of banking can be confusing for non-Colombians. On the plus side, making a deposit directly into the hotel's bank account provides some peace of mind because it will diminish the need to carry large amounts of cash. To make a consignación, you need to know the recipient's bank account and whether that is a corriente (checking) or ahorros (savings) account. You will also need to show identification and probably have to provide a fingerprint. Be sure to hold onto the receipt to notify the recipient of your deposit.

ATMS

The best way to get cash is to use your ATM card. These are almost universally accepted at cajeros automáticos (ATMs) in the country. Cajeros are almost everywhere except in the smallest of towns or in remote areas. Withdrawal fees are relatively expensive, although they vary. You can usually take out up to COP$300,000-500,000 per transaction. Many banks place limits (COP$1,000,000) on how much you can withdraw in a day.

CREDIT AND DEBIT CARDS

Credit and debit card use is becoming more prevalent in Colombia; however, online credit card transactions are still not common, except for the major airlines and some of the event ticket companies, such as www.tuboleta.com or www.colboletos.com. When you use your plastic, you will be asked if it's credito (credit) or debito (debit). If using a tarjeta de credito (credit card) in restaurants and stores, you will be asked something like, "¿Cuantas cuotas?" or "¿Numero de cuotas?" ("How many installments?"). Most visitors prefer one cuota ("Una, por favor"). But you can have even your dinner bill paid in up to 24 installments! If using a tarjeta de debito, you'll be asked if it is a corriente (checking) or ahorros (savings) account.

TIPPING

In most sit-down restaurants in larger cities, a 10 percent service charge is automatically included in the bill. Waitstaff are required to ask you, "¿Desea incluir el servicio?" ("Would you like to include the service in the bill?"). Many times restaurant staff neglect to ask international visitors about the service inclusion. If you find the service to be exceptional, you can leave a little extra in cash. Although tipping is not expected in bars or cafés, tip jars are becoming more common. International visitors are often expected to tip more than Colombians. In small-town restaurants throughout the country, tipping is not the norm.

It is not customary to tip taxi drivers. But if you feel the driver was a good one who drove safely and was honest, or if they made an additional stop for you, waited for you, or was just pleasant, you can always round up the bill: Instead of COP$6,200, give the driver COP$7,000 and say, "Quédese con las vueltas por favor" ("Keep the change"). Note that sometimes a "tip" is already included in the fare for non-Colombian visitors.

In hotels, usually a tip of COP$5,000 will suffice for porters who help with luggage, unless you have lots of stuff. Tips are not expected, but are certainly welcome, for housekeeping staff.

VALUE-ADDED TAX

Non-Colombian visitors are entitled to a refund of value-added taxes for purchases on clothing, jewelry, and other items if their purchases total more than COP$300,000. Save all credit card receipts and fill out Form 1344 (available online at www.dian.gov.co). Submit this to the **DIAN office** (tel. 1/607-9999) at the airport before departure. You may have several hoops to go through to achieve success. Go to the DIAN office before checking your luggage, as you will have to present the items you purchased.

Internet and Telephones

Being connected makes travel throughout Colombia so much easier. Free Wi-Fi is available at most hotels, restaurants, and cafés in major cities. An important Spanish phrase to learn is "Como es la contraseña para el wifi?" ("What's the password for the Wi-Fi?")

Obtaining a SIM card for your cell phone will ensure connectivity in all but the most remote locations. Sometimes low-tech phones work better than smartphones in very rural or remote locations like Providencia. SIM cards (datos de prepago) are available at mobile-phone carriers in all major towns and cities. Three main cell phone companies are Claro, Movistar, and Tigo.

Facebook and WhatsApp are often the best bets for contacting hotels, restaurants, and shops.

The telephone country code for Colombia is 57. Cell phone numbers are 10 digits long, beginning with a 3. To call a Colombian cell phone from abroad, you must use the country code followed by that 10-digit number. Landline numbers in Colombia are seven digits long. An area code is necessary when calling from a different region. To call a landline from a cell phone, dial 03 + area code + 7-digit number. To reach a cell phone from a landline, dial 03 + 10-digit number.

RESOURCES

SPANISH PHRASEBOOK

Knowing some Spanish is essential to visit Colombia, as relatively few people outside the major cities speak English. Colombian Spanish is said to be one of the clearest in Latin America, but there are many regional differences.

Spanish commonly uses 30 letters—the familiar English 26 plus four straightforward additions: ch, ll, ñ, and rr, which are explained in "Consonants" below.

Pronunciation

Once you learn them, Spanish pronunciation rules—in contrast to English—don't change. Spanish vowels generally sound softer than in English. (Note: The capitalized syllables below receive stronger accents.)

VOWELS

a like ah, as in "hah": agua AH-gooah (water), pan PAHN (bread), and casa CAH-sah (house)

e like ay, as in "may:" mesa MAY-sah (table), tela TAY-lah (cloth), and de DAY (of, from)

i like ee, as in "need": diez dee-AYZ (ten), comida ko-MEE-dah (meal), and fin FEEN (end)

o like oh, as in "go": peso PAY-soh (weight), ocho OH-choh (eight), and poco POH-koh (a bit)

u like oo, as in "cool": uno OO-noh (one), cuarto KOOAHR-toh (room), and usted oos-TAYD (you); when it follows a "q" the u is silent; when it follows an "h" or has an umlaut, it's pronounced like "w"

CONSONANTS

b, d, f, k, l, m, n, p, q, s, t, v, w, x, y, z, and **ch** pronounced almost as in English; h occurs, but is silent—not pronounced at all

c like k as in "keep": cuarto KOOAR-toh (room), casa KAH-sah (house); when it precedes "e" or "i," pronounce c like s, as in "sit": cerveza sayr-VAY-sah (beer), encima ayn-SEE-mah (atop)

g like g as in "gift" when it precedes "a," "o," "u," or a consonant: gato GAH-toh (cat), hago AH-goh (I do, make); otherwise, pronounce g like h as in "hat": giro HEE-roh (money order), gente HAYN-tay (people)

j like h, as in "has": Jueves HOOAY-vays (Thursday), mejor may-HOR (better)

ll like y, as in "yes": toalla toh-AH-yah (towel), ellos AY-yohs (they, them)

ñ like ny, as in "canyon": año AH-nyo (year), señor SAY-nyor (Mr., sir)

r is lightly trilled, with tongue at the roof of your mouth like a very light English d, as in "ready": pero PAY-roh (but), tres TRAYS (three), cuatro KOOAH-troh (four)

rr like a Spanish r, but with much more emphasis and trill. Let your tongue flap. Practice with burro (donkey), carretera (highway), and Carrillo (proper name), then really let go with ferrocarril (railroad)

Note: The single small but common exception to all of the above is the pronunciation of Spanish y when it's being used as the Spanish word for "and," as in "Ron y

Kathy." In such case, pronounce it like the English ee, as in "keep": Ron "ee" Kathy (Ron and Kathy).

ACCENT

The rule for accents, the relative stress given to syllables within a given word, is straightforward. If a word ends in a vowel, an n, or an s, accent the next-to-last syllable; if not, accent the last syllable.

Pronounce gracias GRAH-seeahs (thank you), orden OHR-dayn (order), and carretera kah-ray-TAY-rah (highway) with stress on the next-to-last syllable.

Otherwise, accent the last syllable: venir vay-NEER (to come), ferrocarril fay-roh-cah-REEL (railroad), and edad ay-DAHD (age).

Exceptions to the accent rule are always marked with an accent sign: (á, é, í, ó, or ú), such as teléfono tay-LAY-foh-noh (telephone), jabón hah-BON (soap), and rápido RAH-pee-doh (rapid).

Basic and Courteous Expressions

Colombians use many courteous formalities. Whenever approaching anyone for information or some other reason, do not forget the appropriate salutation—good morning, good evening, etc. Standing alone, the greeting hola (hello) can sound brusque.

Hello. Hola.
Good morning. Buenos días.
Good afternoon. Buenas tardes.
Good evening. Buenas noches.
How are you? Colombians have many ways of saying this: ¿Cómo estás/como está? ¿Qué hubo/Qu'hubo? ¿Cómo va/vas? ¿Que tal?
Very well, thank you. Muy bien, gracias.
Okay; good. Bien.
Not okay; bad. Mal.
So-so. Más o menos.
And you? ¿Y Usted?
Thank you. Gracias.
Thank you very much. Muchas gracias.
You're very kind. Muy amable.
You're welcome. De nada.
Good-bye. Adiós.
See you later. Hasta luego. Chao.
please por favor; (slang) por fa
yes sí
no no
I don't know. No sé.
Just a moment, please. Un momento, por favor.
Excuse me, please (when you're trying to get attention). Disculpe.
Excuse me (when you've made a mistake). Perdón. Que pena.
I'm sorry. Lo siento.
Pleased to meet you. Mucho gusto.
How do you say . . . in Spanish? ¿Cómo se dice . . . en español?
What is your name? ¿Cómo se llama (Usted)? ¿Cómo te llamas?
Do you speak English? ¿Habla (Usted) inglés? ¿Hablas inglés?
Does anyone here speak English? ¿Hay alguien que hable inglés?
I don't speak Spanish well. No hablo bien el español.
Please speak more slowly. Por favor hable más despacio.
I don't understand. No entiendo.
Please write it down. Por favor escríbalo.
My name is . . . Me llamo . . . Mi nombre es . . .
I would like . . . Quisiera . . . Quiero . . .
Let's go to . . . Vamos a . . .
That's fine. Está bien.
All right. Listo.
cool, awesome chévere, rico, super
Oh my god! ¡Dios mío!
That's crazy! ¡Qué locura!
You're crazy! ¡Estás loca/o!

Terms of Address

When in doubt, use the formal Usted (you) as a form of address.

I yo
you (formal) Usted
you (familiar) tú
he/him él
she/her ella
we/us nosotros
you (plural) Ustedes
they/them ellas (all females); ellos (all males or mixed gender)
Mr., sir señor
Mrs., madam señora
miss, young lady señorita
wife esposa
husband esposo
friend amigo/a
girlfriend/boyfriend novia (female); novio (male)
partner pareja
daughter; son hija; hijo
brother; sister hermano; hermana
mother; father madre; padre
grandfather; grandmother abuelo; abuela

Transportation

Where is . . . ? ¿Dónde está . . . ?
How far is it to . . . ? ¿A cuánto queda . . . ?
from . . . to . . . de . . . a . . .
How many blocks? ¿Cuántas cuadras?
Where (Which) is the way to . . . ? ¿Cuál es el camino a . . . ? ¿Por dónde es . . . ?
bus station la terminal de buses/terminal de transporte
bus stop la parada
Where is this bus going? ¿A dónde va este bús?
boat el barco, la lancha
dock el muelle
airport el aeropuerto
I'd like a ticket to . . . Quisiera un pasaje a . . .
round-trip ida y vuelta
reservation reserva
baggage equipaje
next flight el próximo vuelo
Stop here, please. Pare aquí, por favor.
the entrance la entrada
the exit la salida
(very) near; far (muy) cerca; lejos
to; toward a
by; through por
from de
right la derecha
left la izquierda
straight ahead derecho
in front en frente
beside al lado
behind atrás
corner la esquina
stoplight la semáforo
turn una vuelta
here aquí
somewhere around here por aquí
there allí
somewhere around there por allá
road camino
street calle, carrera
avenue avenida
block la cuadra
highway carretera
kilometer kilómetro
bridge; toll puente; peaje
address dirección
north; south norte; sur
east; west oriente (este); occidente (oeste)

Accommodations

hotel hotel
Is there a room available? ¿Hay un cuarto disponible?
May I (may we) see it? ¿Puedo (podemos) verlo?
How much is it? ¿Cuánto cuesta?
Is there something cheaper? ¿Hay algo más económico?
single room un cuarto sencillo

double room un cuarto doble
double bed cama matrimonial
single bed cama sencilla
with private bath con baño propio
television televisor
window ventana
view vista
hot water agua caliente
shower ducha
towels toallas
soap jabón
toilet paper papel higiénico
pillow almohada
blanket cobija
sheets sábanas
air-conditioned aire acondicionado
fan ventilador
swimming pool piscina
gym gimnasio
bike bicicleta
key llave
suitcase maleta
backpack mochila
lock candado
safe caja de seguridad
manager gerente
maid empleada
clean limpio
dirty sucio
broken roto
(not) included (no) incluido

Food

I'm hungry. Tengo hambre.
I'm thirsty. Tengo sed.
Table for two, please. Una mesa para dos, por favor.
menu carta
order orden
glass vaso
glass of water vaso con agua
fork tenedor
knife cuchillo
spoon cuchara
napkin servilleta
soft drink gaseosa
coffee café, tinto
tea té
drinking water agua potable
bottled carbonated water agua con gas
bottled uncarbonated water agua sin gas
beer cerveza
wine vino
glass of wine copa de vino
red wine vino tinto
white wine vino blanco
milk leche
juice jugo
cream crema
sugar azúcar
cheese queso
breakfast desayuno
lunch almuerzo
daily lunch special menú del día
dinner comida
the check la cuenta
eggs huevos
bread pan
salad ensalada
lettuce lechuga
tomato tomate
onion cebolla
garlic ajo
hot sauce ají
fruit fruta
mango mango
watermelon patilla
papaya papaya
banana banano
apple manzana
orange naranja
lime limón
passionfruit maracuyá
guava guayaba
grape uva
fish pescado
shellfish mariscos

shrimp camarones
(without) meat (sin) carne
chicken pollo
pork cerdo
beef carne de res
bacon; ham tocino; jamón
fried frito
roasted asado
Do you have vegetarian options? ¿Tienen opciones vegetarianas?
I'm vegetarian. Soy vegetarian(o).
I don't eat . . . No como . . .
to share para compartir
Check, please. La cuenta, por favor.
Is the service included? ¿Está incluido el servicio?
tip propina
large grande
small pequeño

Shopping

cash efectivo
money dinero
credit card tarjeta de crédito
debit card tarjeta de débito
money exchange office casa de cambio
What is the exchange rate? ¿Cuál es la tasa de cambio?
How much is the commission? ¿Cuánto es la comisión?
Do you accept credit cards? ¿Aceptan tarjetas de crédito?
credit card installments cuotas
money order giro
How much does it cost? ¿Cuánto cuesta?
expensive caro
cheap barato; económico
more más
less menos
a little un poco
too much demasiado
value added tax IVA
discount descuento

Health

Help me please. Ayúdeme por favor.
I am ill. Estoy enferma/o.
Call a doctor. Llame un doctor.
Take me to . . . Lléveme a . . .
hospital hospital, clínica
drugstore farmacia
pain dolor
fever fiebre
headache dolor de cabeza
stomach ache dolor de estómago
burn quemadura
cramp calambre
nausea náusea
vomiting vomitar
medicine medicina
antibiotic antibiótico
pill pastilla, pepa
aspirin aspirina
ointment; cream ungüento; crema
bandage (big) venda
bandage (small) cura
cotton algodón
sanitary napkin toalla sanitaria
birth control pills pastillas anticonceptivas
condoms condones
toothbrush cepillo de dientes
dental floss hilo dental
toothpaste crema dental
dentist dentista
toothache dolor de muelas
vaccination vacuna

Communications

Wi-Fi wifi
cell phone celular
username usuario
password contraseña
laptop computer portátil
prepaid cell phone celular prepago
post office correo
phone call llamada
letter carta

stamp estampilla
postcard postal
package; box paquete; caja

At the Border

border frontera
customs aduana
immigration migración
inspection inspección
ID card cédula
passport pasaporte
profession profesión
vacation vacaciones
I'm a tourist. Soy turista.
student estudiante
marital status estado civil
single soltero
married; divorced casado; divorciado
widowed viudado
insurance seguro
title título
driver's license pase de conducir

At the Gas Station

gas station estación de gasolina
gasoline gasolina
full, please lleno, por favor
tire llanta
air aire
water agua
oil (change) (cambio de) aceite
My . . . doesn't work. Mi . . . no funciona.
battery batería
tow truck grúa
repair shop taller

Verbs

Verbs are the key to getting along in Spanish. They employ mostly predictable forms and come in three classes, which end in ar, er, and ir, respectively:

to buy comprar
I buy, you (he, she, it) buys compro, compra
we buy, you (they) buy compramos, compran
to eat comer
I eat, you (he, she, it) eats como, come
we eat, you (they) eat comemos, comen
to climb subir
I climb, you (he, she, it) climbs subo, sube
we climb, you (they) climb subimos, suben

Here are more (with irregularities indicated):

to do or make hacer (regular except for hago, I do or make)
to go ir (very irregular: voy, va, vamos, van)
to walk caminar
to wait esperar
to love amar
to work trabajar
to want querer (irregular: quiero, quiere, queremos, quieren)
to need necesitar
to read leer
to write escribir
to send enviar
to repair reparar
to wash lavar
to stop parar
to get off (the bus) bajar
to arrive llegar
to stay (remain) quedar
to stay (lodge) hospedar
to rent alquilar
to leave salir (regular except for salgo, I leave)
to look at mirar
to look for buscar
to give dar (regular except for doy, I give)
to give (as a present or to order something) regalar
to carry llevar
to have tener (irregular: tengo, tiene, tenemos, tienen)

to come venir (irregular: vengo, viene, venimos, vienen)

Spanish has two forms of "to be":

to be estar (regular except for estoy, I am)

to be ser (very irregular: soy, es, somos, son)

Use estar when speaking of location or a temporary state of being: "I am at home." "Estoy en casa." "I'm happy." "Estoy contenta/o." Use ser for a permanent state of being: "I am a lawyer." "Soy abogada/o."

Numbers

zero cero
one uno
two dos
three tres
four cuatro
five cinco
six seis
seven siete
eight ocho
nine nueve
10 diez
11 once
12 doce
13 trece
14 catorce
15 quince
16 dieciseis
17 diecisiete
18 dieciocho
19 diecinueve
20 veinte
21 veinte y uno or veintiuno
30 treinta
40 cuarenta
50 cincuenta
60 sesenta
70 setenta
80 ochenta
90 noventa
100 cien
101 ciento y uno
200 doscientos
500 quinientos
1,000 mil
10,000 diez mil
100,000 cien mil
1,000,000 millón
one-half medio
one-third un tercio
one-fourth un cuarto

Time

What time is it? ¿Qué hora es?
It's one o'clock. Es la una.
It's three in the afternoon. Son las tres de la tarde.
It's 4 a.m. Son las cuatro de la mañana.
six-thirty seis y media
quarter till eleven un cuarto para las once
quarter past five las cinco y cuarto
hour una hora
late tarde

Days and Months

Monday lunes
Tuesday martes
Wednesday miércoles
Thursday jueves
Friday viernes
Saturday sábado
Sunday domingo
today hoy
tomorrow mañana
yesterday ayer
day before yesterday antier
January enero
February febrero
March marzo
April abril
May mayo
June junio
July julio
August agosto

September septiembre
October octubre
November noviembre
December diciembre
week una semana
month un mes
after después
before antes
holiday festivo
long weekend puente

SUGGESTED READING

History

Bushnell, David. *The Making of Modern Colombia: A Nation in Spite of Itself.* Berkeley, CA: University of California Press, 1993. Mandatory reading for students of Colombian history. Bushnell, an American, is considered the "Father of the Colombianists."

Hemming, John. *The Search for El Dorado.* London: Joseph, 1978. Written by a former director of the Royal Geographical Society, this book explores the Spanish gold obsession in the New World. It's a great companion to any visit to the Museo de Oro in Bogotá.

Lynch, John. *Simón Bolívar: A Life.* New Haven, CT: Yale University Press, 2007. This biography of the Liberator is considered one of the best ever written in English, and is the result of a lifetime of research by renowned English historian John Lynch.

Palacios, Marco. *Between Legitimacy and Violence: A History of Colombia, 1875-2002.* Durham, NC: Duke University Press, 2006. Written by a Bogotano academic who was a former head of the Universidad Nacional, this book covers Colombia's economic, political, cultural, and social history from the late 19th century to the complexities of the late 20th century, and drug-related violence.

The Drug War and Armed Conflicts

Bowden, Mark. *Killing Pablo: The Hunt for the World's Greatest Outlaw.* New York: Grove Press, 2001. This account of US and Colombian efforts to halt drug trafficking and terrorism committed by drug lord Pablo Escobar was originally reported in a 31-part series in *The Philadelphia Inquirer.*

Dudley, Steven. *Walking Ghosts: Murder and Guerrilla Politics in Colombia.* New York: Routledge, 2004. Essential reading for anyone interested in understanding the modern Colombian conflict, this book is written by an expert on investigating organized crime in the Americas.

Gonsalves, Marc, Tom Howes, Keith Stansell, and Gary Brozek. *Out of Captivity: Surviving 1,967 Days in the Colombian Jungle.* New York: Harper Collins, 2009. Accounts of three American military contractors who were held, along with former presidential candidate Ingrid Betancourt, by FARC guerrillas for over five years in the Colombian rainforest.

Leech, Garry. *Beyond Bogotá: Diary of a Drug War Journalist in Colombia.* Boston: Beacon, 2009. The basis for this book is the author's 11 hours spent as a hostage of FARC.

Otis, John. *Law of the Jungle: The Hunt for Colombian Guerrillas, American Hostages, and Buried Treasure.* New York: Harper, 2010. This is a thrilling account of the operation to rescue Ingrid Betancourt and US government contractors held by FARC. It's been called a flip side to *Out of Captivity.*

Natural History

Hilty, Steven L., William L. Brown, and Guy Tudor. *A Guide to the Birds of Colombia.* Princeton, NJ: Princeton University Press, 1986. This massive 996-page field guide to bird-rich Colombia is a must for any serious bird-watcher.

McMullan, Miles, Thomas M. Donegan, and Alonso Quevedo. *Field Guide to the Birds of Colombia.* Bogotá: Fundación ProAves, 2010. This pocket-sized field guide published by ProAves, a respected bird conservation society, is a more manageable alternative to Hilty's guide.

Ethnography

Davis, Wade. *Magdalena: River of Dreams.* National Geographic Books, 2021. Wade's latest tells the story of Colombia's Río Magdalena, which runs from the south of the country to the Caribbean. Although it is the largest and most economically, culturally, and ecologically important river in the country, it is in danger of dying.

Davis, Wade. *One River: Explorations and Discoveries in the Amazon Rain Forest.* New York: Simon & Schuster, 1997. From the author of *The Serpent and the Rainbow,* this is a rich description of the peoples of the Amazonian rainforest, and the result of Davis's time in the country alongside famed explorer Richard Evans Schultes.

Reichel-Dolmatoff, Gerardo. *Colombia: Ancient Peoples & Places.* London: Thames and Hudson, 1965. A thorough anthropological investigation of the Indigenous cultures across Colombia by an Austrian-born anthropologist who emigrated to Colombia during World War II.

Architecture

Escovar, Alberto, Diego Obregón, and Rodolfo Segovia. *Guías Elarqa de Arquitectura.* Bogotá: Ediciones Gamma, 2005. Useful guides for anyone wishing to learn more about the architecture of Bogotá, Cartagena, and Medellín.

Travel

Nicholl, Charles. *The Fruit Palace.* New York: St. Martin's Press, 1994. A wild romp that follows the seedy cocaine trail from Bogotá bars to Medellín to the Sierra Nevada and a fruit stand called the Fruit Palace during the wild 1980s. The English author was jailed in Colombia for drug smuggling as he conducted research for the book.

Photography and Illustrated Books

Often only available in Colombia, coffee-table books by Colombian publishers Villegas Editores and the Banco de

Occidente are gorgeous, well-done, and often in English. Save room in your suitcase for one or two.

Cobo Borda, Juan Gustavo, Gustavo Morales Lizcano, and César David Martínez. *Colombia en Flor.* Bogotá: Villegas Editores, 2009. This book features fantastic photographs of flowers you will see in Colombia.

Davis, Wade, and Richard Evans Schultes. *The Lost Amazon: The Photographic Journey of Richard Evans Schultes.* Bogotá: Villegas Editores, 2009. A fantastic journey deep into the Amazonian rainforest by famed explorer Richard Evans Schultes.

Díaz, Hernán. *Cartagena Forever.* Bogotá: Villegas Editores, 2002. A tiny little book of stunning black-and-white images of the Cartagena of yesteryear, by one of Colombia's most accomplished photographers.

Díaz, Merlano, Juan Manuel, and Fernando Gast Harders. *El Chocó Biogeográfico de Colombia.* Cali: Banco de Occidente Credencial, 2009. A spectacular trip through the unique and biodiverse Chocó region.

Freeman, Benjamin, and Murray Cooper. *Birds in Colombia.* Bogotá: Villegas Editores, 2011. Dazzling photographs of native bird species found in Colombia, a veritable birding paradise.

Hurtado García, Andrés. *Unseen Colombia.* Bogotá: Villegas Editores, 2004. Photos and descriptions of the many off-the-beaten-track destinations in the country.

Montaña, Antonio, and Hans Doering. *The Taste of Colombia.* Bogotá: Villegas Editores, 1994. A thorough survey of Colombian cuisine by region, with recipes included.

Ortiz Valdivieso, Pedro, and César David Martínez. *Orquídeas Especies de Colombia.* Bogotá: Villegas Editores, 2010. Jaw-dropping photos of orchids, from the unusual to the sublime, found in the forests of Colombia.

Rivera Ospina, David. *La Amazonia de Colombia.* Cali: Banco de Occidente Credencial, 2008. An excellent souvenir of your visit to the Amazon region.

Rivera Ospina, David. *La Orinoquia de Colombia.* Cali: Banco de Occidente Credencial, 2005. One of the least visited areas of Colombia is the Río Orinoco basin in Los Llanos and the Amazon regions.

Various. *Colombia Natural Parks.* Bogotá: Villegas Editores, 2006. Gorgeous photos from all of Colombia's spectacular national parks.

Villegas, Liliana. *Coffees of Colombia.* Bogotá: Villegas Editores, 2012. Everything you'd like to know about Colombian coffee in one charming and compact book.

Villegas, Marcelo. *Guadua Arquitectura y Diseño.* Bogotá: Villegas Editores, 2003. Profiles of minimalistic and modern constructions throughout Colombia made from guadua.

INTERNET AND DIGITAL RESOURCES

Birding

ProAves

www.proaves.org

Excellent website for the largest birding organization in the country.

Eco-Tourism

Parques Nacionales Naturales de Colombia

www.parquesnacionales.gov.co

Colombia's national parks website has information on all of the natural parks and protected areas in the country.

Aviatur Ecoturismo

www.aviaturecoturismo.com

Package tours of the Amazon, PNN Tayrona, PNN Isla Gorgona, and more are available from one of Colombia's most respected travel agencies.

Fundación Malpelo

www.fundacionmalpelo.org

This nonprofit organization works to protect Colombia's vast maritime territory, including Santuario de Flora y Fauna Malpelo.

Fundación Natura

www.natura.org.co

Fundación Natura operates several interesting ecotourism reserves in the country.

Embassies and Visas

US Embassy in Colombia

www.co.usembassy.gov

The Citizen Services page often has security information for visitors and is where you can register your visit in case of an emergency.

Colombian Ministry of Foreign Relations

www.cancilleria.gov.co

Offers information on visas and other travel information.

Entertainment, Culture, and Events

Tu Boleta

www.tuboleta.com

The top event ticket distributor in the country, Tu Boleta is a good way to learn about concerts, theater, parties, and sporting events throughout Colombia.

Banco de la República

www.banrepcultural.org

Information on upcoming cultural activities sponsored by the Banco de la República in 28 cities in the country.

History and Human Rights Issues

CIA World Factbook Colombia

www.cia.gov

Background information on Colombia from those in the know.

Centro de Memoria Histórica

www.centrodememoriahistorica.gov.co

Excellent website on the human toll of the Colombian conflict.

International Crisis Group

www.crisisgroup.org

In-depth analysis of the human rights situation in Colombia.

Colombia Diversa

www.colombiadiversa.org

Covers LGBTQ+ rights in Colombia.

Language Courses

Spanish in Colombia
www.spanishincolombia.caroycuervo.gov.co
Official government website on places to study Spanish in Colombia.

Medellín

Medellín Living
www.medellinliving.com
This website run by expats is an excellent purveyor of insider information on the City of Eternal Spring.

News and Media

El Tiempo
www.eltiempo.com
El Tiempo is the country's leading newspaper.

El Espectador
www.elespectador.com
This is Colombia's second national newspaper.

Revista Semana
www.semana.com
Semana is the top news magazine in Colombia.

La Silla Vacia
www.lasillavacia.com
Political insiders dish about current events.

Colombia Reports
http://colombiareports.com
Colombian news in English.

The City Paper Bogotá
www.thecitypaperbogota.com
Website of the capital city's English-language monthly.

Colombia Calling
www.richardmccoll.com/colombia-calling
Weekly online radio program on all things Colombia from an expat perspective.

Transportation

Moovit
This app will help you figure out public transportation in Bogotá.

Tappsi
To order a safe taxi in Colombia's large cities, first download this excellent app.

SITP
www.sitp.gov.co
The official website of the ever-improving (yet confusing) public bus system in Bogotá.

Travel Information

Colombia Travel
www.colombia.travel
This is the official travel information website of Proexport, Colombia's tourism and investment promotion agency.

Pueblos Patrimoniales
www.pueblospatrimoniodecolombia.travel
Find a pueblo that suits your needs at this informative website.

Volunteering

Conexión Colombia
www.conexionla.org
This website is one-stop shopping for the nonprofit sector in Colombia and other countries in Latin America.

INDEX

C

D

E

F

G

H

I

J

KL

M

N

OP

QR

S

T

UV

WXYZ

LIST OF MAPS

PHOTO CREDITS

All interior photos © Ocean Malandra, except: title page © Ulita | Dreamstime.com; pages 6-7 © Sevenkingdom | Dreamstime.com; pages 8-9 © Jkraft5 | Dreamstime.com; page 10 © Iralgo74 | Dreamstime.com; pages 12-13 © Cosmopol | Dreamstime.com; page 14 © (bottom left) Markpittimages | Dreamstime.com; page 15 © Markpittimages | Dreamstime.com; page 16 © (top left) Argolorogerio | Dreamstime.com; (bottom left) Ulita | Dreamstime.com; page 17 © (top right) MalaMaña Salsa Bar; (bottom right) Jhampiergiron | Dreamstime.com; page 22 (left) © Coughlandarragh | Dreamstime.com; page 27 © Nestor Jaime Sanabria Gutierrez; page 30 © (left) Jkraft5 | Dreamstime.com; (middle) Pxhidalgo | Dreamstime.com; page 31 © (middle) Scottiebumich | Dreamstime.com; page 33 © (right) Rechitansorin | Dreamstime.com; page 34 © (left) Jkraft5 | Dreamstime.com; (middle) Tbintb | Dreamstime.com; (right) Jhampiergiron | Dreamstime.com; page 36 © Electropower | Dreamstime.com; page 38 © Nestor Jaime Sanabria Gutierrez; page 39 © Nestor Jaime Sanabria Gutierrez; page 40 © Nestor Jaime Sanabria Gutierrez; page 54 © (left) Rechitansorin | Dreamstime.com; page 69 © Jhampier Giron | Dreamstime.com; page 95 © Vic36 | Dreamstime.com; pages 108-109 © Jkraft5 | Dreamstime.com; page 111 © Wirestock | Dreamstime.com; page 119 © Mineko80 | Dreamstime.com; page 121 © Cristianlourenco | Dreamstime.com; page 132 © Jkraft5 | Dreamstime.com; pages 142-143 © Tbintb | Dreamstime.com; page 152 © Nestor Jaime Sanabria Gutierrez; page 183 © (bottom right) Carolinajc | Dreamstime.com; page 186 © (left) Rchphoto | Dreamstime.com; (middle) Quasarphoto | Dreamstime.com; (right) Ibrester | Dreamstime.com; page 195 © Nestor Jaime Sanabria Gutierrez; page 199 © Pixattitude | Dreamstime.com; page 205 © Nestor Jaime Sanabria Gutierrez; pages 212-213 © Jhampiergiron | Dreamstime.com; page 220 © (bottom right) & 227 (middle) Pxhidalgo | Dreamstime.com; (right) Sevenkingdom | Dreamstime.com; page 280 © (top) Nestor Jaime Sanabria Gutierrez; (bottom) Urosr | Dreamstime.com; page 285 © Nestor Jaime Sanabria Gutierrez; page 286 © (bottom) Ulfhuebner | Dreamstime.com; page 292 © (top left) Nestor Jaime Sanabria Gutierrez; (top right) Salsa Pura; (bottom left) Quasarphoto | Dreamstime.com; page 299 © Jenny37 | Dreamstime.com; page 303 © (top) Jimwaggy | Dreamstime.com; page 319 © Nestor Jaime Sanabria Gutierrez; page 326 © Ilyshev | Dreamstime.com; page 330 © Warren1225 | Dreamstime.com; page 343 © theteamtall | Dreamstime.com; page 346 © (bottom right) Jkraft5 | Dreamstime.com; page 350 © (left & middle) Pxhidalgo | Dreamstime.com; (right) Rjlerich | Dreamstime.com; page 357 © Sdelgadocaicedo | Dreamstime.com; page 369 © (top right) Dshoug | Dreamstime.com; (top left & bottom) Jkraft5 | Dreamstime.com; page 375 © Jhampiergiron | Dreamstime.com; page 376 © (top left) Nestor Jaime Sanabria Gutierrez, (bottom right) Aifeati | Dreamstime.com; page 380 © (left) Kstipek | Dreamstime.com; (middle) MaleoPhotography | Dreamstime.com; (right) © Nestor Jaime Sanabria Gutierrez.

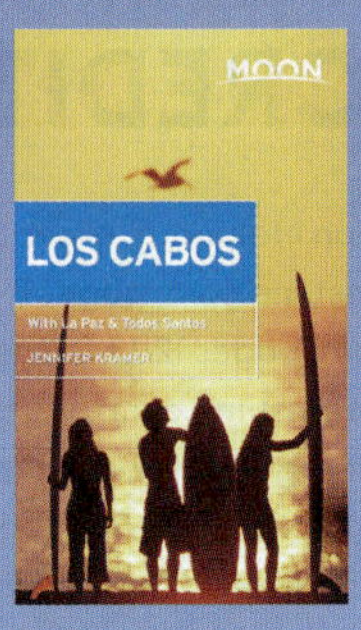

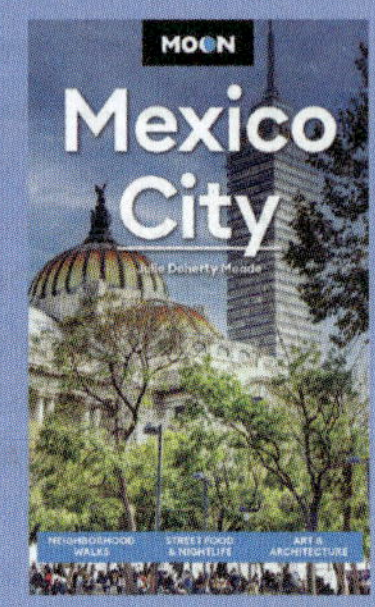

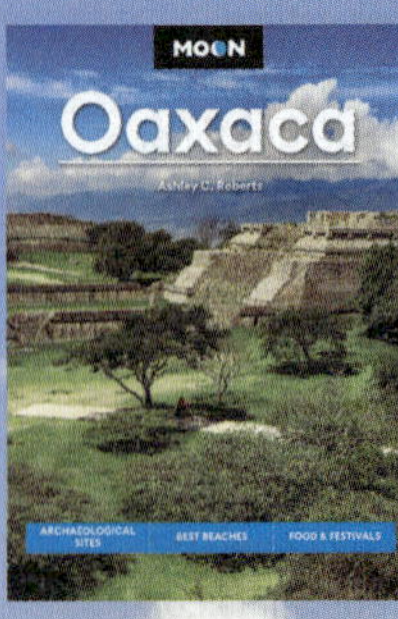

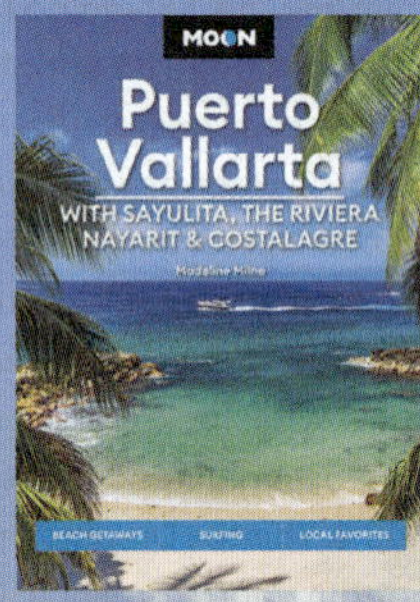

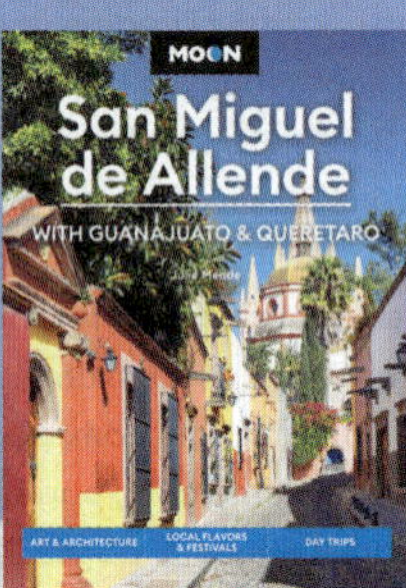

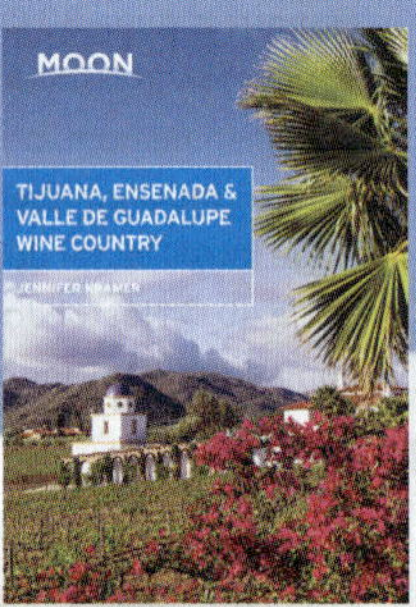

Mexico and Latin America Travel Guides

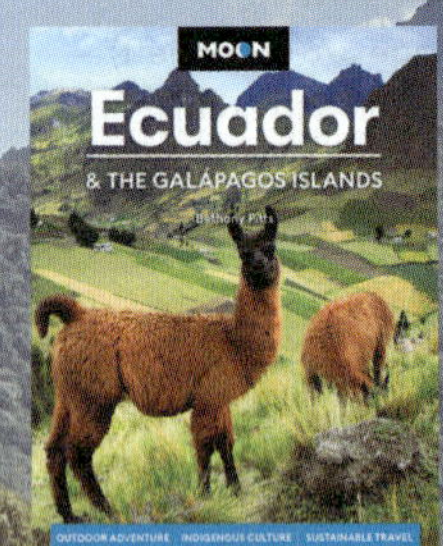

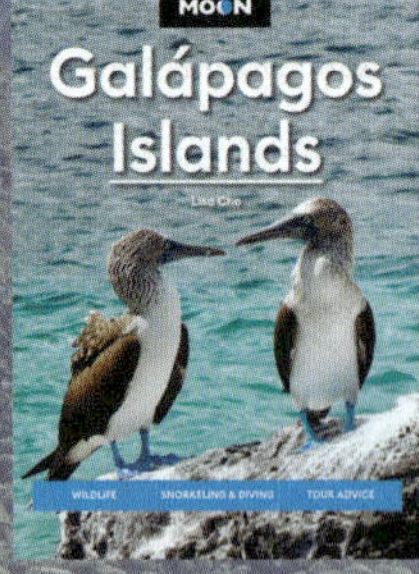

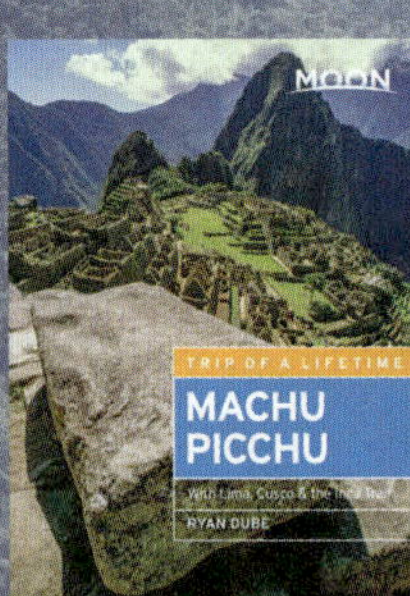